The Good Housekeeping

Woman's Almanac

BY THE EDITORS OF THE WORLD ALMANAC

Published by
NEWSPAPER ENTERPRISE ASSOCIATION, INC.
New York

Library of Congress Catalog Card Number 77-75353
Doubleday and Co., Inc.   ISBN 0-385-13377-4
Soft-Cover Edition: Newspaper Enterprise Association, Inc.
ISBN 0-911818-07-3

Printed in the United States of America

Newspaper Enterprise Association, Inc.
230 Park Avenue, New York, NY 10017

The Good Housekeeping
Woman's Almanac

Editors:
Barbara McDowell Hana Umlauf

Writers: Jan Billingsley
Barbara McDowell Victoria Heller Secunda
Terri Schultz Ann Guerin

Researchers: Phyllis Lester
Stephanie Bernardo Mary Leverty
Susan Bronson Robert Peck
Ann Victoria Cosstick Vivian Scheinmann
Barbara Culbreath Joan Schlissel
Phyllis Dolgin Susan Wallach
Christine Douglas Joyce Wesolowski
Laura James Betty Zoss

Book Design: Jean King **Graphics:** Elke Raedisch

Consulting Editor: David Hendin

The World Almanac Good Housekeeping
George E. Delury, Editor John Mack Carter, Editor

NEWSPAPER ENTERPRISE ASSOCIATION, INC.
230 Park Avenue, New York, NY 10017

Robert Roy Metz, president; Robert J. Cochnar, vice president and editorial director; Michael W. Callaghan, vice president and business manager.

This book is dedicated to
Ellen Browning Scripps (1836-1932),
journalist, philanthropist, and feminist.
"She would not compromise
with ugliness or wrong.
Her life was
an American benediction."

CONTENTS

INTRODUCTION

Survey after survey has reported that women are happier with their lives today than at any time in recent memory. Largely responsible for women's high spirits is the falling of barriers — many of them ages old — that kept our sex in a tightly circumscribed place.

In all the consciousness raising about women's past misfortunes, we have sometimes lost sight of the truly remarkable achievements of women throughout history. That's why one of this book's purposes is to spotlight successful women of today and yesterday: mothers and mathematicians, poets and politicians, actresses and athletes.

We're not making light of the obstacles every successful woman has encountered before reaching the top. Entertainer Dinah Shore, runner Wilma Rudolph, and author-reformer Helen Keller all triumphed over crippling childhood illnesses. Many grew up in poverty, among them singer Loretta Lynn, Congresswoman Shirley Chisholm, and feminist Gloria Steinem. Most encountered some form of sex discrimination; first lady Eleanor Roosevelt, artist Mary Cassatt, and choreographer Agnes De Mille, among others, even fought opposition within their own families. We'll let you in on some of their secrets of success.

But our book is not just about women who have already made names for themselves. Most of all, we're interested in the woman still on her way to the top: You!

What constitutes success for the modern woman? For most of us, the formula for personal fulfillment contains elements both old and new. We are excited — and occasionally a bit frightened — about the array of new opportunities opening up for our sex. At the same time, we welcome our traditional responsibilities to family and community. That's why we tell you about both finding a job and finding a pediatrician, buying cosmetics and buying stocks and bonds.

We hope these suggestions and the examples set by celebrated women will help make your future even brighter. As daring aviator Amelia Earhart insisted, "Women must try to do things as men have tried. When they fail, their failure must be but a challenge to others."

At the outset of this project, filling 576 pages with information about women seemed a difficult task. Time has taught us just how little can fit into a book this size. If we were unable to include one of your favorite women, let us know. We'll try our best to fit her into a subsequent edition.

Barbara McDowell
and Hana Umlauf,
editors

Health

FEMALE HEALTH

Many women know how important it is to compare and ask questions before making a decision about a new car, dress, or piece of furniture. But do most women know how to go about finding a good doctor?

Every woman should have a primary physician to take care of general health needs. This can be a general practitioner, family physician, or internist. This doctor will take a broad overview of your medical history and medical problems and serve as a focal point for all of your health care.

How to Choose a Good Doctor

If you don't already have such a doctor, how can you go about finding one?

Consult a relative or close friend who is in the medical profession. Medical students, pharmacists, dentists, and medical social workers might be able to help you out as well. You might also phone your local medical society, which will give you the names of several doctors who are willing to accept new patients. However, it should be cautioned that medical societies are mainly professional interest organiza-

tions for their members, and are not likely to give you any information that might cast a bad light on one of their members.

If you are searching for a specialist, you can ask your present doctor to refer you. If this is not feasible, you can phone the department head in that specialty at the nearest teaching hospital or medical school.

Today, more doctors are in group practices, consisting of several specialists. Many of these group practices can offer especially good medical care because of the close cooperation of their members.

Once you've got the name of a doctor or doctors, you can check credentials in the *Directory of Medical Specialists,* or a similar reference source. These should be available at your local library and some public ones.

Another element in your decision is whether you choose a man or woman physician. It appears that both men and women are often biased against women doctors. A 1974 study showed that only 17 percent of the women patients and only 5.6 percent of the men surveyed expressed a preference for a woman doctor. Maybe

Every woman needs a trusted primary physician to take care of her general health needs.

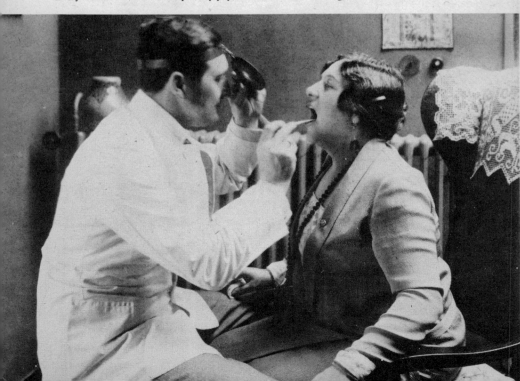

America's First Woman Doctor

Administrators of New York's Geneva College had a good laugh when they received an application to their medical school from a woman. They thought the joke so preposterous that they passed her application along to their students, who added to the hilarity by voting the woman into school.

Elizabeth Blackwell (1821-1910) knew nothing of the circumstances of her admission when she arrived at Geneva in November 1847. But she learned quickly that few at the school took her desire to become the nation's first woman physician seriously. She was barred from classroom demonstrations by teachers who thought it immoral for a woman to study the human body alongside men. She even tried starving herself, because she thought it would keep her from blushing during lectures on the reproductive organs. But so fascinated was Blackwell with her studies, that she managed to bear the torment, and her abilities, determination, and seriousness of purpose turned most of her tormentors into admirers.

She continued her studies in Europe, after graduating at the top of her Geneva class in 1849. Her dreams of becoming a surgeon were dashed when she contracted an eye disease from a patient and lost the sight of one eye. Returning to the United States, Blackwell encountered new discrimination: New York hospitals refused to hire her, colleagues ignored her, and

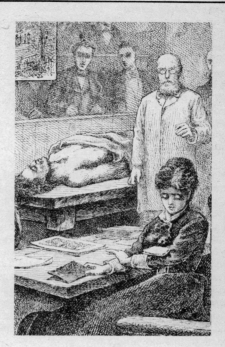

landlords even refused to rent her office space.

In 1853, she opened a small clinic in a tenement area, which eventually grew into the New York Infirmary for Women and Children. She was joined at the infirmary by her sister, Emily, a recent medical school graduate.

Blackwell founded her Woman's Medical College of the New York Infirmary in 1868, a high-quality institution that functioned until women were admitted to Cornell University Medical School in 1899. Blackwell settled in London in 1869, where she had a large, successful practice.

this will change as more women enter the medical profession. According to a recent survey of the deans of American medical schools, about 30 percent of the young doctors studying medicine in 1985 will be women — up from a total of 18 percent in 1975.

Don't wait until an emergency strikes to find a doctor. If you have regular checkups, your physician may be able to uncover some disorders before they even begin to cause you discomfort. Most doctors recommend a general physical and a gynecological examination once a year.

The Physical Exam

The general physical examination generally includes (1) **a medical history,** in which the doctor questions you about any previous illnesses, medications you are taking, and a history of cancer and other diseases in your family; (2) **a check of your overall physical condition,** including height, weight, blood pressure, a stethoscope examination of the heart and lungs, a check of reflexes, and examination of eyes, ears, throat, and nasal passages; and probably (3) several **laboratory tests,** including chest X ray, analysis of blood and urine, and electrocardiogram.

Any woman past puberty should have a gynecological examination once a year. This examination usually includes examination of the breasts and genital area. A woman who doesn't know how to examine her breasts should be taught how to do it, and urged to check them **once a month.**

In the "pelvic" examination, the woman lies on her back with her heels in "stirrups," letting her knees fall out to the sides as far as possible. There are three parts to this examination:

Gynecological exam procedures have changed immensely since the time this lithograph was made.

The external examination — which involves inspection of the labia, the clitoris, and the vaginal opening;

The speculum examination — The speculum is an instrument which holds open the walls of the vagina so the inside can be seen. The doctor inserts the speculum and examines the cervix and vagina. Then the doctor takes a Pap smear to test for uterine cancer.

The manual examination — The doctor inserts two surgically gloved fingers into the vagina, and with the other hand presses down on the lower abdomen. This allows him to feel the shape of the uterus and ovaries and to spot any lumps in the area.

Your Health Is Up To You

Regular checkups help monitor your health, but for the most part, your health is in your own hands. You should not smoke cigarettes, nor should you drink or use drugs other than prescribed medications. Exercise regularly and get proper nutrition.

Women have special nutrition needs. They need more iron than men because of blood loss during menstruation, and they also need an additional iron supply during lactation (secretion of milk from the mammary glands). Girls approaching puberty need extra iron too, because they are growing at a very rapid rate.

The Food and Nutrition Board of the National Research Council has set the Recommended Dietary Allowance of iron for women between the years of ten and fifty-five at eighteen milligrams daily. (After fifty-five, ten milligrams is sufficient). Foods that are high in iron content include liver, some kinds of shellfish, eggs, chocolate, enriched or whole-grain breads, dried fruits, and flour and cereals. Chronic iron deficiency can result in one kind of anemia, called iron-deficiency anemia.

The pregnant woman not only needs extra iron, but extra calcium, protein, and other nutrients as well. This is because she must not only feed herself but must help build her child's bones and tissues. For this reason every pregnant woman should be under the care of a doctor, who regulates her diet during pregnancy.

The Good Housekeeping Institute recommends that a woman include in her daily diet two- to three-ounce servings of meat or the equivalent of other protein-rich foods; four servings of whole grain or enriched breads or cereals; four servings of fruit and vegetables, including one citrus fruit and one green leafy or yellow vegetable; and two cups of milk — four for teenage girls — or the milk product equivalent. Women should consume about 2,000 calories a day; adolescent girls between 2,300 and 2,400.

Menstrual Disorders

Menstrual disorders are among the most common female problems. Here's a rundown on some prevalent ones:

Primary dysmenorrhea — This is characterized by severe cramps in the lower abdomen during menstruation. It is common in teenage girls, women in their early twenties, and single women in their thirties and forties, and is likely to disappear after the first pregnancy (no one is sure why). In more serious cases, it may be accompanied by nausea and vomiting. Treatment includes application of local heat with a hot water bottle or heating pad, massage of the abdomen, or aspirin. Check with your physician if these are not sufficient.

Premenstrual tension — This disorder usually appears several days before the onset of menstruation and is often characterized by pelvic congestion and bloating, a weight gain of up to five pounds, depression, irritability, lethargy, backaches, headaches, and nausea.

As with primary dysmenorrhea, the symptoms are probably due in part to changes in hormone levels during the monthly cycle. Water and salt retention are believed to cause the sense of "bloating" and weight gain, so regular exercise (which helps carry off excess body fluids through perspiration), a high-protein diet (which helps maintain the normal fluid balance of the body), and a salt-free diet (which helps prevent sodium retention) may relieve the symptoms.

Amenorrhea — There are two kinds of amenorrhea, *primary amenorrhea* and *secondary amenorrhea*. Primary amenorrhea is diagnosed when the female fails to have her first menstrual period by age 18. It can be caused by several factors including over-rigorous dieting, a genetic abnor-

mality, or by a form of hermaphroditism.

Secondary amenorrhea — or skipping one or more menstrual periods — is far more common. It may be caused by the onset of menopause, emotional upsets, crash diets, obesity, minor thyroid and adrenal disturbances, ovarian disorders, liver and kidney disease, or birth control pills. (The Pill suppresses the activity of hormones necessary for ovulation, and it may take the body several months after the cessation of Pill-taking to get those hormones going again.) If your period still has not come within six months after you stopped using the Pill, consult a doctor. In some cases, where the doctor suspects an emotional cause for this type of amenorrhea, he usually waits awhile before considering any medication to see if the emotional problems (and the secondary amenorrhea along with them) disappear.

Menorrhagia — or excessive menstruation, may be present when a woman finds she needs to use more than six to eight tampons or sanitary napkins per day during her menstrual period and/or has large blood clots in her menstrual flow. Heavy bleeding may be due to infection, inflammation or benign tumors, emotional upsets, use of the intrauterine device (IUD), organic malfunctioning, and glandular imbalances. If you have excessive bleeding, see your doctor.

Mittelschmerz, or pain at ovulation — At mid-cycle, when the egg bursts out of the ovary, some young women feel a sudden twinge of pain; others experience pain that lasts for a day or two. This is *mittelschmerz,* a disorder often confused with and misdiagnosed as appendicitis. Doctors usually don't treat *mittelschmerz* unless it is chronic and very painful.

Unusual Bleeding — A woman's menstrual flow generally becomes lighter and shorter as she approaches menopause. If yours becomes heavier and longer in duration at this time (approaching menopause), report this to your doctor. If you bleed **after** menopause (defined as six to twelve months with no period), report this to your doctor.

Any bleeding that differs from your normal pattern should be considered unusual. If unusual bleeding persists through two or three menstrual cycles, see your doctor.

Women sometimes bleed midway between periods, at about the time of ovulation, and some women using the Pill bleed between periods too. But bleeding between periods may mean trouble, so see your doctor.

For at least one or two years after the onset of menstruation, it is normal for girls to experience irregular menstrual periods, since it takes a while for the hormones which regulate the monthly cycle to settle into a pattern.

Vaginal Infections

The membranes that line the vagina normally secrete moisture and mucus. Usually this discharge is clear or milky and slippery. It may turn yellow when dry. But when it is accompanied by severe itching and burning of the vulva, or painful or frequent urination, a vaginal infection may be present. These infections can be caused by hormone pills, excessive douching, pregnancy, general lowered body resistance (from lack of sleep, bad eating habits, infection in another part of the body, for example), antibiotics, and diabetes. Two common causes of vaginal infections are: *Trichomonas vaginalis (trich, TV, trichomoniasis)*.

Public health experts estimate that between 75 and 90 percent of all women will develop this infection at some point in their lives. It is the work of a one-celled parasite called *trichmonas vaginalis* that can be found in men and women, and is usually transmitted during genital-to-genital contact. Its home is in the vagina or in the male's urinary tract.

Its main symptom is a thick yellowish-green or gray discharge that often has a foul odor. Burning and itching of the vagina and vulva are also common symptoms. Only a few men have symptoms. If they do, it is usually a burning feeling after urination or ejaculation.

One effective treatment is a prescription drug taken orally called metronidazole (Flagyl), which, if taken as directed, cures 95 percent of the women suffering from this infection. However, women should consult closely with their doctors before taking this drug, since certain experiments on bacteria indicate that use of the drug may entail certain risks. The woman's sexual partner should also be treated for *trichomonas vaginalis* to prevent cross-infection.

Candida vaginalis (candidiasis, moniliasis, vaginal thrush, yeast infection, fungus): This infection is caused by a yeastlike fungus called *candida albicans*. Four out of ten women have this fungus in their vagina, but only under certain conditions will it reproduce itself rapidly enough to cause the symptoms of vaginal infection. These symptoms include intense itching, burning, and swelling. These may be accompanied by inflammation of the vulva, and a thick discharge with the odor of yeast.

This infection is most common among pregnant women, as increased estrogen levels during pregnancy cause larger than usual amounts of sugar to be stored in the cells of the vaginal walls. This "excess sugar" provides the fungus with the food supply needed for rapid growth. The estrogens in birth control pills have the same effect, as does diabetes. Antibiotics can help the fungus to proliferate, because these drugs often kill bacteria in the vagina that might otherwise have checked the fungus' growth.

Candida vaginalis can also strike when the body's resistance has been lowered through fatigue, emotional problems, or bad eating habits. The infection usually is treated with antifungicidal suppositories or cream.

Trichomonas vaginalis and *candida vaginalis* are two kinds of "specific vaginitis" — that is they are caused by a number of readily identifiable organisms. There are, however, some "nonspecific" forms of vaginitis, meaning that there is no known physical or biological cause for the infection.

Cervicitis

Cervicitis is one of the most common disorders of the female reproductive tract — at least 60 to 75 percent of all women suffer from it at some point in their lives. Cervicitis is an inflammation of the cervix, the neck of the uterus. It usually is not a serious condition, but if not treated, can cause infertility, painful or difficult intercourse, and other problems.

It can be caused by a number of things — among them childbirth, general lowered body resistance due to glandular disorders or vitamin deficiencies, poor hygiene, other diseases (like gonorrhea), and possibly birth control pills. It can also develop as a secondary inflammation to *trichomonas vaginalis* and *candida vaginalis*.

Symptoms may not be present, but if they are, they may include an irritating whitish or yellowish discharge, low back pain, pain during intercourse or menstruation, slight fever, burning sensation during urination, and heavy bleeding or spotting between menstrual periods or after intercourse.

Don't worry if you notice a slight increase in a vaginal discharge before and after menstruation or during ovulation (at mid-cycle) — that's perfectly normal. But when this discharge is **continual and irritating,** a doctor should be consulted. Any unusual bleeding, of course, should be reported immediately to your doctor.

Cystitis

Many women suffer from cystitis, or bacterial infection of the bladder. Bacteria enter the bladder from the kidneys, bloodstream, digestive tract, or through the urethra. Ten times as many women as men get cystitis because the female urethra is shorter than the male's and is located close to the vaginal and rectal openings. It is therefore relatively easy for bacteria to travel from the vaginal and rectal areas into the urethra, and up into the bladder.

Symptoms of cystitis include blood and/or pus in the urine and painful and frequent urination. Although you may feel the urge to urinate often, there probably will be very little urine in your bladder. Milder symptoms may include a feeling or discomfort low in the abdomen or a sensation of pressure or heaviness in the groin.

Cystitis usually can be treated successfully by the physician. If it is allowed to persist for a long time, many doctors think serious kidney disease can result.

Good preventive measures are to drink lots of fluids, and to urinate whenever you feel the need. These two measures help wash harmful bacteria out of the bladder.

Venereal Disease

"Venereal disease" (VD) is a term used to describe a group of diseases that are

A fashionable physician of the 18th century takes a female patient's pulse rate.

passed on by sexual contact. They are usually spread through contact of the genitalia during intercourse, but may also be transmitted by kissing or touching the infected area.

VD has been around a long time. The Old Testament makes many references to it. Notables who have suffered from VD include Caesar and Cleopatra, Catherine the Great of Russia, Napoleon, Oscar Wilde, John Keats, and Vincent Van Gogh.

Today venereal diseases are spreading at epidemic rates in the United States. Two of the main venereal diseases are *syphilis* and *gonorrhea*.

Gonorrhea is basically a disease of the linings of the genito-urinary organs and can cause arthritis, sterility, and blindness. If a pregnant woman has gonorrhea, she can pass it to her child during delivery. This can cause blindness in the child.

Gonorrhea is basically a disease of the linings of the genito-urinary organs and can cause arthritis, sterility, and blindness. If a pregnant woman has gonorrhea, she can pass it to her child during delivery. This can cause blindness in the child.

Gonorrhea is especially dangerous to women, because 80 percent of the women who have gonorrhea show no symptoms. If symptoms do appear in the woman they may include painful urination and a slight vaginal discharge. Symptoms of this disease are far more likely to appear in the male, and they are more acute. Urination can be very painful, and there is a thick, milky discharge from the penis.

Anyone who has had gonorrhea should notify all persons with whom he or she has had sexual contact during the month or two prior to the diagnosis.

Doctors diagnose gonorrhea by examining the sexual organs and taking a swab from the discharge of the penis, or cervix and urethra, for laboratory examination.

The usual treatment for gonorrhea is penicillin or tetracycline. Once cured of gonorrhea, the patient is *not* immune.

Syphilis

Syphilis is more dangerous than gonorrhea. It can cause damage to any of the vital organs, cause lesions of the skin, and inflammation of the bones, invade joints, eyes, and especially the brain and cardiovascular system. It can even be fatal if it remains untreated for a long period of time. The untreated pregnant woman can give syphilis to her unborn child.

The first symptom of syphilis, the chancre sore, appears between nine and ninety days after initial exposure. It generally appears at the point where the disease's harmful bacteria entered the bloodstream — usually the genitals. It is painless and resembles a cold sore. Only 10 percent of the women who have this sore notice it, as it is often hidden within the labia (lips of the vagina). The sore can also appear on the fingertips, lips, breast, anus, or mouth. It usually disappears within three or four weeks without treatment.

Syphilis then advances into its second stage. Anywhere from a week to six months later, a rash appears — all over the body, or just on the palms of the hands and soles of the feet — accompanied by mild fever and headache. If untreated at this stage, syphilis enters its third or "latent" stage, where there are *no* outward symptoms. The latent stage may last ten to twenty years, during which the bacteria invade the inner organs, including the heart and brain. After the first few years of the latent stage, the disease is not likely to be spread to others.

Syphilis is fairly easily detected by a blood test, and is treated generally by penicillin, or a substitute like tetracycline for those allergic to penicillin. The disease can be arrested at any stage with treatment, but its damage cannot be undone.

Herpes Genitalis (Herpes Type 2)

Also common in the United States is herpes genitalis, or herpes type 2, closely related to the common cold sore (herpes type 1). Its first symptom usually is a painful, blister-like sore which appears on the genital organs. This may be accompanied by fever, headaches, itching, swelling of the lymph nodes, and general weakness. Although medication may help relieve visible symptoms, the virus can lie dormant in the body with symptoms reemerging every couple of weeks for many years. The disease has been linked to cervical cancer and can seriously harm newborn babies.

Like syphilis and gonorrhea, it is transmitted primarily through sexual contact. There are not yet any safe and effective treatments for genital herpes infections.

Endometriosis

The endometrium is the membrane which normally lines the inner surface of the uterus. Sometimes, however, the cells of the endometrium grow in parts of the body other than the uterus. This disorder is known as endometriosis.

The most common symptoms are pain at the time of menstruation, pain during intercourse, heavy menstrual bleeding, bleeding from the rectum, and severe backache. In some women, these symptoms may manifest themselves only during the menstrual periods; in others, the symptoms will crop up two to three weeks before the menstrual period and continue right through it.

It occurs most frequently in women aged 25 to 45, and most often in childless women. Infertility can result, as the endometrial tissue can attach itself to reproductive organs.

Treatment used to consist mainly of surgery, but recently more and more doctors have begun to use drug therapy.

Breast Cancer

Breast cancer occurs more often than any other form of cancer in women in the United States. There will be an estimated 89,700 new cases in 1977 alone. It is also the biggest cancer killer among women — an estimated 34,000 women will die from it in 1977, according to the American Cancer Society.

Breast cancer can strike at any age, but it usually affects women over thirty-five. It is the leading cause of death for women aged thirty-seven to fifty-five. The average woman in the United States faces a 7 percent chance of developing breast cancer.

Some famous victims of breast cancer are Shirley Temple Black, Julia Child, Betty Ford, "Happy" Rockefeller, Marvella Bayh, wife of Indiana Senator Birch Bayh, and Alice Roosevelt Longworth, daughter of Theodore Roosevelt.

When breast cancer is diagnosed early and treated promptly, it can be cured up to 85 percent of the time. (A "cure" is defined by the American Cancer Society as an absence of symptoms five years after initial diagnosis and treatment of the dis-

ease.) For this reason it is essential that women examine their breasts regularly — once a month. In fact, most cancerous breast lumps are found by women themselves, not their doctors.

Women should check their breasts a week after the menstrual period. After menopause, check your breasts on the first day of each month. If you have had a hysterectomy, check with your doctor or clinic for the appropriate time of the month to check your breasts.

Here are directions from the American Cancer Society on how to practice breast self-examination:

(1) In the shower or bath: Examine your breasts. Your hands will glide easily over wet skin. Fingers flat, move gently over every part of each breast. Use your right hand to examine the left breast, the left hand to examine the right. Check for any **lump, hard knot,** or **thickening.**

(2) Before a Mirror: Inspect your breasts with arms at your sides. Next, raise your arms high overhead. Look for any changes in contour of each breast — a **swelling, dimpling of the skin, or changes in the nipple.** Then, rest palms on hips and press

American Cancer Society advises women to follow this 3-step breast exam procedure monthly.

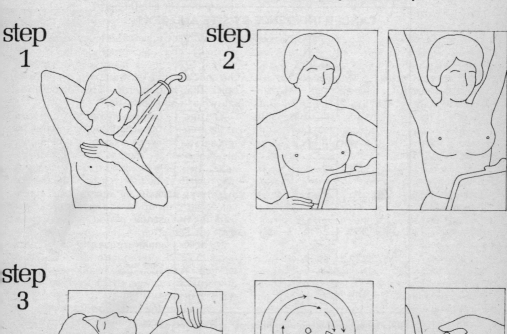

step 1

step 2

step 3

down firmly to flex your chest muscles. Left and right breast will not exactly match — few women's breasts do. Regular inspection shows what is normal for you and will give you confidence in your examination.

(3) Lying Down: To examine your right breast, put a pillow or folded towel under your right shoulder. Place right hand behind your head — this distributes breast tissue more evenly on the chest. With the left hand, fingers flat, at the outermost top of your right breast, make small circular motions all the way around the outer edge of the breast until you reach the top again, pressing gently all the while. (Don't panic if you find a ridge of firm tissue in the lower curve of each breast — it's normal. Then move in an inch toward the nipple and repeat the procedure. You will probably have to circle your breast three additional times so that every part — including the nipple — is examined. Now slowly repeat the whole procedure on your left breast with a pillow under your left shoulder and your left hand behind your head. The whole time, take note of how your breast structure feels.

Finally, squeeze the nipple of each breast gently between the thumb and index finger. Any **discharge, clear or bloody,** should be reported to your doctor immediately. **You are your own best protector against breast cancer. Learn how to examine your breasts today and do it regularly — once a month. This simple procedure could save your life.**

If you discover a lump, a dimple, or a discharge, see your doctor *immediately*. Don't panic. Most breast lumps or changes aren't cancerous, **but only your doctor can make the diagnosis.** Your doctor will perform a biopsy to see if the lump is cancerous. Between 65 and 80 percent of these lumps turn out to be benign, according to the American Cancer Society. A biopsy should be performed and results carefully explained to you before any treatment decision is made.

Breast cancers are not all the same. Increasingly they require individual kinds of treatment. More and more, combined treatments — involving surgery, drug therapy or chemotherapy, and radiation are being used.

The standard surgical treatment for

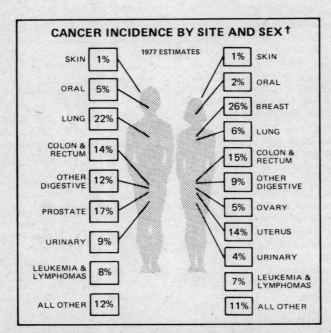

CANCER INCIDENCE BY SITE AND SEX †

1977 ESTIMATES

Male		Female	
SKIN	1%	1%	SKIN
ORAL	5%	2%	ORAL
		26%	BREAST
LUNG	22%	6%	LUNG
COLON & RECTUM	14%	15%	COLON & RECTUM
OTHER DIGESTIVE	12%	9%	OTHER DIGESTIVE
PROSTATE	17%	5%	OVARY
		14%	UTERUS
URINARY	9%	4%	URINARY
LEUKEMIA & LYMPHOMAS	8%	7%	LEUKEMIA & LYMPHOMAS
ALL OTHER	12%	11%	ALL OTHER

† Excluding non-melanoma skin cancer and carcinoma in situ of uterine cervix.

breast cancer has been the radical mastectomy, an operation in which the surgeon removes not only the breast but also other tissue that may have been invaded by cancerous cells: the pectoral muscles which support the breast and the lymph nodes in the armpit. In more serious cases, the internal mammary lymph nodes may also be removed. This operation results in lifelong weakness and periodic swelling of the arm. Much opposition has been voiced in recent years to radical mastectomy — some of it from feminists who say such operations are performed by male doctors who have difficulty fully comprehending the psychological (and physical) trauma some mastectomees suffer. In certain cases, some doctors do advocate less radical surgery — like the *modified radical mastectomy,* which removes the breast and lymph nodes in the armpit, but not the pectoral muscles.

A report released in late 1974 by the National Cancer Institute (NCI) suggested that in certain cases, where the cancer has not spread to the lymph nodes, *total mastectomy* — removal of the breast and no other tissue — may be just as effective as radical surgery.

Some doctors have advocated even less radical surgery — like *lumpectomy,* which removes only the cancerous lump with or without a small amount of surrounding breast tissue or overlying skin; and *partial mastectomy,* which removes the cancerous lump in addition to at least an inch of surrounding tissue, the overlying skin and underlying fascia (connective tissue covering the muscle).

But there has been very limited professional support for operations which remove only part of the breast. The American Cancer Society, for example, has issued an official statement which says, in part: "1) Removal of the entire breast (most often radical or modified radical mastectomy) is recommended for the surgical treatment of operable breast cancer. 2) Limited surgical procedures which remove less than the entire breast have not been scientifically proven to be as effective as mastectomy."

There are marked differences in survival rates between women who have had partial mastectomies and those who have had radicals. Among the 53 women who underwent partial mastectomies over a nine-year period at the Cleveland Clinic in Ohio, for example, only 18, or 34 percent survived ten years. Of the 304 who underwent radical mastectomies in 1960 at New York's Memorial Sloan-Kettering Cancer Center, 185, or 61 percent were still alive ten years later.

The woman who has undergone breast surgery need not be alone. Reach to Recovery, a program begun by the American Cancer Society in 1969, sends volunteers to visit mastectomees in the hospital. These volunteers – mastectomees themselves — comfort the patient, teach her exercises to strengthen the arm and shoulder affected by the operation, and give advice about where the patient can buy breast prostheses and clothing she may need. Consult the branch office of the American Cancer Society in your area for the address of the Reach to Recovery Program nearest you.

Uterine Cancer

There are two kinds of uterine cancer — cancer of the cervix and cancer of the body of the uterus.

Cancer of The Cervix

One of the symptoms of cervical cancer is bleeding between periods. This may be due to menopause, benign polyps, fibroids, or other minor problems. **But let your doctor decide that. Report any unusual bleeding.**

The Pap smear is 95 percent effective in detecting cervical cancer. Pap is short for Papanicolaou, the name of the doctor who developed the test. Don't panic if your Pap smear result is positive. This simply means that some abnormal cells — not necessarily cancerous ones — are present. Remember, there are five classes of Pap smear results, and **only** class 5 reveals definite malignancy. Abnormal cell growth in the other classes may be due to cervical infection, irritation, or inflammation, among other things. If you have a class 5 Pap smear; i.e., if cancerous cells are found, surgical treatment may consist of removal of a cone of tissue *(conization)* from the cervix. If the cancer is more advanced, surgical removal of the uterus — *hysterectomy* — is usually performed. There are basically three kinds of hysterectomy.

Free Cancer Hotlines

There are a number of cancer hotlines throughout the nation. The telephones are answered by trained volunteers who have access to medical consultants and source material about various types of cancer, substances that cause cancer, pain killers, diagnosis, detection, and treatment of cancer. They can also refer you to the best center for care in your area.

Most of the hotlines operate between 9 a.m. and 5 p.m., but if you call outside those hours you will be referred to the backup inquiry system at the National Cancer Institute. All calls to the cancer hotlines are treated as confidential and the anonymity of callers is guaranteed.

Here are the numbers of some of the cancer information services — they are accessible, toll free, to more than 120 million Americans. All the 800 numbers are toll free *for the areas listed.* Other numbers can be reached from any location at the usual long distance rates.

Duke University Comprehensive Cancer Center, in North Carolina, 800-672-0943; 919-286-2266.

Fox Chase and University of Pennsylvania Cancer Center, within Pennsylvania, 800-822-3963; from out-of-state, 800-523-3586; 215-728-2700.

Colorado Regional Cancer Center, in Colorado, 800-332-1850; 303-333-1516.

Comprehensive Cancer Center for the State of Florida, in Florida, 800-432-5953; 305-547-6920.

Howard University, Cancer Communications for Metropolitan Washington, 202-232-2833.

Illinois Cancer Council, in Illinois, 800-972-0586; 312-346-9813.

Johns Hopkins Cancer Center, in Maryland, 800-492-1444; from Pennsylvania and West Virginia, 800-638-1415; 301-955-3636.

Minnesota Cancer Council, in Minnesota, 800-582-5262; 507-282-2511, ext. 8285.

Memorial Sloan-Kettering Cancer Center, in New York City, 212-794-7982.

Roswell Park Memorial Institute, in New York State, 800-462-7255; in Erie County, 716-845-4400; 716-845-4402.

Sidney Farber Cancer Center, in Massachusetts, 800-952-7420; 617-732-3152.

University of Southern California Cancer Center, in California, 800-252-9066; 213-226-2371.

University of Texas System Cancer Center, in Texas, 800-392-2040; in Greater Houston area, 713-792-3245.

University of Wisconsin, in Wisconsin, 800-362-8038, 608-262-0046.

Yale University, in Connecticut, 800-922-0824; 203-436-3779.

University of Alabama, Birmingham, 205-934-2651 or 934-2659.

Fred Hutchinson Cancer Research Center, Seattle, 206-292-6301.

In the partial hysterectomy, the uterus, but not the cervix, is removed. In the *complete hysterectomy,* both uterus and cervix are removed. *Radical total hysterectomy* involves removal of both uterus and cervix as well as the upper portion of the vagina.

Cancer of the body of the uterus

Seventy-five percent of the cases of cancer of the body of the uterus start after menopause. This type of cancer can cause all of the symptoms cited above, but the most common symptom by far is some form of abnormal menstrual bleeding.

Menopause is said to begin when six to twelve months have passed without a period. To be on the safe side, any bleeding after full menopause should be checked by your doctor immediately. It is particularly important to be on your guard for cancer symptoms because the routine Pap Smear (done during your annual gynecological exam) is less effective in detecting cancer of the body of the uterus, than it is in detecting cervical cancer. Treatment may be, either hysterectomy alone, or in combination with radiation therapy.

Cancer of the Ovaries, Vulva, Vagina, and Fallopian Tubes

Cancer of the ovaries can strike at any age, but it is most frequent in postmenopausal women. This is one of the most difficult female cancers to detect in its early stages, according to some doctors. Because the ovaries are located deep in the pelvic cavity, the doctor usually can find a growth only by feeling the ovaries during a regular gynecological checkup. As the cancerous growth gets bigger, a woman may feel a sensation of pressure or "fullness" in the lower abdomen. All of this should be reported to a doctor immediately. (The cause of these symptoms may *also* be benign cysts on the ovaries.)

Several other kinds of cancer peculiar to women are cancer of the vulva, vagina, and Fallopian tubes — although they occur more rarely than cancer of the ovaries. Women who notice a lump or sore at the vaginal entrance should report this to their doctor. But don't wait for symptoms to appear. The best way to protect yourself is to have a gynecological checkup annually.

Follow the American Cancer Society's advice — know cancer's warning signals:

—Change in the bowel or bladder habits

—A sore that does not heal

—Unusual bleeding or discharge

—Thickening or lump in breast or elsewhere

—Indigestion or difficulty in swallowing

—Obvious change in wart or mole

—Nagging cough or hoarseness

If you have a warning signal, see your doctor.

REPRODUCTIVE FREEDOM

A woman's internal sexual organs, the ovaries, are located several inches on either side of the midway point between vagina and navel. When a baby girl comes into the world her ovaries already contain about a half million immature eggs. By the time the girl reaches puberty the number has shrunk to about 30,000. Only a few hundred of them will be capable of fertilization.

From puberty on, once a month one of these tiny eggs reaches maturity and bursts free. This is the process of ovulation; it occurs in alternate ovaries, and usually halfway through the monthly menstrual cycle, about 14 days before the period begins. The brief time during which ovulation occurs lasts only about twenty-four hours. This is the so-called fertile period. It is the time a woman is most likely to conceive.

When the egg — even in its smallness, it is the largest cell in the human body — bursts free from the ovary, it floats into the abdominal cavity. It floats toward the mouth of one of the Fallopian tubes which connect the ovaries to the womb or uterus, a hollow, pear-shaped muscular organ. The diameter of each Fallopian tube is no greater than that of a human hair, but more often than not the egg is wafted into one of them. If the egg is going to be fertilized, it most probably will happen here.

Whether or not the egg is fertilized by the penetration of a sperm, the womb prepares itself each month to receive a growing embryo. During the third week of the menstrual cycle, the lining of the womb grows spongy, thick and rich in tiny blood vessels preparing to nourish a growing embryo, should it arrive. if no embryo is forthcoming, the thickened, blood-rich wall of the womb decays, and is passed out as menstruation.

Contraception

Before discussing specific types of contraception, it is worth making a few general points:

—Estimates of effectiveness of most birth control methods will vary according to the study. We are using the official figures from the Planned Parenthood Federation of America.

—There are two basic kinds of "effec-

GUIDE TO BIRTH CONTROL

METHOD	FAILURES PER YEAR PER 100 WOMEN	COST	ACTION REQUIRED AT TIME OF COITUS
Diaphragm with spermicidal cream or jelly	*Method failures: 2 to 4 **User failures: 10 to 20	Exam: $20 to $65 privately, less at clinic. Diaphragm: $3 to $7.50 and cream or jelly is $3 to $5 monthly.	May be inserted up to 6 hours before coitus (Jelly—not more than 2 hours)
Condom	Method failures: 2 to 4 User failures: 10 to 20	Approximately $1 per package of three plain condoms	Interruption of foreplay
Foam	Method failures: 2 to 4 User failures: 10 to 20	$3 to $5 per month	May be used not more than an hour before coitus
Creams, jellies, suppositories, tablets	Method failures: 10 to 15 User failures: 15 to 30	$3 to $5 per month	Insert not more than 15 minutes before coitus. Tablets and suppositories require brief waiting period
Temperature rhythm	Method failures: 2 to 4 User failures: 20 to 30	Ovulation thermometer costs about $5	None
Calendar rhythm	Mehtod failures: 5 to 10 User failures: 20 to 30	None	None
Cervical (vaginal)-mucus rhythm	Method failures: 5 to 10 User failures: 20 to 30	None	None
Withdrawal	Method failures: 10 to 15 User failures: 15 to 30	None	Interruption before ejaculation
Female or tubal sterilization	Virtually 100 percent effective	$250 to $500 plus hospital stay, if any. Health clinics adjust fees to income	None
Vasectomy	Virtually 100 percent effective after two to three months or 10 to 15 ejaculations after the operation	$75 to $175. Clinics adjust fees to income	None
Oral contraceptive (includes mini-pill, but it is less effective).	Almost 100 percent effective if taken as directed. Method: less than 1 (conventional) and 2 to 3 (mini-pill). User failures: 2 to 4.	About $2 to $3.50 a month; less at clinics.	None
IUD (Intra-uterine devices).	Method failures: 2 to 4. User failures: None, but such device failures as expulsions can be detected early by user regular checking.	Exam, insertion and follow-up visit. Range from $20 to $65 from private doctor.	None

*Method failure means a pregnancy resulting from failure of the contraceptive itself.
**User failure means a pregnancy resulting from failure of the woman (or man) to use the method or device properly.

NEED FOR MEDICAL SERVICES	UNSUITABILITY FOR SOME WOMEN	SIDE EFFECTS OR RISK FACTORS
Yes, initial exam and yearly checkup. Instruction to learn insertion technique	Infrequent medical reasons determined by doctor	Rare instances of allergic reactions, vaginal irritation or vaginal or urinary infection
No	No	Rare allergic reactions to rubber
No	No	Rare allergic reactions
No	No	Rare allergic reactions
Instruction to learn interpretation of temperature chart	Not for women with grossly irregular menstrual periods	None
Instruction to learn computation of "safe" and "unsafe" days	Not for women with grossly irregular menstrual periods	None
Careful instructions needed	Should not be used if infection is present, if drugs are taken or if contraceptive creams or foams are used	None
No	Cannot be used if partner cannot control ejaculation	Possible psychological disturbances
Yes, hospitalization or outpatient surgery center	Not reversible	Recuperative period. Risk associated with any surgery and anesthesia
Yes, minor surgery. Follow-up tests are necessary until no sperm are found	Not reversible	Temporary scrotal swelling; soreness or discomfort. Very rare risk associated with this procedure
Yes, exam and prescription. Regimen instruction. Regular checkups.	Not for women over 40 who smoke heavily or who have diabetes, high blood pressure or blood clots, vein inflammation, serious liver disease or unexplained vaginal bleeding, or certain other medical conditions to be explained by a doctor.	Irregular spotting, nausea or vomiting, weight gain, breast tenderness, bloating, headaches, mood fluctuation, depression. Risk factors: Abnormal sugar metabolism, changes in blood chemistry, high blood pressure. *Rare:* thromboembolic disorders including blood clots in legs, lung, heart, liver or brain; heart attack and stroke, liver tumor.
Yes, exam (and fitting, initially) and annual checkup.	Not for women with pelvic infection, heavy menstrual bleeding, bleeding between periods, cancer or possible malignancy, severe menstrual cramps, venereal disease.	Irregular or excessive bleeding, discomfort or pain from uterine cramps or low backache; chance of miscarriage or serious infection if pregnancy occurs with IUD in place; *rare*, pelvic inflammation, disease which may result in infertility, perforation of the uterus.

NOTE: With the exception of the following, none of the methods described reduce opportunity for coitus. Temperature rhythm: Coitus limited to about 13 days per menstrual cycle. Calendar rhythm: Coitus limited to 5 to 15 days, depending on menstrual cycle. Cervical (vaginal)- rhythm: Coitus limited to about 10 days per menstrual cycle.

Birth Control Pioneer

Working as a nurse in New York's Lower East Side tenement district, **Margaret Sanger** (1883-1966) met women who were already old at age thirty-five from bearing and raising many children in poverty. She nursed one such woman back to health from a near- fatal, self-inflicted abortion, only to see her die following a second such operation. The woman's doctor had refused her any protection against another pregnancy; "Tell Jake to sleep on the roof," was the only help he offered.

"I came to a sudden realization," recalled Sanger, after the 1912 incident, "that my work as a nurse and my activities in social service were . . . futile and useless to relieve the misery I saw all about me." She learned all she could about contraception, and founded a magazine, *Woman Rebel,* to spread the word in 1914. Sanger was arrested soon after under New York's Comstock law, which made it a crime to offer contraceptive information. The indictment was eventually quashed, and the case publicized the issue of birth control through the world. (Sanger herself had coined that term in 1914, in founding the National Birth Control League. That organization, and the American Birth Control League she founded later in her career, joined forces in 1939. They were renamed Planned Parenthood Federation of

America two years later.)

In 1916, Sanger opened the nation's first birth control clinic in Brooklyn. The office functioned only nine days before it was closed by police and Sanger was carted off to jail. She appealed that action, winning an important court decision that allowed doctors to prescribe contraceptives.

Sanger remained in the forefront of the birth control movement for most of the rest of her life. Though shy in her youth, hers became a forceful voice. Policemen were said to blush at the Irish invective that issued from her mouth upon being arrested. Sanger was married twice and had two sons.

tiveness" in contraceptives. First is "theoretical effectiveness," which is the effectiveness of the birth control method if used properly before every instance of intercourse. "Actual effectiveness" takes into consideration the possibility of human error, for example, the woman who forgets to take birth control pills, or the couple that decides that "just this once" they can do without use of a condom or diaphragm. Thus a couple must decide which method of contraception they are going to use *consistently,* since this, obviously, is a major factor.

Abstinence

Abstinence from sexual intercourse is the surest method of birth control. It is 100 percent effective. If there is no meeting between sperm and egg, pregnancy cannot possibly take place. All forms of contraception attempt to place either a chemial or physical barrier between the sperm and egg. Only abstinence never fails. Just one lapse, however, could defeat the purpose of this method of contraception.

Periodic abstinence, or rhythm, is a birth control method used by many Roman Catholic couples, since it is the only method of birth control fully approved by their church. Even when adhered to carefully, the rhythm method often fails.

If a woman decides to use this method of contraception, her physician can help her calculate the days that are supposedly "safe" and those that are not. This method is based on the theory that an egg is released from a normal woman's ovaries regularly, and that "unsafe for sex" days would fall from two to four days before ovulation to several days after ovulation.

In order to determine the day of ovulation in her cycle, a woman must keep a written record of the first days of her menstrual periods for eight to twelve months. This is the calendar system. The doctor may also ask the woman to keep a record of her body temperature, since this is another indication of the day of ovulation.

Even when followed faithfully, periodic abstinence fails 5 to 10 percent of the time. Its actual failure rate among users is 20 to 30 percent. In spite of all the record-keeping, ovulation may not always follow a set pattern. It sometimes occurs during the period when a woman believes she is "safe."

The Pill

Next to abstinence, the Pill is the most effective method of birth control now known. The most commonly used oral contraceptive pill, the combination pill, has a theoretical failure rate of less than 1 percent. Its actual failure rate is 2 to 4 percent, mainly because women forget to take it.

The Pill works in much the same way as a woman's hormones do during pregnancy, when estrogen and progesterone inhibit the chemical messages which cause the ripening and release of an egg. Thus the oral contraceptive pill suppresses ovulation. With no egg to fertilize, conception cannot occur.

The combination oral contraceptive contains both estrogen and progesterone. The first pill is taken on day 5 of a normal menstrual cycle, counting the first day of bleeding as day 1. Usually the pill is taken for twenty-one days, with seven days off.

Two days after the woman has taken the last pill of the cycle, a period of bleeding, similar to menstruation, begins. On day 5 of that period, the woman should resume taking the pills.

Since some women find it more convenient to take a pill **every** day, a twenty-eight-pill package is available, but seven of those pills are "blanks," that is they are inert and serve no contraceptive purpose.

One month's supply of pills costs about three dollars. The pills must be prescribed by a physician, since there are a number of different types available.

The biggest advantage of the Pill is that it has a near-perfect capacity to prevent pregnancy, provided it is taken as directed. It also allows the couple to have sex spontaneously.

Oral contraceptives also have disadvantages. Side effects occur in some women. Sometimes they are minor; at other times they may be more serious. Some women experience nausea and fatigue during the first month or two of taking oral contraceptives. A few women experience persistent side effects, which may include migraine headaches, weight gain, or blood clots, which have been disabling and even fatal. However, there is no conclusive evidence linking use of the oral contraceptive to any form of cancer.

Nevertheless, women who use the oral contraceptive pill — especially women older than forty — run an increased risk of heart attacks and liver tumors which may cause severe bleeding. Recent studies have also found that smoking cigarettes severely compounds the dangers of the birth control pill, and **for women older than thirty who smoke heavily,** the birth control pill is more dangerous than any other method of contraception.

The IUD

The intrauterine device — or IUD — is an effective and popular birth control method. Its theoretical failure rate is 2 to 4 percent; its actual failure rate is slightly higher. About 15 million women throughout the world currently use IUDs.

IUDs come in a variety of shapes, from tiny loops to coils, rings, and spirals.

The devices are inserted in the uterus by a physician, and the IUD remains there until a woman is ready to get pregnant and has it removed. Most of the IUDs are made of flexible plastic, but some also have copper wire wrapped around them.

With the IUD there are rarely serious side effects, it remains in place at all times, and no special act of insertion or application is necessary.

About 20 percent of the women who have had an IUD inserted cannot keep it, either because it is expelled or it makes the woman uncomfortable. Sometimes a woman feels cramps for a few hours after the IUD is inserted. But a woman should **never** attempt to remove an IUD herself.

Another rare problem with the IUD is the possibility that it might perforate the walls of the uterus. There have also been reported infections with certain types of IUDs, but the particular IUDs in question have been removed from the market by the Food and Drug Administration.

The Diaphragm

If it is used properly, the diaphragm can also be a very effective method of birth control. It is widely used by women who are concerned about the unpleasant side effects or health risks of the oral contraceptive or IUD.

If used correctly, the diaphragm has a failure rate of 2 to 4 percent. Unfortunately, many women don't use it correctly, and its actual failure rate can be as high as 20 percent.

The diaphragm itself is a circle of thin rubber stretched over a flexible ring. It is designed to fit over the woman's cervix, thus providing a physical barrier to the entrance of sperm. The diaphragm **must** be used with spermicidal cream or jelly, which kill the sperm on contact. The **combination** of a physical and chemical barrier makes this method of contraception highly effective when properly used.

A diaphragm must be fitted by a physician, since every woman is built differently. The doctor will show women how to insert and remove the diaphragm. The cost of an examination and fitting ranges up to fifty dollars, and the diaphragm itself costs about seven and a half dollars.

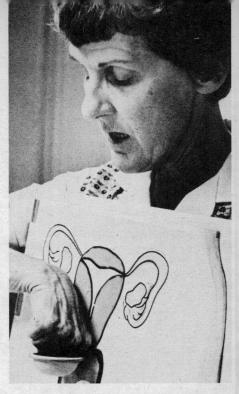

Planned Parenthood worker displays a diaphragm, an effective contraceptive posing few health risks.

The diaphragm can be inserted up to six hours before intercourse, but if intercourse takes place longer than two hours after insertion, additional spermicidal jelly or cream will be needed. The diaphragm should not be removed sooner than six to eight hours after the end of intercourse.

Effectiveness of the diaphragm can be increased to a near-perfect level if the woman's partner uses a condom.

The Condom

Also known as the "rubber," "prophylactic," or "safe," the condom is a sheath made of thin, strong latex rubber or animal membrane. The male slips this over the penis when it is erect, leaving a reservoir at the tip which catches sperm and prevents it from entering the vagina and uterus.

The condom *must* be used before intercourse, since even before a man ejaculates he can release sperm cells which can get into the vagina.

Care must also be taken that the condom does not slip off. This occurs most frequently if the covered penis is not removed from the vagina before erection is

Ten Birth Control Methods of the Past (None Recommended)

1. The Chinese were among the first to come up with a recipe for an oral contraceptive. The *I Ching*, which appeared about 2700 B.C., advised women seeking to avoid pregnancy to: "Take some quicksilver. Fry it for a whole day in oil, take a piece about the size of a lozenge and swallow it on an empty stomach."
2. Chinese prostitures of the same period were urged to drink lead each month to guard against conception!
3. Later, Chinese philosophers believed that women could prevent pregnancy by controlling their passion. Advice offered in 1100 B.C. told women to "draw a deep breath and think of other things" at the moment of ejaculation.
4. A contraceptive method favored by the Egyptians involved inserting a mixture of crocodile dung and honey into the vagina. The goo might well have worked by providing a barrier to sperm.
5. A mixture of honey, oily cedarwood, and pomegranate or fig pulp was prescribed by the Greek physician, Soranus, as a vaginal suppository to forestall conception.
6. Another Greek physician, Aetius, suggested in the sixth century A.D. that women protect themselves by cutting a pomegranate in half, emptying it, and inserting the cup-like gourd into the vagina before intercourse.
7. Women of ancient India sought to keep sperm and egg separated by stuffing their vaginas with bunches of feathers.
8. Many ancient people inserted a sponge into the woman's vagina before intercourse to absorb sperm. Birth control clinics continued to provide sponges as contraceptive devices until the 1930s.
9. In the eleventh century, the Jewish physician Avicenna advised women to prevent conception by standing up immediately after intercourse and take seven progressively higher jumps backward, sneezing all the while.
10. Casanova, the famous eighteenth-century lover, is said to have inserted an 18-millimeter gold ball into each of his partner's vagina before intercourse.

lost. A fresh condom must be used each time the man ejaculates.

Like the diaphragm, the condom is an effective method of birth control, if used properly. Its theoretical failure rate is 2 to 4 percent, but the actual failure rate ranges up to 20 percent. Failures can occur if the condom is not put on soon enough, if it slips off, or if it tears or bursts.

A particular advantage of the condom is that it is both a contraceptive and a method of protecting both man and woman from venereal disease. Condoms do not require a prescription. They cost between twenty-five cents and one dollar each.

Vaginal Foam, Creams, and Jellies
Vaginal foams, creams, and jellies are chemical spermicides designed to cover the cervix and provide a physical and chemical barrier to sperm.

Foam, the most effective of the three, has a theoretical failure rate of 2 to 4 percent. The foam can be a highly effective method of birth control, but its actual failure rate is 10 to 20 percent. Unlike the actual failure rates of the diaphragm and condom, however, many of the actual failures of foam are difficult to prevent. For example, one could mistakenly not use enough foam, or it may not be spread evenly over the cervix. Thus this method of contraception is most effective when used in addition to the condom. (Do not, however, use foam with a diaphragm; use cream or jelly.)

As with other contraceptives, be sure to

explicitly follow the directions on the container of any foam, cream, or jelly that you might use.

Withdrawal

Withdrawal is the most widely used method of contraception in the world. It is also perhaps the least effective. This method, also known as *coitus interruptus,* involves the man pulling his penis out of the vagina before ejaculation. Reliance on this method of contraception should be avoided whenever possible.

Non-Contraception

Douching is not a method of contraception. Neither are having intercourse in different positions, lack of orgasm, or intercourse during breast feeding. Home-made condoms are not effective contraceptive devices.

Voluntary Sterilization

A man or a woman who uses this method of birth control must be certain that he or she does not want any more children. Except in rare cases, sterilization is not reversible in either men or women.

The male operation is called a vasectomy. It involves the cutting and tying of the *vas deferens,* the tubes which carry the sperm from the testicles. Vasectomy is a simple operation and can be performed under local anesthetic in the doctor's office. It costs $50 to $150 when performed by a private physician. The operation can also be obtained at public health clinics or some Planned Parenthood clinics, free or at low cost. Vasectomies will not affect the male's sex drive or performance physically in any way. A few men have negative psychological effects. After the procedure the man will continue to ejaculate at his climax, but there will be no sperm cells present. The operation, however, is not effective immediately. Be sure to check with the doctor about the "fertile" period that remains after a vasectomy. This can be up to six months or even more.

The most widely used form of voluntary sterilization for women is tubal ligation, or cutting and tying of the Fallopian tubes. This operation prevents eggs from reaching the uterus. The traditional method of tubal ligation is major surgery, and re-

quires several days of hospitalization.

Recently, however, an operation called the "laparoscopy" has been developed. This has also been called "band-aid" surgery for female sterilization. In this procedure the physician makes an incision near the navel, and inserts a tube containing lights and mirror. With these he locates the Fallopian tubes, burns them closed, and cuts them. This technique is less expensive than the traditional form of tubal ligation, and can even be performed on an outpatient basis.

Women's sterilization operations cost between $250 and $500, plus the cost of the hospital stay. Some family planning clinics offer these services and adjust rates according to income.

Abortion

Abortion is the least desirable method of birth control. Proper use of contraceptives is less expensive, less dangerous, and less likely to create moral, legal, marital and psychological problems. Abortion, however, is of significant importance in cases where it is determined that a pregnancy could severely damage a mother's health, or when there is medical evidence that the child could be born with a severe genetic or birth defect.

Whether to undergo an abortion is not likely to be an easy decision for any of those involved. You can get free information and counseling about abortion and birth control methods from Planned Parenthood, which you can probably find in your telephone directory. If it is not listed, telephone the national Planned Parenthood office at (212) 541-7800 to find out the location of the affiliate nearest you.

There are several basic types of abortion:

—Very early abortion, which is also called menstrual regulation or mini-abortion. The procedure is usually performed seven to fourteen days after the period was due. Since most pregnancy tests are not reliable before two weeks, some women who undergo this procedure may not be pregnant at all. The very early abortion is usually performed in a doctor's office or clinic. It is a brief and usually painless procedure in which the physician inserts a thin tube through the vagina and into the uterus and draws out the contents

The bitter conflict between abortion proponents and opponents shows no signs of cooling down.

performed after the sixteenth week of pregnancy. It is the most complicated and expensive type of abortion, and should rarely be necessary except in the case of illness in the mother, or prenatal diagnosis of a severe defect in the fetus.

In the late abortion the physician inserts a hypodermic needle into the womb and withdraws a small quantity of amniotic fluid. The fluid is replaced with a saline solution — or sometimes another drug — which will induce contractions within about forty-eight hours. The result will be expulsion of the fetus and placenta. A two- to three-day stay in the hospital is required in this method of abortion. The cost of this procedure runs from $300 to $500.

MALE VS. FEMALE

Two central anatomical differences between males and females are the external and internal reproductive organs, although, as we shall see later, the two sexes have different skeletal structures, sex chromosomes, hormone levels, pulse rates, metabolic rates, and death rates.

In the female, the external sexual organ is called the *vulva,* and it is composed of a *mons veneris, labia majora, labia minora,* a *clitoris* and a *hymen*. The mons veneris is a mound of fat, covered with hair, which lies above the labia majora at the entrance of the vagina. The labia majora, or outer lips, are folds of skin which lie on either side of the vulva. The labia minora, or inner lips (also folds of skin), lie between the labia majora and the vaginal opening. These lips are equipped with excretory glands called *Bartholin's glands,* which secrete a fluid that lubricates the vagina in preparation for intercourse. The clitoris lies about two inches above the entrance to the vagina. When stimulated, the clitoris fills with blood, and becomes firm and erect during sexual excitation. It serves no reproductive purpose. The hymen is a membrane which covers part of the vaginal opening in most female virgins. It is broken either by the first experience of sexual intercourse or by strenuous exercise or masturbation.

The female internal reproductive organs consist of two *ovaries,* two *Fallopian* tubes, a *uterus,* and a *vagina*. The almond-shaped ovaries are located on

by means of suction. The cost of this procedure ranges from $125 to $175 in most clinics, and can cost more if performed by a private physician.

—Early abortion is the most common kind of abortion. it is usually performed up to the twelfth week after the first day of the last menstrual period. It is usually performed in a clinic or a hospital. The operation takes about ten minutes and is relatively free of risks for the woman. The early abortion is most frequently performed by dilatation and evacuation (D & E) also called vacuum curettage. Less often the older method of dilation and curettage (D & C) is used.

In the D & E, a tube is inserted into the uterus, after dilating the cervix, and the contents are removed by vacuum.

In the D & C, the cervix is dilated and the contents are scraped out.

Both procedures usually require only a local anesthetic. The costs range from $125 to $175, and can go higher depending on the physician.

—The late abortion is also frequently known as the saline abortion and is usually

First Woman Dental School Graduate

Thwarted in her efforts to gain entry to medical school, **Lucy Hobbs Taylor** (1833-1910) settled on dentistry instead. In the mid-nineteenth century, dentists were not the high-status professionals they are today. They were in a class with traveling medicine salesmen, often following the same routes from town to town, armed with little more than a file, a few excavators, and bit of silver coin and mercury. Dentistry lacked the status of medicine, thus it was easier for a woman to gain a foothold in that field.

Because no dental school would admit her, Taylor studied privately with practising dentists. She opened her first practice in Cincinnati in 1861, then moved on to Iowa one year later, winning patients through their curiosity, but keeping them through competence. Her skill won her membership in the Iowa State Dental Society, one of the groups formed to improve the stature of dentistry. The society aided Taylor in gaining admission to the Ohio College of Dental Surgery, the school that had earlier rejected her application. Due to her previous work, Taylor had to attend only one college session before receiving her degree. She became the first woman

to graduate from dental school.

Diploma in hand, Taylor moved her practice to Chicago, where she met and married a painter in a railroad car shop. She taught her husband dentistry, and the two remained partners in work as well as matrimony, until his death in 1886. By the turn of the century, nearly 1,000 women had followed Taylor into dentistry, which was rapidly gaining professional stature.

either side of the uterus. They are about one to two inches long and produce the female hormones estrogen and progesterone. The ovaries each release one egg every other month, hence the availability of one egg each month.

The uterus is about the size of a pear. It is located directly above the bladder. It narrows at its lower end to form the cervix, or neck of the uterus. The uterus is rarely more than three inches long in non-pregnant women. The cervix leads directly into the vagina, which leads out to the vulva.

The vagina is a canal — usually three to four inches long — that stretches from the vulva to the opening of the uterus. It plays a role in sexual pleasure, serves as a receptacle for the male sperm, and is the passageway through which children are born. The vaginal walls — made of tough muscular tissue — can be stretched greatly.

The female breasts, which develop at

Accident Injury Rates
Per 1,000 persons per year

■ Female
▨ Male

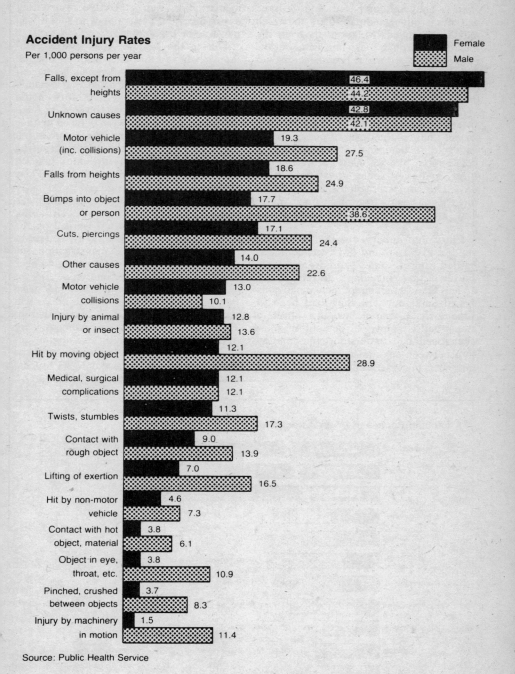

Cause	Female	Male
Falls, except from heights	46.4	44.2
Unknown causes	42.8	42.1
Motor vehicle (inc. collisions)	19.3	27.5
Falls from heights	18.6	24.9
Bumps into object or person	17.7	38.6
Cuts, piercings	17.1	24.4
Other causes	14.0	22.6
Motor vehicle collisions	13.0	10.1
Injury by animal or insect	12.8	13.6
Hit by moving object	12.1	28.9
Medical, surgical complications	12.1	12.1
Twists, stumbles	11.3	17.3
Contact with rough object	9.0	13.9
Lifting of exertion	7.0	16.5
Hit by non-motor vehicle	4.6	7.3
Contact with hot object, material	3.8	6.1
Object in eye, throat, etc.	3.8	10.9
Pinched, crushed between objects	3.7	8.3
Injury by machinery in motion	1.5	11.4

Source: Public Health Service

puberty, are sometimes called *mammary glands*. They are composed of fatty tissue and numerous glandular lobes in which milk is produced. Milk travels from the milk ducts through these lobes and out the nipple when a woman is breast-feeding her child. The *nipple* is in the center of the breast. The round pigmented area around the nipple is called *areola*.

Onset of Puberty

In our culture, the onset of puberty isn't, as a rule, recognized by common ritual or celebration, unlike many primitive cultures, and even some other societies today. The adolescent in America, for the most part, comes to terms with maturing body and emerging sexuality totally on his or her own.

Entry into puberty for the female is a sudden event. Many girls are confused, baffled, upset, and ignorant about the causes of this "bleeding." In one survey, no less than 39 percent of the women questioned said they felt they had been inadequately prepared for the onset of menstruation. Only 25 percent of those questioned had understood the relationship between sex and reproduction when they began menstruating; and for every

female who said *menarche* or the onset of menstruation was a positive or exciting experience, there was one who said it was negative or frightening.

During the Middle Ages it was commonly believed that menstruation was the undeniable proof that woman is the essence of evil or sin, a belief that extends back to the Adam and Eve story in the Book of Genesis. During the Middle Ages menstruating women were allowed neither to attend church nor to take communion. This prejudice persists; menstruating women of the Russian Orthodox Church traditionally have not been allowed to kiss the cross or take communion.

Intercourse during menstruation was long thought to be dangerous. Orthodox Jewish women were often warned not to make themselves sexually attractive to their husbands during menstruation for fear they might have intercourse and bear unhealthy or defective children.

Even today the women of Indonesia may not enter the tobacco fields or work in the rice paddies during menstruation. In Saigon, menstruating women were excluded from working in the opium factories. It was thought they might turn the opium bitter. All of these dangers to local

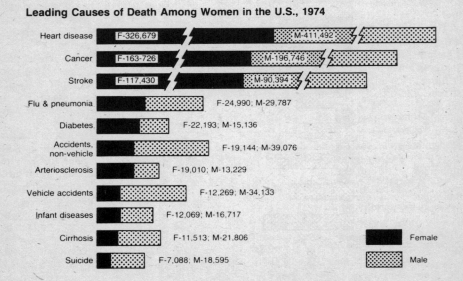

Leading Causes of Death Among Women in the U.S., 1974

Cause	Female	Male
Heart disease	F-326,679	M-411,492
Cancer	F-163-726	M-196,746
Stroke	F-117,430	M-90,394
Flu & pneumonia	F-24,990	M-29,787
Diabetes	F-22,193	M-15,136
Accidents, non-vehicle	F-19,144	M-39,076
Arteriosclerosis	F-19,010	M-13,229
Vehicle accidents	F-12,269	M-34,133
Infant diseases	F-12,069	M-16,717
Cirrhosis	F-11,513	M-21,806
Suicide	F-7,088	M-18,595

■ Female   ▦ Male

industry are considered particularly acute if the female is experiencing her first menstruation.

The Male

The male external sexual organs are the *penis*, the *scrotum*, and the *testicles*. The penis is made up of erectile tissue which, stiffens when the male becomes sexually aroused. The scrotum consists of two connected skin pouches which lie below and on either side of the penis and contain the testicles, or testes. The testicles are small glands, which correspond to the ovaries in the female. The testicles produce sperm cells, each of which is only 1/50,000 the size of a single female egg.

Other Differences

At any age, the male's death rate is higher. About 20-25 percent more males than females are conceived, but only about 5 to 6 percent more are born. During the first few years of life and thereafter males have a consistently higher death rate than females. The male also lives a shorter life than the female. The male is more prone to physical defects.

According to the *Vital Statistics of the United States* (U.S. National Center for Health Statistics) the life expectancy in 1973 for white men was 68.4, and for non-white men 61.9, while the life expectancy for white and nonwhite woman was 76.1 and 70.0, respectively.

The male and female show significant differences in their skeletal structures too. The most obvious differences is in the shape of their pelvises. The male's pelvis is funnel-shaped, whereas the female's is shaped like a basin. The main opening of the female pelvis is also wider to permit passage of an infant at birth. The pelvis is the most reliable part of the skeleton for determining the sex of an individual, but there are other basic — though less universal — differences.

The male skeleton is usually larger than the female, and more massive and rugged in appearance. The male's cheekbones are usually more massive and point outward, while the female's are lighter and more compressed. The "orbits," or eyesockets, tend to be smaller and square-shaped in the male, and larger and round in the female. The knees and elbows usually are "knocked" in the female — the shape of the elbows makes it easier to cradle a baby and the knee configuration stabilizes her stance, in conjunction with her broader hip-n-pelvic-anatomy.

Here are some other physical sex differences:

— The average pulse rate of an adult male at rest is 72 beats per minute; in the adult female at rest, it is, on the average, 80 beats per minute. The incidence of elevated blood pressure is higher in the male than it is in the female up to age 40, but after that age, high blood pressure occurs more frequently in women.

— Males and females differ in their basal metabolism rates, i.e., the rate at which food is absorbed and used by the body. Men absorb and use food more quickly than women, therefore they can consume more calories than women without gaining weight.

— While men are stronger and faster than women in neuromuscular performance, women have greater ability to endure physiological and mental hardships, like fatigue, exposure to shock, and starvation.

— The average male heart and brain weigh more than those of the average female. Contrary to popular myth, however, there is *no* correlation between brain size and intelligence!

— A larger percentage of the male's total body weight is made up of water and muscle, while fat forms a larger percentage of the female's body weight.

— The male's spine is longer, his number of red blood cells per cubic millimeter greater, his total lung capacity greater, and his average intake of air greater. Women take on the average two to four more breaths per minute.

— The average newborn male is usually slightly longer and heavier than the female, a trend which applies throughout life except during adolescence, when girls for a time are taller and heavier than boys.

The female develops more quickly and in a more consistent growth pattern year-by-year than does the male. At any age, therefore, girls have arrived at a larger percentage of their final weight and height than boys. They are more likely at any age to be more physically mature than boys. Some researchers have suggested that the girl's advanced physical development may have a correlation in the area of mental development, although evidence is less convincing for this hypothesis.

By age thirteen, girls have passed their peak in weight and height gain, while boys have yet to attain theirs. From age thirteen to the end of his growth, the average boy gains 10 to 11 inches, while the average girl gains only about 3 or 4 inches. Also, between the ages of thirteen and seventeen the average boy can gain up to 50 pounds, while the average girl won't gain more than about 35 pounds.

THE MYSTERIOUS FEMININE MIND

Many feminists rank Sigmund Freud as Public Enemy Number One. Were the eminent father of modern psychiatry still alive, he would no doubt retort that they were merely immature victims of unresolved penis envy — and suggest that they return home and get pregnant in short order.

A woman's unique problems begin, said Freud, when she discovers at some point between the ages of three and five, that she lacks a penis. Distraught over being thus mutilated and deprived of a "superior endowment," the girl experiences the "penis envy" which — however sublimated — sets the course for all her future psychological development.

Seeking to take out her disappointment on her mother, the girl transfers her erotic feelings to her father. Her wish for a penis is thus turned into the wish to bear her father's child. In this transference, Freud believed, the girl changes active, masculine strivings (penis envy) into passive, feminine ones (the wish to be impregnated). Her feelings of inadequacy are usually resolved later in life when she gives birth to a child — especially if it is a boy, who "brings the longed-for penis with him."

Any attempt by women to participate in the competitive professional world indicated to Freud their inability to repress masculine-active impulses. Only through passively accepting her traditional maternal role, he believed, could woman find true happiness.

According to Freud, masochism — the acceptance and even enjoyment of pain — was an important feature in the normal woman's psychological makeup. Her masochism evolved from her need to turn her masculine-active impulses in upon herself *and from* her acceptance of the discomforts of such female functions as childbirth and menstruation.

Freud also believed women have a weaker superego — or conscience — than men. Thus, women are more dependent than men on punishments or rewards doled out by a parent or other "authority figure." Men, by the same token, are more inclined toward independent thought and action.

Women analysts — such as Helene Deutsch and Marie Bonaparte — were among the most loyal of Freud's many followers. But another group, calling themselves "interpersonal relations theorists," arose in the United States during the 1930s to challenge Freud's doctrines. They argued that social relations and culture — not anatomy — were the major determinants of human behavior.

One of the most influential members of this school was Karen Horney, a German emigre, who asserted that specific cultural

Karen Horney argued that culture — rather than anatomy — was the prime determinant of behavior.

conditions make women and men act in different ways. She believed that a woman's wish to have a penis was often symbolic of her legitimate desire to occupy an equal place in society with men. (While not denying the existence of penis envy, Horney suggested that men experience an even more intense envy of the female's child bearing potential!)

In an argument that would be echoed by later feminists, Horney declared that, like culture at large, psychological theory was biased toward men. A woman's perspective had been lacking too long in the field of psychoanalysis, she said, and women had been too quick to accept theories about themselves dreamed up by men.

Horney's challenges to the biological bedrock of Freudian theory brought her into serious conflict with the psychoanalytic establishment. She was dismissed from her position as training analyst at the New York Psychoanalytic Society. In protest, she and four other members — analyst Clara Thompson among them — resigned altogether from the Society and founded their own American Institute for Psychoanalysis, and Association for the Advancement of Psychoanalysis.

Between 1941 and 1950, Thompson wrote a series of papers interpreting the female personality in terms of Western woman's historically second-class status and shame about her sexuality.

Anthropologist Margaret Mead supplied evidence to support the emphasis Horney and her followers placed on cultural influence in the development of personality. In 1935, Mead published a study of behavior in three primitive New Guinea tribes.

In one society, both men and women exhibited high degrees of the nurturance and responsiveness, traits traditionally associated with the female. In another society, members of both sexes showed great ruthlessness and aggression. The women of the third tribe were dominant and impersonal, while the men were emotionally dependent and less responsible.

Concluded Mead, "Many, if not all, of the personality traits which we have called masculine or feminine, are as lightly linked to sex as are the clothing, the manners and the forms of headdress that a society at a given period assigns each sex."

Modern Feminism and Psychology

Following a twenty-year lull, interest in the psychology of women reawakened with the feminist movement of the sixties and seventies. Psychologist Naomi Weisstein's views are typical of those shared by most critics of Freud in the women's movement: "I don't know what differences exist between men and women apart from their genitals. . . . But it is clear that until social expectations for men and women are equal, until we provide equal respect for both men and women, our answer to this question will simply reflect our prejudice."

Feminists have attacked not only Freudian concepts, but the technique of psychotherapy itself. Critics from Betty Friedan (*The Feminine Mystique,* 1963) to Phyllis Chesler (*Women and Madness,* 1972) have argued that psychoanalysis — in which a woman becomes dependent on still another male authority figure, her analyst — might do women patients more harm than good. "For most women," says Chesler, "the (middle-class oriented) psychotherapeutic encounter is just one more instance of an unequal relationship."

Still, women outnumber men by 57 to 43 percent among patients of psychiatrists in private practice. According to a National Institute of Mental Health study, there were 45,800 more female than male admissions to mental hospitals, mental health centers, hospital psychiatric units, and outpatient psychiatric services in 1970, a ratio of 96 men to 100 women. However, if Veterans Administration hospitals had been included in the study, the ratio of females to male in psychiatric facilities would have shifted to 100:104. Census Bureau figures for all mental institutions in 1970 show 56,000 more men than women residents.

Some feminists have suggested that many women have been *classified* as mentally ill when they simply rebelled against an unappealing role assigned them by society. If so, future years should see a shift in the types, symptoms, and prevalence of mental disorders suffered by women.

Among female admissions to psychiatric facilities in 1970, depressive disorders — extreme feelings of sadness, inadequacy, helplessness, and hopelessness — were the most frequently reported diagnoses. In second place was schizophrenia, a large group of mental illnesses characterized by disjointed and inappropriate thoughts, emotions, and behavior.

By contrast, the leading diagnosis among male admissions was alcohol disorders, followed by schizophrenia and depression.

According to psychiatrist Ruth Noulton of New York's Columbia University, the common complaints of female psychiatric patients have changed in recent years. During the 1950s and early 1960s, women most often sought help for sexual and child rearing problems, she told the 1976 American Psychiatric Association Convention. Today, their problems center on the work place. They worry about their ability to perform their jobs well, about their unavailability to their families, and their difficulties in dealing with the competitive feelings of their husbands and co-workers.

Though more men than women commit suicide, more women than men attempt suicide, but fail. White men commit suicide three times as often as white women and black men, and black women have the lowest suicide rate of all. But it has recently been found that professional women have a suicide rate as high or higher than that of professional men. One theory has it that suicide results when a person's actual life circumstances do not measure up to his or her expectations. Perhaps working women expect more from life than women who remain at home, and, consequently, run a greater risk of letdown if their plans go awry.

Men and women even differ in their physical manifestations of psychological stress. Peptic ulcers and skin disorders are more common among men, while women more often have such symptoms as headaches, backaches, and insomnia.

The area of female psychology is, of course, far too complex to discuss thoroughly in a single article — or a single book. Psychology, which set out to simplify our understanding of human behavior, sometimes seems only to have added to the confusion. In Freud's day it was believed that biological traits were responsible for many of the vagaries of human conduct. Today we realize we cannot study behavior except as a complex interaction of biology, personality, social organization, and cultural beliefs. Thanks to renewed interest in the subject sparked by the women's movement, studies are currently underway across the nation which may furnish many new insights into the mysteries of the female — and male — minds.

UNHEALTHY HABITS

Smoking

Teenage girls and young women are today more likely to smoke cigarettes than ever before, according to a 1975 study by the American Cancer Society. According to the report, half a million more teenage girls were smoking cigarettes in 1975 than were smoking in 1969.

Even more striking is the fact that the number of pack-a-day-or-more teenage-girl smokers quadrupled between 1969 and 1975. The same statistic for teenage boys remained stable.

Women, on the average, live longer than men, but according to the ACS, by the year 2000, women may die **sooner** than men, mainly because of cigarette smoking. Health experts say that cigarette smoking is more dangerous for women, since their lung capacities are smaller, and women thus get more concentrated doses of the toxic substances in cigarettes than men.

The death rate from lung cancer among women has doubled in the past ten years; lung cancer is now the third largest cancer killer among women.

Heavy smoking during pregnancy can cause damage to the fetus, increasing the risk of spontaneous abortion and premature birth, the risk of stillbirth, and the risk of giving birth to a smaller baby, or a baby with low intelligence and slower physical development.

Alcohol

The percentage of adult women who drink alcohol has been increasing steadily since World War II, and the trend seems to be continuing.

In 1975, Dr. Robert L. DuPont, director of the National Institute on Drug Abuse, reported the percentage of ninth grade girls who had used alcohol 50 or more times in a year was two-and-a-half times greater in 1975 than in 1970. The number of boys who were regular users of alcohol, by

Cigarette Smokers
Percentage of population

Men ━━━━ Women ━━━━

Source: The Tobacco Institute, Gallup and Roper polls and Public Health Service surveys
* Caution notices placed on cigarette packs.

the same criterion, was only twice as great. The increase in alcohol use by *both* sexes presents a serious problem. In 1975, in Los Angeles County alone, there were 28 chapters of Alcoholics Anonymous for teenagers alone.

Today men are twice as likely to be moderate drinkers, and three times as likely as a woman to be heavy drinkers. But preliminary results from a 1974 government survey of junior and senior high school students indicate that the number of girls who drink is rapidly approaching that of boys.

According to the National Institute on Alcohol Abuse and Alcoholism (NIAAA), ten years ago, one of every six alcoholics was a woman. Today the gap has narrowed to one in three. There are an estimated 10 million alcoholics in the United States.

Dr. Morris Chafetz, former director of the NIAAA, says that "Just as youth drink to achieve a demonstrable measure of adulthood, it may be that women who are confused about their current role are drinking heavily as a measure to indicate they have achieved equal status with men."

Liquor poses serious threats to the health of the alcoholic and her children. In less than ten years female deaths from alcohol-related diseases, such as liver and intestinal disease, have risen from 6.3 to 8 per 100,000 deaths. Several studies have shown that alcoholism can cause serious problems in the development of a fetus, and even alcohol addiction of the infant.

Other Drug Abuse
The National Institute on Drug Abuse (NIDA) reported in 1975 that the percentage of women who use pills to cope with stress increased almost 30 percent between 1972 and 1974, but there was no similar increase among males.

These drugs include the major and minor tranquilizers, sedatives, stimulants, hypnotics, and antidepressants, which are obtained with a doctor's prescription.

The NIDA study found that the greatest prevalence of female-over-male use of these drugs was in the thirty to fifty-nine-year-old age bracket. The most commonly prescribed drugs were minor tranquilizers, such as Valium, Librium, Serax, Tranxene, and Miltown. These are used to treat anxiety, mild depression, muscle pains, headaches, irritability, tension, and insomnia.

One reason the NIDA study offers to explain the higher number of women who use these drugs is that females tend to visit doctors more frequently than men, and thus have more opportunity to obtain such prescriptions. Second, it has been more acceptable for a woman, especially a middle-aged woman, to seek medical help for symptoms of psychic distress.

However, men clearly have a different pattern of drug use than women. If alcohol had been considered in this study of American patterns of anti-anxiety drug use, men would have surpassed women in the use of drugs.

The image of the pill-popping middle-class housewife is false, according to the NIDA study of national patterns of psychotherapeutic drug use. The percentage of "high level" users of minor tranquilizers and sedatives is equal among working women (whether full- or part-time) and full-time housewives. About one in twenty women in both groups is a "high level" user. The study shows that long-term use of these drugs is *not* most prevalent among well-to-do and well-educated women, whether working or full-time housewives, but among poorer and less well-educated housewives.

Another popular belief — that anti-anxiety drugs are generally prescribed by psychiatrists — also has no basis in fact. They are far more often prescribed by family doctors. The use of minor tranquilizers has several hazards. Both drugs can be used for suicide. And if used for an extended period of time in large doses, both can become physically and psychologically addicting.

Prescribing these drugs, according to Milton Silverman and Philip R. Lee, in their book, *Pills, Profits, and Politics,* "may lead to the dangerous belief that one of these agents not only will alleviate the symptoms for a brief period, but will actually solve the woes, griefs, and problems of everyday living. The attitudes surrounding the prescribing and use of these drugs can lead to a way of life based on the conviction that all personal and interpersonal relations can be readily and safely regulated by chemistry."

Drowsiness is a common side effect of the minor tranquilizers and sedatives. This drowsiness has been cited as the cause of auto accidents and household mishaps. Because of their depressive effect on the nervous system, both kinds of drugs can also cause lethargy, slurred speech, and loss of ability to coordinate muscles.

Amphetamines — a kind of stimulant some women have used to lose weight — can also be dangerous if used over a long period. Amphetamines can not only cause psychological dependence and possible physical addiction, but also interfere with other body functions. The drugs can also cause mental changes related to paranoid states.

Among adults over eighteen, almost twice as many men as women have ever used marijuana or are currently using it. And, according to the U.S. Drug Enforcement Administration, about 84 percent of active narcotics users in 1974 were men, while only about 16 percent were women.

However, the trend among females is definitely headed toward more widespread use of marijuana. Among adolescents aged twelve to seventeen, for example, nearly equal numbers of boys and girls — about one out of five — have used marijuana, and about one-half of them, regardless of sex, are continuing to use marijuana.

There is some evidence that heroin addiction among females may also be on the upswing. Data from Texas Christian University's Institute on Behavioral Research shows an increasing pattern of female admission to treatment programs for heroin addiction between 1969 and 1973. In 1969, clients admitted to treatment were 83 percent male and 17 percent female. By 1973, the percentage of female admissions has increased to 28 percent. While this last change could be interpreted as the outcome of attempts to make treatment more acceptable to women, it could also mean a relative growth in the population of female heroin addicts.

Girls

GAMES AND TOYS

Most children's games are sophisticated versions of primitive religious, agricultural, and hunting rituals. "Ring Around the Rosy," "The Farmer in the Dell," and "Drop the Handkerchief," for example, are all derived from ancient adult games that symbolized marriage by capture, in which the bride was caught and carried away. In "Ring Around the Rosy" ("Ring around the rosy/A pocketful of posey/ashes, ashes/We all fall down"), the "falling down" refers to the sexual consummation of the marriage and to the early funerals of many girl brides who died young in childbirth. Later, when flirtation was an accepted form of courtship, more obvious games like "Spin the Bottle" and "Post Office" gained popularity.

During Hippocrates' time, Greek children rolled flaming hoops, called "fire wheels," down the hills each autumn, hoping their brightness would hold back winter. These early hoop rutuals led to other hoop games, right up to the twentieth century phenomenon of the Hula Hoop. Making a cat's cradle — by looping and crossing a piece of string until a figure appears between your hands — goes back to the Stone Age.

Hand-clapping games like "Pease Porridge Hot" and "Pat-a-Cake" originated when the hands and voice were still used like musical instruments to keep rhythmic time to early drumbeats. Archeologists have found hand-changing games like "Button, Button, Who's Got the Button?" portrayed on Egyptian and Grecian pottery thousands of years old.

Until the nineteenth century, children were generally considered little adults, without any special "right" to play. But children, of course, found ways. The first mention of girls playing a game is found in Homer's *Odyssey,* where little Nausicaa and her maidens are described as "playing at ball." Another favorite was Fivestones, an imitation of men's gambling, played with pebbles; today we call it jacks.

In Western societies, the earliest children's games usually imitated adult life: while mother worked a large loom, her daughter played with yarn and sticks in the corner; while father hunted, son trudged alongside with a smaller bow and arrow. In 1775, a ten-year-old American girl who made a list of what she had done in one

Refined little girls of the 1800s did not know their favorite game stemmed from bride capture.

Through the ages, a girl's closest confidant has often been a favorite, well-worn doll.

day included no mention of play: she had spun twine, carded wool, sewed, made cheeses, ironed, read sermons, milked cows, made a broom, dyed cloth, and scoured pewter.

In colonial America, Puritan children had few toys and were discouraged from laughing, dancing, and singing. Puritan preacher Cotton Mather said parents who showed their children too much love were sinners; if they put too much emphasis on earthly possessions God would punish them by taking away the child. In Mather's conversations with his own four-year-old daughter, Katy, he instilled a "healthy" fear of God and father. Katy suffered from a nervous condition all her life.

Toys were not high on the list of necessary imports. After searching for a gift for her niece Patty, Martha Washington wrote to her brother in 1778: "Please give little Patty a kiss for me. I have sent her a pair of shoes . . . there was not a doll to be got in the city of Philadelphia." Even without store-bought toys, colonial children played happily — when they had time — with sticks, rope, and mud.

In rural areas, the intricate and vigorous four-couple square dance was popular, and the entire family could eat, laugh, and do-si-do the night away. Despite the restrictions on them, even the Puritan children managed to "dance" by inventing party games like "Paw Paw Patch" and "Shoo Fly," which they played to their own singing.

Dolls

Dolls, among the oldest of human inventions, were used originally in magic ceremonies or as religious icons. Small figures of wood, clay, bone, and ivory are found in Egyptian, Roman, and Greek tombs, and dolls made of sticks, stones, bones, and mud existed even before then.

In ancient Japan, women made "scapegoat dolls" from willow sticks, with string for hair and paper clothes. These dolls were dressed, fed, and treated as if they were living children in the belief that they would attract evil that might otherwise go to the real child. Infertile women also made scapegoat dolls, dressing and tending them as if they were alive. They would then present the "nourished" doll at a shrine, hoping this would qualify them to receive a living child in exchange.

Child brides in Arab countries always brought a collection of elaborately dressed dolls as part of her dowry, defying Mohammedan prohibition against creating images of human beings. In certain African tribes, each girl is given a doll when she reaches puberty, and she must cherish it until she has her second living child. Early European Christians modeled their dolls after saints, and the first dollhouses were replicas of the Christmas crèche.

American Indian children were given dolls portraying powerful spirits. Hopi Kachina dolls, given to each girl at puberty, were considered powerful messengers to the spirits and were so feared by the Navajos that they invented their own dolls of weathered wood to protect them from the Kachina magic.

In Western Europe and the American colonies, early dolls were almost always portrayed and dressed as adults, reflecting the attitude that girls were simply miniature women. The first dolls were made primarily of wood with facial features painted on. Later, dollmakers experimented with wax, terra cotta, and alabaster — but the most popular were made of porcelain. Most girls, unable to afford the delicate porcelain dolls, settled contentedly for dolls with stuffed cloth torsos, their head, hands, and feet made of china or clay.

The first modern dollhouse was made in Germany in 1558 for the daughter of Duke Albert V of Bavaria; scholars believe it was destroyed during a fire in his Munich castle. Dollhouses were luxuriously furnished and served as status symbols and to help teach girls about good taste and domestic duty. In 1572, Anna, electress of Saxony, provided her daughters' dollhouse with seventy-one tiny pewter bowls, forty meat dishes, one hundred six plates, twenty-eight egg dishes, tables, chairs, cupboards, pin-cushions, bathtubs, and a poultry yard. It, too, has been lost. One of the oldest dollhouses to be preserved, displayed in the Germanische National Museum in Nuremberg, dates from 1639; it contains more than one thousand objects in its fifteen rooms.

In the 1700s, a German princess named Augusta Dorothea spent her thirty-five years of widowhood supervising the construction of an entire doll's town, "Mon Plaisir", with twenty-six houses inhabited by four hundred dolls.

Paper dolls first appeared in Germany in 1791; they were modeled in the round and, although quite expensive, they soon became popular. Around 1880, Heinrich Stier of Sonneberg made a major breakthrough in doll production when he used the cup-and-ball joint to make movable limbs, and counter-weights to make eyes open and shut. By 1900, dollmaking had reached a peak of perfection which declined quickly with the onset of mass production.

Today, most dolls are made of rubber or plastic; the "baby" dolls eat, cry, wet, and talk. The lovable Raggedy Ann and Kewpie doll, followed by the more chic corkscrew-curled Shirley Temple doll in the 1930s and the Barbie doll in the 1950s, became best-sellers. During the Depression of the 1930s, paper dolls also became a popular substitute for the real thing. Girls who could not afford even a dime to buy paper dolls created their own by cutting comic strip figures like "Boots" from the newspapers and by improvising dresses from things like silver candy wrappers.

Best Books, Best Toys

Each adult remembers her or his favorite childhood toy: they were almost always simple, durable, comforting, and a springboard for the imagination — a rag doll, a set of blocks, even a blanket. Today, the basic rules of buying toys — like the basic joy of playing with toys — remains unchanged. The best toys give children a framework in which to be creative.

Toys should be safe: metal edges should be rolled under; wooden toys should be smooth and splinter-proof, covered with nontoxic paint or varnish. All electrical toys, such as trains, should be approved by Underwriters Laboratory (UL). Toys should also be long-lasting: the most durable ones are made of wood and heavy metal rather than plastic or tin.

Whenever possible, mothers or fathers should encourage their children to create their own toys, and help them by providing materials and working alongside. Store-bought toys should be suitable to the age of the child: when parents choose toys beyond their child's understanding, the child feels frustrated rather than challenged. Toys should stimulate creativity and promote physical coordination and emotional development.

Some suggested toys are:

Infancy to two: mobiles, such as the Wind-Me-Not 3-in-1 Electric Mobile made by Dolly Toys and those made by

Kenner or Childcraft, for form and color; stuffed toys (Ideal, Amsco, Knickerbocker) for cuddling; Five-Finger Exerciser (Creative Playthings) to help focus eyes and coordinate fingers.

Two to six: Romper Stompers (Romper Room) for balance; Gym-ee (Gym-Dandy) for climbing; simple puzzles that require a child to fit shapes into matching spaces; hand puppets, alphabet blocks, blackboard and chalk, and building blocks are also fun and educational.

Six to ten: Magnetic Boards (Child Guidance) can be combined with Flashcards (Milton Bradley) for help in math and reading; musical instruments with true tones (Childcraft, Creative Playthings) for an introduction to music; larger gym sets for muscle coordination; and construction sets, such as the Erector Set (Gilbert) or Plastic Blocks (Halsam), for creativity.

Ten and over: Chemcraft Labs (Porter Science) and Chemistry Modulab (Gilbert) foster interest in science. Games such as Herstory, Endangered Species, Famous Black People, and Guinness Game of World Records also help give children access to a wide range of ideas and cultures.

Books are also an important part of a child's life, starting with picture books and continuing through the classics. Books should contribute to a child's understanding of herself or himself and of society. They should stimulate the imagination and be printed in clear type with attractive illustrations.

Some suggested books are:

Toddlers: *Golden Block Books* (Western); *Best Word Book Ever* (Richard Scarry, Western); *The Cat in the Hat Beginner Book Dictionary* (Dr. Seuss, Random House); and *Goodnight Moon* (Margaret Wise Brown, Harper and Row).

Two to three: *Brian Wildsmith's ABC* (Brian Wildsmith, Watts); *ABC of Cars and Trucks* (Ann Alexander, Doubleday); *The Indoor Noisy Book, The City Noisy Book, The Country Noisy Book* (all by Margaret Wise Brown, Harper and Row); and *The Tale of Peter Rabbit* (Beatrix Potter, Warne).

Three to six: For this age range, the Harper and Row series is suggested, including *I Can Read Books* and *I Can Read Science Books; Where the Wild*

Books should contribute to a child's understanding of herself and her society.

Things Are (Maurice Sendak, Harper and Row); and *Free to Be You and Me* (Marlo Thomas, et al., McGraw-Hill).

In addition, the Children's Services Division of the American Library Association and the Children's Literature Association include the following in their recommended lists:

Five to Eight: *The Biggest Bear* (Lynd Ward, Houghton-Mifflin); *A Child's Garden of Verses* (Robert Louis Stevenson, Walck); *The Courage of Sarah Noble* (Alice Dalgliesh, Scribner); *The Golden Book* — including the "Golden Goose", the "Three Bears", the "Three Little Pigs", "Tom Thumb" (Warne); *The Little House on the Prairie* and *The Little House in the Big Woods* (Laura Ingalls Wilder, Harper and Row); *Winnie-the-Pooh* (A. A. Milne, Dutton).

Nine to Eleven: *Alice's Adventures in Wonderland* and *Through the Looking Glass* (Lewis Carroll, World); *The Borrowers* (Mary Norton, Harcourt Brace

Jovanovich); *Charlotte's Web* (E. B. White, Harper and Row); *The Children's Homer* — the adventures of Odysseus and the tale of Troy (Padraic Colum, Macmillan): *Johnny Tremaine* (Esther Forbes, Houghton-Mifflin); *Mary Poppins* (P. I. Travers, Harcourt Brace Jovanovich); *Stories of King Arthur and His Knights* (Barbara L. Picard, Walck); *Tales from Grimm* (Wanda Gag, translator, Coward-McCann); *The Wind in the Willows* (Kenneth Graham, Heritage Press); *The Wizard of Oz* (L. Frank Baum, various editions).

Twelve to Fourteen: *The Adventures of Tom Sawyer* and *The Adventures of Huckleberry Finn* (Samuel L. Clemens alias Mark Twain, various editions); *Better Known as Johnny Appleseed* (Mable Leigh Hunt, Lippincott); *The Incredible Journey* (Sheila Burnford, Atlantic-Little Brown); *Island of the Blue Dolphins* (Scott O'Dell, Houghton-Mifflin); *Lassie Come Home* (Eric Knight, Holt Rinehart and Winston); *Little Women,* (Louisa May Alcott, Crowell); *The Merry Adventures of Robin Hood* (Howard Pyle, Scribner); and *Treasure Island* (Robert Louis Stevenson, Grosset & Dunlap).

100 YEARS OF FADS

1870s: Young people sipped newly invented ice cream sodas after a hot game of lawn tennis. Girls prepared luscious picnic baskets to be raffled off at church socials. The height of adventure was a journey on the new railroads that crisscrossed the nation.

1880s: Schoolmates declared their undying friendship on the pages of autograph albums. Wild West shows packed 'em in, and croquet was the new sports rage. Even little girls were caught up in the patriotic spirit of the times; many marched down Main Street in red, white, and blue bunting on the Fourth of July.

1890s: The front parlor piano was never a more popular gathering place. Bicycles filled the streets, and adventurous fairgoers took a whirl on the new ferris wheel. Youngsters sneaked a peep at the best-selling

sex education manuals, "What A Young Boy Ought to Know," and "What A Young Girl Ought To Know."

1900s: Popular reading matter for young folks were adventure-packed dime novels and the comics that began to appear in Sunday newspapers. High-spirited Alice Roosevelt (Longworth) was the girl of the hour.

1910s: The automobile was quickly becoming a more common sight around town. Everyone with five cents to his or her name headed for the flicks; the first movie serial, *The Adventures of Kathlyn,* debuted in 1913. During World War I, "victory gardens" sprouted everywhere.

1920s: Short-skirted flappers slipped out of the house to dance the Charleston and sipped illicit liquor at the local speakeasy. Thousands strummed "Yessir, That's My

Siblings Frank and Marie Micholowsky were champion marathon dancers of the 1930s.

Baby'' on their ukuleles. Bridge was on its way to becoming a national addiction. Dance marathons began as good fun, but grew to exhausting lengths. Betty Boop's ''Boop Boop Ba Doop'' was the ''in'' phrase.

1930s: Shirley Temple was the nation's sweetheart; countless girls in corkscrew curls tapped their way through look-alike contests. The English princesses, Elizabeth and Margaret, also had a sizable following. The radio had become the center of family entertainment, and youngsters cherished ''Little Orphan Annie'' premiums, like mugs and wrist decoders. The chain letter and the Dionne quints were born.

1940s: Every single woman over age fifteen had a faraway soldier boyfriend to pine over — even if she had to invent him. ''Mairsy Doats'' was the nonsense song of the era, and big band sounds filled radio airwaves. ''Frankie'' Sinatra won the hearts — and squeals — of millions.

1950s: Elvis — and his gyrating pelvis — made young women's hearts throb; they duplicated his moves with their Hula Hoops. Other girls twirled batons and dreamed of leading the Homecoming Parade. Television replaced radio, and growing up meant transitions from ''Mickey Mouse Club'' to ''American Bandstand'' to ''Father Knows Best.'' Teenagers lived on cola, French fries, and rock 'n' roll.

1960s: The surfer with sun-bleached hair and sun bronzed skin opened the decade. When the surf wasn't up, a volleyball usually was. Farther inland, a skateboard had to suffice. Then came Beatlemania, and every craze before or since palled by comparison. Youths followed their idols into Mod fashions, psychedelic drugs, and transcendental meditation. Other faddish offshoots included granny glasses, blue jeans decorated in every conceivable manner, guitars, and Frisbees. Demonstrations replaced

Though one hoop was enough for most girls, this expert twirled more than a dozen at once.

drive-ins as places to see and be seen at. For stay-at-homes, ''Get Smart'' (''Would you believe. . . ?''), ''Batman'' (''Biff. . . Bang . . . Pow!''), and Rowan and Martin's ''Laugh In'' ('Sock it to me!'') were top-rated television shows.

1970s: Fads of the Fifties were resurrected by Seventies youths; heart throb of the era was Henry Winkler, ''The Fonz'' of television's ''Happy Days.'' In a continuation of the Sixties back-to-the-earth movement, Frye boots, down jackets, house plants, and vegetarianism won many young adherents. Being scared out of one's wits — by the devil in *The Exorcist,* by a shark in *Jaws,* by a giant ape in *King Kong,* or by one of the new loop-the-loop roller coasters at amusement parks — was a popular pastime. Backgammon won favor among those with weaker stomachs. Streaking enjoyed a moment of glory, though it was more popular among young men than young women. (As feminist Gloria Steinem commented, while a naked young man streaked through a conference she was addressing, "I guess, for men, streaking is liberation. For women, it's not having to streak.")

THE "BEST YEARS"?

If a girl sheds a few tears on her way to womanhood, she is in good company.

When she met husband-to-be Carlo Ponti at fifteen, says actress Sophia Loren, "I was very skinny and very ugly and everyone said I looked like a giraffe." Ponti told her she had no future in movies.

Adolescent Helen Gurley Brown saw herself as "flat-chested, pale, acne-skinned, terrified." The *Cosmopolitan* editor went through eighteen secretarial jobs before she was twenty-five.

Model Lauren Hutton wore falsies in high school to compensate for her lack of natural endowments. A fellow student discovered Hutton's secret and passed the padding around the school. The future cover girl had to rely on a sympathetic teacher to arrange her date to the prom.

According to Ralph Keyes, in *Is There Life After High School?*, the ranks of self-described teenage wallflowers include Joan Baez, Mia Farrow, Betty Friedan, Ali McGraw, Joan Rivers, Buffy St. Marie, and Barbra Streisand.

Though many women recall the high school years as "the best years of my life," puberty is for many a time of aching loneliness. "My folks keep telling me these are the best years of my life," one 16-year-old wrote to columnist Ann Landers. "If they are right, I hate to think what the rest of my life is going to be like."

The adolescent girl wrestles with the physical and emotional manifestations of newly-active sex hormones; with conflicting social pressures to date and be popular on the one hand, but to retain her virginity and "reputation" on the other; and with a restless desire to find herself and escape from the parental yoke.

A common teenage refrain is, "Nobody understands me." She often cannot even understand herself. "Adolescents feel so intensely," says Dr. Gerald Dabbs of New York City's Payne Whitney Psychiatric Clinic, "that they can't imagine everyone doesn't know how miserable they are."

The thrill of seeing the idolized Beatles moved more than one 1960s teenager to tears.

More often than not, the budding woman is embarrassed by her body; she fears she is too tall or too short, too thin or too heavy, too flat-chested or too well-endowed. Psychologists urge parents to prepare their children well in advance for the changes their bodies will undergo during the teen years. No amount of sex education pamphlets, educational films, or exchanges of misinformation with the girls can replace a sensitive, down-to-earth mother-daughter chat.

Menstrual irregularities, acne, dramatic mood changes, and growth that seems to come too quickly or not quickly enough, are some of the most tear-provoking by-products of the teen years. All but the most severe of these disorders pass with time.

Mothers accustomed to keeping careful watch over their children's diets and bedtime throw up their hands in despair during the teen years. It is especially important for maturing women to get adequate rest and nutrition, though strident maternal nagging on those topics has been known to do more harm than good. Mothers should be especially alert for sudden changes in their teenager's behavior; the youngster who begins starving herself or spending half her days in bed may be a victim of severe physical or emotional problems.

Parent-Child Conflict Normal

A woman never needs her parents more than during the teen years. Yet she never treats them worse! Psychologists postulate that a change in the parent-child relationship begins in early adolescence, when the child realizes that mother and father are not perfect. Adolescents often overreact by staging a full-scale rebellion against many of the values their elders hold most dear. They charge parents with hypocrisy for condemning marijuana (with martini glass in hand) or demanding respect for authority, while cheating on their income tax. And, to a certain extent, they are right.

So long as it stays within bounds, parent-child conflict is a normal — even healthy — part of growing up. "Rebelliousness against parents is a natural, built-in aspect of adolescents," says baby doctor Benjamin Spock. "It assists them in giving up the comforts and security of home and achieving real independence."

Andrea Boroff Eagan, who tackles the problems of growing up from an adolescent's perspective, in *Why Am I So Miserable If These Are The Best Years Of My Life?*, advises teens to "handle" parents by trying to see them in a more objective light. She suggests her readers determine if their fights with parents are necessary, or picked merely for the sake of being disagreeable. "If you can figure out where they're coming from, why they're doing what they're doing, and not accept or reject them automatically, it will make your life with them a bit easier," she counsels. Parents would do well to follow the same advice with regard to their children. "If all else fails," says Eagan, "just remember that most relationships between parents and kids improve enormously all by themselves by the time the kids are 21 or so."

Friends — male and female — rightly play a greater role in a girl's life as she grows older. Many parents are miffed when their daughters seem to prefer friends' company to that of family members; fathers, especially, tend to see each young suitor as a rival for their daughters' affections. Though parents should learn to accept their children's longer flights from the nest, they should not neglect their responsibilities over such matters as curfews and chaperonage. According to psychologists, youngsters want their parents to exert some authority over their comings and goings. "Parents should never assume that because youths ask for more freedom they necessarily want it," says Spock.

Rules should be clear, logical, and sufficiently flexible to accommodate special events like all-night proms. As for younger children, teenagers' punishments should be meted out quickly and should fit the transgression.

Money is a frequent arena of contention between teens and their parents. Experts suggest teens be given a clear understanding of family finances, including how much they can regularly expect to cover their own needs and whims. Youngsters should be involved early in financial planning for their post-high school education.

Discovering Boys

Girls realize early in adolescence that boys are more than classroom teases and neighborhood playmates. Complicating this new sexual awareness is the fact that boys usually do not "discover" girls until two or more years later.

Once the attraction becomes mutual, girls have new problems. While they are usually seeking love and companionship in a male-female relationship, boys are more preoccupied with its sexual aspects. The "new morality" has often had a less than liberating impact on young women. "The effect of declaring sex healthy and necessary, and women 'free' to do it," states Shere Hite in her nationwide study of female sexuality, "was to take away women's right *not* to have sex. Women lost their right to say 'no.' "

Despite the greater availability of birth control information to teenagers, the number of unwed teenage mothers is rising. In 1977, about 600,000 babies will be born to unwed women under the age of nineteen; from 1968 through 1973, the pregnancy rate increased 13.1 percent among black and Hispanic teenagers and

By the time a woman leaves her teens, relations with her mother have usually turned upward.

50 percent among white teenagers. Epidemic venereal disease rates among teenagers are another result of increased sexual activity.

"What will I be when I grow up?" is another question that plagues adolescents. Relatives, high school counselors, and college admissions officers all press youngsters for career commitments they are not yet ready to make. From ninth grade on, students must contend with the fact that their grades "count" for college. SAT tests throw many youngsters into panic. Though attitudes are improving, girls still encounter biases from elders who try to channel them into traditional female roles. Many parents and teachers remain unconvinced that girls need college educations as much as their brothers and male classmates.

While most teenage girls wage their battles quietly in their rooms, some seek other ways of release. More than half a million girls run away from home each year, prompting parents to place ads like this one in the *New York Times:* "Karen, don't call, come home. We love you. We want you with us. Grandma is dying. She wants to see you. Love, Mom, Dad, Jennie, Peter."

Suicide is the second greatest cause of death among adolescents (accidents are first). Teenage suicides have increased more than 200 percent in recent years, compared with a 20 percent increase for the population at large. Ninety percent of failed adolescent suicide attempts are by girls, though girls commit only 30 percent of the successful suicides.

Teenage Delinquency

From 1960 to 1974, the rate of girls under eighteen arrested for delinquent behavior jumped 245 percent. For boys under eighteen, the rate was up less than half that amount.

And there are other disturbing statistics. For example, more than 1.3 million preteen and teenage girls and boys have serious drinking problems — a trend not unnoticed by liquor companies, that have begun to sell milk shake-flavored alcoholic beverages.

But adolescence is by no means a decade or so of unremitting loneliness, rebellion, and acne. The mere fact that most adults remember the period as "the best years" suggests that good memories outlive the bad. The teen years cap a period in an individual's life of unequaled physical, mental, and emotional growth. A girl enters her teens still largely defined and sustained by her parents; she emerges well on her way to becoming an independent, self-confident woman.

Perhaps the best thing about adolescence is that it does not go on forever. Like Hutton, Brown, and Loren, most women are able to look back from success on the years they sometimes felt ugly and unloved. *Is There Life After High School?* suggests that some of the most unpopular teenagers grow up to be life's greatest successes.

Though the heartaches of high school are best filed away in the back recesses of memory, a woman is never so old that she must relinquish her teenage inquisitiveness, scepticism of authority, and zest for life. After years of defining herself solely as wife or mother, feminist Betty Friedan experienced a period of self-discovery in her forties that she termed "a second adolescence," one that was "much more interesting and fun" than the first. Along with many women who have held on to the best of adolescence in later life, Friedan could rejoice upon turning fifty, "I feel more like 18 than when I was 18."

CHILD CELEBRITIES

Historical Girl Prodigies

Pocahontas, daughter of the Tidewater Virginia Indian chief Powhatan, became legendary for saving the life of Captain John Smith by throwing her body over his in 1607 when he was about to be tomahawked by her tribe. She was about twelve years old. Smith became her immediate friend. Soon after Smith's return to Jamestown a few days later, Pocahontas began to supply his struggling colony with food. For the next year, she acted as emissary between the Indians and settlers.

In 1613, Pocahontas was taken hostage by Captain Samuel Argall, an Englishman, and held in exchange for English prisoners and materials seized by the Indians. She was treated as a guest rather than a captive, and, at her request, she began to learn the English language and religion. While prisoner, she met John Rolfe, a wealthy colonist ten years her senior who later founded Virginia's tobacco industry. They were married in April 1614, after Pocahontas had been baptized. Because of the marriage, relations between the colonists and Indians improved. Pocahontas visited England to meet King James I, and died there of fever when she was twenty-two years old.

The exotic Pocahontas caused a great stir in high society during her 1616 visit to London.

Another Indian girl, **Sacajewea,** when in her late teens, accompanied two men, Meriweather Lewis and William Clark, on their search for the Northwest Passage and is credited with guiding their expedition between the Rocky and Cascade mountain ranges. She also acted as an emissary to other Indians they met along the route.

Before joining Lewis and Clark, Sacajewea, a Shoshone Indian, had been captured at age twelve and sold to a French Sioux, Toussaint Charbonneau, who took her as his second wife. In 1804, Charbonneau was hired by the Lewis and Clark team to guide them on their journey, and he insisted on bringing his wife. Sacajewea proved much more valuable than her husband. Along the way, she often sang in response to bird calls, and the explorers named her "Bird Woman." During the trip, she gave birth to a son, and Clark later sponsored his education. Her life after the expedition is unknown, but she is believed to have died in the Dakota territory in about 1884.

Several girls have passed in and out of history. Among them:

Lady Jane Grey, born in 1537 in Leicestershire, England, is known as the "Nine Days Queen" because at age seventeen she ruled England for nine days before being beheaded for treason on Tower Hill. A brilliant and beautiful girl, she read Plato for recreation. Through a series of political meneuvers by her father, Henry Grey, marquis of Dorset and later duke of Suffolk, and by her father-in-law, John Dudley, duke of Northumberland, she succeeded her cousin Edward VI to the throne. However, the country preferred the rightful heir, her cousin, Mary Tudor, for queen. Palace intrigues and popular feeling ousted the teenaged queen: Jane Grey and her husband were beheaded on February 12, 1554.

On August 18, 1587, **Virginia Dare** became the first English child born in America. She was the granddaughter of John White, governor of 150 colonists who had settled in Roanoke. Nine days after the birth, Governor White sailed to England to seek aid for the new colony. The Spanish War interrupted his return, and no one was able to travel to Roanoke for sixty-four years. When colonists did return in 1651, they found no trace of those who had been left behind, including America's first baby, Virginia Dare.

Linda Brown, a little black girl who got tired making the long daily trek to her segregated school, more recently gained a place in history. Linda had to walk five blocks and ride a bus two miles to her all-black elementary school, even though a school for white youngsters was only four blocks from her home. Her mother and father thought the segregated school system deprived Linda of her rights, so they brought suit against the Topeka, Kansas, Board of Education. The result was the U.S. Supreme Court's landmark *Brown v. Board of Education* decision, which directed school districts to open classrooms to black and white students, alike, "with all deliberate speed." Now the mother of two school-aged children, Linda Brown Smith believes much of the promise of the 1954 *Brown* decision has gone unfulfilled. "A lot of people around here don't remember me and aren't even aware of the decision at all," she said in 1974. "I guess I'm a symbol lost in the crowd."

Young Literary Lights

Brief fame also struck two young letter writers. When she was eleven years old, **Grace Bedell Billings** wrote to the future President Abraham Lincoln, telling him he would look better with a beard. Lincoln agreed, grew one, and wore it from then on. Eight year old **Virginia O'Hanlon** wrote to *The New York Sun* in 1897 asking if Santa Claus really existed. *Sun* editor Francis P. Church responded with the now-famous essay, "Yes, Virginia, there is a Santa Claus".

Other young women achieved fame through more poignant writing. One teenager, **Anne Frank,** kept a secret diary from 1942 to 1944 while she hid with her family from the Nazis who were rounding up Dutch Jews. Non-Jewish friends sheltered them in an attic in Amsterdam and brought them food and books. But the Franks were discovered and sent to concentration camps. Anne Frank, then sixteen, her older sister, and her mother died in Bergen-Belsen. Only her father lived to return to the attic, where he found his daughter's notebook hidden in a cupboard. *The Diary of Anne Frank,* origi-nally entitled *Diary of a Young Girl,* was published in 1947; it was a testament of courage, strength, and the will to live. Trying desperately to lead a normal life under abnormal circumstances, Anne Frank wrote: "In spite of everything, I still believe that people are really good at heart."

"Any kid who thinks he can write a book should do it," believes **Alexandra Sheedy,** "even if grown-ups don't think they can." At thirteen, Sheedy published her first book, *She Was Nice to Mice: The Other Side of Elizabeth I's Character Never Before Revealed by Previous Historians*. The 1975 book offered an account of Elizabeth's reign from the perspective of a palace mouse. The historical novel was illustrated by Sheedy's young friend, Jessica Levy.

Stars in the Performing Arts

Despite old taboos on performing in public, girls have excelled in all branches of the performing arts. **Maria (Nannërl) Mozart,** born in 1751 in Salzburg, composed and played her own works on the harpsichord before she was seven. When her baby brother, Wolfgang, was three, they played duets. Encouraged by their father Leopold, himself a composer and gifted violinist, the children played in Paris for Marie Antoinette and in London for the royal family. Nannërl was soon overshadowed by her genius brother; she was, however, one of the first females to break tradition by playing in public.

Another older sister, **Fanny Mendelssohn,** born in 1805 in Germany, was a gifted composer and musician, but spent most of her life being musical consultant to her younger brother, Felix. Sister and brother were devoted to one another, and when people would praise Felix's piano skill, he would boast: "But you should hear my sister, Fanny!" However, both brother and father disapproved of women playing music in public or publishing their works. Fanny married when she was twenty-four, and, with the support of her husband, did give a charity concert in Berlin.

Today, girls who want to play music have an easier time finding an audience. **Kirsten Agresta,** of Bloomfield Hills, Michigan, sang in perfect pitch when most babies are learning to talk, played piano at age two, and wrote a love song at four. By the time she was six, in 1977 Agresta played the harp and the marimba, and had started violin lessons. She wants to begin guitar when her hands get bigger. Her mother, who holds a masters degree in music, plans to wait until her daughter is a few years older before accepting the concert offers already coming in. Agresta's favorite composers: Mozart, Chopin, and John Denver.

Sixteen-year-old **Lilit Gampel,** of Los Angeles, has already been a violin soloist with the Boston Pops Orchestra, the Los Angeles Philharmonic, the Vienna Symphony, the New York Philharmonic, and the Cincinnati Symphony. "I'm never nervous. Why should I be? If I were, it wouldn't be fun," she told an interviewer.

At thirteen, **Janis Ian** wrote the song "Society's Child" while waiting to see her high school guidance counselor. Though the bitter song about interracial love was banned from the airwaves by many radio stations, the record became a million seller.

But Ian's fortune dipped. "I was sixteen and on the road by myself," she recalled. "Everybody I met was much older and no one related to me. There was nothing to do except make myself crazy."

She dropped out of music completely at twenty. But she returned four years later with her Grammy-winning "At Seventeen," a wistful song of teenage loneliness. Hers was not a comeback, Ian insisted, "It's more like two separate lives. But I know one thing — this life is much better. I know what I'm doing now."

Child Stars of the Silver Screen

It has been easiest for girls to earn fortune and fame on the silver screen. **Shirley Temple** was Hollywood's favorite by the time she was three years old; she made more than three million dollars before she reached puberty. Born in 1929, she became imitated and admired through the 1930s for her performances in films like *Bright Eyes* (1934) for which she won a special Oscar.

Her career faded with maturity. Married twice, Temple concentrated on rearing children and working with the Republican Party until 1969, when she was appointed a U.S. representative to the

Shirley Temple was at the height of her screen popularity when she starred in *Dimples*.

United Nations. She was named as ambassador to Ghana in 1974; and, in 1976, President Gerald Ford appointed her the first woman chief of protocol.

Another child star, **Patty Duke,** was thirteen when she opened on Broadway in *The Miracle Worker* in 1959. She played the young Helen Keller, a blind-deaf mute who was guided by her teacher into making contact with the world. In 1961, she co-starred with Anne Bancroft in the film version of the play and won an Oscar for best supporting actress. She went on to star as "identical cousins" in her own television series, "The Patty Duke Show," which ran for several seasons.

Duke, the daughter of a New York cab driver-alcoholic father, once said, "If I hadn't become a child star. . . , I might have turned into a prostitute." At the age of seventeen, she dropped out of films "to grow up, to function for myself." During the next few years, she went through divorce, annulment, miscarriage, psychoanalysis, and had a much-publicized affair with Desi Arnaz, Jr. and bore his child. When she did work again, she was ridiculed for her role in the film *Valley of the Dolls*. She is now married for a third time, to actor John Astin, and appears on television periodically.

In 1974, ten-year-old **Tatum O'Neal** became the youngest person to win a Best Supporting Actress Oscar, for her performance in *Paper Moon*. Daughter of actress Joanna Moore and actor Ryan O'Neal, she became an overnight celebrity for her portrayal of a precocious 1930s con artist; later, she starred in *The Bad News Bears* and *Nickelodeon*.

Tatum has led a stormy life: her parents separated when she was two, and she spent some years with her mother on a San Fernando Valley ranch, where Moore became addicted to methadrine and Tatum grew flowers in a wrecked car in the front yard. When she was eight, Tatum went to live with her father. "She really hated me," her mother said at the time. "She spit in my face." Tatum now watches jealously over her father's social life. Tatum's director on *Paper Moon*, Peter Bogdanovich, says the secret of Tatum's success is that "It's always amusing if a child behaves older than she is by about thirty years."

Tatum O'Neal's chief young rival is

Jody Foster, who played the female lead in the short-lived television version of *Paper Moon*. At thirteen, Foster already had several sophisticated roles to her credit, including a precocious prostitute in *Taxi Driver* and a gangster's moll in *Bugsy Malone*. "The only doll I ever played with was a G.I. Joe," recalls Foster of her childhood.

Olympic Heart Throb

No child since Shirley Temple has captured the world's hearts like the somber, fourteen-year-old **Nadia Comaneci.**

Comaneci somersaulted to fame at the 1976 Montreal Olympics. She scored three perfect tens in her gymnastics routines, surpassing the performance of Olga Korbut, the young sweetheart of the 1972 Olympics.

Daughter of a Romanian auto mechanic father and office-worker mother, Comaneci was discovered at six while playing in a school yard. The intense child soon began training three to four hours a day after classes.

What makes Comaneci great? A lithe, slender body (five feet tall, eighty-six pounds at the Montreal Games). Self-discipline. Tremendous power of concentration. And, adds coach Bela Karolyi, "She has no fear."

Besides gold medals, Comaneci collects dolls. She now has more than 200 of them from 60 countries. Her favorite is an Eskimo doll of fading sealskin which she takes with her everywhere. Coach Karolyi gave it to her to overcome her bad luck at finishing thirteenth in her first Junior National Championships of Romania eight years ago. The doll did its work well.

Comaneci is not the only young woman making sports history. Back in 1958, eight-year-old **Joy Foster** of Jamaica became her country's singles and mixed doubles champion in table tennis. In 1975, eleven-year-old **Karen Stead** became the first girl to win the All American Soap Box Derby. Stead built her car herself and steered it to a photo finish victory over two boy finalists.

And sixty-pound **Amber Edwina Hunt,** a pre-teen Junior Golden Gloves boxer, says she is already in training for the 1984 Olympics. "I'll be tough like a boy but act like a girl," declares Hunt.

Nadia Comaneci offered a rare smile after receiving her first Olympic perfect score.

GROUPS FOR GIRLS

Millions of American girls belong to all-female organizations. Some of these groups were founded as social clubs, some as part of more serious feminist reform efforts.

Nineteenth century feminists who were concerned about the safety and living conditions of young immigrant women working in city factories established America's first **Young Women's Christian Association** in 1858 to provide a cheap, clean place for women to sleep. It was modeled after the British YWCA founded three years earlier. The American "Y" offered its young women classes in English and taught them the fundamentals of American citizenship. As the needs of women changed, the curriculum has expanded. Today, many YWCAs offer physical education — dance, yoga, swimming — along with art, gourmet cooking, consciousness-raising sessions, and weekend outings. Along with their male counterpart, the YMCA, they often serve as community centers.

There are 8,000 YWCAs in the United States, with 2.5 million members. The group lists the "elimination of racism" as its major priority. Although the YWCA remains centered on the Christian ethic, it is open to all young women, regardless of religion, over the age of twelve. The national headquarters is at 600 Lexington Avenue, New York, NY 10022.

Its Jewish counterpart, the **YWHA,** or **Young Women's Hebrew Association,** was founded in 1888 as a "ladies' auxiliary" by the Young Men's Hebrew Association. The early centers provided reading rooms, physical education, and cultural events. Today, the YWHA, like the YWCA, offers a wide range of classes, is inter-denominational, and is well-integrated with its male counterpart. Almost half a million women belong to the YMHA-YWHA, also known as the Jewish Community Centers. The national headquarters is at the National Jewish Welfare Board, 15 East 26th Street, New York, NY 10010.

On March 12, 1912, Juliette (Daisy) Gordon Low founded the first unit of the **Girl Scouts of the USA** with sixteen girls in Savannah, Georgia. Low, a native of Savannah, had married a wealthy Georgian and lived with him in England. The marriage was unhappy, and her husband filed for divorce. He died in 1905, before divorce proceedings were finished. Left with little to do, Low drifted between America and England until 1911, when she met Sir Robert Baden-Powell and his sister, Agnes Baden-Powell, founders of the English Boy Scouts and Girl Guides.

Inspired by them, she set up Girl Guide

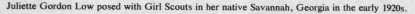

Juliette Gordon Low posed with Girl Scouts in her native Savannah, Georgia in the early 1920s.

units among the poor in Scotland and London, and then turned her energy, wealth, and influence to establishing a similar group in America. Today there are 3.2 million Girl Scouts in the U.S., and Girl Scouting is the largest voluntary activity of girls around the world.

Girl Scouts are divided into groups by age: the youngest are Brownies, followed by Juniors, Cadettes, and Seniors. Each age group wears a distinctive uniform. Many people are familiar with Girl Scouts only through their annual fund-raising cookie sales. The group's main purpose, however, is to learn to serve others, respect authority, be cheerful and friendly, and improve the world. The original Girl Scout pledge, "to be clean in thought, word and deed," was omitted in a 1970 revision of Girl Scout laws. The national headquarters is at 830 Third Avenue, New York, NY 10022.

Girl Scouts do not welcome boys as members. In 1974, however, the Explorers' division of the Boy Scouts of America began to admit women aged fifteen to twenty. Early in 1977, Boy Scouts changed its name to Scouting/USA to reflect this changing membership. Today there are 230,000 women Explorers.

The first **4-H Club** began in Douglas County, Minnesota, in 1904 as a corn, potato, and tomato growing contest. No girls entered these first displays of agricultural prowess, but female participation in 4-H has grown rapidly through the years. 4-H is largely under the auspices of the U.S. Department of Agriculture. Today, 4-H membership is 5.5 million, and more than half its members are female.

The 4-Hs stand for "head, heart, hands, and health". The 4-H pledge is: "My head to clearer thinking, my heart to greater loyalty, my hands to larger service, and my health to better living for my club, my community, my country, and my world". Each state has its own 4-H headquarters, and the national mailing address is: Extension Service, U.S. Department of Agriculture, Washington, DC 20250.

Camp Fire Girls was founded in 1910 by Dr. Luther Halsey Gulick and his wife, Charlotte Vetter, based on their work in child development and their belief in the value of outdoor recreation and social action. Today, there are 625,000 Camp Fire Girls; the program is open to anyone — boys as well as girls — up to the age of twenty-one. The national headquarters is at 1740 Broadway, New York, NY 10019.

In 1945, the United States Office of Education sponsored the creation of **Future Homemakers of America,** the female counterpart to Future Farmers of America. Current membership in FHA is 439,000 girls and 16,000 boys. The national headquarters is at 2010 Massachusetts Avenue, NW, Washington, DC, 20036.

Nineteen girls' clubs formed the **Girls' Clubs of America** in 1945. The organization remains one of the most active in women's rights and is concerned with the rising pregnancy rate among young teenagers, the increasing number of runaways and school dropouts, and the small amount of corporate and foundation money given to girls' groups. The Girls' Clubs provide places where girls and young women can go for daily tutoring, job training, and counseling on health, sex, or drug problems. The national headquarters is at 133 East 62nd Street, New York, NY 10021.

A less socially aware group is the **Supreme Assembly International Order of the Rainbow for Girls,** which has 175,000 members. The "Rainbow Girls" are part of the Masonic Order. They raise money for philanthropic projects but some chapters seem to emphasize social activities, especially formal ceremonies.

In 1976, twenty-seven Rainbow Girls in Iowa voted unanimously to admit a twelve-year-old black friend into their group, violating a 56-year-old whites only policy. When the international organization threatened to cancel the Iowa charter, the Iowa group retaliated by threatening to form its own nondiscriminatory Rainbow club. The issue was finally resolved when the Masons agreed to allow black Rainbow Girls.

The national headquarters is at 315 Carl Albert Parkway, MacAlester, OK 74501.

Lovers

LOVE AND MARRIAGE: ANCIENT TIMES THROUGH 1600

In the first marriage, a man crept into a woman's cave, captured her, and dragged her away. He chose his "wife" not for her beauty, but for her willingness to be a submissive worker.

Later, a man purchased a wife, rather than capturing one, a practice that continues today in many parts of the world. A suitor paid for her with goods, money, or property, to compensate her father for the loss of her free labor. Even the word "wedding," in many languages, originally meant "bride price."

If a man were wealthy enough, he could afford to increase his "stable" of wives. Solomon had 700 wives and 300 concubines, for status; to prove he could support all of these women and their children. Akbar the Great, Emperor of India, advised every man to have at least four wives: ". . . a Hindu to bear children, a Persian for conversation, an Afghan to keep house, and a Turk to beat up as an example to the other three." Polygamy was also a necessity where large numbers of men had been killed in hunting or war; women depended on men, and sharing a husband was preferable to having no husband at all.

A few ancient societies also practiced polyandry, where one woman had several husbands. She did not, however, have the right to choose her husbands — she was shared among several men who agreed to choose her. Polyandry was rare: anthropologist George P. Murdock studied 250 ancient cultures and found that while 193 practiced some polygamy, only two sanctioned polyandry.

Greek Women Married Young

In ancient Greek society, women in their early teens were married to men in their mid-thirties because, Euripedes explained, "a man's strength endures, while the bloom of beauty quickly leaves the woman's form." Immediately before marriage, Greek women cut off their hair and gave up their "maiden girdle" and toys, dedicating them to a goddess. In some arranged marriages, the bride wore a heavy veil, and the groom did not even see her face until the time for sex. After marriage, a wife became her husband's chattel, and could be lent or sold.

Spartan women had more freedom. They married when they were about twenty years old, and the wife could appear in public with her husband. Before the wedding ceremony, the Spartan couple often wrestled in public in the nude, for the Spartans believed that thirty minutes of athletic competition teaches more about a person than years of cohabitation.

Roman matrons were the most liberated of all: they could appear in the streets, even without escort, inherit property, and run the house while their husbands were at war.

But marriage, especially among the upper classes, lost popularity as Roman moral codes relaxed. Women, having little else to occupy their time, indulged in sexual escapades. They practiced birth control — usually coitus interruptus — and even underwent abortions. Many Roman men chose not to marry at all, settling instead for the company of prostitutes and concubines.

Early Christian Customs

In response to the loose morals of the time, the early zealous Christians taught their converts that passionate sex, even in marriage, was sinful. Women, represented by Eve in the Garden of Eden, were portrayed as evil temptresses. The Church exalted celibacy, and warned that sex was only for procreation. Church fathers even banned the burial of female and male corpses next to one another, fearing that some sexual energy would flow between them. Christian weddings were solemn affairs, without feasting or celebration.

In medieval days fathers were forced to offer dowries to help marry off their daughters. If the marriage proved unsuccessful, the groom often had to return the dowry, along with the wife, to her father's home. Dowries grew so large at this time that a man with many daughters usually put at least one of them in a convent. The nunnery was, for some women, preferable to living with a husband who believed in a popular proverb: "A woman, a dog, and a walnut tree. The more you beat them, the better they'll be."

Despite these continuing abuses, the Church declared marriage to be one of its seven sacraments — meaning it was made in heaven and could not be dissolved. Church fathers also decided that parental consent was no longer necessary for marriage. Most parents were not yet ready for this radical change in tradition, and managed to avoid it by marrying off their children when they were still too young to find other mates. In one account, a five-year-old girl was carried to the altar for her marriage, in the arms of a priest; her equally young groom was promised that, if he could sit still during the tedious ceremony, he would afterwards be allowed to go out and play.

With the new freedom of marital choice, granted by the Church, courtship came slowly into vogue; especially among the lower and newly developed middle classes, where political and economic alliances were less important.

The Game of Courtly Love

During this time, the game of courtly love was invented as a playful prelude to what is now the more serious preoccupation of romantic love. Courtly love originated in southern France, where it was probably brought by the Arabs, and it flourished in castles occupied by bored young women whose husbands were away fighting in the Crusades. These noblewomen flirted with the young troubadours and squires, who, in turn, wrote poems and songs honoring their ladies' love. This romanticism was certainly more exciting than anything most of these women had ever experienced in marriage. Before long, courtly love was touted as being more exalted than married love, for it was spontaneous and passionate rather than dutiful.

In theory, courtly love was "pure": a couple would kiss, or even embrace without clothing, but consummation of sexual passion was forbidden, and sometimes impossible because of the chastity belts desperate husbands soldered onto their straying wives. Wives titillated, teased, and frustrated their attentive suitors. For the first time, love became widely equated with suffering. Love was associated with impossible ideals, unobtainable goals, and a constant sense of longing.

Soon, this new concept of romantic love was incorporated into marriage.

THE AMERICAN WAY: 17TH AND 18TH CENTURIES

Love American-style was different from anything immigrants had known in their homelands. Courtships were short, dowries uncommon, women more accessible, chaperones often absent, and parents were left with little to say about mate selection. In this young and mobile society, tradition, money, and prestigious family titles lost some of their immediate importance because few pioneers married for those reasons.

Instead, they married to survive. A household needed at least two people to perform the duties of housekeeper, handyman, cook, and farmer; two people to share long winters and to produce children who could help with chores. Love was expected to grow with the passing years, but not necessarily to be present at the time of the wedding ceremony. In choosing his mate, a man would find someone nearby whom he "cottoned to," and the couple would set up housekeeping. Many settlements had no clergy, so the couple would live together in common-law marriage with no special social stigma.

Because more settlers were needed to share the work and populate the land, white women were a valued commodity, and were imported from England. In the 1600s, the first load of ninety women, advertised as "handsome, honestly educated maids of honest life and carriage," were shipped to Virginia to become settlers' wives. Each woman's "bride price" was the cost of her passage to America, which was paid after her arrival by the man she chose as her mate. This practice run was a great success, and importing wives became a regular commercial venture.

Out of necessity, many courtships were pursued in bed. Bundling was one of the few ways a young couple could get acquainted, for there was little free time and less privacy during the day; often, one-room cabins had no lights, and everyone went to bed shortly after dark. When a young woman "bundled," she dressed in a garment that resembled a laundry bag, encasing her up to her armpits, and then slept with her suitor. Actual sexual relations were an exception.

Bundling apparently produced few illegitimate births until its later years, and even then a debate raged over whether the blame lay with bundling, or with the newer phenomenon — the private parlor sofa. By the time of the Revolutionary War, bundling was generally out of vogue.

America's Blatant Sexual Behavior

Visiting Europeans were sometimes shocked by Americans' blatant sexual behavior, especially in the North. Even the early Puritans displayed their affection openly; causing a visiting French noblewoman to comment on the, "extreme liberty that prevails in this country between the two sexes, as long as they are not married," and to note with some wonder that, "it is no crime for a girl to kiss a young man" in public.

It was understood, however, that below the surface appearance of this "new morality," women were to remain virginal until they married. The French political philosopher Alexis De Tocqueville, visiting America, was amazed that young American couples could be left alone without fear that sex play would follow.

Every well-bred Victorian lady learned to flirt, tease, and blush to get her man.

He decided this must be because American women were more equal, and because American men were too concerned with building up a nation to waste their time in idle romance. In fact, it probably had more to do with fear of getting caught.

Double standards flourished here, as they had in Europe. America adopted English common law; which made two married persons as one, and that one was the husband. Colonial physician Dr. Benjamin Rush told a woman who was about to be married that from the day of the wedding, ". . . you must have no will of your own. The subordination of your sex to ours is enforced by nature, by reason, and by revelation . . . The happiest marriages I have known have been those where the subordination I have recommended has been most complete."

Modern Courtly Love

Women's work became less valued as society became more fragmented and complex. Like the bored medieval noblewomen, abandoned in their castles while their husbands fought in the Crusades, American women were left home while their husbands went off to work. As women became less essential to a man's economic survival, they became more isolated from the "man's world" and from each other.

Gradually, a new kind of male-female relationship developed, based on an elaborate ritualistic courtship. It was the modern version of courtly love. But, unlike the medieval love games in which both the married noblewoman and her handsome troubadour knew their escapades were fantasy, Americans approached it with dead seriousness. The stakes were high. Courtship was the proper way for a young man and woman to behave toward one another, and it was a sure road to the one thing each young American woman wanted: marriage. Unmarried women were considered "old maids" by the age of twenty, and ridiculed. A North Carolina newspaper, of 1790, described them as "ill-natured, maggotty, peevish, conceited, disagreeable . . . good for nothing."

To avoid these insults, a well-bred woman learned to flirt, tease, and blush to get her man. Her status was measured by the number of men cooling their heels on her front porch or in her parlor. According to the rules, her job was to coax each young man into declaring his affection, while she refrained from expressing any interest in him. When a man proposed, she was supposed to pretend surprise, embarrassment, even anger. She was always supposed to turn him down the first time. If a young man persisted despite such obstacles, it was a sign that his intentions were honorable and his love was true.

Southern plantation women, "Southern belles," were especially noted for their skills in this area. The real-life counterpart of Scarlett O'Hara was always above politics, business, intellectual discussions, and, of course, sex. The Southern belle was known for her untouchable virginity, a stereotype which probably originated among white plantation owners whose sexual attentions often focused on the black slave women rather than their wives.

These relationships were usually ignored by white women. As one Southern wife wrote: "Any lady is ready to tell you who is the father of all the mulatto children in everybody's household but her own." Whites often ignored the marriage vows and love bonds of their slaves. Certain parts of the slave marriage ceremony were deleted, including the phrase "till death us do part," for a master could part the couple at his whim. Black women became prized for their breeding potential, and white masters would often pair them with black men to improve the plantation's slave stock, regardless of their marital status or personal preference.

THE VICTORIAN AGE

By the early 1800s, most American women had learned to pretend sex did not exist. Victorianism, which originated in England as a reaction to the licentiousness of previous years, captured the imagination of American women, who were always ready to follow the fashions and trends of the motherland. Young women were told to not sit with a man, "in a place that is too narrow, read not out of the same book, let not your eagerness to see anything induce you to place your head close to another person." They were told

to not wear tight corsets because their blood would concentrate in their sex organs and arouse their passions.

Even library shelves were to be demure. In 1863, Lady Cough's *Etiquette* text advised: "The perfect hostess will see to it that the works of male and female authors be properly separated on her bookshelves. Their proximity, unless the authors happen to be married, should not be tolerated."

Decent women were not supposed to enjoy sex. To buttress that "fact" the United States Surgeon General, William Hammand, announced that in only one time out of ten do women experience even a slight bit of pleasure during intercourse. In 1891, Hermann Fehling, of the University of Basel, went even further and declared that, "the appearance of the sexual side in the love of a young girl is pathological." It is no wonder that, by 1880, there was one prostitute for every fifteen adult males in New York.

During this period, romantic love became more and more separate from sexual passion, resulting in a below-the-belt/above-the-belt schizophrenia that persists today. Men were supposed to flatter and woo women with words and attention, but not to touch them. Women were supposed to indulge in their romantic illusions, and suppress their sexual feelings. By the middle of the 1800s, romantic love had become so idealized that it was exalted as the primary reason for marriage.

LOVE IN THE TWENTIETH CENTURY

Until the 1900s, most social activities centered around church and home, and most courting was done on the front porch. By the turn of the century, however, young unmarried couples could go out dancing, go skating, attend the theater, or even ride bicycles, far away from the watchful eyes of parents. This new freedom was accelerated during World War I. For the first time, women went to work in large numbers; soldiers from farms and small towns went to Europe and found a rich and different culture, prompting a popular song of the time: "How you gonna keep 'em down on the farm/After they've seen Paree."

Jitterbuggers, 1944: Women began to smoke, drink, paint their lips, show their legs, use slang.

Women began to smoke, drink in public, paint their lips, show their legs, use slang, and even move into apartments of their own. Contraceptives became more available — especially for men — and Freudian psychology began to be popular. For the first time, young people heard that sexual repression could lead to psychological problems. The automobile, a "bedroom on wheels," offered a new and total privacy when parked on back country roads.

By the end of World War II, even long engagements lost some of their popularity. Instead, young people began to "go steady," swapping fraternity pins or high school rings as a token of temporary fidelity. In 1953, Dr. Alfred C. Kinsey published his landmark report on sexuality, revealing, among other items, that 50 percent of the 8,000 young American women he surveyed had engaged in premarital sex, sparking talk of a "sexual revolution."

Until the late 1960s, pre-college dating remained firmly structured: the boy asked the girl out, and then picked her up at home, preferably in a car. He took her to a social event, paid for her entertainment and showered her with attention. In return, he had the right to try and coax from her some sexual favor, if only a "good night kiss."

Seventies Bring New Dating Patterns

By the 1970s, however, this pattern had changed. A survey conducted by *Seventeen* magazine, in 1975, showed that 93.4 percent of the young women surveyed had taken the initiative, at least once, and asked a young man for a date. Young people are also more likely to go out in groups rather than pairs, a custom long practiced in Europe. Young women often pay their own way on dates — partly because activities are expensive, partly because they are likely to have jobs where they can earn spending money. Most young women still approve of traditional male courtesies, such as having doors opened for them, but they also feel more free to do untraditional things, like give men gifts on romantic occasions.

Two other modern phenomena are the singles bar and computer-arranged dating. Many single women who live alone — especially in urban areas — find singles bars are a "safe" way to scout for a partner: you can meet men, talk to them — usually under cover of loud music — but don't have to feel obliged to go home with them. Others, however, feel singles bars cheapen sex and love. One woman said of her experience: "I felt as if I were a piece of sirloin steak hanging in the butcher's window."

Computer dating began in 1965, when two Harvard students started Operation Match. For a three-dollar fee, a college student could receive the names of at least five members of the opposite sex whose interests were matched to his by computer. It was a resounding success. Within nine months, Operation Match had arranged dates for 90,000 students. Others began to offer computer dating as well, but in most cases the computer company had more success than the people it paired up. Early systems, like Operation Match, concentrated on students — who had a great deal in common simply by virtue of being students. But when computer-dating became big business, typical clients became lonely women in their forties and fifties; more variables were involved and expectations were probably higher. Many clients complained that they had been mismatched, even in obviously important areas like age or religion.

In an article in *The Nation* in 1970, Linda Mason concluded: "The fact is that the only true love around these firms is the love of money — and for that, hearts are broken." But psychologists point out that the fault does not always lie with the computer. Compatibility tests assume that two people with the same traits will like each other when, in fact, people who are too much alike sometimes detest each other. They dislike in the other person the same traits they dislike in themselves; because of this, opposites do, in fact, sometimes attract.

Video-dating tries to offset some of the risk of mismatches by allowing each client to watch videotaped interviews with potential dates the computer has selected. The client sees the tape, and then receives only the names and addresses of those persons she likes. Fees range from $75 to $135 for three months, during which time a client can view a minimum of three potential dates.

Is Marriage Passé

It is true that more people are living together without marriage. The United States Census Bureau reported that the number of men and women living together, in unwedded bliss, was 17,000 in 1960; zoomed to 654,000 by 1970; and doubled again to 1.32 million in 1976. Perhaps such statistics prompted President Jimmy Carter, a Baptist, to comment in 1977 to one thousand government employees that: "Those of you who are living in sin, I hope you'll get married." The comment drew laughter and applause.

As the costs of living rise, more elderly, unmarried men and women live together to avoid loneliness, and to share their Social Security checks. Since 1969, new laws, providing tax relief to singles, have also encouraged people to live together out of wedlock to save tax dollars.

But a 1971 study of Cornell underclassmen revealed that the most important reason young people live together is to try and develop a meaningful relationship. The Cornell men said they are tired of the dating game, and want to test the strength of an already close relationship.

Other studies show that co-habitors are quite faithful to each other, and tend to drift into marriage when they leave college, or when the woman gets pregnant. Financial columnist Sylvia Porter calls these couples "mingles": mingling is just another stepleading to marriage. The main difference is that the young wait longer to wed — the average age for women is now 21.3 years; for men, 23.8 years — and when they do marry, they have a better idea of what it is really like to share a home.

In fact, all signs indicate that Americans continue to believe fervently in marriage. A recent Gallup Poll shows that three out of four women in the United States say marriage and children are among the most important elements that they need for an ideal life; 44 percent of the women would prefer not to have a job outside the home — they want to be full time wives and mothers. A 1974 Virginia Slims opinion poll found that almost 90 percent, of both sexes, do not believe society could survive without marriage. Feminist Betty Friedan agrees: "I cannot believe that the need for marriage is over. But marriage is changing, as it had to, and like a broken bone that has healed it may emerge stronger than ever."

The new shape of marriage remains to

be seen. Many feel that we must begin by readjusting our romantic attitudes about what married life should be like. Dr. Selma G. Miller, president of the New York chapter, American Association of

Marriage and Divorce rates

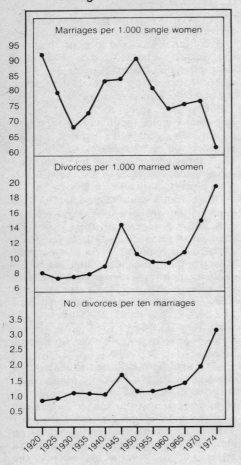

Marriages per 1,000 single women

Divorces per 1,000 married women

No. divorces per ten marriages

U.S. Statistical Abstract.
National Institute for Health Statistics

Marriage and Family Counselors, says: "People expect storybook marriage, all love and wonder. When it isn't all love and wonder, it leads to shock, and, worse, a feeling of failure."

MARRIAGE CUSTOMS: HOW THEY STARTED

Many of today's popular wedding rituals date back to the days when humans dwelt in caves. Among the warlike tribes which practiced bride capture, best men and ushers evolved from the confederates of the groom, who fought off the abducted woman's relatives while the couple made their get-away. The original bridesmaids surrounded the woman to try to prevent her kidnap. (Later, the best man became the go-between for consenting couples, who were not allowed to see each other for a designated time before the wedding.) Less than 100 years ago, wedding guests in southern Russia staged mock fights between friends of bride and groom.

According to *Bride's Book of Etiquette*, the honeymoon did not start out as a romantic vacation. Instead, it was the period during which the groom hid with his captured bride until the excitement had died down and they could return to his village. The actual term "honeymoon" originated later among the Teutons, who, after the ceremony, drank a honey substance until the moon waned.

Engagement and wedding rings nowadays symbolize love. But they began as ropes or shackles used to subdue the abducted woman. Later, the ring was placed on the left hand — rather than around her ankle or through her nose — because that hand was considered weaker. (In some European countries, however, the ring is worn on the right hand.) The third finger was chosen because it was thought a vein from that finger led directly to the heart.

The earliest wedding gifts were tokens with which the groom appeased his new father-in-law for the loss of his daughter. Later, it became customary for the groom to pay his bride's father a "bride price," which started out as a useful gift, like a cow, and later became money. (Still later, the gifts were presented to the bride instead of her father.) "Giving away the bride" marked the official transfer of ownership from father to husband. Russian men added one more step; to make sure that the woman knew her place, the father would gently beat his daughter with a new whip, then give the whip to her husband.

Tradition holds that the woman who catches the bride's bouquet will be the next to marry.

The wheat and grains used in cake have often been present at weddings as fertility symbols. In old England, the bride and groom first kissed over a stack of little cakes, an early version of the modern tiered wedding cake. In ancient Rome, a thin loaf of bread was broken above the bride's head during the ceremony. The guests saved the crumbs as good luck tokens. Other signs of prosperity and happiness which have received prominent places at weddings include orange blossoms, fruit, and the rice or other seed-bearing plants thrown at the bridal couple.

Early wedding guests feared demons would dampen the couple's happiness, and did their best to ward them off. In Jewish marriages, the *chupa*, or canopy, was originally a sanctuary from evils that hovered above the young couple who, in their innocence and happiness, were most vulnerable. The canopy's shape also symbolized the groom's tent, where the bridal deflowering would take place. In other ceremonies, guests threw old shoes after the couple in the belief that the spirits feared leather.

Veils were traditionally worn as a sign of virginity, but the first American woman to insist on a veil for her wedding did so for a different reason. Nelly Custis wanted to please her fiance (an aide to President George Washington) who had complimented her appearance when he glimpsed her face behind a lace curtain at the window. From time to time, other American women also defy tradition by holding unusual wedding ceremonies, and the practice is becoming more common.

10 Unusual Weddings

• Evangelist Sun Myung Moon officiated at history's largest multiple wedding, which took place in Seoul, South Korea, in 1975. Some 1,800 couples responded "ye" to Moon's query, "Will you swear to love your spouse forever?"

• Irwin Allen relied upon the expertise he gained producing *The Towering Inferno* to stage his 1976 wedding to Sheila Matthews. Allen created an exotic Arabian Nights scene in the Grand Ballroom of Los Angeles' Beverly Wilshire Hotel and proceeded to "direct" his own wedding.

• A wedding doubleheader took place in 1976 when two sets of identical twins married in a ceremony attended by 60 other sets of twins. The ceremony included twin bridesmaids, twin matrons of honor, twin flower girls, and twin organists. The happy couples honeymooned together and took up residence in one big house.

For modern marrying couples, almost anything goes: This couple heads for the golf course.

• "Babes in Toyland" was appropriately chosen as the wedding march for the 1976 marriage of Caroline Pool and Alan Turoff, two toy designers, in New York's F.A.O. Schwarz toy store. The two met five years before when both sighted smoke coming from the store and called the fire department. Among the prominent guests at the wedding were stuffed versions of Snoopy, Winnie the Pooh, and Raggedy Ann.

• David Carter apparently wanted to make sure he didn't miss the starting flag of 1975's Purolator 500 Race at Pennsylvania's Pocono International Raceway. So he married Nina Johnson in the victory lane before the start of the race. Auto racing great Richard Petty, whose fan club Carter headed, was best man.

• "Health spa" managers Donald Scott and Tobi Eiferman married in 1970 at Nevada's first nudist wedding. The couple, their attendants, and guests were required to strip before the ceremony. Only the justice of the peace who united the two was permitted to keep his clothes on.

• Steven Cranfill and Dana Taggart had spent many hours in the Wyoming state capitol, he as a state representative and she as daughter of a state senator. So they chose the capital rotunda for their 1977 nuptials. (Ironically, Cranfill is a Democrat while Taggart's father is a Republican.)

• A Swedish woman and a Detroit man were united in 1933 in the world's first transatlantic telephone wedding. The ceremony was relayed by radio across the ocean via Scotland and England.

• The nuptials of Tom Basham and Peggy Donovan were ordinary enough: a traditional Catholic ceremony followed by an old-fashioned Polish reception. But the date they chose was not: July 4, 1976. They picked the nation's 200th birthday, said Basham, "in order to form a more perfect union." "And to insure domestic tranquility," added Donovan.

• Sherry Lee Clarke, who kept a ten-foot cardboard cut-out of King Kong in her bedroom, informed her fiance — Albert Jackson, that they could be married on the observation deck of New York's Empire State Building — or not at all. So the two were united eighty-six floors above the ground in a 1977 ceremony. The minister who performed the marriage had previously officiated at a horseback wedding and at a ceremony aboard a 747 at Kennedy Airport.

PLANNING A WEDDING

If you plan to have a traditional-style wedding with invited guests, there are certain timetables you should follow and costs you should know about.

Six months before the ceremony, you should select the location, date, and time for the marriage and the reception; decide how many guests to invite, and how formal you want the occasion to be. Hotels, clubs, and caterers generally need this much advance notice. If you prefer a religious ceremony, choose the clergyman or woman you want, and ask if he or she will be available. If you are planning to make changes in the standard marriage ceremony, or intend to write your own, tell the minister, priest, or rabbi at this time. Discuss the kind of music you like, and make sure the musicians are available. Select your attendants — the bride and groom

Marriage Information

Marriageable age, by states, for both males and females with and without consent of parents or guardians. But in most states, the court has authority, in an emergency, to marry young couples below the ordinary age of consent, where due regard for their morals and welfare so requires. In many states, under special circumstances, blood test and waiting period may be waived.

State	With consent		Without consent		Blood test		Wait for license	Wait after license
	Men	Women	Men	Women	Required	Other state accepted*		
Alabama (b) 17	17	14	21	18	Yes	Yes	None	None
Alaska 18	18	16	19	18	Yes	No	3 days	None
Arizona 16²	16²	16	18	18	Yes	Yes	None	None
Arkansas 17	17	16⁴	18	18	Yes	No	3 days	None
California ....—²	—²	—²	18	18	Yes	Yes	None	None
Colorado 16	16	16	18	18	Yes	...	None	None
Connecticut 16	16	16(q)	18	18	Yes	Yes	4 days	None
Delaware ....—(q)	—(q)	16⁴	18	18	Yes	Yes	None	24 hrs. (c)
District of Columbia ...18	18	16	21	18	Yes	Yes	3 days	None
Florida 18	18	16	21	21	Yes	Yes	3 days	None
Georgia 18	18	16	18	18	Yes	Yes	None (b)	None (o)
Hawaii 16	16	16	18	18	Yes	Yes	None	None
Idaho 16	16	16	18	18	Yes	Yes	None (p)	None
Illinois (a) ....—(e)	—(e)	15(e)	18	18	Yes	Yes	None	None
Indiana 17	17	17	18	18	Yes	No	3 days	None
Iowa ....16(e)	16(e)	16(e)	18	18	Yes	Yes	3 days	None
Kansas ....—(e)²	—(e)²	—(e)²	18	18	Yes	Yes	3 days	None
Kentucky 18	18	16	18	18	Yes	No	3 days	None
Louisiana (a) 18	18	16	18	18	Yes	No	None	72 hours
Maine 16	16	16	18	18	No	No	5 days	None
Maryland 18	18	16	21	18	None	None	48 hours	None
Massachusetts ....—²	—²	—²	18	18	Yes	Yes	3 days	None
Michigan (a) ....—	—	16	18	18	Yes	No	3 days	None
Minnesota ....—	—	16(e)	18	18	None	...	5 days	None
Mississippi (b) 17	17	15	21	21	Yes	...	3 days	None
Missouri 15	15	15	18	18	Yes	Yes	3 days	None
Montana ....—²	—²	—²	18	18	Yes	Yes	5 days	None
Nebraska 18	18	16	18	18	Yes	Yes	5 days	None
Nevada 18	18	16	21	18	None	None	None	None
New Hampshire (a) ...14(e)	14(e)	13(e)	18	18	Yes	Yes	5 days	None
New Jersey (a) ......—	—	16	18	18	Yes	Yes	72 hours	None
New Mexico 16	16	16	21	21	Yes	Yes	None	None
New York 16	16	14	18	18	Yes	No	None	24 hrs. (h)
North Carolina (a) ...16	16	16	18	18	Yes	Yes	None	None
North Dakota (a) .....—²	—²	15	18	18	Yes	...	None	None
Ohio (a) 18	18	16	18	18	Yes	Yes	5 days	None
Oklahoma 16	16	16	18	18	Yes	No	None (f)	...
Oregon ....18 (e)	18 (e)	15 (e)	18	18	Yes	No	7 days	None
Pennsylvania 16	16	16	18	18	Yes	Yes	3 days	None
Rhode Island (a) (b) ..18	18	16	18	18	Yes	No	None	None
South Carolina 16	16	14	18	18	None	None	24 hrs.	None
South Dakota 18	18	16	18	18	Yes	Yes	None	None
Tennessee (b) 16	16	16	21	21	Yes	Yes	3 days	None
Texas 16	16	16	18	18	Yes	Yes	None	None
Utah (a) 16	16	14	21	18	Yes	Yes	None	None
Vermont (a) 18	18	16	18	18	Yes	...	None	5 days
Virginia (a) 16	16	16	18	18	Yes	Yes (r)	None	None
Washington 17	17	17	18	18	(d)	...	3 days	None
West Virginia 18²	18²	16	18	18	Yes	No	3 days	None
Wisconsin 18	18	16	18	18	Yes	Yes	5 days	None
Wyoming 18	18	16	21	21	Yes	Yes	None	None
Puerto Rico 16	16	16	21	21	(f)	None	None	None
Virgin Islands 16	16	14	21	18	None	None	8 days	None

Many states have additional special requirements; contact individual state.

(a) Special laws applicable to non-residents. (b) Special laws applicable to those under 21 years; Ala.: bond required if male is under 21, female under 18. (c) 24 hours if one or both parties resident of state; 96 hours if both parties are non-residents. (d) None, but male must file affidavit. (e) Parental consent plus court's consent required. (f) None, but a medical certificate is required. (g) Wait for license from time blood test is taken; Ariz., 48 hours. (h) Marriage may not be solemnized within 10 days from date of blood test. (j) If either under 21; Ida., 3 days; Okla., 72 hrs. (x) May be waived. (1) 3 days if both applicants are under 18 or female is pregnant. (2) Statute provides for obtaining license with parental or court consent with no state minimum age. (3) If either party is under 18, 3 days. (4) Under 16, with parental and court consent. Del.; female under 18. (o) All those between 19-21 cannot waive 3 day waiting period. (p) If either under 18—wait full 3 days. (q) If under stated age court consent required. (r) Va. blood test form must be used.

Source: Compiled by William E. Mariano, Council on Marriage Relations, Inc., 110 E. 42 St., New York, N.Y. 10017 (as of Oct. 1, 1976)

usually have at least one each — and plan your guest list.

Three months before, order the invitations and announcements and, if you wish, personal stationery for thank-you notes. Order your bridal gown and select the bridesmaids' dresses. Dresses usually require at least six weeks for delivery, plus additional time for fittings. Choose your rings, especially if they are to be engraved. Also pick out the china, silver, and other gifts you want, and register your preferences with a convenient store that will keep your needs on file.

Two months before the wedding, choose a photographer to take candid shots during the day and/or do a formal portrait; make medical and beauty-shop appointments; select the gifts for your attendants; arrange delivery for floral decorations, and make transportation and hotel arrangements for the wedding party and parents.

Mail out the invitations at least three weeks ahead. During the last month, you should also record all wedding gifts you receive in advance, and start mailing thank-you notes. Prepare a list of the clothing you want to take on your honeymoon. Verify all final arrangements with the clergy, caterers, florist, and photographer. Send out wedding announcements to local papers, and include pictures where they will use them. Get blood tests and the marriage license.

With this careful groundwork, any wedding should go smoothly and be as worry-free for the bride and groom as it is for their guests.

Money-Saving tips

Marriage is big business. Each year, Americans spend more than five billion dollars on weddings. Brides spend $160 million on trousseaus alone. Weddings vary widely in cost, depending on whether you have the ceremony in a church before 300 guests, or with a justice of the peace before two witnesses, whether you have the reception in someone's living room, with homecooked food, or in a hotel, with caterers.

Elizabeth Post says the price of most weddings ranges from $500 to $4,000. Two thousand dollars is a typical budget for a formal wedding with four to six attendants and one to two hundred guests invited to a reception in a hotel or club for a light buffet. This includes $400 for wedding clothes; $760 for the reception (food, beverages, wedding cake); $200 for the photographer; $160 for flowers; $160 for music; $80 for bridesmaids' gifts; $80 for invitations; $100 to transport the bridal party to church and reception; and a $60 contingency fund for unforeseen expenses.

Costs can be cut without detracting from the beauty of the occasion. You can, for example, but a less expensive ring.

If you buy a diamond, insure it: stones can fall from mountings, and they can be lost or stolen. Before you buy, select a reputable jeweler; once you are in the store, speak with the jewelry expert, not just a part time salesclerk. The four basic characteristics of gems are color, clarity,

Americans spend more than $5 billion on weddings each year — and love it!

cut, and weight. Weight is the least important; color is the most important. Stay away from merchants who offer ridiculous bargains and, when you make your purchase, get a written guarantee of its value.

Most people choose 14-carat gold bands. If you choose 18-carat, you should know that it tarnishes less but dents more easily. White gold is also popular. It looks like platinum, but after a few years the yellow gold in it may discolor the ring.

You can also cut costs on wedding invitations. Engraved invitations are more expensive than printed invitations. It is also usually 10 to 20 percent cheaper to order printed invitations from a retail store than from a local printer. Some people write their own invitations, and, for small weddings, even invitations by telephone are acceptable.

Wedding gowns are an expense many women would prefer to avoid, knowing they will probably never wear the dress again. The average bride spends $600 on her gown. If you don't want to spend that much money, you might consider checking local papers or second-hand stores for a dress-shop sample or a once-used gown. Ask friends or relatives if they could lend you their wedding dress; most women are honored by the request. If you do buy your own dress, look for something you might be able to wear again as a party dress. If you can sew, make your own, and instead of buying a veil, wear flowers in your hair.

Some ways to reduce the flower budget are: mix inexpensive flowers, like carnations or chrysanthemums, with your bouquets; carry a bouquet of greenery with no flowers at all; carry a single rose; use fresh garden flowers; or use silk or dried flowers you can keep later in your home. You can also save money on photographs by hiring a photographer from a local paper, or asking a friend with professional equipment to help you out. In any case, be sure you see samples of the photographer's work ahead of time, to avoid disappointment.

Today's brides and grooms often share, equally, the cost of the wedding. But, traditionally, the responsibility for expenses has been split along clear lines. If you wish to follow the old way, you should know that the bride or her parents pay for invitations, flowers, music, transportation for the bridal party, reception, gifts for the bridesmaids, photographer, rental of the church or hall, the groom's ring, lodging for out-of-town bridesmaids; and wedding gown, veil, and trousseau.

The groom, or his parents, pay for the bride's engagement and wedding rings, marriage license, clergyman's fee (they usually run $20 and up), accessories for the men in the wedding party, including the boutonnieres, accommodations for out-of-town male attendants and the honeymoon.

DIVORCE: HOW TO HANDLE IT

Divorce is always a painful process. It is a time when women need financial, legal, and emotional help, and are often unable to find it. If you are planning to file for divorce, a few basic pieces of information can smooth your transition.

In most states, you can divorce on grounds of mental or physical cruelty, adultery, abandonment, alcoholism, drug addiction, impotence, or insanity. California was the first state to introduce no-fault divorce, and other states have followed suit. No-fault divorce means the marriage has simply broken down, and there is no guilty party. If you are in a hurry, you can get a fast Nevada divorce after residing there for six weeks. You must prove that Nevada is your legal residence — which you can do by registering to vote, getting a new driver's license, and changing the addresses on your credit cards.

But, despite these precautions, the divorce may not be considered valid in your home state. Even with proof of residency, an out-of-state divorce, especially in Nevada or Mexico, may run into legal snags if your spouse contests it. If you want a decree that includes alimony or child support, it is safer to stay in your home state. If your husband flies to Nevada for a divorce you want to contest, see your lawyer immediately.

Regardless of the special arrangements you have to make with your church or synagogue, you remain married in the eyes of the state until a divorce decree is signed by a judge. If the breakup is friendly, you can use do-it-yourself kits and divorce without a lawyer in California, New York,

Grounds for Divorce

State	Cruelty	Desertion	Non-support	Alcohol	Felony	Impotency	Pregnancy at marriage	Drug addiction	Fraudulent contract	Other causes	Residence time	Time between interlocut'y and final decrees
Alabama	X	X	X	X	X	X	X	X		Q-K-W-F-MM	1 year*	None-R
Alaska	X	X		X	X	X		X		F-K-B	1 year	None
Arizona										QQ	90 days	None
Arkansas	X	X	X	X	X	X		X		B-Y-K-DD	3 months*	None
California										K-KK	6 months	6 months
Colorado										QQ	90 days	None
Connecticut	X	X		X	X				X	K-F-QQ	1 year*	None
Delaware										QQ	2 years	3 months
Dist. of Columbia	X								X	Y-Z	1 year	None
Florida										QQ-K	6 months	None
Georgia	X	X		X	X	X	X	X	X	K-M-AA-QQ	6 months	1
Hawaii										QQ	1 year	1
Idaho	X	X	X	X	X					X-K	6 weeks	None
Illinois	X	X		X	X					DD	6 months*	None
Indiana	X	X			X					K-QQ	6 months	None
Iowa										MM	1 year*	None-S
Kansas	X	X		X	X	X	X		X	K-CC-DD	60 days	None-T
Kentucky										QQ	180 days	None
Louisiana					X					X-Z	1 year*	None
Maine	X	X	X	X	X			X		X-KK	6 months	None
Maryland		X		X						Y-K	1 year	None
Massachusetts	X	X	X	X	X					LL	2 years*	6 mos.
Michigan										MM	1 year*	None
Minnesota				X	X			X		K-W-OO-QQ	1 year*	None-T
Mississippi	X	X		X	X	X	X	X		K-M-DD	1 year*	None-U
Missouri	X	X	X	X	X	X	X			B-J	1 year	None*
Montana	X	X	X	X	X	X				QQ	1 year	6 months
Nebraska										K-Y-F	6 weeks	None
Nevada		X				X				D-GG-HH-II-KK	1 year*	None
New Hampshire	X	X	X	X	X	X		X		NN-K-Y	1 year*	None
New Jersey	X	X						X		F	6 months	None
New Mexico	X	X	X							X-Z*	1 year	
New York	X				X					Q-K-X	6 months	None
North Carolina	X	X								Q-K-X	6 months	None
North Dakota	X	X	X	X	X			X		K-KK	1 year	None
Ohio	X	X	X	X	X	X		X		BB-CC-DD	6 months	None
Oklahoma	X	X	X	X	X	X		X		F-K-BB-CC	6 months	None
Oregon	X				X					KK	6 months*	90 days
Pennsylvania	X	X		X	X		X			B-M-DD-K-Y	1 year*	None
Rhode Island	X	X	X	X	X	X		X		H-X	2 years*	6 months
South Carolina	X	X	X	X						Y	1 year	None
South Dakota	X	X	X	X	X					Y	1 year*	None
Tennessee	X	X	X	X	X	X	X			A-DD-EE	6 months*	None
Texas	X	X		X	X					K-X-F-PP	1 year	None-T
Utah	X	X	X	X	X					W-K	3 months	3 mos.*
Vermont	X	X	X	X	X					Y-K	6 months	3 mos.-O*
Virginia		X				X				B-X	1 year	None-U*
Washington									X	QQ	6 months	None
West Virginia	X	X	X	X	X			X		X-K	2 years*[2]	None
Wisconsin	X	X	X	X	X	X	X			Y-Z-K	6 months	None-T
Wyoming	X	X	X	X	X	X				B-J-K	60 days	None

(1) Determined by court order. (2) No minimum residence required in adultery cases. (A) Violence. (B) Indignities. (D) Joining religious order disbelieving in marriage. (F) Incompatibility. (H) Any gross misbehavior or wickedness. (J) Husband being a vagrant. (K) 5-yrs. insanity; permanent insanity in Utah; incurable insanity in Cal. Exceptions 1 yr. Wis.; 18 mos. Alas.; 2 yrs. Ga., Ha., Ind., N.J., Nev., Ore., Wash., and Wyo.; 3 yrs. Ark., N.C., Fla., Tex., Minn., Col., Kan., Ha., Md., Miss., W. Va.; 6 yrs. Ida. (M) Consanguinity. (O) Plaintiff, 6 mos.; defendant 2 yrs. to remarry. (Q) Crime against nature. (R) Sixty days to remarry. (S) One year to remarry; Ha. one year with minor child. Except Ia. 90 days. (T) Six months to remarry; in Kan. 60 days. (U) Adultery cases, remarriage in discretion of court. (W) Separation for 2 yrs. after decree for same in Ala. and Minn.; 3 yrs. in Ut., 4 yrs. in N.J.; 18 mos. in N.H.; 5 yrs. in Md. (X) Separation, no cohabitation—5 yrs. Exceptions La., Va., Wyo., W. Va. 2 yrs.; Tex. and Me. 3 yrs.; Nev. and N.C. 1 yr. and R.I. 10 yrs. (Y) Separation, no cohabitation--3 years. Exceptions Vt., Wash., 2 yrs.; Del., Mo., and N.J. 18 mos.; N.Y., Nev., Va., D.C., and Wis. 1 yr. (Z) Separation for 2 yrs. after decree for Dist. of Col.; 1 yr. for N.Y., Wis., and La.; per decree in Ha. (AA) Mental incapacity at time of marriage. (BB) Procurement of out-of-state divorce. (CC) Gross neglect of duty. (DD) Bigamy. (EE) Attempted homicide. (GG) Treatment which injures health or endangers reason. (HH) Wife without state for 10 yrs. (II) Wife in state 2 yrs.; husband never in state and has intent to become citizen of foreign country. (KK) Irreconcilable differences. (LL) Life sentence dissolves marriage. (MM) Breakdown of marriage with no reasonable likelihood of preservation. (NN) Deviate sexual conduct. (OO) Course of conduct detrimental to the marriage relationship of party seeking divorce. (PP) Incompatibility without regard to fault. (QQ) Marriage irretrievably broken.

Adultery is either grounds for divorce or evidence of irreconcilable differences and a breakdown of the marriage in all states. The plaintiff can invariably remarry in the same state where he or she procured a decree of divorce or annulment. Not so the defendant, who is barred in certain states for some offenses. After a period of time has elapsed even the offender can apply for special permission. The U.S. Supreme Court in a 5 to 4 opinion ruled April 18, 1949, that one-sided quick divorces could be challenged as illegal if notice of the action was not served on the divorced partner within the divorcing states, excepting where the partner was represented at the proceedings. **Enoch Arden Laws.** Disappearance and unknown to be alive—Conn., 7 years absence; N.H., 2 years; N.Y., 5 years (called dissolution); Vt., 7 years.

Source: Compiled by William E. Mariano, Council on Marriage Relations, Inc., 110 E. 42 St., New York, NY 10017 (as of Oct. 1, 1976).

Persons contemplating divorce should study latest decisions or secure legal advice before initiating proceedings since different interpretations or exceptions in each case can change the conclusion reached. *Exceptions are to be noted.

and the state of Washington. In most cases, however, a lawyer's services are required. Select your attorney carefully. A family lawyer who is friendly with both you and your husband may not be the best person to represent your interests. Ask your friends for recommendations, or call the local bar association.

Once you have selected the lawyer, discuss the fee immediately. Lawyers may charge in one of four different ways: retainer, contingent fee, hourly rate, or flat fee. For divorces, the flat fee is best. This can range from $400 for uncontested divorces, to $1,000 for contested ones, plus $300 court costs for each day of the trial. A retainer means you will pay the attorney a fee in advance to handle all your legal work for a year — a much longer commitment than is needed for most divorces. Most states forbid attorneys to charge a contingent fee in divorces because the fee depends on how much she or he recovered for the client; in these cases, lawyers will be more likely to turn the divorce into a legal battleground than to try for an equitable settlement. An hourly rate will average forty to fifty dollars, and is not recommended; if the trial is prolonged, the bill could be huge.

How to Meet Divorce Costs

If you have no income of your own, the court will order your husband to pay your legal fees. There are also ways to cut divorce costs. First, be realistic when asking for alimony and child support. Contrary to popular belief, alimony and child support are granted in only a small percent of cases, and are very difficult to collect. Judges are denying alimony to women who have continued to maintain careers while married; on January 20, 1977, a New York state judge ruled that, in some cases, men can collect alimony from their working wives. Many states also consider alimony only as a reward, to be paid to "ideal" wives for services rendered.

Because of existing laws, divorced women usually suffer more financial hardship than do divorced men. In forty-one states, all money earned by a husband during marriage belongs entirely to him, and the housewife is not entitled to financial compensation for doing the housework and caring for the children. In the other nine states, money earned and purchases made during marriage are "community property," owned by both spouses, but only two of those states require that such property be divided equally in case of divorce. In most states, property purchased by the wife with her own earnings is considered the husband's property unless she holds a record of ownership.

Another way to reduce divorce costs is to try to reach an agreement with your husband before you go into court, or even before you hire a lawyer. You can do this by either talking it out or, if that fails, by using a professional arbitrator. You can find an arbitrator by contacting the American Arbitration Association, 140 West 51st Street, New York, N.Y., 10020.

Several laws have been passed, or proposed, to help divorced mothers make ends meet. More than half the states have enacted the Uniform Reciprocal Enforcement of Support Act, which means that when a man owing alimony or child support, leaves the state where the divorce was awarded, he can be brought to court in the state where he now lives and forced to pay. If your ex-husband leaves town and owes you money, see your lawyer. Yvonne Burke, a representative from California, has a bill before Congress that would guarantee unpaid homemakers the same economic rights now enjoyed by paid workers: unemployment compensation, Social Security, and the right to job training. This bill would be especially important to housewives who get divorced after many years of marriage.

In addition to financial problems, most divorced women feel a terrible sense of failure, loneliness, and confusion once the relationship is ended. Many feel unwanted by their still-married friends. If you want to save your marriage, or need help resolving some of the emotional problems that have come with divorce, you can contact the American Association of Marriage and Family Counselors, 41 Central Park West, New York, New York.

REMARRIAGE

Three-fourths of the women who divorce, remarry eventually, often within three years. Many of these second marriages are happier and longer-lasting than the first ones. However, second marriages often involve new emotional and financial pressures. If you marry a man who has children by a previous marriage, he may have large alimony and/or child support payments. If he is supporting two households, chances are you will have to work — especially if his children, by the previous marriage, are still young, and his first wife is unable to work. You should try to remain objective about the rights and demands of his ex-wife, and help him maintain good relations with his children. If her alimony, custody, visitation, or child support demands are unreasonable, you can encourage your husband to take legal action. You can also suggest he finance education or job training for his ex-wife, so she can learn to support herself.

THE EROTIC WOMAN

Sex, somebody once said, is the most fun you can have without laughing. With the publication of the Kinsey report on female sexuality in the 1950s, it became a matter of public record that this sexual enjoyment

Most women enjoy the intimacy and closeness of sex more than the orgasm.

applied to women as well as men. Before then, it was no laughing matter. Women were taught it was unladylike to experience sexual pleasure. In the last half of the nineteenth century, doctors even performed clitoridectomies — removal of the highly sensitive clitoris — to prevent women from masturbating. At that time, masturbation was considered an unhealthy practice that might unleash a woman's insatiable sexual desires. The operation was also considered a cure for many physical and psychological problems.

By the 1920s, attitudes towards sex began to change, but the "sexual revolution" began for real in 1937, when Indiana University offered its first undergraduate course in marriage. The professor of that class was Dr. Alfred C. Kinsey, and for the next decade he recorded how men and women behaved sexually, through case histories and direct observation. In 1948, Kinsey published *Sexual Behavior in the Human Male;* in 1953, he followed up with *Sexual Behavior in the Human Female.* The Kinsey team rejected the notion that women were passive sex partners, and found that many women not only enjoy sex but have multiple orgasms. This discovery was so revolutionary that the researchers were immediately attacked by other doctors for telling "fantastic tales."

Five gynecologists, working with the Kinsey team, also tested the clitoral sensitivity of nearly 900 women and found, "considerable evidence that most females respond erotically . . . with intensity and immediacy, whenever the clitoris is tactilely stimulated." In an age when sex was rarely talked about, many women were leading fairly active sex lives. Kinsey found that half of the 8,000 women he surveyed had engaged in premarital sex, more than one-fourth had engaged in extramarital sex, and 62 percent had masturbated.

Two other leaders in the field of sex research, Dr. William Masters and Virginia Johnson, reported their findings on human sexuality to the New York Academy of Sciences in 1959, and generated little interest. However, after six more years of work they published their medical textbook, *Human Sexual Response,* in 1966. It quickly became a bestseller, despite its technical language. Their research was the first based on direct observation of sexual physiological response between men and women. Some of the most revealing findings included:

— almost all female orgasm involves some form of clitoral stimulation.

— women feel more intense orgasm through masturbation than during intercourse.

— women have as definite an orgasm as men and, in general, have greater potential for sexual responsiveness than men because they can experience several orgasms within a short period of time.

— sex drive in pregnant women often increases in the last three months, and to ban sexual intercourse during this time can do more harm than good.

— menopause does not blunt a woman's sexual capacity or drive. For the first time, physicians had information that could help them treat sexual problems, and that could be used as a basis for sex education.

What is Sexual Liberation?

The work of Masters and Johnson opened a Pandora's Box of other surveys on female sexuality, creating as much confusion as enlightenment over the meaning of "sexual liberation." Dr. Helen Singer Kaplan, sex therapist and an associate clinical professor of psychiatry, explained in a 1976 "New York Times Magazine" article: "To some extent, sexual freedom has become confused with high levels of sexual performance. Both men and women have come to feel new pressure to meet these standards — and the pressures have proved destructive to their fundamental relationships."

The largest survey on women and sex was made in 1975, when *Redbook* polled 100,000 of its readers; most of them ages twenty to thirty-four, white, middle-class, and married. It found that 80 percent of the women had had premarital sex, beginning at the average age of seventeen, usually with two to five different men. Ninety percent of the women reached orgasms, usually within ten minutes, and 65 percent masturbated occasionally or frequently. Almost 40 percent complained that they didn't get enough sex.

A 1976 poll by *Good Housekeeping* found that 38 percent of the two thousand readers surveyed had slept with their husbands before their marriage. More revealing was that 44 percent of those surveyed said they would do the same again today.

More than one third of the women in the *Redbook* survey said they wanted to have an extra-marital affair. But in the *Good Housekeeping* survey only three percent of the readers would have considered having an affair, while 12 percent admitted already having had an affair with "another man."

In another major study, *The Hite Report*, a book published in 1976, 3,000 American women described in detail their sexual experiences. The material was compiled and interpreted by Shere Hite, a doctoral candidate at Columbia University. The women reported everything from preferred positions during masturbation to their feelings about oral sex. Among the most surprising results:

— only 30 percent of the women claimed to reach orgasm during intercourse without clitoral stimulation.

— almost all could achieve orgasm through masturbation, but felt guilty and ashamed of it.

— many women felt the new sexual permissiveness put uncomfortable pressure on them to have more sex, and to have more orgasms during sex.

— contrary to myth, these women said, orgasms do not involve violent thrashing or writhing; most women become very still and tense at the moment of orgasm.

— most women had heightened sex drive immediately before and during menstruation — the times when they are infertile.

Hite notes that women have been made to feel they *must* have orgasms, which leads to greater tension when they cannot. According to her, almost every woman has faked orgasm at least occasionally. She suggests that women can learn to reach orgasm by knowing more about their own bodies and what pleases them; by talking with female friends about their own bodies and what pleases them; by talking with female friends about their sexual experiences; and by experimenting with masturbation.

Almost all the women in *The Hite Report* enjoyed sex, whether they had orgasms or not. Most enjoyed the intimacy and closeness even more than the orgasm, and liked giving pleasure to their partners. For most women, this attitude is the opposite of what they were taught: 95 percent of the women said they had been brought up to feel sex was "dirty."

Lesbianism, a fact of human sexuality still frowned on by many, is nonetheless being discussed more openly. For some women, being gay is as much a matter of feminist politics as of sexual preference. During a 1976 Gay Liberation Day, in New York's Greenwich Village, young women sported shirts proclaiming: "A woman without a man is like a fish without a bicycle," and female couples wore matching T-shirts explaining: "We're more than just best friends."

Dr. Paul Gebhard, director of the Institute for Sex Research started by Dr. Kinsey, estimates that at least one million American women, ages eighteen and over, are predominantly homosexual. Because of strong social prejudice against them, however, gay women often have trouble finding jobs and housing. Many lose custody of their children after a divorce. In 1972, forty-two states still banned private homosexual activities between consenting adults. In 1977 the White House acknowledged, for the first time, the presence of a gay constituency, when President Jimmy Carter's staff met with fourteen gay rights activists.

LOVING COUPLES

Heloise and Abelard: Star-Crossed

Peter Abelard, philosopher and theologian, and Heloise, an eighteen-year-old maiden, were star-crossed lovers of the twelfth century. Heloise's uncle, Canon Fulbert, invited the middle-aged Abelard to his Paris home to tutor his brilliant niece. Student and teacher soon fell in love and, wrote Abelard, "more words of love rose to our lips than of literature, kisses were more frequent than speech." When Uncle Fulbert finally realized what was going on, he ordered Abelard to leave. But it was too late. Heloise, already pregnant, escaped with her lover to his native Brittany, where she gave birth to his son. The two were married secretly in Paris, although Heloise continued to deny it, knowing marriage would ruin Abelard's future in the Church.

Heloise's relatives, outraged by these events, hired a band of men to castrate Abelard. After his castration, he became a monk at the monastery of St. Denis and ordered his wife Heloise to enter the convent at Argenteuil, where she later became abbess. She was twenty years old. Later in his life, Abelard wrote to Heloise about his disgust over their earlier sexual activities, regretting he had let himself "wallow in that filth." Heloise, however, continued to long for him, writing back that "when I ought to lament for what I have done, I sigh rather for what I had to forego."

Abelard was unpopular even with the monks he supervised, and they tried unsuccessfully to poison him. He died in 1142. Heloise, much-beloved in her convent, died in 1164. They were buried beside each other.

Mary and Maximilian I: Diamond Ring

Maximilian I, an Austrian prince, originated the tradition of the diamond engagement ring in 1477 when he brought one to his bride whom he had never seen. She was Mary of Burgundy, daughter of Charles the Bold. The couple had fallen in love through letters. Mary's father wanted her to wed Charles, the boy dauphin of France, but she resisted. Instead, after her father died in battle, she married Maximilian by proxy. Then the bridegroom traveled to Burgundy to claim his bride.

Austrian wars had depleted the royal coffers, and Maximilian was penniless when he started out on his journey. But as he traveled through the Austrian villages, people gave him gold and silver gifts for his marriage, and he used them to buy a diamond ring. After four months of travel, he arrived in Burgundy where he and Mary were married again — in a church. Their union is considered one of the most important in European history, for it established Maximilian as an independent prince, later to become the Holy Roman Emperor, and it insured that vast territories, including the Netherlands, would be under Hapsburg dominion. The marriage of their son, Philip the Fair, later brought Spain into the Hapsburg dynasty.

Mary lived only five years after their marriage; she died in 1482 after falling from her horse. Maxmilian died in 1519, but his romanticism lived on. Before a century had passed, noblemen and commoners alike were giving diamond betrothal rings to their beloved.

Priscilla and John: Puritan Love

Priscilla Mullins reportedly came to America on the Mayflower along with **John Alden** and a married couple, Mr. and Mrs. Miles Standish. Unknown to them, their romantic fates were linked. Few people survived these first years in the colonies. The 18-year-old Priscilla's entire family died during the first bitter winter, and she was cared for by Governor John Carter, who also died. Miles Standish, too, became a widower.

Standish wanted to remarry, and chose the young Priscilla, but he was afraid his proposal would not be eloquent enough. Instead, he asked his still-single friend, John Alden, to propose on his behalf. Alden, a cooper, was also in love with Priscilla and delivered the proposal with such passion that when he had finished she asked: "Why do you not speak for yourself, John?" He did, and the two were married sometime between 1621 and 1623.

Standish eventually forgave his brash friend and married someone else. The two families remained close, and one of the Aldens's daughters (they had eleven children) eventually married Standish's oldest son. The incident was commemorated in Henry Wadsworth Longfellow's 1858 poem, *The Courtship of Miles Standish*. Inherent in Longfellow's verse was the implicit message that if you want the job done right you must do it yourself.

Concha Arguello: Stead Fast Lover

Concepcion "Concha" Arguello was the flirtatious and beautiful daughter of a Spanish commandant stationed in California in the early 1800s on the site of what is today San Francisco. The sixteen-year-old girl was bored with life in the Spanish outpost until she met a tall dark stranger named **Nikolai Petrovich Rezanoff,** the middle-aged Russian ambassador to Japan. He had come to California to trade cloth produced by Russian settlements farther north for fresh fruits and vegetables. It was also thought he might be plotting to run the Spanish out of California and declare it Russian territory.

Concha and Nikolai soon fell in love. After overcoming her parents' strong objections to their daughter marrying someone of a different religion and moving far away, the couple got their consent to a betrothal. But before he could marry, Nikolai also had to obtain permission from the Russian tsar, the king of Spain, and the pope. He vowed to do so, and set sail for Russia.

He never came back. Rumors spread that he had taken ill on the homeward voyage and later died in Siberia, in a peasant's cabin. Concha, heartbroken, swore she would never marry. She eventually joined the Third Order of St. Francis, caring for the sick and poor, and became loved and admired throughout California. She entered the first convent established there, and died at the age of sixty-six.

Baby Doe: No Golddigger

In one of the most unlikely matches ever made, the young, golden-haired, and seductive **Elizabeth "Baby" Doe** married **Horace Tabor,** an uncouth gambler more than twice her age who had mined a fortune from the Colorado silver lode during the late 1800s. Everyone assumed she had married for his money and would leave him if times got rough. But they misjudged her.

Baby, one of fourteen children of an Irish immigrant tailor, had moved to Denver from the East with her first husband, Harvey Doe, who had trouble finding and keeping a job. Tabor, known for lusting after beautiful women, saw Doe's wife and offered him $1,000 in exchange for an introduction. Later, Tabor arranged for Harvey Doe to be caught in a "compromising position" — presumably in someone else's bed — and gave him $5,000 as an additional bribe to divorce Baby. Once that was taken care of, Tabor arranged a divorce from his own wife, Augusta, and married his new twenty-year-old sweetheart, first secretly in 1882, then publicly one year later, with President Chester A. Arthur as guest of honor.

The elite of Denver shunned the new couple, but Tabor didn't seem to mind. He bought jewels, Paris dresses, and the finest home in Denver for his bride. For himself, he bought the lieutenant governorship of Colorado and, later, a United

States Senate seat. They had two daughters and named the youngest Silver Dollar.

In the 1890s, Tabor's luck changed. He speculated in worthless mines and railroads, and sacrificed his sound investments to pay for foolish ones. After the crash of 1893, he and Baby moved to a shack near the Matchless Mine, where Tabor had made his first fortune. She was thirty-three and still beautiful; he was almost seventy. She surprised everyone by staying with him while he tried to work the mines and then, later, took a job as Denver postmaster, working in the post office built on land he had donated to the city. When Tabor died in 1899, Baby kept the family together. She spent her last years living austerely and alone, trying in vain to interest people in prospecting for new deposits. She was desperately poor but never asked for charity. In 1935, she was found in her shack frozen to death.

Lunt and Fontanne: 'Divorce, No'

For forty years, **Alfred Lunt** and **Lynn Fontanne** were the Great Couple of the theater. When Lunt first met the young actress, he bent to take her hand, slipped, and toppled down the rickety staircase on which he was standing. Despite this inauspicious beginning, they were married in 1922, and even then, before they became famous, their charisma was so strong that photographers followed them on their honeymoon.

When they made their theater debut two years later in *The Guardsman,* a critic wrote: "They have youth and great gifts and the unmistakable attitude of ascent." From then on, plays in which they appeared were almost guaranteed to be hits by their very presence. Their stage performances deepened with their relationship, until one critic remarked that their greatest gift was their "psychic ability to time, within a split second, each other's reactions."

"I just love to play opposite Lynn . . . there is nobody else I want to play with," Lunt once said. But their life together was not all roses, and they reportedly argued intensely over interpretations of scenes in which they appeared together. Fontanne, asked if she had ever contemplated divorce, replied: "Murder yes, but divorce, no." They retired in 1960 but still take an occasional turn on the stage.

The Fyodorovas: Russian Drama

The love stories of **Zoya Fyodorova** and her daughter, **Victoria,** are as filled with as much drama as the Russian classic *War and Peace.* Zoya, a famous Russian actress in the 1930s and 1940s, fell in love in 1945 with **Jackson R. Tate,** an American navy captain assigned to the United States Embassy in Moscow. When Soviet officials learned of the affair, they expelled Tate and sent Zoya to prison.

The love affair had produced a child, Victoria — named for the Allied victory — who was reared by an aunt while Zoya was in prison. Ten years later, mother and daughter were reunited, and Victoria learned for the first time about her father. For several years, Victoria tried unsuccessfully to find out more about him, and a sympathetic American visiting Moscow finally agreed to help. Tate was found in Florida, and father and daughter exchanged letters. Tate, now a retired admiral, was ailing and wanted to see his daughter, but Soviet authorities dragged their feet. Finally, in March 1975, she received a visa, and the two shared a tearful reunion.

Three months after her arrival in America, Victoria met a Pan American copilot, Frederick Pouy, at a party; they fell in love and within a month were married. The moved to Stamford, Connecticut, where he taught her to speak English and she bore him a son, Christopher. Zoya arrived from the Soviet Union just in time for the birth of her new grandchild. Hollywood heard of the mother-daughter story and began to talk about making a movie, with Zoya and Victoria playing themselves. Meanwhile, the house of Alexandra de Markoff, a cosmetics line owned by Lanvin-Charles of the Ritz, signed a five-year contract with the beautiful Victoria to advertise their Russian-named makeup.

Zoya soon returned to Russia, but her daughter writes regularly and sends her Frank Sinatra records. Victoria's father is too ill to visit his newfound daugher but keeps in touch by telephone. "My feeling is very strong for him," Victoria says. "I need him always."

Mothers

PREPARING FOR MOTHERHOOD

Despite the barrage of anti-baby propaganda of the early 1970s, babies are as
popular as ever. A 1974 poll of women
found that only 1 percent of all women
surveyed were opposed to having children, and 95 percent of all married women
expected to have children — but perhaps
not as many as once was popular.

The news may come as a surprise to
some. During the early 1970s, some
feminists suggested that the burdens of
motherhood were a major reason for women's oppression. Organizations like the
National Organization for Non-Parents
touted the virtues and freedom of remaining childfree. Zero population growth advocates called for fewer children because
the diminishing resources available on the
planet could not support them.

Many young women appeared to be
more interested in careers than in marriage
or children. Statistics also painted a picture of declining interest in mothering. Although the number of women of childbearing age has increased by 13.3 percent
in the last five years, the birth rate has
dropped each year, to a low in 1977 of 1.8
babies per woman. (At the height of the
baby boom in 1957, the birth rate was 3.7
children per woman.) The number of
young wives who anticipate a childless
marriage grew from one in every 100 in
1967 to four per 100 in 1974.

Nevertheless, women still look forward
to becoming mothers. The reasons are as
old as time itself: wanting to add joy to a
happy marriage; a way of immortality;
confirming femininity; or, for a religious
woman, fulfilling God's will. Other, less
sound, but prevalent, reasons are: wanting
never to feel lonely; competing with one's
mother; boredom with a job; insecurity
and the feeling that motherhood is the only
role one can do well.

But some of today's attitudes toward
motherhood *are* different from those in
previous generations. While many women
in earlier decades approached motherhood

"An Increase Of Family": Women thoughout the ages have looked forward to becoming mothers.

U.S. Birth Rate

Live births per 1,000 population

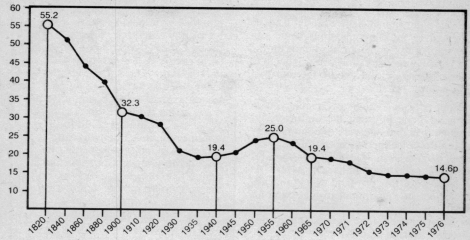

p=preliminary

Source: U.S. Census Bureau

with a sense of duty and self-sacrifice, submerging themselves in the care of their children, today's mother feels that her own fulfillment is as important as her children's and considers her needs as carefully as theirs.

She is aided in her independence by the variety of effective birth control methods available. A woman and her husband can choose if and when they want to have a baby — parenthood is seldom an unexpected "mistake".

The liberating option of choosing whether or not to have a baby can be a troublesome one. Dr. Elizabeth Whelan, executive director of New York's A Baby? . . . Maybe Services, a parenthood counseling service, offers these guidelines:

• Don't be pressured into a decision — whether from potential grandparents, zero population growth advocates, or the fact that you're getting older.

• Make sure your reasons for having or not having a child are valid — not just excuses for masking more serious problems.

• Realistically evaluate your resources — emotional, physical, and financial. Study your professional and social calendar for the previous two weeks, and think about what modifications would have been necessary if you had had a child.

Motherhood

So you've decided to have a baby. If you're like most mothers-to-be today, you've had more formal education than women of earlier generations. You'll probably read up on childbirth and child-rearing, and attend prenatal classes, usually with your husband. You'll also be alert to newspaper and magazine articles on any subject and new developments related to motherhood.

You will pick an obstetrician whom you trust. The obstetrician will probably give you a physical, Pap smear, and prenatal blood test as soon as the pregnancy is confirmed, and will tell you to maintain your normal activities, including most sports and exercise, but to make sure you eat sensibly and get enough sleep. You'll see the obstetrician once a month until your seventh month, when you will make more frequent visits. Among the doctor's "don'ts" for you probably will be: don't smoke; don't take any medication, even aspirin, without checking with the doctor; avoid activities that overstress stomach and back muscles; and don't eat for two — it isn't necessary.

During the first three months, you might get morning sickness. Doctors suspect it is a result of hormonal change, and it's not as common as most people think. You can also expect to gain about 25 pounds during the whole pregnancy, and you will begin to need maternity clothes about the fourth or fifth month.

Your husband might even join you in some of your physical discomforts. According to a Yale University doctor, many fathers-to-be experience morning sickness, dizziness, nausea, cravings for exotic foods, even labor pains. Dr. Morris A. Wessel says the physical symptoms reflect the man's emotional struggle with his wife's pregnancy, and he encourages men to participate in their wives' pregnancy through prenatal classes.

Preparing yourself emotionally for motherhood is as important as attending to your health. In psychological terms, a prospective mother must prepare herself for the sudden shift from a self-image of a non-parent to that of a parent. The slow preparation for this change of the self-image is one of the primary experiences of pregnancy. There are many books that explore the emotional side of pregnancy, but one recommended for both parents-to-be is *Preparing for Parenthood,* by Dr. Lee Salk.

Like everything else, your baby will cost money. It has been estimated that a baby born in 1976 will cost the parents nearly $65,000 in food, clothing, shelter, education and recreation before she graduates from college.

Your first worry, however, is the approximately $2,000 it costs for the goods and services of a baby's first week of life.

Obstetricians' rates across the country vary between $400 and $800. Pediatricians charge between $30 and $75 for hospital checkups for the newborn. Nationally, the average cost of a maternity ward bed is $130 daily, and most women with routine deliveries stay for four days.

Delivery room charges, medications, hospital supplies, and lab tests will add several hundred dollars to your bill. Most health insurance plans cover at least some of these costs.

Family budget should also provide

Rod Laver in the Delivery Room

Australia's Rod Laver may rank as one of the greatest tennis players in the history of the sport, but his delivery room performance leaves a bit to be desired. According to Jeanne Parr's *The Superwives,* Mary Laver unwittingly doubled her trouble by picking an obstetrician as crazy about tennis as her husband. While she moaned and groaned on the delivery table, the two men sat with eyes glued on a telecast of a Stan Smith-Pancho Gonzalez tennis match. The only notice they took of the soon-to-be mother was to ask her to keep down the noise.

"'I think it's going to three sets,' Rod shouts, all excited, to the doctor," Mary Laver recalled. "Then he turns to me, cool as ice, and has the nerve to ask if I can hold out for one more set. You want to know what it's like to be married to a tennis champion? THAT's what it's like."

With a welcoming committee like that, Rickie Laver is bound to follow in father Rod's famous footsteps.

---

about $200 for maternity clothes, $300 or more for nursery furniture and supplies, $200 for baby clothes, $350 for a baby's food for a year, and money for diapers (disposable are more expensive than cloth), toys, pediatrician's bills, and miscellaneous items.

Help for Genetic Illnesses

The growth of obstetrics has led to several advances in techniques to help insure better health in infants. Some hospitals have fetal-heart monitors, which record the heartbeat of the child during a mother's labor and enable the medical staff to spot any danger instantly. A test called amniocentesis can determine many genetic abnormalities in a fetus during pregnancy.

An estimated 15 million Americans have a genetic illness of one sort or another. These are passed from generation to generation, the same way hair color and physical stature are. One of every 250 newborn babies has a genetic disorder. One out of every three hospital admissions of infants or children occurs because of a genetic or genetically-related problem.

Until recent years there was little more than sympathy to offer the couple whose child was born with a genetic disease, or the person with a genetic disease.

Today, however, through prenatal tests, laboratory studies, physical examinations, and review of family history, experts called genetic counselors can often help alleviate problems of genetic diseases in some individuals. They can also help prevent many types of genetic birth defects in offspring. These counselors are usually physicians with a special expertise in genetics.

A genetic counselor can tell you whether you ought to have blood tests for specific ethnic diseases such as Tay-Sachs disease, which strikes Jewish people of Eastern European origin; Cooley's anemia, which strikes persons of Mediterranean extraction; and sickle cell anemia, which primarily affects blacks.

Genetic diseases include Down syndrome (mongolism), cystic fibrosis, hemophilia, Huntington's disease, many forms of mental illness, and certain types of deafness and blindness, just to name a few.

If you are expecting a child and are worried about a specific genetic problem, the counselor can allay your fears or confirm your situation and help you examine the alternatives.

The experts say that you can benefit from genetic counseling if:

• You are the parents of a child with a genetic disease or birth defect and are thinking about having another child.

• Your family has any history of genetic disease and you are considering having children.

• You have taken drugs, had X rays or been exposed to a virus (such as rubella) at or near the time of conception of a child you are now carrying.

• You are a mother-to-be older than 35 years of age.

• You are a pregnant woman whose mate is 55 years of age or older.

• You are not thinking of having chil-

dren, but you may have a genetic disease yourself. The genetic counselor can help you learn more about and better cope with your situation.

There are several hundred centers in the United States and Canada that offer genetic counseling and testing. You can get free advice and referral to the nearest appropriate center from either the National Foundation-March of Dimes, 1275 Mamaroneck Ave., White Plains, N.Y. 10605; or the National Genetics Foundation, 250 West 57th St., New York, N.Y. 10019.

Choosing a Delivery Method

Ironically, in spite of modern medical advances, the trend today is toward less mechanized, more natural childbirth techniques.

The most popular natural approach for delivery is the Lamaze method, which aims to reduce the pain of labor and delivery through exercises and breathing rather than by drugs. Started by Fernand Lamaze, the course involves the husband as helpmate during labor and delivery of the baby, and permits the woman to participate fully in her baby's birth.

The Lamaze method teaches the woman exercises to strengthen her leg and pelvic muscles so she can push the baby down the birth canal. She also learns three breathing techniques, one to help her through each stage of labor. When she is in labor, her husband helps her with the breathing exercises and gives her moral support during the delivery.

Many woman who have had their babies this way, with their husbands present, are very enthusiastic about the warmth and intimacy of the experience.

Another approach recently introduced in this country is that devised by Frederick Leboyer, a French doctor. He condemns the standard delivery room practices, claiming that they are too violent for the child, and advocates delivery of a child in a dimly lit, quiet room.

The Leboyer method has had limited acceptance in the United States, although some doctors have adopted modifications, like putting a baby in a warm incubator right after birth — Leboyer recommends putting the baby in a basin of warm water.

A small number of women are advocat-

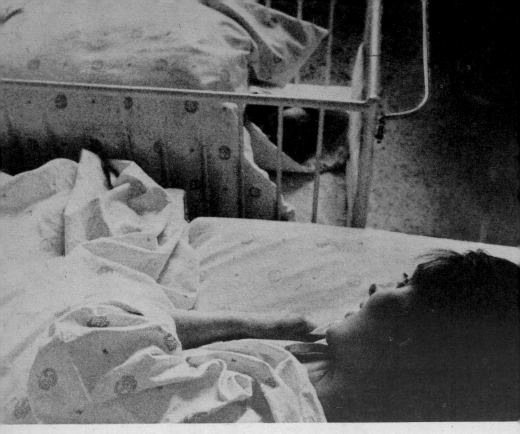

The sudden shift in self-image from non-mother to mother is a primary experience of pregnancy.

ing home births assisted by midwives. And some hospitals, like Roosevelt Hospital in New York City, have midwives on staff who take care of routine births but defer to a doctor if a complication arises.

Another decision you must make is whether or not to breast-feed your baby. As the popularity of natural childbirth has grown, the incidence of breast-feeding among American women also has increased — 40 percent nurse their babies today, compared to half that number fifteen years ago.

Among the reasons for the popularity of breast-feeding is that it creates a pleasing intimacy between mother and child, it's convenient, and it's cheaper than bottle-feeding. Studies also show that breast-fed babies have more resistance to disease than bottle-fed babies because they get from their mother's milk antibodies that immunize them against many illnesses for several months. Mothers, however, can also pass along harmful chemicals to their baby through breast-feeding. Your doctor can tell you specifically which drugs and other substances to avoid while breast-feeding.

However, if you are going back to work right away, or don't feel comfortable with breast-feeding for one or another reason, your doctor will probably recommend that you bottle-feed your baby. Children should be fed in a relaxed manner that allows for development of security and intimacy, and women shouldn't feel pressured into a method of feeding with which they are uncomfortable. Experts agree that your child will be well nourished by either method.

SIZE OF FAMILIES AND SPACING OF CHILDREN

Smaller families are becoming increasingly popular among both women and men. According to the 1974 Virginia Slims American Women's Opinion Poll, nearly half of all Americans thought a family of two children was ideal, compared with only one in four Americans in 1952, and in 1941. The main reason given by those polled were the high cost of living.

The desire for fewer children coincides with the current claim that spacing children three or four years apart improves each child's emotional and intellectual growth.

Two in every five American women in 1941 and 1952 — and nearly as many men — desired four or more children. Today fewer than one woman in four wants that many. Interestingly, *men* have consistently desired smaller families than women.

In addition to the high cost of living — cited by 82 percent of the women and 78 percent of the men — three out of five women, and nearly as many men, considered the threat of overpopulation sufficient reason to have fewer children.

Though few persons said they would limit family size because of the inability to give sufficient attention to each child, several professionals in the child-care field cite child-spacing as an important developmental factor.

Pediatrician Dr. Lee Salk, and psychologist Dr. Burton L. White, both agree that toddlers need one-on-one attention from a parent without the strain of sibling rivalry. Being a parent's prime concern for the first three or four years gives a child stability and support harder to come by if the child must compete with a new baby.

BRINGING UP BABY

Now you have a baby. What do you do next? If you read all the books in the library on child care, you will probably retreat into a corner and cry. There are so many do's and don'ts expounded by batteries of learned doctors, psychologists,

Mother's Day

Mother's Day — a worthwhile and touching tradition, or a perfect example of commercial exaggeration, depending on your point of view — was first celebrated on the second Sunday of May 1914, when President Woodrow Wilson proclaimed "a public expression of our love and reverence for the mothers of this country."

A spinster teacher from Philadelphia, **Anna M. Jarvis** (1864–1948), is credited with launching the idea of Mother's Day, some years after the death of her own mother, to whom she was very devoted.

On the second Sunday of May, 1907, Miss Jarvis told visiting friends of her plan to create a Mother's Day, and one friend, prominent Philadelphia merchant John Wanamaker, suggested she start a national campaign to garner support for the idea. She took his advice and conducted a massive letter-writing crusade throughout the country.

Her object was to make observance of Mother's Day a religious event. Ceremonies were held in honor of her late mother at a hometown church in Grafton, Pa., and in Philadelphia. From Jarvis came the tradition of wearing a pink carnation to honor a living mother; a white one for the dead.

The idea caught on quickly. The governor of West Virginia issued the first Mother's Day proclamation in 1910. By 1912 every state was observing it.

In this country, Mother's Day quickly became more than a religious holiday. Jarvis was appalled to note that there were fewer and fewer church services for mothers, while more and more advertising urged families to buy flowers and candy for Mother. In 1961, an estimated 55 million families spent $875 million on gifts for this occasion; in 1976, $200 million was spent on flowers alone.

psychiatrists, and social workers, that the bewildered mother faces a maze of often contradictory advice.

History of Child Rearing

Despite the fact that Western civilization sometimes thinks it invented cultivated behavior, like the stable family group, all human societies since the beginning of time have raised children in small groups of blood relatives. Few doubt that the intimacy and love a family provides create the best environment in which to raise a child as a normal human being, capable of playing adult roles.

In earlier years, and even today in some areas of the world, women were considered too valuable as able-bodied workers to spend all their time taking care of babies. Baby sitting has often been left to younger brothers and sisters, or the elderly, and there were no assumptions that the mother was neglecting her child.

Similarly, the idea of spending time pondering proper techniques for raising children, is a contemporary one. In ancient Greece and Rome, the child was considered primarily as a member of a political state. Young males were simply trained to be good citizens, capable of serving the state; girls were trained to serve the citizen-men. In the Middle Ages, childhood was not regarded as a developmental phase of life; children were simply miniature adults.

It wasn't until the Renaissance, from the fourteenth to sixteenth centuries, that children were thought to be at all special. They were given their own toys, games, and wardrobes, and reaped other benefits of the times, including a more enlightened attitude toward education and welfare.

In Puritan New England, under the chilling tenets of Protestant Calvinism, children, like their parents, were considered innately evil. Parents were exhorted to break a child's will which was in *thrall* to the devil.

As the American frontier expanded, children became an important part of a family's work force; they were expected to share in the chores of running a farm or put to a trade.

But the precursors of today's child-raising attitudes were waiting in the wings. In 1834, Theodore Dwight wrote *The Fathers Book,* which urged fathers to evaluate their commitment to their offspring by asking themselves: "What is my business, and ought it to engross me so as to make me a stranger to my children?"

Burgeoning interest in the science of psychology in the 1930s and 1940s strongly affected child-rearing techniques. Parents read that their behavior toward their children was as important as the physical care of their bodies. Difficulty in interpreting these somewhat nebulous "proper" psychological attitudes attitudes caused much anxiety for parents who wanted to raise their children correctly.

The "Dr. Spock" Revolution

Dr. Benjamin Spock's 1946 book, *Baby and Child Care,* was revolutionary. Spock told parents to relax, and to rely on their own instincts and on common sense in raising their children.

His advice is based on the conviction that children are friendly, reasonable, and loving creatures. He suggests following the child's natural appetites and needs to best regulate eating and sleeping habits and growth.

Dr. Spock, and his frequently updated book (which has sold more than 28 million copies) have become synonymous with permissive child-rearing, because he argues against repressive treatment of children and blames excessive parental discipline for flawed child development.

At the same time, he advocates firmness with children and believes that children should be punished for wrongdoing. Spanking and sending a child to sit in a corner for a few minutes have a definite place in discipline, he says.

Dr. Spock has been criticized in recent years as a sexist for placing all responsibility for child-rearing on the mother. Sensitive to this, in 1976 he published a newly revised *Baby and Child Care,* which attempts to eliminate sex stereotyping by referring to a baby as "she," as well as "he," discussing the importance of the father's role in child-rearing, and the situation of the working mother.

In the 1970s, the psychoanalytic approach to child rearing receded. It has been replaced by "behavior modification," which uses play therapy and reward systems to reinforce *desired behavior.*

The Parent Involvement Program is one example of a behavior modification approach. Advocated by Los Angeles psychiatrist Dr. William Glasser, the program stresses the value of dealing with visible behavior rather than dwelling on feelings and motivations. It is founded on mutual respect between parents and child. The first rule for parents in dealing with a troubling situation is to calm the youngster down by asking: "What are you doing?" This approach avoids assigning guilt at the outset. It encourages youngsters to look at themselves and their actions with a view toward finding out if they have done something that is harmful to another person or is considered wrong. The important thing, according to Dr. Glasser, is "What the child did and what is he or she willing to do to change," rather than the deep motivations for the action.

Another technique for improving a child's adjustment is Parent Effectiveness Training, (PET) originated in 1963 by Thomas Gordon, a clinical psychologist. Termed the "no-lose program for raising responsible children," PET advocates "active listening" on the parents' part. By repeating in your own words what you think your child is trying to tell you, you open up communication with your child, Gordon says.

Some general do's and don'ts for successful child rearing have been developed by behavioral psychologist Burton L. White of Harvard University. The guides are geared to a child at the age of eight months, which Dr. White considers the beginning of its most formative development period, which it lasts until 24 months of age, he says.

Do: Respond promptly and favorably as often as possible when the child seeks attention; make an effort to understand what the child is doing; set limits; provide encouragement, enthusiasm, and assistance whenever possible; talk to the child often to encourage verbal response; encourage make-believe activities, as well as others.

Don't: Confine the child physically for extended periods; allow child to keep close to you constantly; worry that the baby won't like you if you say "No" occasionally; take a full-time job or otherwise prevent yourself from being available

to the child for at least half its waking hours; try to force toilet training.

Parents today are a pretty savvy group. To be sure, there are many stereotypes of mothers — the "Jewish" mother, holding power over her child by inducing guilt over parental self-sacrifice; the "Italian momma," who spends all her time either having babies or cooking for them.

But the picture that emerges from surveys of parents shows them, in fact, to be thoughtful, concerned, and eager to avoid the pitfalls to which their own parents may have succumbed.

Discarding some of the old parent-child roles has made parents much more open with their children than was the case in previous generations. According to another survey, communication between parents and children is of paramount importance to parents in their twenties and thirties. Parents are making intense efforts to listen to their children, and both parents and children feel more comfortable about expressing their emotions than did the previous generation. Also, parents are more willing to own up to their mistakes.

One of the most dramatic changes of all between generations is the freer attitude about girls' roles. The image of what is

The intimacy and love a family provides is the best environment in which to raise a child.

"proper" for girls has expanded to include sports of every type, mastery of math and science, and work in previously all-male occupations.

The definition of what constitutes "making it" is different for today's generation. Although monetary comfort is still prominent, parents today say they are more concerned about the quality of life, and insist on finding time to enjoy themselves and their families.

The result of all these changes seems to be a fairly relaxed and open parent, one who realizes there is no "ideal" parent, and who follows her instincts, rather than strict societal mores.

Child rearing is a happier job in the 1970s, a choice rather than a duty, and children can't help but benefit from the newly available parental warmth and guidance.

ADOPTING A CHILD

Adoption is one of the more loving and beneficial concepts in our culture. Adults who want to share their love with children are matched with homeless children who need attention and security.

Adoption has long been practiced, though not always for the most altruistic of motives. In ancient Greek and Roman societies, families might adopt boys to be sure of heirs; the adopted child acquired all the rights of natural offspring.

In the early years of this country, homeless children were placed in poorhouses. Some were subsequently taken in by relatives; others were hired by tradesmen as indentured workers — they worked in exchange for room and board. Other unclaimed youngsters might be shipped out to the Western frontier. Jammed into railroad cars, at each stop they would be marched out on the train platform where local townsfolk could "adopt" any they thought likely to work out as unpaid labor.

The first law to protect homeless children was passed by Massachusetts in 1851. At the same time, private social agencies tried to better the plight of children in orphanages by introducing foster care. Rather than have children spend years in a cold, impersonal institution, reasoned Protestant minister Charles Loring Brace, founder of the New York Children's Aid Society, why not subsidize families to take homeless children into their homes, where, under the care of foster parents, they would get more attention.

Until some fifteen years ago, the workings of orphanages, foster care, and adoption remained unchanged. In a typical adoption, a young, married couple, most often white, who couldn't have their own children, submitted to an exhaustive investigation of their financial and personal condition, including proof of infertility. If the investigation was completed in their favor, they could adopt a newborn, healthy, white baby.

The dramatic change in life styles in the past decade, however, has completely altered the adoption picture. Historically, almost nine out of ten children offered for adoption were illegitimate. With widespread use of effective birth control, and legalized abortion, the supply of illegitimate babies has nearly dried up. Also, social mores have relaxed to the point that women who do bear illegimate children no longer feel uncomfortable about keeping their babies.

With the decrease in the number of healthy, white newborns, which are the most desirable adoptees, older, nonwhite, and handicapped children, once considered unadoptable, have moved into the front ranks of the adoption market.

To find homes for such children, restrictions on parents who want to adopt have relaxed significantly. Older people and single people can now adopt, and interracial and interreligious adoptions are also possible.

Adoptions, perhaps because of more open attitudes, have increased significantly; from 57,800 in 1960, to 809,200 in 1970.

"Gray" and "Black Market" Adoption

But people who still want to adopt healthy, newborn whites must often turn to sources other than public or private adoptive agencies, where the wait for a white baby can last seven years.

Legal in all but a few states are "gray market" adoptions. These are independent adoptions arranged outside the jurisdiction of adoption agencies, but at normal fees. Lawyers, clergymen, doctors, social workers, and others serve as intermediaries. "Gray market" babies are found in this country or through legitimate channels elsewhere, such as orphanages in South America.

The law of short supply and high demand always has an underside, however, and there is a notorious "black market" for healthy white babies, which can cost prospective parents anywhere from $4,000 to $40,000.

Witnesses at a 1975 Congressional hearing on the subject testified to the existence of "baby farms," operated by Miami lawyers for unwed mothers who would agree to give up their babies. One enterprising lawyer, it was reported, flew West German women to this country to deliver their babies who would then be United States citizens and consequently easier to adopt.

"Black market" adoptions and legal inconsistencies among the various states adoption laws have led reformers to call for standardization and a nationwide adoption network.

Liberalized attitudes toward adoption have affected thinking about a basic dilemma faced by parents adopting newborns — to tell or not to tell their children that they are adopted, and what to do if the adoptee wants to find the biological parents.

The consensus among adoption professionals is that the parents should eventually tell the child he or she is adopted. There is still intense controversy surrounding the problem of discovering the real parents of an adopted child.

Most states seal birth records at the time of adoption, with the intention of protecting the child from the social pressure or emotional problem of learning, that in nine out of ten cases, the birth was illegitimate.

MEDICAL ADVICE FOR MOTHERS

Childhood accidents and diseases can be among the most frightening things a parent must face. Watching your own child being rushed to the hospital, or even just suffering with a bad case of the sniffles, can be more painful for the parent than for the child.

Fortunately, there is a lot a parent can do to arm herself with information that can not only allay these anxieties, but can help the sick child as well.

A matter of primary importance to both you and your child is the choice of a physician. Consider a pediatrician rather than a family physician — at least for the child's first few years. The reason for this is straightforward. Since a pediatrician sees only children she or he has far more experience with the particular problems a youngster may face. Many diseases run different courses in children than in adults. Furthermore, since pediatricians treat many other youngsters in the community, they can spot disease trends, or local epidemics such as various virus infections, and treat them quickly.

How should you choose your pediatrician? There are several matters to consider. Of course, you will want a physician who is fully qualified, preferably board certified or board eligible in pediatrics — although there are many excellent pediatricians who are not board certified. You will also want a physician whose philosophy of child rearing meshes nicely with your own. And, of course, you

Both parents and children feel more comfortable about expressing their emotions than ever before.

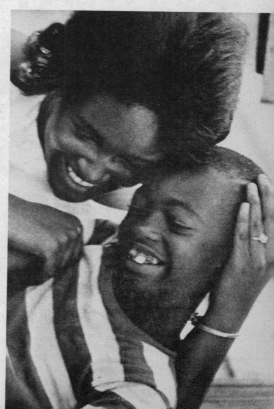

will want a physician who is nearby and available when needed.

If you are in a position to do so, you ought to interview more than one pediatrician before deciding on the right one to care for your child.

While in a doctor's office, carefully observe the waiting room equipment and atmosphere. It will tell you a lot about the doctor and the office procedure itself.

What is the tone of the nurses and other office staff? Are they polite and friendly, or cold and quick-tempered? More than one mother has changed pediatricians because of an unfriendly nurse.

You may have a choice between a pediatrician who practices alone and a group of doctors practicing together. All other things being equal, the group practice may be best for you since you can be sure one of the doctors will always be available in spite of vacations or unusual hours.

One good way to find a pediatrician is to ask friends and neighbors. If several of them have had good experiences with one doctor or group, there is every chance that you will have the same kind of experiences.

Immunizations Still Vital
We have come a long way from the days when polio, diphtheria, whooping cough, smallpox, and tetanus were common. Now we have vaccinations against all of those diseases and, in fact, the smallpox vaccination has been so successful in wiping out that disease that the vaccination is no longer even recommended in the United States and most other countries.

Here are the immunizations that *are* recommended:

— DPT (diphtheria-pertussis-tetanus) inoculations at two, four, six, and eighteen months, and a booster when the child begins school.

— Polio vaccine either oral (Sabin) or injected (Salk), at times specified by your physician.

— MMR (measles, mumps, rubella) at age one year to 15 months.

— Tetanus-diphtheria booster at 14 to 16 years of age, and tetanus boosters thereafter as required.

If money is a problem for you, these vaccinations are usually available free or at very low cost from your local department of public health.

In Case of Illness
Every parent should have in the home and have studied beforehand at least one good book on childhood illness. Such books can both reassure parents and warn them when to check with their physician about problems that may be more serious.

Two of these books are Dr. Spock's *Baby and Child Care,* and *Childhood Illness: A Common Sense Approach,* by Jack Shiller, M.D., a pediatrician on the clinical faculty of the Columbia University College of Physicians and Surgeons.

Do not try to doctor your child yourself. Home remedies that seem to work for adults may not be indicated for children.

A good book, like the two mentioned above, will give you some idea of the kinds of home remedies that may be valuable for youngsters, and the circumstances in which to use them. Otherwise, or when in doubt, telephone your physician. That will ensure the best advice.

Save Your Child's Life
Although home remedies for various diseases are not generally advisable, we strongly urge parents to learn a lot about first aid. First aid is the immediate treatment of accidental injuries or other health emergencies. It is usually practised on the scene by a lay person who has been trained in proper first-aid procedures. All parents would be wise to enroll in at least one adult education first-aid course. If that is impossible, study and keep at hand a good first-aid book.

One is *Save Your Child's Life,* by David Hendin. (Order from P.O. Box 489, Radio City Station, New York, NY 10019. Enclose one dollar plus 25 cents for postage and handling. Other first-aid books may be obtained from your library, pharmacy, or local Red Cross office.

In Case of Poisoning
It's a sad and little realized fact that fully 95 percent of the reported cases of accidental poisoning of children take place when the youngsters are supposedly under the supervision of parents or other adults.

Every year between 500,000 and a million children swallow poisons. Most of them will be under five years of age.

You must poison-proof your home, and do it today! Get *all* poisonous substances out of the reach of children.

Remember — in the case of poisoning, PREVENTION IS THE ONLY SURE CURE!

Nevertheless, accidents may happen. Here are some important signs of poisoning. Watch for them: overstimulation, drowsiness, shallow breathing, unconsciousness, nausea, convulsions, stomach cramps, heavy perspiration, burns on hands and mouth, dizziness, changes in skin color.

Also, be on the lookout for: unusual stains on skin or clothes, sudden changes in a child's behavior, open bottles of chemicals, or medicines out of place.

If you suspect a child has ingested a poisonous substance you must:

— Call the doctor, hospital, or poison-control center immediately. Give them all the information you have about the poison and the child. Write down and follow their directions.

— If you cannot reach any of the above, don't waste any more time trying. If another person is available, let him do the calling while you *dilute the poison*. Do this by giving the child a glass or two of milk or water. It is important to dilute the poison before you induce vomiting.

— Make the child vomit if you have been directed to do so by doctor, hospital, or poison-control center.

Do not induce vomiting if:

— The child is unconscious or having fits.

— The swallowed poison is a strong corrosive (such as ammonia, bleach, lye products, sulfuric, nitric, or hydrochloric acids).

— The swallowed poison contains kerosene, gasoline, or other petroleum products (unless it also contained a dangerous insecticide which must be removed). Some common petroleum products include benzene, liquid furniture and metal polish, turpentine, and oven cleaners. Do not make the child vomit if he has eaten any of the above. Instead, if he is conscious, give him a glass of milk (fresh or canned) and get him to the nearest hospital. Vomiting should not be induced in these cases because the strong chemicals may cause more harm when they are re-

gurgitated. Lye may cause the food pipe to rupture and petroleum products may damage the child's lungs.

If the situation calls for you to make the child vomit:

— Give one tablespoon of syrup of ipecac to a child older than one year. Also give the child at least one cup of water. If no vomiting occurs after twenty minutes this procedure may be repeated, but repeat it only once unless otherwise directed by a doctor.

— If you do not have syrup of ipecac, then you can try to make the child vomit by tickling the back of his throat with a finger or spoon after having him drink lukewarm water.

— Do not waste time waiting for the child to vomit if he does not do so right away. Take him immediately to a doctor or hospital emergency room. Bring the container or package from which the poison came, and leave any remaining sample of the poison intact.

— After the child has vomited you may give him a glass of milk or water to help dilute any remaining poison and protect his stomach.

When taking your child to the hospital, keep him warm and comfortable. Keep airways open and be sure the child does not choke on vomit.

Keep yourself calm. If you are excited, your child may also panic and be more seriously harmed.

Other Injuries
Here are some first-aid steps to take in case of other injuries.

Burns
Never underestimate the severity of a burn. Burns are usually larger and more severe than you think.

In case of burns from fire, here is what to do:

1. Get the victim out of the burning area. If clothes are on fire, put it out by wrapping the victim in a blanket, rug, or other heavy material at hand.

2. If the burn is minor, immerse it in clean ice water, or apply ice packs to the area. Keep it cold for ten to fifteen minutes. Cover the burn with a clean gauze or cloth dressing, or a thin, no-stick plastic covering (clean plastic kitchen wrap works very well). Consult a physician.

3. If the burn is more serious, keep the victim lying down. Try to keep the head and chest slightly lower than the rest of the body. Keep the victim warm.

4. If the victim is conscious and can swallow, give him nonalcoholic liquids to drink.

5. Take the victim to a doctor or hospital immediately.

Important note: Do NOT use butter, grease, ointments, or powders on burns. These increase the danger of infection and make treatment more difficult later.

Cuts

When a child scrapes or skins the knee or other part of the body, gently clean the area with soap and water. Apply a sterile dressing, bandage, or film-type gauze pad (which will prevent the dressing from sticking to the wound). (The American Medical Association does not recommend use of antiseptics for minor cuts and scrapes.)

If the cut is larger, and spurts blood or bleeds for a long time, apply direct pressure to the wound. Prompt medical attention is needed.

Choking

To save a choking victim you must take steps to remove the obstruction as quickly as possible. Pull the victim's tongue forward while slipping the middle and index fingers into the throat to grasp the obstruction and remove it.

A small child may have a mouth that is too small for adult fingers. An attempt should be made to clear the airway with the fingers first, but if this isn't successful, hold the child upside down by the heels or over your knee and pound him on the back between shoulder blades. Be careful, however, since pounding on the back can cause an obstruction to become lodged more firmly unless the person is held upside down so that gravity can help.

Another method that has recently received publicity is the "bear hug" maneuver, invented by Dr. Henry Heimlich of Cincinnati. This technique pushes out the air remaining in the victim's lungs with enough force to dislodge the obstruction.

You do this by standing behind the victim, with your arm under his arms, tightly clasped just below the rib cage. Pressure is applied quickly and forcefully.

In many cases this will cause the foreign matter in the throat to pop right out.

Convulsions

Call a doctor. Have the child lie down with the head lower than the hips. Apply cold cloths to the head. Do not give the child anything to eat or drink.

Drowning

Remove victim from water. Let water drain out of victim. Begin mouth-to-mouth breathing and external cardiac massage if necessary.

Foreign Body in Eye

If you can see the object, gently remove it with a moist cotton swab. If severe, seek medical help. Never rub or press on the eye.

Head Injuries

Check bleeding, but use common sense in doing this, since there may be a fracture. Don't move the victim. Ask him a few simple questions to check coherence, speech, and alertness. Watch for shock. Call a physician, police, or an ambulance, depending on severity.

Nosebleed

Have the victim sit erect. Apply pressure to the outside of the nostril for five minutes. If bleeding continues, call the doctor.

Stomach Ache

Keep patient quiet. No laxatives should be given except on the doctor's orders. If stomach ache persists, or other symptoms such as fever accompany it, call physician.

WORKING MOTHERS

Does a mother who works harm her child's development? Even in the liberated 1970s there's a lot of opposition to mothers who work — especially if their children are infants and toddlers.

Recent research has found that an infant's development is not harmed by the mother's absence during the day. In fact, according to the 1974 study which compared children in a South Boston day care center with those raised at home by their mothers, there was no difference at all between the children.

After making the decision to work, a

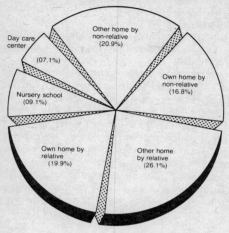

Type of Child Care for Children Receiving 10 or More Hours per Week

Day care center (07.1%)

Other home by non-relative (20.9%)

Own home by non-relative (16.8%)

Nursery school (09.1%)

Own home by relative (19.9%)

Other home by relative (26.1%)

Source: Department of Health, Education and Welfare, National Childcare Consumer Study: 1975

mother faces the dilemma of finding the best possible child care at an affordable price. Her choices are several: public or private day care centers; nursery schools; or baby sitters.

Day Care Centers and Nurseries

A day care center is a facility where pre-schoolers are cared for in a group. Usually nonprofit, except for those that are franchised by corporations, they provide basic care — food, shelter and recreation — from early morning to early evening, for children of working parents, usually with lower- and middle-incomes.

Nursery schools are privately owned and operated for profit, and their pupils are generally from families in the upper-income bracket.

Costs for day care and nurseries seem to have no direct connection to quality of care, but a 1974 survey gave the following cost estimates for annual care: $1,245 for minimal care; $2,320 for adequate care, and up to $4,000 for full-time, top-quality care.

Public day care centers are run by state or city agencies and supported by the federal government, which pays three dollars for every dollar of state money. The federal government permits the states to give free day care to children whose parents

earn only 80 percent of the median income in their state, although the state can charge fees to this group if it wishes. The federal government allows some day care subsidies for children of families whose median income is between 80 and 115 percent of the median income, but none to children from families earning over 115 percent of the state's median income.

Other day care centers are run by churches, universities, charitable groups, profit-making franchise owners, and co-operatives organized and run by parents.

Experts in early childhood education describe the best day care centers and nursery schools as dedicated to children's security, self-esteem, and social growth. A good day care center will have a staff willing to work cooperatively with parents in mapping programs, qualified teachers, and programs tailored to individual needs.

A highly rated nursery school would have roomy outdoor play areas, and outdoor play equipment which provide for motor skills development, like crawling, jumping, and balancing; a good selection of reading material and a place to sit quietly; painting easels, and a variety of games and puzzles.

Baby Sitting

Some mothers prefer having a baby sitter take care of their children in their familiar home setting.

Finding a good baby sitter is a combination of perseverance and luck. There are agencies in some cities which match baby sitters to families. Or you can place an ad in a newspaper, being sure to ask for references; or you can ask for suggestions from your friends. Some parents form baby-sitting cooperatives to provide a pool of baby sitters with no fees, but this is tricky if you have a full-time job.

Once you find a baby sitter, members of a Brooklyn, New York, baby-sitting pool recommend the following guidelines:

Tell the sitter how long you expect to be gone, and call if you're going to be late; tell her of any special duties to be carried out, like bathing the baby, or feeding children dinner; tell her about any emotional or physical problems your child has; leave her with a complete list of telephone numbers — where you can be reached, your child's doctor, the poison-control center, and the name and telephone number of a neighbor.

Tax Credits for Child Care

Where both parents work, or for families where one works and one is a full-time student, a change in the 1976 tax law affecting child care expenses saves them tax money.

The new tax law treats child care expenses as a tax credit, rather than an itemized deduction. This means parents can subtract 20 percent of their employment-related child care expenses directly from the total tax due. The maximum credit is $400 for one dependent, and $800 for two or more dependents. The credit is applicable, also, to care for a disabled older dependent or spouse.

Also eligible for the tax break is a divorced or separated single parent who has custody of the child.

MEMORABLE MOTHERS

Kennedy: Molder of Statesmen

Rose Fitzgerald Kennedy (1890-   ), mother of nine, including two U. S. Senators and one American President, is one of the most celebrated mothers in the world today. She is well known for the strength she has shown in the face of multiple tragedies — the loss of her eldest son, Joseph, in World War II; the assassination of her two sons, John F. and Robert; the death of a daughter in a plane accident, and another daughter's mental retardation.

Her recipe for molding successful children has been untiring diligence to make them independent, competitive, and unafraid. Her efforts included everything from guiding their education to watching them dance at country club get-togethers, and correcting the sloppy dancers the next day.

Although her husband, the late Joseph Kennedy Sr., was often credited for his sons' drive and accomplishments, he was away during much of their youth. His wife took the leading role in their upbringing. It has been said that "Joe provided the fire in the family, but Rose provided the steel."

A religious woman, who ascribes her strength to her faith, Rose Kennedy is a slim, impeccably-dressed woman. Seven years ago she went to Ethiopia to have a joint 80th birthday celebration with Emperor Haile Selassie; today she is still going strong.

Churchill: More than a Mother

Another mother of a famous politician, but cut from a different cloth, was **Jennie**

Rose Kennedy and children, 1938. From left: Kathleen, Robert, Mrs. Kennedy, Ted, Patricia, Jean.

Jerome Churchill (1854-1921), the flamboyant but affectionate mother of Sir Winston Churchill.

At the age of thirteen, this native Brooklynite went to live in Paris with her two sisters and her mother, who had separated from husband Leonard Jerome. At nineteen, the startlingly beautiful young woman met Lord Randolph Churchill, a prominent Englishman. She married him a year later.

Although her mother-in-law, the Duchess of Marlborough, frowned on the match, Jennie soon played a prominent role in London society. Her marriage to Lord Randolph was not very successful. His contraction of syphilis cut short a brilliant political career, and he died a slow, difficult death.

Her son Winston inherited Jennie's indomitable courage and energy. Although she was not the most constant of mothers in his early life — neglecting to visit him at boarding school — her drive and support was to help launch him on his successful political career.

She used her social contacts quite regularly to help him get jobs, like that of foreign war correspondent early in the century, and secure him a place in Parliament. Sir Winston was very devoted to his mother and appreciative of her abilities.

Carter: "Miss Lillian"

The newest political "Mama" (as her son calls her) is **Lillian Carter**, (1898-   ) President Jimmy Carter's mother. A spirited octogenarian, "Miss Lillian" raised four children during her thirty years of marriage. After her husband's death, she took on a series of new ventures, including jobs as fraternity house-mother and nursing home administrator.

Most venturesome, however, was her enlistment at age 67 in the Peace Corps. She applied, she said, half thinking her children would never let her go, but then found they loved the idea. "I had to go into the Peace Corps to keep from losing face with my children," she has said.

Her Peace Corps experience in a family planning center was exciting, but the intense poverty of India so depressed her that she changed her own eating habits and, today, is unable to eat between meals.

Jennie Jerome Churchill: Sir Winston was appreciative of his mother's encouragement.

The President's mother says she prefers to stay in Plains, Georgia, during her son's administration rather than do a lot of traveling.

"I'm a country hick," she said. She wears slacks unless it's absolutely necessary to wear a dress, she admits.

Hovick: Stage Mother

Politicians aren't the only people who have strong mothers. **Rose Hovick** was the driving force behind the show business careers of daughters Rose and June, better known as Gypsy Rose Lee and June Havoc. Their mother enrolled them in dancing school when they were toddlers, and they soon appeared professionally at a Knights of Pythias celebration.

At the height of their careers as child stars, they earned $1,250 weekly.

Hovick was a determined stage mother, her daughter, "Gypsy" reported in a 1943 interview: "When we played on the same bill with another kiddie act, things always seemed to go wrong — for them. Pieces of their wardrobe would be missing. A toe shoe would get burned. Mother was always 'very sympathetic' when these misfortunes happened."

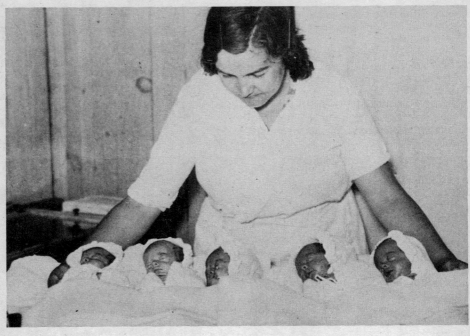

Dionnes: "The smell of greed must have hung in the air like hot dogs and popcorn."

Gilbreth: Cheaper by the Dozen

Taking care of not one, but twelve children, was the awesome achievement of **Lillian M. Gilbreth** (1878-1972) and her husband Frank B., who had five boys and seven girls. The family was immortalized in a book *Cheaper by the Dozen* written by two of the Gilbreth children. It later also became a movie.

Both parents were industrial engineers, specializing in time/motion studies, which they used to manage their house. They took films of their children washing dishes so they could learn how to speed up the task.

Dionne: Once in 57 Million

A much grimmer story of life in a large family was told by the quintuplets born to **Elzire** and **Oliva Dionne** in Ontario, Canada on May 28, 1934. From birth, Marie, Cecile, Emilie, Annette, and Yvonne were treated as lucrative freaks rather than people. Their father, who already had four other children, barely eked out a living as a farmer. He decided to try to make his fortune by turning the quints into a sideshow attraction.

Because of the public outcry against that plan, the girls were named wards of the British Crown. A trust fund was set up for them, and they were moved across the street from their parents' shack into a new, nine-room nursery.

Elzire Dionne, apparently resentful of her daughters' attachment to their nurses, rarely visited them. When she did, she bribed her daughters with candy to tell reporters they wanted to come home. After a seven-year battle, the quints were returned to their parents. But, according to the sisters, their homecoming was far from happy. Oliva Dionne forced them to work as servants in the new house built with their money; the quints recalled that they dined downstairs on cold cereal while the rest of the family ate steak in the dining room above.

The three surviving quints — Yvonne, Cecile and Annette — remain bitter about their experiences. Of their childhood, they wrote in their autobiography, "The smell of greed must have hung in the air like hot dogs and popcorn the peddlers sold to the neighbors."

Emilie died in 1954 and Marie in 1970.

Older Women

THE BEST IS YET TO BE

In *Gone With the Wind,* Scarlett O'Hara's pea-green eyes turned red from weeping because she thought she was over the hill at twenty-eight. And she had good cause for concern — at the time of the Civil War, the average American woman could expect to live only forty years. Even at the turn of the century only three million people or 4.1 percent of the total United States population were sixty-five years of age or older. Today, women approaching thirty — although they may still shed a tear on seeing the first gray hair or hint of jowl or sag in chin — can look forward to at least forty more active years.

As a result of better sanitary conditions and modern medical techniques, women now live an average of seventy-five years, exceeding the average life-span of men by almost eight years. Twenty-two million or 10.5 percent of the total United States population are sixty-five or older. Women older than seventy-five now constitute one sixth of this elderly population.

Gerontologists forecast that in the 1990s the average life span will lie somewhere between 90 and 105 years of age. And, based on present death rates, the total United States population over sixty-five is expected to increase to thirty-one million by the 1990s.

To some women the statistics are down-

Gerontologists say that before too long the average life span will lie between 90 and 105 years.

right frightening. It's great to survive to 105 if you're healthy, wealthy, wrapped in love, and confident you're wanted and needed. But nobody wants to be old, ill, poor, alone, and unwanted in a country where the accent is on youth.

The solution is to be prepared. Don't be like Scarlett O'Hara who said, "I'll worry about that tomorrow." Start planning for your old age immediately, and you'll agree with Robert Browning that "the best is yet to be."

Aging Isn't a Disease

First, abandon the misconception that aging and illness go hand in hand.

Barring accidents and other major catastrophes, it's possible to slow the aging process by taking certain precautions. The old adage "An apple a day, keeps the doctor away" is not just poppycock. Eating proper meals is a good way to stay young. An improper diet accelerates the body's decline. Overweight requires the heart to work harder to pump blood to the larger body and can contribute to high blood pressure. High blood pressure can adversely affect the heart and brain. Statistics show that individuals 20 percent or more overweight have a mortality rate almost 50 percent higher than persons of average weight. Experts advise keeping weight as close as possible to that maintained in good health at age twenty-five.

Hardening of the arteries, once considered a natural occurrence of old age, is now known to be related to high cholesterol levels in the blood. Avoid foods high in cholesterol such as egg yolks, fatty meats, and butterfat, use less fat in all foods, and substitute oils such as safflower or corn oil for solid fats and you can lower your blood cholesterol count.

Age Changes Vary

Although it's true that the body changes — and not for the better — with age, it's important to keep in mind that the degree of change varies with each individual. Not too many years ago, a woman died in jail at the reputed age of 113. She had been arrested for horse thievery and for practicing medicine without a license. It seems that the life she had led agreed with her because an autopsy revealed very few of the changes commonly associated with old age. Although a career in crime

How Long Will You Live?

Want to know how long you can expect to live? First, write down the average expected life span for your sex — seventy-five for women, sixty-seven for men. (Women and men in their fifties and sixties should add ten years to this figure because all of you have already proven to be healthy.) After you have answered each question below, add the total pluses to the average span, subtract the total minuses, and you'll end up with your personal life-expectancy score. This quiz was taken from *Good Housekeeping*, and was prepared in cooperation with Drs. Richard H. Davis and Diana S. Woodruff of the Ethel Percy Andrus Gerontology Center at USC.

Are you a light drinker (2 drinks a day)?	+2	A little alcohol aids relaxation;
Are you a heavy drinker (more than 2)?	−8	too much is harmful; teetotalers'
Are you a teetotaler?	−1	values may be too rigid.
Do you smoke 2 or more packs of cigarettes daily?	−8	Studies show chemicals in cigarettes cause lung cancer.
Do you smoke 1 to 2 packs?	−4	
Do you smoke less than a pack a day?	−2	
Are you a nonsmoker?	+2	
Do you exercise moderately (jogging) 3 times weekly?	+3	Exercise keeps muscles strong.
Are you happily married?	+3	The presence of a "significant
Are you single and between 26 and 35?	−1*	other" in one's life is a major plus.
Is your job active (housework, sales work, etc.)?	+3	Physical activity is essential for maintaining good muscle tone.
Is your job sedentary (secretarial, other seated work)?	−3	
Do you sleep 9 hours a day?	−4	Too much sleep
Do you sleep 10 or more hours a day?	−6	saps energy.
Have you lived most of your life in an urban environment (e.g., New York)?	−1	Urban living creates stress through competition for space, etc. Rural living is more
Have you lived most of your life in a rural environment (e.g., the Dakotas)?	+1	leisurely.
Is your family's income over $40,000 per year?	−2	Success often brings stress.
Do you have less than a high-school education?	−2	Education usually creates increased awareness of proper
Do you have 4 years of school beyond high school?	+1	health care and life-planning.
Do you have 5 or more years beyond high school?	+3	
Are you over 60 and still active?	+2	This enhances quality of life.
Is your home's thermostat set at no more than 68°F.?	+2	Low temperatures slow body aging.
Are you a reasoned, practical person?	+1	Stress caused by aggression and
Are you aggressive, intense and competitive?	−1	competition shortens life.
Are you basically happy and content with life?	+1	Stress from unhappiness
Are you often unhappy (worried, tense and guilty)?	−1	shortens life.
Do you use seat belts regularly, and obey speed limits?	+1	Shows a concern for safety.
Are you at least 10 pounds overweight?	−1**	The heart works harder to pump
Are you over 40 and not overweight?	+3	blood through a fat body.
If you're a woman over 30, do you give yourself a monthly breast self-examination, have your doctor give you a periodic breast exam and Pap smear?	+2	Treatment of cancer is most effective when the disease is caught at an early stage.
If you're a man over 40, do you have an annual medical examination and proctoscopic exam every 2 years?	+2	Checkups aid early detection of life-threatening diseases.
Have 2 of your grandparents lived to 80, or beyond?	+5	Longevity is hereditary.
Has any parent, grandparent, sister or brother died of heart attack or stroke before 50?	−4	Heredity increases chances of suffering one of these diseases.
Has anyone died from these diseases before 60?	−2	
Have there been any cases of diabetes, thyroid disorders, breast cancer, cancer of the digestive system, asthma, emphysema or chronic bronchitis among parents or grandparents?	−3†	There is a genetic predisposition to these diseases, so odds of getting one are greater— but not inevitable.

TOTALS:

*If you're 36 to 45, it's −2; 46 to 55, −3, etc.   **For each additional 10 pounds subtract another point.
†Subtract 3 points for *each* such case.

after fifty isn't a sure way to stay fit, a career that requires movement and fast thinking is. Youthfulness at an older age is no accident. People who stay young follow the principle that physical or mental functions which are exercised tend to persist. Others tend to disappear.

One of the most encouraging notes about aging is, contrary to popular belief, that learning abilities do not necessarily diminish with time.

Dr. Wayne Dennis of Brooklyn College, in a study of works completed by 738 creative persons who lived to be at least seventy, found that scholars, scientists, writers, artists, and other creative individuals reach their peak of productivity in their forties or later and remain prolific through their eighth decade.

What Is Menopause?

Menopause, literally an end to the menses, or monthly bleeding, is one true physical change that women experience with age. According to the 1970 census, some twenty-seven million women in the United States are at or beyond the average age of menopause — about fifty years of age or a little older.

Life after menopause is nothing to dread. The menopause need have no effect on a woman's femininity; it merely marks the end of her child-bearing years. Menopause occurs when ovulation — and, thus menstruation — permanently ceases. Irregular or missed menstrual periods *may* be a signal of the onset of menopause. However, there can be *many other causes* of missed or irregular menstrual periods besides the onset of menopause.

In a normal woman of reproductive age, the ovaries continually produce the hormones estrogen and progesterone in amounts which fluctuate each month in relation to the cyclical development of new eggs. The gradual decline and, finally, the cessation of the ovaries' production of estrogen is another part of menopause.

At the same time production of estrogen by the ovaries drops, there is also a decline in production of progesterone, the other female hormone. Each month before the menopause, progesterone had prepared the lining of the uterus to receive a fertilized egg.

Unlike menstruation, which begins abruptly, the menopause usually occurs so gradually that there are no clear markers for its beginning and end. A woman may begin producing less estrogen before there is any irregularity in her periods. However, via the adrenal glands, women may produce estrogen after the menopause.

Many women worry a lot about the variety of symptoms related to the menopause. Their fears are usually exaggerated. Although certain discomforts often accompany menopause, not all women suffer from them. Less than half of the women going through menopause even consult a physician about it.

Two characteristic signs of the menopausal period are hot flashes and mild genital atrophy. Hot flashes, or sudden waves of heat, are generally felt on the upper chest and arms, neck, and head. This sensation usually is accompanied by reddening of the skin and is followed by profuse sweating. In most instances these symptoms are more inconvenient than anything else. Occasionally they can become severe and frequent enough to interfere with a woman's sleep or work routine.

Genital atrophy is one discomfort of menopause. The vagina gradually shortens and becomes narrower and less elastic. Its lining undergoes cellular changes and loses its thickness. Vaginal secretions lose their normal acidity, and susceptibility to vaginal infections increases. The tissues and structures of the external sex organs shrink and lose some of their fat. However, unless a woman finds intercourse painful or notices a lack of vaginal lubrication, she will not be aware of these changes.

Other discomforts that may accompany menopause are: migraine headaches, pains at the back of the neck and in the chest, insomnia, irritability, depression, nausea, and constipation. Women who suffer any of these symptoms can help alleviate them by careful attention to diet, particularly by increasing their calcium intake, exercising, and keeping active mentally as well as physically.

If Symptoms Persist

If the symptoms persist, it's time to see the doctor. He may prescribe aspirin, tranquilizers, sleeping pills, or he may suggest estrogen therapy. Remember, it may be wise to seek an additional consultation on health problems that are especially troublesome. It has been said that some doctors prescribe drugs for all women whatever the complaint or dismiss menopausal problems as temporary and psychologically based.

Experts now hold that estrogen replacement therapy (ERT) is a reasonable treatment for relief of some menopausal symptoms — specifically severe hot flashes and genital atrophy — as long as the dosage is moderate and the patient is checked regularly by her physician. Since women vary in their degree of estrogen deficiency, a routine vaginal smear test helps the physician evaluate the need for estrogen therapy and the effectiveness of treatment. Researchers are in the process of developing even more sensitive tests to allow the doctor to precisely determine the need for estrogen therapy.

Because of possible health risks involved in taking estrogens, a physician may suggest less aggressive measures unless menopausal symptoms are unusually severe.

Although some doctors are currently using estrogens to relieve a wide variety of symptoms which may be associated with menopause it is felt that more research is needed to validate such uses of ERT.

Before beginning estrogen therapy, a woman should make sure her doctor evaluates her carefully and, if she decides to take the treatment, gives her regular checkups during the course of the therapy. Physicians have been cautioned against using ERT as a cure-all for aging and for the emotional and psychological disturbances that can occur after the menopause.

AGE IS NO BAR TO BEAUTY

Europeans, particularly the French, have always found women "of a certain age" more attractive than young girls. But in America the ideal has long been to stay twenty-one forever. However, a relentless pursuit of the fountain of youth is absurd.

To look and feel good at forty-plus, the first thing to do is get rid of excess weight. As a woman grows older, her body requires fewer calories. Between the ages of thirty-five and fifty-five, a woman needs 10 percent fewer calories than at age twenty-five, and in the years from fifty-five to seventy-five, 16 percent fewer. The average woman of this age group needs only 1,700 calories each day to maintain her current weight. Eating properly may help her live beyond seventy-five years, when her body will require 1 percent fewer calories per year.

The biggest mistake in dieting is to set impractical goals. Most women need to lose only fifteen to twenty pounds to get back in shape, and they can do it by selecting a well-balanced diet and sticking to it. Once unnecessary weight is lost, a woman can keep it off by watching calorie consumption and exercising regularly.

Exercise is the closest thing to the fountain of youth. It improves muscle tone, aids digestion, and helps maintain other body functions. Lack of exercise leads to flabbiness and tired muscles, which in turn may cause abnormal posture and eventually may even cause spinal curvature or rounded shoulders. Regular moderate exercise, whether it is gymnastics, swimming, sports, dancing, jogging, or just walking, is preferable to violent exertion performed sporadically. Always check with your doctor before starting any type of new diet or exercise program.

Beware of Shortcuts

"No-exercise" products, advertised heavily, should be approached with caution. These products range from creams to vibrator belts to inflatable belts that supposedly take off inches while the user does nothing. Some such products have already been seized by the Federal Trade Commission on grounds of false advertising.

Above all, exercise should begin before age sixty-five. Building a level of conditioned fitness is one of the essential ingredients in combating premature old age.

Once a good diet and exercise program are underway, the next step is to control the wrinkles. Unfortunately, there's no magic potion for removing lines. Regardless of the amount of cream a woman slathers on her face or the hormones she swallows, wrinkles will still appear because the skin gradually loses elasticity. Nevertheless, facial exercises can help slow down lining of the skin and improve its color, texture, and elasticity. They must be done regularly to obtain any benefit.

In addition to facial exercises, wrinkles can be postponed with plenty of sleep and lots of water to keep the skin from drying out and to rid the system of impurities. Investing in a humidifier to combat dry winter air, and pampering the skin with a regular pattern of care can also help combat wrinkles. A moisturizing beauty mask is an extra-kind treatment for facial skin. It's also a fact that smokers get more severe "crow's feet" sooner than nonsmokers.

To look beautiful, a woman must feel beautiful. If exercise, proper diet, and skin nourishment don't seem to improve the image in the mirror, it may be the time to give serious thought to a face-lift. However, a face-lift won't produce miracles. An ideal face-lift is one that doesn't do anything drastic. There shouldn't be a new face, just one that looks like it's been given new life. Don't delay a face-lift until the whole face is heavily lined. Best results may be obtained between the ages of forty and forty-five. There are many types of face-lifts and obviously many prices. (See section on cosmetic surgery.)

LOVE LIFE AFTER MENOPAUSE

Often more terrifying than wrinkles is the fear of losing love. Menopause, if it arouses anxieties about age and sex, can be a critical period for a woman. She begins to feel inadequate, to worry about her husband losing interest in her, to fear possible rejection, even to doubt her own ability to enjoy sex. Such fears are best dispelled by a loving, understanding husband.

In *Human Sexual Inadequacy,* Dr. William H. Masters and Virginia Johnson state: "There is no reason why the milestone of the menopause should be expected to blunt the human female's sexual capacity, performance or drive. The healthy aging woman normally has sex drives that demand resolution. The depths of her sexual capacity and the effectiveness of her sexual performance, as well as her personal eroticism, are influenced indirectly by all of the psycho- and sociophysiologic problems of her aging process . . . in short, there is no time limit drawn

by the advancing years to female sexuality. We must, in fact, destroy the concept that women in the 50–70 year age group not only have no interest in but also have no facility for active sexual expression. Nothing could be further from the truth than the often-expressed concept that aging women do not maintain a high level of sexual orientation.''

Use It or Lose It
Masters and Johnson stress the importance of maintaining regular sexual contact. They found that women who had not engaged in an active sex life over the years lost their enjoyment of sexual activity with the onset of their mature years. Other medical authorities support this conclusion. Dr. David Reuben summed it up succinctly: "Use it or lose it."

There is no valid reason why sex should not continue into advanced old age. It gives a sense of personal importance and of being wanted, and it is a source of comfort and joy. Asked at what age a woman loses interest in sex, the Princess Metternich promptly replied: "You must ask someone else; I wouldn't know. I am only sixty years old!"

Use it or lose it: There's no reason why older people should not lead active sex lives.

FACING FINANCIAL PROBLEMS

Financial insecurity is one of the biggest worries of old age. In 1974, one of every five couples with a husband sixty-five or older received an income of less than $4,000. On the other end of the scale, one of every four elderly couples had incomes of $10,000 or more. About 15.7 percent of 3.3 million persons sixty-five or older were below the poverty level. Among elderly whites, one out of every seven was poor, but over one third of all elderly blacks fell below the poverty level.

The reason for much of this poverty is that most people over the age of sixty-five are not working. In 1975, only 14 percent of older people were in the labor force. This includes 20 percent of the older men (1.9 million) and 8 percent of the elderly women (1.0 million).

A retired woman's income may come from several sources, which are listed here:

Social Security is a form of retirement, disability, or life insurance administered by the federal government through the Social Security Administration.

Nearly two thirds of aged single beneficiaries and one half of elderly couple beneficiaries depend upon Social Security for over half their income; female Social Security beneficiaries outnumber male beneficiaries by a ratio of 149 to 100.

At the same time, women continue to receive lower Social Security benefits than men. This is a reflection of long-standing sex differences in work opportunities and work patterns. For example, in June 1975, average monthly benefits for male retired workers amounted to $225, compared with $180 for female retired workers.

As a group, aged widows have traditionally been the most economically deprived segment of the aged population. There are twelve million widows in the country, many of whose husbands made no financial provision for them. Widows receiving Social Security benefits in June 1975 numbered 4,287,000, and their average monthly benefit was $187. Older women living alone, the overwhelming proportion of whom are widows, had median incomes of $2,642 in 1973; 33.4 percent of these American women were living below the poverty level.

Supplemental Security Income is an income maintenance program for the aged, blind, and disabled, funded by the federal government. Under SSI, the federal government also administers a number of state income maintenance programs; payment amounts and eligibility requirements under these programs differ from state to state. To meet requirements for the federal portion of the program, older persons must be at least sixty-five years old with incomes below $167.80 a month for an individual or $225.00 for a couple.

Even though the Social Security Administration runs the federal program, supplemental security income is not the same as Social Security. People who get Social Security checks can get supplemental security income checks as well if they are eligible for both. If you think you may be eligible for SSI, contact your local Social Security office.

In addition to these federal programs, you may also be eligible for one of the following:

Veterans Benefits: For information, contact the local Veterans Administration office or the Veterans Administration, 2033 M Street, N.W., Washington, D.C. 20036.

Private Pension Plans: For information, Ralph Nader and Kate Blackwell's book *You and Your Pension* offers details on different types of plans.

Retirement Savings Plans: For detailed information, see chapter on "Women and Money."

HOW TO SPEND YOUR MONEY AND WHERE TO SAVE

Retirement income goes to five basic areas — housing, food, transportation, and medical and personal expenses. Because these items are costly, suggestions on how to trim some costs in each area are included here.

The first thing a retired woman should do to cut costs is find a bank that provides free checking accounts to older citizens. She would also be wise to have Social Security checks mailed directly to her bank, thereby protecting herself against theft and eliminating the worry of carrying a large amount of money.

Housing After Retirement

According to the Bureau of Labor Statistics, a retired woman can expect to spend close to 40 percent of her annual budget on housing costs. This, of course, depends on where she lives and whether she owns her home or rents a house or an apartment. Where a retired woman lives will be determined by many factors, of which marital status is most significant.

Problems increase when the absence of a husband or friend places a retired woman in the category of "women living alone." More than one third of all older people, including five million women, lived alone or with nonrelatives in 1974.

Choosing an Institutional Home

About 5 percent or approximately one million older people lived in institutions of all kinds in 1974. Although some older people need the care, comfort, and security of nursing homes and similar institutions, most authorities feel that 25 to 30 percent of those currently in nursing homes could survive well in the community if provided with necessary services. Alternatives to nursing homes include senior citizen residences, geriatric daycare centers, and home health-care programs.

A woman who wants to move to a retirement community or to an area which is set aside for elderly people should first investigate the following:

• Climate: Does it suit her health and can her body adjust to the change in the climate from her present location?
• Privacy: Is participation in all events required or does the community allow time for her own hobbies and interests?
• Ease and cost of maintenance: How much will it cost and will transportation to and from places she may want to visit be included?
• Accessibility to neighbors, relatives, and professional help: Will she be too far removed from the people and things she enjoys?
• Entertainment: Will she be able to entertain guests if she wishes?
• Pets: Whether she likes or dislikes them, this may be an important factor.
• Prejudices: What is the composition of the community and is it right for her?
• Morale: Are the residents depressed or enthusiastic? Are the physical surroundings cheerful or depressing?
• Ease of breaking contract: Is the con-

tract binding for life or too restrictive in other ways for her life-style? In addition, she may want to verify, or have someone with legal knowledge verify, the dependability of the promoters, the tax rate (this applies for independent housing within a community), and the security system within the community.

For detailed information on special housing, the National Council on the Aging, 1828 L Street N.W., Washington, D.C., publishes a *National Directory of Housing for Older People*, available for $2.50.

Geriatric day-care centers provide a partial or full program of medical services for the elderly person with special needs. These include health evaluation and nursing or physical, occupational, and speech rehabilitation therapy for those who have had strokes or disabling illnesses. Many of these centers also provide mental-health counseling and educational, recreational, and service activities. Other centers are affiliated with hospitals, often called day hospitals. Local offices on aging or city departments of social or health services will provide information on such centers.

The home health-care program provides nurses as well as physical, occupational, and speech rehabilitation professionals and trained aides who assist with nursing care and other personal services. There are more than 2,200 such agencies, sponsored by public, voluntary, and private agencies in the United States. The National Council for Homemaker-Home Health Aide Services, Inc., 67 Irving Place, New York, N.Y. 10003, will, upon request, provide a free list of such agencies around the country.

Smart Food Shopping Is a Must

Although food costs tend to vary, they average out over a few months. The Bureau of Labor Statistics estimates that a retired couple on a moderate income spends roughly 30 percent of it on food.

However much a retired woman can afford to spend on food, the money-saving tips in the chapter "Women and Money" will help her get good nutritious meals within her budget.

Food stamps can also help balance the food budget. Food stamp eligibility is not based on age, but on income, so anyonwho is below certain levels is eligible. Under this program, the retired woman pays cash for the stamps, but receives stamps worth about 30 percent more in purchasing power than she pays for them. They may be exchanged for the food of her choice at most grocery stores. Even if you think your income is too high to qualify you for food stamps, you should investigate the rules in your area. Many people in special circumstances are eligible, and it will pay you to be informed in advance if your financial situation changes. Local offices on aging or the welfare bureau can supply information on current laws and where to apply for food stamps.

If a retired woman's budget doesn't allow for nutritional meals, or if she is homebound and can't prepare her own meals, or if she simply doesn't like to eat alone, various programs sponsored by the Administration on Aging may solve her problem. Approximately 228,000 meals are being served daily at some 4,400 sites through federal funds. Hot meals, delivered to older persons' homes, are popularly known as "Meals-on-Wheels." They often consist of a hot noon meal and a cold supper for evening use. Sometimes the volunteer who delivers the meals stays to chat during the meal. Local social service agencies can provide information on availabilities and requirements for inclusion.

Transportation Opportunities

Most older people don't drive. Taxis are too expensive, and public transportation in non-urban areas either doesn't exist or is too expensive or difficult to use.

Some help is on the way. At least fifty cities with public transportation systems have made available reduced fares for older people during nonrush hours. Pennsylvania has even begun a statewide free-fare program for senior citizens. Other cities throughout the country have special buses or vans to take older people on needed trips.

Information on special programs in specific areas or reduced-fare information on public transportation is available from local offices on aging.

Cutting Medical Expenses

Approximately 11 percent of a retired woman's budget will go toward medical expenses, according to the Bureau of Labor Statistics. In 1974, older people had about one chance in six of being hospitalized during a year, and, on the average, paid over one third more visits to the doctor than did persons under sixty-five.

Those eligible for Social Security benefits are also eligible to use Medicare to help pay for health care. Medicare hospital insurance covers three kinds of care: inpatient hospital care and, when necessary after a hospital stay, inpatient care in a skilled nursing facility, and home health care. More details of the Medicare program are available from local Social Security offices.

Medicaid is another government health program for low-income persons, which is financed by federal, state, and county government grants. There is no one basic Medicaid program; each state sets up its own. A woman who thinks she is qualified for Medicaid should contact her local welfare office to find out how to apply.

Private health insurance (generally Blue Cross and Blue Shield) is often provided to a worker under group coverage and can be continued on an individual basis after retirement, for a slightly higher premium. If a woman can afford to keep her existing policy after retirement she should. Medicare helps pay medical bills, but a long illness can ruin her financially.

At least fifty cities already have reduced fares for senior citizens on public transportation.

AVOIDING LONELINESS

If I had my life to live over again, I
would start barefoot earlier in the
Spring
And stay bare much later in the Fall.
I would go to more dances, would ride
more merry-go-rounds
I would pick more daisies.

Written by an eighty-five-year-old woman, this poem gives a clue on how to
have a happy, fulfilling old age. An active
interest in the world around her helps keep
the older woman vital.

Several existing government programs
provide jobs and opportunities to meet
people. They are listed here:

Retired Senior Volunteer Program (RSVP)

Persons sixty or older are placed in
community activities suited to their interests. Contact: State Agency on Aging (in
your state capital) or ACTION, Washington, D.C. 20525.

Foster Grandparent Program

Persons sixty or older and on a low income can serve as foster grandparents to
children on a one-to-one basis four hours a
day, five days a week. Contact: AC-
TION, Washington, D.C. 20525.

**Service Corps of Retired Executives
(SCORE)**

Persons retired from business volunteer
to help owners of small businesses or
community organizations that are having
problems with management. Contact: any
Small Business Administration regional or
district office.

Senior Companion Program

Senior Companions serve adults with
special needs. Contact: ACTION, Washington, D.C. 20525.

The Peace Corps and Volunteers in
Service to America (VISTA) are also
open to older people. Information is available from ACTION.

The following Department of Labor
projects also offer part-time employment
to older people:

Green Thumb, sponsored by the National
Farmers Union, provides part-time work
in conservation, beautification, and community improvement in rural areas or in
existing community service agencies.
Contact: GREEN THUMB, Inc., 1012

Mrs. Adela Hein, 81, beats out rhythm for the
"Kitchen Kettels" at a Milwaukee performance.

14th Street, N.W., Washington, D.C.
20005.

Senior Aides, administered by the National
Council of Senior Citizens, offers part-
time work in community service agencies.
Contact: National Council of Senior Citi-
zens, 1511 K Street, N.W., Washington,
D.C. 20005.

Senior Community Aides, sponsored by
the National Council on the Aging, provides part-time work in Social Security
and state employment service offices, public housing, libraries, hospitals, schools,
food and nutrition programs. Contact: National Council on the Aging, 1828 L
Street, N.W., Washington, D.C. 20036.

Senior Community Aides, sponsored by
the National Retired Teachers Association and the American Association of Retired Persons recruits, trains, and finds
part-time work for aides in public or private service programs. Contact: NRTA/
AARP, 1909 K Street, N.W., Washington, D.C. 20006.

Operation Mainstream Program, administered by the U.S. Forest Service, employs
older persons on an average of three days

a week in conservation and beautification projects. Contact: USDA Forest Service, Room 3242, South Agriculture Building, 12th and Independence Avenue, S.W., Washington, D.C. 20250.

If getting a job or working with one of these programs is not for you, or if you are physically incapable of working, there are other services available which can bring you companionship.

Senior Centers are gathering places for older people and some also serve as central umbrella agencies for all services relating to older people. A directory prepared by the National Council on the Aging, Inc., in Washington, D.C., lists over five thousand senior centers and clubs in the United States.

Telephone Reassurance Programs provide a daily telephone contact for an older person who might otherwise have no touch with the outside for long periods of time. If the person does not answer at a predetermined hour, help is immediately sent to his or her home. Contact: Area Agency on Aging.

It's never too late to learn, and wise oldsters know it. They are flocking back to college. Many public and private institutions across the country offer special programs for older adults at little or no cost. Others open regular courses to older adults tuition free or at specially reduced costs.

Organizations

Several independent groups have been formed to aid the elderly.

The **American Association of Retired Persons** (AARP) is a nonprofit organization that offers many services including health, life and automobile insurance, a low-cost tax-aid program, a consumer information program, and help in preretirement planning. Members must be fifty-four or over, either working or retired, and pay a nominal fee. Contact: AARP, 1225 Connecticut Avenue, N.W., Washington, D.C. 20036.

The **National Council of Senior Citizens** is a nonprofit organization that aims to restore the dignity and independence of older people by such measures as adequate income levels, comprehensive health services, decent housing at decent prices, adequate low-cost transportation,

and good nutrition. Contact: NCSC, 1511 K Street, N.W., Washington, D.C. 20005.

The **Gray Panthers,** originally known as Consultation of Older Adults, is a network of social activists who act as organizers at the grass-roots level, making older people conscious of the discrimination they suffer, and encouraging reform. Contact: Gray Panthers, 3700 Chestnut Street, Philadelphia, Pennsylvania 19104.

Senior Advocates International works toward reform in health insurance, pensions, and employment. For a small fee, members are offered insurance, drugs, travel, and other services at discount prices. Contact: 1825 K Street, N.W., Washington, D.C. 20006.

The National Organization for Women established a **Task Force on Older Women** in 1973, which aims to remove sexist inequities in almost all areas affecting the older woman. Contact: your local NOW chapter or the NOW Task Force on Older Women, 434 66th Street, Oakland, California 94609.

Former U.S. Senator Joseph S. Clark talks with Maggie Kuhn, founder of the Gray Panthers.

The **Institute of Gerontology** has a variety of publications aimed mainly at professionals, but some may be of interest to you. Contact: The Institute of Gerontology, University of Michigan/Wayne State University, 543 Church Street, Ann Arbor, Michigan 48104.

SUCCESSES PAST SIXTY

Brico: Seventy-two-year-old Prodigy

Antonia Brico (1903-   ), an extraordinarily gifted conductor, was rediscovered at age seventy-two in Judy Collins' film *Antonia: A Portrait of the Woman*.

In 1930, Brico was the first woman to conduct the Berlin Philharmonic. In 1934, she founded the Woman's Symphony in New York to prove that women could play every instrument in the orchestra. But America was not yet ready for a female conductor.

Her early success blighted by prejudice, Brico moved to Denver, where she conducted the semiprofessional Denver Businessmen's Orchestra and taught piano.

Since the appearance of the film, which won an Academy Award nomination in 1974, Brico's schedule has been booked solid, and when not conducting, she is teaching, lecturing, and coaching opera.

Delaunay: A Painter with Plans

One of the most distinguished women artists of the twentieth century, **Sonia Delaunay** (1885-   ) is still hard at work as she approaches her ninety-second birthday.

Born Sonia Terk in the Ukraine, she was raised in St. Petersburg. In 1905, she moved to Paris. There in 1910, she married Robert Delaunay under whose tutelage she took up abstract painting.

It was not until after her husband's death in 1941 that Delaunay began to attract serious attention in her own right. During the 1950s and 1960s her designs and paintings achieved international fame.

Age has not soured Delaunay's outlook on life. She terms her painting "optimistic," and in 1975 she said she wanted to get back to painting "large pictures."

Fenwick: Grandmother in Congress

A pipe-smoking grandmother of eight, **Millicent Fenwick** (1910-   ) was elected

Congresswoman Fenwick: "Older women like me are more independent, we know how to cope."

U.S. representative from New Jersey's Fifth Congressional District in 1974 when she was sixty-four. She beat out a thirty-seven-year-old male opponent.

Strong-minded and outspoken, Fenwick believes the political arena needs mature women. "I don't think we should be encouraging so many young people to get involved in politics," she says. "Older women like me are more independent, we know how to cope."

Fuldheim: Television Pioneer

The first woman to anchor a television news show, **Dorothy Fuldheim** (1893-   ), now in her ninth decade, has been a television regular since 1947, longer than any other personality, local or network. Her hair is as red and her tongue as sharp as ever they were.

Besides hosting a weekday interview show on WEWS, Cleveland, and doing two commentaries daily on the station's news programs, Fuldheim has written several books.

During her long career, Fuldheim has interviewed the famous and the infamous from Adolf Hitler to Jerry Rubin, whom she threw off her show when he attempted to show her a nude photograph.

Gordon: Discovered at Sixty

In 1966, when **Ruth Gordon** (1896-   ) received an Oscar nomination for her performance in *Inside Daisy Clover,* her husband, playwright-director Garson Kanin said, "Suddenly Hollywood has discovered Ruth, and it's only taken them fifty years."

In 1968, Gordon won the Academy Award for "Supporting Actress" in *Rosemary's Baby.* Accepting the Oscar, the seventy-two-year-old remarked, "I can't tell how encouraging a thing like this is." She has also won success as a playwright and scenarist.

Far from a shrinking violet, Gordon believes in the power of positive thinking. "My talent, of which there is a great deal, has just been training itself for seventy years. I think I'm terribly attractive," she says.

Kuhn: The First Gray Panther

A retired social worker, **Maggie Kuhn** (1906-   ) was sixty-four when she organized the Gray Panthers in 1970. A network of highly vocal older people in the United States, the group is dedicated to improving conditions for Senior Citizens. "It's demonic," says Kuhn. "Our society segregates the elderly with bricks and mortar. We take them away from their friends, their way of life, their feelings of personal power." She is determined that no person over retirement age will be "isolated by government policy."

Asked how she finances herself and her organization's multitude of activities, she said proudly, "By hustling."

Lindbergh: Woman of Fortitude

Shy, gentle **Anne Morrow Lindbergh** (1906-   ) has withstood trials that might have destroyed lesser women: her highly publicized courtship and marriage to America's foremost hero, Charles A. Lindbergh; the kidnapping and murder of her infant son followed by the sensationalized trial of his abductor; widespread ostracism brought on by her husband's isolationist views in the years prior to World War II, and widowhood in 1974.

Despite raising five children, Anne Morrow Lindbergh had the energy to write more than a dozen books, ranging from autobiography to poetry. She hopes to write a book on her widowhood and about the period in a woman's life when the children leave the nest because she says, "It could be a constructive period, but a lot of women don't use it well because they're often discouraged."

Moses: Rural American Genius

Anna Mary Moses (1860-1961) is better known to her myriad admirers as Grandma Moses, America's foremost primitive painter. Anna Moses left home at thirteen to become a hired hand. She married young, bore ten children, raised the five who survived, and worked long hours farming in the Shenandoah Valley and New York State. For many years, she embroidered on canvas during her few leisure hours, but at seventy-eight her fingers became too stiff to use a needle so she began to paint.

On Masonite panels, using paints she found in the barn, she created brilliantly colored, precisely detailed scenes of country life. Her works were either given away or sold for a pittance until 1939, when she was "discovered."

In all, Grandma Moses produced two thousand paintings. At the age of one hundred she illustrated an edition of Clement Moore's "T'was the Night Before Christmas," which was published after her death.

Peck: Octogenarian Mountain Climber

Annie Smith Peck (1850-1935). A classics scholar and lecturer, Annie Peck did not let a trifling matter like age interfere with her determination to reach a height "where no man has previously stood." An accomplished mountain climber, she first won attention when she scaled the Matterhorn at age forty-five.

Annie Peck climbed the Matterhorn when she was 45; by age 82 she was still scaling mountains.

In 1908, she became the first to scale Peru's Mt. Huascaran, then believed to be the highest mountain in the Western Hemisphere. Four years later, at age sixty-two, Peck returned to Peru and climbed the 21,250-foot Mt. Coropuna, planting a "Votes for Women" pennant at the summit. She scaled her last mountain, New Hampshire's Mt. Madison, at age eighty-two.

Reynolds: Songwriter Turned Singer

Malvina Reynolds (1900-   ) is best known as the composer of the modern folk song, "Little Boxes." Her songs — including "Turn Around" and "What Have They Done to the Rain?" — have been recorded by Pete Seeger, Judy Collins, Joan Baez, Harry Belafonte, the Kingston Trio, and the Limeliters.

But it was not until she was past sixty that Reynolds got up the courage to sing her own songs. She has since recorded six albums, published five songbooks, and appeared for a season on the renowned children's television show, *Sesame Street*.

Growing old doesn't trouble her a whit, she told Amie Hill of *Ms*, "Now I'm usually so occupied with things that I never really think of my age; sometimes I'm even mildly surprised when I look in the mirror."

Warren: Historian of the Revolution

Mercy Otis Warren (1728-1814). Past fifty when she set out in the late 1770s to write a history of the American Revolution, Warren worked nearly thirty years and produced three volumes.

Published in 1805, Warren's *History of the Rise, Progress and Termination of the American Revolution* is still valued by scholars for its keen perceptions of the characters of the founding fathers.

An acquaintance of most of the young nation's leading patriots, Warren had helped popularize the cause of independence by penning sharply satirical poetry and plays which ridiculed the Redcoats and their ladies. She has been called the "Mother of the American Revolution."

More "Young" Oldsters

Although the aforementioned women are remarkable, there are many less celebrated oldsters putting the youngsters to shame today. One example is a young-old couple, Harold and Bertha Soderquist, who joined the Peace Corps in 1974 when he was eighty and she was seventy-six. They pulled top honors in the Corps' two-and-a-half-months training program, shattering the myth that "older people can't learn new languages."

Seventy-six year-old Hattie Carthan is known as "Brooklyn's Tireless Tree Lady." In 1964, she convinced Mayor John Lindsay to help her get trees planted in her neighborhood. After fifteen hundred trees were planted in one-hundred blocks, Mrs. Carthan received a grant from the New York State Council on the Arts to organize the Neighborhood Tree Corps, a group that puts young boys and girls to work after school caring for the trees.

Older people are even invading the college social scene. Just two years shy of her sixtieth birthday, Rita Reutter was elected 1976 Home-coming Queen of Florida Technological University in Orlando. "It proves that just because you're fifty-eight years old, you don't have to jump in a box and hide," said the grandmother.

Fancy Ladies

FIVE THOUSAND YEARS OF FASHION

Had the earth's climate been universally hospitable, humans might never have bothered with clothing at all. But scorching sun, drenching rains, and bitterly cold winds made covering up essential for survival.

The fur stole was by no means only a twentieth century phenomenon; the first articles of clothing were crudely fashioned from animal hides. Other people protected themselves from the elements by draping their bodies with foliage and long grasses. Feathers, shells, and polished bones, worn as charms against evil, were the first pieces of jewelry.

Cloth weaving developed among Mediterranean people as a concession to their warm, humid climates. Once knowledge of the craft spread, two styles of dress appeared that remained in vogue for the next several thousand years. One was the long, draped shawl or sari of the Babylonians and Indians, a single piece of fabric that wrapped the wearer from head to toe. The tunic, two pieces of cloth sewn together at the shoulders and belted at the waist, was the style preferred by the Greeks and Romans.

Egyptians Go Topless

Egyptian noblewomen, who had plenty of leisure time to devote to their toilettes, were the fashion plates of the ancient world. Dyes, embroidery, and fringes embellished their delicately woven garments. A popular fashion was a length of fabric wrapped below the breasts, held up by no more than a narrow strap that ran between them and attached to a collar.

The height of an Egyptian's hairdo indicated his or her social status. The nobility wore elaborately plaited and piled coiffures, with hair pieces and wigs taking over where nature left off. Everyone but slaves wore gold earrings and bracelets. The royalty added enameled gold, gems, and heavily-beaded collars.

The Egyptians were the first to use cosmetics and perfumes to make themselves more alluring. Cosmetics were used in religious rites and for protection from the elements. Perfume was first used in the Egyptian death ritual of mummification. By the first millennium B.C., the toilet box of every Egyptian noblewoman

Statue of Egyptian girl bearing basket and live duck. From The Metropolitan Museum of Art.

held perfumes of musk and rosewater, pencils for applying eyepaints made of kohl and pulverized ants' eggs, and lipsticks composed of animal fat and pigment.

Greek Dandies

The stylish Greeks were men rather than women. Men — and an occasional courtesan — curled their hair and used cosmetics and perfumes. The good housewife did not. She wore her hair pulled back in a modest chignon and dressed in the simplest of costumes, indicative of her lowly position in Greek society.

Though fashion remained in the drape-and-wrap stage, a forerunner of the "layered look" became stylish. A short tunic might be worn over a longer one, or a woolen garment over one made of linen. Sleeves began to be defined where once fabric had been caught only roughly at the shoulders and left to fall. The Greek concept of beauty shunned the ornate in favor of simple and uncluttered styles.

What You Wear Is What You Are

A Roman's style of dress was an absolute indication of his or her social rank. The ancient Roman law set specific standards — ranging from the length and color of garments to the number of thongs on a sandal — according to the position of status the person held in society.

Within these strict bounds, fashion changed primarily in terms of refinement during the course of the empire. The time-consuming process of weaving and sewing by hand also discouraged faddish style changes.

Roman women powdered their faces with ceruse, a ground white lead, and colored hair with imported dyes. Judging from the composition of their dyes, Roman women were apparently convinced blondes had more fun. The results achieved, however, were unpredictable, sometimes creating unwanted colors or even causing hair to fall out. Wigs, consequently, were a staple of Roman fashion.

By the end of the fourth century A.D., the Romans had settled on a style of women's dress that varied little for the next nine hundred years: a long tunic — usually made of linen — with tight, wristlength sleeves. It was worn beneath another tunic, with loose sleeves and a belt set at or just above the waist. A long veil, either attached by a headpiece or draped around the head and left to flow down the back, completed the costume.

Sensuous East Meets Drab West

The simple Roman tunic was scarcely recognizable after the flamboyant Byzantines added their elaborate embellishments. Women of Byzantium, which flourished in the East after the fall of Rome, fashioned their garments from cloth woven with colorful designs, brocaded with gold thread, or encrusted with jewels.

Meanwhile, the women of India were pouring over the "Kama Sutra," a detailed study of love and its pursuit. Apart from its sexual content, the "Kama Sutra" was perhaps the first widely disseminated collection of beauty tips. The Sanscrit treatise encouraged women to use cosmetics for the sole purpose of increasing their attractiveness to men.

The First Crusade, in the twelfth century, reopened ties between East and West. The idea of using clothing and cosmetics to enhance sexual allure then began to take hold among the comparatively drab women of Western Europe. Women started paying more attention to appearance: dresses were fitted, cut was more precise, and colors were more varied.

Medieval Unisex

The medieval woman dressed in a voluminous skirt that trailed behind her as she walked. She couldn't run — nor was she supposed to. The bodice of her gown was fitted tightly from shoulder to waist, and its sleeves were likewise confining. She alternated this costume with a bliaut, a meticulously pleated gown that was worn with only minor variation in style and length by both men and women.

Men's and women's fashions remained

Medieval gowns made running nearly impossible. Tapestry detail from The Metropolitan Museum of Art.

similar throughout the Middle Ages. The most notable difference was in the length of garments. Although a man might wear a pair of breeches under his gown, he did not yet substitute them for a gown.

Women parted their hair in the center and coiled or plaited it near each ear. They plucked their eyebrows and shaved or plucked their hairlines far back from their foreheads. Any remaining hair was often concealed under a headdress, a jeweled headpiece from which trailed a short veil called a wimple. The headdress took an extreme turn in style as the Middle Ages drew to a close, growing into a gaudy, fantastically shaped cap piled with gold netting, jewels, and veils.

The Church, the most powerful force in medieval society, slowed the development of fashion consciousness by condemning emphasis on personal appearance. The Church feared such interest would lead believers to forsake the spiritual for the carnal. (The same view was held by the seventeenth and eighteenth century Puritans.) Although modest dress and simple coiffure were extolled, an increasingly independent middle class was growing more and more fascinated with its reflection in the looking glass.

Steel-Girded Finery

By the 1540s, the upper class had a new look. Women's dress became exceptionally restrictive. Dresses had high, stiff ruffs at the neck, ballooning sleeves, rigidly boned corsets and farthingales — petticoats reinforced with steel that gave skirts added fullness and the wearer added discomfort. A velvet gown laden with pearls and bits of silver plus its accompanying farthingale added many pounds to a woman's weight.

The cumbersome fashions of the sixteenth century were not designed for the woman who liked to do things for herself. Their weight and complexity encouraged a quiet, dignified life — exactly the sort of life women were supposed to lead. Women who could not afford the idle life of the rich dressed more simply in plain gowns of inexpensive material. While upper-class fashion flirted with changes in neckline and waist placement, the dress of the working class remained much the same for centuries. However, the time involved

The heavy, constricting fashions of Elizabethan England discouraged an active life.

in hand spinning, hand weaving, and hand sewing dictated that even the ladies of the court keep their gowns until they were worn out.

Cosmetics first gained wide acceptability under Elizabeth I in England and Catherine de Medici in France. Both men and women wore cosmetics, and the ravaging effects of prolonged use were visible on the skins of both sexes. Deaths from lead poisoning were common among those who powdered their noses with ceruse. Perfumes also appealed to Elizabeth, who used them to cover the odors caused by poor sewage systems and haphazard bathing habits.

Enter the Cavalier

The peacock of the seventeenth century was male. With the passing of the ruff and farthingale, women's fashions declined in outlandishness. But men's fashions, except for a brief span of Puritan restraint at mid-century, escalated in grandeur. Decked out in plumes, ruffles, ribbons, and false curls, the dandy easily outdid the damsel in sheer visual effect.

By century's end, Paris had become the

fashion capital of Europe as well as its economic and political hub. More than 2½ centuries passed before Paris began to share its dominance in the fashion world with New York.

Corsets Loosen — Briefly

A well-to-do woman of the early eighteenth century dressed in a painted taffeta or satin gown with a fitted bodice. The décolletage was either daringly bare or filled in with a fabric panel. She wore a boned corset, laced in the back, underneath her dress. The skirt was wide, supported by a bell-shaped hoop petticoat. In her closet hung at least one sacque dress, a waistless full-skirted gown with deep oval neckline, worn with an underdress.

Her hair was worn either in a high chignon or parted in the center and rolled back over padding. There were still only minor distinctions in men's and women's footwear; shoes for both sexes had long vamps; pointed toes, and low heels.

Her granddaughter at century's end could breathe and move more easily in a high-waisted Empire gown with an unstructured bodice. The dress was fashioned in a soft, flowing fabric, often muslin. Hoops had been dispensed with, though they reappeared as part of the

Flowing Empire gown shown in a detail from a Charpentier in The Metropolitan Museum of Art.

nineteenth century crinoline. The gown had puffed or fitted sleeves and few embellishments beyond an ornamental ribbon bordering the oval neckline. Hair was often worn in ringlets.

The French powdered wig, despite its presence in nearly every movie made about pre-twentieth century France, actually had about a twenty-year lifespan that ended at the time of the French Revolution. Though full wigs were often used to create the massive pompadour favored by both men and women, many coaxed their own hair into that extravagant style. The hair was lacquered with pomatum, powdered, blended with false hair, and wrapped over poufs to form a coiffure of startling height and width. Because creation of a pompadour required so much skill and effort, the hair was not combed — much less washed — for weeks on end. Spiders — and sometimes even a rat — were found nesting in the hairdos. Because the fashion ruined many heads of hair, the century closed with shorter styles in vogue. Elaborate hats perched on heads that a short while before had sported elaborate curls.

Hoops and Bustles

After a brief flirtation with freedom in the late eighteenth and early nineteenth centuries, women's fashions again grew restrictive. The Empire gown of the Classical Revival was replaced by the tightly-corseted bodices and wide skirts of the Victorian era. By the mid-1800s, fashionable women dressed in long-sleeved gowns with high round necks and wide collars. The gown had a minutely smocked or tucked bodice, a wide bell-shaped skirt buoyed by several petticoats atop a wooden hoop frame. And she wore a corset to draw in her waist, a breathtaking endeavor. Little wonder the comfortable dressing gown became popular at-home attire.

The mid-nineteenth century woman wore her long hair combed into a chignon or plaited and coiled at each ear. If she went out, she covered her hair with a small, flower-trimmed bonnet.

Unlike the fashionable women of Paris and New York — fashion had by this time begun to cross the Atlantic — pioneer women on the American frontier dressed

"Winding Up The Ladies (A Slenderizing Machine)". From a 19th century engraving.

more practically in homespun and buckskin. Only a few women dallied with the "bloomers" — a divided skirt gathered at each ankle — which Amelia Bloomer and her followers introduced in 1841.

Emphasis in fashion had moved downward from the Restoration cleavage to the Victorian wasp-waist. The 1870s and 1880s focused attention still lower and to the rear, where the bustle sat ready to make up for any deficiency of nature. Skirts grew narrower to accommodate the newly popular means of travel, the railway.

Fashion for the Masses

Elias Howe's invention of the sewing machine, patented in 1846, democratized fashion by giving birth to the ready-to-wear industry. Manufacturers quickly began to produce low-cost copies of the latest designs. Once, only women wealthy enough to afford dressmakers could follow fashion's whims. Now, anyone from a schoolteacher to a maidservant could wear low cost facsimiles of the exotic creations current in Paris. From about 1860 on, thanks to pattern makers like Ellen Demorest, a woman could sew even stylish gowns on her home sewing machine.

Not everyone, however, liked the new democracy. *Vogue,* the arbiter of fashion, wrote: "The greatest lesson our women have to learn is to dress according to their

"The Grecian Bend: Fifth Avenue Style" — the bustle carried to a ridiculous extreme.

position in life. If they have no great fortunes summing up to millions, why follow suit with a woman who has?'' Needless to say, the newly fashionable class paid little heed to *Vogue*'s admonition.

The Gibson Girl

Born in the drawings of Charles Dana Gibson, the Gibson Girl was the quintessential figure of the Gay Nineties. She dressed in a shirtwaist ensemble: a gathered skirt and high-necked, lace-trimmed blouse with long, mutton-chop sleeves. Hardly an inch of her costume lacked some sort of decoration. Though the bustle had gone the way of hoops and overblown petticoats, her whalebone corset still controlled where nature didn't. Figures were tugged into the hour-glass shape, an exaggerated conception of the female form best exemplified by actress Lillian Russell. The ideal woman of the era was no longer dainty and plump, but tall and willowy. Her hair was caught up in a tall, loose pompadour, whose height was achieved by backcombing or pinning hair

The willowy Gibson Girl was the pinnacle of Gay 90s feminine perfection.

over small rolls of lamb's wool called ''rats.''

Early feminist Elizabeth Cady Stanton once said, ''Many a woman is riding to suffrage on a bicycle.'' Likewise, the bicycle fad of the late nineteenth century did much to liberate women's fashions. Though Ellen Penrose was arrested at Coney Island in 1887 for wearing bloomers while bicycling, they and knickerbockers were considered proper attire for female bikers by the turn of the century. ''To wheel far, one must breathe,'' cautioned an opponent of corsets and tight clothes for bicyclers at an 1896 meeting of the New York Academy of Medicine.

Goodbye Child, Hello Woman

After one last outburst of Victoriana, the first half of the twentieth century saw an almost continual pruning of the Gibson Girl silhouette.

The Art Deco period and the popularity of the streamlined, curvilinear design opened the century. The 1910 woman dressed up in floor-length, low-necked columns of silk and wool embellished with finely hand-sewn details. Her accessories were likewise streamlined: stoles, long necklaces, trailing silk scarves, and handbags suspended by long cord handles. Her hats were wide brimmed, heavily plumed, and frequently veiled. (When automobiles replaced carriages, dust-coats as well as veils came into vogue, more because they were practical than fashionable.) Fashions, like the woman who wore them, were becoming more worldly.

For everyday wear, tailored ready-to-wear ensembles were popular. Such suits were pared-down versions of the Gibson Girl's shirtwaist, minus ruffles, pleats, trains, and other fluff. Skirt lengths had just begun their ascent, hovering in the vicinity of the ankle. Though the whalebone corset was gone, woman's freedom of movement was still limited by her long, narrow ''hobble skirt.''

As new modes of transportation and communication shrank the globe, fashion changed more quickly than ever. Despite increasingly swift production, a new look was often old by the time it reached ready-to-wear stores in the far reaches of the United States.

As   the   theater — and   soon   the

Six "bathing beauties" illustrate the evolution of women's swimwear from 1900 to 1920.

movies — gained respectability, the influence of theatrical costume design increased. For example, the motif of Lev Bakst's costumes for *Scheherazade* turned up in the sashes, fringes, braiding, and strong colors of 1914 street wear and negligees.

Makeup was in accepted — if subtle — use. A woman could choose cosmetics from the offerings of Yardley, Helena Rubinstein, or Cheeseborough-Ponds, much as she might today. Her hair was still long, most often swept back into a knot.

Flapping to the Speakeasy

The 1920s began quietly enough with a post-war dip in skirt lengths. But by 1925, things were roaring. Skirts rose steadily, from mid-calf in 1920 to the knee several years later. Corsets flattened the bust and hips and obliterated any hint of a waistline, creating a boyish silhouette compatible with the low- or no-waisted garments then in fashion. The flapper didn't care for the full, loose styles and staid colors her older sister had chosen in 1920. She preferred a daring sleeveless chemise with boat neck, a beaded geometric pattern on the bodice, and pleated flounce from hip to knee. She might also have owned a dress with a handkerchief hemline, or a two-piece jersey suit topped by a cardigan jacket such as that introduced by Gabrielle "Coco" Chanel. Silk stockings became an important accessory as more of the leg was bared.

Like Irene Castle and Clara Bow, the flapper bobbed her hair and combed it flat against her head. A deep-crowned cloche, adorned at most with a feather or bow, hugged her head. The obviously painted face was now popular. The flapper liberally applied rouge, powder, and mascara. She painted her lips into a bright red cupid's bow.

Jaded Elegance

The 1930s woman projected a more mature image. Unlike the frenetic flapper, she was coolly sophisticated — sometimes even jaded. The Great Depression

Flappers danced the Charleston in sleeveless chemises with pleated flounces from hip to knee.

that followed the stock market crash of 1929 was not an era for conspicuous grandeur; fashion elegance was in the cut and hang of a garment rather than in lavish embellishments.

Women of the early thirties wore clinging, bias-cut dresses of crepe, jersey, and rayon. (Synthetic textiles had been available since the end of World War I.) Neutral colors regained popularity, and skirts fell abruptly to mid-calf. V-necklines, collared and accented with a brooch or artificial flower, came into vogue. Cap sleeves were seen along with long, tight ones. The college girl look — skirts, sweaters, and blouses — gave limited wardrobes mix-and-match flexibility.

By the mid-thirties, the clingy dress had been replaced by an updated tailored suit with a narrow skirt and close-fitting jacket. For day, the suit was made of linen or wool; for evening, it was velvet or lamé with appliqué or sequin decorations. Hems moved upward along with the nation's economy. Women began to wear trousers on the golf course — but not yet

on the street unless the woman was Katharine Hepburn.

Women often emulated the look of their favorite screen stars: Greta Garbo's trench coat and slouch hat, Jean Harlow's halter-necked satin evening gown, and Joan Crawford's padded shoulders were frequently copied.

The flat, linear look in female bodies remained fashionable throughout the thirties. Women wore corsets or the new one-piece foundation garment to minimize bust and hips.

Shoes — sometimes with platform heels — received much attention from designers of the thirties; low-heeled sports oxfords, "barefoot" sandals with ankle straps, t-straps, and suede pumps were popular styles.

The face of the thirties had pale cheeks, thin-plucked eyebrows, and deep red or burgundy lips. Nails, too, were painted. The hair was Harlow's: longer, freer, and platinum blonde. Popular hats were the beanie, the draped turban, and the "halo hat" with turned-up brim.

Jean Harlow's was the face of the 30s: red lips, thin-plucked brows, platinum blonde hair.

Wartime Austerity

Fashions had to be simple during World War II; U.S. law limited the number of yards of fabric used in clothing. Many French fashion houses closed during the German occupation, and imports from those that remained open were banned.

The tailored shirtwaist dress with A-line skirt was the standard costume of the woman who went to work during World War II. Skirts had risen to knee level, and the natural curves of the female body received more attention than they had in recent decades. Influenced by the military uniforms of their men, women sprouted wider shoulders with the help of triangular pads of fabric pinned or sewn inside their dresses. A version of the waist-length, patch-pocketed battle jacket worn by General Dwight D. Eisenhower appeared on many American women. Trousers — belted and pleated at the waist — had finally become acceptable for casual wear.

With the advent of pancake makeup in 1938, the suntanned look was in. Women combed their hair up into pompadours or wore their curls long and loose à la Rita Hayworth.

Back to Femininity

With the war over, men returned to the workplace. Women returned to the home — and to restrictively feminine fashions. Christian Dior more than made up for wartime yardage restrictions in 1947 with his "New Look": longer, fuller skirts, cinched waists, rounded soft shoulders, petticoats, and corsets. Hems plunged to no more than eight inches off the floor. Shoes had high heels and pointed toes. Nylon stockings appeared on the market for the first time. In terms of comfort and convenience, the New Look was a regression into the old idea that women's clothing should be pretty — even if impractical. The stylish figure had a high bust, tiny waist, and curved hipline. Women donned padded bras and Banlon sweaters to compete with voluptuous Hollywood stars like Jane Russell.

The sheath dress and stiletto heels of the early fifties insured that women would continue walking — and wobbling — like ladies. The sheath, often made in a knitted material, fell straight from the shoulders and was belted at the waist. Every fashionable woman's wardrobe included a "little black dress," short white gloves, bandeau hat (almost always veiled), and two-tone patent leather or black suede heels.

Beatniks and Teenyboppers

The "beatnik" look was popular among women who read Camus and listened to jazz — and those who wanted to give the impression that they did. Though their garb started out as a rebellion against fashion, "beatnik" jumpers, black tights, and turtle-necked tops soon appeared in abundance on department store racks.

For the first time, teenagers developed a style of dress all their own. The young woman of the era danced to rock 'n roll played on American Bandstand, while wearing pegged jeans, a large white oxford shirt from father's or brother's bureau with sleeves rolled to the elbow, bobby socks, and penny loafers. For school, she wore a dirndl dress or a pleated or gathered skirt — sometimes with poodle appliques — topped by a pastel sweater set or Peter Pan collared blouse. She showed her luck at puppy love by wearing her boyfriend's class ring on a chain around her neck. Sometimes she talked him out of his letterman's jacket or sweater as well.

When the senior prom rolled around, the fifties miss donned a strapless gown with layered tulle skirt and bodice supported by bone stays. She wore a strapless bra (no girl older than age thirteen went braless, and lingerie counters did a steady business in 32AAA's) and a girdle with stockings attached by garters. Pumps and a small handbag, dyed to match, completed the ensemble. And, Amy Vanderbilt cautioned, her escort had better know the color of her gown when picking out the corsage.

The pony tail was the hairdo of the bopping teen, while her mother favored a short, curly style. Many women followed Mamie Eisenhower's lead and adopted bangs. As the decade wore on, Audrey Hepburn's gamin look came into vogue and women cut their hair into the shorter "pixie" do.

Both hairspray and rollers came into widespread use during the decade, making possible the teased bouffant styles like the beehive that gained popularity in the late fifties and early sixties.

Up, Up, and Away

The sixties were as inventive as the fifties had been traditional. The loose but still

Young women of the 50s had a fashion all their own. Many dreamed of becoming cheerleaders.

Minis had more in common with medieval man's tunic than with anything woman had ever worn.

lengthy silhouette that entered the decade culminated in the micro-miniskirt, a design that had more in common with men's tunics of the fourteenth century than with anything women had worn before.

The first miniskirts, matched with over-the-knee boots, appeared in Pierre Cardin's 1961 collection. Most women, however, were initially unimpressed, content with the less drastic styles that were just nearing the knee. They followed the lead of Jacqueline Kennedy with bouffant hairdos, pillbox hats, mammoth sunglasses, and shifts.

As with most changes in fashion, the young were the first to wear the short skirts topped with revealing body suits, poorboy sweaters, or see-through blouses. However, women of various ages and proportions adopted the fashion — sometimes mistakenly. Even more than the clinging dresses of the thirties and the wasp-waisted dresses of the fifties (which often covered a sturdy corset), the mini required a slender, well-built body; maximum flesh is attractive only when teamed with minimum flab.

With the advent of pantyhose in the

early sixties, women began to discard girdles, panty girdles, and garter belts. Before the decade was out, many shed their bras as well. As hems crept upward, legs received more and more attention. No longer did stockings come only in shades ranging from beige to coffee bean; wildly colored and patterned hose appeared on the market. Boots reaching anywhere from ankle top to above the knee were popular complements to the mini.

On the beach, clothing was similarly minimized. The two-piece bathing suit shrank to the brief bikini. Some women were arrested for indecent exposure after appearing in Rudi Gernreich's 1964 topless swimsuit.

As the sixties marched on, the trend toward individuality in appearance became more pronounced. Boutiques specializing in the unusual and unique sprang up. There were many inexpensive ways to dress — variations on Thrift Shop Chic, Army-Navy Surplus Chic, and Grandma's Attic Trunk Chic. No longer were garments made only of fabric; the use of plastic, paper, leather, and metal chain link reflected the experimental flair of the sixties.

Class distinctions in fashion practically disappeared. Ready-to-wear manufacturers freely adopted the latest Paris and New York designs, and even employed some big name designers to create outfits specifically for mass-market reproduction. If an original Halston was too expensive, a copy could usually be found at the local department store. Couture patterns were even available for the home seamstress.

Still, the upper crust found means to set themselves apart from the crowd. One way was through "signature" accessories emblazoned with such elite trademarks as Gucci, Hermès, Pucci, and St. Laurent.

Black women let their hair go *au naturel* and wore caftans and dashikis in traditional African prints. "Natural" became the byword for young men and women alike, and most wore their hair long and loose with a center part. Curlers, permanents, and hair straighteners fell into disfavor. Wigs and hairpieces made manes even longer and thicker.

Women experimented with more fantastic makeup, with emphasis placed on the eyes. Many wore false lashes — Twiggy used three sets at once — and paler lips. Before the decade was out, some women — and men — painted not just their faces, but their entire bodies. Though most body painting washed off with soap and water, some daring women — like singers Janis Joplin, Grace Slick, and Joan Baez — had themselves tattooed.

Whatever Goes Up . . .

Though a 1967 attempt to introduce a *Dr. Zhivago*-inspired, mid-calf-length skirt fell flat, designers were showing little but the midi in 1970. Women rebelled. Rather than acceding to the new, longer lengths, they dressed in the slacks, jumpsuits, and pantsuits that became acceptable attire for work, school — even church. The hippie's blue denim jeans — embroidered, appliqued, patched, or faded — were now a status costume. Minidresses were recycled as tunics and overblouses. Workshirts, decorated T-shirts, and halters were other popular jean toppers. Legs still remained in view with the hot pants craze of the early seventies. If a woman wore a skirt at all, it was likely as not a floor-length maxi.

As The Pill was leading to a unisex moral standard, the similar tailoring of men's and women's pants, shirts, and jackets led to a unisex fashion look. While women of twenty-five wore pantsuits that could have come from Brooks Brothers, the sixteen-year-old dressed in jeans, boots, and down jackets that could have come from her boyfriend's closet.

The Skirt Reappears

By the mid-70s, women were again wearing skirts. Lengths varied from just below the knee to mid-calf. Blue jeans turned into denim skirts, and hot pants became longer, looser fitting gauchos.

The design credited with putting women back into skirts was Diane von Furstenberg's flattering jersey wrap dress. Other popular looks of mid-decade were the scoop-necked T-shirt with floral print skirt, the sashed "big dress," and the man-tailored three-piece suit. Big sellers in casual wear were sweatsuits in winter and tennis dresses in summer.

Shoe fashions, following a dangerous flirtation with platform sandals in the early seventies, became lower and sturdier. In keeping with women's newly awakened interest in sports, sneakers gained popularity.

Redder lips and cheeks characterized the face of the seventies. Nails were painted blue, green, and purple, as well as the more traditional red, pink, and peach shades. Cosmetic counters began to carry lines especially for black skins. Hair was shorter and often curlier; favorite styles included skater Dorothy Hamill's wedge cut, Farrah Fawcett-Majors' long layered look, and singer-actress Barbra Streisand's short ringlets.

After the come-as-you-are party of the late sixties and early seventies, a return to a more refined concept of fashion was due. Yves St. Laurent's 1976 collection was termed as precipitous as Dior's 1947 "New Look." The motif was Russian peasant, with a return to tiny waists, big skirts, and higher heels. Though women adopted many of St. Laurent's ethnic touches, they showed little inclination to return to the restrictive fashions and lifestyles of the 50s.

Few popular fashions have had only one life. The last decade has seen revivals of twenties bobbed hair, thirties platform sandals, forties shoulder pads, and fifties

Tiny waists, big skirts, and high heels characterized St. Laurent's 1976 collection.

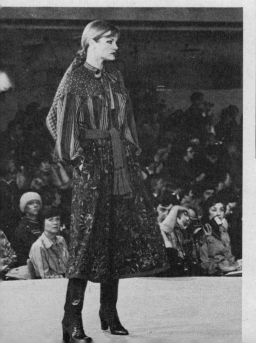

TWENTIETH CENTURY FASHION HEADLINES

1900 Corsets Mold S-Shaped Torsos; No Stylish Woman Can See Her Feet

1905 After 300-Year Reign, Nightgown Loses Preeminence to Pajamas

1914 V-Neckline Is Introduced; Health and Morals Are Feared Threatened

1925 Red Lips Are In: Husbands' Collars Searched For Telltale Lipstick Stains

1927 Flappers Bare Their Knees; Silk Stockings Become Fashion Essential

1930 Economy Plunges — So Do Hemlines; Subtle Elegance Is Look of Decade

1935 Backless Evening Gowns Are The Latest; Platinum Blondes Boost Peroxide Sales

1942 Short, Skimpy Skirts Help War Effort; Stocking Shortage Puts Women in Pants

1947 Women Wobble Back Home In Dior's "New Look"

1955 Teenagers and Beatniks Set Anti-Fashion Fashion

1961 Jackie Moves Into White House; Becomes Fashion's First Lady

1964 Women Arrested for Wearing Gernreich Topless Swimsuits

1967 Twiggy Arrives in U.S. With Long, Long Lashes and Short, Short Skirts

1970 Women Rebel Against Midi Length; Trousers, Trousers Everywhere

1975 The Skirt Returns — Along With More Elegant Fashion

strapless gowns. Even Turkish trousers, an updated version of 1841's shocking bloomers, were born again in the seventies. Little wonder antique clothing stores are doing a booming business.

Fashion in 2076

What's in store for the future? In 1976, New York's Bonwit Teller department store asked America's leading women's designers to assemble a Tricentennial fashion collection.

Jumpsuits were foreseen by many as a popular 2076 style. Patti Cappalli and Victor Joris both designed them in clear plastic. Alice Blaine created a short work suit for women maintenance workers on space stations.

Silver sequined pants with feet like Doctor Dentons are seen by Bill Blass as the wave of the future. If Kasper's design becomes popular, separate wardrobes will no longer be needed for winter and summer; his white plastic pantsuit is lined with curving glass tubes that can carry either a heating agent or coolant.

Von Furstenberg's mannequin did not wear a stitch of clothing. Instead, it was painted all over in warm jungle colors.

Believing comfort and practicality will be the hallmarks of a 2076 wardrobe, Calvin Klein designed a stretch jumpsuit with attached bag to enable the wearer to tote her necessities without carrying a pocketbook. "By that time," Klein suggested, "I don't think what's on the outside will be as important as what's on the inside, in the head."

No one will argue that brains will be more important than ever in the world of the future. But considering fashion's long and colorful history, it's unlikely to lose its important place in the lives of men and women the world over. As German sociologist René Konig notes, "Fashion is as profound and critical a part of the social life of man as sex."

THE PAINTED LADY

Which came first, the lipstick or the looking glass? Like the old chicken and egg riddle, the verdict is still in doubt. We do know, however, that both mirrors and make-up first appeared on the scene about four thousand years ago.

Ancient men and women used cosmetics in religious rituals and for protection from nature's elements. From the American plains to darkest Africa, warriors and witch doctors painted fierce masks on their faces to frighten enemies and ward off evil.

The early Egyptians shielded their eyes from the sun with eye shadow concocted from kohl (a lead ore) and greenish malachite. People later realized that cosmetics could beautify as well as protect, and added pulverized ants' eggs to their eye paints for a touch of frosted glamour. From that time on, cosmetics have been fun.

Unlike the ballyhooed "organic" preparations of recent years, the first cosmetics were truly natural: juices of crushed berries reddened lips and cheeks, charred wood darkened lashes, and olive oil smoothed ancient dishpan hands.

By the first century A.D., a vast array of cosmetics enabled a Roman woman of the leisure class to devote as much attention to fixing her face as does the modern society matron. She could lighten her skin with powders and shade her eyelids with kohl. Rouge, hair dyes, perfume, bath oil — even an abrasive for cleaning teeth — were already on the market.

Northern Europeans of both sexes embraced cosmetics as soon as the Crusades opened up trade with the East in the thirteenth century. The protective function of the earliest cosmetics had long since fallen by the wayside. In fact, lead pastes and mercury compounds became real dangers to their user's health. Toothless mouths, hairless heads, and inflamed and pitted skin were common cosmetic results among European nobility of both sexes.

A seventeenth century poison epidemic among users of a popular arsenic face wash stimulated concern with the safety of cosmetics. Italy responded in 1633 by requiring that poisons be registered, the first in a string of modern cosmetics laws.

A Slow Start in America

Early American women were too preoccupied with keeping johnnycake on the table and kindling in the fireplace to pay much attention to cosmetics. Besides, their Puritan upbringing stressed that adornment of the body was considered foolish pleasure in the eyes of God.

Cosmetics thus remained largely in the make-it-yourself stage until the beginning of the twentieth century. Even in great grandmother's day, use of more than a discreet veil of rice powder was sufficient to brand one a "painted lady" of questionable repute.

But World War I and the Jazz Age lib-

FIRE! FIRE!!

HEALTHY GROWTH.

BEWARE OF PREPARATIONS THAT BURN THE HAIR.

NOTHING MAKES HAIR SO SOFT AND FINE, AS "DOBBINS' VEGETABLE Hair Renewer

As this advertisement indicates, 19th century cosmetics were sometimes dangerous.

erated women's fashions, faces, and lifestyles. And cosmetics rapidly became big business. Within a generation, American women used enough lipstick annually to paint forty thousand barns red.

Today, cosmetic sales in the United States total $7.2 billion annually — $35 a year for every American man, woman, and child.

And spending on make-up and toiletries soars ever higher, affected little by the ups and downs of the nation's economy. By 1882, annual purchases of cosmetics are expected to exceed $10 billion.

The Allergy Factor

It's not only the old witches' brew that contained things like castor oil, scales of herring, virgin beeswax, Brazilian palm leaves, and lanolin. These are some of the sources of an ordinary tube of frosted pink lipstick.

Although its recipe is nothing to tempt finicky appetites, lipstick is at least as safe as any food you put in your mouth. Most American women can cheerfully use their lipstick, mascara, and deodorant without fear of unfavorable reactions to the variety

of chemicals from which they are made. A recent Food and Drug Administration (FDA) poll found that only seven persons in ten thousand suffered adverse reactions to any cosmetic within a one-month period. Most of these reactions were labeled "mild," with only 3 percent — about 20 per million cosmetic users — being serious enough to warrant any medical attention.

Antiperspirants and deodorants caused the highest rate of adverse reactions, followed by depilatories, moisturizers and lotions, hair sprays, mascara, bubble bath, eye cream, hair coloring, skin cream, and nail polish. Safest of all, said the FDA, was good old lipstick.

Today's most frequent causes of adverse cosmetic reactions are allergies. Since allergies are often unique to the individual, they are hard for cosmetic companies to uncover in pre-market testing. Common allergy symptoms include skin irritation, dry or cracked lips or cuticles, swollen or watery eyes, runny nose, headaches, and stomach distress.

Fortunately, most allergic reactions are quickly cleared up by ceasing to use the particular brand. Anyone with further problems should see her physician.

The allergic woman is seldom doomed to a cosmetic-less existence. With twenty-five thousand different cosmetic formulas currently on the market, simply switching brands may solve the allergy problem.

Unscented products are often kinder to sensitive skins than fragrant ones.

What about the new "hypo-allergenic" cosmetics? The FDA has yet to set uniform standards for testing whether a product is any less likely than its competitors to cause adverse reactions. But "hypo-allergenic" does not mean "non-allergenic," so the individual still needs to exercise care to choose brands that suit her skin. Of course, the major cosmetic firms do their best to keep customers happy and reaction-free.

An Ounce of Prevention

Before a woman douses herself from head to toe with a new cosmetic, the FDA recommends that a small amount of the product be applied to the forearm as a sensitivity check. If no adverse reactions —

redness, itching, or blisters, for example — appear within twenty-four hours, the product is probably safe for use. Package directions for testing of such hair preparations as dyes, permanents, and straighteners should be followed to the letter.

A woman should stop using a cosmetic at the first sign of an allergic reaction. (It is possible suddenly to become sensitive to a cosmetic one has used safely for years.) If the condition persists, a trip to the doctor is in order.

Report any cosmetic injuries to the FDA, the manufacturer, and the store where the offending product was purchased. Manufacturers are eager to hear your complaints, and can often recommend substitute cosmetics if the problem stems from an allergy.

A boon for the allergic is the FDA's new cosmetic labeling law, which requires that ingredients be listed prominently on cosmetic packages to help consumers comparison shop and avoid substances to which they are allergic.

But the new regulation has its loopholes: So-called "secret" additives need not be divulged, and fragrances and flavors — which can contain as many as 20 components each — may simply be listed as "fragrance" or "flavor."

The Cost of Beauty

Mascara: $3.50. Eye Shadow: $2.75. Liquid Foundation: $3.00. Blusher: $2.65. Lipstick: $3.20.

The cash register totals $15.10 in cosmetic sales — 15 percent of the typical working woman's weekly take-home pay. True, this batch of cosmetics may last her for several months. But seldom does a week go by when her supply of at least one beauty aid — from shampoo to nail polish — is not depleted. And advertisements and store displays constantly entice her to buy the very latest — and costliest — in make-up and toiletries.

The price of a cosmetic increases 500 to 1,000 percent between the factory where it is made and the retail store where it is sold. Hence, ingredients may account for only 30 cents of that $3.00 bottle of foundation: the remaining $2.70 is divided among manufacturer, packager, shipper, wholesaler, advertiser, and retailer.

A hefty price tag is no indication that a cosmetic is any better than its more moderately priced competitor. As former Congresswoman Leonor K. Sullivan, a long-time crusader for tougher cosmetics laws, noted several years ago, "Most of us know that $5.00 jar of cream will do no more for us than the 50-cent jar . . . Those who can afford the $5.00 jar, and some who cannot, buy it on the outside chance that perhaps it might be a bit more effective. At least they feel better about it."

The American Medical Association agrees that "price is not always the best guide to buying cosmetics. Several low-priced products have proved, through years of satisfactory use, to compare favorably with similar but more expensive items."

Scientists can tell us whether cosmetics are pure and safe. But the subjective judgment about which cosmetics are really best is, and will always remain, a private matter between each woman and her make-up mirror. And women's opinions on cosmetic brands are as diverse as their views on politics, hair styles, and children's names. One woman might swear by Brand Plain and Cheap, while her sister prefers — and is willing to pay for — the shades, textures, packaging, and general prestige of a more expensive line.

And the benefits of cosmetics are many. They can accentuate positive features while playing down the negative. They can help the harried young mother look like she just spent the week sunning at Saint-Tropez. They can transform a woman's image from schoolgirl to sophisticate in a matter of minutes. And some moisturizing cosmetics can even slow — though, unfortunately, not stop — the march of time.

Most of all, cosmetics help a woman feel good about herself. A new lipstick is cheaper than a psychiatrist, healthier than a martini, and more fun than a consciousness-raising group.

Remember, though, that the most effective beauty aids have always been a healthy body, a balanced diet, and a good night's sleep. And don't forget a big, sunny smile.

Shop for Safety — and Savings

A woman should comparison shop for cosmetics, taking price, quality, and quantity into consideration. She should buy a cosmetic because she wants it, not because it is on sale or because the salesperson pressures her to do so.

The proper time for reading labels and directions is before a cosmetic is purchased. Many women discover only after they return home that a cosmetic is wrong for their skin type or allergic sensitivities.

Much valuable information on cosmetics can be obtained from consumer publications and reputable women's magazines. But beware of periodicals that do no more than repeat the optimistic advertising claims of cosmetic manufacturers.

Department store cosmetic clerks and consultants can be a fountain of advice on new make-up products, techniques, and trends, and can help a woman identify her skin coloring and type. But the consumer should listen to their advice with a skeptical ear, remembering that their first concern is with racking up sales.

Cosmetics are often less expensive at self-service discount and drug stores than at high-overhead boutiques and department stores. Some women have even formed cooperatives so they can buy cosmetics at low bulk rates. A few exclusive brands of cosmetics, however, are sold only in certain stores.

A lipstick is a lipstick, whether it comes in a plastic container or one made of solid gold. Don't judge a cosmetic solely by the opulence of its cover.

A woman should not invest in the large, economy size of a cosmetic she has never before tried. A small, sample container will enable her to judge whether the new product is all it is cracked up to be.

Women should be especially careful when it comes to their eyes. They should use only cosmetics specifically labeled for use on or near the eyes. Women with sensitive eyes — especially contact lens wearers — should beward of false eyelashes and bits of fuzz from lash-lengthening mascara, which can fall into the eyes and irritate them.

The "neither a borrower nor a lender be" adage goes double with regard to cosmetics. Though most cosmetics contain preservatives to help them withstand contamination, shared cosmetics could result in shared infections. And cosmetic containers should be closed immediately after use to avoid contamination from bacteria in the air. Moisten make-up, if need be, with water — never saliva.

Before attempting a radical change of hair color, a woman should assess whether the new shade is right for her by trying on wigs or using a temporary color rinse. Having one's first hair coloring done professionally is money well spent. Frosting or tipping are more economical ways to change hair color than complete dye jobs because fewer touch-ups are required.

The Egyptians had a wise idea in wearing cosmetics to protect themselves from the sun. So use a moisturizer or a sunburn preventive if you are planning to spend time in the sun. You might wish to eschew colognes and perfumes while you suntan; these preparations can lead to splotching and irritation of sensitive skin.

So-called feminine sprays are designed for application to the external genital area only. All the current products are formulated to be a supplement to, not a substitute for, simple washing. The same goes for douches. Vaginal odors and discharges that regular bathing cannot control should be investigated by your doctor.

A little dandruff is common, though severe itching and flaking warrant a doctor's scrutiny. If you wash your hair every day or two, most shampoos will help keep dandruff away. For more effective control, the special anti-dandruff preparations contain ingredients to discourage the surface cells of the scalp from flaking. But there is still no permanent cure for this condition.

Cosmetics and children should be kept separated. Even the gentlest of cosmetics can irritate children's skins. And some products — colognes, for example — are easily ignited.

DIETING: THE GREAT NATIONAL OBSESSION

The great national obsession? It's not baseball, or tennis, or even sex. The pastime which modern Americans — especially female Americans — seem to engage in most frequently is sweating, stretching, and starving themselves into new figures. Or at least vowing to do so starting tomorrow.

A recent government survey indicated that 42 million Americans are worried about their weight. And that 37 million more are not but should be.

What's wrong with being pleasingly plump? Even Venus di Milo would never make it as a modern-day fashion model.

First, excess pounds can make a woman look and feel years older than she really is. Flab can subtract years from life expectancy; an overweight woman runs a greater risk of heart attack, stroke, diabetes, high blood pressure — even accidents. Heavy women are more prone to menstrual pain, and special problems during pregnancy, including toxemia, delivery complications, and stillbirths.

The emotional aches and pains of being overweight are often as bad as the physical ones. Fat women have more difficulty than their slender sisters at finding everything from jobs to lovers to pantyhose. Despite the image of the jolly fatty, many heavy men and women are loners, convinced that their low opinion of themselves is shared by the rest of the world.

Most women don't need more than a good, hard look in the mirror to tell if they are overweight. But if you are in doubt, it is wise not to rely on the average weight charts which frequently crop up in diet books and doctors' offices. These charts fail to take into account individual differences in body build; any correspondence to a person's truly desirable weight is mainly coincidental.

A better indicator is the pinch test. Simply pinch the skin at the back of the arm between elbow and shoulder. If the skin and fat below it measure one inch or more, it is time to start dieting.

There are hundreds of diets on the market designed for every taste: milk and banana diets, grapefruit and egg diets, lollypop-before-each-meal diets, rice-and-rice-alone diets. Most of these fad diets are dangerous, as well as silly, for they fail to provide the dieter with nutrients the body needs.

The best diets aim for gradual weight loss — about two pounds a week — through sensible, balanced eating. Meals should include foods from the four basic groups: (1) milk and milk products; (2) meat, fish, poultry, eggs, and legumes; (3) fruits and vegetables, and (4) breads and cereals. Vitamin supplements should be taken while dieting to make doubly sure you receive all necessary nutrients. Iron is especially important for females, dieters and non-dieters alike.

The best reducing diet is relatively high in proteins and low in fats — especially saturated fats — and carbohydrates. A good example is Dr. Norman Jolliffe's Prudent Diet, offshoots of which include the Weight Watchers and Diet Workshop diets. Simply counting calories is not enough. Count nutrients, too. Consuming 500 calories worth of chicken, green beans, and milk is vastly better than wolfing down 50 potato chips.

Many popular diets are silly, impossible to follow, or just plain dangerous to the health. Beware of The Drinking Man's Diet; Dr. Atkins' Diet Revolution; Dr. Stillman's Inches-Off Diet (this is *not* Dr. Stillman's Weight Loss "Water" Diet): Candy Diet; Grapefruit Diet; Ice Cream Diet; vegetarian diets; Zen Macrobiotic Diet, and fasting.

Women who are older than fifty, considerably overweight, or afflicted by serious illnesses should consult a knowledgable doctor before beginning a diet or exercise program. Insist upon receiving a thorough medical checkup, including medical history, physical exam, and lab tests.

"Fat Doctors" and "Diet Factories"

A relatively new phenomenon is the "fat doctor," a physician who specializes in treating overweight persons. Though some fat doctors are reputable, others are simply out to make a buck.

Beware of "diet factories" where doctors have so many patients they can only give a minute or two to each. Such doctors cannot give a dieter the individual attention needed to lose weight safely and effectively.

Some doctors prescribe drugs or hormones to help with weight loss. HCG (human chorionic gonadotropin), a hormone extracted from the urine of pregnant women, is frequently prescribed along with a dangerously low low-calorie diet. According to such reliable sources as the Food and Drug Administration, HCG is virtually useless.

Occasionally women gain weight because of a malfunctioning thyroid and

Working Off The Chocolate Bar

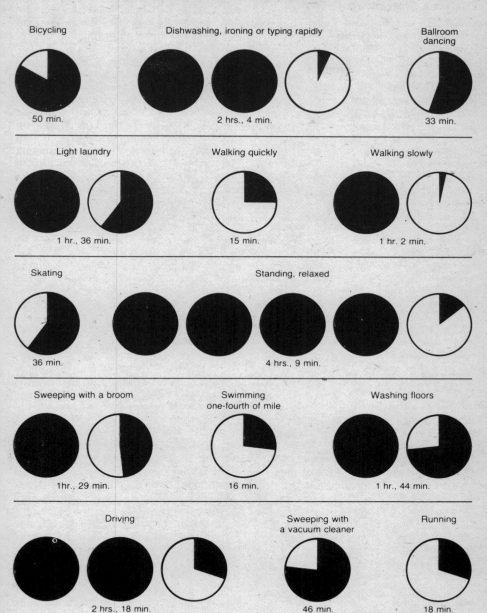

Bicycling

50 min.

Dishwashing, ironing or typing rapidly

2 hrs., 4 min.

Ballroom dancing

33 min.

Light laundry

1 hr., 36 min.

Walking quickly

15 min.

Walking slowly

1 hr. 2 min.

Skating

36 min.

Standing, relaxed

4 hrs., 9 min.

Sweeping with a broom

1hr., 29 min.

Swimming one-fourth of mile

16 min.

Washing floors

1 hr., 44 min.

Driving

2 hrs., 18 min.

Sweeping with a vacuum cleaner

46 min.

Running

18 min.

It requires 15 minutes to 24 hours of common daily activities or exercise to burn off the 145 calories found in a 1 ounce bar of chocolate.

If the chocolate bar eater gets no exercise at all, but spends the entire time in bed, resting and sleeping, it will take at least 24 hours for the 145 calories to be used up by the body.

Nutritive Value of Foods
(Calories, Proteins, etc.)

Food	Measure	Water %	Food Energy (calories)	Protein (grams)	Fat (grams)	Carbohydrate (grams)	Calcium (mg)	Iron (mg)	Vit. A (I.U.)	Thiamin (mg)	Riboflavin (mg)	Niacin (mg)	Ascorbic acid (mg)
Milk, Cream, Cheese													
Milk, fluid, whole, 3.5% fat	1 cup	87	160	9	9	12	288	0.1	350	0.07	0.41	0.2	2
Milk, fluid nonfat (skim)	1 cup	90	90	9	T	12	296	.1	10	.09	.44	.2	2
Buttermilk, fluid, cultured, made from skim milk	1 cup	90	90	9	T	12	296	.1	10	.10	.44	.2	2
Cheese, Roquefort type	1 oz.	40	105	6	9	1	89	.1	350	.01	.17	.3	0
Cheese, Cottage, creamed	12 oz.	78	360	46	14	10	320	1.0	580	.10	.85	.3	0
Cream, half-and-half	1 cup	80	325	8	28	11	261	.1	1,160	.07	.39	.1	2
Cream, heavy	1 cup	57	840	5	90	7	179	.1	3,670	.05	.26	.1	2
Custard, baked	1 cup	77	305	14	15	29	297	1.1	930	.11	.50	.3	1
Yoghurt, whole milk	1 cup	88	150	7	8	12	272	.1	340	.07	.39	.2	2
Eggs (large)													
Raw	1 egg	74	80	6	6	T	27	1.1	590	.05	.15	T	0
Scrambled (milk and fat)	1 egg	72	110	7	8	1	51	1.1	690	.05	.18	T	0
Meat, Poultry													
Bacon	2 sli.	8	90	5	8	1	2	.5	0	.08	.05	.8	
Beef, lean and fat	3 oz.	53	245	23	16	0	10	2.9	30	.04	.18	3.5	
Hamburger, regular	3 oz.	54	245	21	17	0	9	2.7	30	.07	.18	4.6	
Steak, broiled, lean and fat	3 oz.	44	330	20	27	0	9	2.5	50	.05	.16	4.0	
Corned beef	3 oz.	59	185	22	10	0	17	3.7	20	.01	.20	2.9	
Chicken, cooked:													
Flesh only, broiled	3 oz.	71	115	20	3	0	8	1.4	80	.05	.16	7.4	
With bone, ½ breast, fried	3.3 oz.	58	155	25	5	1	9	1.3	70	.04	.17	11.2	
Chicken, potpie, baked	8 oz.	57	535	23	31	42	68	3.0	3,020	.25	.26	4.1	5
Lamb chop, thick with bone	4.8 oz.	47	400	25	33	0	10	1.5		.14	.25	5.6	
Lamb, lean and fat	3 oz.	54	235	22	16	0	9	1.4		.13	.23	4.7	
Liver, beef, fried	2 oz.	57	130	15	6	3	6	5.0	30,280	.15	2.37	9.4	15
Ham, light cure, lean	3 oz.	54	245	18	19	0	8	2.2	0	.40	.16	3.1	
Boiled ham, sliced	2 oz.	59	135	11	10	0	6	1.6	0	.25	.09	1.5	
Pork roast, lean and fat	3 oz.	46	310	21	24	0	9	2.7	0	.78	.22	4.7	
Frankfurter, heated	2 oz.	57	170	7	15	1	3	.8		.08	.11	1.4	
Veal cutlet	3 oz.	60	185	23	9		9	2.7		.06	.21	4.6	
Veal roast	3 oz.	55	230	23	14	0	10	2.9		.11	.26	6.6	
Fish													
Bluefish, baked with fat	3 oz.	68	135	22	4	0	25	.6	40	.09	.08	1.6	
Clams, raw, meat only	3 oz.	82	65	11	1	2	59	5.2	90	.08	.15	1.1	8
Crabmeat, canned	3 oz.	77	85	15	2	1	38	.7		.07	.07	1.6	
Oyster, raw, meat	1 cup	85	160	20	4	8	226	13.2	740	.33	.43	6.0	
Salmon, pink, canned	3 oz.	71	120	17	5	0	167	.7	60	.03	.16	6.8	
Shrimp, canned, meat	3 oz.	70	100	21	1	0	98	2.6	50	.01	.03	1.5	
Swordfish, broiled with butter	3 oz.	65	150	24	5	0	23	1.1	1,750	.03	.04	9.3	
Tuna, canned in oil	3 oz.	61	170	24	7	0	7	1.6	70	.04	.10	10.1	
Nuts													
Almonds, shelled, whole	1 cup	5	850	26	77	28	332	6.7	0	.34	1.31	5.0	T
Cashew nuts, roasted	1 cup	5	785	24	64	41	53	5.3	140	.60	.35	2.5	
Peanuts, roasted	1 cup	2	840	37	72	27	107	3.0		.46	.19	24.7	0
Pecans, halves	1 cup	3	740	10	77	16	79	2.6	140	.93	.14	1.0	2
Walnuts, black or native, chopped	1 cup	3	790	26	75	19	T	7.6	380	.28	.14	.9	
Vegetables & Products													
Asparagus, cooked, spears	4 sp.	94	10	1	T	2	13	.4	540	.10	.11	.8	16
Asparagus, canned	1 cup	94	45	5	1	7	44	4.1	1,240	.15	.22	2.0	37
Beans, lima, immature, cooked	1 cup	71	190	13	1	34	80	4.3	480	.31	.17	2.2	29
Beans, snap, green, cooked	1 cup	92	30	2	T	7	63	.8	680	.09	.11	.6	15
Beans, snap, canned, green	1 cup	94	45	2	T	10	81	2.9	690	.07	.10	.7	10
Beans, snap, yellow or wax	1 cup	93	30	2	T	6	63	0.8	290	.09	.11	.6	16
Beans, sprouted mung, cooked	1 cup	91	35	4	T	7	21	1.1	30	.11	.13	.9	8
Beets, cooked	2 beets	91	30	1	T	7	14	.5	20	.03	.04	.3	6
Broccoli, cooked	1 stalk	91	45	6	1	8	158	1.4	4,500	.16	.36	1.4	162
Brussels sprouts, cooked	1 cup	88	55	7	1	10	50	1.7	810	.12	.22	1.2	135
Cabbage, raw, shredded	1 cup	92	15	1	T	4	34	.3	90	.04	.04	.2	33
Cabbage, cooked	1 cup	94	30	2	T	6	64	.4	190	.06	.06	.4	48
Carrot, raw 5½ by 1 in.	1	88	20	1	T	5	18	.4	5,500	.03	.03	.3	4
Carrots, cooked, diced	1 cup	91	45	1	T	10	48	.9	15,220	.08	.07	.7	9
Cauliflower, cooked, flower buds	1 cup	93	25	3	T	5	25	.8	70	.11	.10	.7	66
Celery, raw, stalk, large	1 stalk	94	5	T	T	2	16	.1	100	.01	.01	.1	4
Corn, cooked, ear 5 × 1¾ in.	1 ear	74	70	3	1	16	2	.5	310	.09	.08	1.0	7
Corn, canned	1 cup	81	170	5	2	40	10	1.0	690	.07	.12	2.3	13
Cucumbers, raw, pared	10 oz.	96	30	1	T	7	35	.6	T	.07	.09	.4	23
Lettuce, Boston type	1 head	95	30	3	T	6	77	4.4	2,130	.14	.13	.6	18
Mushrooms, canned	1 cup	93	40	5	T	6	15	1.2	T	.04	.60	4.8	4
Onion, mature, raw, 2½ in.	1	89	40	2	T	10	30	.6	40	.04	.04	.2	11
Peas, green, cooked	1 cup	82	115	9	1	19	37	2.9	860	.44	.17	3.7	33
Peas, green, canned	1 cup	83	165	9	1	31	50	4.2	1,120	.23	.13	2.2	22
Potato, medium, baked	1	75	90	3	T	21	9	.7	T	.10	.04	1.7	20
Potato, medium, boiled in skin	1	80	105	3	T	23	10	.8	T	.13	.05	2.0	22
Potatoes, mashed, milk added	1 cup	83	125	4	1	25	47	.8	50	.16	.10	2.0	19
Potato chips, medium	10 chips	2	115	1	8	10	8	.4	T	.04	.01	1.0	3
Sauerkraut, canned	1 cup	93	45	2	T	9	85	1.2	120	.07	.09	.4	33
Spinach, cooked	1 cup	92	40	5	1	6	167	4.0	14,580	.13	.25	1.0	50
Squash, summer, diced, cooked	1 cup	96	30	2	T	7	52	.8	820	.10	.16	1.6	21
Squash, winter, baked, mashed	1 cup	81	130	4	1	32	57	1.6	8,610	.10	.27	1.4	27
Sweet potato, baked	1	64	155	2	1	36	44	1.0	8,910	.10	.07	.7	24
Sweet potato, candied 3½ by 2¼ in.	1	60	295	2	6	60	65	1.6	11,030	.10	.08	.8	17
Tomato, raw, medium	1	94	40	2	T	9	24	.9	1,640	.11	.07	1.3	42
Tomato catsup, tablespoon	1 tbsp	69	15	T	T	4	3	.1	210	.01	.01	.2	2
Tomato juice, canned	1 cup	94	45	2	T	10	17	2.2	1,940	.12	.07	1.9	39

Food	Measure	Water %	Food Energy (calories)	Protein (grams)	Fat (grams)	Carbohydrate (grams)	Calcium (mg)	Iron (mg)	Vit. A (I.U.)	Thiamin (mg)	Riboflavin (mg)	Niacin (mg)	Ascorbic Acid (mg)
Fruits and Fruit Products													
Apple, medium, raw	1	85	70	T	T	18	8	.4	50	.04	.02	.1	3
Apple juice, bottled or canned	1 cup	88	120	T	T	30	15	1.5		.02	.05	.2	2
Applesauce, canned, sweetened	1 cup	76	230	1	T	61	10	1.3	100	.05	.03	.1	3
Banana, raw 6 by 1½ in.	1	76	100	1	T	26	10	.8	230	.06	.07	.8	12
Blueberries, raw	1 cup	83	85	1	1	21	21	1.4	140	.04	.08	.6	20
Cantaloupe, raw, medium	½ melon	91	60	1	T	14	27	.8	6,540	.08	.06	1.2	63
Cranberry sauce, sweetened, canned	1 cup	62	405	T	1	104	17	.6	60	.03	.03	.1	6
Grapefruit, raw, medium, white	½	89	45	1	T	12	19	.5	10	.05	.02	.2	44
Grapefruit juice, canned, unsweetened	1 cup	89	100	1	T	24	20	1.0	20	.07	.04	.4	84
Grapes, raw, American type	1 cup	82	65	1	1	15	15	.4	100	.05	.03	.2	3
Grapejuice, canned	1 cup	83	165	1	T	42	28	.8		.10	.05	.5	T
Lemon, raw, medium	1	90	20	1	T	6	19	.4	10	.03	.01	.1	39
Lemon juice, raw	1 cup	91	60	1	T	20	17	.5	50	.07	.02	.2	112
Lime juice, fresh	1 cup	90	65	1	T	22	22	.5	20	.05	.02	.2	79
Orange, raw, 2⅝ in.	1	86	65	1	T	16	54	.5	260	.13	.05	.5	66
Orange juice, frozen, undiluted	6 oz. can	55	360	5	T	87	75	.9	1,620	.68	.11	2.8	360
Peach, raw, whole, medium	1	89	35	1	T	10	9	.5	1,320	.02	.05	1.0	7
Peaches, canned halves or sliced	1 cup	79	200	1	T	52	10	.8	1,100	.02	.06	1.4	7
Pear, raw, 3 by 2½ in.	1	83	100	1	1	25	13	.5	30	.04	.07	.2	7
Pineapple, canned, sliced	Large sli.	80	90	T	T	24	13	.4	50	.09	.03	.2	8
Plums, raw, 2 in. diam.	1 plum	87	25	T	T	7	7	.3	140	.02	.02	.3	3
Prune juice, canned	1 cup	80	200	1	T	49	36	10.5		.03	.03	1.0	5
Raisins, seedless, pkged. ½ oz.	1 pkg.	18	40	T	T	11	9	.5	T	.02	.01	.1	T
Strawberries, raw, capped	1 cup	90	55	1	1	13	31	1.5	90	.04	.10	1.0	88
Watermelon, raw, wedge	1 wedge	93	115	2	1	27	30	2.1	2,510	.13	.13	.7	30
Grain Products													
Bagel, 3 in. diam. egg	1	32	165	6	2	28	9	1.2	30	.14	.10	1.2	0
Biscuit, baking powder	1	27	105	2	5	13	34	.4	T	.06	.06	.1	T
Bran flakes (40% bran)	1 cup	3	105	4	1	28	25	12.3	0	.14	.06	2.2	0
Bread, cracked wheat	1 loaf	35	1,190	40	10	236	399	5.0	T	.53	.41	5.9	T
Bread, enriched, French	1 loaf	31	1,315	41	14	251	195	10.0	T	1.27	1.00	11.3	T
Bread, enriched, Italian	1 loaf	32	1,250	41	4	256	77	10.0	0	1.32	.91	11.8	0
Bread, raisin, loaf	1 loaf	35	1,190	30	13	243	322	5.9	T	.23	.41	3.2	T
Bread, American, rye	1 loaf	36	1,100	41	5	236	340	7.3	0	.82	.32	6.4	0
Bread, white, enriched	1 loaf	36	1,225	39	15	229	381	11.3	T	1.13	.95	10.9	T
Cake, angel food	1 cake	34	1,645	36	1	377	603	1.9	0	.03	.70	.6	0
Cupcake, small, choc. icing	1 cake	22	130	2	5	21	47	.3	60	.01	.04	.1	T
Cake, Boston cream pie	1 pce.	35	210	4	6	34	46	.3	140	.02	.08	.1	T
Cake, pound	1 loaf	17	2,430	29	152	242	108	4.1	1,440	.15	.46	1.0	0
Saltines	4	4	50	1	1	8	2	.1	0	T	T	.1	0
Danish Pastry, round piece	1 pastry	22	275	5	15	30	33	.6	200	.05	.10	.5	T
Doughnut, cake type	1	24	125	1	6	16	13	.4	30	.05	.05	.4	T
Macaroni, enriched, cooked	1 cup	64	190	6	1	39	14	1.4	0	.23	.14	1.8	0
Noodles, enriched	1 cup	70	200	7	2	37	16	1.4	110	.22	.13	1.9	0
Oatmeal, or rolled oats, cooked	1 cup	87	130	5	2	23	22	1.4	0	.19	.05	.2	0
Pie, apple, ⅐ of 9-in. pie	1 sector	48	350	3	15	51	11	.4	40	.03	.03	.5	1
Pie, custard, ⅐ of 9-in. pie	1 sector	58	285	8	14	30	125	.8	300	.07	.21	.4	0
Pie, lemon meringue, ⅐ of 9-in. pie	1 sector	47	305	4	12	45	17	.6	200	.04	.10	.2	4
Pie, mince, ⅐ of 9-in. pie	1 sector	43	365	3	16	56	38	1.4	T	.09	.05	.5	1
Pie, pumpkin, ⅐ of 9-in. pie	1 sector	59	275	5	15	32	66	.7	3,210	.04	.13	.7	T
Pizza, (cheese) ⅛ of 14 in. diam.	1 sector	45	185	7	6	27	107	.7	290	.04	.12	.7	4
Popcorn, plain	1 cup	4	25	1	T	5	1	.2			.01	.1	0
Roll, home recipe	1 roll	26	120	3	3	20	16	.7	30	.09	.09	.8	0
Spaghetti, enriched, cooked	1 cup	72	155	5	1	32	11	1.3	0	.20	.11	1.5	0
Fats and Oils													
Butter, regular	½ cup	16	810	1	92	1	23	0	3,750				0
Lard	1 cup	0	1,850	0	205	0	0	0	0	0	0	0	0
Vegetable fats	1 cup	0	1,770	0	200	0	0	0	0	0	0	0	0
Margarine	½ cup	16	815	1	92	1	23	0	3,750				0
Salad dressing, French, regular	1 tbsp.	39	65	T	6	3	2	.1					
Salad dressing, mayonnaise	1 tbsp.	15	100	T	11	T	3	.1	40	T	.01	T	
Salad dressing, T,000 Island	1 tbsp.	32	80	T	8	3	2	.1	50	T	T	T	T
Sugars, Sweets													
Candy, milk chocolate, sweetened	1 oz.	1	145	2	9	16	65	.3	80	.01	.10	.1	T
Candy, plain fudge	1 oz.	8	115	1	4	21	22	.3	T	.01	.03	.1	T
Chocolate syrup, fudge type	1 oz.	25	125	2	5	20	48	.5	60	.02	.08	.2	T
Honey, strained or extracted	1 tbsp.	17	65	T	0	17	1	.1	0	T	.01	.1	T
Jellies	1 tbsp.	29	50	T	T	13	4	.3	T	T	.01	T	1
Sugar, brown	1 cup	2	820	0	0	212	187	7.5	0	.02	.07	.4	0
Sugar, granulated	1 cup	T	770	0	0	199	0	.2	0	0	0	0	0
Miscellaneous													
Barbecue sauce	1 cup	81	230	4	17	20	53	2.0	900	.03	.03	.8	13
Beer	12 oz.	92	150	1	0	14	18	T		.01	.11	2.2	
Alcoholic beverage, 86-proof	1½ fl. oz.	64	105			T							
Cola-type beverage	12 fl. oz.	90	145	0	0	37				0	0	0	0
Ginger ale	12 fl. oz.	92	115	0	0	29				0	0	0	0
Soup, cream of chicken	1 cup	85	180	7	10	15	172	.5	610	.05	.27	.7	2
Soup, tomato	1 cup	84	175	7	7	23	168	.8	1,200	.10	.25	1.3	15
Beans with pork	1 cup	84	170	8.	6	22	63	2.3	650	.13	.08	1.0	3
Clam chowder	1 cup	92	80	2	3	12	34	1.0	880	.02	.02	1.0	

T indicates a trace.

Source: U.S. Department of Agriculture.

can safely reduce by taking thyroid hormones — under strict medical supervision, of course. But heart and circulatory problems have arisen among thyroid users whose flab is solely a result of overeating, so let the doctor decide. Don't tell him what to prescribe!

Some doctors continue to prescribe amphetamines and appetite suppressants, despite tighter federal controls. These pills are effective only briefly — if at all — and carry with them a list of possible side effects ranging from increased heartbeat to drug dependence.

Unless one leads the active life of Chris Evert or "Moolah the Lady Wrestler," exercise unaccompanied by a diet will melt pounds away only very slowly. But that is no reason to languish in front of the TV salivating over macaroni commercials. A religiously followed exercise program will tone flabby muscles and bring new color to pale cheeks. A good workout also strengthens the heart and other body organs, and helps relieve the tensions which build up during a long day at the office or with the baby.

The best regimen exercises the entire body; swimming, jogging, and walking are excellent all-over conditioners. Start an exercise program slowly and do a little more each day. Make exercise a part of your daily routine. Set the alarm clock ahead fifteen minutes to squeeze in some wake-up calisthenics. Get off the bus a few stops before your destination and walk the rest of the way. Climb the stairs, instead of taking the elevator.

Exercise need not be limited to dreary toe-touching and situps. And it can be a lot more fun when one has company. Challenge your husband to a Billie Jean King-Bobby Riggs-style battle of the sexes on the tennis court. Organize a belly-dancing class for the women on your block.

Dieting Clubs

On the theory that misery loves company, clubs of dieters have sprung up across the nation. And much to the surprise of many first-time visitors, misery is largely absent from the rollicking meetings of TOPS, Weight Watchers, The Diet Workshop, Diet Watchers, and Overeaters Anonymous. Members of these groups prod and encourage one another to reduce to a weight goal through weekly weigh-ins, in-

spirational talks, and individual counseling. As William G.Shipman, an expert on the psychology of women dieters, notes, diet groups are among "the most successful techniques to date in treating" overweight.

According to *Consumer Guide,* the five groups are equally good, though each has different strengths. Weight Watchers, with its magazine, newspaper column, and diet-food line, is the slickest of the groups; TOPS and Overeaters Anonymous are more folksy; The Diet Workshop and Diet Watchers provide the most individual attention.

To find the diet groups in your community, consult the phone directory, or their national headquarters:

Weight Watchers
800 CommunityDrive
Manhasset, Long Island, NY 11030

TOPS
4575 South 5th St., P.O. Box 4489
Milwaukee, WI 53207

The Diet Workshop
28 Merrick Ave.
Merrick, Long Island, NY 11566

Diet Watchers
39 S. Main Street
Spring Valley, NY 10977

Overeaters Anonymous
P.O. Box 2613
Hollywood, CA 90028

Remember that most of these groups are not just in business for your health. Be prepared to pay a nominal membership fee and regular dues to each organization, except Overeaters Anonymous, which is free. You might wish to save the extra money for your new, Size-9 wardrobe, and organize your own group of fellow dieters. Remember, all five of the above groups were founded by formerly fat women.

"You can never be too thin or too rich," socialite Babe Paley supposedly remarked. For those who are rich and want to be thin, "fat farms" — elegant camps for the overweight — may be the answer. They offer outright supervision of every bite one puts in the mouth, as well as a variety of diet plans (averaging a too-low 800 calories a day), and assorted amenities. Whether they are worth the cost — about $1,000 per week — is up to the patron to decide. The woman of average means might be better advised to formulate her own program of exercise, facials, herbal soaks, and diet meals.

Forming Good Eating Habits

The key to keeping weight off lies in permanently changing the bad eating habits that made you fat in the first place. If dieting is not to be in vain, one must adopt *for keeps* a new, thin life-style: learn to savor one piece of bread rather than the whole loaf, to opt for fresh fruits over deep dish apple pie a la mode, to enjoy the morning jog around the block. You will appreciate that occasional pizza or banana split all the more for having to "save up" for its calories.

One final word of caution. In a diet-conscious society like ours, there are bound to be some people overly preoccupied about their weight. Starving oneself sick in pursuit of bony beauty is just as unhealthy as filling one's face with cream puffs. (*Anorexia nervosa,* a form of self-starvation predominantly afflicting teenage girls, is a potentially fatal illness which demands immediate medical attention.) After all, even Twiggy has put on a good 20 pounds since her fashion model days, and looks none the worse for it.

The most important dieting secret is to prevent food from running your life. A happy person actively involved in the world around her is too busy to think about hunger pangs. Nobody says losing excess weight is easy, but the rewards — a slender figure, a better self-image, maybe even a longer life — make it well worth the effort. Good luck!

TRENDSETTERS

Arden: She Sold Prestige

Elizabeth Arden (1878-1966) believed so fervently in her own products that she insisted her stable of race horses be rubbed down with Ardena Cream. She might have had something there; her horse "Jet Pilot" won the Kentucky Derby in 1947.

Arden's real name was Florence Nightingale Graham and like her famous namesake gave nursing a whirl. But she lit off for New York at age thirty with a new name and a satchelful of fluffy face cream and astringent, her first products. By the time of her death, Arden's business was producing 450 different products in 1,500 assorted shades.

Arden sold prestige as well as cream in her little pink jars. Everything from her posh Fifth Avenue address to her products' evocative names breathed snob appeal. Reversing the law of competitive trade, Arden deliberately priced her products dollars above the competition. She may have sold less in terms of volume, but she more than made up for it in terms of profit.

There was a glimmer of principle behind her financial ambition. Arden sought to improve the safety of cosmetics and taught her customers to care for their bodies with exercise and lotions. She beautified the international jet set for $750 a week at her Maine and Arizona "health spas."

In keeping with her products' claims of indefinitely prolonged youth and beauty, the strong-willed Arden kept her birth date a closely guarded secret. Her age was disclosed only after her death.

Ayer: Puffery and Practicality

Modern newspaper readers are bombarded with hints on losing weight, powdering noses, and shopping for face lifts. But at the turn of the century, only one newspaper columnist was offering beauty advice to American women.

She was the beautiful, tenacious **Harriet Hubbard Ayer** (1849-1903).

A penniless but socially prominent divorcée, Ayer entered the fledgling beauty industry by marketing a facial cream. She claimed the concoction was the invention of one Madame Recamier, an ageless beauty who had plotted against Napoleon. Ayer pulled out all the stops in advertising her product: she daringly put her own picture and coat of arms on the jars and forged testimonials from unnamed socialities. Actress Lily Langtry — who was said to roll naked in morning dew to preserve her unblemished skin — endorsed Ayer's cream.

But Ayer's success was fleeting. A disgruntled suitor and former financial backer convinced Ayer's daughter to have her committed to an insane asylum. Business had slumped by the time attorneys gained her release fourteen months later. Claiming she had been perfectly sane all the while, Ayer lectured far and wide on the abysmal treatment of the insane and organized legal aid for others unjustly committed.

Ayer arrived in the office of *New York World* Editor Arthur Brisbane in 1896 to apply for a reporting job. She dashed off a column of health and beauty tips, and he hired her on the spot. Ayer's columns offered few outright beauty secrets, but her common-sense endorsements of fresh air, exercise, and healthy eating were considered novel in her day. By her example and by her writing, Ayer encouraged her readers to move away from the constraints on nineteenth-century women.

Bloomer: Fashion Rebel

Poor **Amelia Bloomer** (1818-1894): She spent her life crusading for temperance, abolition, and women's rights. But she is chiefly remembered for the gathered trousers which came to bear her name.

Thanks to Amelia Bloomer's active pen, the new trouser costume came to bear her name.

"BLOOMERISM,"
OR THE
NEW FEMALE COSTUME OF 1851,

As it has appeared in the various Cities and Towns.

BOSTON: S. W. WHEELER, 66 Cornhill—1851.

Bloomer was editor of the *Lily*, newspaper of the Seneca Falls (N.Y.) Ladies Temperance Society, when Elizabeth Smith Miller apeared on the streets of the town wearing — horrors! — Turkish pantaloons topped with a short overskirt.

The *Lily* quickly jumped to the costume's defense. Bloomer declared Miller's garb a sensible alternative to the heavy petticoats, floor-length skirts, and tight corsets that helped keep nineteenth-century women in their place.

Newspapers across the nation picked up on Bloomer's articles, creating a fad for the costume. Because of the proselytizing editor, these trousers came to be known as "bloomers."

"For some six or eight years," Bloomer recalled, "I wore no other costume." But along with other early feminists, she came to realize that bloomers were distracting attention from more important women's rights issues.

Though reconciled to wearing long skirts and petticoats, Bloomer continued to wield her pen for the cause of women well into her seventies. She deserves a place in the annals of womankind — not for the short-lived fad she promoted — but for introducing America's pioneer feminists, Susan B. Anthony and Elizabeth Cady Stanton, to one another.

Chanel: It Began At A Polo Match

Gabrielle "Coco" Chanel (1883-1971) designed her first dress at a polo match. Shivering with cold, she donned a man's polo sweater and tied it at the waist with a scarf. Encouraged by the compliments her creation received, she set out to transform the hat shop her lover had bought for her a few years earlier.

Timeless simplicity became the hallmark of the mighty House of Chanel in Paris. She replaced the cumbersome frivolity of women's fashions — the corset was just then pinching its last — with simple lines reminiscent of men's attire.

"A dress made right," said Chanel, "should allow one to walk, to dance, even to ride horseback." And women agreed. By 1938, the milliner-turned-designer was employing 400 workers who turned out more than 28,000 dresses a year.

Chanel changed black from a color of mourning to one of utmost elegance with

In classic suit, Coco Chanel watched the unveiling of her spring 1969 collection.

design their own gowns and cut them to size. Demorest took the guesswork out of fitting by developing standard sizes. And her modish styles, which she picked up on her semi-annual trips abroad, brought Parisian **haute couture** to the Midwestern front porch.

Demorest spread news of her patterns in *Mme. Demorest's Mirror of Fashion,* a quarterly she published with her husband. The magazine also offered mail-order fashion accessories created by Demorest: "the first . . . really excellent cheap hoopskirt," the "most elegant . . . most comfortable corsets," and an "Imperial dress elevator" to raise long skirts above muddy sidewalks. But the popular magazine dealt with far more than fashion; under Demorest and her able editor, Jennie June Crosby, it crusaded for woman's equality in education and in business.

By bringing inexpensive chic to the average American woman, Demorest democratized fashion as Thomas Jefferson and Andrew Jackson had democratized politics.

her creation of the little black dress, often embellished with white collar and cuffs. The cardigan jacket, sometimes trimmed with a fur collar, was another Chanel trademark.

World War II closed the House of Chanel, and the designer decided to live out her days on proceeds from her lucrative perfumes. But she made a comeback in 1954 with an updated Chanel suit — spare, ageless, always correct. In short, classic Chanel.

Demorest: Fashion's Jefferson

The American small town woman of a century ago might not have known whether she wanted the vote, but she knew she wanted to dress just like the fine ladies of New York and Paris.

Ellen Demorest (1824-1898) made it possible for her to do so by devising the mass-produced home dressmaking pattern.

Prior to Demorest's innovation, women who could not afford seamstresses had to

Lauder: Doorstep to Boardroom

The name **Estee Lauder** conjures up visions of chandelier-lit department stores studded with diamond-dripping matrons. But this modern cosmetics queen got her start peddling her Viennese uncle's facial preparations Avon Lady-style to friends and neighbors.

Retail stores received their first line of Lauder products in 1946: a facial mask, an all-purpose cream, cleansing oil, powder, red lipstick, and turquoise eye shadow. The line took up only a fraction of the cosmetics counter space which Lauder products demand today.

Lauder faced a more competitive cosmetics industry than that which confronted Elizabeth Arden and Helena Rubenstein at the beginning of their careers. She fought back with new ideas.

Lauder scooped everyone on men's cosmetics (Aramis), scented bath oil (Youth Dew) and a "hypo-allergenic," youth-oriented line (Clinique).

Only Estee Lauder-Clinique, of all the top cosmetic companies, remains family owned. Lauder herself, however, has handed over day-to-day control of the firm to her son.

Nidetch: Dieting Evangelist

The Billy Graham of the dieting set is Weight Watchers' **Jean Nidetch** (1923-   ).

Nidetch began eating compulsively in childhood. "Whenever I had a fight with the little girl next door, or it was raining, and I couldn't go out, or I wasn't invited to a birthday party, my mother gave me a piece of candy to make me feel better," she claims.

The chubby child ballooned into a 214-pound adult. After unsuccessfully trying every fad diet and appetite-suppressing pill around, the gregarious Nidetch realized it was more difficult to cram cookies into her mouth if it was busy talking.

So she summoned six overweight friends to her home and began confessing her secret food cravings and indulgences. With their encouragement, and a sensible, low-calorie diet, Nidetch began to lose weight. And so did her friends. By the time she reached her ideal weight of 142 pounds, meetings had grown so large that they had to be moved from her living room to the basement of her apartment building.

Two of those she helped, Arnold and Felice Lippert, saw gold in the mountains of melting flab, and convinced Nidetch to go into business. Weight Watchers was incorporated in 1963 with Nidetch as its symbol.

Within a decade Weight Watchers had helped more than five million people shed excess pounds. And keep them off. As Nidetch noted at the organization's ten-year reunion, "What makes Weight Watchers different is that ten years later we can stage a big reunion and 20,000 people will show up still keeping their weight off."

Rubinstein: Hard Work and Chutzpa

Helena Rubinstein (1872-1965) sailed into New York harbor in 1914 and promptly declared the appearance of American women "appalling." Their noses were purple, she said, and their cheeks dead white.

But four years later, as her vials of creams, perfumes, and lotions graced department store counters from coast to coast, she was seeing only green as the dollars rolled in.

Cosmetics queen Helena Rubinstein was too busy making money to worry over her own looks.

Polish-born Rubinstein entered the beauty business in Australia, where she had gone in 1902 to visit relatives. Noting the dry, weather-beaten condition of Australian women's skin, she wrote home for a supply of the cold cream she had used since childhood. Aussies flocked to the door of her Melbourne shop, and similar scenes were repeated at the shops she then set up in London — where lipstick was just gaining respectability — and Paris.

Rubinstein attributed much of her success to plain, unglamorous hard work. "You must work 24 hours a day and 300 years in a lifetime," she remarked.

And "a little *chutzpa*" never hurt, she added. The queen of *chutzpa,* Rubinstein even hired the ex-husband of her arch rival, Elizabeth Arden, to manage her firm.

Rubinstein was too busy running her empire to waste time on her own appearance. Violating the rules of beauty, she wore her hair skimmed back severely in a tight knot.

Rubinstein left an estate of $100 million when she died.

Trigère: Genius With Scissors

A shopper once complained that a dress designed by **Pauline Trigère** (1912-   ) did nothing for her. "What is it supposed to do, tickle?" the designer retorted.

Trigère can afford a bit of sass. The French-born designer has been one of the most influential figures in American fashion since she pawned her diamond brooch and set up shop in 1942.

Trigère's elegant tailoring — perhaps carried over from family members who made uniforms for the Russian aristocracy — has won her a devoted cult of followers. Unlike most designers, Trigère creates her designs by cutting directly into fabric without using a pattern. "I can't draw. I can't paint. I can't even sew. But put a piece of fabric in my hands and magic happens," she once commented.

"Never say 'never' in business," is a Trigère maxim. Though no faddist, the designer has shown an ability to change with the times. She once declared trousers inappropriate for street wear, but has since reversed herself and included them in her collections. She was a major influence behind the reintroduction of split skirts — or culottes — in the Seventies.

Trigère was the first New York designer to employ a black model, Beverly Valdes, in 1961. Though hate mail at first streamed into her studio, the action signaled a breakthrough for blacks in that area of the fashion world.

More recently, Trigère has worked with Israeli craftspeople to develop an indigenous clothing industry. She also helped found New York City's First Women's Bank.

Twiggy: "Not Really A Figure"

Britannia ruled the waves of Sixties pop culture, through the music of the Beatles, the Mod fashions of Mary Quant, and the Cockney charm of **Twiggy** (1949-   ).

Leslie Hornby's 5'6", 92-pound frame won her the nickname "Sticks" at school, which she left at fifteen after discovering "boys and dances." Her boy friend Justin de Villenueve renamed her "Twiggy," had her hair and makeup styled, and masterminded her quick climb to the top of the modeling ladder. In little more than a year she was commanding fees of $240 an hour during a highly publicized 1967 tour of the United States.

Soon the market was flooded with Twiggy dresses, Twiggy dolls — even Twiggy ballpoint pens. One commentator suggested to the model that her 31-22-32 figure might be the shape of the future. "It's not really what you call a figure, is it?" she responded.

Twiggy let her hair grow and removed her three sets of false eyelashes the following year. She gave up modeling soon after, but not before her likeness had been added to Madame Tussaud's famed wax museum.

Twenty pounds heavier, Twiggy resurfaced in 1976, singing a Cockney-accented brand of Country Western music.

Von Furstenberg: Chanel of the '70s

"I never pretended I was a fabulous designer," says Princess Diane von Furstenberg (1946-   ). "I am a woman who makes clothes."

Regardless of what von Furstenberg calls herself, others have christened her the Chanel of the seventies, the designer who put women back in dresses.

The key to von Furstenberg's success is her now-classic V-neck, wrap-around knit dress. By 1976 — only six years after she arrived in New York with her three first efforts — von Furstenberg was marketing 20,000 dresses a week.

At the height of her fame, Twiggy modeled a pant suit from her own fashion line.

Seven years ago, nobody in the fashion world but *Vogue*'s prophetic Diana Vreeland would give the princess (titled by virtue of her unsuccessful marriage to Prince Egon von Furstenberg) the time of day. Now, manufacturers are lining up along New York City's Seventh Avenue to get the designer's million-dollar name on their products. In addition to the dress, cosmetics, and Tatiana fragrance enterprises she owns (the last named after her daughter), von Furstenberg has lent her name and aura to everything from eyeglasses to lingerie. Add a pair of shoes, and a woman would never have to buy another label. She has even written *Diane von Furstenberg's Book of Beauty* to help women put it all together.

All told, von Furstenberg's activities are expected to gross $100 million in sales this year. Little wonder she once commented, "Sometimes I wake up in the night in terror of all I carry on my shoulders."

As *Vogue* editor, Diana Vreeland helped decide the latest styles, colors, and models.

Vreeland: Doyenne of Fashion

Diana Vreeland (1904-   ) wore sensible black skirts and sweaters as a virtual winter uniform during her editorship of *Vogue*. But she was a trend setter all the same.

Vreeland emerged as an arbiter of chic during her 1936-to-1962 tenure as a *Harper's Bazaar* editor. She declared which styles would be emphasized, which colors would be "new," which hair lengths would be fashionable, and which accessories would be "in" during the season ahead.

While at *Bazaar* she wrote a column titled "Why Don't You. . ." which made little suggestions with a tone of command. "Why Don't You," Vreeland urged: "Knit yourself a little skullcap? Tie black tulle bows on your wrists? Put all your dogs in bright yellow collars and leads like all the dogs in Paris?" The implication was that if you didn't, there was something wrong with you.

Vreeland's influence on all things fashionable increased even more when she became editor-in-chief of *Vogue* in 1962. Her influence helped make Verushka, Twiggy, and Penelope Tree the super-models of the Sixties, establishing a taste for strikingly individualistic looks that transcend mere prettiness. And the career of Lauren Hutton, who would later become Revlon's million-dollar baby, was launched when Vreeland put her face on a *Vogue* cover.

Since retiring from *Vogue* in 1971, Vreeland has supervised fashion exhibitions at New York's Metropolitan Museum of Art, including "The World of Balenciaga," "The Tens, the Twenties, the Thirties," "Romantic and Classic Hollywood Design," and "The Glory of Russian Costume."

Walker: Washerwoman Makes Good

Sarah Breedlove Walker (1867-1919) spent eighteen years washing white folks' clothes. But she died a millionaire in her "colored woman's palace" on the Hudson River.

Walker's ticket to success was the hair straightening method which she said was revealed to her in a dream in 1905. The three-step method itself was simple: vigorous shampooing of the hair, brushing with a special "hair growing" pomade, and, lastly, straightening with hot iron combs.

Walker's earliest products were blended in washtubs with kitchen utensils. She demonstrated the method door-to-door to her neighbors. Many of Walker's clients were recruited into her corps of Walker agents, who eventually spread the mes-

The Glamorous Life

There's a popular belief that a model's life is a continuous flow of glamorous parties, beautiful clothes, and evenings spent with famous and dashing men. But it's largely a myth. Instead of the glamorous life, here's what to expect if you set out to be a model:

7 A.M.: Awake to a feast of juice, one egg, and coffee, or an equally low-calorie meal.

7:30: Calisthenics, unless an exercise class can be slipped in during the day. Afterward, hair, makeup, and nails are done, all very carefully.

8:30: If you're new in town but lucky enough to have signed with an agency, you probably face a day of "go-sees" — the model's equivalent of the job interview. Armed with a portfolio containing a collection of photographs showing you in various poses, styles, and moods, designed to show your range, you'll be sent to perhaps ten of your agency's clients and photographers every day. Appointments usually begin at 9 A.M. If you aren't being handled by an agency, the day is spent looking for one that will take you on because most work is available only through the agencies.

11:00: You may have already seen three clients. One appointment may have been a "cattle" or mass call for a certain look. You sat in a room filled with other 5-feet-9-inch, blond, long-haired, European sophisticated types, and every time you lifted your head, you had the feeling you were looking into a mirror.

11:30: Check in with the agency. The agency gets 10 percent of whatever you earn and all your bookings are made through it. They make sure each booking is legitimate and set your hourly rate.

Lunch: Lunch is light. You can choose freely between the diet platter or chef's salad, but no dressing. Photographs add weight and emphasize extra bulges, a problem you're learning to keep always in mind. Although you can make sixty to seventy-five dollars an hour once you're working, at this point an inexpensive lunch is probably also best for your budget. Signing with an agency, even the best, is no guarantee of immediate steady work. It may take months. It may never happen. A successful model can "easily" earn $50,000 a year for the duration of her brief career. At twenty-eight, a model is approaching retirement, and few are in demand past age thirty.

1 P.M.: You probably face an afternoon with more go-sees. If you get work, it's not easy. For each picture you see in a magazine, dozens of poses were tried and dozens of photographs taken. Studio lights are hot, the clothes — often pinned to give the illusion of fit — are uncomfortable, heavy make-up is stifling, and the work is exhausting and repetitious. Shots of fur coats are often made on summer beaches, with models in mink sweating in August heat.

Evening: Dinner is spartan. Bedtime is early because bleary eyes photograph badly, and you don't often meet eligible men on the job. If you've been hired by a client and your day begins with a shooting, you will get up several hours before you are scheduled to arrive at the studio. You may forgo makeup if the client provides a makeup person or go to the studio early enough to do your hair and makeup there. Besides your portfolio, you'll carry your makeup kit. An assignment may last an hour or a day, occasionally several days. Then it all begins again. Your life won't seem glamorous to you, but those who see your picture in *Vogue* won't believe it isn't.

sage through the United States and the Caribbean, wearing characteristic costumes of black skirts and white shirtwaists. Even dancer Josephine Baker had her hair styled à la Walker.

Walker — or "Madame Walker" as she later preferred to be called — was one of black America's first philanthropists. The National Association for the Advancement of Colored People (NAACP) was a frequent recipient of her generosity, as were young women in need of scholarships, homes for the aging, and Christmas funds for the needy. "Cleanliness and loveliness," Walker believed, would help blacks gain self-confidence and the respect of white society.

First Miss America Margaret Gorman, 30-25-32, did not stack up to her modern counterparts.

THERE SHE IS . . . MISS AMERICA

Miss America sweeps down the runway, tears falling freely into her bouquet of roses, young womanhood incarnate and, in the words of Bernie Wayne who wrote her theme song, "the queen of femininity." And she's probably a queen of competition as well. Before being crowned, Miss America has demurely edged out approximately seventy thousand other women in the pyramid of three thousand local and state contests which, according to Frank Deford (*There She Is: The Life and Times of Miss America*, 1971), yearly takes two hundred thousand volunteers working a total of six million hours to produce.

"Miss America," said 1951 winner Yolande Betbeze, "is the kind of girl who would go into a bar and order orange juice in a loud voice." Very loud, lest any potential judges should be within earshot. As a contestant, however, she isn't even allowed near a bar, nor may she smoke or drink at all, and she is constantly chaperoned to make sure she doesn't slip — there is no honor system in Atlantic City, New Jersey.

She must maintain this attitude throughout her reign, because most of her income during her year as Miss America comes from bookings with church groups, civic organizations, and state pageants.

Tawny Godin, Miss America of 1975, lost an estimated $20,000 in personal-appearance fees during her reign. Godin

outspokenly admitted she had tried marijuana and neglected to take the obligatory stance against premarital sex and abortion (women who have been pregnant are barred from the contest). While Godin's attitudes are no longer radical, they are still too controversial for the basically conservative Miss America ideal.

The first pageant was held in Atlantic City, where it's held still. Bert Parks, whose toothy grin has become as much a part of the ritual as the crown, the roses, and the tears, began hosting the show in 1955, the second year the pageant had been televised.

Everybody's Every Girl

Every girl can aspire to be Miss America, because Miss America is Every Girl, a compilation of best qualities. That Every Girl measures 5'6", 34.9", 23.9", 35.4", weighs 119, has brown hair and blue eyes, and is 19.35 years old. Because the first Oriental competed in 1948, and the first blacks entered only in 1970, it isn't surprising that this composite contestant should have a fair complexion. Bust measurement didn't equal hip measurement until 1959. A little padding often went a long way to help a middling body appear to be a good one.

A feminist group which staged a counter-pageant on the boardwalk in 1968 obviously felt the Miss America contest was antifeminist. Nevertheless, the pageant does offer more scholarships than any other private institution. Imagine a similar contest to win a Rhodes scholarship.

Although most Miss Americas take their scrapbooks and head for home once their year has ended, some continue in the limelight:

Bess Myerson (1945), the only Jewish Miss America, became a television personality and consumer advocate.

Phyllis George (1971) is a sportcaster for CBS.

Maria Fletcher (1962) became a Rockette.

Jean Bartel (1943) became vice president of a documentary film company. She

---

Miss America Winners

Prior to 1950 the selection of Miss America was for the year in which she was selected. Starting with 1950 she became Miss America of the following year; as a result there was no Miss America for 1950.

		Height	Bust	Waist	Hips	Wgt.	Age	Hair
1921	Margaret Gorman, Washington, D.C.	5-1	30	25	32	108	16	Blonde
1922-23	Mary Campbell, Columbus, Ohio	5-7	35	26	36	140	16	Brown
1924	Ruth Malcolmson, Philadelphia, Pa	5-6	34	25	34	137	18	Brown
1925	Fay Lanphier, Oakland, California	5-8	35	26	37	138	19	Blonde
1926	Norma Smallwood, Tulsa, Oklahoma	5-4	33	25	34	118	18	Brown
1927	Lois Delaner, Joliet, Illinois	5-5½	33	25	34	115	17	Brown
1933	Marion Bergeron, West Haven, Conn	5-4½	32	26½	37½	112	16	Blonde
1935	Henrietta Leaver, Pittsburgh, Pa	5-6½	33	23	35½	120	19	Brown
1936	Rose Coyle, Philadelphia, Pa	5-6	34	23½	34½	114	22	Black
1937	Bette Cooper, Bertrand Island, N.J.	5-6	32	26	36	120	17	Blonde
1938	Marilyn Meseke, Marion, Ohio	5-7	34¼	26	35½	128	20	Blonde
1939	Patricia Donnelly, Detroit, Michigan	5-7	36	25	34	126	19	Brown
1940	Frances Marie Burke, Philadelphia, Pa	5-9	34	23	35	120	19	Brown
1941	Rosemary LaPlanche, Los Angeles, Calif	5-5½	34	24	36	120	18	Blonde
1942	Jo-Carroll Dennison, Tyler, Texas	5-5	34	22	34½	118	18	Brown
1943	Jean Bartel, Los Angeles, Calif	5-8	36	23	35	130	19	Brown
1944	Venus Ramey, Washington, D.C.	5-7	37½	25	36½	125	19	Auburn
1945	Bess Myerson, New York City, N.Y.	5-10	35½	25	35	135	21	Black
1946	Marilyn Buferd, Los Angeles, Calif.	5-8	35½	25½	35	123	21	Brown
1947	Barbara Walker, Memphis, Tennessee	5-7	35	25	35	130	21	Black
1948	BeBe Shopp, Hopkins, Minnesota	5-9	37	27	36	140	18	Brown
1949	Jacque Mercer, Litchfield, Arizona	5-4	34	22	34	106	18	Black
1951	Yolande Betbeze, Mobile, Alabama (Postdated)	5-5½	35	24	35	119	21	Brown
1952	Colleen Kay Hutchins, Salt Lake City, Utah	5-10	36	24	36	143	25	Blonde
1953	Neva Jane Langley, Macon, Ga	5-6¼	35	23	35	118	19	Brown
1954	Evelyn Margaret Ay, Ephrata, Pa	5-8	37	24	36	132	20	Blonde
1955	Lee Meriwether, San Francisco, Calif	5-8½	34½	22	35	124	19	Brown
1956	Sharon Ritchie, Denver, Colorado	5-6	35	23	35	116	18	Brown
1957	Marian McKnight, Manning, S.C.	5-5	35	23	35	120	19	Blonde
1958	Marilyn Van Derbur, Denver, Colorado	5-8½	35	25	36	130	20	Blonde
1959	Mary Ann Mobley, Brandon, Miss	5-5	34½	22	35	114	21	Brown
1960	Lynda Lee Mead, Natchez, Miss	5-7	36	24	36	120	20	Brown
1961	Nancy Fleming, Montague, Michigan	5-6	35	22	35	116	18	Brown
1962	Maria Fletcher, Asheville, N.C.	5-5½	35	24	35	118	19	Brown
1963	Jacquelyn Mayer, Sandusky, Ohio	5-5	36	22	36	115	20	Brown
1964	Donna Axum, El Dorado, Arkansas	5-6½	35	23	35	124	21	Brown
1965	Vonda Kay Van Dyke, Phoenix, Ariz	5-6	36	24	36	124	21	Brown
1966	Deborah Irene Bryant, Overland Park, Kansas	5-7	36	23	36	115	19	Brown
1967	Jane Anne Jayroe, Laverne, Oklahoma	5-6	36	24	35	116	19	Brown
1968	Debra Dene Barnes, Moran, Kansas	5-9	36½	24	36½	135	20	Brown
1969	Judith Anne Ford, Belvidere, Ill	5-7	36	24½	36	125	18	Blonde
1970	Pamela Anne Eldred, Birmingham, Mich	5-5½	34	21½	34	110	21	Blonde
1971	Phyllis Ann George, Denton, Texas	5-8	36	23	36	121	21	Brown
1972	Laurie Lea Schaefer, Columbus, Ohio	5-7	36	24	34	118	22	Auburn
1973	Terry Anne Meeuwsen, DePere, Wisconsin	5-8	36	25	36	120	23	Brown
1974	Rebecca Ann King, Denver, Colorado	5-9	36	24	36	125	23	Blonde
1975	Shirley Cothran, Fort Worth, Texas	5-8	36	23	36	119	21	Brown
1976	Tawney Elaine Godin, Yonkers, N.Y.	5-10½	36	24	36	128	18	Brown
1977	Dorothy Benham, Edina, Minn.	5-7½	35	22	35	120	20	Blonde

owns a travel business, has sung opera, and was chairman of the Television Academy of Arts and Sciences, Hollywood chapter.

Mary Ann Mobley (1959) appeared in films, including several beach party movies.

Vonda Kay Van Dyck (1965) wrote best-selling children's books.

Lee Meriwether (1955) costarred in *Barnaby Jones* on CBS.

Rosemary La Planche (1941) had an extensive film career and is now a painter.

Some contestants, however face grimmer futures: Janice Hansen, who competed as Miss New Jersey in 1944 but lost, was later suspected of being a Mafia drug courier. Her body was found in 1958, riddled with bullets.

FOURTEEN COMMON AND UNCOMMON WAYS WOMEN HAVE SUFFERED FOR BEAUTY

1. **Bound Feet:** In pre-Communist China, girl's feet were bound in infancy to inhibit their growth. Foot muscles and bones became so mutilated that walking was an excruciating process. Helpless, tiny-footed women were considered a sign of a family's wealth.
2. **Corsets:** Often stiffened with whalebone, corsets helped many nineteenth century Scarlett O'Haras achieve seventeen-inch waistlines. The most beauty conscious women even slept in their tightly laced cinchers.
3. **Dazzling Smiles:** The Mayans of Mexico filed their teeth into points and inlaid them with jewels.
4. **Decorative Scars:** Peoples of equatorial Africa adorned their scantily-clad bodies with scars. Even in recent times, many Africans were scarred to indicate tribe or clan membership.
5. **Elongated Lips:** Beginning at age four, women of central Africa's Saras-Djinges tribe had their lips stretched with wooden discs. Eventually, their lips became large enough to accommodate fourteen-inch soup plates. The women could consume only liquids and were barely able to talk.
6. **Hair Rollers:** First popular during the 1950s, hair rollers produced headaches and scalp indentations when slept on overnight. But worse than the pain were the snide remarks heard from men when rollers were worn to the grocery store.
7. **Hoopskirts:** This fashion was not made for the incautious woman. The wooden hoop which held wide a woman's skirt could fly up and break her nose if she sat down too quickly.
8. **Pierced Ears:** Ears were originally pierced to let the demons out of one's head. Today, the purpose is decorative and the process is relatively painless — unless a woman tries to do the job herself with painful self-piercers, designed to slowly poke their way through the wearer's ear lobes.
9. **Re-shaped Heads:** The heads of women from the Congo's Mangbettu tribe were tightly bound during childhood to achieve an elongated shape. The Mayans tied boards to their children's heads to flatten them. During the heyday of the powdered wig in France, girls' heads were laced to form ridges upon which wigs could rest.
10. **Silicone Injections:** Under-endowed women of the 1960s hailed liquid silicone as salvation from a lifetime of 32-A padded bras. But their problems increased more than their bust measurements when the silicone began to solidify and travel through the body, threatening infection, gangrene, and odd lumps in areas that would have been better off flat.

Plate-lipped women of central Africa were thought very beautiful by their tribesmen.

11. **Starvation Diets.**

12. **Stretched Necks:** The Burmese piled brass or iron rings — each about one-inch thick — around girls' necks. Eventually, necks reached lengths of up to fourteen inches.

13. **Tatoos:** Though most frequently associated with drunken sailors, tatoos have been popular among witches and women of the sixties counterculture. More painful than getting a tatoo is trying to get rid of it. Most methods involve surgery or skin planing, and usually leave a scar.

14. **Unsteady Stilts:** Stiletto heels and the platform sandals which succeeded them were not intended for women who had to run for the bus. If they tried anyway, a sprained or broken ankle was the frequent result.

WHAT PRICE BEAUTY?

If given the choice, most women would opt for a longer (or shorter) nose, a larger (or smaller) bust, a more (or less) prominent chin. Though the majority still settle for making the best of what nature gave them, more and more women are considering cosmetic surgery to remedy facial and figure flaws.

Cosmetic surgery, the correction of minor abnormalities, and reconstructive surgery, the correction of major birth defects or injuries, are both varieties of plastic surgery. Both were practised as far back as 600 B.C. by the Hindus, without the modern comfort of anesthesia.

Cosmetic surgery is still far from painless, and recovery periods can stretch to as long as six months. The high cost of most procedures can add to the patient's discomfort.

Medical experts also caution that cosmetic surgery will not give a woman a new face — or a new life. She will remain herself, with a slightly smaller nose or a few less wrinkles. As one woman who had just had a face lift put it, "If you looked like Phyllis Diller, you're not going to wind up like Shirley Temple."

The same problems the patient took with her into surgery will be waiting for her when the anesthetic clears. Her husband will not love her more, and her friends will not treat her differently, simply because of an operation.

Doctors suggest that the best cosmetic surgery patient is the woman who wants to feel better about herself, not the woman who wants to change herself to please others. Some people, they say, may be better off seeking psychotherapy than cosmetic surgery.

If you think cosmetic surgery is for you, the first step is to find a reputable and sympathetic physician. Your own family doctor, or a friend who has had a similar operation, may be able to provide the names of several good plastic surgeons. You might also check with a nearby medical school to see whether they have a department specializing in cosmetic surgery.

Good cosmetic surgeons have long preliminary sessions with each patient to discuss what surgery, if any, needs to be done. Be sure to express yourself clearly during this discussion. It often helps to bring along written notes and pictures to help explain what you want. Insist that the physician describe the medical procedure he or she plans to use; be sure to find out the total cost of the surgery, the length of the recovery period, and the results you can expect.

Feel free to change your mind if the consultation raises second thoughts about the surgery. If the doctor gives you "bad vibes" or tries to talk you out of the operation, you are perfectly justified in obtaining a second opinion. (Remember that you will be charged for each consultation.)

Cosmetic surgery is excluded from most medical insurance plans, unless it is medically necessary.

Some of the most popular kinds of cosmetic surgery are:

The *total face lift,* which can remove up to about ten years from a woman's visual age, has become the "did she or didn't she" of the 1970s. Sagging skin on the face, chin, and jowls is pulled taut, and the excess removed. The edges of the skin are then stitched at the hairline so that the scars are hidden. The total face lift requires about four hours of surgery, a week of hospitalization, and another month of recovery at home. Cost of the surgery averages $1,000 to $4,000 depending on the physician and area of the country. The patient is usually ready for a repeat operation five to ten years later.

A cheaper, simpler, and less dramatic

procedure is the *mini face lift,* sometimes performed by the surgeon in his office. The surgery lifts the lower part of the face; usually only slight improvement is noted in the eye area and forehead.

Superficial chemosurgery has recently been used in the fight against wrinkles. In this procedure, caustic agents are applied to the skin to burn away its wrinkled upper layers. This must be done only by a doctor expert in the technique. Newly-treated skin must be handled gently and kept out of harsh sunlight. Only some people benefit from chemosurgery, and improvement may be evident for no more than a few months.

Blepharoplasty is the procedure used to correct eye wrinkles and reduce bags. Separate operations exist for upper and lower lids, each of which requires about one and one-half hours of surgery. Often, both procedures are performed at once. The patient is usually home from the hospital in three days, and swelling subsides by two weeks after surgery. The cost of a blepharoplasty on both upper and lower lids ranges from $750 to $1,500. The operation seldom needs to be repeated since the skin on the upper part of the face stretches less than the cheeks and jowls.

One of the most popular cosmetic surgery procedures for younger women is *rhinoplasty,* better known as a "nose job." The operation can reduce or reshape the nose and correct broken capillaries near the surface of the skin. A five- to six-day hospital stay is usually required. Most swelling and bruising disappears in two weeks, though the nose is not completely "settled" until six months after surgery. The surgery is seldom performed on persons under sixteen because the nose has not yet reached its adult size and shape. The cost of a rhinoplasty ranges from $750 to $2,000.

A flabby chinline can be corrected with a *submandibular lipectomy,* often done along with a total face lift. The incision is made along natural skin folds so that scars are hardly visible.

Mammoplasty is a general term for operations which reduce or increase breast size. Augmentation is the simpler and more popular of the two; more than 100,000 such operations were performed in the United States between 1965 and 1975. The procedure involves the insertion of a silicone pouch beneath the breast to push it outward. There is little scarring and the breast looks and feels normal afterward.

Reduction mammoplasty, a costlier and more involved procedure, corrects overlarge, sagging, and asymmetrical breasts by removing excess fatty tissue. Doctors frequently recommend reduction surgery to relieve the strain on supportive muscles and bone structure caused by excessively heavy breasts.

Women are usually discouraged from undergoing mammoplasty until age twenty, when breasts have stopped developing. Operations range in length from four to six hours, after which a one- to two-week hospital stay is required. A breast augmentation operation averages $1,000 to $2,000, and a reduction $1,200 to $2,500. Mammoplasty patients are no more likely than other women to contract breast cancer and have no greater difficulty in breast feeding.

Other surgical procedures can reduce the size of stomachs, arms, and thighs. But the long-range success of such operations depends on dieting and exercise.

The stomach reduction operation removes fatty tissues by horizontal incisions across the abdomen in folds of skin or below the bikini line. The operation is performed most frequently after pregnancy or extensive weight loss. A one-week hospital stay is normally required.

Operations to remove fat from arms and thighs vary in success. Incisions are made on the insides of limbs so scars are not as noticeable. (Heavy ankles cannot be helped by the procedure.) One to two weeks in the hospital is typical.

Dermabrasion, or skin planing, is a nonsurgical technique used to improve the appearance of scarred and pitted skin. The skin is anesthetized and the upper layers removed with a rapidly rotating brush. Within a day or two swelling and crusting develop. The crusts are shed in about two weeks. Skin begins to look normal from six weeks to six months later. Dermabrasion is most often performed in the doctor's office, though patients are occasionally hospitalized. Costs vary, depending upon the severity of the problem and the area of skin to be treated.

Scholars

THE EDUCATED AMERICAN WOMAN

The 1970's have seen a tremendous boom in the educational opportunities open to women in this country, thanks to the women's movement and subsequent anti-discriminatory legislation.

In 1900, only 9 percent of women high school graduates graduated from college; today that figure is 25 percent. Women cadets march with their male colleagues at West Point, 18 percent of today's medical students and 22 percent of first-year law students are women — thirteen women received Rhodes scholarships in 1975, the first time in the seventy five-year history of the famous scholarships that any woman has received one.

Clearly, a heady time for women students and scholars is at hand. Never have so many women been free to pursue so wide a variety of educational goals, from traditionally female service jobs like teaching and social work to the previously all-male pursuits of law, medicine, and college teaching.

Ironically, recent successes tend to blur the bleak history of women's educational efforts in this country. In the Dutch colonies in the New York area in the seventeenth and eighteenth centuries, 60 percent of the women were illiterate. And in Puritan New England, 40 percent of the women were unable to write their own names.

Poet Anne Bradstreet, who lived in the Massachusetts Bay Colony, wrote in 1650: "For such despite they cast on female wits. If what I do prove well, it won't advance, They'l say its stoln, or else it was by chance."

Education was at the bottom of the priority list for American girls in the colonies. While boys were often sent to public schools or had private tutors, girls were taught at "mother's knee" the tasks of domesticity: sewing, cooking, cleaning, and child care. An educated woman was considered a threat to a tranquil home and a well-run family. People were seriously concerned that women with schooling would stop having children and would abandon their household duties.

Interestingly, it was the Protestant religion, conservative in the area of women's education, that gave the first big boost to women's literacy by urging mothers to learn to read so they could read the Bible to their children. During the nineteenth century, several European countries mandated some education for girls.

But such encouragement hardly opened the floodgates for women in America. While the Pilgrims opened a school for boys in 1635, less than twenty years after landing in this country, girls in the colonies were dependent on the whims of kindly fathers, brothers, or uncles to help them with their alphabet and sums, or they went to dame schools. Though often heralded as early coeducational schools for children, dame schools seem to have been little more than glorified day care centers, where a poor woman earned some money and taught what little she knew to her charges.

Things loosened up somewhat after the Revolutionary War, and girls were occasionally allowed to use boys' classrooms.

Natural affinity for children — and willingness to accept low pay — won woman teaching jobs.

Bachelor's Degrees Conferred, by Sex and Field of Study

Source: **National Center for Education Statistics, U.S. Dept. of Health, Education and Welfare.**

Field of study	1947-48[1]			1964-65			1973-74		
	Men	Women	Percent Women	Men	Women	Percent Women	Men	Women	Percent Women
Agriculture	5,225	177	3.3	5,026	168	3.2	14,684	1,569	9.6
Anthropology	79	89	52.9	598	605	50.3	2,669	3,323	55.5
Architecture	943	131	12.2	558	50	8.2	4,215	298	6.6
Biology	4,294	2,445	36.3	10,293	5,258	33.8	24,661	11,527	31.8
Business and commerce	32,260	6,111	15.9	54,925	5,067	8.4	28,381	4,281	13.1
Chemistry	5,361	2,068	27.8	8,106	1,931	19.2	8,287	2,070	20.0
Computer sciences	—	—	—	63	4	6.0	3,976	780	16.4
Economics	7,684	1,318	14.6	9,836	1,039	9.5	12,205	2,080	14.6
Education	8,393	21,301	71.7	27,900	90,634	76.5	49,141	136,040	73.5
Engineering	30,905	191	0.6	34,743	125	0.4	49,490	796	1.6
English	4,392	8,222	65.2	12,360	23,823	65.8	16,650	29,682	64.1
Fine arts	967	2,689	73.5	2,149	2,292	51.6	1,765	3,108	63.8
Foreign languages	1,197	3,044	71.7	4,154	9,937	70.5	4,529	14,311	76.0
History	5,669	3,576	38.7	16,824	9,030	34.9	24,660	12,389	33.4
Home economics	97	7,204	98.7	109	5,099	97.9	553	14,783	96.4
Journalism	2,016	1,334	39.8	1,615	1,112	40.8	3,641	3,069	45.7
Library science	417	1,194	74.1	49	574	92.1	86	1,078	92.6
Mathematics	2,619	1,647	38.6	12,858	6,398	33.2	12,791	8,844	20.0
Music	1,766	3,518	66.6	1,417	1,966	58.1	3,549	4,316	54.8
Nursing	27	3,324	99.9	77	7,658	99.0	750	18,535	96.1
Philosophy	1,397	329	19.1	2,106	606	28.7	4,383	1,408	24.3
Physical education	3,174	2,042	39.1	8,070	4,636	36.5	15,979	11,744	42.4
Physics	1,962	164	7.7	4,679	245	4.9	3,600	326	8.3
Political science	3,727	1,147	23.5	10,654	3,035	22.2	24,594	6,150	20.0
Psychology	2,808	3,594	56.1	8,688	6,033	40.9	25,705	26,116	50.4
Religion and theology	2,990	980	24.7	2,407	1,204	33.3	3,027	1,191	28.2
Sociology	1,787	4,484	71.5	5,123	7,773	60.3	15,199	20,292	57.2
Speech and Dramatic arts	826	1,662	66.8	2,016	2,873	58.8	2,299	3,098	57.4

[1]In addition to B.S. and B.A. degrees, also includes first professional degrees.

New World Experiments

By the 1830s, most states offered primary school education to girls. There were several experiments with secondary education for girls, but they often ran into a wall of male prejudice. A girls' high school was opened in Boston in 1826 and was so popular that the town fathers closed it down two years later, claiming it was an "alarming success."

But a number of canny women succeeded in surmounting male opposition and opened their own schools for girls. In 1821, Emma Willard opened the Troy Female Seminary, now called the Emma Willard School, and in 1828 Catharine and Harriet Beecher opened the Hartford Female Seminary.

The latter resorted to subterfuge to be allowed to teach substantial academic subjects. To explain instruction in chemistry and mathematics, the Beechers told worried parents that knowledge of the subjects was necessary to good cooking and home management.

Mary Lyon mapped out a careful dip-

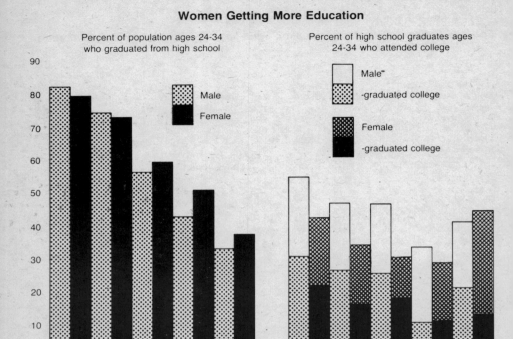

Women Getting More Education

Percent of population ages 24-34
who graduated from high school

Percent of high school graduates ages
24-34 who attended college

Adapted from U.S. Census Bureau data.

lomatic course in seeking approval for the Mount Holyoke Female Seminary in 1834:

"It is desirable," she wrote, "that the plans relating to the subject should not seem to originate with us, but with benevolent gentlemen. If the object should excite attention there is danger that many good men will fear the effect on society of so much female influence and what they will call female greatness."

In addition to these enterprising educators, certain religions sects, particularly the Quakers and Moravians, believed in education for women.

As the idea of women's education slowly gained acceptance, so did the idea of women as educators. They were encouraged to teach because of their alleged affinity with children. And, because men refused to accept teaching jobs in the deso-

late prairie states, where the pay was poor and living conditions often worse, women were hired in those areas.

Women also moved into nursing jobs — nursing schools were opened in New York City, New Haven, and Boston in the late nineteenth century. Mary Seymour, in 1879, and Katharine Gibbs, in 1911, opened secretarial schools to train women for the burgeoning businesses of the day.

If it was difficult to persuade parents to allow their daughters a primary and high school education, it was next to impossible to convince them of a daughter's need for a college education.

Women Enter College

Feminist Lucy Stone paid her own way at Oberlin College, Ohio, until her father, who had paid for the college educations of her brothers, was convinced she was serious about her education and gave her financial help.

Before the Civil War, Oberlin and Antioch colleges, both in Ohio, were the only ones to allow women to matriculate, but women were offered a special program, separate from the men.

In 1862, the Morrill Land Act improved the situation somewhat. It established land grant colleges that accepted anyone who could pay, including women.

The increase in educational opportunities open to women continued into the twentieth century, with the founding of women's colleges and coeducational universities.

But women still faced conflict in pursuing educational and career plans. The problem was two-pronged. First, there was real discrimination against women who were professionally competitive with men. These women also had to cope with the practical logistics of juggling a career and a home life.

More subtle was the prejudice against intelligent and ambitious women. Educated women were stereotyped as owl-eyed, unattractive bookworms, pushy, and badly dressed. Femininity, grace, and wit were the provinces of the bubbly coed, whose dates were more important than her studies, and whose goal was to find a husband and have children. Educated women were seen as anti-family.

The feeling that a woman's primary role was that of a wife and mother was reflected in discriminatory educational and business policies against women. These laws have only recently been challenged by new laws and court cases.

New Rights

In 1972, educational amendments to the 1963 Equal Pay Act prohibited discrimination in admissions policies to any federally assisted educational program. Undergraduate institutions are exempted from the law — all-male or all-female colleges do not have to become co-educational — but graduate programs must open equally to both sexes. Consequently, the number of women enrolled in graduate law, medicine, allied health and technological fields, business, and

theological schools has increased substantially. Also mandated in the amendments was the guarantee of equal pay for equal work in educational institutions.

Federal law forbids discrimination in employment by any holder of federal contracts. Under this provision, the Women's Equity Action League has brought class action suits against 250 colleges and universities for allegedly discriminatory practices.

The Women's Education Equity Act of 1974 may have the most far-reaching effects. The act provides funding for studies of educational conditions for women, workshops, and a central bank for women's educational information. It also calls for model programs in career preparation and more opportunities for unemployed and underemployed women.

The results have been dramatic. Women comprised 35 percent of the enrollment at Columbia University's business school in 1976, compared with only 5 percent in 1970. The entering business school class at Stanford in 1974 was 20 percent women. One third of the nation's medical students are likely to be women by 1986, compared with 18 percent in 1976, according to a medical school survey. A 1974 survey of college freshmen at over three hundred colleges in the United States found that 17 percent of the women planned careers in busines, engineering, law, or medicine — a 300 percent increase from 1964.

Discrimination is still in evidence, however. The Department of Health, Education and Welfare reported in March 1977, that two thirds of the nation's schools and colleges failed to meet legal requirements for banning sex discrimination.

In higher education fields, women comprise only 8 percent of full professorial appointments of religious and community colleges, and only 2 percent of appointments in the most prestigious universities.

Clark Kerr of the Carnegie Commission on Higher Education has estimated that it will take until the year 2000 or beyond to achieve a balance of men, women, and minorities in the educational institutions.

But professionals monitoring the increase of women's educational opportunities are optimistic. Patricia McGrath, a Worldwatch Institute researcher who studies the education of women wrote,

"Many obstacles remain to be overcome. Yet on the basis of the gains that have already been made, it seems fair to predict that equal education for women will shape the future, perhaps profoundly, for men as well as women . . . the doors now opening will never be closed again."

WHICH SEX IS SMARTER?

The provocative question of which sex is smarter has happily become obsolete. Studies show that while women's achievement declines after the age of nine, their "negative growth" is due to social conditioning rather than to less brain power.

Society has traditionally encouraged girls to be obedient and passive — qualities that work against intellectual questioning. Women were discouraged from competing — ambition was frowned on. While women were expected to get good grades, they weren't supposed to concentrate on education at the expense of their more important goal of marrying and raising a family.

A recent study by the National Assessment of Educational Progress (NAEP) found that although the performance levels of men and women in most academic areas was similar, performance levels for women decreased as they got older, while men's educational performance increased. This has been labeled as "negative growth" and "positive growth," respectively.

Most dramatic are the disparate achievements in math. Up to the fourth grade, girls are as good at math as boys, according to another NAEP study. But at adulthood, women experience a drop in their performance level while men's performance has increased.

Even traditionally feminine subjects like writing, reading, literature, and music reflect women's "negative growth." According to the NAEP, girls at age nine perform on a higher level than boys, but again, by the time they have reached adulthood, women have declined in the performance level while men have bettered their skills.

The Pressure to Fail

"The immorality of these sex differences," wrote Prof. John Ernest in a 1976 University of California study on math performance, "lies precisely in the fact that they are the result of many subtle and not so subtle forces, restrictions, stereotypes, sex roles and parental-teacher-peer group attitudes."

Matina Horner, president of Radcliffe College, studied the "negative growth" of women, and thinks it is a result of women's "motivation to avoid success." She claims that many women fear that being too smart and ambitious will render them unfeminine and unfit in the traditional roles of wives and mothers. As a result, they develop many anxieties and unconsciously underachieve to avoid the stigma of independence.

Fortunately, younger women — products of the feminist movement of this decade — are less afraid of success, and are equaling and surpassing men academically.

WOMEN'S COLLEGES

The names Barnard, Radcliffe, Bryn Mawr, Vassar, and Smith carry prestige and clout among Americans. Gloria Steinem and Betty Friedan of Smith College, Margaret Mead of Barnard, and Katharine Hepburn of Bryn Mawr all attest to the high caliber education offered to women at all-female colleges. These women's colleges are respected equally with the traditionally male colleges and universities like Yale, Harvard, and Princeton.

But such respect is a relatively recent phenomenon. For years, women's colleges were luxuries for daughters of the wealthy, and the concept of education for women was treated with skepticism, at best.

Indeed, when ambitious female educators started their schools for women in the nineteenth century, they used the words seminary or academy rather than the bold appellation "college," which would have been considered presumptuous for a womens' school. Further, teaching "male" subjects like math required subterfuge by women educators, lest parents feel their daughters were being dangerously over-educated.

Emma Willard opened the first all-female school in 1821. Her school, the Troy Female Seminary, offered the ad-

Barnard's Class of 1910: The feminist movement has brought new life to women's colleges.

vanced curriculum that previously had been available only at men's schools.

More women's colleges were founded as the century continued, until by 1870, six out of seven female college students attended women's colleges. The most famous, eventually called the "seven sisters," were Vassar (1861), Smith (1875), Wellesley (1875), Bryn Mawr (1885), Radcliffe (1879), Mount Holyoke (1888), and Barnard (1889).

Women's Colleges Today

During the freewheeling 1960s, enrollments at women's colleges dropped as women sought coeducational colleges or universities. Women's colleges, created to fill an educational void for women, were thought to be obsolete. Between 1960 and 1972, about half the women's colleges in existence became coeducational or were closed. By 1972, the number of women's colleges had been reduced from 185 to 73, and accounted for less than 10 percent of female college students.

But with the femininism of the 1970s came a resurgence of interest in single sex women's colleges. Although women now had other educational options, women's colleges offered a haven from traditional male/female roles, and women were thought to be freer in their educational pursuits.

Proponents of women's colleges claim that women are less reluctant to display knowledge in the all-female atmosphere, and have no fears of losing their femininity. Also, they have more opportunity to assume leadership roles without having to compete with men. A number of studies have shown that the performance of women at all-girls schools has exceeded that of those at coed schools.

On the other hand, some argue that coeducational schools are more like the "real world," and that women's activities at single sex schools are too passive.

Some women's colleges, and all-male colleges too, are seeking the best of both alternatives by maintaining their autonomy but participating in inter-college arrangements, where students can take courses at a number of neighboring schools. Wellesley shares a cross-registration program with the Massachusetts Institute of Technology, and Smith, Mount Holyoke, Amherst, the University of Massachusetts, and Hampshire College have a Five College Conference system of busing and cross-registration.

Whatever the reasons, enrollment at all-female schools is once again rising, according to recent studies.

Said a former student council president of Bryn Mawr, which has a "brother" relationship with neighboring Haverford College: "We are not Haverford coeds.

We can live a quiet, single-sex life or choose a coeducational environment. It reduces academic tension and encourages a meeting of minds on an equal basis. It would be ludicrous to lose this."

SORORITY ROW: ALIVE AND GROWING

Historically, sororities have had two distinct images. Sororities have been fun, solid social units with charitable intentions, or they have been inane and often discriminatory cliques.

Both images have held sway at different periods in the one-hundred-year history of college sororities in the United States. Modeled on college fraternities in the middle nineteenth century, sororities began as literary societies as groups of women tried to circumvent the restrictive social policies of their colleges.

As they evolved, turning into active social clubs, associated with fresh-faced girls, pony tails, convertibles, and fraternity pins, sororities came to monopolize the social life of many college campuses. Still, some colleges, like Barnard and Mount Holyoke, abolished them.

Where they were active, sororities served many functions. On a large, impersonal university campus, they offered a small compatible unit of friends to young women who otherwise might feel quite lonely. They also participated in charitable functions in addition to their social activities.

During the 1960s, sororities and fraternities became an endangered species. Women and men working for the causes of the decade often felt their social clubs were frivolous.

Changing life-styles, increased dormitory facilities, coeducational dormitories, and off-campus privileges provided attractive options to the sorority as a home away from home. In 1969, sororities at Northwestern University (Illinois) accepted nonmembers in residence, just to keep the houses open.

The decrease in sorority membership continued into the early 1970s, until the pendulum began to slowly swing back toward tradition. The ranks of sororities began to grow again. In 1975, for the first time in eight years, there was an increase (3.5 percent) in college sorority membership.

There is no country-wide pattern to participation in the Greek letter societies. Percentages of women in sororities range from 45 percent at Duke University to 1 percent at the University of North Carolina, with 5 to 9 percent membership at Indiana State University, University of California at Los Angeles, University of Wisconsin, and the University of Tennessee. Many colleges, especially in the northeast, have no sororities at all.

The stereotype of a sorority member as a bubbly, but brainless, rah-rah girl is hard to crack. Nevertheless, many of today's prominent American women have been sorority members. They include:

Alpha Chi Omega: Jean Saubert, Olympic medalist; Georgia Anne Geyer, newspaper columnist; Jane Jayroe, Miss America; Dr. Irene Carswell Peden, Antarctic researcher.

Alpha Omicron Pi: Margaret Bourke-White, photographer.

Kappa Alpha Theta: Agnes DeMille, dancer/choreographer; Nancy Hanks, head, National Endowment for the Arts; Marlo Thomas, actress; Joan Ganz Cooney, children's television innovator; Mary Louise Smith, former Republican Party chairperson.

Kappa Kappa Gamma: Jane Pauley, "Today" hostess; Kate Jackson, actress; Jane Blalock, golfer; Candice Bergen, actress/photographer; Nancy Dickerson, television newswoman.

Zeta Tau Alpha: Virginia Knauer, consumer advocate; Phyllis George, Miss America/television sports commentator; Lynda Johnson Robb, magazine editor.

Other prominent sorority women are Georgia O'Keeffe, painter, Kappa Delta; Pearl Buck, author, Kappa Delta; Margaret Chase Smith, former U.S. senator from Maine, Sigma Kappa; Joyce Carol Oates, author, Phi Mu; Sylvia Porter, financial writer, Phi Sigma Sigma.

Also, Cloris Leachman, actress, Gamma Phi Beta; Eva Marie Saint, actress, Delta Gamma; Carol Lawrence, entertainer, Alpha Xi Delta; Frances Neff, former treasurer of the U.S., Alpha Delta Pi; Sandra Palmer, golfer, Alpha Delta Pi; Dr. Ruth Patrick, environmental scientist, Alpha Xi Delta.

And Dr. Jane A. Hall, first woman recipient of Atomic Energy Citation, Alpha Gamma Delta; Frances Willard, Temperance crusader, Alpha Phi; Claire C. Weintraub, originator of Mother's March on Polio, Delta Phi Epsilon; Charlotte Reid, Federal Communications Commissioner, Gamma Phi Beta; Cynthia Clark Wedel, president of National Council of Churches and first woman elected to World Council of Churches, Kappa Delta.

WOMEN'S STUDIES GROW

Most people remember studying about Florence Nightingale, Susan B. Anthony and Madame Curie in their school days. Joan of Arc, Amelia Earhart, and perhaps Louisa May Alcott were also familiar names. But these women's lives and works were usually treated as sidelights to historical events that were conducted by men.

But the feminist movement of recent years has turned the tables and stirred an interest in women's history and an attempt to recover the neglected past of women in the United States.

The interest has sparked, in a time of budget cuts in all areas of education, a proliferation of women's studies programs in American colleges. Women's studies, during the 1973/74 academic year, numbered forty-six hundred courses in twenty-five hundred colleges and universities. The programs vary from single course offerings to part of an interdisciplinary studies program to a major course of study in itself.

The programs aim to explore women's participation in history, trace the history of sex roles, give women a sense of their own worth, and show them they can change society through collective effort.

"Women's studies," says Linda Gordon, historian at the University of Massachusetts, "is an attempt to transform the contemporary study of human life and culture by rescuing it from the culture of male supremacy."

In addition to exploring the history of women in our culture, many colleges aim courses at understanding and improving the role of today's women. Purdue University's "Span Plan" sponsors conferences for women to plan future roles for themselves, and offers financial aid to students' wives to start their own academic programs.

Claremont College in California has an internship program to train women in science and technology, and Mount Vernon College in Washington, D.C., has the same kind of work study program for public service and political careers.

Where the Action Is

Across the country, centralized collections of materials on women are being set up. Northwestern University and the University of Wyoming share a women's history research library begun in Berkeley, California.

Radcliffe's Schlesinger Library has one of the largest collections of source materials from the beginning of the nineteenth century to the present. Manuscript collections of individual women and publications of major women's organizations dating back to 1865 are part of the Sophia Smith Collection at Smith College.

Other important source materials for women's studies are at: Barnard College, New York; University of Kansas; Swarthmore College, Pennsylvania (Lucretia Mott collections); Scripps College, Claremont, California. (MacPherson collection, which has information of women's suffrage, history of domestic employment, and women in California); Tulane University, Louisiana, (women in medicine), and Bennett College, North Carolina (Afro-American women).

Major studies on women, presently under way, include research on women in American history (at Berkeley), and research on health careers for women, family planning, and career planning for women (at the Radcliffe Institute). The Radcliffe Institute has also published a three-volume Who's Who of American women, called *Notable American Women*. The Association of American Colleges published in 1975 a "Survey of Research Concerns on Women's Issues," which proposes areas of research and analysis in history, economics, sociology, psychology, and physiology.

Foundations and private industry have also gotten involved in women's studies. A Mount Holyoke College program to prepare women for high business positions has the backing of the Carnegie Corporation, Andrew Mellon Foundation, International Business Machines, General Motors Corporation, and Monsanto Fund.

The Lilly Fund gave Radcliffe $386,000 to spend two years preparing case studies on American women and their careers, and the Ford Foundation has sponsored college research projects on women's studies.

Despite recent developments, women's studies is still an undeveloped discipline. Large gaps exist in research in some areas, especially the sciences and social sciences. But it is one of the fastest growing subjects on all educational levels and, if handled with a minimum of exploitation and a sense of serious scholarship, could dramatically improve upon the traditionally male slant that has permeated almost all areas of learning for generations.

BACK TO SCHOOL

One of the biggest changes in the educational world in recent years is the number of older men and women going back to school. Housewives with school-age children, women who are suddenly self-supporting after many years of marriage, and retired men and women are returning to studies for fun, fulfillment, and profit.

An estimated 650,000 women have gone back to school in recent years. And colleges are welcoming them. Perhaps because of shrinking enrollments of younger students, colleges are offering varying curricula specifically for older students — two thousand schools across the country have fifty thousand courses for adults.

Older students tend to be shy about their abilities, feeling that their study skills are rusty after twenty years of nonacademic activity. But figures show that their performance excels that of younger students in almost all areas, as they are often more committed to their studies than younger students are, and can successfully integrate their life experiences into the learning process.

Psychologically, returning to school can be an invigorating experience. Charting a new life course, being exposed to new ideas, and meeting new friends is exciting and energizing.

Getting Started

But before a woman launches headlong into an expensive new educational career, she should consider some basic questions.

What are your educational goals: Preparation for a career, or a new career? Completing an unfinished degree? Interest in a particular subject?

If you are interested in a career, what kind of career, and will there be a market for your skills? (In the 1960s, mature women filled thousands of teaching vacancies as postwar babies flooded the school system. Today there are few vacancies for teachers.) Do you need a college degree, business or secretarial training, or vocational training of another kind? How quickly do you need a job? What are your present skills?

If you're not sure of all the answers, you might take a career workshop course, which helps you sift through your skills and interests to find a practical and fulfilling career.

You can check on the practicality of different careers through varying counseling services. Women's centers, community action programs, state employment services, the civil service commission, and the U.S. Labor Department's publication *Vocational Outlook* can all steer you toward a profitable career.

How to Do It

Next explore the schools that offer you what you want, comparing entrance requirements, course options, facilities, and expenses. Most schools will send you a free catalogue, or you can buy one of several comprehensive guides to colleges, junior colleges, and vocational schools.

Some returnees will need a "high school equivalency diploma," offered by state departments of education to persons nineteen and over. The diploma is given for passing general education development tests, which measure the ability to think and to reason rather than just factual information. Your local high school can give you information on this. Another route to high school and college diplomas is through programs offered on education television stations — for information, write to Manpower Education Institute, 450 Lexington Ave., N.Y., N.Y. 10017; Great Plains Institutional T.V., Library,

University of Nebraska, Lincoln, Neb. 68508 or to Dr. Catherine G. Nichols, College of Education, Arizona State University, Tempe, Ariz. 85281.

Similar to the high school equivalency test is the College Level Examination Plan (CLEP), which tests general education acquired in living and working. Passing the tests gives you college credits that can be applied toward a degree in more than thirteen hundred schools in the United States. Also available at some colleges are home-study courses and curricula for part-time students. For information on all these programs, write to the National University Extension Association, Suite 360, 1 Dupont Circle, N.W., Washington, D.C., 20036.

Other alternatives are designed especially for older students who must juggle their schoolwork with home and family responsibilities. "Repentant Dropouts" (Mundelein College, Chicago), "My Fair Lady Program" (Miami Dade Junior College, Miami), "Discovery Program" (City University, New York City), and "While You Were Away" (Syracuse University, Syracuse) are innovative programs that offer flexible work schedules for women returning to school.

Other courses of study are conducted outside of conventional classrooms. Supervised, independent study is the focus of the "Classroom without Walls" program at the University of Minnesota and "Open University" at the University of Maryland. Write to the National University Extension Association at the above address for further information.

Continuing education outside of degree programs can be found in seminars, workshops, short-term courses, and intersession weekends that are growing in popularity. They are conducted by libraries, adult schools, the YMCA, YWCA, and YWHA, as well as by colleges and universities.

More directly job-oriented than many college degree programs are vocational schools. About seven thousand private vocational and trade schools offer programs that can run anywhere from two weeks to three years, and train women for jobs in computer technology, medical and dental techniques, electronics and engineering, cooking, and other skills.

What Kind of School?

Before signing up for what sounds like an enticing course, check the accreditation of the school, because a certificate from a nonaccredited school will be useless to you in applying for a job. The Better Business Bureau, state employment services and offices of education, the Veteran's Administration of the National Association of Trade and Technical Schools, and the National Home Study Program are all sources for information about accredited vocational courses.

Vocational schools have long been the Cinderellas of the education world. But the federal government recently committed millions of dollars to a five-year program to upgrade the entire system of vocational education. Programs include grants for the disadvantaged, bilingual vocational education, and work/study programs. The program also provides for an "Office for Women" in every state, which is aimed at opening career possibilities to the unemployed, underemployed, and disadvantaged.

In addition to government-sponsored and privately-run vocational schools, private industry offers many training programs to train new employees and retrain other employees for higher positions. General Motors, Sperry-Rand, International Business Machines, Polaroid, and Eastman Kodak all have training programs. American Telephone and Telegraph has 139 standardized training programs.

Other places to look for vocational training are union apprenticeship programs, on-the-job work/study programs, and adult education programs at local high schools.

Money and Child Care

Older students, like their younger colleagues, must find money for their education, but they also often have the additional problem of getting child care. Although some communities offer good day care, and even some colleges have babysitters for faculty and student children, availability and quality of day care are erratic and require some ingenuity as well as money on the part of the back-to-school parent.

Financial aid, too, must be diligently

sought. Most readily available are guaranteed student loans. Individual colleges may reduce the tuition for older students, and in some cases tuition may be reduced in exchange for work at the college.

An additional source of funding is Clairol, which gives grants to women over thirty through the Business and Professional Women's Foundation. Clairol also offers free *"Educational Financial Aid Sources for Women"* from the Clairol Scholarship Program, 375 Park Avenue, New York, N.Y. 10022.

Some states aid adults who want to attend state universities. Some businesses and private companies underwrite courses for their employees, especially if courses will benefit an employee in her job.

Because of the variety of financial assistance available, be sure to check with the financial departments of the schools you are interested in to see what aid you might qualify for.

Returning to school to pursue an old dream or a new vocation can be a very stimulating experience. Older students sometimes work too hard at their studies, so education professionals recommend that they relax, avoid becoming overly grade conscious, and avoid dominating classroom discussion with too many insights based on past experiences. The older student's views can complement the class's topic, but it is important to know when to stop. Enjoying the experience is as important as the results of academic effort.

SCHOLARS AND SCHOOLMARMS

The history of women's education in this country is the story of dedicated and shrewd women who combined diplomacy with a sense of mission to prove that women were as bright as men, and as capable and deserving of a good education.

Willard: Women's Education Radical
Emma Hart Willard (1787-1870) was one of the first women educators to challenge traditional educational attitudes toward women. Founder of the Troy Female Seminary in 1821, she insisted on teaching women "nonornamental" courses, like math and science, and her school grad-

uated some of the first multi-disciplined women teachers in the country.

Born on a farm in Berlin, Connecticut, Willard was encouraged by her father to develop her intellect to the fullest, and gained from that atmosphere a thirst for knowledge and a passion to encourage other women to make use of the full range of their mental capacities.

She began teaching when she was seventeen; three years later, she was the preceptress of the Female Academy in Middlebury, Vermont. At twenty-two, she married an elderly widower, Dr. John Willard, and they had a son, John Hart Willard, a year later. Excluded from classes at the all-male Middlebury College, she became determined to provide women with a "male" education.

It wasn't until 1821, however, when Willard was thirty-four, that she was able to implement her plan with the founding of the Troy Female Seminary, a school to train women as teachers. The seminary, now called The Emma Willard School, was a model for girls' boarding schools. It offered instruction in traditional feminine subjects like deportment and baking, but also taught subjects previously offered only to men. The seminary's science course, for example, was more advanced than many similar courses at men's schools. Her school proved that girls can perform equally with boys when given equal opportunity.

Interestingly, she was not at all radical in other areas. Willard was not a feminist: she based her arguments for state support of female education on the proposition that women teachers could be paid less than men teachers. She did, however, advocate removing girls from factory work and training them as teachers.

Willard wrote a number of school textbooks and a journal, and published a volume of poems, in addition to her administrative work.

Lyon: Mount Holyoke's Founder
Mary Lyon (1797-1849) founded Mount Holyoke College in 1837.

Despite the fact that she was one of seven children in a poor Massachusetts family, Lyon received a solid and varied education, and started teaching when she was only fourteen. From then on, she al-

Mary Lyon feared too much "female greatness" would erode male support for her school.

ternated teaching with study. At twenty, she was accepted into the all-male Sanderson Academy, a privilege given to exceptionally bright young women, and continued her education at Amherst Academy and Byfield Female Seminary with subjects such as Latin, science, and history.

At age thirty-seven, after more than twenty years of teaching, she became convinced of the need of a permanent institution for women's education, and began a three-year lobbying campaign that resulted in the opening of Mount Holyoke Female Seminary with eighty students in South Hadley, Massachusetts.

The seminary's curriculum was a three-year program to train women as teachers and to instill in them a deep sense of Christianity. Many of the courses offered were part of the neighboring Amherst College curriculum, and the seminary enjoyed visiting lecturers from the Amherst faculty, as well as from preachers from all over New England. Seventy percent of the school's graduates of the first forty years taught at one time or another. Lyon was convinced that effec-

tive teacher training would improve the general educational system.

Lyon was shrewdly aware of the need to cater to her male benefactors. She guarded her institution and its students from any activities that would draw negative attention to them, lest the "benevolent gentlemen," on whom she relied, should accuse the seminary of too much "female influence" and "female greatness" and withdraw their support.

Mary Lyon was the principal of Mount Holyoke until her death.

Beecher: Crusading Educator
Catharine Beecher (1808-1878), the sister of Harriet Beecher Stowe, was a very successful crusader for training women as teachers, and was responsible for preparing numerous female teachers who taught in the West.

She was lucky to be born into a stimulating family; most of her education, which included philosophy and mathematics, was taught her at home. Her father, Lyman Beecher, a Yale Divinity School graduate and a successful preacher, was particularly close to his daughter and influential in her liberal education.

Imbued with the idea of education for women and the belief in their value as teachers (she felt women were innately better teachers than men), she opened the Hartford Female Seminary in 1823. In addition to teacher training, she introduced physical education and domestic science courses into her curriculum, both innovative concepts for women in the nineteenth century.

She wrote several books on domestic science, including *Treatise on Domestic Economy*, which explained how to systematize skills and stressed thrift, comfort, and harmony over elegance and fashion.

In 1832, she opened the Western Female Institute to train teachers for the vast reaches of the western United States. Through her own school, and organizations she set up throughout the country, thirty thousand teachers were trained for western schools. Her work led her to found the American Women's Educational Association.

In other areas, Beecher was more conservative. She opposed women's suffrage and believed women should not display themselves publicly — she always had a male relative accompany her on her business trips.

Thomas: Feminist and Educator

The president of Bryn Mawr College for twenty-eight years, Quaker **Martha Carey Thomas** (1857-1935) was an outspoken feminist who combined politics with activism.

"My one aim and concentrated purpose shall be and is to show that women can learn, can reason, can compete with men in the grand fields of literature, and science and conjecture . . . without having all [their] time engrossed by dress and society," she wrote in her diary.

Educated at Friends' schools and Cornell University, she pursued a Ph.D. degree at the University of Zurich because no graduate school in the United States would admit a woman. She graduated summa cum laude.

On her return, she got a job as dean and professor of English at Bryn Mawr. Ten years later, after much lobbying on her part, she was named president and for twenty-eight years advocated a rigorous academic curriculum for her students which allowed no free electives or vocational training.

A fiery speaker for women's suffrage, she believed that only one half of all women should marry and that all women should have careers. Called "triumphantly sexless" and "militarily individualistic," Thomas was an inspiring, opinionated educator.

Montessori: Child Education Pioneer

Although she was the first woman in Italy to receive a medical degree (in 1896), it was in the field of early childhood education that **Maria Montessori** (1870-1952) established an international reputation, founding the schools that bear her name.

As a young doctor working with "subnormal" children, Montessori found that stimulating educational programs, rather than medical treatment, were most successful in rehabilitating the children.

She perfected her "Montessori Method" in 1907, in a tenement section of Rome. She worked with normal children, ages three to seven, with no previous education and illiterate parents. As a result of her work, they learned to read and write

Daughter of slaves, Mary McLeod Bethune founded a college and influenced Franklin Roosevelt.

and progressed with ease to botany, mathematics, zoology, and geography.

The "Montessori Method" is designed to encourage the development of a child's initiative by allowing freedom of action; to improve sense perception through training; and to develop coordination through activity, exercise, and games. The teacher is a guide and supervisor rather than a director.

Although some claim her method is too rigid, Montessori precepts are the backbone of many preschools throughout the country. Her book, *The Montessori Method,* was published in English in 1912.

Bethune: Black Educator

Mary McLeod Bethune (1875-1955), black educator and administrator, devoted a lifetime to the improvement of the educational and vocational opportunities for black youth.

Bethune was born into a slave family, of which she was the first freeborn member. Her mother was from Africa, and Bethune was proud of her African heritage; she rejected the idea of black inferiority.

Educated in mission schools, she applied for missionary service but was twice rejected. Instead, she chose the teaching profession.

Following marriage to Albertus Bethune and the birth of a son, she moved to Florida, where, in 1904, she opened a school for the children of black families who worked for the wealthy whites living in the state's resorts. It was called the Daytona Educational and Industrial Training School for Negro Girls, and Bethune, by then widowed, was teacher, fund raiser, and construction foreman for the little school.

The school prospered, expanded, and in 1923 was joined with the Cookman Institute, a men's college. It is now called the Bethune-Cookman Institute, a junior college training teachers, homemakers, and Christian leaders. Bethune was president of the institute until 1942.

Bethune was an influential member of many organizations for black women. Former President Franklin D. Roosevelt appointed her a special assistant on minority affairs; and in 1936, she served as director of the Division of Negro Affairs of the National Youth Council. She also had a consulting position at the conference to draft a United Nations Charter.

Keller and Macy: Pioneers for the Handicapped

Helen Keller (1880-1968) was imprisoned in a dark, silent world when an illness left her blind and deaf at the age of eighteen months. Often taken for an idiot, she grew into a spoiled, willful child, frustrated by her total inability to communicate.

Enter **Anne Sullivan Macy** (1866-1936), a young teacher from an impoverished background whose own eyesight had been only partially restored through surgery. She believed that handicapped persons needed to develop their independence and should not be coddled out of pity. So she went to work on young Helen, teaching her manners, self-control, and self-reliance. She unlocked the child's prison by teaching her to understand words spelled out on her hand; the first word Helen understood was "water."

The two became inseparable and embarked on Keller's impressive academic career. Macy accompanied Keller to Radcliffe in 1900, serving as her companion and reader. Four years later, Keller graduated from Radcliffe *cum laude* with studies in Greek, Latin, German, French, and English.

Afterward, they went to live on a Massachusetts farm, though their worldwide

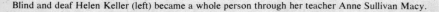

Blind and deaf Helen Keller (left) became a whole person through her teacher Anne Sullivan Macy.

travels to raise money for the blind and other causes frequently took them away from home.

Macy's eyes, which had grown steadily worse because of overuse, failed her totally in 1935. She died in 1936 after training another person to help her student.

Keller paid tribute to her friend in her book *Teacher:* "Anne Sullivan Macy was one of the pioneers in civilization for the blind and deaf. She saw the usefulness of whole souls in imperfect bodies."

Horner: Radcliffe Head

Matina Souretis Horner (1939-   ) was the youngest president in Radcliffe College's history when she was appointed in 1972 at the age of thirty-two.

A gifted child, she was encouraged academically by her father, a professor. She graduated from Bryn Mawr *cum laude* in 1961 after studying psychology, and married Joseph Horner, an engineering student. They went together to graduate school at the University of Michigan.

At Michigan, Horner developed her provocative "fear of success" theme, based on studies she did on motivation and achievement in women. The theory proposes that highly intelligent women fear that academic or business success will undermine their femininity, and that they will be criticized, rather than encouraged, for their ambition. Such women develop strong anxieties and unconsciously underachieve. Her work received wide acclaim and has been included in many women's courses.

Horner then taught at Harvard before being appointed Radcliffe's president. She foresees a time when Harvard and Radcliffe will merge, but wants to forestall the assimilation until attitudes toward women have changed and women are free of male dominance.

Sandler: Equal Education Activist

Bernice Sandler (1928-   ) is an activist working inside and outside the government to promote educational equality for women. After an impressive academic career as both a student and a teacher, Sandler was refused a faculty appointment at the University of Maryland in 1969 because, according to university officials, "she came on too strong for a woman."

At that time, sex discrimination lawsuits were rare, but after considerable legal research, Sandler invoked a provision of Executive Order 11246 that stipulated that organizations receiving federal funds, as did the University of Maryland, cannot discriminate.

Her case opened the floodgates for similar class action suits against 250 colleges and universities in the United States.

Sandler is a strong believer in the need for academic women to band together to protest sexual discrimination; she is a member of the Women's Equity Action League, founded in 1968 to fight for equality for academic women. WEAL is now involved in many other feminist issues as well.

Since her landmark case, she has been involved in many other pro-women activities. She presided over the President's Advisory Council on Women's Education Programs, which oversees the Women's Educational Equity Act. She is director of the Association of American Colleges Project on the Status and Education of Women and also served on the Advisory Committee on the Economic Role of Women of the President's Council of Economic Advisers.

Mattfield: Ivy League First Lady

Jacquelyn Mattfield (1925-   ) is a strong proponent of all-female colleges, and, as president of Barnard, since 1976, she has dedicated herself to keeping the college autonomous from Columbia University, the brother college that is seeking to assimilate it.

Mattfield has an impressive track record of teaching and administrative jobs at prestigious eastern colleges, including her recent job as professor of music, associate provost, and dean of academic affairs at Brown University.

Her aim at Barnard is to sustain the high quality of education offered at the college and keep the present percentage of women faculty members at the college. Women's colleges have *30 to 60 percent* women professors, compared with 3 to 10 percent women faculty members at other colleges. She has challenged the "wisdom of dissolving the very faculties where women still have the highest probability of being offered regular appointments and tenure."

PER SONS
M̶E̶N̶
WORKI

Workers

WORKING WOMEN IN AMERICA

"A caress is better than a career," American theatrical agent Elizabeth Marbury wrote in her book, *Careers for Women,* in the late 1800s. Many still argue that a woman is happier when she chooses the caress.

Frontier women never faced such a choice. They had to work hard to survive, and their work was as important as the men's. No one was idle: women spun yarn, wove cloth, made soap and candles, gardened, tended animals, cooked, and produced a large enough family to assure a continued labor supply. The early rural economy was, for most families, hand-to-mouth, and men and women both worked long, hard hours to produce all they needed. For most rural families, any income — through the sale of crops, animals, or craft items — was often the result of shared labor between the husband and the wife.

Colonial women followed the work patterns of the Indian women whose lands they gradually occupied. Indian women, too, took care of all household needs, and in addition wove baskets, made pottery, dressed animal skins, fished, trapped small animals and birds, gathered nuts and berries, and irrigated the land. Some Indian women among the Prairie tribes even built their own homes: they assembled tipis or molded earth-and-thatch dwellings.

Even for those colonialists in settled areas, most businesses were family-operated, and located in or near the home. Money earned was used to support the household and keep the business running. "Mom-and-Pop" operations were common, with women sharing equally in the work and the rewards, although married women were also required to continue caring for the house and children. Women who had paying jobs were often widows who had inherited businesses from their husbands: some kept inns, ran farms, published books or newspapers, and managed retail businesses. Others worked out of their homes as seamstresses, milliners, or midwives.

One woman who earned money at home, **Eliza Lucas Pinckney,** supervised her father's South Carolina plantation whenever he went off to fulfill his duties as an army colonel. In 1744, at age twenty-one, she introduced the cultivation of indigo, a blue dye, to America. This was an important venture for it meant that the colonies no longer had to depend on imported dye from the French West Indies. On Nantucket Island, seventy women took care of business matters when their husbands went to sea.

Woman Indentured Servants

Women working with the blessings of their husbands often fared better than unmarried women who, in the 1700s, were limited to jobs such as wet nurse, dairymaid, governess, or cook. Ironically, this situation was to reverse itself in the 1800s, when it became more acceptable for single women to work. Not all women, of course, worked out of choice. Those who had come to the colonies as indentured servants were forced to work for nothing, either to pay off the cost of their voyage from England or as punishment for some crime. They could not quit until their contract expired, usually a period of seven years. Newspapers of the mid-1700s were filled with ads in search of information about indentured servants who had run away. Black women brought

Frontier women worked long hours spinning . . . cooking . . . gardening . . . producing large families.

Matchmakers, 1871: The first to leave the hearth for work were young, unmarried women.

to the colonies as slaves worked in the fields side-by-side with black men, or in the "master's" house.

The first women to leave the hearth in large numbers were the young single daughters of New England farm families, who were paid by the textile factories to do the same sewing, spinning, and weaving they had done for nothing at home. By 1811, these mills employed 3,500 women and children, and 500 men. Although the pay was low and the hours long, conditions were, in the beginning at least, not as bad as they were later to become. Factory work gave young women a taste of freedom. They usually lived away from their families in carefully supervised rooming houses provided by the mills.

Harriet Hanson Robinson, who began working in 1835, at age ten, in a mill in Lowell, Massachusetts, wrote that she worked from 5 a.m. to 7 p.m., with half an hour for breakfast and dinner. After room and board was deducted from her pay, she earned two dollars a week.

Men and women were usually assigned different kinds of work in these factories, but in the few cases where work overlapped, men always earned more. In 1837, suffragist Sarah Grimké wrote, ". . . in tailoring, a man has twice or three times as much for making a waistcoat or pantaloons as a woman, although the work done by each may be equally good."

In 1834, more than 1,200 of the mill women in Lowell, Massachusetts, went on strike to protest a salary cut. It was one of the first organized labor protests in the United States. After a march and a few speeches, however, they returned to their jobs. The strikers lacked the organization, the financial support, and the will they needed to have any real effect. This impotence soon grew worse.

By 1840, new waves of married immigrant women, most of them Irish and French-Canadian, began competing for available jobs. As the labor supply rose, wages fell, and conditions deteriorated. Factory bosses had little respect for the married "foreigners" they hired; sexual advances were not uncommon. In addition to a plentiful supply of cheap labor, an important new mechanical discovery also changed the face of the textile industry.

Sweat Shops Open

Shortly before the Civil War, Isaac Singer invented the foot treadle for sewing machines; he quickly sold six million of these new machines, most of them to factories. Jobs became more mechanized, and the noise in factories was often deafening. Hundreds of women were jammed into stifling rooms and were divided into competing teams controlled by a male supervisor called a "sweater." As the women left work each day, they filed past a guard with their pocketbooks open to prove they weren't stealing any thread. Many were fined for talking, laughing, or singing. Factory owners fought every reform the workers proposed, from better wages to better lighting, from shorter hours to a place to eat.

As transportation improved, industry expanded, and women began working in cigar factories, paper mills, and printing plants as well as in textile mills. By 1860, 65 percent of all jobs in Atlantic Coast factories were held by women and children.

Despite their prevalence — or because of it — women were systematically excluded from unions by working men who feared threats to their own jobs and wage scales. Actually, women were rarely hired for the same jobs as men and, when they were, generally earned half as much. By the 1880s, the average factory girl earned five to six dollars for a 60-hour week. But many earned less.

A few women tried to organize — shoe top stitchers formed a short-lived union called the Daughters of St. Crispin — but most women were too poor to pay regular dues, and many still hoped to escape work through marriage. In the 1880s, the Knights of Labor hired **Leonora Barry** as the first woman to investigate female working conditions. She found that while male bosses mistreated women, women themselves were apathetic. Many women had developed the "habit of submission and acceptance, without question, of any terms offered them." These were traits employers liked. In 1895, when questioned by the United States Bureau of Labor, employers said they valued women workers because they were "more reliable, more easily controlled, cheaper . . . more polite, less liable to strike."

Of course, not all working women worked in factories. Nearly half of all American women in the 1890s still lived on farms. Black women were often excluded from factory jobs and turned to domestic work where they often put in 100 hours a week. They had little privacy,

lived in a maid's room, and earned two to five dollars a week. Domestics found their jobs through employment agencies, which often defrauded them by charging a fee, hiring them for a day, and then firing them without pay.

White, middle-class, single women who wanted to work had other options: they could become teachers, nurses, or social workers, but were expected to quit working once they married. Women teachers, especially in small towns, could not go to the theater, attend dances, or play cards. They were paid one-half to one-third the wages of their male counterparts. Nurses were expected to live at the hospital, and were on call 24-hours-a-day. Most social workers were volunteers for charity organizations, and received no pay.

Young women who dressed neatly and spoke reasonably good English were hired to work in department stores. However, they were not given important jobs. In 1895, E. W. Bloomingdale boasted that there was not a woman in his New York department store who did the same work as a man. The women were change girls, stock clerks, package wrappers, and occasionally sales clerks in the "bargain basement." The men were sales clerks in the other departments, buyers, managers, and supervisors.

Keeping Women at Home

Most Americans felt it was immoral for women — especially married women — to want to work outside the home. Women, it was argued, were intellectually inferior and physically delicate. Grant Allen, a well-known science popularizer in the 1880s, wrote, "All that is distinctly human is man . . . all that is truly woman is reproductive . . . (women) who prefer to follow male avocations . . . for the most part unsex themselves." This attitude was espoused by many women as well.

As a result of this stigma on working women, and as a paternal attempt to protect them, Illinois passed, in 1879, the first of what would become a nationwide blanket of protective legislation: it prohibited women from entering the state's coal mines. It is questionable whether

Women's Work and Wages
Source: U.S. Census Bureau, 1970 Census

	Number employed		%	%+/− 1960- 1970[1]	Avg. income[2]		% dis- parity
	Women	Men	Women		Women	Men	
Total employed	29,170,127	48,138,665	37.7	+4.9	$3,646	$7,620	52.2
Professional, technical, etc.	4,314,083	6,516,610	39.8	+1.4	6,030	10,617	43.2
Accountants	183,078	520,752	26.0	+9.6	5,796	10,677	45.7
Architects	1,981	54,253	3.5	+1.5	6,995	13,188	47.0
Lawyers, judges	13,196	259,264	4.8	+1.4	8,974	18,870	52.4
Librarians	102,225	22,047	82.3	−3.2	6,203	7,727	19.7
Mathematics specialists	12,048	23,052	34.3	−0.9	7,135	11,993	40.5
Physical and life scientiest	26,615	175,963	13.1	+4.8	7,518	12,025	37.5
Doctors, dentists, etc.	45,722	493,215	8.5	+2.6	7,831	19,337	59.5
Registered nurses	807,825	22,444	97.3	−0.2	5,603	7,013	20.1
Social and recreation wkrs.	156,500	110,447	58.6	−1.4	6,172	7,939	22.3
College teachers	138,136	348,265	28.4	+4.7	6,220	11,248	44.7
Secondary school teachers	491,857	510,339	49.1	−0.2	6,724	9,036	25.6
Elem., pre-kind. teachers	1,306,498	234,132	84.8	−1.9	6,253	8,095	22.8
Engineering & science techs.	87,963	715,759	10.9	+1.9	5,433	8,699	37.5
Writers, artists, entertainers	228,375	528,722	30.2	+1.7	4,170	9,430	55.8
Managers and administrators	1,013,843	5,125,534	16.5	+1.8	5,494	11,012	50.1
Sales workers	1,999,794	3,267,653	38.0	+2.4	2,316	8,447	72.6
Demonstrators, hucksters, peddlers	127,806	28,369	81.8	+10.5	1,041	4,859[3]	78.6
Retail clerks	1,481,981	769,008	65.8	+3.7	2,208	5,482	59.7
Retail salesmen	59,581	401,462	12.9	+2.2	3,092	7,839	60.6
Clerical workers	9,582,440	3,452,251	73.5	+5.5	4,228	7,259	41.8
Tellers and cashiers	910,179	171,393	84.2	+8.7	2,835	3,682	23.0
Bookkeepers, billing clerks	1,346,790	296,052	82.0	−1.4	4,225	6,925	39.0
Receptionists	288,326	16,046	94.7	+1.7	3,376	4,281	21.1
Secretaries	2,640,740	64,608	97.6	+0.5	4,803	7,536	36.3
Telephone operators	385,331	22,696	94.4	−1.4	6,469	4,241	−52.5
Typists	922,804	57,272	94.2	−0.9	4,042	6,025	32.9
Craftsmen	494,871	9,501,588	5.0	+1.9	4,450	8,176	45.6
Operatives except transport)	3,719,842	6,096,313	37.9	+2.4	3,634	6,737	46.1
Assemblers	455,272	490,247	48.2	+7.2	4,145	6,988	40.7
Checkers, examiners, inspec.	327,836	362,872	47.5	+3.7	4,359	7,955	45.1
Graders and sorters, mfg.	24,410	13,811	63.9	−3.9	3,103	5,635	44.9
Laundry and drycleaning	108,542	62,001	63.6	+2.0	2,789	4,830	42.3
Packers, wrappers (except meat and produce)	315,041	203,170	60.8	+1.9	3,516	5,336	34.1
Textile operatives	232,955	197,232	54.2	+2.0	3,905	5,228	25.3
Transport operatives	121,819	2,644,368	4.4	+2.9	2,481	6,923	64.2
Laborers (except farm)	268,505	2,944,649	8.4	+3.2	2,927	4,614	36.6
Farm laborers, paid	99,379	680,609	12.7	+2.3	992	1,496[3]	60.2
Farm laborers, unpaid and fam.	38,930	68,146	36.4	−8.0	768	1,000	30.2
Service workers (except private household)	4,424,030	3,640,487	54.9	+3.4	2,323	5,086	54.3
Cleaning service	601,929	1,295,731	31.7	−0.9	2,288	4,636	50.6
Food service	1,943,325	916,426	68.0	+0.4	1,808	2,899	37.6
Health service	1,044,944	139,760	88.2	+5.1	3,247	4,448	27.0
Health aides (except nursing)	101,157	18,501	84.5	−2.5	3,460	4,354	20.5
Practical nurses	228,762	8,579	96.4	+1.1	4,205	5,745	26.8
Personal service	776,222	393,273	66.4	+13.3	2,735	5,072	46.1
Hairdressers, barbers, cosmetologists	433,466	206,382	67.7	+10.0	3,049	5,927	48.6
Private household workers	1,051,803	37,312	96.6	+0.2	981	1,712	42.7

(1) Increase or decrease, 1960 to 1970, of per cent of women among total employed in that occupation.
(2) Average earnings in 1969.
(3) Men tended to work a significantly greater number of weeks in the year than women in these occupations. The men's income figure has been adjusted downward to allow comparison with women's income.

Everyday Adventurers
Women in Some Unusual
Occupations

Occupation	Number	%
Auctioneers	237	4.6
Baggage porters, bellhops	441	2.3
Blacksmiths	346	3.3
Blasters, powdermen	305	4.1
Boatmen, canalmen	397	7.7
Bootblacks	336	8.7
Brick, stonemasons	2,054	1.2
Cabinet makers	3,301	4.9
Carpenters	11,110	1.3
Construction foremen	1,416	0.9
Construction laborers	9,206	1.7
Crane, derrick, hoist operators	1,931	1.3
Earth drillers	3,629	6.3
Earthmovers: bulldozer drivers	1,245	1.4
other heavy equip.	2,360	1.0
Electricians	8,283	1.7
Embalmers	158	3.2
Engineers: aero-, astronautical	974	1.4
mining	54	1.2
petroleum	102	0.9
Firemen	2,157	1.2
Flight engineers	124	1.9
Forge, hammermen (metals)	834	5.3
Forklift, towmotor operators	3,699	1.7
Garage, gas station attendants	11,947	2.8
Garbage collectors	950	1.3
Lathe, milling mach. operators	7,347	5.3
Locomotive engineers	456	0.9
Locomotive fireman	228	1.8
Longshoremen, stevedores	826	1.8
Lumberman	1,892	2.3
Machinists	11,560	3.0
Marshals, constables	228	4.1
Mechanics, repairmen:		
air cond., heat., refrig.	1,074	0.9
aircraft	4,304	3.0
auto body	1,055	1.0
auto	11,228	1.4
heavy equipment	10,884	1.9
railroad and car	486	0.9
Millwrights	975	1.2
Miners: coal	681	1.4
petroleum	3,244	4.9
Plumbers, pipefitters	4,048	1.1
Police, detectives (public)	10,869	3.1
Pressmen, printers	12,585	7.9
Railroad brakemen	597	1.3
Railroad switchmen	987	1.9
Riveters	11,051	43.5
Sailors, deckhands	454	1.8
Smelter, furnacemen; pourers	2,486	3.9
Stone cutters, carvers	511	8.0
Structural metal workers	1,060	1.3
Truck drivers	20,275	1.5
Telephone linemen	671	1.3
Telephone repair, installation	8,064	3.4

U.S. Census Bureau, 1970 Census.

these laws served their original protective purposes. In 1911, Louis Marion Bosworth, a settlement worker in Boston, found factory girls earning three dollars a week, huddled into cold, tiny rooms in boarding houses, often without water or enough food. During World War I, while the men went to war, women as taxi driver and elevator-operator. After the war, the old protective laws and male-dominated unions were used to remove women from their new jobs and to deny them night work and overtime.

Despite these hurdles, with immigration rising and industry booming, the number of women working continued to swell. In 1850 there were 226,000 women working in manufacturing; in 1900 there were 1,313,000; by 1930 there were ten million, and one-third of all working-class women were earning money to supplement their husbands' income, although most of them continued to work at home, sewing buttons on cards and trim on clothing, doing janitorial work in their apartment buildings, or taking in lodgers.

Rosie the Riveter

During the Depression of the 1930s, many women lost their jobs and some local, state, and federal governments even

World War II drill operator: Even married women were told it was patriotic to work.

re-imposed bans on hiring married women for government jobs. Yet, as husbands and fathers joined the unemployment lines, wives and daughters continued to seek out work. By 1940, the number of women in the labor force had grown to fourteen million. Slowly but surely, unions began to open their doors to female members. This trend peaked during World War II, when even married women were told it was patriotic to work, and "Rosie the Riveter" became the symbol of the new, strong female who was now welcomed into vacant jobs once held by men. In Detroit, 350,000 women joined the United Auto Workers in 1944, a 112 percent increase in female membership.

When the war was over, most women wanted to keep their jobs, but once again they had no luck. Almost all were fired or demoted to lower-paying jobs and company and union officials began reminding women that, in normal times, their places were in the home. This attitude, prevalent in large parts of the country even today, has failed to stop the flow of married women into the job market. In the 1950s, many older married women, with grown children, went to work. In the late 1960s, influenced by the declining birth rate, rising inflation, and women's liberation, more young married women began to work as well. Today,

Twenty feet above ground, a telephone "lineperson" leaves her mark on a formerly all-male field.

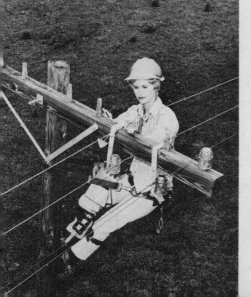

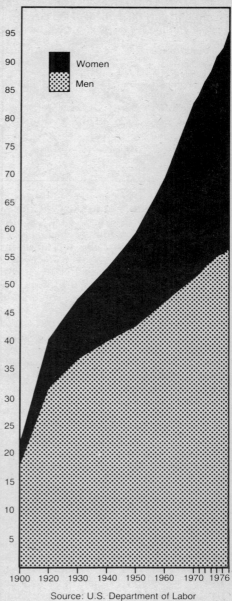

Women in the Labor Force
Total labor force in millions

Women
Men

Source: U.S. Department of Labor

more than 35 million women work outside the home.

Many jobs, however, remain defined by sex: men are doctors, women nurses; men are school principals, women

Woman's Pay

For the last twenty years, the median pay for year-round full-time working women has averaged only 60 percent of the pay men receive. As more women enter the labor force, usually in the lower-paying jobs, their share of the median pay dollar declines.

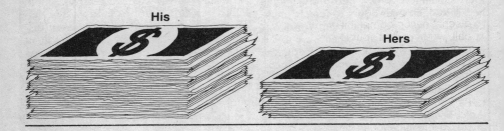

His

Hers

teachers; men are executives, women secretaries. Even when most of the people in a profession, such as library science, are women, the top positions are held by men. A few women now climb telephone poles and trade stocks on the floor of the New York Stock Exchange. Yet in spite of rumors of equality, fewer than one in twenty women work in skilled crafts and trades that require training and apprenticeship — such as airline pilots, typesetters, or welders, or hold executive or middle-management positions. Women make up almost half of the work force, yet they comprise only 7 percent of America's lawyers and judges; and only 10 percent of its physicians and surgeons. One result of this de facto segregation is that most women earn considerably less than men. In 1974, the average earnings of year-round full-time workers aged fourteen and older were $12,104 for white men, $8,524 for minority men, $6,823 for white women, and $6,258 for minority women.

Why does this pattern persist? First, many employers still think of women as temporary workers: they believe a single woman will marry and quit; and they believe a married woman's primary commitment is, or should be, to her family. Because of this, they argue, women are absent more frequently and quit more often than men. Government figures, however, show that women and men today have about the same job-turnover rate.

Industrial health problems have caused further discrimination patterns. Many substances such as benzene, lead compounds, polyvinylchloride, and anesthetics can harm the fetus of a pregnant woman. In an effort to protect their female employees, many companies have banned all women — including single women and women who do not plan to have any children — from areas where exposure is greatest. As a result, women have often been transferred to departments with lower-paying jobs, and have lost their seniority.

Another major stumbling block to work equality is male attitudes. Men sometimes feel threatened when women enter traditionally male fields. Barbara Reighard, a dentist, says that in dental school men resented the three women in their class because they felt "we were in direct competition for their jobs . . . they (also) assumed we were husband-hunting and they were the trophies we were looking for." After her graduation, a dental equipment company balked at leasing her equipment, fearing she "might get pregnant" and quit dentistry.

Until the mid-1960s, women who were discriminated against had little recourse. In 1963, Congress passed the Equal Pay Act, an amendment to the Fair Labor Standards Act, which forbids wage discrimination based on sex. Women and men in the same company who perform substantially equal (not necessarily identical) work on jobs requiring comparable skills and responsibility must be paid the same wages. This act covers everyone except household workers, employees in retail establishments grossing less than $250,000 a year, and employees of state and local governments.

> If you have a wage discrimination complaint, you can call, write, or visit your local representative of the United States Labor Department's Wage and Hour Division. There are no forms or affidavits to fill out. Ninety-five percent of the cases are resolved without going to court; those that do go into litigation are usually won by the Labor Department.

In 1964, Congress passed an even more sweeping piece of legislation: the Civil Rights Act. Title VII of that act prohibits discrimination in employment because of sex, race, color, religion, or national origin. This act covers all employers with fifteen or more employees, labor unions, and employment agencies; it forbids discrimination in almost every aspect of work, including hiring, firing, recruitment, promotion, working conditions and assignments, seniority and pensions.

> If you have a complaint about sex discrimination at work, you must file charges in writing with your local Equal Employment Opportunity Commission office within 180 days after the discriminatory act. EEOC investigates the charges, and, if reasonable cause for the complaint is found, it then tries to conciliate. If that fails, EEOC attorneys bring civil action in Federal Court against the employer on your behalf. The EEOC has a backlog at this time, and it can take up to four years to clear up a complaint.

One form of discrimination women are complaining about more frequently is sexual harassment, which may range from blatant sexual propositions to hugs and pinches disguised as friendly gestures. Working Women United, a feminist group, found in 1975 that 70 out of 155 women they interviewed had experienced some abuse of this kind. EEOC is trying to include sexual harassment in its list of illegal forms of discrimination. Most state unemployment officials, however, don't recognize sexual harassment as a serious problem. If you leave a job because of it, they will usually refuse to give you unemployment compensation.

Pat Schnabel, a female crane operator on the Trans-Alaska pipeline, says: "At work I de-emphasize my femininity. I have to. The first three weeks on the job, every man I saw tried to gross me out. Dirty stories. Snickers. Propositions. They totally resent the thought of any woman making as much money as a man." She puts up with it because she can earn more than $56,000 a year, working twelve hours a day, seven days a week. Some women have banded together to help each other cope. Women Working in Construction — a group composed largely of apprentices in carpentry, plumbing, and cement finishing — provides mutual support for its members and encourages other women to enter these fields, in spite of harassment they might suffer on the job.

Eager for more pay and a chance for promotion, women continue to flock to "men's jobs" in increasing numbers. There were, for example, 6,200 women police officers in America in October 1976—double the number four years earlier. The trend appears irreversible. Although private employers often hesitate to train women for jobs they consider too dirty, or too heavy, some women can now get the needed training elsewhere. Since 1974, the National Urban League has placed women in apprenticeships as tile-setters, machinists, electricians, pipe-fitters, and truckdrivers. Employers who *want* to train women can also get outside help. Wider Opportunities for Women (WOW) — located in the C.F. Hurley Building, Government Center, Cambridge and Stamford Streets, Boston, Massachusetts, 02202 — has helped the Xerox Corporation train women to repair office machines and has helped Sears teach women to repair major appliances.

Government pressure also aids women in finding the jobs they want. The U.S. Department of the Interior, for instance, must enforce laws against sex discrimination in any project it oversees, and one of those projects is the Trans-Alaska pipeline. As a result, the number of women in blue-collar construction jobs working for the Alyeska Pipeline Service Company, the contractor building the pipeline, soared from 21 in July 1974 to 1,702 in December 1975.

THE HOUSEWIFE

In 1973, John Kenneth Galbraith described housewives as a "crypto-servant class" — meaning that every man, rich or poor, could own a female servant simply by getting married. It is a common misconception that feminists dislike women who are housewives: in fact, feminists object to only the stigma housewives bear. Since the turn of the century, the function of housewives has been viewed increasingly as childlike, menial work that women perform out of a sense of duty rather than choice. Feminists believe the labor that goes into homemaking should be valued as highly as other, paid, jobs.

In colonial days, housewives took great pride in their work: in the clothing they made, the food they canned, the poultry they raised. Cooking in itself was a big responsibility, for middle-class diets were monotonous and scurvy was a constant threat. Often, housewives had to educate and nurse their own children. In 1869, *The American Woman's Home,* written by Catharine Beecher and Harriet Beecher Stowe, preached thrift and productivity, and offered practical tips on plumbing, heating, and construction as well as family health and child education.

The work of a housewife in those days was physically exhausting as well as time-consuming. Women not only kneaded dough, but also hauled water from the well, mended and laundered their clothes by hand, beat the carpets, stoked the oven, and bore large numbers of children. In the late 1880s, **Ellen Swal-**

"Shake Hands?": The 1854 housewife's work was physically exhausting as well as time-consuming.

low Richards created the field that was to become known as home economics. Born in Dunstable, Massachusetts, in 1842, she was to change irrevocably the nature of housework before her death in 1911. At the age of twenty-five, after working to save money for tuition, she entered Vassar College; two years later she became the first woman allowed to study chemistry at Massachusetts Institute of Technology. Richards' main concern was using science to help the housewife.

She organized a Woman's Laboratory at MIT, where she tested wallpapers and fabrics for arsenic content, examined the contents of drinking water, and studied the causes of spontaneous combustion. She wrote a pamphlet for housewives stressing the importance of intellectual interests to provide a balance to household routine. Richards wrote some of the first United States Department of Agriculture pamphlets on nutrition, and helped Boston set up one of America's first school lunch programs. She was among the first housewives to use a vacuum cleaner, a shower, a hot water heater, and a telephone.

In 1890 Richards set up the first public kitchen, where she demonstrated how to prepare a balanced meal. There was no reliable cookbook for daily use until 1896, when Fannie Merritt Farmer published *The Boston Cooking-School Cook Book,* which eventually sold four million copies. For the first time, housewives could prepare meals following specific directions and using level measurements. In 1901, the Good Housekeeping Institute, soon to become a first-rate investigatory facility, was started.

In the last 150 years, the tasks of the housewife have been revolutionized. The first gas stove went on sale in 1826; the first commercially produced electric light bulb, in 1880, and the first ready-to-eat breakfast cereal, Shredded Wheat, in 1893. The first electric washing machine was sold in 1925; frozen food appeared in the stores in 1930; the first automatic clothes dryer debuted in 1955; and wash-and-wear clothing came out in 1964. During the Depression of the 1930s, many housewives gave up the new conveniences, but not for long. After World War II, consumer spending, long dammed by war shortages and sacrifices, rapidly increased in volume. The housewife had become the family's number one spender.

Technology Comes Home

Ironically, the technological advances so eagerly promoted by early housewives ended up, in many ways, diminishing the value of homemaking. The housewife could buy things instead of make them, and she became a consumer rather than a producer. As income became the measure of a person's importance and success, the housewife's importance diminished. She spent money but did not make any. She worked but did not get paid. She was considered in many statistics to be unemployed. Her work, if less exhausting than before, was also less creative and fulfilling.

Strangely enough, however, technology did not reduce the amount of time needed to run a house. Despite smaller families and time-saving appliances, housewives today spend even more time doing the housework than their foremothers did. In 1924, non-employed women spent about fifty-two hours a week doing housework. In the 1960s, they spent about fifty-five hours per week. Joann Vanek reported in *Scientific American,* in 1974, that while housewives may need less time to produce food and clothing, they need more time to shop. In the 1920s, women averaged less than two hours a week in stores; today, they spend eight hours a week shopping. Washing and ironing is less of a burden today, yet women report they spend more time with their laundry — apparently because they have more clothes and wash them more often. Mothers also spend more time on child care. In the post-Spock era, they worry about mental and social development as well as discipline and cleanliness.

This work pattern, however, changes once a housewife gets an outside job. Employed women spend only about twenty-six hours a week doing housework, even if they have the same size families as the nonemployed housewife. This phenomenon, Vanek suggests, shows that "since the value of household work is not clear, nonemployed women feel pressure to spend long hours at it," especially when others are around to notice.

Despite modern appliances, women spend more time on laundry today than they did years ago.

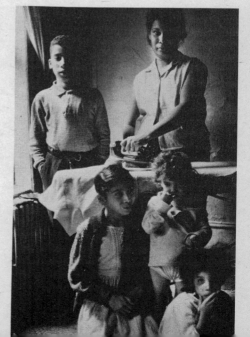

Invisible Profession

Nonetheless, housewifery often remains an invisible profession: nobody notices the work that is done until it suddenly stops being done. To raise the housewife's status, some have suggested she be paid for her services. Mike McGrady, who switched roles with his wife and became a "househusband" for a year, believes no salary could be too high for the housewife. "This is a job," he said, "that should not be done by any one person for love or for money." The Chase Manhattan Bank has calculated a housewife's value — including her roles as nursemaid, hostess, dietition, chauffeur, and laundress — to be at least $13,391.56 a year.

Some Enjoy Housewifery

Most housewives claim not to be upset by their neglected status. Recent surveys by Good Housekeeping, McCalls, and Virginia Slims show that the majority of housewives like what they are doing, don't receive or expect much help from their husbands, and are unwilling to accept the idea of a salary for their services.

The Good Housekeeping poll, conducted in June, 1975, showed that 85 percent of the housewives polled *wanted* to stay at home, and tended to feel that being with their children was as challenging as other work. The poll also found that most women no longer view themselves as lifelong housewives. Only 41 percent of those polled agreed that "a woman's place is in the home." Most wanted to alternate outside work with housework, depending on the ages of their children and their need for more income.

The major factor in any woman's job is pride. As **Betty Ford** said at the International Women's Year Conference in October, 1975: "We have to take the 'just' out of 'just a housewife' . . . A liberated woman is one who feels confident in herself and is happy in what she is doing. A woman who is satisfied with her life at home is just as liberated as a woman with a career outside the home. What is important is that a person has the option to decide the direction of her own life and that she makes that decision herself, without pressures restricting her choice."

WOMAN'S WORK

Many outside jobs are also considered "woman's work": they usually involve helping or serving others. Often, they are low in pay, status, and promotion possibilities. Today 3.3 million people, nearly all of them women, work in secretarial jobs. They type, take dictation, answer mail, get coffee, file, greet people, and operate office equipment. Jobs as secretaries and clerks were held by men until Philo Remington invented the typewriter in 1867. From that time on, secretarial work gradually dropped from a highly skilled, high-paying job that often led to executive positions to a lower-level, often dead-end, job.

Secretarial Work

There are more than 300 secretarial schools in the United States. The most famous is the Katharine Gibbs School, which opened in 1911 and now offers one-year secretarial and two-year liberal arts-secretarial programs in six locations on the East Coast. Most colleges and universities also offer classes in business and secretarial skills. The advantage of being a secretary, says Shirley Englund, editor of *The Secretary* and spokeswoman for the National Secretaries Association, International, is that while "a secretary doesn't take home the highest paycheck, she doesn't take home management's night work or worries, either." Some secretaries are promoted into management positions as they become more experienced, and the NSA gives a series of tests which qualify the most competent as Certified Professional Secretaries.

A high school degree is almost always required for secretarial work, but some companies have their own training facilities. U.S. government offices and many private firms usually require that stenographers be able to take dictation at a minimum of 110 words per minute, and secretaries be able to type at least forty to fifty words per minute. Men are entering the secretarial field in small numbers; they generally earn at least 20 percent more than women doing the same job, despite legislation barring such discrimination. For women, $3.50 to $5.00 an hour is

Western Freight Office secretaries, 1911: Neither the boss's worries — nor his paycheck.

For further information on careers in secretarial work, you can write to: National Secretaries Association (International), 2440 Pershing Road, Suite G10, Kansas City, Missouri, 64108. For a directory of business schools, write: Association of Independent Colleges and Schools, 1730 M Street NW, Washington, D.C., 20036.

considered a typical beginning wage. The need for secretaries is expected to increase in the 1980s. •

Nursing

Nursing, another traditionally female profession, was considered a disreputable occupation in the 1800s. Hospital nurses were often accused of drinking too much, and of being prostitutes and thieves. Hospital conditions verged on the barbaric: in the 1870s, investigators could not find a single bar of soap in all of Bellevue Hospital in New York City. Florence Nightingale began the reform of nursing in the 1850s and made it into a respectable profession: she encouraged discipline and obedience and "lady-like" behavior.

Today, nearly 860,000 people are registered nurses, and almost 99 percent of them are women. Another 495,000 persons, also mostly women, are licensed practical nurses who have less medical training and less responsibility than the registered nurse. Most nurses work in hospitals and nursing homes, and the rest work in medical offices, private homes, and the public health and nurses' training fields. About one-third work part time.

Women who want to become registered nurses have a choice of taking a two-year associate degree program in a junior or community college, or a four-to five-year baccalaureate program in a college or university. The latter is often required to enter administrative and management positions. Licensed practical nurses must complete a one-year, state-approved training program. Many of these programs do not require a high school diploma for admission.

Registered nurses who work in hospitals now earn an average starting yearly salary of $9,100. Nurses employed in federally owned hospitals average about

For information on nursing schools and careers, you can write to: American Nursing Association Committee on Nursing Careers, 2420 Pershing Road, Kansas City, Missouri, 64108.

$14,700 a year. Licensed practical nurses in hospitals begin at about $6,700 a year; in federal hospitals starting salaries are slightly higher.

Employment opportunities for nurses are expected to be good through the 1980s, but competition will probably increase for the more desirable positions as more women enter nursing schools.

Airline Opportunities

From the onset of the first scheduled airline passenger flights, women have served as flight attendants. "Sky girls," as they were called, were introduced on United Airlines' Chicago-to-Oakland run in 1930. The first was Ellen Church, a nurse who convinced the airline to hire her. For $125 a month, she not only made passengers comfortable but also carried their baggage, helped pull the airplane out of the hangar, cleaned the plane's interior, and refueled it.

Despite the initial hard labor, the profession quickly began to resemble a training ground for future Miss Americas. A good figure and a pretty face were basic requirements for the job. TWA even dictated the shade of lipstick and the maximum hip span of its female crew. Serving drinks was given priority — at least for publicity purposes — over the fact that the stewardess's main function was to save lives if the plane crashed.

As a result of litigation and government pressure, airlines had to remove the restrictions which had allowed them to fire stewardesses who married or reached their early thirties. Today the airlines must also provide maternity leaves, and hire more black women and more men as flight attendants.

Today, beginning pay for a flight attendant is around $500 a month for seventy to eighty-five hours of flying time, travel layovers, and ground duties. Flight attendants must be at least twenty years old, and have some college or work experience before taking the five-week flight-training course.

More equality is being urged by groups like the Stewardesses for Women's Rights, of Alexandria, Virginia. They point out that among the country's six largest airlines, only 6.4 percent of the people in management are women. There were no women airline captains on scheduled flights in the United States until 1976, when Emily Howell, a pilot for Frontier Airlines, was promoted.

Teachers

This same inequality is found among school teachers. Women have been school teachers since America was founded. Today, there are 1.3 million elementary school teachers, and 85 percent of them are women. They usually instruct twenty-five to thirty children in several subjects, introducing them to mathematics, language, science, and social studies, although more elementary school teachers are beginning to specialize the same way high school teachers do.

Elementary school teachers work about forty-six hours a week, mostly in the classroom. The remainder of the time they attend faculty meetings, prepare lessons, work with students who need special help, and confer with parents. A teacher must have a bachelor's degree and a state-approved teaching certificate. Thirteen states also require that teachers get a master's degree or complete a fifth year of study within a few years after certification.

Unlike most other female-dominated jobs, teachers at all levels tend to belong to fairly strong unions. Most states now have laws that require collective bargaining in teachers' contracts, and because of that, wages and benefits are usually good. The National Education Association reports that public elementary school teachers earn about $11,234 for a nine-month teaching year.

However, opportunities for advance-

For information on local teaching requirements, you can contact your local school board or your state department of education. For information on internships and graduate fellowships for teachers, write to: The United States Department of Health, Education and Welfare, National Center for Education Statistics, Washington, D.C., 20202.

ment in elementary teaching are limited; the job of principal usually is awarded to a man. Also, kindergarten and elementary school teachers will have a harder time finding jobs during the next decade. The birth rate, and the number of teachers needed, is declining while the number of women graduating with teaching degrees continues to rise.

Waiting Tables

Waitressing is another job women often take. Co-eds working their way through college and married women with small children often opt for this time-honored way of earning money. Waitresses, however, remain excluded from most luxury restaurants, which prefer waiters. In 1975, the American Civil Liberties Union charged sex bias against ten of New York City's most exclusive restaurants which refused to use waitresses — including the "21" Club and Sardi's. Rather than go to court the restaurant owners gradually relented, but many expensive restaurants continue this segregation.

Waitresses usually receive the minimum wage — $2.30 an hour — and rely on tips to bolster their income. Tips average ten to twenty percent of the cost of dinner and drinks.

Job opportunities in your area are probably listed in local restaurant windows and the classified ads. The larger, higher-priced restaurants are usually unionized, and your local branch of the Hotel and Restaurant Employees and Bartenders International Union would know about available jobs. For general information on waitress jobs, write: National Institute for the Food Service Industry, 120 South Riverside Plaza, Chicago, Illinois, 60606; or the Council on Hotel, Restaurant, and Institutional Education, 1522 K Street NW, Washington, D.C., 20005.

Today almost two million people in the United States work as waitresses or waiters. Most of them work part time. Waitressing jobs are usually available in most neighborhoods. Employers prefer to hire people who have at least a few years of high school education, are good at arithmetic, and like working with people. Although serving meals is her main function, a waitress may also suggest wines, and

Turn of the century waitresses: The most prestigious jobs still go to men.

clear and set up tables, especially in smaller restaurants.

Retailing

When retail stores first came into existence, most of the sales clerks were men. Today, that situation has reversed: 2.8 million sales people are employed in retail stores, and three-fifths of them are women. Men continue to dominate the door-to-door jobs, selling products like encyclopedias and kitchenware, but even this is changing with campaigns in which women sell house-to-house to other women.

The advantage of the retail trade is that women sometimes have chances for advancement, even without college degrees. Although many businesses hire college graduates as management trainees, sales people can also be promoted to jobs as buyers or managers. In smaller stores, women who begin as sales clerks may even have the opportunity to take over the shop when the owner retires or quits.

Beginning sales clerks usually earn only the federal minimum wage; some also get a commission on what they sell. Retail workers also get discounts on merchandise from their stores.

You can receive information on careers in retailing by writing to: The National Retail Merchants Association, 100 West 31st Street, New York, N.Y., 10001; or from your local branch of the Retail Clerks International Association, a union for sales people.

Beauticians

Many women have been attracted to jobs as beauticians which, like retail sales, can sometimes offer the chance for advancement without a college degree. Of the half million beauticians in this country, more than one-third of them own and operate their own businesses. Many female beauticians, however, see their work as part time and temporary.

Each beautician must be licensed by the state in which she works; qualifications for licensing vary from state to state. Most states require graduation from a state-

For information about careers in cosmetology you can write to: National Beauty Career Center, 3839 White Plains Road, Bronx, New York, 19467; or, National Hairdressers and Cosmetologists Association, 3510 Olive Street, St. Louis, Missouri, 63103.

approved cosmetology school and a minimum age of sixteen. Most full-time school programs take six months to a year to complete. Experienced beauticians can earn $250 to $300 a week, including tips, in urban areas, and the selected few who set trends as well as hair can earn $1,000 or more a week. Success often depends on building up a regular clientele.

A Stitch in Time

The garment industry was the first to hire women *en masse* in this country, and it remains a popular source of income for women. Common jobs are sewing machine operation or hand-sewing to put the finishing touches on more expensive clothing. Each sewing machine operator specializes in one facet of putting together a garment: one sews the shoulder seams,

From the opening of the first clothing factories, most garment workers have been women.

In the early days of telephones, the operator was the center of the local gossip mill.

another makes sections like pockets, collars, or sleeves, and others join completed sections to the main garment.

About half of the 1.3 million people in this industry — most of them women — work at these jobs each day. Many of the rest are pattern-makers, who use the finished experimental garment to make a paper pattern for mass-production; hand-spreaders, who lay out bolts of cloth into precise lengths for cutting; or markers who trace the pattern pieces onto the cloth. Most women learn these skills on the job, where they are taught how to perform each task with minimal finger, arm, and body movement.

Despite the presence of powerful unions, like the International Ladies' Garment Workers Union (ILGWU) and the United Garment Workers of America, earnings in the garment industry are relatively low. The estimated average hourly wage of all clothing production workers in factories in New York is $3.79. Sewing machine operators average slightly more, $3.84 to $4.10 an hour. In addition to low wages, many sewers are forced to work less than full time during slack periods, which further reduces their paycheck. The employment rate for the apparel industry is expected to grow more slowly than other industries during the 1980s.

Ma Bell

The greatest oppressor of working women, according to a 1971 report by the Equal Employment Opportunity Commission, was the Bell Telephone System, owned by the American Telephone and Telegraph Company. The Bell System is also the largest private employer of women. In 1878, Emma Nutt became the first woman telephone operator. Although men were considered most capable of handling this new technology, they tended to get too rowdy sitting in a confined space all day. Thirty-three years later, Nutt still held the same job.

The telephone company's sex bias continued into the early 1970s, when 99.8 percent of the secretaries and 99.9 percent of the operators were women; in the higher-paying craft jobs such as installer or switchman, the figure was reversed: only 1.1 percent were women. All Bell companies maintained separate hiring offices for men and women.

Telephone operators had to be women, Bell argued, because the company had invested money in its image of "the voice with a smile." But the Equal Employment Opportunity Commission (EEOC) was not sympathetic. As a result of its 1973 settlement with the EEOC, Ma Bell agreed to pay $38 million in back pay and

These maids, cooks, and laundresses made up the domestic staff of a single, wealthy household.

wage increases to its female employees, and to change its practice of discriminating against women (and men) in hiring, promoting, and training. More men have been hired as telephone operators, but change is slow. In 1975. AT&T agreed to pay an additional $2.5 million in compensation and penalties for failing to comply fully with the 1973 consent order. In addition, male-dominated unions like the Communications Workers and the Electrical Workers, as well as the Alliance of Independent Workers, have challenged some of the anti-sex discrimination agreements, saying that they violate union contracts.

Domestic Workers

Domestic workers are the lowest paid of all female workers. The average income in 1974 for the two million household workers in this country — 97 percent of them women — was $2,243 a year. Most are black women who work in urban areas. The "servant" status of domestic workers has helped keep them underpaid and unorganized. In 1911, the attitude towards maids as a throwaway luxury item was made clear in an advertisement in the New York Times. Housewives who found their maids chipping glasses and nicking plates were advised to "change the housemaid instead of the plates. It's less expensive, and good housemaids are

easier to find than cherished patterns in china." To this day, women who are paid to do housework tend to be less respected than women who do it for free.

Carolyn Reed, a household worker for twenty years, is trying to win the right of collective bargaining for domestic workers. In 1960, Reed was paid fifteen dollars a week and given a basement room in exchange for washing, cleaning, and cooking ten to fourteen hours a day. Now she has founded Household Technicians of America, a union with 800 members in Ohio, North Carolina, Alabama, and New York.

> The National Committee on Household Employment, 7705 Georgia Avenue NW, Suite 208, Washington, D.C., 20012, provides information on laws affecting household workers.

UNION WOMEN

Working women have fought long and hard for the right to organize, struggling against the apathy and fear of other women, the hostility of employers, and the antipathy of male unions. The earliest unions began as male social clubs that met in neighborhood saloons. Women were not welcome. In the 1860s, women formed "sister chapters" and union men voiced support for principles such as equal pay for equal work. Support seldom extended to the picket line, however, and only since the 1940s, as men began to view women as a permanent and potentially powerful part of the labor force, have women been accepted in large numbers into unions.

The earliest women to organize worked in the textile factories of New England. During their first strike in 1828, 300 to 400 women in Dover, New Hampshire, walked out to protest low wages, expensive rooming charges, and a thirteen-and-a-half hour work day. But the spontaneous walk-out soon fell apart and the women returned to work without gain.

This pattern of impotent protest continued until 1844 when the Massachusetts legislature appointed a committee to investigate working conditions. **Sarah G. Bagley,** who worked in a cotton mill in Lowell, founded the Lowell Female Labor Reform Association, an auxiliary of the all-male New England Workingmen's Association, and quickly rounded up several hundred members from New England mills. She gathered 2,000 signatures petitioning the legislature to limit the working day to ten hours, and worked full time to organize female factory workers along the East Coast, until her health failed.

Changes were slow to come. Many women ruined their health trying to organize. And other leaders gave up union work for the sanctuary of marriage. In 1868, a reporter and typesetter named **Augusta Lewis Troup** formed the Working Women's Association and the Women's Typographical Union — a sister chapter of the International Typographical Union (ITU) — to regulate women's wages and working conditions. As a typesetter, Troup gained a reputation for being able to set the entire text of Rip Van Winkle in six and a half hours. As an organizer she became equally respected for her tact and firmness in working with male union leaders. Her union, however, never had more than forty members, and was resented by male union foremen who didn't believe in equal pay for equal work.

Despite hostility from many members,

the ITU elected Troup corresponding secretary in 1870, and by 1878 the ITU began to admit women into locals. The women were an unwelcome minority, however, and their problems were usually ignored. In 1874, Troup married, moved to New Haven, and left unionizing to rear seven children, support woman's suffrage, and do charity work in New Haven's Italian community.

Another union leader, **Leonora Kearney Barry,** was born in Cork, Ireland, and came to America as a young child. She went to work in a hosiery and men's underwear factory in 1881, at the age of thirty-two, after her husband and a child had died, leaving her with two children to support. Her first week's wages were sixty-five cents: outraged, she turned to the local union, the Knights of Labor, to protest. One year later, the Knights voted to admit women members. Barry was soon elected head of the new Department of Women's Work for the Knights and spent four years traveling around the country, investigating working conditions, and organizing. Employers would not let her in their factories, and women were afraid to talk to her, but her determined persistence made her the conscience of the female labor movement.

In 1886, the union had 50,000 women members — 9 percent of its total membership. But the Knights' popularity declined soon afterwards. The Haymarket Square incident on May 4, 1886 — a violent eruption between Chicago police and labor protesters in which several people on both sides were killed — fostered bad public feeling towards the unions. With the Knights' decline, the cause of union women also faded. Most other unions did not want to bother organizing the low-paid, unskilled trades where women were concentrated. In 1890, Barry remarried and resigned her labor duties; she worked, instead, for woman's suffrage and for temperance.

Mother Jones Organizes

One of the most colorful and effective women in the turn-of-the-century labor movement was **Mary Harris Jones,** known as "Mother Jones." She, too, was from Cork, Ireland, and came to America when she was ten years old. When her husband,

Mother Jones, who lived to be 100, advised, "No matter what your fight, don't be ladylike."

a union official in the Knights of Labor, and her four children, died of yellow fever in Memphis in 1867, Mother Jones opened a dressmaking shop in Chicago. The Chicago Fire of 1871 destroyed all she owned, and the Depression of 1873 prevented her from finding work. She began attending meetings in the Knights' fire-scorched building in Chicago, and soon became an organizer for them and, later, for the United Mine Workers.

In 1877, she was involved in her first strike, against the Baltimore & Ohio Railroad. She soon went out to help organize in the coal fields. Coal operators jailed her three times, but each time she returned to their property to organize. At each strike she lifted morale by moving in with the strikers' families, caring for the sick and injured, laying out the dead, and keeping the men out of saloons. When she had succeeded in organizing enough people, she would pay for a new union charter if they had no money.

In 1911, Mother Jones was sentenced to twenty years in prison for conspiracy to commit murder in a West Virginia coal strike. The West Virginia governor released her soon after sentencing. In 1914, when the Colorado National Guard machine-gunned twenty strikers, she told the story of the massacre around the country, until President Woodrow Wilson proposed that the union and owners create a grievance committee at each mine. She also led a march of child laborers from their textile plant in Kensington, Pennsylvania, to Oyster Bay, New York, near President Theodore Roosevelt's home, explaining that she wanted the President to hear "the wail of children who never had a chance to go to school." Soon after, the Pennsylvania legislature passed a child labor law barring children under fourteen from factory work.

Mother Jones advised women that, "No matter what your fight, don't be ladylike," yet she disapproved of violence. When women in Greensburg, Pennsylvania, were arrested for yelling at the scabs who were taking their husbands' jobs, she encouraged the women to sing in their prison cells twenty-four hours a day. After five days, during which time everyone in town was kept awake, the judge ordered their release.

After Mother Jones

With the inspiration of women like Mother Jones, other women began to stand up for their rights. The first major all-woman's strike was held by the shirtwaist workers in New York and Philadelphia in 1909 and 1910, organized by union locals that were to become part of the International Ladies' Garment Workers Union. Between ten thousand and thirty thousand women — no one knew the exact number — struck for better factory conditions and higher pay. After thirteen weeks, settlements were made shop by shop, usually with few gains. But never again would it be easy to argue that it was useless to try to organize women.

The shirtwaist workers strike led, in 1910, to a five-month woman's strike in

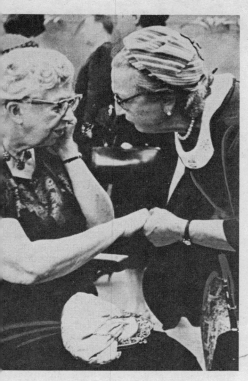

Amalgamated Clothing Workers founder Bessie Hillman (right) greeting Eleanor Roosevelt.

Chicago against the clothing manufacturer Hart, Schaffner and Marx. The strike grew to include 30,000 cutters and male tailors in other factories as well. One of the strike leaders, **Bessie Abramowitz Hillman,** an immigrant from Grodno, White Russia, later founded the Amalgamated Clothing Workers of America. For twenty years she was the only female union leader in the clothing industry, even though most of the workers were women. Today, the ACWU has more than 400,000 members.

On March 25, 1911, 145 women, aged sixteen to twenty-eight, died in the New York Triangle Shirtwaist Factory fire. The only fire-escape in the ten-story building was locked. Most of the women had been the sole supporters of their families. The tragedy highlighted the conditions of factory women, and strengthened the cause of the National Women's Trade Union League, which had been formed in 1903 as a "friend to the [male] unions" to improve working conditions, provide bail, raise strike funds, investigate police brutality, and mobilize public support for women in unions. As a result of the fire, the New York State legislature finally passed an Industrial Code regulating working conditions. The code became a model for other states.

One League member, **Rose Schneiderman,** a Polish immigrant who worked in a factory making linings for men's caps, helped organize a mass funeral and a relief committee for the families of the dead women. Schneiderman was later appointed to the U.S. Labor Advisory Board under Franklin D. Roosevelt, and ran for the U.S. Senate on the New York Labor Party ticket. In 1937 she became secretary of the New York State Department of Labor. She also founded the Bryn Mawr Summer School for Working Women, which was incorporated, in 1952, into Rutgers University's program on labor management.

In the 1930s, under the influence of Roosevelt's New Deal, attitudes towards organized labor improved. The Wagner Bill, signed on July 5, 1935, upheld the rights of workers to organize and bargain. The Fair Labor Standards Act, passed in June 1938, established a minimum wage, a 44-hour work week, and some child labor regulations. It wasn't until World War II, however, that women joined male unions in great numbers. Folksinger Woody Guthrie marked the active female participation in unions with his classic folksong "Union Maiden."

By 1944, 21.9 percent of working women were union members, but twenty-five national unions still excluded women. And even those unions that did support equal pay for equal work still accepted sex-segregated jobs.

Today, more women than ever belong to unions, but union membership has not kept pace with the numbers of women in the job market. In 1972, only 12.6 percent of working women were active union members, and the percentage continues to fall. Thirty million working women do not belong to unions. And most union women are concentrated in a few industries: they belong to the apparel unions; to the Hotel and Restaurant Workers; to the International Brotherhood of Electrical Workers, which includes telephone operators; and to the Retail Clerks. Most major unions now support the Equal Rights Amendment, but only one, the United Auto Workers, has set up a Women's Department to lobby internally for women's interests; to organize working women conferences; to research and publish material on working women; and to work for fair employment legislation. Almost all union apprenticeship programs have excluded women, and women in executive union positions are rare.

To combat this discrimination, the Coalition of Labor Union Women (CLUW), based in Detroit and headed by **Olga Madar,** a retired vice-president of the UAW, now has more than 2,800 members working to get more women in unions. CLUW makes sure women are recalled after layoffs, in line with their seniority; that they get more government jobs; and that their children get better day care. CLUW says protective legislation, such as weight limits and night work, should be extended to include men.

Progress has been even slower for women — and men — who are migrant farm workers. **Dolores Huerta,** vice-president of the United Farm Workers, and UFW leader Cesar Chavez have waged a bitter two-edged struggle against the growers over the right to unionize, and against the powerful Teamsters over who should control that union. In March 1977, an agreement was reached between the UFW and the Teamsters. It established jurisdictions for each union's recruitment drives, and the 30,000 members of the UFW may now be able to devote themselves to settling long-standing disputes with growers.

Huerta was born in 1930 in Dawson, New Mexico; she has been married twice, and has ten children. In 1955, she began working to organize the Mexican-American communities of California for the Community Service Organization. In 1962, she left the CSO and began organizing farm workers. For the last fifteen years, she has earned five dollars a week, plus room and board. She negotiated the first contracts with growers, and has been arrested eighteen times.

"I consider myself a feminist and the women's movement has done a lot toward helping me . . ." Huerta says. "But among poor people, there's not any question about the women being strong. They work in the fields right along with the men. When your survival is at stake, you don't have the questions middle-class women do."

WOMEN AT WORK

Female Entrepreneurs

"The business of women going into business is booming," **Jeanne Wertz,** a business consultant, told the Joint Economic Committee of the 93rd Congress. "This phenomenon is a fallout from the women's movement, the result of new options, new freedoms, new lifestyles." Today, the woman who wants to go into business on her own has more resources, but still faces severe sex discrimination.

On the plus side, government agencies are more responsive to women. The federal Small Business Administration made 2,050 loans to women between June 1974 and June 1975, totaling $102 million. And new agencies have been created to help. The American Woman's Economic Development Corporation (AWED), 250 Broadway, Washington, D.C., sponsored by the U.S. Department of Commerce, six corporations, and two foundations, encourages and helps women to start and to expand their own companies, and encourages companies to expand opportunities for women in their organizations.

Still, Arthur S. Fleming, chairman of the U.S. Commission on Civil Rights, says that female-owned firms encounter "problems of staggering proportions" in obtaining government contracts and the capital they need for effective marketing and bidding. Lending institutions still consider women's work a risky business.

Nevertheless, more women now own their own businesses such as restaurants, retail stores, personal services like beauty shops, real estate, grocery stores, and hotels, than ever before. In 1972, 402,025 businesses were owned by American women, and they grossed $8.1 billion. This figure is impressive, but it still represents less than 5 percent of the 8 million small businesses in this country.

Among the most successful women entrepreneurs today is **Marion O. Sandler,** vice-chairman of Golden West Financial Corporation in Oakland, California, a company she formed with her husband in 1963 in order to acquire Golden West Savings & Loan. She has built its assets from $38 million to $1.8 billion. In October 1976, the corporation merged with Trans-World Financial Corporation and is now the second largest savings and loan branch network in the country, with 107 branches in California and Colorado.

Another successful entrepreneur is **Olive Ann Beech,** chairman of the Beech Aircraft Corporation in Wichita, Kansas. Beech began running the company in 1940 when her husband became ill with encephalitis. She soon developed a reputation as a tough boss, and when her husband died in 1950 she became president, chairman of the board, and chief executive officer. Under her guidance, company sales rose from $74 million in 1963 to $267 million in 1975. Although she retired in 1968, she remains active in day-to-day operations.

Behind each of these successful women there was — in the beginning, at least — a man. The same seems true for some of the best-known businesswomen of the past, such as **Henrietta Chamberlain King,** who amassed an estate of $5.4 million, and more than one million acres in Texas, before her death in 1925 at age ninety-two. She was born in Brownsville, Texas, taught school, and at twenty-two married Richard King and moved to his ranch near Corpus Christi. He hoped to build a beef cattle empire, but he died deeply in debt.

His widow got out of debt by selling several thousand acres of his ranch land. She then encouraged a rail line to run through her ranch by contributing land for the right-of-way as well as for a new town called Kingsville. She used the railroad to ship her cattle cheaply. Later, she planned most of the town, owned and ran its lumber company and weekly newspaper, and owned nearly all the cotton gins between Corpus Christi and Brownsville.

King seemed unafraid to try any new scientific venture. She was among the first to dip cattle in a chemical solution to protect them from tick fever. The King Ranch also produced the only authentic new breed of cattle to be developed in North America, the Santa Gertrudis. And King eventually bought or bred three Kentucky Derby winners — Bold Venture, Assault, and Middleground.

In 1907, King turned down a $10 million offer for her ranch. When she drew up her will in 1919, she made sure her holdings would be kept intact for a decade after her death. Soon after she died, oil was discovered on her land, and $12 million to $18 million extra annual income went to the corporation that was formed by her grandchildren. In the 1970s, the King Ranch has become a multinational corporation, raising cattle on 11.5 million acres of land in Australia, South America, and Texas.

Maggie Lena Walker made a splash in banking and insurance circles. She grew up in Richmond, Virginia, and in 1883, at age nineteen, quit a teaching career to marry Armstrong Walker and rear three children. While a housewife, she became active in the Independent Order of St. Luke, a black group organized to provide low-cost cooperative life insurance. In 1899, with $31.60 left in the treasury, Walker became secretary-treasurer of the group. Membership doubled during her first year in office. She refused to insure anyone who didn't believe in God, and she encouraged children to save their money. In 1903, Walker convinced the group to sponsor what was to become the St. Luke Bank and Trust Company, and she became the first woman bank president in America. When Richmond's white banks could lend no more money to help keep the Richmond public schools open, her bank financed a $100,000 loan.

The insurance company also flourished. By 1924 it had grown from 57 to 1,500 chapters, from 3,400 to 50,000 members, and had acquired $400,000 in assets. When she died in 1934, Walker left a personal estate of $40,000. Her insurance company had sold more than $3 million in premiums, and it owned a four-story building where it employed black women as clerks at a time when most blacks were barred from white-collar office jobs. Despite her success, Walker was an unassuming, well-loved figure in Richmond. She helped found a school, a sanatorium, a nursing program, as well as a black community center.

Company officials believe a Tupperware party starts somewhere in the world every 10 seconds.

Home Retailers

Today, there is a new category of businesswoman as well, but few of them are likely to be wealthy through their labor. Housewives can earn cash by selling products like Avon and Tupperware to neighbors and friends. Fifty thousand women sell Tupperware, and it is estimated that every ten seconds a Tupperware party is beginning somewhere.

Tupperware dealers can earn about $100 a week through these parties, but turnover is high because dealers get discouraged after a few parties with low sales.

A Tupperware dealer can move up in company ranks, and become a distributor. However, the Tupperware company requires that all distributorships be run by partners rather than just one person, and the partner is usually the woman's husband. A distributorship may be invited to sell out and join the company payroll, but when this happens it is the husband who joins officially. Although the wife is told she is part of the team, her husband gets the paycheck.

The Avon Lady sells cosmetics door-to-door. She is usually a housewife and mother in her mid-thirties who wants to make money without disrupting her family schedule. To earn a 40 percent commission, she must place orders every two weeks totaling at least $100; if she drops below this, her commission drops to 25 percent.

If you are interested in going into business for yourself, here are a few places you can contact. The Small Business Administration has a management assistance program, and also publishes free and for-sale booklets on every subject of interest to small-business persons. You can contact the SBA through your local federal government offices. Three other groups are: The Office of Minority Business Enterprise (OMBE), U.S. Department of Commerce, Washington, D.C., 20230; the Association of Women Business Owners, 1000 Connecticut Avenue, N.W., Suite 1101, Washington, D.C., 20036; and Advocates for Women, 593 Market Street, Suite 500, San Francisco, California, 94105.

Today, 450,000 women are Avon Ladies, and their average earnings for part-time work are $52 every two weeks. After expenses, this profit shrinks. An Avon Lady from a Minnesota farm, for instance, earned almost $500 commission during nine months, and found the sum was reduced to $150 after she deducted expenses like gasoline and auto depreciation.

At both the Avon and Tupperware corporate levels, few executives are women. An affirmative action program for women and minorities was begun at Avon in 1974 as a result of several sex and race discrimination complaints.

FINDING A JOB

Looking for work, especially when the economy is in a decline, can be a frustrating, ego-shattering experience. But you can increase your chance of finding the kind of job you want. Whether you are just beginning your first job, or a housewife, widow, or divorcee re-entering the job market, you should pinpoint the kind of work that interests you, learn how to write a resume, and work on how to handle an interview.

Before you begin your search, take a close look at what *you* want out of working. In *The Woman's Work Book* by Karin Abarbanel and Connie McClung Siegel, a questionnaire asks you to examine:

— Which is more important to you in looking for work: Salary? Responsibility or job title? Advancement?

— Do you prefer to work with people? With information? With ideas? In a large organization, or a smaller company? In an efficient work situation, or a flexible one? With energetic people, or low-key, quiet ones?

— Do you expect to be working one year from now? Five years? Are you willing to relocate? Would changes in your lifestyle, such as marriage or children, make you decide to stop working?

Your answers to questions like these will help define your job goals. If you are looking for a short-term job to help put a child through college, pension benefits might not interest you as much as good immediate income, and perhaps a chance for overtime. If you are planning a career,

the starting salary might not be as important as the promotion possibilities. Remember, your goals may change over the years. A single woman who plans to quit when she marries, and then doesn't get married, may find herself locked into a job she hates. A married woman who plans to work for only a short time may, in cases of divorce or death, find herself the sole supporter of her family.

The next step is to identify your skills, which may be simple for some career women, but more difficult for a housewife who has been out of the job market for twenty years. Housewives tend to underestimate their skills because their work has been unpaid or underpaid. But if you have coordinated a fund-raising drive, planned a testimonial dinner, or organized a tour, you have already developed skills that can be listed on a resume.

Resume Tips

When writing your resume, it is important to keep in mind exactly the kind of job you're looking for, and then tailor your resume to fit that job. There are two basic kinds of resumes: chronological, which lists paid or unpaid work beginning with the most recent; and functional, which organizes your work experience by category rather than date. A chronological resume might be easier to compile, but a functional resume allows you to focus on specific skills which would qualify you for the job you want.

Resumes should include personal information, such as: education, age, hobbies, travel, and club memberships. Be sure to also include your name, address, and telephone number. If you wish to list references, ask your references in advance if you may use their names. If you prefer not to list references, you can say they're available on request. A resume should be no longer than two pages. Type it neatly, with wide margins, double-spaced. If you wish to make copies, use a good duplicating machine rather than carbons.

If you mail the resume to potential employers, enclose a short three- or four-paragraph letter describing the position you seek and why you are applying. Find out exactly who to address your letter to.

If you have no "in" with a company, and no knowledge of available jobs, you

More job information is available from:

- The U.S. Department of Labor, Women's Bureau, Branch of Labor Force Research, Room 1322, Washington D.C., 20036, offers information on job opportunities.
- Federally Employed Women, 621 National Press Building, Washington, D.C., 20004, publishes a newsletter listing job openings in federal government. It charges ten dollars annually.
- The National Organization for Women (NOW), 5 South Wabash, Suite 1615, Chicago, Illinois, 60603, has 800 local women's groups. Many of them provide employment seminars and job referral services.
- Local branches of the YWCA/YMCA and YWHA/YMHA are scattered across the country; many offer career-counseling services.
- Women's centers also exist nationwide, and every state has at least one center that can give practical advice on the local employment situation. If you cannot locate a women's center near you, write: Project on the Status of Education of Women, Association of American Colleges, 1818 R Street N.W., Washington, D.C., 20009.

Associates, says the job market is like an iceberg — only 25 percent of the jobs are visible, advertised by newspapers or agencies. If you don't know any people in the field that interests you, get to know them. Ask the owner of the local garden shop how landscape designers are hired. Call the union local that represents electricians, and ask about apprenticeship programs.

Employment agencies can often find jobs, but there are several things to guard against. Every year, 10,000 agencies place about four million people. Some require that you pay a fee for placement, while others charge the fee to the employer. If you get a high-paying job, the agency fee will be from 5 to 15 percent of your first year's salary. For jobs in the lower $6,000 to $10,000 range, you will have to pay 25 percent or more of your first month's earnings. Good agencies will review both the applicant's and the company's needs, to find the best matches. Other agencies, however, run "lure" ads, touting non-existent glamour jobs to get people to come in and sign up with their firm.

If you respond to a specific job ad, and find yourself being offered only lesser positions, you should report the incident to the Better Business Bureau. Agencies also can not specify sex preference in a job, unless sex is a bona fide occupational qualification — such as a locker room attendant, or a model for women's bikinis. **If you are qualified for a job and are denied it because you are a woman, you have the right to file a complaint with the Equal Employment Opportunity Commission under Title VII of the 1964 Civil Rights Act.**

There are several organizations that can guide you in finding a job. Catalyst, 14 E. 60th Street, New York, New York, 10022, is a nonprofit, nationwide program that helps college-educated women with career planning and job placement.

If you want to become a businesswoman, get to know other women in business by getting in touch with their organizations. Two of them are The Business and Professional Women's Foundation; and the National Federation of Business and Professional Women's Clubs, which has given $250,000 in grants to help women receive the training they need to re-enter the job market. Both are located at 2012

can call employers directly. Do not ask if there are openings; simply ask for an interview. If she or he refuses, ask if you can call again at a later date. Meanwhile, send in your resume. Be bold and assertive, even if you don't feel that way.

Look for job openings in the want ads of local newspapers, trade magazines, and newsletters — especially women's newsletters. The local branch of your state employment office can often help. Carl Bielby, a career counselor for Mainstream

Massachusetts Avenue, N.W., Washington, D.C., 20036.

For reading material, the Women's Bureau of the U.S. Department of Labor offers *Occupational Outlook Quarterly,* a how-to-do-it magazine covering new occupations, training and education opportunities, salary trends, and job prospects. For three dollars you can get a two-year subscription. Contact the Department of Labor office near you to subscribe. It also publishes each year the *Occupational Outlook Handbook* which covers 850 occupations in 35 industries, including training requirements for each job, earning potential and working conditions. It is available at your public library.

Your library or bookstore should also have helpful books such as: *The Working Mother,* edited by S.D. Callahan; and *How to Go to Work When Your Husband Is Against It, Your Children Aren't Old Enough and There's Nothing You Can Do Anyhow,* by Felice N. Schwartz, Margaret H. Schiften and Susan S. Gillotti.

The Crucial Interview
The most harrowing part of job-hunting can be the interview. It is natural to feel insecure when going for an interview — so accept your nervousness, but take steps to make your interview as successful as possible. Dress neatly: avoid attention-getters like low-cut blouses, heavy makeup, and clinking jewelry. Be friendly, but businesslike. Pay attention to the questions the interviewer asks, and respond in the same natural manner you would respond to a friend. Take your time to answer thoughtfully. Be sincere, and brief.

Watch for danger signs. If the first question is "How fast can you type?", promotion for women may be limited. Interview your interviewer: ask questions about the firm and your potential job. Your first question, however, should not be about salary. Remember that employers rarely hire on the spot. Ask the interviewer when she or he plans to make a decision, and call back on that date.

Once you have the job you like, pay attention to office politics and establish bonds to other women in the organization. Risk making mistakes. Keep your relations with male co-workers on a profes-

sional basis. Control your emotions while on the job, and accept criticism as a learning tool rather than a personal insult. When you feel you are ready for promotion, or salary increases, say so. Concentrate on your long-term goals, and look at each job as a step along the way.

UNEMPLOYMENT

Under the Social Security Act of 1935 and subsequent social legislation, most out-of-work Americans can now collect tax-free income for up to fifty-two weeks, ranging from an average of $48.80 a week in Mississippi to an average of $95.90 in the District of Columbia.

About 70 percent of working people are covered by unemployment insurance. Exceptions are domestics, farm workers, and state employees. Although state eligibility rules vary, you can usually collect benefits if you: have lost your job through no fault of your own; have been willing and able to work again but simply could not find a job; have worked a minimum number of weeks during the last year; and if your former employer was a member of the unemployment insurance program.

Unfortunately, more than twenty states still disqualify pregnant women from all unemployment benefits, even where the woman has medical approval to work. Sexual harassment is also not considered a valid reason for leaving a job, and most state departments of labor will refuse unemployment insurance to women who say they quit for that reason. Fifteen states also deny benefits to those who leave work for marital or domestic reasons — such as quitting to move with your husband to his new job location. This may soon change, however. In a precedent-setting decision, the California Unemployment Insurance Board granted benefits to Kay Drewa, who left her job as a waitress in Fallbrook, California, to move with her husband to his hometown of Menasha, Wisconsin. The California Unemployment Insurance Board said that "maintenance of the marital relationship" was good cause for leaving her job. The same rule would apply if a husband moved to accompany his wife.

Before leaving your job, check into your eligibility for unemployment benefits.

Find a New Job First

It is better, before quitting a job, to try to find a new one rather than rely on unemployment benefits to tide you over. If you do think you may soon leave your job, first find out whether you are covered by unemployment insurance; what are considered justifiable reasons for leaving that will qualify you for that insurance; where to file a claim; how long it takes to receive payments, and how long you will be eligible to continue receiving them. If you think you may be fired and don't want to be, find out whether you can appeal a decision to fire you. Also, try to learn what becomes of your unused vacation and sick pay, whether you can maintain your group health insurance coverage on your own, and whether you can still get a good reference for your next job.

Eight million women also stay in the job market by working part time, and some firms that cannot afford to hire a full-time person will consider someone for part-time work. Pay tends to be low, and fringe benefits almost non-existent, but part-time work does offer more flexibility and freedom. Some effort is being made to experiment with part-time jobs. For example, in a "paired job," two part-time workers fill one full-time job. This is used most often in "team" teaching where one person teaches mornings and the other afternoons. About 1,000 companies have also begun to use three- to four-day work weeks, totalling thirty-six to forty hours. Unions generally oppose this, because they fought long and hard for the shorter eight-hour day. But many workers enjoy the long weekend, and the reduction in commuter and child care costs. Other companies are experimenting with "flexi-time," in which employees can arrive at and leave work within certain flexible hours, as long as they put in eight hours each day.

Money

THE POWER OF THE PURSE

Women control 47 percent of the nation's wealth, according to Internal Revenue Service statistics. Among people with an income of $60,000 a year or more, women hold 52 percent of all bonds, 49 percent of all cash, and 47 percent of all corporate stock. And, in 1975, there were 90,836 women millionaires as compared to 89,164 men millionaires.

But, unfortunately, statistics don't give the whole story.

Even in the case of wealthy women, most of the money has been transferred to them from men. Since women generally live longer than men, estates of deceased husbands often revert to their wives. The estates are then usually controlled by other men: trust officers and executors who invest the money conservatively, with the aim of preserving rather than increasing the widows' estates.

But none of these facts or statistics deny the tremendous influence women have in spending money. Married women are pur-

A woman stuffs her shirt with part of $25,000 spread over the Atlanta Braves' diamond in 1975.

chasing agents for more than 46 million households, with income of $626 billion. A 1974 Chase Manhattan Bank survey of couples with joint checking accounts found that women paid the bills 60 percent of the time.

In addition, 27.8 million single women make personal and family economic decisions, according to a 1972 survey.

Women and the Household Budget

What decisions do they make? According to Sylvia Porter's *Money Book* (1976), Americans spend the most money, 22.3 cents of every dollar, on food, alcohol, and tobacco. Next on the list is housing, including owned and rented, which costs 14.5 cents of each dollar. Another 14.4 cents goes to household operation, including furniture, kitchen and other appliances, china, glassware and tableware, household utilities, and telephone and domestic service.

Transportation, including car purchase, insurance and upkeep, and local and intercity travel, accounts for 13.6 cents of each dollar.

The rest of a family's budget, which is strongly influenced by the woman in the household, goes to, in order: clothing, including accessories and maintenance; medical care; recreation, which includes reading material, television and radio, musical instruments, spectator admissions, club dues and membership costs; personal business, such as legal services, funeral and burial services; private education; personal care, including toilet articles and beauty and barber shop costs; religious and welfare activities and foreign travel.

But women have a long way to go before reaching economic parity with men, according to figures from the U.S. Bureau of the Census and the Internal Revenue Service. In 1974, a man's median income was $13,288, almost double that of a woman's $7,236. In 1975, while the man raised his median income by $831 to $14,119, a woman's median income grew only $558, thus increasing the disparity between a man and a woman's median salary to $6,325.

Also, women who do the same work as men only get paid 57 percent as much, according to 1974 statistics. This represents a backward step. In 1964, women made 59 percent as much as men.

The picture is not all bleak. In professional and technical work, female earnings rose from 72 percent of male pay in 1974 to 73 percent in 1975. In crafts, sales, and farming, they also made moderate advances, But elsewhere, they suffered offsetting comparative declines.

The fact remains that women cannot have equal economic clout without equal earnings. Money is power, and women have a way to go, in terms of fiscal realities and attitudes, before they can take direct control of their economic lives.

HOUSEHOLD BUDGETING

In a 1976 *Good Housekeeping* poll of 1,700 women, almost half reported that they had increased their weekly household budgets between eleven dollars and twenty dollars over the previous year's budget. Fifty-three percent of the women surveyed reported that their budgets "just barely" covered their costs. Fifth-six percent said they try to limit their expenses to their budget, but "go over if necessary."

More than half of the women responding to the survey spent between twenty-one and sixty dollars weekly which covered all food costs, more than half the expenses for cleaning supplies, laundry and dry cleaning, and personal items such as stockings. Half the women also included the cost of newspapers and magazines. Less than half the women included the cost of cigarettes, shoe and clothes repair, school lunches, and the beauty parlor. The "Good Housekeeping" poll illustrates a well-known fact: setting up a workable household budget is an awesome task. The following guidelines, however, can help the homemaker create a flexible and reasonable budget.

Building a Budget
First: Determine your actual income. In addition to your take-home pay from your job, include any income from bonuses, commissions, interest, dividends, rents, gifts, tips, tax refunds, and benefit payments. Also add any profits you expect from the sale of securities, home, car, or other major items.

When in doubt about potential income, always underestimate it. If your income is irregular — from part-time or free lance work — estimate your profit for the time period of the budget, but keep the estimate low.

Second: Itemize expenses. Include fixed expenses, flexible but regular expenses, then miscellaneous and luxury expenses.

Fixed expenses are rent or mortgage payments, insurance premiums, installment payments, commuting costs, and tuition payments. Somewhat flexible, but regular expenses are food, household goods, utilities, foreseeable medical and dental expenses, entertainment, clothes, and minor home maintenance costs.

For major expenses that arise each year, like tuition bills, divide the sum due by twelve and set aside that amount each month to cover the expense when it comes due.

Savings should also be included as a fixed expense. Sylvia Porter recommends saving 5 percent of your monthly income. Savings should equal two months' income to cover emergency expenses.

To force yourself to save money, you should consider an automatic deduction plan from your checking account, a payroll savings plan where a part of your salary check is deposited in a savings account, or is invested either in U.S. savings bonds, mutual funds, or corporate stock.

To help in budgeting for more flexible, but regular expenses — like food, clothing, and household goods — keep a careful list of how you spend your money for several weeks. Use that list as a guide for setting up a personalized budget that will reflect your priorities.

It Has to Balance
Now comes the sticky part of budget making. After adding up your income and adding up your expenses, you may find that the latter exceeds the former. When this happens, you must reduce your expenses to meet your income. According to a 1972 survey, 46 percent of women who keep budgets report that they sometimes run over their allotment.

Today, living within a budget requires keeping your dreams in check, a restraining hand on your checkbook, and a back drawer of savings for a rainy day.

COST CUTTING TIPS

Convinced you'll never save up for the Florida vacation? The new living room rug? Junior's orthodontia? Just figure out the great things you could afford by setting aside another five dollars a week. Then start observing the following cost cutting tips, and you'll be sunning at Miami Beach in no time.

General Tips

• Plan ahead before embarking on a shopping spree. Watch newspaper and television advertisements for news of specials.

• Keep track of how much the items you buy normally cost so you can tell which items are really on sale. Remember that you are getting no bargain if you buy something you don't need.

• Don't buy a twenty dollar embroidered lace handkerchief when plain cotton broadcloth will do. Buy the quality of product that is right for you — no better and no worse.

• Make financial management a family affair. Enlist your husband, children, or roommate in the battle against household costs.

• Make a shopping list and stick to it. Keep a continuous list in a convenient spot and add items as soon as they start running low. Limit your impulse buying.

• Investigate store brands, local brands, and other brands you don't see advertised on the national market. Buying these labels can save you money if their quality is adequate for your needs.

• Consider convenience when evaluating products. You can often save money by buying items that require more effort from you.

• Compare stores not only for price but also for service. Check into store policies for repairing damaged products and replacing unwanted ones.

Cutting Food Costs

• Plan meals for the whole week at one time.

• Never shop when you're hungry.

• Limit shopping trips to once a week, except for necessary fill-ins like milk.

• Best food shopping days are Thursday, Fridays and Saturdays, when advertised "specials" are available.

• Read labels to find out what you're

Soup: 11 cents. Toilet paper: 8 cents. Prices — as well as fashions — have changed since the 20s.

really paying for. Ingredients must be listed in decreasing order of weight.

• Unit pricing can help you compare various brands and sizes of the same product.

• Watch carefully when food is being weighed at the market. Don't end up paying for the package along with the product.

• During sales, stock up on several months' worth of staples and canned goods.

• Use coupons and cents-off offers only when you would have purchased the product at full price anyway.

• If you have a large family, buy by the case on discount, or get together with friends and relatives to split a case of canned foods.

• Don't overbuy expensive protein foods. Even the most active members of the family require only the amount of protein in four ounces of cooked meat and three glasses of milk per day.

• When comparing the costs of meat, fish, and poultry, always consider servings per pound. Boneless lean meat, fish, and poultry give three to four servings per pound. Steaks and chops, fish steaks, and cut-up chicken pieces give two to three servings. Fatty or bony meats — spareribs, whole fish, and chicken wings, for example — yield one or two servings.

• Large cuts of meat often cost less per pound. Plan several meals using meat from one roast, ham, or turkey.

• Learn to recognize cuts of meat and how they should be cooked. Often, less expensive cuts can be substituted in recipes.

• Dried beans, peas, and lentils are economical main dishes. For efficient use of vegetable protein, combine them with small amounts of meat, fish, poultry, eggs, milk, or cheese.

• Substituting reliquefied nonfat milk for whole milk can save about twenty cents a quart.

• Note which fruits and vegetables are in season; these will generally be cheaper. But be sure to compare even seasonal fruits and vegetables with their canned and frozen counterparts.

• Growing your own fruits and vegetables in your backyard — or even your windowsill — is both economical and fun.

• Chopped, sliced, or cut vegetables usually cost less than those packaged whole.

• Save about one-fourth on baked goods by buying "day old" products at supermarkets or outlet stores.

• Bread you are not able to use immediately can be kept in the freezer for up to three months.

• To keep fruits and vegetables in peak condition longer, do not wash them until just before using.

• Serve a lower cost but filling and nutritious first course, like soup or salad, to take the edge off appetites.

• Cut down on foods that provide only empty calories, such as carbonated drinks, candy, and many other popular snack items.

• Save from one-third to one-half on mayonnaise and on French and Italian salad dressings by making your own.

• Sometimes you pay no more for a convenience product: instant coffee, frozen French fries, "complete" pancake mixes, and many cake mixes, for example.

• Whipped butter or margarine is easier to spread, so it goes further.

• Be kind to both health and pocketbook by pan-frying foods in small amounts of oil rather than deep-frying. When you do deep fry, strain the oil, cover, and refrigerate for use again.

• Cut costs on non-food items, which amount to about 25 per cent of the average grocery bill. With paper goods, stick to simple basics. Whenever possible, compare the cost per towel or sheet.

• Choose multipurpose cleaning supplies rather than many special-purpose items.

• Additional food buying tips can be found in publications of the U.S. Department of Agriculture. For information on pamphlets currently available, write to the Superintendent of Documents, Washington, D.C. 20402.

Food Co-ops

By far, the most dramatic savings in food costs are found through food cooperatives — groups of people who join together to buy their weekly groceries in bulk at wholesale food markets. Food prices of co-ops in the New York City area are about 42 percent below retail supermarket prices, according to the city's Consumer Affairs

Food co-ops vary in size from five families to four hundred. In most co-ops, members take turns buying and delivering the week's food supply to other members. There is usually a membership fee.

For further information on co-ops, write the Cooperative League of the USA, Suite 1100, 1828 "L" Street, Washington, D.C. 20036.

Savings on Clothing

• The most economical wardrobe sticks to coordinated basics. Interchangeable separates of good quality and compatible colors can take you anywhere in style, especially when accentuated with an interesting scarf, belt, or other low-cost accessory.

• When shopping, look for garments to supplement your existing wardrobe.

• Buy clothing that fits you properly — not that size eight skirt that you will have to lose ten pounds to get into.

This smart shopper found a mountain of $1-per-pair shoes on a sidewalk of New York's garment district.

• Look for all-season items, like raincoats with detachable linings.

• Examine clothing for quality before you buy, checking the width of seams, size of hems, and security of buttons. If you notice a rip in a garment you want to buy, tell a salesperson and the store may fix it for you at no cost.

• Buy bargain-priced items — such as underwear — in quantity. Patronize economical clothing stores for staples like underwear, nightwear, belts, and work clothes.

• Check the bargain departments of your favorite stores, but keep a wary eye. You may get better quality — and a better price — in a regular department. Check the "seconds" or "irregulars" for good buys; flaws may be barely noticeable or easily repaired.

• Children outgrow and wear out play clothes so fast that it's more economical to buy cheaper brands. Do the same for casual sportswear for the whole family.

• "Vintage" clothing stores, where you can purchase "gently worn" clothes for excellent prices, are gaining in popularity.

• Sewing is a big money saver. Making your own clothes can cut their price in half, and you are assured of quality.

• Do not wear the same dress or pair of shoes day after day; clothing that gets a rest lasts longer.

• Follow cleaning directions on your clothes. Keep clothing in a dry, airy place.

• With a little ingenuity, old clothing can be recycled to look like new.

• One of the best ways to cut clothing costs is to buy off-season. A general month-by-month off-season sale guide follows:

January — men's coats, costume jewelry, dresses, furs, handbags, men's hats, infants' wear, lingerie, men's shirts shoes, sportswear, and toiletries.

February — millinery and sportswear.

March — hosiery, infants' wear, and children's shoes.

April — women's and children's coats, dresses, millinery, and men's and boys' suits.

May — handbags, lingerie, and sportswear.

June — dresses and fabric.

July — bathing suits (after July 4), children's clothing, handbags, hats, infants' wear, lingerie, men's shirts, shoes, sportswear, and toiletries.

August — back-to-school clothes, bathing suits, coats, and furs.

September — children's clothing and fabric.

October — back-to-school clothes, and hosiery.

November — children's clothing, women's and children's coats, dresses, men's and boys' suits, fabric, and shoes for adults.

December — children's clothing, women's and children's coats, children's hats, men's and boys' suits, and shoes for adults.

Buying a Car

If you need a car, new or used, here are some guidelines to help you choose an automobile: Decide on the type of car you need, depending on the size of your family, the weather conditions you will be driving in, and whether the car is for work, commuting, or family use.

Decide how important the status-value of your car is to you and what extras you need and want. Investigate gas mileage and maintenance costs of different cars. Time your purchase to get the best deal — winter is usually a good time. Also, look for special spring cleaning sales and rebate offerings.

Study publications that compare prices and performance of different cars. A look at Consumer Reports *Buying Guide,* published every December, for instance, will allow you to shop around for the best auto bargain for your needs.

After you've bought a car, proper upkeep will prolong its life. Take it in for check-ups regularly, and use the proper gas and oil. Familiarize yourself with the owner's manual and warranty, and perhaps invest in a layman's auto repair book or in a simple auto repair course.

Smooth, steady driving saves gas. Keep tires inflated to two or three pounds above lowest pressure recommended in the owner's manual. Turn off the engine instead of idling it — it takes less gas to start the engine again than to keep the car idling. Don't trade your car in too soon — it's usually cheaper to run a car into the ground than to trade it in for a new one.

Also, report every accident to your insurance company, regardless of how minor it may appear or how much the other driver was at fault. Otherwise, you may not be covered if the accident turns out to be more serious than originally thought.

Renting and Leasing

Owning a car is not the only solution to transportation needs. If you only need a car occasionally, you can rent. Check the budget car-rental companies in your area for special weekend or business day rates. Mileage is often free.

Another increasingly popular alternative to owning a car is leasing one. Nationally, 25 percent of all cars are leased, and it is estimated that figure will rise to 40 percent by 1980.

Air Travel

When you leave your car for air travel, don't leave your consumer nose at home. There are many cost cuts in flying that are well worth the time it takes to find out about them.

Never fly first class, where seats cost much more than those in the coach section. Check on special discount fares available by booking ahead or flying at mid-week or at night. Recent Civil Aeronautics Board decisions have opened up good bargains in the air charter business — look into them through a travel agent. For an information sheet on air travelers' rights, write to Aviation Consumer Action Project, Washington, D.C. 20036. Or for a free sixteen-page booklet "Air Travelers' Fly-Rights," write to Consumer Information Center, Pueblo, Colorado 81009. Ask for Booklet 608-E.

THE ROOF OVER YOUR HEAD

Most people will both rent and buy during a lifetime. Renting a home is usually more economical for the short term, and buying is better for a long-term investment.

The main advantage of renting is mainly financial flexibility — there is no large down payment, and the financial commitment is only as long as your lease. Also, major household repairs and maintenance are the landlord's responsibility. For a young couple with no children and limited money, renting is probably preferable to buying.

Buying a house requires a higher initial outlay than a rental, but it becomes more economical as the years pass. The money you pay for the house in down payment, mortgage payments, and home improvements, becomes an investment that pays dividends when you sell the house at a higher price than you bought it.

Another advantage to buying a house is the tax advantage you receive. The interest paid on a mortgage is tax deductible. The local real estate taxes are also deductible.

If you want to further explore the facts of buying and maintaining a home, you can write for the U.S. Department of Agriculture's "Handbook for the Home," from the Superintendent of Documents, Washington, D.C. 20402.

What's in a Lease?

Good Housekeeping suggests that before you sign a lease for an apartment, house, or vacation cottage, be sure you understand *all* the rights you are entitled to and the limitations you must accept. In particular, get the answers to these important questions.

Rent. Does the lease spell out the exact amount due each month, when it is due, and whether or not there is a grace period (usually ten days) in which to pay before the rent becomes overdue? Is there a clause allowing your landlord to increase the rent before the lease expires?

Security And Damage Deposit. Does the landlord require a deposit as security in the event you break the lease or damage his property? Will you get all, a portion, or none back when you move?

Services. Does the rent include utilities, or must you pay for them separately? If utilities are included, can your rent be increased if utility rates go up? Will the landlord repair holes, cracks, etc., and paint before you move in, or must you rent "as is"? Are laundry facilities, garbage removal, and yard work and window-washing services provided?

Subletting and Sharing. Can you sublease the unit you are renting? If you are con-

sidering a roommate, can a name not on the lease share with you?

Other
- Are promises and agreements made to you verbally also spelled out in the lease? (Additions to, as well as deletions from, the text should be initialed by both you and the landlord.)
- Must you give advance notice of your intention to move when the lease expires? And what happens if you move *before* the lease expires?
- Does your landlord have the right to enter your apartment whenever he wants to?
- Is the landlord given a lien on your personal property that lets him hold your furnishings and belongings until you pay any money you owe him?

Cut Fuel Costs

By now you've probably completed major heat-saving projects like insulating the attic or installing storm windows and doors. But even if you're the proverbial grasshopper instead of the provident ant, there are still some things *Good Housekeeping* suggests you can do to keep fuel bills down:
- Have your heating system serviced annually. Clean or replace dirty furnace filters.
- Keep the door to an attached garage closed.
- It's best to remove any window air-conditioning units. But if you keep them in, cover them tightly.
- Keep closet doors closed — you'd be surprised at the amount of heat wasted on heating closets.
- If you don't have storm windows, cover your windows — including those in the basement — with cut-out sheets of polyethylene and seal with tape. It may not look elegant, but it helps hold in heat.
- Check weather-stripped windows and doors every so often to make sure the weather stripping is in good shape.
- Check to make sure that rugs, furniture, or draperies are not covering baseboard heat outlets, heaters, and hot-air registers.
- During the day, set the thermostat at sixty-eight degrees; at night, or when you plan to be away from home during the day, turn it down to sixty degrees — simple

steps that can save you from 10 to 15 percent annually on fuel bills. If you have radiators, put metal reflectors behind them to reflect the heat back into the room.

- Fix leaky hot-water faucets and take showers instead of baths. To save further on hot water, install a flow restrictor on your showerhead.
- Run dishwashers and clothes washers and dryers only with full loads. Whenever possible, use cold water to wash clothes.

Running Your Home

Telephone, heating, and electricity are the major utilities, whether you rent or own your own home.

To save on telephone bills, follow these few hints: dial long distance calls yourself and only when they are cheapest; on weekends and late in the evening. When you dial a wrong number, call the operator immediately and get a credit for your call. Report an out-of-order phone immediately — in some areas you get credit for the time your phone is broken. Extra phone extensions cost money, so choose them carefully. Ask the phone company's sales person whether you are indeed buying the least expensive service available.

To save money on electric costs: don't buy more air conditioning units than you need, and keep your air conditioning thermostat down; defrost your refrigerator before the ice on the coils is one-quarter-inch thick; restrict your cooking to a minimum in hot weather; and avoid buying small appliances you don't really need.

To cut down on your heating bills, be sure your home is properly insulated. Keep your thermostat down, especially at night.

AFTER YOU'RE RETIRED

Retirement pension plans, unlike Social Security benefits, are not automatically guaranteed to every worker. They are not mandated by law, and only 50 percent of the nation's employers offer pension plans at all. Also, unlike the fixed Social Security formula, there are numerous pension plans with widely differing benefits.

A key to varying pension plan benefits is the federal Pension Reform Law.

Tips on Tipping

In a restaurant, a waiter or waitress receives 15 percent of total food and beverage check, less tax, and a wine steward fifty cents per person. A captain should get a dollar for two persons if special service is received, and a bartender 15 percent of bar bill.

A taxi driver gets twenty-five cents on a fare of a dollar or less, and about 20 per cent of all larger fares. A doorman expects twenty-five cents for calling a cab and more if he helps with bags or provides other services.

A hotel doorman expects 50 cents for carrying your luggage to the registration desk, a dollar for more than three suitcases. If he calls a cab, tip him twenty-five cents. Porters receive fifty cents a bag, chambermaids fifty cents per night's stay or $3 a week.

If you order from room service in a hotel, tip fifty cents for a delivery, but more if the waiter brings ice and drink mixers. If you have a meal in your room, tip as you would in a restaurant.

When traveling abroad, tip in amounts comparable to those in this country, but be aware of differing tip customs. In France, for instance, ushers in theaters and movie theaters are tipped. Tip in local currency whenever possible.

Most important of all, remember that tipping is a courtesy based on the quality of service you receive and need not be automatic.

Passed in 1974, it outlines the basic requirements the employer must meet in his pension plan. (A booklet entitled "Often Asked Questions About the Employees Retirement Income Security Act of 1974" can be obtained from the U.S. Department of Labor, Labor-Management Services Administration, Office of Employee

Benefits Security, Washington, D.C. 20216.)

What the law does not require is the following: it does not guarantee a pension to every worker. It does not set a specific dollar amount to be paid to workers, nor is it concerned with whether or not the benefits are adequate. It does not guarantee benefits to all widows. It does not provide that an employee can automatically transfer pensions if changing jobs. It does not restore benefits lost before its enactment.

Among the things it does require is that an employee be guaranteed 50 percent of the money she and her employer have invested in the pension plan after she has worked for an employer for ten years, and 100 percent of her pension money if she has worked for the same employer for fifteen years. The employee's guarantee of her share of the pension money is called "vesting" — one says, so and so is "50 percent vested."

Also, the law states that an employee must generally be allowed to participate in a pension at age twenty-five when one year of service is completed. But, the law also allows pension plans that exclude new employees who are within five years of retirement age.

Pointing out these variables is not meant to scare you, but to send you to your employer to find out exactly what your pension plan, if there is one, includes. Make a list of what you think you and your dependents will need in retirement, and find out if your employer's pension plan answers those needs.

Also keep up to date on changes in your pension plan. Your employer must furnish you with notice of these changes. Make sure you read them. In addition, if your pension claim is denied, your employer is required to give you an explanation in writing.

Profit-Sharing and Stock Bonus Plans

Some companies offer profit-sharing plans, in which a percentage of the company's profits each year are put into a pool for employees. Usually the employees must have worked for the company for a certain number of years before they become eligible for profit-sharing, and there are varying regulations, depending on the company, covering how soon employees become vested for profit-sharing benefits. Investigating your company's profit-sharing means finding out the vesting requirements, the percentage of the profit that goes into the plan, and your eligibility requirements.

Stock-bonus plans are similar to profit-sharing, but employees receive company stock instead of a percentage of the profits.

Individual Retirement Accounts and Keogh Plan

Prior to 1977, housewives, because they had no earnings of their own, were unable to open their own retirement accounts. Now they are able to do so under certain conditions. If a husband isn't covered by a pension plan at his job, he may open an Individual Retirement Account for himself and a separate one for his wife.

The 15 percent limit on tax free annual deposits in the account, however, must be spread out over both accounts. He can have up to $1,750 in one account or $875 in two separate accounts.

Similar to the individual retirement account is the Keogh Plan, designed specifically for self-employed people. Eligible people can set aside and deduct up to $7,500 a year on income tax returns. The money can be reinvested and, like the individual retirement account, is not taxable until you start receiving the benefits, from age 59½ to 70½.

Social Security

Even if your retirement is decades away, it is wise to prepare for the future by familiarizing yourself with the Social Security system. If you have questions about benefits to which you might be entitled, Social Security officials suggest you save yourself time and trouble by contacting them by phone. The number of your local Social Security office is listed in the phone book under "United States Government."

A working woman pays 11.7 percent of her income up to $16,500 a year into Social Security; 5.85 percent is deducted from her paycheck and 5.85 percent is paid by her employer. She cannot receive worker's retirement benefits until she reaches retirement age and puts in a specified amount of time in jobs covered by Social Security. Today, most jobs in which people work for wages or salaries, as well as most work of self-employed persons, is covered. Housewifery, however, is not. Just how long one must work depends upon age; generally, a person is eligible if she has one quarter of coverage for every year after 1950 or the year she reached age twenty-one.

You may begin collecting retirement benefits at age sixty-two, but you then receive only 80 percent of the benefits you would be entitled to if you waited until age sixty-five. The nearer you are to sixty-five when you begin to collect payments, the larger they will be.

If you become so disabled that you cannot work, you may be eligible for Social Security benefits if you worked at least five of the ten years prior to the disability.

Wives receive benefits based on their own earnings or those of their husbands, whichever is greater. The working wife, although paying her own Social Security, will collect only one benefit. The standard wife's benefit is 50 percent of the husband's benefit.

You will not be entitled to a wife's benefit until you reach age sixty-five — or age sixty-two for a reduced benefit — and until your husband begins collecting his own Social Security. If your marriage ends in divorce before your twentieth anniversary, you lose any wife's benefit to which you otherwise would have been entitled. Your husband's new wife, however, immediately becomes eligible. There have been proposals for modifying this arrangement.

Survivor benefits are paid to the spouses and minor children of workers who die while insured. Mother's benefits are paid a widow if children under eighteen are left in her care. Her benefits continue until the youngest child reaches eighteen, and resume when she reaches age sixty. If childless, she will receive widow's payments for the first time at age sixty for reduced benefits or age sixty-five for full benefits. If she is disabled, she can receive widow's benefits at age fifty. By remarrying, a woman forfeits her right to benefits based on the late husband's earnings. Survivors of women workers receive benefits on the same basis as those of survivors of men workers.

Persons receiving old-age benefits cannot earn more than $3,000 a year (in 1977) without losing $1 for every $2 earned. However, persons over age seventy-two receive full benefits regardless of outside income.

BANKING AND CREDIT

For four out of five American families, basic banking starts with a checking account. An average family writes about twenty checks a month, and pays for more than 90 percent of its goods and services by check.

In a regular checking account, also called a minimum balance plan, you have to maintain a minimum cash balance in the bank. The minimum varies from bank to bank and from $100 to $500. With this balance you can then write checks without paying a monthly service charge, but will be charged a fee if your balance falls below the minimum. Since the balance you keep in a regular checking account doesn't earn any interest, you are probably better off with another type of account, unless you write a lot of checks and can afford to keep a non interest-bearing balance in the bank.

A special checking account, or a "per check" plan is an account with two charges — a monthly maintenance fee and a charge for each check. No balance is required.

(If you write fewer than five checks a month, your best bet is to keep your money in a savings account and write money orders.)

There are several other, less common types of accounts. Some banks offer free checking with no minimum balance. Package accounts offer a variety of services in addition to checking for a flat monthly fee, but be careful of these accounts because you could end up paying for a lot of services you never use.

When looking for a checking account, shop around for the best deal — banking is as much a service as dry cleaning and shoe repair.

Savings Account Options
Once you have opened a checking ac-

count, it's time to look into the equally important area of savings. There are a number of ways to put your savings money to work for you, from a standard passbook savings account to U.S. Savings Bonds. The investments discussed here are conservative investments and guarantee certain monetary growth with virtually no risk (unlike investing in the stock market, discussed later in this chapter, where profit can't always be assured).

For a start, most financial analysts recommend keeping the equivalent of between two and six months salary in a "liquid" account — one that allows you to withdraw money any time you need it. A passbook savings account is the most common liquid account. For the privilege of easy access to your money, you receive lower interest than in other accounts: 5 percent at commercial banks and up to as much as 6 percent or more in other savings institutions.

In addition to different interest rates, however, there are significant variables in how the interest is paid in regular savings accounts, and it is worth your while to comparison shop.

First you should find out how often the interest on your money is compounded (to compound interest means to pay interest on interest). The more frequently the interest is compounded, the better. If the interest rate is the same, daily compounding is most profitable for you

You should also ask when the bank starts to tabulate its interest. The best method for you, and the one used in half of all commercial banks and 60 percent of savings and loan banks, is when interest is paid from the day-of-deposit-to-day-of-withdrawal. Many banks advertise this plan by using just that name. Other interest periods are quarterly, semi-annual, or annual.

You should also know whether the bank pays interest on the most money you have in the account during the interest period, the least, or some amount in between. Surprisingly, 30 percent of commercial banks pay interest on the least amount of money in your account for the interest period.

Other Savings Accounts

Other savings accounts offer higher interest rates if you can commit money to them for a specified time period. Called time deposit accounts and certificates of deposit, these accounts generally call for minimum deposits of $500 to $5,000 to remain in the bank from one to seven years, although certificates of deposit usually require much higher minimum deposits, about $10,000. The latter are used more often by institutional investors than individuals.

There is a stiff penalty for withdrawing money from these accounts before they mature — about 25 percent of the interest you've earned. Before opening such an account, be sure you won't need the money for the duration of the deposit.

When looking for a savings account, also consider these questions: does the account offer a grace period — days when you can deposit or withdraw money from your account without jeopardizing the interest due you; is there a charge for excess withdrawals or for premature closing of an account; is a minimum balance required; in whose name or names do you want the account?

Other Conservative Investments

In addition to banking your money, you can deposit it with a credit union: a nonprofit savings and loan organization owned by its depositors. Credit unions are not as accessible as banks — most are formed by people who share a common bond of work or other affiliation. If you can participate in one, they usually pay interest as high as seven percent. Most of them are insured by the federal government as are banks.

U.S. Savings Bonds are another no-risk investment. There are two types of savings bonds — Series E and Series H. Both pay 6 percent interest if you hold them to maturity, and are non-negotiable, which means you can't use them for collateral for loans.

The most familiar is the Series E bond, which you buy at a discount and redeem at its face value five years from its purchase date. Series H bonds are sold at face value, and you receive semi-annual interest payments on them until they mature, ten years from issue date.

Interest on savings bonds is exempt from state and local taxes, but is subject to federal income tax. On the E bonds, the tax may be deferred until the bonds mature or are cashed. The tax-deferral option is used by some people to build up education or retirement funds. Under certain circumstances, they can then avoid having to pay taxes on their investment.

Credit

To some people, buying things on time, or using credit, seems to go against the grain. It seems slightly irresponsible to buy something when you don't have the money to pay for it. But be assured that credit is the American way. Without it, you may not be able to buy a house, car, boat, or other major item, and there is really nothing wrong with using the bank's money as long as you are borrowing for sound reasons and expect to pay the money back.

To get a big loan from a bank, one must have a good credit rating. The best way to accomplish that is to open charge accounts in your own name, charge items, and pay your bills promptly. (Housewives, beware. Using Mrs. John Smith on credit cards establishes your husband's credit, not yours. Use your own first name and maintain your own checking account.)

Recent legislation has made it easier for women to get credit. Stores, national credit card companies, and other lending institutions cannot deny you credit on the basis of sex or marital status if your credit record is acceptable.

If you are rejected for credit, you must be told why, and should ask for an explanation in writing. If you suspect an error in your credit status, you may see your credit file by checking with your Chamber of Commerce or nearest credit bureau. The service is free if you are challenging a credit denial — otherwise there is a small charge.

If you can't pay your bills, it's best to call your creditor and explain why. Usually, if you show good faith, you can work something out and your credit rating won't be damaged.

Loans

Once you've established a good credit rating, getting a loan is a matter of shopping around for one that best suits you.

There are two types of bank loans. A secured loan requires that you provide collateral, like a savings account passbook. An unsecured loan requires a pledge to repay the borrowed money. Payment schedules vary from bank to bank, and interest on loans from commercial banks can range from 8 to 14 percent, so before you borrow, compare costs.

You can also borrow money against the paid-up cash value of a life insurance policy, usually at between 5 and 6 percent interest.

Credit unions provide loans to members at interest of about 12 percent or less, and consumer finance companies will also lend you money. The latter, although they often do not demand collateral, charge up to 43 percent in interest.

When taking out a loan, ask if you will be penalized for early repayment. Creditors who don't give finance charge refunds for early repayment must say so before a lending agreement is signed.

FINDING THE BEST INSURANCE BUY

As women take more responsibility for their own financial affairs, it follows that they must also look out for themselves and their dependents in the event that something should happen to them.

Not all women need life insurance. If you are young and single, with no dependents, you can put off getting a life insurance policy. But everyone should have health insurance, and the majority of women should have both. A sorting out of the labyrinth of insurance policies is in order.

Life Insurance

To decide how much life insurance to buy, try to put a dollar figure on your value to the rest of the your family. In doing this keep in mind the salary you contribute from outside work and your housekeeping and child-rearing chores. You should be insured for the amount it would cost to replace you for the number of years your services are essential to the family — a young housewife with two small children might insure herself for the price of a housekeeper for ten years.

Once you decide how much insurance you need, you must begin shopping around. There are two main types of life insurance. Term insurance is the cheaper and provides coverage for a certain time period, usually a year or five years, after which time it is renewable for a higher premium (because you are older). The advantage of term is that it is a simple protection policy with no frills. Also, your premiums are cheaper when you are young, when your income is less and you need your money for other things.

Whole-life, or straight-life, is the other type of insurance, which combines protection with a savings plan. It is more expensive than term, but the premium is fixed at the time you purchase the insurance and never increases. You may borrow against the cash value of a whole life policy at a reasonable interest rate, and can cash in the whole policy at anytime.

Both policies come with a variety of options. Keep your specific needs in mind when you see these options — don't buy something you don't need.

A wide range of prices are offered by different companies for similar insurance. In a 1974 cost comparison of insurance policies by *Consumer Reports,* annual premiums for a $25,000-life insurance policy for a thirty-five-year-old-man ranged from $460 to more than $600 for the same basic policy.

Because of this wide price span, go beyond the insurance agent. Contact local consumer groups, or call your state insurance department to see if they offer any guides to life insurance. To find out about companies that deal specifically with women's insurance needs, write to Bernice J. Malamud Associates, a private referral service at 450 Seventh Ave., New York, N.Y. 10001.

In addition to finding the best insurance policy for your own needs, check your husband's policy to insure that you and your children are adequately provided for in case of his death. If you are getting a divorce remember that, if your husband dies, any child support and alimony he pays will cease. You should request that the court order a policy on your husband's life to guarantee income for you and your children.

Annuities: Income for Life

Life insurance companies also sell annuities. Unlike life insurance, which pro-

tects your survivors if you die, an annuity provides you with a steady, monthly income until you die, usually as a supplement to your Social Security or other pension payments. Since women live longer than men, their annuity payments are spread out over a longer period than the same priced annuities owned by men, and are therefore smaller.

When your annuity comes due, you can either get it in monthly payments or in a lump sum. The latter is more economical if you transfer the money to a savings account where it will earn interest, but the former provides a specific monthly income you don't have to think about.

Health Insurance

Health costs are this country's fastest growing personal expense. With the average cost of a bed at a community hospital higher than $100 a day, rising doctor's bills, and the high cost of medication, no one can afford to be without some form of health insurance.

Unfortunately, health insurance policies are often so complicated one could get ill trying to read them. There are three main areas of insurance — basic hospitalization coverage, general supplementary coverage (called Major Medical), which covers medical bills; and disability insurance, which replaces part of your income if you are disabled and can't work. The cheapest health insurance is group insurance, available through your job or other organization. If you and your husband both work, compare your companies' respective policies and choose the one most beneficial to you both. Do not maintain two policies. If you do, each policy may pay only 50 percent of the bill if there is a claim, even though each policy is often supposed to cover more.

If you're not covered by a group plan, choose a plan carefully. Check the following points. What are the per-day limits on hospital costs (many policies pay for less than the daily cost of hospital care). Can you get a percentage contract so rising costs won't lower your benefit? How much do you have to pay for medical expenses before any expenses are reimbursed?

Also, what is the benefit limit, in case you incur a major medical expense? Avoid policies that place a limit on the time benefits will be paid for a single illness. Look for non-cancellable policies. Find out what medical treatment is excluded from the policy and if there is coverage for psychological treatment and convalescent care.

The better policies cover complications of pregnancy and, for an additional premium, offer coverage of normal pregnancy.

If You Are Disabled

If you are a working woman and are not covered at your job by disability insurance, it is important to get it through a private plan. This insurance provides you with an income if you are disabled and cannot work.

Some states provide disability benefits for women absent from work for childbirth, so check with the Human Rights Commission in your state to find out if you can collect such benefits.

For more information about disability insurance, especially pertaining to special problems you may have as a woman, write to Bernice J. Malamud Associates, 450 Seventh Ave., New York, N.Y. 10001.

INVESTING YOUR MONEY

For many people, the term "stock market" conjures up an image of intricate high finance on Wall Street, get-rich-quick schemes, and vast amounts of money changing hands.

That thinking is unfortunate, because there is good money to be made by small investors who take the time to familiarize themselves with the logical and relatively simple workings of buying and selling stocks and bonds, called securities.

If you have taken care of all living expenses and already have money in a savings account and a life insurance policy, it could be worthwhile to invest extra money in stocks, bonds, or other securities.

Stocks

When you buy a share of common stock, you are buying part ownership in a company. Since one share of stock can range in price from a few cents to more than $250, you can easily find a number of stocks to buy in your price range.

Next, do your homework. There are numerous guides to investing, but one of the best for a novice investor, often recommended by brokers to their clients, is *How to Buy Stocks,* by Louis Engel. You can also take courses offered through brokerage firms or write to the New York Stock Exchange, 11 Wall St., New York, N.Y. 10005, for an "Investors Information Kit," which costs two dollars. Start to read the financial sections of your newspaper and tune in to finance shows on radio and television.

When you have a general idea of what you're looking for in your investments, you must find a stock broker to transact your business for you — you can't do it yourself.

You want a broker who works for a brokerage firm that is a member of the New York or American Stock Exchange, the primary marketplaces for the securities business.

When you call or visit a firm, unless you ask for someone you know, you will probably be assigned to a broker. Even if you like the broker who you get at one firm, shop around at other firms before choosing a broker. You want one who is reasonably cautious, who doesn't make promises of easy money, who doesn't talk down to you (some male brokers tend to do this).

When you've picked a broker, probably a man, and told him what you'd like to do with your money, he will give you some suggestions. If you're interested in safeguarding your money, he might recommend buying stock in an established, financially solid company that will increase your investment at a slow, steady rate. If you want bigger money faster, he might suggest investing in a young company that could grow quickly and give you a landfall return on your investment. This is a riskier investment, called speculative, because you are investing your money on what you think a company will do, rather than on known past performance. As easily as you could make a lot of money on your investment, you could lose it.

If you want something in between, a safer investment but with more immediate earning potential, he might recommend buying stock in a utility, which usually increases in value at a very slow rate, if at all, but which usually pays a higher dividend.

When you and your broker have picked

a stock to buy, he will place the order for you, charging you about one percent in commission.

There is no definite rule about when to sell your stock to make the best profit. You must follow your own instincts and listen to your broker's advice. There are tax reasons, however, for selling stock at certain times, and you should definitely ask your broker, accountant, or attorney to explain them to you.

Corporate bonds

When you buy a corporate bond you are lending money to a private company; rather than buying part ownership in the company, as you do when you buy stock shares (municipal bonds are discussed under "government securities"). Bond buying is a more conservative investment than stock purchase. Shares of stock represent ownership in a company, and rise and fall with the company's profits; but bonds must be paid back in full at a specified time and pay the bondholder interest in the interim.

The minimum price for a corporate bond is usually $1,000, and interest is paid either annually or semi-annually. Before buying a bond, you can check its quality through two rating systems, Moody's or Standard & Poor's. Your broker, through whom you must buy the bond, can check its rating for you.

Mutual Funds

Mutual funds have been growing in popularity over the past twenty years. Individuals pool their money in a mutual fund, which is invested in different securities by a money manager. There are about 600 mutual funds in the U.S.

Their strength lies in their diversity. By federal law, the money invested in mutual funds must be divided among various stocks, bonds, and other securities, which lessens the risk of the investment.

Also, mutual funds free individuals from the decision-making of where to invest. This is good if you don't have the time to research different investments yourself, or if you lack investing confidence. But you should follow your investments carefully, and not succumb to the let-someone-else-take-care-of-it philosophy.

When selecting a mutual fund, look for one that doesn't charge a commission,

called a no-load fund. Commissions can range from 1 to 9½ percent.

For information on mutual funds, write to: Wiesenberger Services, Inc., 1 New York Plaza, New York, N.Y. 1005, which publishes past and present performances of mutual funds; No-Load Mutual Fund Assn., 475 Park Ave. S., New York, N.Y. 10004; Forbes Magazine, 60 Fifth Ave., New York, N.Y. 10011, which has an annual issue on mutual fund performance; Moody's Bank and Finance Manual, Moody's Investors Service, Inc., 99 Church St., New York, N.Y. 10004.

Government Securities

In addition to stocks and corporate bonds, which finance the growth of private companies, federal, state, and local governments must sell securities to raise money for public projects, like schools and public works projects.

The federal government finances its projects through selling treasury bills, notes, and bonds. Interest on these securities is fairly high, all payment is guaranteed by the federal government, and they are exempt from state and local taxes.

The minimum purchase for treasury bills is $10,000. They are bought at less than face value and when they mature, in three to twelve months, they are redeemed at face value. Treasury notes cost a minimum of $1,000, pay interest semi-annually, and mature in one to seven years. Treasury bonds also cost a minimum of $1,000 and pay semi-annual interest, but their maturation date ranges from seven to twenty-five years.

Things to note when you buy treasury securities: you lose money if you sell before the maturation date. The investing benefits are over at maturation date, so get your money into something else immediately. Keep the securities in a safe place, because they are not registered and do not bear your name. They are negotiable as cash and anyone can cash them in.

State and local governments sell municipal bonds, which pay relatively high interest rates and are exempt from federal taxes. Although municipal bonds have gotten a lot of bad publicity recently, because of New York City's financial instability and attendent worry about the value of its bonds, municipal bonds are a conservative and usually safe investment. Like corporate bonds, you can check a municipal bond's rating with a rating agency before you buy the bond.

WILLS AND WIDOWHOOD

Where there's a will, there's a way," goes the old homily, which aptly points out the importance of drawing up your own will. Where there's no will, there's no way to be sure your survivors get your belongings according to your wishes.

A will should name at least two people, called executors, to administer the will. It should state who will take custody of your children, and who will get your property, cash, securities, and other assets, and in what proportion.

Get a lawyer to draw up your will. Hand-scribbled, homemade wills have dubious legal standing if there is a dispute among survivors. An estate lawyer will also be familiar with your state's tax laws, and can set up your will to save your survivors from heavy inheritance taxes.

Your lawyer, whom you usually name as one of the executors of your will, will take charge of expediting your will after your death, at a time when your family shouldn't have to think about technical legal matters.

As important as writing a will is keeping it up to date. Suppose you provided in your will for your mother to take custody of your children in case of your, and your husband's, death. In the meantime, your mother has moved to a retirement community. Your brother, however, has married, has a family of his own, and you would rather your children go to him. If you don't change your will to specify that, there could be a long delay in getting your children in a suitable home, especially if someone disputes it.

Widowhood

When you are widowed, the world often seems to be crashing down around you, and you may feel helpless about your future. There are some things you can do, however, to take stock of your situation and begin to plan for yourself.

Get a copy of your husband's death certificate — you'll need it to apply for most benefits. Check with your attorney to handle probate proceedings, and to guide you with respect to other legal matters; including creating trust funds, handling your tax situation, changing your own will, and conserving your property. Be sure to take an active part in these proceedings.

Check with your bankers about how much money you have access to, and when and how to get it. Inquire about credit life insurance on any outstanding loans before paying any bills. Notify creditors about your husband's death. Check with your husband's insurance company to get details on insurance benefits to which you are entitled. Do the same for pension, Social Security, and veterans benefits. Notify your husband's stockbroker to freeze your husband's account.

HOW TO COMPLAIN

The average family may lose as much as several hundred dollars a year by not complaining, or not complaining through the proper channels, about shoddy goods and services.

The first thing to do, if something doesn't live up to your expectations, is to return it to the dealer from whom you bought it. Tell her what is wrong with the product and whether you want it repaired, replaced, or your money returned. Be armed with your receipt and the item itself, or its serial number. Be calm and polite, but firm. Most complaints can be settled at this stage.

If you have no luck, however, the next step is to contact the manufacturer's customer relations department. Many large companies have special toll free telephone numbers you can call or people to write to with complaints. A partial list appears at the end of this section. Provide all relevant information, including photocopies (not originals) of cancelled checks and correspondence.

Find out the name of the person to whom you should address the letter — a personal contact is more efficient. Similarly, keep track of the names and positions of people you speak to on the phone, so you can call them back if necessary.

If you are still dissatisfied, write to the president of the company. If you can't get the president's name from company personnel, most libraries have copies of *Poor's Register of Corporations, Directors and Executives,* or *Moody's Industrial Manual,* which list corporate executives. Send copies of the letter to local, state, or national consumer agencies, Better Business Bureaus, or local newspapers. And indicate that you have done so in your letter to the company president.

For government help in pursuing your claim, decide if your problem lies under local, state, or federal control. If it is local, contact your city's Chamber of Commerce, Better Business Bureau, and the consumer affairs office, which are listed in the telephone book under "city government." Local consumer affairs departments, depending on their power, can investigate the complaint, then try to work out a settlement; it may sue on behalf of a consumer, issue violations notices, hold hearings, fine a company, or revoke or suspend a company's license to operate in the city.

Many towns and counties also have consumer protection agencies. States, too, offer aid to dissatisfied consumers. Usually, it is a part of the Attorney General's office. Write or phone the Attorney General (attention Consumer Protection Office), in your state.

Nationally, one may write to the Bureau of Consumer Protection, Federal Trade Commission, Washington, DC 20580, or to the nearest Federal Trade Commission office.

The Consumer Product Safety Commission, a federal agency created in 1973, has a toll-free number, (800) 638-2666, where you can find out if a particular product has been declared unsafe or file a complaint about one you believe is hazardous.

Also, try contacting your local Better Business Bureau or, if there is no bureau in your area, the Council of Better Business Bureaus, 1150 17th Street, NW, Washington, DC 20036.

For a complaint against an airline (fares, baggage, service, delays), write Office of the Consumer Advocate, Civil Aeronautics Board, Washington, DC 20428.

Within industry groups there are industry and trade associations which may be helpful. One with a good track record of solving complaints is the Major Appliance

Consumer Action Panel (MACAP), 20 North Wacker Drive, Chicago, IL 60606. You may write, or make a collect phone call to (312) 236-3156, if you don't get satisfaction from a manufacturer of home laundry equipment, range, refrigerator, freezer, room air conditioner, water heater, dehumidifier, dishwasher, disposer, gas incinerator, or humidifier.

A similar organization is the Carpet and Rug Industry Consumer Action Panel (CRICAP), Box 1568, Dalton, GA 30720.

Some industry complaint centers sponsored by the U.S. Chamber of Commerce are: *American Apparel Manufacturers Assn.,* 1611 N. Kent St., Arlington, VA 22209; *American Footwear Manufacturers Assn.,* 342 Madison Ave., New York, NY 10017; *Direct Mail Advertising Assn.,* 230 Park Ave., New York, NY 10017; *Direct Selling Assn.,* 1730 M St. NW, Washington, DC 20036 (on door-to-door sales); *Master Photo Dealers and Finishers Assn.,* 603 Lansing Ave., Jackson, MI 49202.

In addition, *Mobile Homes Manufacturing Assn.,* 14650 Lee Rd., Chantilly, VA 22021; *National Assn. of Furniture Manufacturers,* 8401 Connecticut Ave., Suite 911, Washington, DC 20015; *National Employment Assn.* (for employment agencies) 2000 K St. NW, Washington, DC 20006; *National Automobile Dealers Assn.,* 2000 K St., Connecticut Ave., Suite 911, Washington, DC 20015; *National Consumer Finance Assn.,* 1000 16th St., NW., Washington, DC 20036; *National Institute of Drycleaning,* 909 Burlington Ave., Silver Spring, MD 20910.

Here's what some big companies suggest you do if you can't get satisfaction from your local dealer:

Ford — Phone or write Ford Parts & Service Div., district office (see phone book or ask local Ford dealer); or phone (800) 648-4848 (toll-free call) for all vehicles made by Ford (from Nevada, phone (800) 992-5777).

Chrysler — Phone or write Chrysler Corp., Customer Service (ask dealer or see phone book); or write to: Consumer Affairs, Chrysler Corp. P.O. Box 856, Detroit, MI.

General Motors — Phone or write Divisional Owner Relations Office (listed in owner's manual); or GM Owner Relations, Central Office, 3044 Grand Boulevard, Detroit, MI 48202.

American Motors — Contact zone office (see owner's manual); then write Harry Allen, Owner Relations Manager, AMC, 14250 Plymouth Rd., Detroit, MI 48232.

Volkswagen — Try Customer Assistance Dept. at Volkswagen regional office (see owner's manual); or write Customer Assistance, Volkswagen of America, Englewood Cliffs, NJ 07632.

J.C. Penney — See store manager; if unsatisfied, write Patricia Ludorf, Customer Relations Dept., J.C. Penney Co., 1301 Ave. of the Americas, New York, NY 10019.

Woolworth's — See store manager; if not satisfied, write F. W. Woolworth Co., 233 Broadway, New York, NY 10007; Attention: Consumer Relations Dept.

Kresge's — See section supervisor; then store manager; finally get the address of S.S. Kresge Co., regional office from store manager and write to Customer Relations there.

Avis — Write Customer Service Dep't., Avis Rent A Car System, World Headquarters, 900 Old Country Road, Garden City, NY 11530.

Hertz — Phone 212 598-4921; or write Consumer Relations, RCA Corp., 30 Rockefeller Plaza, New York, NY 10020.

Kodak — See phone book under Eastman Kodak Co. for Kodak Consumer Center (in some thirty-five cities) for free minor adjustments and advice; write Eastman Kodak Co., 343 State St., Rochester, NY 14650, attention-Dept. 841.

For information on consumer service at other companies, check *The World Almanac,* under the heading "Personal Finance-Consumer Complaints."

If all the above channels still leave you unsatisfied, you could try contacting a consumer reporter or "action line" at your local newspaper or television station.

Remember to keep copies of correspondence and of all other relevant materials needed to substantiate your claims. Be persistent — don't worry about complaining long and loud when you have a justifiable gripe.

WOMEN'S BANKS

Banking by women for women is not a new idea in the United States. In 1919, the year women won suffrage, a group of women in Clarksville, Tenn., formed a women's bank. In 1926, it merged with the male-run First Trust and Savings Bank, which is still operating.

Decorating the First Women's Bank is a dollar bill poster with the Mona Lisa in place of George Washington.

It took the feminist mood of the 1970s, however, to reawaken the urge to dismantle discriminatory banking traditions by breaking away from male-dominated banks.

As the feminist movement gathered steam, some banks, like Bank of America and Citibank, began to aim marketing techniques at attracting more women customers.

But it was the splashy, 1975 opening of New York City's First Women's Bank, in its lush Park Avenue office, that trumpeted the idea of women as suitable bankers and desirable bank customers.

Started by fifteen women prominent in politics, such as New York City councilwoman Carol Greitzer, in business, such as designer Pauline Trigere; and in feminism, such as Betty Friedan; and headed by a female former Federal Reserve Bank officer; the First Women's Bank seemed a sure success.

When it opened on October 16, it had $3 million in capital, and 7,000 shareholders, 81 percent of whom were women. Three hundred and fifty depositors arrived that day to open accounts and, by the following August, the bank had $13 million in deposits.

What it didn't have, unfortunately, was good management. President Madeline H. McWhinney had had little experience in commercial banking and the bank's board had none. It is reported that McWhinney's ill-advised business decisions were followed without question and put the bank deeply in the red by the end of 1976. The bank's image was also troubling. Identifying itself strongly with the feminist movement, the bank was not taken seriously by big investors. In 1976, 70 percent of the bank's 4,000 savings accounts had balances below the $300 minimum necessary for the bank to break even on an account.

It is now headed by a new president, Lynn Salvage, who is determined to give the bank a new image — "We're playing up the business, and playing down the cause," she says.

The First Women's Bank's losses have been other women's banks' gains. In March of 1976, a second women's bank was opened in San Diego, California. It has avoided any association with the feminist movement and, while having a woman chairman, named a man as chief executive officer.

Similarly, the Western Women's Bank, scheduled to open in San Francisco, California, sometime in 1977, will be run by a man, because the bank's women organizers found no women who were qualified.

Both banks, though eschewing the feminism that hurt the First Women's Bank, do hope to reach out to those who have not traditionally used banks, whether for business or philosophic reasons. The San Diego Bank offers financial counselling, especially for young, widowed or divorced persons. The San Francisco bank hopes to help people establish credit for the first time.

Following these pioneers are women's banks, in various stages of planning, in six other cities — Los Angeles, Seattle, Boston, Chicago, Greenwich, Conn., and Washington, DC.

Credit Unions

While women's banks have made the headlines, other women, mostly younger and less established, have organized some twenty credit unions across the country since 1973.

Credit unions, where women can keep their savings and take small business loans, are small operations, often run in basements by volunteers. Unlike banks, they don't require a lot of initial capital or experience, and most have less than a half million dollars in assets.

However, since the women's credit unions aren't tied to any organization, such as a private firm, they do have some problems. There are no financial sponsors, no set up offices, and no payroll deduction plan to encourage savings and borrowing. The women, too, sometimes differ on whether the union should be a financial institution or a feminist organ.

The largest feminist credit union is the Feminist Federal Credit Union in Detroit, MI, with $1.3 million in assets. An offshoot group is the Feminist Economic Alliance, located in the same city.

In addition to the credit unions in Detroit, there are credit unions in Harrisburg, PA; Connecticut, New York, Chicago, San Francisco, Los Angeles, San Diego, Miami, Seattle, Dallas, Houston, Washington (State), Pittsburgh, Cambridge, Mass.; Charleston, S.C., and Denver.

In addition, there is a Feminist Economic Network; which encourages the formation of feminist credit unions in every state, and the pooling of experience to help new credit unions. For more information about this network, or to find out about a feminist credit union near you, write the Feminist Economic Network, P.O. Box 20008, Detroit, MI 48220.

WOMEN IN ADS

Life was easy for the 1950s housewife. Dressed to the hilt in shirtwaist frock and high-heeled pumps, she operated push-button appliances with the greatest of ease. Rarely did she do anything as unglamorous as scrubbing the floor on hands and knees clad in grubby dungarees. And she was always waiting dutifully to give her tired husband a peck on the cheek when he arrived home from the office.

At least, that is the image of the 1950s women perpetrated by advertisements of the period. The househusbands and working wives in contemporary television and magazine advertisements indicate just how much times have changed.

Happy Housewives and Office Slaves

Thanks to women as much as men, advertising came of age in the post-World War II years. The young suburban population had more time and money than before to spend on newspapers, magazines, radio — especially the newly popular television.

Then as now, advertising performed an important public service. In the late forties and fifties, it alerted Americans to the new and improved products that had just come on the market after years of wartime scrimping. But some critics charged that advertising also distorted Americans' opinions of themselves.

"An American woman no longer has a private image to tell her who she is, or can be, or wants to be," wrote Betty Friedan in *The Feminine Mystique* (1963). "As the motivational researchers keep telling the advertisers, American women are so unsure of who they should be that they look to this glossy public image to decide every detail of their lives."

Unlike the happy housewife of the fifties, the working woman of that era was pictured chained to her typewriter or cash register with a male boss hanging over her shoulder. According to one study, only 13 percent of all women in 1958 advertisements worked outside the home. All but 15 percent of working women held low-paying factory, secretarial, or clerical jobs. Not one woman in the ads studied held an executive position. By contrast, only 25 percent of working men in 1958 ads worked in similarly low-status jobs.

Ads directed at female audiences urged them to buy the relatively inexpensive items that promised to clean their homes, nourish their families, and beautify their bodies. Men, Madison Avenue implied, made the decisions on major expenditures for items like insurance and automobiles. Though a woman might adorn a liquor or cigarette ad, the message was directed primarily to men.

Liberation Leaves Its Mark

Women's life-styles had changed by the late 1960s, and advertising changed along

Coffee ad, 1886: Advertisements have traditionally used women as sex objects.

GRANULATED 7 O'CLOCK BREAKFAST COFFEE.

Flour ad, 1895: Women have usually been depicted as housewives or in low-status jobs.

with them. Women had more economic clout because of their increased presence in the nation's work force and as heads of households. Advertisers recognized they risked alienating an important segment of their market if they did not revise their concept of women.

But some observers do not believe advertising has changed quickly enough. A 1972 study found that the percentage of women shown working outside the home was up only 6 percent over 1958. Blue-collar and nonprofessional white-collar jobs still claimed more than half the working women in advertisements. Though 15 percent were middle-level executives, no woman had yet reached the upper echelons of management.

But greater advances have occurred since that study was published. A major airline has begun telling female business travelers, "You're the boss." Josephine the Lady Plumber has boosted the entry of women into jobs traditionally held by men. Commercials of the nation's leading soup manufacturer depict a singing husband preparing dinner for his working wife.

Though women still clean house, they at least get to wear comfortable blue jeans.

Rena Barton, vice president of the large J. Walter Thompson agency, has urged advertisers to avoid the simple solution of replacing one distorted image with another. She fears commercials will soon be invaded by legions of househusbands and working women still as mindlessly concerned with waxy, yellow buildup and ring around the collar as pre-liberation housewives. "And while we're at it," she adds, "Let's get rid of all those ads which cast the man as old dumb-dumb."

As important as woman's new image in advertising is the expansion in the variety of products being offered specifically to female audiences. Banks, auto manufacturers, and insurance companies are now fiercely competing with one another on the pages of women's magazines.

Advertisements of Tomorrow

Wendy Wilkenson, promotion director of KHJ Radio in Los Angeles, believes that both working woman and housewife will seek "timesaving, informative commercials that pinpoint and explain, not talk down to her."

Marketing experts forecast that woman's changing role will influence the products as well as the tone of future advertisements. With more women — especially the wives and mothers at whom much advertising is directed — entering the work force, greater emphasis will be given conveniences like slow cookers, fast food restaurants, and easy-care clothing. A 1975 study by the William Esty Company's Marketing Information Center predicts that women will become an ever greater target of advertisements for products "once thought to be the almost exclusive preserve of males," like life insurance, credit cards, and rent-a-cars.

"Overmanned and Undergirled"

Healthy changes in advertising for and about women will be speeded along by the growing number of women in the advertising profession. Ad writer Tricia Ingersoll claims, "When a woman is not involved in the design, positioning, and headline writing of a product, the ad is behind the times."

As in most lines of work, it took women

Who Was the Gerber Baby?

Before **Ann Turner Cook** revealed her identity and received $7,500 from the baby food company in 1951, a number of far-fetched stories had circulated about the bright-eyed, rosebud-mouthed infant. It was even rumored that the drawing was made by artist Maude Humphrey of her son, who went on to become screen star Humphrey Bogart.

Cook posed for the Gerber portrait painted by neighbor Dorothy Hope Smith in 1928. She grew up, married, and had four children, all of whom were raised on Gerber baby foods. After thirteen years as a housewife, Cook returned to school and eventually became chairman of a large high school's English department.

a long time to move in force into top advertising jobs. But a few women have always beat the odds. **Helen Lansdowne Resor,** the dean of women in advertising, campaigned for more opportunities in the profession for women in the 1920s. Using the skill with which she coined such slogans as "The Skin You Love to Touch" for Woodbury Soap, Resor exhorted, "If You Want More Legal Tender, Hire More of the Female Gender." Advertising, she frequently said, was "Overmanned and Undergirled."

Another female trailblazer in the advertising field was **Mabel Hill,** who started her own ad agency in New York City and later edited a major women's magazine. **Bernice Fitz-Gibbons** fueled the feud between New York's leading department stores by coining the phrase, "It's Smart to be Thrifty," for Macy's. The store's arch rival, Gimbels, lured her away with a ninety thousand dollar salary offer. There she came up with the slogan, "Nobody, but Nobody, Undersells Gimbels."

Among today's leading ad women are **Shirley Polykoff,** creator of "Does She

. . . or Doesn't She?" for Clairol; **Reva Korda,** executive vice president of Ogilvy and Mather, Inc., New York City; **Barbara Proctor,** president of Chicago's Proctor and Gardner Advertising, and **Joan Satin,** founder and president of Throckmorton-Satin Associates of New York City, which handles clients like Time, Inc. and Doubleday Book Clubs.

Lawrence: "Love Is The Key"

The queen of contemporary advertising is **Mary Wells Lawrence,** partner in New York City's Wells, Rich, Greene, Inc., the fastest growing firm in advertising history. Within two months of its opening in 1966, the agency had billings of $30 million. The three partners jokingly came up with a slogan for their firm: "If we were modest, we'd be perfect."

Lawrence made her reputation with the highly successful "End of the Plain Plane" campaign she designed in the mid-sixties for Braniff Airlines. She convinced the airline's management to paint their planes bright colors and dress their flight attendants in layered, Pucci-designed uniforms. Ads featured beautiful stewardesses shedding layers of clothing as flights progressed. Though some found the commercials too provocative, they were credited with greatly increasing the company's revenues.

Mary Wells Lawrence designed an ad campaign for Braniff — and won herself a husband.

Mary Wells married Braniff President Harding Lawrence in 1967. At the time she observed, "I lost an account but gained a husband."

Lawrence says her advertising philosophy is keyed to the word "love." "Too many ads are cold, too filled with jargon," she believes. "You have to talk person-to-person, use people terms . . . touch them, show humanness and warmth . . . You have to make them feel good about a product so they'll love you."

THE ECCENTRICITIES OF THE RICH WOMEN

Rich women are fascinating. Traditionally protected from ever having to earn their money, they seem privileged indeed; particularly if they are young and beautiful.

Yet there is a poignant side to many of these women. Difficult family lives, too much sheltering from reality, or personal instability, have produced many eccentric rich women, who would probably be called crazy if they weren't wealthy.

One of the richest and most eccentric was **Hetty Green** (1834-1916), a ruthless American businesswoman, whose assets at her death were estimated at $100 million.

Born into a wealthy, and very strict, Quaker family in Massachusetts, the young Hetty was introduced to the business world at an early age, when she read the stock quotations to her weak-eyed grandfather.

With inheritances from her family of over five million dollars, she launched a successful business career by investing in railroads, real estate, and government bonds. When she was thirty-two, she married millionaire Edward Henry Green.

It was for her eccentricities, however, that Green was best known. After her husband died, she often wore rags, lived in run-down boarding-houses, and fought with shopkeepers over petty purchases. Because of numerous newspaper accounts about her, she earned the nickname, "the witch of Wall Street."

Another eccentric, and one of several very rich women who owed their wealth to the Standard Oil Company, was **Edith**

Rockefeller McCormick (1872-1932), who had an estate of about $40 million.

One of John D. Rockefeller's (the oil company's founder) four children, Edith was an artistically-inclined girl, described by biographers as the most unconventional member of the family.

In 1895, she married reaper heir Harold Fowler McCormick, and the two were known as the Queen of Standard Oil and the Prince of International Harvester. Edith became very extravagant when the couple moved to Chicago, entertaining in great splendor, and feeding her guests off Napoleonic gold plate. She was also a generous benefactor to the city, contributing over $10 million during her lifetime to the arts and civic projects in Chicago.

But she was prone to emotional instability, and the latter part of her life was marked by a nervous breakdown in 1911; an extended stay in Switzerland to study psychoanalysis with Carl Jung; divorce; and alienation from her three children. She developed phobias, like fear of water; cel-

Miserly millionaire Hettie Green haunted Wall Street in a black, forbidding costume.

ebrated Christmas on December 15; and was fascinated with offbeat cults.

A second wealthy Rockefeller woman, **Geraldine Rockefeller Dodge** (1882-1973), was the daughter of the president of the Standard Oil Company, but acquired additional wealth when she married multimillionaire Marcellus Hartley Dodge.

When she died at the age of ninety-one, her personal fortune was estimated at about $85 million, and included a forty-five-room mansion in New Jersey; a thirty-five-room mansion on Fifth Avenue in New York City; $31 million in tax free bonds; and an art collection and furnishings worth $4.5 million.

Dodge was a recluse and, after the death of her son in 1930, stayed primarily at her 415-acre New Jersey estate, where she bred dogs. Every year she had an extravagent dog show at her estate. The "Morris and Essex" dog shows were the fanciest, most famous, and largest one-day dog shows in the world.

At the age of eighty-one, Dodge was declared incompetent. Her estate administrator continued to maintain the more than 100 dogs who lived on the New Jersey estate, at a cost of $50,000 in food bills alone. Only one dog is alive today and lives in grand style.

When **Caroline Webster Schermerhorn Astor** (1830-1908) wed William Backhouse Astor, she married into what was to become one of the nation's richest families. Her own father was worth a half million dollars, so she was not a rags-to-riches heroine.

Mrs. Astor was the grande dame of New York City society during the late nineteenth century. Invitations to her home — located on 34th Street, where the Empire State Building stands today — were coveted, and the term, "The Four Hundred," referred to the number of people she could fit into her ballroom for her annual winter ball.

She was considered regal rather than pretty, and wore lavish clothes and jewels; the most famous of which was a diamond stomacher (a triangle that's set into the bodice of a dress and narrows to the waist or below) said to have belonged to Marie Antoinette.

Called "*The* Mrs. Astor" and "The Queen," Astor closed down her 34th Street house in 1895. *Town Topics* commented, "If the Executive Mansion at Washington has been the center of the nation's political life, the Astor house has been, since 1870, the center of fashionable life in America."

One of America's leading feminine benefactors was **Margaret Sage** (1828-1918), who gave about $80 million to various charitable causes.

She was married at age forty-one to widowed businessman Russell B. Sage, whose first wife had been one of her school friends. Sage, who made a vast fortune in railroad stocks and money lending, was known as a tightwad.

When he died in 1906, Mrs. Sage set about to improve his reputation, and eventually rivaled Andrew Carnegie, John D. Rockefeller, and J. P. Morgan in her contributions to good works, mostly in the Northeast.

Among the recipients of her generosity were hospitals, religious societies, nearly a score of colleges; and New York City cultural institutions, like the Metropolitan Museum of Art, the American Museum of Natural History, the New York Zoological Society, and the New York Botanical Garden.

In addition, in 1970, she gave $10 million to establish the Russell Sage Foundation which continues today to contribute to improving social and living conditions in the United States.

Less lofty, but equally generous was **Lillie Hitchcock Coit** (1842-1929), a wealthy San Francisco woman. As a little girl she liked chasing fire wagons, and she continued to do so throughout her life. She was made an honorary member of San Francisco's Knickerbocker Engine Company 5, and often signed "5."

Her life in San Francisco was an eccentric one, attending the fire company's annual birthday banquet, riding in the fireman's parades, wearing a variety of hair wigs, and giving much aggravation to her husband.

Coit left one-third of her large estate to the city of San Francisco. San Francisco commissioned the construction of an observation tower in her name, which opened in 1934.

Barbara Hutton (1912-   ), heir to the Woolworth fortune, is a wealthy woman

Once a gay debutante, Barbara Hutton spends most of her time in hospitals nowadays.

whose main charity seems to be alimony to her seven husbands. The only one of her husbands — who have included European princes, counts and playboys — who did not get a big settlement from her was Cary Grant. During their marriage, they were known as "Cash and Cary."

Hutton gained a reputation for living the role of the rich heiress to the hilt — during the Depression she spent $10,000 to fly an orchestra from London to Paris to celebrate her birthday. At this same time, clerks at her family's store, Woolworth's, were earning $11 weekly. She became so disliked that she was once attacked by a screaming, clawing crowd as she entered a theater.

She now spends much of her time in hospitals; her poor health is said to be the result of strained nerves and years of over-dieting on black coffee and orange juice.

Perhaps the richest woman in the world today is twenty-six-year-old **Christina Onassis.** When her father, Greek shipping magnate Aristotle Onassis, died in 1975, he left the bulk of his estate, estimated at between $400 million and one billion dollars, to his daughter.

Onassis, an intense young woman with the haunting, Greek looks of an Irene Pappas, has thrown herself into her father's business. The day he died, she told a reporter, "I'm going to run the business and give my life to it." The business is practically all that's left of her family.

The young Christina, and her brother Alexander, were raised in sumptuous wealth in various residences in Paris, Athens, and the French Riviera, and were educated in exclusive European schools. The two were brought up largely by servants.

At twenty, Onassis married a California realtor twenty-seven years her senior, but her family strongly disapproved of the match, and she was soon divorced.

Two years later, in 1973, her brother was killed in a plane crash. A year later her mother died suddenly and Christina, distraught, tried to take her own life.

Now twenty-six, with a second marriage behind her — to Alexander Andreadis of another powerful Greek shipping family — Onassis owns 47.5 percent of all her father's assets, 75 percent of his interest on the island of Scorpios, the yacht named after her, and an annual income of $250,000.

Christina Onassis vowed to "give my life" to the business her father built.

TEN IMMORTAL IMAGES

Woman — the mystery, the goddess, the virgin, the mother, the courtesan, the symbol of liberty, the wanton. Artists have been obsessed by the female image throughout the ages. In every museum and every major city in the world, there are paintings and sculptures of women that justly can be described as magnificent. Each person, no doubt, has her favorite painting or sculpture. But only a few such works of art have universal appeal — these are the immortals:

The Sphinx

In ancient Egypt, the sphinx personified the rising sun and symbolized royal majesty. It had the body of a lion and the head of a man, often, as in the case of the famous Sphinx of Gizeh, a representation of Egypt's current ruler. Then, in Greek art, the sphinx reappeared as a female hybrid, a virgin with the body of a lioness. The Greek sphinxes, such as the winged sphinx from Delphi and the sphinx on the Temple of Aphaea at Aegina, wear the inscrutable smiles some critics believe influenced Leonardo da Vinci's painting of the Mona Lisa. "Like the sculptors who carved smiles on Greek sphinxes," Leonardo "was striving to penetrate the double mystery of the cosmos and of consciousness, and at the same time to create an illusion of reality," says art historian Roy McMullen in *Mona Lisa, The Picture and the Myth*.

Nike of Samothrace

Discovered in 1863 in the Sanctuary of the Great Gods at Samothrace, the Winged Victory — or Nike — is possibly the finest surviving example of Hellenistic sculpture. Excavations revealed the Greek goddess of victory had been depicted alighting on a ship's prow projecting over a large pool. The goddess was of pure white marble; the prow was of gray marble. Rippled marble slabs placed beneath the water gave it a shimmering and sparkling effect.

Her great wings spread wide, the Nike is partly airborne, advancing against a powerful head wind that shapes every fold of her thin clinging garment. Because this invisible onrush of air balances the Nike's forward movement, the statue seems inseparable from the space around it.

The Nike was apparently made to celebrate the Rhodian victory over a Persian-Carthaginian fleet led by Hannibal in 190 B.C. She is attributed to an unknown Rhodian sculptor.

Venus de Milo

Many who have been captivated by the Venus de Milo don't realize they have fallen before the charms of Aphrodite, ancient Greek goddess of love. Indeed, the Venus de Milo is one of the most famous surviving Greek statues of Aphrodite.

The softness of the Venus' flesh, modeled in Persian marble by an unknown Greek genius, and the gentle nuances of light and shadow that mold her torso have enchanted countless admirers. Her pose, with one leg raised slightly higher than the other, subtly reveals the curves of the body.

Found by a peasant on April 19, 1829, on the Aegean island of Melos, the sculpture was armless and broken in several pieces. The fragmented stone goddess was purchased on behalf of the Marquis de Riviere, the French consul in Constantinople, who presented her to Louis XVIII for the Louvre. The Venus was first thought to date from the classical period of ancient Greece. Then, in 1897, the German art scholar Furtwängler attributed it to the Hellenistic period circa 150 B.C. His statement caused a furor because the Hellenistic period was considered one of decline and dissolution. Scholars feared the prestige of the Venus would suffer. But she withstood the controversy.

Various reconstructions of the missing arms have been offered — perhaps holding a shield in which she views her reflection or possibly spinning threads. Although it is generally accepted that her right arm crossed her body and the left arm was raised, even the greatest art historian can no more than speculate what Venus de Milo was doing with her hands.

The Birth of Venus

According to Greek mythology, Aphrodite (the Roman Venus) was born fully grown from the foam of the sea near the island of Cythera. That bubbling birth of

Boticelli's *The Birth of Venus:* Akin to the Madonna, she is "more virginal than voluptuous."

the goddess of love and beauty was celebrated by Botticelli in his masterwork painted about 1480. Today the painting is at the Uffizi Gallery in Florence.

Botticelli's painting was the first portrayal of the pagan goddess since Roman antiquity and thus is of major historical importance. It was executed as a visual sermon in philosophy for a fourteen-year-old boy, Giovanni di Pierofrancesco. Botticelli's Venus illustrates one of the basic humanist tenets which held that physical perfection was the emblem of a noble spirit. Her beauty did not symbolize lust or sensual pleasure, but pure intelligence and the highest attainments of the mind. Botticelli's Venus, though nude, is closer to the Christian Madonna than the pagan deity. "Botticelli's Venus may be the loveliest ever created," wrote art critic John Canaday, "but she is also the least fleshly, more virginal than voluptuous."

Mona Lisa

Her unfathomable smile has been the focus of attention for hundreds of years. But a Japanese heart specialist says he knows one thing Leonardo da Vinci's *Mona Lisa* wasn't smiling about: her health.

A bit of yellow coloring in Mona Lisa's left eye tipped Dr. Haruo Nakamura to the possibility that this "certain Florentine lady" suffered from high cholesterol. The yellowing of an eye is one known symptom of excessive indulgence in rich foods and coronary heart disease. Art experts at the Louvre, where the *Mona Lisa* hangs, confirm that the yellow in her left eye is part of the original painting.

Accounts of meals served on the tables of wealthy families in Leonardo's day tell of such cholesterol-laden fare as pork, lamb, and partridges stewed in heavy cream or smothered in lard.

In spite of the subject's poor health, the *Mona Lisa,* painted about 1503, is the most famous painting in the history of the visual arts.

Even while it rested unfinished in Leonardo's studio, the work was imitated by fellow artists, among them Raphael. By the end of the sixteenth century, the painting was declared a divine work.

The subject of the painting is commonly held to be the Lady Lisa, daughter of Antonio Maria di Noldo Gherardini, a Florentine notable, and wife of Francesco di Bartolomeo di Zenobi del Gioconda, one of the city's leading citizens. But the

Leonardo's *Mona Lisa:* Seductive, mysterious, all-seeing — and a victim of high cholesterol?

Mona Lisa is far more than the portrait of a particular woman. Leonardo, the genius of the High Renaissance, gave a particular warmth and intimacy to this lady seated against an eerie landscape of mountains, valleys, and deep sky. He accomplished it by a remarkable use of *sfumato,* an effect suggesting fine haze. But more fascinating than the master's technical expertise are the psychological depth and mystery of the Mona Lisa's personality. With her seductive yet disturbingly omniscient smile, the *Mona Lisa* hovers tantalizingly between the human and the divine. Perhaps art critic Walter Pater described it best: "The fancy of a perpetual life, sweeping together ten thousand experiences, is an old one. . . . Certainly Lady Lisa might stand as the embodiment of the old fancy. . . ."

Grand Odalisque

When first shown at the 1819 Salon in Paris, Jean-Auguste Dominique Ingres' *Grand Odalisque* scandalized critics of the day. They picked at the seeming arbitrariness of her anatomy, protesting that she had three vertebrae too many and lacked certain bones and muscles. But Ingres had deliberately used abstract anatomy to heighten the languorous erotic effect of his work.

The enduring fascination of the Ingres

Ingres' *Grand Odalisque:* For mortals, an erotic delight forever out of reach.

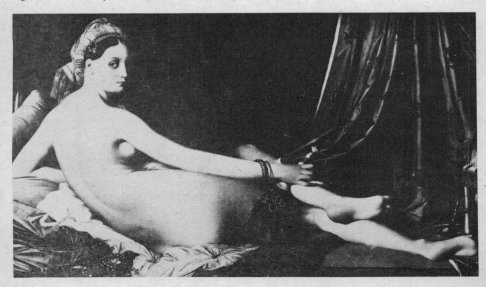

nude, which was commissioned by Napoleon's sister, Queen Caroline of Naples, lies in its contradictions. Stretched out passively on a silken couch, the first lady of the harem appears soft, supple, as inviting as a kiss. Yet there is tension in her attitude. Her wary gaze belies an Oriental languor. More goddess than odalisque, she draws back even as she entices. And the seductive trappings of the harem, executed with almost photographic detail, serve to emphasize her inaccessibility. For mere mortals, Ingres' *Grand Odalisque* remains an erotic delight forever out of reach.

Arrangement in Black and Gray No. 1: The Artist's Mother

A friend of James Abbott McNeill Whistler once laughingly remarked that it was hard to believe that he had a mother. The artist retorted, "Oh, but I do, and a pretty bit of color she is, I can tell you." Yet when he decided to put her on canvas, he chose to do it in subtle shades of black and gray. The exact year Whistler painted his mother is not known, but as early as 1867 in a letter to Fantin-Latour, the artist wrote: "I'll have the portrait of my mother photographed and will send you a print."

Five years passed before Whistler sent the completed picture to the Royal Academy in 1872. The academy rejected it and only the intercession of his fellow artist William Boxall, who threatened to create a scandal by resigning from the academy, won the painting entry to the show. A few chosen friends saw the work prior to the opening, and one commented, "It has a holy expression. Oh, how much sentiment."

The words must have struck terror into Whistler's heart because sentiment was precisely what he had tried to avoid. He had attempted to strip the work of all personal connections and to focus attention on its purely aesthetic qualities. "An Arrangement in Gray and Black. Now that is what it is," he said. "To me it is interesting as a picture of my mother; but what can or ought the public to care about the identity of the portrait."

From the first the public did care. The dignity and strength of Anna Mathilda McNeill Whistler at rest in her chair, hands folded in resignation with an air of patient endurance, attested to a life well-lived, a job well-done. Visitors flocked to see her, first in London in 1872, then in America nine years later, and in Paris, Dublin, Glasgow, and Amsterdam in the late 1880s. They still pay her homage at the Louvre today. In the United States, she has become the national symbol of motherhood. Her image has appeared on candy-box lids, playing cards, greeting cards, and in 1934 it was reproduced on a three-cent postage stamp issued "in memory and honor of the mothers of America."

Even Whistler in later years accepted her popularity and lightly remarked; "One must always do best by one's Mummy."

Statue of Liberty ("Liberty Enlightening the World")

Not comparable in beauty to Nike of Samothrace or the Venus de Milo, the Statue of Liberty towers above them, both literally and figuratively. She stands as the symbol of a nation which fought to ensure every one's right to be free. She was, perhaps, the dearest work of art to every tired, hungry, battered refugee who, on first beholding her torch in New York harbor, took a breath of hope.

The Statue of Liberty was a gift from the French people to the United States in honor of the one hundredth anniversary of the signing of the Declaration of Independence. She was unveiled on October 28, 1886, and was dedicated by President Grover Cleveland. *The New York Times* trumpeted the event as the day "a hundred Fourths of July broke loose."

Lady Liberty is made of sheets of hammered copper, about as thick as a silver dollar, welded over an iron-and-steel framework constructed by Gustav Eiffel, the man who later designed Paris' famed Eiffel Tower. She stands 151 feet, 1 inch from torch to toe.

Noted French sculptor Frederic Auguste Bartholdi designed the statue and recommended the twelve-acre Bedloe's Island as its site. Bartholdi first sculpted a fifty-inch figure. He modeled the face of the goddess after his mother's, but it was his mistress, Jeanne-Emilie Bheux de Pusieux, who posed for the body. After enlarging the model's various sections point by point through four plaster

Construction of the Statue of Liberty: Bartholdi's mother's face, but his mistress's body.

models, the final model was used to shape the metal sheets of the statue itself.

In 1884, the statue was completed and presented to the American minister in Paris on July Fourth. Lady Liberty was then dismantled, packed into 214 wooden crates, and shipped across the Atlantic. In June of the following year, she was unloaded on Bedloe's Island. When reassembled, the statue was placed on a pedestal (paid for by the American people), which brought the total height to 305 feet, 1 inch. New Yorkers marveled. The statue towered twenty feet above the steeple of old Trinity Church, then the tallest structure on the Manhattan skyline.

In 1903, a bronze plaque inscribed with Emma Lazarus' sonnet, "The New Colossus," was placed inside the pedestal. Part of the classic verse: "Send them, the homeless, tempest-tossed to me, I lift my lamp beside the golden door." In 1956, Congress officially changed the name of Bedloe's Island to Liberty Island.

The Tub

By painting **The Tub,** Edgar Degas showed his respect for Ingres' dictum that

The Tub: Degas showed that the unposed figure was beautiful, even when performing homely acts.

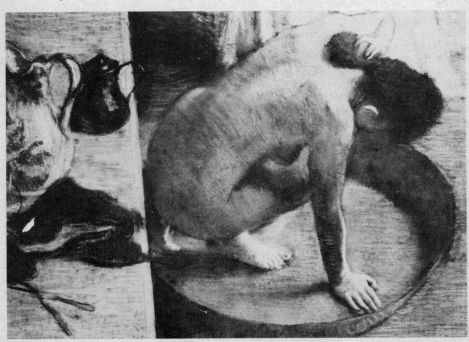

Pablo Picasso's *Les Demoiselles d'Avignon* (1907), oil on canvas, 8' x 7'8". Collection, the Museum of Modern Art, New York. Acquired through the Lillie P. Bliss Bequest.

if you make lines and then make more lines, you will become an artist. He also realized that lines are most evident when the body is in action. Unlike other great artists of the Realist-Impressionist school, Degas did not paint pretty models in leafy arbors dappled in shadows, nor did he work outdoors, painting luminous landscapes. "Movement in things and in people . . . consoles me," he wrote in a letter to his friend Henri Rouart in 1886, the same year he did this beautiful pastel of a woman in her bathtub.

Although as obsessed with the female form as any of his contemporaries, Degas loved to paint women involved in their daily activities. He did hundreds of studies of the dancers in the corps de ballet at the old Opera House in the Rue Le Peletier in Paris. Music-hall artists, circus ladies, milliners, laundresses, and nude women at their toilet were his subjects. He spent hours watching them work, making notes and sketches. Then he went back to his studio and began to paint.

Degas constantly tried to show that the unposed figure was beautiful, even while performing simple, homely acts. His success is no better illustrated than in the round forms and lyrical rhythms of the nude bather in her tub.

Les Demoiselles d'Avignon

Pablo Picasso, the many-sided genius of the twentieth century was twenty-five when he painted **Les Demoiselles d'Avignon**. He had already produced the romantic works of his Blue and Rose periods, which he later dismissed as "all sentiment." Working now under the influence of primitive Negro sculpture, Picasso was reaching out for new, less sensuous styles of expression.

During the winter of 1906–7, Picasso began work on a canvas of female nudes in an interior. The painting was intended to be a temptation scene in a brothel. Picasso's *demoiselles* were not the pretty maidens from the town celebrated in the old French song, "Sur le pont d'Avignon,'' but ladies of the night who lived in Avignon Street, a notorious section of Barcelona. But, before long, any theme or content was obliterated. The figures became angular, their proportions distorted, and color was limited to blue, pink, and terra cotta. The three figures on the left, although distorted, are reasonably naturalistic, but the violently dislocated features and bodies of the two on the right have all the barbaric qualities of primitive art. When first shown, the painting outraged even Matisse, and one critic has said that *Les Demoiselles d'Avignon,* ''resembles a field of broken glass.''

Beyond its importance as the major work of Picasso's early artistic maturity, many art historians hold that the painting, in large part, sparked the Cubist revolution. Talking of his painting in later life, Picasso said, ''Reality must be torn apart in every sense of the word. What people forget is that everything is unique. . . . I want to draw the mind in a direction it's not used to and wake it up. I want to help the viewer discover something he wouldn't have discovered without me.''

WOMEN IN THE ARTS

In the first century, Pliny the Elder wrote about a woman who painted pictures that ''had such merit that they sold for higher prices than those of Sopolis and Dionysos, well-known contemporary painters, whose works fill our galleries.''

By Pliny's day, women artists had already been in business for perhaps as long as seven thousand years. Scholars credit women with developing domestic arts such as weaving, pottery, and straw-plaiting.

However, as the golden rays of history moved toward the male-dominated civilizations of Egypt and Mesopotamia, women as artists became less important and, besides Pliny's statements, little is known about women's contributions to the artistic life of Greece and Rome.

The Middle Ages offered women greater opportunities in the arts. During the thirteenth and fourteenth centuries they worked as silk spinners, embroiderers, lace-makers, linen manufacturers, goldsmiths, and even sculptors. But it was not until the middle of the sixteenth cen-

tury that women finally emerged as serious professional artists.

FEMALE ARTISTS

Sofonisba Anguissola (1535-1625) was the most famous of women painters of the Renaissance and is best known for her portraits.

Artemisia Gentileschi (1593–?), a baroque artist, was noted for her full-figure compositions of biblical and historical events involving women.

Rosalba Carriera (1675-1757) was a pastelist and miniaturist whose work is noted for its delicacy of color.

Elizabeth Vigee LeBrun (1775-1842) was the most famous woman artist of the late eighteenth century, portraitist of Queen Marie Antoinette, the Prince of Wales (George IV), and European aristocracy.

Julia Margaret Cameron (1815-74) was one of the best of the early photographers, known for her portraits of Alfred Lord Tennyson, Robert Browning, Ellen Terry, and others. She was a great-aunt of Virginia Woolf.

Rosa Bonheur (1822-99), a painter and advocate of full equality for women, was born Marie Rosalie in Bordeaux, France, the daughter of landscape painter Raymond Bonheur. She was known for the accuracy and detail of her portrayals of animals.

A life-long outdoorswoman, Rosa Bonheur was best known for her detailed portrayals of animals.

Morisot's *Hortensia:* The artist is more acclaimed today than during her lifetime.

Morisot: Early Impressionist

Berthe Morisot (1841-95) is described by one art historian as "the most fascinating figure of Impressionism" and is more acclaimed today than she was during her lifetime.

The youngest of three daughters of an upper middle-class family, Morisot was born in Bourges, France. When she was seven, her father, a civil servant, was transferred to Paris. She early showed signs of unusual artistic ability and was encouraged by her parents in the study of art.

In 1861, Jean Corot, then sixty-four and the leading landscape artist of the day, urged her to·paint out-of-doors, directly from nature. Morisot entered two landscapes in the Salon of 1864 and continued to exhibit there until 1874, at which time she helped organize the first Impressionist exhibition. Nine of her pictures were included in that show along with works by such masters as Monet, Degas, Cezanne, Sisley, Renoir, Pissarro, and Guillaumin.

Under the guidance of Edouard Manet, one of the leading lights in the artistic avant-garde, whom she met in 1868 and whose brother she later married, Morisot's work became freer in execution and bolder in palette. In 1892, she had her first one-woman show at the Boussod and Valadon galleries in Paris, and in 1894 her painting of a *Young Woman Dressing for a Ball* was purchased by the French government for the Luxembourg Collection.

Financially unsuccessful in her lifetime, Morisot was honored by a retrospective at the Orangerie in Paris in 1941. In 1952 her paintings from the Rouart Collection were seen in a traveling exhibition in the United States and Canada.

Cassatt: Cool Tenderness

Mary Cassatt (1844-1926) was born in Pittsburgh and brought up in Philadelphia. At age seventeen, she announced to her father that she was going to Europe to study art. "I'd almost rather see you dead," he replied and refused to let her go. After spending what she considered four fruitless years at the Pennsylvania Academy of Fine Arts, she won her father's reluctant support for her European dream.

Cassatt's *The Bath:* "A point of view which is full of tenderness and comprehension."

Cassatt studied in Europe from 1866 to 1870, spending most of her time in Paris. In 1872, she returned to Europe, living in Parma, Italy, where she painted *On the Balcony*, which she submitted to the Paris Salon using the name Mary Stevenson. To her delight, it was accepted. Even this recognition did not overly impress her family. Her brother Aleck said, "I suppose she expects to become famous, poor child."

Edgar Degas invited her to join the Impressionist exhibition of 1879, and from that time until 1886 she was an active member of the movement. During those years her most frequent models were members of her family, particularly her father, mother, and sister Lydia, who came to live with her in Paris in 1877.

After 1886, Mary Cassatt began to concentrate more and more on the mother and child theme. These paintings, art critic Allen S. Weller wrote, "exploit all that is most observant and precise in a draftmanship of impeccable skill, in a radiant use of color, particularly in the flesh areas, and in a point of view which is full of tenderness and comprehension but without sentimentality or overemphasis."

Mary Cassatt was also a fine printmaker, and a series of color etchings executed in 1891 is regarded by many historians as one of her finest achievements. By the time of her death in 1926, she was recognized as the outstanding American painter of the nineteenth century.

Hoxie: Lincoln Sculptor

Vinnie Ream Hoxie (1847-1915) was one of the few American women sculptors of the late 1800s.

Born in Kansas, Ream moved to Washington, D.C., in 1861. There, her father who was seriously strapped financially, made maps for the War Department, and she augmented the family income by working in the Post Office. Soon after arriving in the capital, Ream became friendly with the well-known sculptor Clark Mills, who suggested she try modeling in clay. From the first, Ream showed marked talent and, perhaps because of her youth, was made much of by some of Washington's leading politicians. While in her teens, she sculpted the bust of Representative Thaddeus Stevens.

The only criticism of Hoxie's sculpture was that Lincoln looked better than he had in life.

More than anything else, she yearned to do a sculpture of her hero, Abraham Lincoln. Through her influential friends, her desire was fulfilled. In later years she recalled: "When friends of mine first asked him to sit for me he dismissed them wearily until he was told that I was but an ambitious girl, poor and obscure. Had I been the greatest sculptor in the world I am sure I would have been refused."

After Lincoln's assassination, Ream was given a $10,000-commission to sculpt his statue for the Capitol building — the first woman to win so signal an honor. Unveiled in January of 1871, the sculpture was instantly acclaimed a success. The only complaint was that she had made the craggy, ungainly Lincoln look better than he had in life. Today the statue stands in the Great Rotunda of the Capitol.

Although known primarily for the statue of Lincoln, Vinnie Ream, who became Mrs. Richard L. Hoxie in 1878, sculpted many prominent figures of her day, including Admiral David Glasgow Farragut.

Kollwitz: Prints of Pain

Käthe Kollwitz (1867-1945) was one of the finest graphic artists of the early twentieth century. Her reputation rests solely on her prints. Their power is in their compassion and humanity. "It is my duty," she said "to voice the sufferings of men, the never-ending sufferings heaped mountain-high."

Born in Königsberg, East Prussia, Kollwitz was the daughter of a stonemason and the granddaughter of a Protestant minister. In her memoirs she writes, "From my childhood on my father had expressly wished me to be trained for a career as an artist. . . . And so after my fourteenth year he sent me to the best teachers."

In 1891, she married Karl Kollwitz, a

doctor, and moved to Berlin. There she witnessed the hardships of the lives of the poor and she embodied their pain in her art. "Middle-class people held no appeal for me at all," she said. "The proletariat, on the other hand, had a grandeur of manner, a breadth to their lives." Her first great print cycle, *The Weavers' Uprising*, based on a play by Gerhart Hauptmann, was recommended for a Gold Medal at the Berlin Free Art Exhibition in 1898, but it was ruled out by the Kaiser because of its political content.

Kollwitz was the first woman to be elected a member of the Prussian Academy of Arts, where she held the directorship of graphic arts from 1928 until she was forced to resign by the Nazis in 1933. A lifelong pacifist, her hatred of war was strengthened by the battlefield death of her son, Peter, in World War I. The depth of her feelings is expressed in her haunting postwar lithograph, *Never Again War!*

Brooks: Loneliness on Canvas
Romaine Brooks (1874-1970) was a skilled portraitist possessed of a highly individualistic style.

She was born into a wealthy American family in Rome. Her father deserted the family before her birth, her mother was unbalanced and unloving, and her brother was mad. A classic case of the poor little rich girl, Romaine found her only solace in her drawing.

After completing her formal schooling, she returned to Rome in 1896 and studied art at the Circolo Artistico and the Scuola Nazionale. On the death of her mother in 1902, she inherited a fortune, but could not rid herself of a sense of doom. She wrote that "the demon ever hanging over massed humanity is more active for evil than for good." The main theme of her work is the loneliness of the human condition.

Following her marriage to John Ellingham Brooks, the artist lived briefly in England and finally settled in Paris. There, in 1910, she had her first one-woman show which was extremely successful. In the years that followed she painted portraits of many of the leading figures of the day — Gabriele D'Annunzio, the poet and playwright, the dancer Ida Rubinstein, and Jean Cocteau.

Although acclaimed in Europe, Romaine Brooks won little recognition in the United States during her lifetime. In 1971, the year following her death, a retrospective exhibition was held at the Whitney Museum in New York, and in 1977 her works were included in the first international exhibition of art by women, assembled by the Los Angeles County Museum of Art.

Cunningham: Photographic Art
Imogen Cunningham (1883-1976) one of America's greatest photographers, was elected a fellow of the National Academy of Arts and Sciences in 1967.

Born in Portland, Oregon, Cunningham moved to Seattle when she was six, and lived most of the remaining eighty-seven years of her life on the West Coast. She had set her mind on photography as a career in 1901 when she saw Gertrude Kasebier's photographs in a magazine. She majored in chemistry at the University of Washington, learned commercial platinum printing at the Curtis Studio, and studied photographic chemistry at the Technical College in Dresden, Germany.

On her return to America, she opened her own studio in Seattle. At first she did studies in the romantic, soft-focus style of the period, then began experimenting with new techniques. In 1915, she married fellow artist Roi Partridge; they had three sons. It was during their early nuisance years that she did a brilliant series on plants, the beauty of which strongly argues for the importance of photography as an art. Besides her flowers, leaves, and plants, Cunningham is best known for her portraits, among them Gertrude Stein, Upton Sinclair, Edward Weston, Alfred Stieglitz, and Minor White.

O'Keeffe: Landscape of the Mind
Georgia O'Keeffe (1887-   ) is acknowledged as America's foremost woman artist. "I realized that I had a lot of things in my head that others didn't have," she said. "I made up my mind to put down what was in my head." O'Keeffe grew up on a large farm in Sun Prairie, Wisconsin, and by age ten, had decided to be a painter. She began her formal art training in a convent school in Madison in 1901. She studied at the Art

Institute in Chicago, the Art Students League in New York, and for two years at Teacher's College at Columbia University. Shortly before her thirtieth birthday, she destroyed all her early work and began sketching in charcoal the abstract shapes and forms that came from her own mind.

In 1916, she had her first exhibition in New York at the 291 Gallery directed by Alfred Stieglitz, whom she married in 1924. Stieglitz continued to exhibit her work until his death in 1946.

Georgia O'Keeffe has drawn inspiration from many landscapes — Lake George, New York (where she spent many summers), the central Wisconsin of her childhood, and the Gaspé region of Canada. But the Southwest has been her background of choice since she first visited Taos, New Mexico, in 1929. For two decades she spent several months each year there and, following Stieglitz's death, settled in Abiquiu, New Mexico in 1949. "I came out here," she told a *Newsweek* reporter in 1976, "because of the earth colors — the ochres and the reds. They are the same colors that are on my palette."

Honors bestowed on O'Keeffe include five full-scale retrospectives, election to the National Institute of Arts and Letters, the American Academy of Arts and Letters, and the American Academy of Arts and Sciences, and, in 1970, the Gold Medal for Painting from the National Institute of Arts and Letters.

O'Keeffe's *Goat's Horn With Red:* "I had a lot of things in my head that others didn't have."

Abbott: Portrait of New York

Berenice Abbott (1898-   ) set out in 1935 to document New York City in photographs "before the old buildings and historic spots were destroyed." The result, *Changing New York,* published in 1937, records the old landmarks, the new skyscrapers, the squalid slums, and the electric vitality of America's largest city. It is a mammoth achievement by one of this country's finest photographers.

Abbott was born in Springfield, Ohio, and attended Ohio State University for a year and a half, before dropping out in 1918 to become an artist. She studied in New York, Paris, and Berlin, concentrating on the traditional arts, particularly sculpture. In Paris, while working in the studio of the Dadaist Man Ray, she decided to become a portrait photographer. Over the next few years, her studies of famous people in literary and artistic circles included James Joyce, Marie Laurencin, Jean Cocteau, and André Gide, and gained her a reputation as a skillful delineator of character on film.

Real fame came to Abbott with the publication of her series of New York, but since that time she has made further significant contributions to photography. She brought the work of the great French photographer Atget to the attention of the American public, wrote several photography manuals, and taught at the New School of Social Research in New York.

Nevelson: Abstract Sculpture

Louise Nevelson (1899-   ) was born Louise Berliawsky in Kiev, Russia. She emigrated with her family to America in 1905. She grew up in Rockland, Maine, and went to the local public schools. At age eighteen, she married Charles Nevelson, who was in the shipping business in New York, and moved with him to the city with the full understanding that she was to become an artist. She studied voice and dramatics, played the role of a fashionable young matron, bore a son, and studied at the Art Students League.

In 1931, she left her husband; over the next ten years, she studied under Hans Hofmann and Diego Rivera, took up modern dance, and began to work on her distinct abstract sculptures.

In 1941, she had her first show at the

Black, sculptor Louise Nevelson believes, is "the most aristocratic color."

Nierendorf Gallery in New York. Critics applauded the eerie sculptures of boxes within boxes, mostly painted black, "the most aristocratic color," she says.

It was not until the late 1950s that she was recognized as an artist of the first rank. In 1959, her work was included in the Museum of Modern Art's show "Sixteen Americans." Two years later she was invited to exhibit in the U.S. Pavilion at the Venice Biennale. She was the first woman and the first sculptor to be asked to join the Sidney Janis Gallery, one of the most prestigious galleries in New York. Today, Louise Nevelson is at work on a new project, designing the interior of a Lutheran church in New York.

Hepworth: Sculpture as Landscape

Barbara Hepworth (1903-75), a major sculptor of the twentieth century, won recognition with her first one-woman show in 1928, when she was twenty-five. She spent her early life in her birthplace, Wakefield, Yorkshire, England.

She studied at the Leeds School of Art where she met Henry Moore, who exercised an important influence on her work, and later at the Royal College of Art in South Kensington, where her interest in the modern abstract movement was strengthened. In her early sculptures, the human figure was clearly visible, but over the years her works became more and more abstract. Although obviously rooted in nature, they appeared part of a world of pure form. Her native Yorkshire terrain was her inspiration. She wrote in her *Pictorial Autobiography*, published in 1970, "The hills were sculptures; the roads defined the form . . . there was the sensation of moving physically over the contours of fullnesses and concavities, through hollows and peaks. . . . This sensation has never left me. I, the sculptor, am the landscape. I am the form and I am the hollow, the thrust and the contour."

From the time of her first show in 1928, Hepworth's sculptures were seen in numerous exhibits in England and outside her own country. In 1959, she won the Grand Prix at the São Paulo Biennale, and in 1968 was awarded a major retrospective at the Tate Gallery in London. She also had the signal honor of being commissioned by the United Nations to design the memorial to its late secretary-general, Dag Hammarskjöld.

From 1939 until her death, Barbara Hepworth lived in St. Ives, Cornwall, with her second husband, the British abstract painter Ben Nicholson.

Da Silva: Brazilian Painter

Maria Helena Vieira da Silva (1908-   ) is one of the first important female artists to emerge from South America.

Born of Brazilian parents in Lisbon, Portugal, she studied with Leger, Friesz, Bissiere, and Stanley William Hayter in his world-famed Atelier 17. She married the Hungarian painter Arpad Szenes in 1930, and they continued to live and work in France until the beginning of World War II. She spent the years between 1940 and 1947 in Rio de Janeiro, and her work was included in the Brazilian section of the UNESCO show of 1946.

Now based in France, she became internationally famous during the 1950s, when her works appeared in exhibits in Paris, New York, London, Stockholm, and Lisbon.

Arbus: Eye of the Beholder

Diane Arbus (1923-71) is not only a cult figure, but is regarded as the most important photographer to emerge in the '60s. Born in New York City, Arbus was the daughter of David Nemerov who owned Russeks, a women's fashion store. The poet Howard Nemerov is her brother.

Educated at the Ethical Culture and Fieldston schools in the city, she married Allan Arbus, at the age of eighteen, and had two daughters. For nearly twenty years, the Arbuses worked as fashion photographers for her father's store.

In 1959, Arbus began working on her own. Four years later, she received a Guggenheim Fellowship to do a project entitled "The American Experience." A second grant followed in 1966. Only an occasional Arbus photograph made it into print because she was reluctant to show her work, but the impact of the few that were seen was staggering. Her pictures of freaks, sexual deviates, and the mentally retarded were compelling in their honesty.

"Most people go through life dreading they'll have a traumatic experience," said Diane Arbus. "Freaks were born with their trauma. They've already passed their test in life. They're aristocrats." Intuitively, photographer Diane Arbus knew society's outcasts were God's favorites and tried to celebrate their intrinsic beauty on film. In 1971, Diane Arbus killed herself by slashing her wrists. The following year the Museum of Modern Art gave her a retrospective which was one of the most successful exhibitions in the museum's history.

Marisol with one of her wooden "people sculptures," *The Kennedy Family*.

Frankenthaler: The Form of Color

Helen Frankenthaler (1928-   ) is established as one of the finest of the young painters in the second generation of the New York School. She was born into a upper middle-class New York City family. She attended the best schools — Dalton, where she studied under the Mexican artist Tamayo, and Bennington College, where her mentor was Paul Feeley. The two major influences on her early work were Kandinsky and Pollock.

She had her first one-woman show in 1951 at the Tibor de Nagy Gallery in New York, and by age twenty-five, her works were included in exhibits at the Jewish Museum and the Whitney Museum of American Art. Using lyrical color and free-flowing forms, her work shows the influence of abstract expressionism refined by a delicate and subtle sensibility. In 1966, she was one of four American artists chosen for representation at the Venice Biennale, and in 1969, was given a retrospective at the Whitney Museum at the age of forty.

Marisol: Wooden People

Marisol (1930-   ) is now established as one of the most outstanding of the younger American sculptors.

Born in Paris of Venezuelan parents, Marisol Escobar spent her childhood in Caracas, but later moved to Los Angeles. At age sixteen, she decided to be an artist and studied at the Jepson School in Los Angeles. After further study at the École des Beaux-Arts in Paris and the Arts Students League in New York, she worked under the tutelage of Hans Hofmann from 1951 to 1954. During that early period, she concentrated on painting, but her dissatisfaction with her work caused her to turn to sculpture.

Her life-size wooden figures, frequently with painted faces, caught and held public attention. Witty, original, almost "pop" in quality, they were photographed and written about in all the major news and fashion magazines as well as the art journals.

Since her emergence on the art scene in the early 1960s, Marisol has been classified as a Neo-Dadaist, a New Realist, and as a Pop artist, but her style continues to evolve, and it's impossible to fit her sculptures into any set category.

MEMORABLE HEROINES

Alice: In Wonderland
Nothing, no matter how fantastic, rattles the no-nonsense **Alice.** She has a positive genius for getting out of jams in Lewis Carroll's *Alice's Adventures in Wonderland* (1865).

Alice's troubles in a topsy-turvey world begin when she follows a time-conscious White Rabbit down the rabbit hole. Soon she locks horns with a parade of bizarre characters: the punning Mock Turtle, with whom she dances the Lobster Quadrille; the Cheshire Cat, whose smile lingers after his body dissolves; the Mad Hatter, who poses rhetorical riddles and wears a watch that gives the day rather than the time; and the March Hare who, naturally, butters the Hatter's watch. Alice even maintains her poise when her body changes its shape — it shrinks when she drinks a potion, enlarges when she eats a piece of cake. She manages to keep her head despite the Queen of Hearts' order to the contrary.

Amanda and Laura Wingfield: Unreal
In Tennessee Williams' play, *The Glass Menagerie* (1944), both **Amanda Wingfield,** the mother, and her crippled daughter, **Laura,** lived in a dream world.

Alice and friends dance the Lobster Quadrille: "Will you, won't you, will you join the dance?"

Amanda, a fading southern belle, lives a life of shabby gentility and bitterness, the product of her husband's desertion. She dwells in the past, endlessly repeating stories of her popular, flirtatious youth. Her children are her life, and her overpowering presence causes son Tom to rebel, and Laura to withdraw further into herself.

Laura is painfully shy, as fragile as the little glass figurines with which she plays. Concerned about her daughter's future, Amanda sends Laura to secretarial school. But Laura, ill-equipped to handle the outside world, only pretends to attend classes.

When Amanda learns the truth, she decides Laura's only hope lies in, "a gentleman caller." Love seems to enter Laura's life when a friend of brother Tom's comes to dinner. But, after gently kissing Laura, the caller announces that he is already engaged. Amanda's anger at Tom for bringing home an already encumbered caller causes him to leave home. Amanda and Laura are left to continue their bleak existence together.

Anna Christopherson: Golden Heart
Eugene O'Neill's play about the prostitute with a heart of gold, *Anna Christie* (1922), won a Pulitzer Prize.

Anna Christopherson's father is a sea captain who hates, "dat old devil sea," and has a rigid sense of morality. Anna and her father, after thirty years of separation, are re-united and live together on a coal barge. The harmony of their lives is disrupted when Matt Burke, a shipwrecked sailor, comes along. Anna wounds her father doubly: she falls in love with Matt and with the sea.

In a spasm of candor she confesses her former profession. Her father repudiates her and Matt decides against marriage. Anna realizes that she, like all women, is considered the property of men. Matt and her father decide to go back to sea. They eventually reconsider and forgive Anna. She is reborn through the love of her father and Matt.

Anna Karenina: Nothing Right
Anna Karenina is a beautiful, passionate, noblewoman married to a public official driven solely by ambition.

In Leo Tolstoy's *Anna Karenina*

(1873–76), Anna falls in love with Alexander Vronsky, a handsome, young officer. Caught between her internal, emotional needs and societal expectations, she ends up doing nothing right. She leaves her husband and child for Vronsky, has an illegitimate child, and is ultimately rejected by Vronsky. With no future or past to turn to, she commits suicide by throwing herself under a train.

Antigone: Oedipus' Daughter
Antigone, in Sophocles' play *Antigone* (about 441 B.C.), is the classic noble-but-fatally-flawed figure of Greek drama.

Antigone's brothers are fighting on opposite sides of a civil war in Thebes. Eteocles sides with their uncle, Creon, King of Thebes, while Polynices supports the rival King of Argos. The brothers kill each other in hand-to-hand combat. Eteocles is given a hero's burial, while Polynices is left to rot in the fields. In ancient Greece, failure to be buried meant eternal damnation. Knowing that she is risking her life, Antigone gives her brother a ritual burial. "I dared — it was not God's proclamation," she declares. Creon sentences her to be buried alive, but, before the punishment is carried out, she commits suicide with her fiance, Haemon, Creon's son.

Antonia Shimerda: Rewarded
In *My Antonia* (1918), **Antonia Shimerda** epitomizes the qualities of the immigrant farmers that Willa Cather so admired. When Antonia's impractical, musician father, a disillusioned immigrant from Bohemia, commits suicide, it is the ever vital and optimistic Antonia who assumes the burden of heavy physical labor on the family's Nebraska farm.

Eventually, she finds work as a hired girl in Black Hawk, where her zest for life leads her into an unpleasant involvement with a deceptive railway conductor. When he spends all her money and refuses to marry her, Antonia returns to the country to give birth to her illegitimate child.

Twenty years later, when the narrator next sees her, the unselfish Antonia has married comfortably and settled down to raise a large family. Because of her inner strength, she has managed to make a good life for herself, and has enriched the heritage of Nebraska's pioneers.

Auntie Mame: Lovable Flake
The term "Auntie Mame" has become part of the American vernacular and means: Lovable flake, generous spendthrift, glamourous iconoclast, energetic philosopher.

Auntie Mame's popularity has been sustained through several incarnations. It began with Patrick Dennis' book, *Auntie Mame* (1955), about his real-life aunt; and grew as it became a play, a film, and a Broadway musical. Mame battles the bad guys with consummate good taste and style.

When Patrick's prospective in-laws are horrified that the property next to their exclusive Connecticut home might be sold to Jews, Mame buys the land herself, planning to use it to house Jewish refugees from World War II. She makes mincemeat of the bigoted friends of her Southern fiancee. She advises her homely secretary, Alice Gooch, on how to be attractive to men. Soon Alice becomes gloriously pregnant. During the war, Mame temporarily mothers a brood of English children, including a nymphomaniac and a kleptomaniac. However Mame — through it all — never loses her dignity, her cool, or her daring.

Bathsheba Everdene: Three Lives
Bathsheba Everdene is blessed with beauty, brains, physical strength, and at least three lives.

In Thomas Hardy's novel, *Far From the Madding Crowd* (1874), she inherits a farm from her uncle which she puts in the charge of a rejected suitor, Gabriel Oak. She is wooed by a wealthy neighbor, William Boldwood, but she marries Francis Troy, a handsome soldier whom she loves but distrusts. Troy, a fortune hunter and unfaithful to boot, disappears and is presumed dead.

Bathsheba welcomes Boldwood's attentions out of pity. When Troy re-appears, Boldwood shoots him. Bathsheba's grief is enormous, but when Oak, who has loved her throughout, says he is leaving England, she realizes she loves him and accepts him — and herself.

Becky Sharp: No Principles
Becky Sharp, *Vanity Fair* (1848), is William Makepeace Thackeray's answer

Becky Sharp rises from rags to riches via flirtation, seduction, and marriage.

to the pretensions of middle class England, in the early nineteenth century.

She uses her assets to acquire that which the upper class has by birth. Her beauty, humor, and native intelligence help her achieve the trappings of aristocracy — and Becky is smart enough to know that the trappings are all she needs. Her vanity and selfcenteredness pull her out of the orphaned, impoverished life of her youth, and into a series of flirtations, seductions, and marriages.

Sharp becomes a governess and marries her employer's son, Rawdon Crawley, who is disinherited. Their elegant lifestyle is maintained with the aid of her admirer, Lord Steyne. When Crawley learns of their affair, Sharp is rejected by friends and family, although Crawley does not throw her out. Her despair is brief; a former suitor of means helps her out. She spends his money at a prodigious rate, including the insurance benefits when he dies suspiciously.

Blanche Dubois: Faded Belle

Blanche Dubois, in Tennessee William's *A Streetcar named Desire* (1947), is a Southern belle no longer in the bloom of youth.

She comes to the French quarter of New Orleans from a small Mississippi town to visit her sister, Stella, and her Polish brother-in-law, Stanley. Flirtatious Blanche strives to make a refined appearance, but she is an alcholic and a nymphomaniac, on the verge of a nervousbreakdown. The woman is haunted by the suicide of her young, homosexual husband years earlier, for which she bears responsibility.

Stan's friend Mitch accepts Blanche despite her confession; but when Stanley learns of her debauchery and that she was practically run out of her home town, he spitefully tells Mitch, who then spurns her. When her sister goes to the hospital to have her baby, Blanche provokes Stanley into ravishing her.

Blanche breaks down completely, and must be taken away to a mental hospital when her delusions of grandeur can no longer sustain her.

Carol Kennicott: Nowhere to Go

In Sinclair Lewis' *Main Street* (1920), **Carol Kennicott** is a misfit. After graduating from college, she becomes a librarian in St. Paul, Minnesota. There she meets and marries Will Kennicott, a doctor from Gopher Prairie.

Small town life is stifling to Carol — her world of ideas does not match the cloistered, provinciality of its people. In an effort to raise their cultural consciousness, she tries unsuccessfully to introduce experimental theater, poetry, and the art of conversation to a community that is content with its unenlightened state. To alleviate the dreariness and frustrations of her life she has a mild flirtation with a Swedish tailor, Erik Valborg. Village gossip forces the Kennicotts to take a trip to California.

Upon her return Carol realizes that her disenchantment with Gropher Prairie is permanent. She leaves her husband and takes her child to Washington, D.C., only to discover she has brought her malaise as well. Carol returns to Gopher Prairie because, emotionally and practically, there is no place else for her to go.

Caroline Meeber: Materialist

Carrie's only abstract thought, in Theodore Dreiser's *Sister Carrie* (1900), is a vague unease about the present. Every other aspect of her life is immediate and material.

An innocent ingenue from Wisconsin, she goes to Chicago, in 1889, to find work. Her short tenure in a shoe factory is degrading, but no less so than her escape with a traveling salesman; and her marriage to George Hustwood, who is a thief and a parasite. Carrie becomes successful an an actress, but still is unable to find happiness. At the conclusion of the book, she is sitting in a rocking chair contemplating her next conquest.

Catherine Earnshaw: Enslaved

Cathy Earnshaw is innocence to Heathcliff's evil, in the convoluted morality of Emily Bronte's, *Wuthering Heights* (1847).

Her childhood is jolted when Heathcliff, an uncouth gypsy orphan, is brought into the Earnshaw family. The two children form a symbiotic, passionate bond, which enslaves and terrifies Cathy, because she cannot resist it. Heathcliff's demonic, vengeful will is as awesome as his love for Cathy is suffocating. Despite her passion for Heathcliff, Cathy rejects him as her social inferior and marries Edgar Linton.

Still, her selfless loyalty to Heathcliff possesses and ultimately destroys her. She dies in premature childbirth, her mind and strength dissolved by Heathcliff's curious, cruel love.

Cinderella: The Shoe Fit

There's nothing wrong with **Cinderella's** life that a little magic dust won't fix in a jiffy.

In the traditional folk tale, her prospects look pretty grim: she's got no daddy, her stepmother exploits her terribly, and her ugly and mean stepsisters are jealous of her.

The stepsisters each want to marry the prince. He's giving a ball to look over the

Cinderella has the only foot in the land dainty enough to fit the magical glass slipper.

market of eligible females. Cinderella wants to go too, but she hasn't a thing to wear. Enter the fairy godmother who, quick as you can say *bibbidibobbidiboo*, transforms Cinderella from frump to fashionplate, and her pumpkin into a plush coach. The catch is that she must return from the ball by midnight, when everything will regress to its original state. She charms the prince, but at the stroke of midnight, she sprints to her coach, losing a glass slipper en route.

The Prince, by then smitten senseless by his love for her, takes the slipper from foot to foot throughout the kingdom. Naturally, it fits only Cinderella's dainty foot. They get married and live happily ever after.

Daisy Buchanan: Gatsby's Great

In *The Great Gatsby* (1925), **Daisy Buchanan** epitomizes the frenzied, vain, pampered world of the Jazz-Age rich.

Daisy was once in love with Jay Gatsby (neé Gatz) but, because he was poor, rejected him for a wealthy, amoral boor, Tom Buchanan. To Gatsby, Daisy is the ideal woman—beautiful, unattainable, brittle, cool. In his mania to win her, he makes a fortune as a bootlegger and, by buying an enormous mansion on Long Island, tries to purchase his way into her world. Gatsby and Daisy renew their romance. Returning from an assignation in New York, Daisy, driving Gatsby's car, runs over Tom's mistress. Tom tells the woman's husband that Gatsby was driving the car and, in grief-stricken rage, the man murders Gatsby. Daisy leaves on a trip with Tom before the funeral, never acknowledging her guilt.

Dorothy: Adventures in Oz

L. Frank Baum's *The Wonderful Wizard of Oz* (1900), is a whimsical tapestry of fantasy, homilies, humor, and adventure.

The practical **Dorothy,** and her faithful dog, Toto, have been transported by a cyclone to the Land of Oz. Dorothy's virtue and spunk are perfect complements to the eccentricities of three friends she meets, as she tries to find her way home to Kansas. The scarecrow is highly flammable and has the wisdom to want a brain. The rustable tin man cries at the drop of a hatchet because he lacks a heart. The outwardly ferocious lion wants courage.

Dorothy, Scarecrow, and Tin Woodsman run into trouble in a scene from the 1939 Judy Garland film.

Only the Wizard of Oz can grant this charming quartet its wishes, but wishes are not free.

The supplicants must earn them by bringing to Oz the broom of the wicked witch. Glenda the Good helps Dorothy escape from the winged monkeys and the witch. The lovable quartet's wishes are granted and Dorothy returns to Kansas.

Eliza Doolittle: Fair Lady

In George Bernard Shaw's *Pygmalion* (1913), Professor Henry Higgins thinks it might be fun to prove his theory; that the only thing separating a lady from a gutter-snipe is phonetics.

On a bet, he persuades a street-wise Cockney flower girl, **Eliza Doolittle,** to allow him to transform her into a lady simply by teaching her to speak the King's English and to dress properly. He proves his point admirably, and she breezes through a ball, not only undetected, but presumed to be a princess.

Eliza falls in love with her mentor, but, because of her innate dignity, refuses to be bullied into dependency. She marries an impoverished aristocrat, Freddy

Eynsford-Hill and, combining her new polish with an old dream, opens a successful flower shop.

Eliza Harris: Runaway

Eliza Harris is a beautiful slave who decides to bolt when she discovers that her master plans to sell her five-year-old son.

In Harriet Beecher Stowe's *Uncle Tom's Cabin* (1852), Eliza outwits the slave catchers by carrying her son across the frozen Ohio river. She manages to find her husband with the help of the Underground Railroad. The family escapes to Canada and finally to Nigeria, where they hope to build a black nation.

Elizabeth Bennet: Perfect Lady

Elizabeth Bennet is a perfectly wonderful woman in almost every way. The heroine of Jane Austen's *Pride and Prejudice* (1813), she's spirited, beautiful, clever and thoroughly pleasant. But she tends to believe too much of what she's heard, and what she's heard about Fitzwilliam Darcy from Mr. Wickham is not terrific. Poor Darcy, who is smitten by Elizabeth, has a tough time trying to prove himself to her.

On the other hand, Darcy has his own personality defects. He's a snob. When he

Brave Eliza carries her child to safety across the frozen Ohio River.

first proposes marriage to Elizabeth, his awareness of her social inferiority seeps through and that doesn't tend to endear him to her. In matters matrimonial, however, he has proven himself. Elizabeth's sharp tongue smoothes the rough edges of his superiority. "By you I was properly humbled," he says at last. On second thought, at his second proposal, Elizabeth decides to marry him after all.

Emily Webb: American Dream

Thornton Wilder's Play, *Our Town* (1938), is about life, death, and the loss of innocence in a small New England town.

Emily Webb, whose father is editor of the town's newspaper, epitomizes the great American dream. She is studious, eager to become a cheerleader, and in love with the local baseball hero, George Gibbs. They marry, and Emily dies in childbirth.

In the final act, set in a cemetery, Emily observes — but cannot communicate with — her loved ones.

She grieves, because she knows in death what they cannot in life — that every moment and small happiness in life should be savoured.

Emma Bovary: Victim of Greed

The tragedy of **Emma Bovary,** in Gustave Flaubert's *Madame Bovary* (1857), is that she is long on sensuality and short on sensibility.

In her rural youth, Emma fantasizes about luxury and romance which, because of her limited intelligence, she acquires in a limited way. Emma marries Charles Bovary, a well-meaning but inept doctor, whom she torments financially and emotionally. She collapses and takes to her bed when she does not get what she wants. To placate her, Charles moves to a larger town, which gives her greater options. She opts for an affair with Leon Dupuis, a relationship as tacky as her taste.

When Leon goes to Paris to study, she falls into an even less satisfying affair. She takes to her bed again and Charles decides to move with her to Rouen. There Emma is reunited with Leon and their affair escalates as do her gambling and purchasing debts. When she can put off the bill collector no longer, she turns to both her husband and her lover for help, but their tolerance has run out. Emma poisons herself and dies a long, painful, ugly death.

Evangeline: Gabriel's Girl

Evangeline Bellefontaine is the beautiful heroine of *Evangeline, a Tale of Acadie* (1847), by Henry Wadsworth Longfellow. Her fortunes in love are shattered by the misfortunes of war.

Evangeline is the daughter of the wealthiest farmer in Grand Pre, French Acadia. Her plans to marry Gabriel Lajeunesse are ruined when the British Commander orders the confiscating of the farmer's lands and the scattering of the population. Evangeline is sent to New England, Gabriel to Louisiana. As the years pass, they continue to search for each other.

Eventually, Evangeline becomes a Sister of Mercy and, while nursing epidemic victims in Philadelphia, she finds Gabriel. He dies, and the strength which has sustained her through her trials gives out. They are buried together.

Hester Prynne: Gets an "A"

Hester Prynne is one of the most admirable women in American literature. For nobility under pressure, she wins an "A," but the wrong kind.

In Nathaniel Hawthorne's novel, *The Scarlet Letter* (1850), the rigid morality of

Evangeline's romantic plans are shattered when the British order the Acadians scattered.

the 1650s is pilloried in Boston along with the heroine.

The lovely and passionate Hester, secretly married to an aging doctor, falls in love with a young clergyman, Arthur Dimmesdale, who fathers her child, the elfin Pearl. Because Hester will not reveal the name of the father, the Puritan community puts her in a pillory and forces her to wear an "A" for adulteress.

Dimmesdale, tortured by conflicting virtues, finally confesses under the torment of Roger Chillingsworth, Hester's long absent husband who has turned up to seek his revenge. Dimmesdale then publicly acknowledges his guilt, and dies in her arms, finally escaping Chillingsworth's evil hold on him.

Hester lives a long and admirable life and, because of Dimmesdale's acknowledgement of paternity, the elfin Pearl becomes human.

Isabel Archer: Determined Lady

The nice thing about **Isabel Archer** is that she has the courage to make mistakes. "I always wanted to know the things one shouldn't do . . . ," she says in Henry James' *The Portrait of a Lady* (1881), "so as to choose."

At twenty-three, she is temporarily penniless, but supremely confident. Her aunt takes her to Europe where she is courted by three suitors. When she inherits a considerable fortune, Isabel travels to Italy where she is pursued by a sinister, egocentric fortune hunter, whom she marries.

The marriage is not a success—her strong, independent mind is more than her husband bargained for — but Isabel stays with him to protect his illegitimate daughter Pansy, whom he schemes to marry off for money despite the girls' feelings.

Despite her adversities, Isabel remains the mistress of her fate.

Jane Eyre: Victorian Cinderella

The story of Charlotte Brontë's *Jane Eyre* (1847), is that of Cinderella in a minor key. **Jane Eyre** is not beautiful,but is she bright. She also has spine and ironclad integrity.

After a bleak childhood as an orphan, she becomes governess to the daughter of the enigmatic, brooding Edward Rochester. Jane falls in love with Edward, but on their wedding day discovers he already

Jane Eyre's youthful timidity is evident in this scene from the 1943 Joan Fontaine movie.

has an insane wife confined to a locked room in his mansion. Jane leaves Edward, becomes wealthy and independent, but continues to love him. Later she returns to Edward, finds him blinded and widowed, and marries him.

Jane Marple: Disarming Sleuth

Jane Marple may be dotty but she isn't stupid. She made her debut as the aged sleuth in Agatha Christie's *The Murder at the Vicarage,* in 1930.

Miss Marple is armed with endless patience, total recall, and a sharp sense of humor, to say nothing of her disarming white hair. Her understanding of human nature, grounded in her observation of her fellow residents in the English village of St. Mary Mead, makes her a natural for solving mysteries.

Marple continued to stalk the bad guys in a collection of short stories in 1932 and in *The Body in the Library,* in 1942, and nearly got rubbed out in *A Murder is Announced,* in 1950. Marple made her final appearance in *Sleeping Murder* (1976), published after her creator's death.

Jo March: Gutsy Little Woman

Jo March is happiest under trial. In Louisa May Alcott's autobiographical *Little Women* (1868, 1869), she is the central figure of four sisters who, with their mother, struggle to survive in a New England town in the absence of their father, a chaplain, in the Civil War.

No tree is too tall for Jo to climb, and no problem is too great for her to solve. In

Katharine Hepburn starred as the rambunctious Jo in the 1933 film version of Little Women.

her attic hideaway, she churns out "blood and thunder" stories for sensational magazines, to fill the family coffers. At one point she even sells her hair. Her Puritan upbringing precludes greed, so when her stories are successful, she stops writing. Jo's wit and good sense continually aid the family during their trials.

Jo is closest in temperament to Alcott, who brilliantly established a four-part counterpoint among the sisters. Meg is the pretty one; Beth is the musical but fragile one; Amy is the vain, remote one. Unlike the author, Jo gets married — to Professor Bhaer, with whom she opens Plumfield, a school for boys.

Jo appears again in two sequels — *Little Men* (1871), and *Jo's Boys* (1886), set at Plumfield.

Juliet: Romeo's Own

William Shakespeare's *Romeo and Juliet* (1596), is probably the most poignant tragedy, about social manipulation, in literature.

Fourteen-year-old **Juliet,** a member of the Capulet family, falls in love with Romeo at her father's great ball. But Romeo is disguised because of the bitter enmity between his family, the Montagues, and the Capulets. A marriage has been arranged for Juliet by her family, but she secretly marries Romeo instead.

To save her family's honor and still have a life with Romeo, she drinks a potion which gives the illusion of death. Romeo doesn't know about the plan and when he sees her apparently lifeless body, he poisons himself. When Juliet awakens and sees what has happened, she stabs herself. The two families learn the truth, and in their considerable shame they reconcile.

Lady Godiva: Naked Rider

It is not wise to make light of a woman's beliefs, particularly if that woman is **Lady Godiva** in Alfred Lord Tennyson's, "Godiva, A Tale of Coventry" (1842).

Lady Godiva is outraged at the oppressive tax her husband, Earl Leofric of Mercia, has imposed on the people of Coventry. Her husband jokingly agrees to repeal the tax if she will ride naked through the town marketplace at high noon. To his surprise, Godiva does it. But she takes the

Romeo believes Juliet dead in a scene from the 1968 film featuring Olivia Hussey.

Lady Godiva rode naked through the marketplace to save her people from an oppressive tax.

precaution of draping her abundant tresses over her body and, as insurance, orders that the doors and windows of the houses be closed.

Only Peeping Tom the tailor looks out. For his quick leer he is struck everlastingly blind. Lady Godiva's husband keeps his part of the bargain.

Lorelei Lee: Diamonds Forever

Anita Loos' play, *Gentlemen Prefer Blondes* (1925), is a satirical, seductive romp about how to steal legally.

Lorelei Lee is a spectacular blonde who is just smart enough to get what she wants. "Kissing her hand can make a girl feel very good," she says, "but a diamond bracelet lasts forever."

Lorelei proves that a fat cat who succumbs to the googly eyes of a blonde deserves exactly what's coming to him. She dispatches her rich husband elsewhere to perform good deeds, while she does a little performing of her own, with another man, Montrose, a brilliant scenario-writer. Moral: Pay now, play later.

Hedda Gabler: Manipulator

Henrik Ibsen's *Hedda Gabler* (1890), was to Sweden what *Madame Bovary*, was to France. Lacking an outlet for her promethean energies, **Hedda Gabler** manipulates two men, in an effort to better her position and satisfy her whims.

Married to a plodding professor, she stews about the creature comforts she might lose if he fails to win a professorship at the university. Hedda renews acquaintances with a former lover, Eilert Lovberg, an unstable writer and drunk who has been reformed by the good, timid Thea Elvsted. Hedda lures him back to his former dissipated lifestyle. She discovers the manuscript of his new book, written with the encouragement and help of Thea. Hedda considers it the symbolic child of Thea and Eilert and burns it, telling him it is lost.

When Eilert threatens suicide, Hedda offers him one of a set of her father's pistols and suggests he, "die beautifully." Judge Brack, a family friend, learns of Hedda's role in Eilert's suicide, and tries to blackmail her into becoming his mistress. Refusing to submit to a life of boredom as the slave of an old man, she takes the other pistol and puts a bullet through her own head, "Beautifully."

Lara: Romantic Victim

Lara, the supremely romantic victim, in Boris Pasternak's *Doctor Zhivago* (1957), seems always to be caught in the middle.

As a school girl, Lara is seduced by her mother's lover, a prominent and powerful lawyer. Later she tries to shoot him. Next she marries an earnest young man who goes on to become a key strategist of the Bolshevik forces. But when she and Zhivago meet, they cannot forget one another.

Lara, whom Zhivago constantly seeks, finds, then loses after a few brief months, is like the good things in life which run through one's fingers. The horrors of the conflict in Russia between White and Red can only momentarily be blocked out by Zhivago.

Before they part for the last time, Zhivago writes his greatest poems for her.

Lena Younger: Mother Courage

In Lorraine Hansberry's play, *Raisin in the Sun* (1957), **Lena Younger** (Mama) discovers that money can be more trouble than it's worth.

Three generations of her family are sandwiched into three rooms in Chicago. When Lena's husband dies, he leaves $10,000 in insurance money. Family tension over how to spend the money renders the bequest a mixed blessing.

Lena wants to move to a small house in

the suburbs. Her married son, Walter, wants to use the money to open a liquor store. Her daughter wants to go to medical school. Rather than see the family fragmented, Lena decides to satisfy all three desires. But Walter's partner disappears with the $6,500 remaining after the down payment on the house.

Nevertheless, the family decides to move into the house and to try to find the future that Mama steadfastly believes will be better.

Ma Joad: 'We Go On'

Large of body and spirit, **Ma Joad,** in John Steinbeck's *The Grapes of Wrath* (1939), is the hard working, indomitable matriarch of a family of "Oakies," who leave the parched earth of Oklahoma during the Depression to start again in California.

Because of her, the family survives the death of the grandparents; Tom Joad's murder of a man during a strike; exploitative employers, harrassing law officers, and disdainful native Californians. "All we got is the family unbroke," she says. "They ain't gonna wipe us out. Why, we're the people — we go on."

Madame Defarge: Knit One

Madame Defarge makes Medea look like Little Bo Peep.

In Charles Dickens' *A Tale of Two Cities* (1859), she is the wife of a revolutionary leader who is a wine shop owner. Madame Defarge urges her husband to violence with curious gusto. She is the literary personification of the *tricoteuses* (the name derives from the French word, "tricotage," which means "knitting"), a group of women who encouraged revolutionary bloodletting. The Royalists called the tricoteuses, "furies of the guillotine." Defarge is their supreme example. Woven in her knitting were the names of people she felt worthy of the blade.

Her blood-thirst was not merely supportive: she was instrumental in having one of the book's heroes, Charles Darnay, sentenced to death. His crime: that he was related to St. Evremond, who attacked her sister.

Maggie Tulliver: Nothing Right

The anomaly of **Maggie Tulliver,** in George Eliot's *The Mill on the Floss*

(1860), is that she is noble in the face of trouble that is of her own making.

The daughter of a miller, she is too creative and too passionate to be content with provincial life; and yet too needy of her family's approval to escape it.

She falls in love with Philip Wakem, the crippled son of her father's arch enemy. Her brother, whom she adores, becomes hostile and makes her romance impossible. When she has an unconsummated dalliance with her cousin's fiance, her brother treats her like a sinner.

Just as she begins to resign herself to her roots, there is a flood. When she attempts to save her brother from the waters, the two are reconciled, but they both drown. They are buried together beneath a tombstone that reads: "In their death they were not divided." The book is said to be semi-autobiographical, paralleling Eliot's relationship with George Lewes, and with her brother, Isaac.

Martha: Vicious Destroyer

Thanks to Edward Albee's play, *Who's Afraid of Virginia Woolf* (1962), **Martha** is a fixture of the American theater. Martha's relationship with her husband, George, raises love-heat symbiosis to a fine art.

Martha's father is president of the college at which George is an associate professor. Because she could never totally please her father, she can never be totally fulfilled, and her rage is combustible. She attacks George with blood-curdling ingenuity at every opportunity.

In the play, she uses and nearly destroys a visiting young couple to humiliate George. She and George feed off one another through their imaginary son, who represents their emotional sterility. Martha's strength, her weakness, and her appeal is her undiluted adrenalin, which she finds impossible to channel constructively. She is a pathetic, though appealing, destroyer in the tradition of Hedda Gabler.

Mary Poppins: Nice Nanny

If everyone had a **Mary Poppins** in their lives, there would be no wars, no poverty, no boredom, and no psychiatrists. She simply wouldn't permit it.

The English nanny to the Banks' children, Mary Poppins has charmed children since the first of P. L. Travers' series of four books appeared in 1934.

Mary's great appeal is that she is no-body's fool. She arrives at the Banks' on a gust of wind hanging, ever so primly from her umbrella. When the children have to take their medicine, it suddenly becomes their favorite flavor. When Mary takes the children for a walk, and they spot a street-artist's landscapes, the group is suddenly transported to the countryside portrayed in chalk.

When she feels she is no longer needed, she disappears as mysteriously as she arrived, leaving the children, and the reader, scratching their heads, wondering if she was just a dream after all.

Medea: Kills Kids
A woman scorned is not to be taken lightly. At least not **Medea.**

In Euripides' Greek play, *Medea* (431 B.C.), Medea will do anything for her man. She helps her husband, Jason, steal the Golden Fleece by murdering her half-brother. She disposes of Jason's enemy, Pelias, by tricking Pelias' children into killing him. But, as thanks, Jason finds another woman.

Fury overwhelms mother love, and Medea murders their two children in revenge against Jason. She also kills Jason's new bride and father-in-law. At the play's end, she is carried off to Athens by winged serpents.

Moll Flanders: Penitent's Tale
Moll, in Daniel Defoe's *Moll Flanders* (1722), is a thief, harlot, and bigamist, but emerges ultimately penitent.

The full title of this early social novel, written in the form of an autobiography, neatly sums up its plot: THE FOR-TUNES AND MISFORTUNES OF THE FAMOUS MOLL FLANDERS, ETC. WHO WAS BORN AT NEW-GATE, AND DURING A LIFE OF CONTINUED VARIETY FOR THREESCORE YEARS, BESIDE HER CHILDHOOD, WAS TWELVE YEAR A WHORE, FIVE TIMES A WIFE (WHEREOF ONCE TO HER OWN BROTHER), TWELVE YEAR A THIEF, EIGHT YEAR A TRANS-PORTED FELON IN VIRGINIA, AT LAST GREW RICH, LIV'D HONEST, AND DIED A PENITENT. WRITTEN

FROM HER OWN MEMORAN-DUMS.

Molly Bloom: Universal Woman
In James Joyce's *Ulysses* (1922), **Molly** is Leopold Bloom's wife, a modern day counterpart to Penelope, in Homer's *Odyssey.*

If Leopold is Ulysses, the wanderer searching for fulfillment, Molly is Penelope, the woman who affirms life and love. But, unlike her ancient counterpart, Molly is unfaithful to her advertising canvasser husband.

She is Joyce's representation of the universal woman. In the final section of the book, in a stream-of-consciousness monologue, Molly talks with humor and gusto about her past, her loves, and her jealousies. She ends the single-sentence discourse with the word, "yes," her affirmation of life and love despite the frustration and isolation gone before. She is sensual, intuitive, a symbol of regeneration.

Mrs. Ramsay: Perfect Woman
Beautiful **Mrs. Ramsay,** the self-sacrificing "perfect woman," in Virginia Woolf's *To the Lighthouse* (1927), wonders about life and whether it is worth living.

She is the warm, creative, center of the household, a contrast to her cold, logical husband. Always questioning life, she doubts that God could have made a world so full of misery and injustice.

Her love of life and respect for elemental virtues influence all those around her.

Even after her death, Mrs. Ramsay's compassion lives. Her younger son James and his father achieve the harmony she had sought to give them.

Nancy Drew: Teenage Sleuth
The dauntless **Nancy Drew** has a natural talent for getting to the bottom of a mystery.

The teen-aged sleuth is blessed with endless curiosity, brains, energy, and steel nerves. Edward Stratemeyer, with the help of his daughter, Harriet Stratemeyer Adams, wrote fifty-seven books under the name Carolyn Keene. Nancy has never aged, nor have generations of readers tired of her capers.

Nancy first appeared in *The Secret of the Old Clock,* in 1930. Hidden staircases, secret messages, missing maps, phantoms, and dubious characters lie at the heart of puzzles she solves. Occasionally her cousin and closest friend, George Fayne, helps get her into scrapes. Occasionally, her boyfriend, Ned Nickerson, and widowed father, Carson Drew, a criminal attorney, are summoned to get her out.

Natasha Rostov: Russian Beauty
Perhaps Leo Tolstoy's greatest creation, **Natasha Rostov,** in *War and Peace* (1864-1869), is the beautiful and ethereal daughter of an influential wealthy nineteenth century Russian family. Her growth from a delightful ingenue to a mature, insightful woman is set against Tolstoy's dissection of the flaws of Russian society and of the weakness of human beings.

Natasha falls in love with Andre Bolknoski, but is not permitted to marry him until she is older. Andre rejoins the army and, in his absence, Natasha is mesmerized into an affair with an unsavory rogue, unaware that he is married. Andre returns to comfort the grieving Natasha.

When he is wounded fighting Napoleon's forces, she cares for him until he dies of his wound. When her brother Nilolai's friend, Pierre Bezukhov, returns from battle, he and Natasha become friends, marry, and Natasha becomes a good manager of her husband's fortune.

Nora Helmer: Unwilling Doll
At the time of its presentation in 1879, Henrik Ibsen's play, *A Doll's House,* was the most devastating blow to male chauvinism ever written.

Like most middle class women of her time, **Nora Helmer** was raised to be a toy. Torval Helmer, newly appointed manager of a bank, calls his wife "my singing lark."

To camouflage her intelligence and her ability to make hard decisions, she forges her dying father's signature on a bond and thereby acquires the money needed to take Torvald to Italy for his health. Krogstad, a bookkeeper at the bank, discovers her secret, and threatens to expose her if she does not persuade Torvald to give him a promotion. When Torvald finds out about the forgery, he tells Nora that she is no longer his wife but that they will live together for the sake of appearances. Krogstad, repentent, returns the bond and

Torvald decides to renew Nora's wifely bondage.

But it is too late. Nora realizes she is simply Torvald's doll and does the unthinkable: she leaves her husband and her children. No longer willing to be an appendage, she decides to seek a way to become a person in her own right.

O-Lan: Exploited Woman
In Pearl Buck's *The Good Earth* (1931), the hardworking **O-Lan** is the most exploited of women. Her courage and strength are exceeded only by the laziness and shallowness of her husband, Wang Lung, a Chinese peasant.

To bring her family out of poverty, she works alongside her husband in the fields. When their first child is born she stops working for only two days. She chokes another child because they cannot feed it. They move to the city because the land cannot provide enough for them. During the civil war she robs a wealthy man, using the gems to buy more land.

But with wealth comes Wang Lung's realization that O-Lan was never beautiful, and has now been coarsened by years of back-breaking labor. He brings a concubine into the household. Despite her husband's unfaithfulness, she patiently serves her family until she dies.

Penelope: Loyal Lady
Penelope's faithfulness to her husband, Odysseus, in Homer's *Odyssey* (6th century B.C.), is heroic.

During his long absence following the Trojan war, she fends off suitors whom she must by custom entertain. She tells them she must finish weaving a shroud for her father-in-law before accepting any proposals. Every day she weaves, and every night she unravels.

Her servants are less faithful than she is, and reveal her secret. But Odysseus, disguised, returns to Ithaca in the nick of time. He slays the suitors and is reunited with his loyal wife.

Pollyanna: Undying Optimist
In Eleanor H. Porter's *Pollyanna* (1913), the perennially optimistic **Pollyanna Whittier** is so good, she's exasperating.

Most people facing her adversities would become suicidal or a homocidal maniac: Not Pollyanna. Her answer to life's miseries is the "Glad Game." She always finds something to be glad about.

She melts the hearts of the heartless; finds a home for Jimmy Bean, an orphan she found in the street; is a marriage counselor and full-time social worker. Then she is run over by a car. Her optimism is not daunted, even when she overhears a doctor say she will never walk again. Wrong. She gets right up and walks into Porter's sequel, *Pollyanna Grows Up* (1915).

Portia: Agile Attorney

In William Shakespeare's play, *The Merchant of Venice* (1595), **Portia** wins her case not because she is beautiful, which she is; nor because she is wealthy, which she is; but because she is wise.

Disguised as Balthazar, a lawyer, she defends Antonio against Shylock's lawsuit for nonpayment of a debt. Shylock wants either payment or a pound of flesh. She appeals to Shylock's sympathy: "The quality of mercy is not strain'd/It droppeth as the gentle rain from heaven . . ."). Shylock is unmoved, but Portia brilliantly wins the case by an argument in logic. Shylock may exact his pound of flesh, but only if he does not spill a drop of blood which is, after all, a capital offense. She shows her capacity for forgiveness when she asks for mercy for Shylock.

Scarlett O'Hara: Belle

Scarlett O'Hara, heroine of Margaret Mitchell's *Gone With the Wind* (1936), and of the film based on that book, is one of the most popular heroines in American fiction.

The vain, beautiful, quintessential southern belle, raised on a southern plantation called Tara, finds in the face of adversity that she is made of sterner stuff. She loves Ashley Wilkes, a scholarly, spineless man, who chooses to marry his sweet cousin Melanie. Scarlett marries Melanie's brother, Charles Hamilton, out of spite. After his death and amidst the ravages of the Civil War, Scarlett becomes mistress of the decaying Tara.

She marries her sister's beau, Frank Kennedy, for money. He dies too, but Scarlett and Tara endure. She meets her match in, and marries, Rhett Butler, a wealthy blockade runner. But his love for her is exhausted by her nostalgia for Ashley, her stubborn mania about Tara and the fading Old South, and by her inability to face reality.

Study in contrasts: Sweet Melanie (Olivia de Havilland) and fiery Scarlett (Vivien Leigh).

Scarlett realizes, too late, that it is Rhett she loves more than Ashley. When Rhett abandons her, her reaction is predictable: "I'll think about it tomorrow. Tomorrow is another day."

Sonya Marmeladova: Saint

In *Crime and Punishment* (1866), Fyodor Dostoevsky's novel of sin, suffering and regeneration; it is the gentle young **Sonya,** the prostitute, who works to save her starving family: her drunken father, Marmeladov; her step-mother and, their children. Sonya convinces Raskolnikov to confess his murder of the woman pawnbroker and her sister, and accompanies him when he is sent to Siberia as punishment. It is through the saintly Sonya that Raskolnikov finally learns about goodness and the need to repent.

Tess Durbeyfield: Society's Victim

Thomas Hardy's *Tess of the D'Urbervilles* (1891), is a moving and tragic social comment on the sexual double standard.

Tess Durbeyfield is sent, by her dissipated and impoverished father, to become a servant to the wealthy Mrs. D'Urberville. Her mistress' son, Alec, seduces Tess. She becomes pregnant and the child dies. Tess becomes a dairy maid and meets Angel Clare, whom she agrees to marry.

On their wedding night Angel tells Tess he is not a virgin. When Tess makes the same confession, he rejects her. Tess maintains her dignity and manages to support herself, until Alec reappears in her life. She agrees to live with him, but only if he supports her family. Clare then recognizes his own hypocrisy and returns to Tess. When he does, Tess kills Alec in a frenzy and is ultimately hanged for the murder.

Karen Wright, Martha Dobie: Social Victims

Lillian Hellman's play, *The Children's Hour* (1934), devastatingly shows how social opinion has the power to destroy lives.

Karen Wright and **Martha Dobie** are two unmarried women who run a boarding school for girls. A spiteful and emotionally corrupt student spreads the rumor that the two women are homosexuals. Enraged, the parents withdraw their daughters, forcing the school to close. For Martha, the demise of the school is almost retributive. She admits her "unnatural" feelings to Karen, and then commits suicide.

Ursula Brangwen: High Hopes

Ursula Brangwen is a women in search of unattainable fulfillment. While her disappointments are largely of her own making, one cannot help but admire the effort she puts into life.

In D. H. Lawrence's *The Rainbow* (1915), Ursula is the daughter of a dominating mother, and a father who is a frustrated artist. She despises her rural background and manages to persuade her parents to give her a good education.

After becoming a school teacher Ursula postpones marriage, preferring a variety of life experiences. Ursula tires of teaching and attends college, where she has an affair with Anton Skrebensky. She has loved him for a number of years, many of which Anton spent fighting in the Boer War in Africa. In his absence she had only one experience with love — an affair with Winifred Inger, one of her high school teachers.

In all her relationships, Ursula expects too much. She rejects Anton because his passion and energy do not match her own. Her focus is on the future rather than on the present. Lawrence developed her character further in *Women in Love* (1916).

The Wife of Bath: In Control

Alice, the wife of Bath, in Chaucer's *The Canterbury Tales* (1380's), is a clothmaker five times widowed, well versed in marriage and love making.

In the prologue to her tale, she tells about her rather lusty life with her five successive husbands, making a case against celibacy. She proclaims marriage to be best when the woman holds sway. It worked with her first four husbands whom she married for money. The fifth, a young man who was half her age, she married for love. When he tried to keep her in her place, she staged a fight and pretended that he had nearly killed her. He was so remorseful that he offered to let her run things from then on, and they were a loving couple thereafter.

The Wife of Bath advises that marriage works best when the woman is in control.

Fifty Twentieth Century Best-Sellers Written by Women

Polly Adler, A House Is Not a Home, 1953

Enid Bagnold, National Velvet, 1935

Peg Bracken, The I Hate to Cook Book, 1960

Pearl S. Buck, The Good Earth, 1931

Taylor Caldwell, Captains and the Kings, 1972

Agatha Christie, Curtain, 1975

Vivian Connell, The Chinese Room, 1942

Adelle Davis, Let's Eat Right to Keep Fit, 1954

Daphne du Maurier, Rebecca, 1938

Joyce Elbert, The Crazy Ladies, 1970

Edna Ferber, Giant, 1952

Leonore Fleischer, Benji, 1974

Anne Frank, Diary of a Young Girl, 1952

Betty Friedan, The Feminine Mystique, 1963

Elizabeth Goudge, Green Dolphin Street, 1944

Joanne Greenberg, I Never Promised You a Rose Garden, 1964

Edith Hamilton, Mythology, 1930

Laura Z. Hobson, Gentlemen's Agreement, 1947

Xaviera Hollander, The Happy Hooker, 1972

Kathryn Hulme, The Nun's Story, 1956

Rona Jaffe, The Best of Everything, 1959

Erica Jong, Fear of Flying, 1973

Bel Kaufman, Up the Down Staircase, 1965

J. Kerr, Please Don't Eat the Daisies, 1957

Frances Parkinson Keyes, The Royal Box, 1954

Marie Killilea, Karen, 1952

Harper Lee, To Kill a Mockingbird, 1960

Betty MacDonald, The Egg and I, 1945

Catherine Marshall, Christy, 1967

Rosamond Marshall, Kitty, 1943

Grace Metalious, Peyton Place, 1956

Mary McCarthy, The Group, 1963

Margaret Mitchell, Gone With the Wind, 1936

Marabel Morgan, The Total Woman, 1973

Jean Nidetch, The Weight Watchers Program Cookbook, 1972

Kathleen Norris, Mother, 1911

Gene Stratton Porter, Freckles, 1904

Katherine Anne Porter, Ship of Fools, 1962

Ayn Rand, The Fountainhead, 1943

Rosemary Rogers, Dark Fires, 1975

Françoise Sagan, Bonjour Tristesse, 1955

Annemarie Selinko, Désirée, 1953

Anya Seton, The Winthrop Woman, 1958

Betty Smith, A Tree Grows in Brooklyn, 1943

Lillian Smith, Strange Fruit, 1944

Jacqueline Susann, Valley of the Dolls, 1966

Tereska Torres, Women's Barracks, 1950

Kate Douglas Wiggin, Rebecca of Sunnybrook Farm, 1904

Laura Ingalls Wilder, The Little House on the Prairie, 1953 ed.

Kathleen Winsor, Forever Amber, 1944

Pulitzer Prizes Won By Women Authors
Fiction

1921 Edith Wharton, The Age of Innocence. Wharton's best about New York high society and a man and woman rigidly enmeshed in it.

1923 Willa Cather, One of Ours. A novel of defeat about Claude Wheeler, a creative spirit in a philistine world.

1924 Margaret Wilson, The Able McLaughlins. Tale about a Scottish community in the post-Civil War Middle West.

1925 Edna Ferber, So Big. Life story of Selina Peake, her travels with a gambler-father, teaching job, marriage to a farmer, and subsequent widowhood.

1929 Julia Peterkin, Scarlet Sister Mary. Mary grows more independent and her life becomes more involved with other people.

1931 Margaret Ayer Barnes, Years of Grace. The story of Jane Ward, a college girl of the 1890's, her engagement, marriage, love for another man, and her daughter Cicily.

1932 Pearl Buck, The Good Earth. Story of impoverished Chinese couple and their hard work to achieve wealth.

1934 Caroline Miller, Lamb in His Bosom. Rural Georgia before the Civil War and one woman's life to her old age.

1935 Josephine Johnson, Now in November. Marget's ten years on her family's farm in the Middle West and the hardships they endure.

1937 Margaret Mitchell, Gone With the Wind. The South during the Civil War and Reconstruction with the unforgettable Scarlett and Rhett.

1939 Marjorie K. Rawlings, The Yearling. Young Jody and his growing up with Flag, his pet fawn, who has to be killed when the deer ruins the farm crops.

1942 Ellen Glasgow, In This Our Life.

Virginia society in the late 1930s and the Timberlake family as the world seems to come apart.

1961 Harper Lee, To Kill a Mockingbird. An eight-year-old's viewpoint of an incident in a small Southern town and a plea for racial justice.

1965 Shirley Ann Grau, The Keepers of the House. A troubled southern white woman must face her family and community when she learns something of her family history.

1966 Katherine Anne Porter, Collected Stories.

1970 Jean Stafford, Collected Stories.

1973 Eudora Welty, The Optimist's Daughter. The judge dies and leaves a middle-aged daughter and much younger second wife.

Plays

1921 Zona Gale, Miss Lulu Bett. Single woman in a small town finds love, marries, but wonders whether her husband has another wife somewhere?

1931 Susan Glaspell, Alison's House. Alison Stanhope leaves unpublished poems which young Elsa believes belong to the world not to the family.

1935 Zoë Akins, The Old Maid. Adaptation of Edith Wharton novel concerning the illegitimate daughter of Charlotte Lovell, the old maid, and Charlotte's sister who wins the child's love.

1945 Mary Chase, Harvey. Elwood and his invisible rabbit have fun, but Elwood's sister winds up in a sanitarium for treatment.

1956 Frances Goodrich (and Albert Hackett), Diary of Anne Frank. Dramatization of Anne's last days hiding from the Nazis in Holland with her family and other Jews.

1958 Ketti Frings, Look Homeward, Angel. Eugene Gant and his growth into manhood in relation to his parents and brother.

WOMEN OF LETTERS

Alcott: Little Women's Jo
Louisa May Alcott (1832-1888), most of whose 270 published works were observations on nineteenth century family life, was a socially privileged maiden with true grit.

Alcott was born in Germantown, Pennsylvania. Although her father, eccentric educator and transcendentalist Bronson Alcott, could only provide Louisa and

Louisa May Alcott crusaded in and out of print for temperance and women's suffrage.

her three sisters with genteel poverty, she grew up with a wealth of literature. Raised in Boston and Concord, Massachusetts, she was educated by her father, tutored by her neighbor Henry David Thoreau, and influenced by Ralph Waldo Emerson. Nurtured by her mother, a woman of strong social conscience (she was a city missionary to the poor in Boston), Alcott became the family breadwinner. At eighteen, she taught in Boston, and later worked as a seamstress, domestic, and governess. She began writing poems and novelettes and, by 1860, was published in the *Atlantic Monthly*. In 1862 she became an army nurse, and wrote of the horrors she witnessed in "Hospital Sketches," which appeared in *Commonwealth* and was published later that year as a book.

In 1867 she became editor of *Merry's Museum*, a girls' magazine. That year, at the age of thirty-five, she wrote *Little Women*, her most successful and cohesive work. The book appeared in two parts, in 1868 and 1869, followed by *An Old Fashioned Girl* (1870), and *Little Men* (1871).

Considered a writer of novels for juveniles, she wrote a few "adult" novels, including *Work* (1873), an autobiographical chronicle of a young working woman.

Despite her world fame, Alcott clung to her role as family supporter and leader, grinding out book after book. She also became an outspoken leader of the suffrage and temperance movements.

Austen: Drawing Room Wit

Jane Austen (1775-1817) has been called "the mother of the English nineteenth century novel." She was a witty, no-nonsense writer, whose ability to see humor in the tug-of-war between formality and feeling produced some of the finest novels in English •nineteenth century literature.

She grew up with style, if not wealth, the seventh of eight children. Her father was rector of a country parish and taught at Oxford; her mother was a literate woman of gilt-edged lineage.

The affection, cheerfulness, and energy of her family, provided her with the setting and characters for her novels. Her life was no more adventurous than that of her characters, and she had the good sense to write only about that which she knew. As a young woman, she was flirtatious and vivacious, and had several romantic attachments, but she never married.

Her first novel, *Sense and Sensibility,* was written in 1797 but was not pub-

Jane Austen had the good sense to write only about that which she knew.

lished until 1811. It brought sedate irony and realistic romanticism to the novel form.

Her other major works were *Pride and Prejudice* (1813); *Mansfield Park* (1814); *Emma* (1816); *Northanger Abbey;* and *Persuasion* (published posthumously in 1818).

The Brontës: Tragic Romanticists

The tragic romanticism of the novels of **Charlotte, Emily,** and **Anne Brontë** is strikingly paralleled in their own lives. Their mother died in 1821, their two older sisters died in adolescence, and their brother died in 1849 of drink and drug addiction.

All three writers were born in Thornton, Yorkshire, daughters of an Anglican minister. Shortly after Anne (1820-1849) was born, the family moved to Haworth where they lived out their lives. Raised by their aunt, Elizabeth Branwell, a well-meaning but austere Methodist; and their eccentric father, the children used their imaginations to fill the gap in their lives. They created a fantasy existence in miniature books, a life they preferred to the outside world they called the Kingdom of Angria.

Charlotte Bronte and her equally shy sisters spoke to the world through their novels.

In 1846 the Brontë sisters published *Poems* under the pseudonyms "Currer, Ellis and Acton Bell." Currer was Charlotte, Ellis was Emily, and Acton was Anne. The first novels of each of the sisters were also published under these pen names, but the secrecy was relaxed by 1848 when Anne's second novel, *The Tenant of Wildfell Hall,* met with great success.

Emily (1818-1848) had a breakdown at seventeen during her second attempt at formal schooling. Charlotte (1816-1855), the strongest of the three, taught school for three years at Roe Head. Anne was a student there, but her ill health, and both sisters' melancholia, drove them back home.

Their crippling shyness and the isolation of the moors imprisoned the Brontë sisters at home. Writing became their major source of communication with the outside world. Emily's *Wuthering Heights* (1847) was explosive in its passion, the safety valve of an unlived existence. Anne's *Agnes Grey* (1847) was the least successful of the Brontë books, although *The Tenant of Wildfell Hall* (1848), her second novel, sold well. Charlotte's *Jane Eyre* (1847) was an enormous success; but what pleasure Charlotte may have felt was darkened by the death of her two sisters within the year.

Charlotte continued to write (*Shirley,* published in 1849 and *Villette* published in 1852). In 1854, she married her father's curate, Arthur Bell Nicholls. She was the only one of the sisters to wed.

Brooks: Voice of Black America

Gwendolyn Brooks (1917-   ) received the Pulitzer Prize for her second volume of poetry, *Annie Allen,* in 1950.

She was the first black woman to receive the prize. Her work, which chronicles her feelings about the black experience, has universal appeal.

Born in Topeka, Kansas, Brooks was raised in Chicago. Her artistic family encouraged her writing — her father worked for a music house, her mother is a composer, and her brother is an artist. Her first published poems appeared in *American Childhood* when she was thirteen.

Brooks has been a prolific writer and

has won many awards. She won several first prizes for her poetry from the Midwestern Writers' Conference in the forties. In 1945, her first book of poetry, *A Street in Bronzeville,* was published. In 1946 *Mademoiselle* named her one of their "Ten Women of the Year." That year she also won an award from the Academy of Arts and Letters and the first of two consecutive Guggenheim Fellowships. In 1966 she was the first of her race and sex to be elected to the National Institute of Arts and Letters, and in 1968 she succeeded Carl Sandburg as poet laureate of Illinois.

Other books of poetry by Brooks include *The Bean Eaters* (1960); *Selected Poems* (1963); *In the Mecca* (1968); and *Riot* (1970). She has written one novel, *Maud Martha* (1953), and a children's book, *Bronzeville Boys and Girls* (1956).

Browning: Love's Triumph

The high romance of the life of **Elizabeth Barrett Browning** (1806-1861) is as well known as her work.

Born in Durham, England, the oldest of eleven children, she spent her childhood in Herefordshire. She was an exceptionally precocious child and at the age of eight she read Greek. Her mother died when Browning was twenty, and, because of financial difficulties, the family moved to 50 Wimpole Street, in London. There, her life-long bout with tuberculosis and the domination of her tyrannical father kept her an invalid.

In 1833, Browning's "Miscellaneous Poems", and her translation of "Prometheus Bound", were published anonymously. In 1838, she published *The Seraphim and Other Poems* under her own name.

The publication of *Poems,* in 1844, led to a joyous upheaval in her life. It brought her fame — and Robert Browning, about whom she had written lines of praise in the book. When her father refused to allow her to go to Italy for her health, they married secretly in September 1846, and moved to Pisa. Her father refused ever to see them again because he did not believe any of his children should marry.

Prior to their marriage, Elizabeth had written "Sonnets from the Portuguese"

Elizabeth Barrett Browning triumphed over both ill health and an overbearing father.

(Browning called her his "Portuguese") as a surprise for her husband, but it was not published until a revised edition of *Poems* was issued in 1850. *Aurora Leigh* was published in 1856.

During her marriage, Elizabeth's health improved sufficiently for her to give birth to a son in 1849. The Brownings spent most of their married life in Italy, where they wrote of their interest in the Italian struggle for unity and independence.

Buck: West Meets East

Although she spent the last forty years of her life in the U.S., **Pearl S. Buck** (1892-1973), Nobel Prize-winning author, was best known as an interpreter of life in the East to those living in the West.

She was born in Hillsboro, West Virginia, while her parents, Presbyterian missionaries, were on furlough from China. Growing up in China, she learned Chinese before English, and became, in her own words, "mentally bifocal." After graduation from Randolph-Macon College in Virginia, Buck taught psychology for a year, then returned to China where she taught English literature at Chinese universities. She married Dr. John Lossing Buck, an agricultural missionary to China.

They returned to the U.S. in 1925, and she earned an M.A. in English at Cornell in 1926.

Her first novel, *East Wind, West Wind,* appeared in 1930. She won the Pulitzer Prize for *The Good Earth* (1931); the first part of a trilogy, followed by *Sons* (1932), and *A House Divided* (1935). Her prolific literary output in the next few years was rewarded by a Nobel Prize in 1938.

She moved permanently to the U.S. in 1934, and earned a second M.A. from Yale. In 1935 she divorced Buck, and married Richard J. Walsh, a publisher. She and her husband lived, with their five adopted children, and her retarded daughter from her first marriage, in Bucks County, Pennsylvania.

Most of Buck's books — she wrote over 40 — centered on the Orient, as did the bulk of her activities. In 1941 she founded the East and West Association, to promote understanding between Asia and the U.S. In 1949, she founded Welcome House, an adoption agency for children of Asian-American descent.

Cather: Champion of Courage
Willa Cather (1873-1947), is best known for her straightforward and sensitive novels about fading frontier America.

Raised in a spacious farmhouse in the Back Creek Valley in Virginia, Cather and her family moved to the Nebraska plain in 1883. Uprooted herself, she admired the courage of immigrant Europeans who made their lives and homes out of the harsh Nebraska earth.

She worked her way through the University of Nebraska, then wrote for the *Daily Reader* in Pittsburgh. In 1901 she became a school teacher. In 1903, she published a book of verse, *April Twilights*. From 1906 to 1912 she was managing editor of *McClure's Magazine* in New York. She resigned to devote all her time to writing fiction, beginning with *Alexander's Brigade* (1912).

The struggle for achievement at the expense of dignity and love was the theme of many of her novels. *O Pioneers!* (1913) and *My Antonia* (1918) were her finest novels about the prairie. *The Song of the Lark* (1915) reflected her love of music.

She won the Pulitzer Prize for *One of Ours* (1922), but became famous with *A Lost Lady* (1923). She was a best-selling author of books about courage — *Death Comes for the Archbishop* (1927) and *Shadows on the Rock* (1931).

Cather's interest in the frontier struggle caused her to seek out heroes and heroines and define hardy enduring virtues. Her best writing was about the contrast between courage and cowardice; dignity and whining. "The history of every country," she wrote, "begins in the heart of a man or a woman."

Chopin: A Scandal in Her Time
Kate Chopin (1851-1904) published only four novels. She is known primarily for her Creole and "Cajun" stories.

After a privileged childhood and youth in St. Louis, she married Oscar Chopin, a Creole and moved with him to Louisiana, where they lived for ten years. Oscar Chopin died of swamp fever in 1882, and in 1884 Kate moved back to St. Louis. It was then that she began to write, and her first stories appeared in *Harper's* and the *Century*.

When her first novel, *At Fault* (1890), was an artistic failure, she tried to improve her skills by reading such French masters as Daudet, Flaubert, and De Maupassant. She succeeded particularly in portraying the dialects and mannerisms of Creoles. Many of her stories appeared in collected form in *Bayou Folk* (1894), and *A Night In Acadie* (1897).

Chopin's finest book was also her last, *The Awakening* (1899). Its literary merits, today considered enormous, were unrecognized because of their controversial themes: mixed marriage, a wife's adultery, sexual awareness, and the treatment of women as property. The sting of unfavorable criticism was paralytic: she never wrote another book.

Christie: Mystery's First Lady
Agatha Miller Christie (1891-1976) wrote her first story as a child to take her mind off a cold. Her first novel was a response to her sister's challenge to write an irresistible detective story. That book, *The Mysterious Affair at Styles* (1920), about a tantalizingly elusive wrongdoer, had nearly as elusive a publisher. After several rejections, Christie

forgot about the book until a year later when a publisher finally accepted it.

During her lifetime she wrote some 90 books, which sold over 400 million copies and were translated into 103 languages. Her play, *The Mousetrap*, opened in London in 1952 and is still running. By all odds, she is the most successful writer in the English language. Christie was born in Devon, England. Her American father died when she was a child and she was raised and educated by her mother, who encouraged her to write and to think. In 1914 she married Archibald Christie. While he served in the Royal Air Corps in France, during World War I, she became a Red Cross volunteer at a hospital in Torquay, Devon. During that time she became a qualified pharmacist and could name her poisons in prose. She also wrote her first book, introducing Hercule Poirot, the cerebral detective who has possibly upstaged Sherlock Holmes forever.

Dame Agatha (she was named a Commander, Order of the British Empire, in 1971) divorced her husband in 1928. In 1930 she married archeologist Max Mallowan, and for many years took annual trips with him to Iraq and Syria, settings for *Murder in Mesopotamia (1936)* and *Death on the Nile* (1937).

Christie wearied a bit of Poirot and invented an eccentric spinster busybody, Jane Marple, to represent the distaff side of detecting. In addition, she wrote non-detective stories under the pseudonym Mary Westmacott. Under her own name she wrote several plays, including *Witness for the Prosecution*, which won the New York Drama Critics Award for the best foreign play of 1954-1955.

When Poirot was killed off by his maker in 1975, it made page one of the New York Times, as did Dame Agatha, when she died the following year.

Colette: The Prolific Sensualist

Colette (Sidonie Gabrielle, 1873-1954) once said that, for her, writing was as easy as "frying eggs."

Her later skill as a writer of fiction, drama, criticism, and journalism was nurtured during her childhood in Burgundy. At age twenty, she married Henri Gauthier-Villars who forced her to collaborate with him on several slightly risqué books. The first, *Claudine a L'École* (1900), was a best seller.

In 1906 Colette divorced her husband,

A registered pharmacist, Agatha Christie brought realism to her fictional poisonings.

The novels of Colette have been rediscovered by a new generation of American women.

became an actress of moderate success, and continued to write. The first book under her maiden name, *Dialogues des Bêtes,* appeared in 1904.

She became a literary correspondent in 1910 for the newspaper, *Le Matin.* In 1912 she married her editor in chief, Henri de Jouvenal. The marriage (and her job) dissolved after twelve years; but they were her most productive, and established her as a writer of extraordinary insight, sensitivity, and sensuality.

Colette's third marriage, in 1935, to journalist Maurice Goudeket, was her happiest and lasted until her death. Although she suffered from arthritis, her writing continued into old age — at the rate of nearly a novel a year. Her most famous is *Gigi* (1944), but her most important books are *The Vagabond* (1912), *Chéri* (1929), and *The Last of Chéri* (1932).

De Staël: An Emperor's Adversary

Madame de Staël, born Anne Louise Germaine Necker, (1766-1817) as historian, literary critic, political essayist, and novelist, was perhaps the most extraordinary woman of her time.

Lacking in beauty but possessing undisputed genius, she counted as admirers the greatest minds of the day, and as face-to-face enemy, Napoleon. Her personality was as powerful as her intellect, and her life was filled with passion and upheaval.

Her father, a Swiss banker who was Louis XVI's finance minister, indulged her. As a child she was surrounded and stimulated by intellectuals, and she was given a superb education. At fifteen she began writing novels, essays, and tragedies. She was married at twenty to the Swedish Ambassador to Paris, Baron Erik Magnus Staël-Holstein, a suitable, if unsatisfying, match. Madame de Staël's *Letters on Jean-Jacques Rousseau* was published in 1788, on the eve of the French Revolution.

During the Revolution she helped friends and members of the royal family to escape, and she was forced to go to Switzerland and later, England. In 1794 she began a twelve-year affair with Benjamin Constant, a fellow writer.

De Staël returned to Paris when Napoleon took power, but her espousal of political reform, in *A Treatise on Ancient and Modern Literature* (1800), irritated him. Napoleon lost his temper over *Delphine* (1802), a novel critical of Roman Catholicism, and he expelled her from Paris. A year of travel in Italy resulted in a second novel, *Corinne* (1807).

Her masterpiece, a three-volume study of northern and southern European literature, *About Germany* (1811), also didn't meet with Napoleon's approval.

Dickinson: Recluse of Amherst

The pulse of **Emily Dickinson** (1830-1886), one of the finest lyric poets of the English language, is found in her 1,775 poems. Like the Brontë sisters, her passion was inner and untried, her adventures literary only.

She was born in Amherst, Massachusetts, in the same house in which she died. Her father, a lawyer, was as austere as her mother was remote. Emily's older brother, Austin, married and moved next door. Her sister, Lavinia, like herself, never married and rarely left the house. Emily attended Mt. Holyoke Female Seminary for one year and came home for good. Her mentor was Thomas Wentworth Higginson, a literary critic

Reclusive Emily Dickinson declared, "When I die, they'll have to remember me."

whose essays she had read in *The Atlantic*. In 1862, she wrote to him asking if her work was "alive," beginning a correspondence that spanned twenty years. Although charmed by her poems, he encouraged her not to publish. In fact, only seven of her poems appeared in print during her lifetime, all over her objections and all altered by editors.

Emily, who always dressed in white, died in 1886. After her death her sister, Lavinia, discovered hundreds of her poems. After unskillful and often unnecessary editing by Higginson, *Poems by Emily Dickinson,* was published in 1890. The critics were cool but the public was enthusiastic. *Poems: Second Series* (1891), and *Poems: Third Series* (1896) followed.

The risks Emily could not take in life she took in dying. "I have a horror of death," she once wrote, "the dead are so soon forgotten. But when I die, they'll have to remember me."

George Eliot received her encouragement — and pseudonym — from her lover, George Lewes.

Eliot: A Double Life
The name of **Mary Ann Evans** (1819-1880) appeared only once on a title page, when her translation of Feuerbach's *Essence of Christianity* (1854) was published. As **George Eliot,** she embarked on the second of two lives.

As the devoted daughter of a Warwickshire estate agent she was a pious, plain, inhibited woman. After her father's death, Eliot, at age thirty lost her taste for Christianity and for isolation. In 1851, after a year in Geneva, she became an editorial assistant on the liberal *Westminster Review,* where she learned every phase of editorial work and met the most important writers of the day.

Eliot also met George Henry Lewes, editor of *The Leader,* physiologist, biographer, and essayist. Literature has Lewes to thank for "George Eliot," the pen name he gave to Mary Ann. The connection between the two was profound and lasted until his death in 1878. Unable to marry Eliot because his wife was insane (English law precluded divorce under the circumstances), they lived together in Germany and London, ignoring Victorian disapproval.

With Lewes' encouragement, Eliot wrote some of the greatest novels in the English language, among them: *Adam Bede* (1859); *The Mill on the Floss* (1860); and *Silas Marner* (1861). *Middlemarch* (1871) is considered her masterpiece.

In May 1880, Eliot married John Walter Cross, but she died of pneumonia the following December.

Ferber: The American Dickens
When **Edna Ferber** (1885-1968) was a child in Kalamazoo, Michigan, she longed to be an actress when she grew up. Economic realities suspended her aspirations when her father became blind.

At seventeen, she had to take a job as a reporter on the *Appleton Daily Crescent* because the family needed the three dollar weekly salary. She later worked for the *Milwaukee Journal* and the *Chicago Tribune*.

However, the hiatus in her theatrical ambitions was temporary. Ferber wrote *Show Boat* (1926) (made into a musical play and movie), *Cimarron* (1929), *Giant* (1952), and *Saratoga Trunk* (1941) (all also made into films). In collaboration with George S. Kaufman she wrote several plays — *Dinner at Eight* (1932), *The Royal Family* (1927), and *Stage Door* (1936). All but the last were made into films.

She once said she had never written a book with which she was totally satisfied. Although the critics usually agreed,

With *Raisin In The Sun*, Lorraine Hansberry tried to destroy stereotypes about blacks.

A frustrated actress, Edna Ferber went on to write plays, films, and historical novels.

the public did not. William Allen White, however, called her "the legitimate daughter of the Dickens dynasty."

Ferber won the Pulitzer Prize for *So Big*, in 1925. Her other historical novels included *American Beauty* (1931); *Come and Get It* (1935); and *Great Son* (1945). Her two autobiographies were *A Peculiar Treasure* (1939), and *A Kind of Magic* (1963).

Hansberry: Gifted and Black
Lorraine Hansberry (1930-1965) was the first black woman to write a Broadway play. She tried to destroy black stereotypes by writing about people who "happen to be Negroes."

A brilliant playwright whose career was cut short by cancer, she was born in Chicago, the daughter of a wealthy real-estate broker. As a young woman she wanted to become an artist and studied at the Chicago Art Institute and the University of Wisconsin. There she also studied theater, and discovered that her ability to put one word after another surpassed her ability to paint.

In 1950, she moved to New York, where she met and married music publisher and song writer Robert Nemiroff.

Her play, *Raisin in the Sun*, written in the early 1950s, opened on Broadway in 1959 to superb reviews, and received the New York Drama Critics Circle award. The play introduced Sidney Poitier, and had the first black Broadway producer in fifty years, Lloyd Richards. She hoped *Raisin* would counteract the stereotypical books and plays about blacks she called "bad art."

Her second play, *The Sign in Sidney Brustein's Window*, appeared on Broadway in 1964. She died three months after it opened. Her husband put together a memoir of her writings called *To Be Young, Gifted and Black*, in 1969. It was made into an off-Broadway and television play.

Hellman: Respected Maverick
Lillian Hellman (1905-   ) is one of America's most respected mavericks.

Her career as a writer has been a stunning series of successes. Her plays include *The Children's Hour; Little Foxes; Watch on the Rhine;* and *Toys in the Attic,* all of which have been made into films. In 1969 she won the National Book Award for her memoir, *An Unfinished Woman. Pentimento* and *Scoun-*

drel Time, both autobiographical works, were best sellers.

Hellman was born in New Orleans, and in 1910 her family moved to New York City, where she later attended New York University and Columbia University. She worked as a play reader for Liveright Publishers and reviewed books for the New York Herald Tribune.

Hellman has visibly stalked society's bullies and taken their heat. After a month in Spain in 1937 she spoke vehemently against Franco's fascist regime upon her return to the United States. She was a first-hand front line witness of the Russian war in 1945.

In 1952, before the House Un-American Activities Committee, she refused to answer questions about either her alleged membership in the Communist Party or about the political activities of her friends. She was blacklisted for her leftist interests, and her McCarthy era experiences are detailed in *Scoundrel Time.*

Lagerlöf: Swedish Legend

Selma Lagerlöf (1858-1940) was the first woman to win the Nobel Prize for Literature. It was the highlight of a life that was outwardly ordinary but brilliantly creative.

An early bout with polio left her permanently lame. That handicap, as well as her love for her ancestral home in Varmland, Sweden, left their mark on her work. Her father became ill and lost the estate in her youth, necessitating her decade of work as a schoolteacher.

Her grandmother had entertained her with local legends while she recovered from polio. Her later ability to make a fable seem real, doubtless stemmed from those convalescing years. Reworked, the legends appeared in *Gösta Berling's Saga* in 1891. It is considered a masterpiece, as is *Jerusalem* (1902), a two-volume account of Swedish peasants who left their farms to live and work in the Holy Land. *The Wonderful Adventures of Nils* (1907) is one of literature's finest children's books.

The success of Lagerlöf's books made it possible for her to write full-time. But her true passion was to regain her father's home. With the money awarded with the Nobel Prize in 1909, she was able to buy back Marbacka Manor, where she lived until her death.

Lazarus: Lady Liberty's Poet

The early poetry of **Emma Lazarus** (1849-1887) was distinguished, but she is primarily remembered for her sonnet, "The New Colossus," inscribed on the Statue of Liberty. The daughter of a wealthy New York Jewish family, she was surrounded with literature, music, and fine art all her life. A shy and introverted child, she found satisfaction in writing. Her first volume of verse was published at seventeen. Ralph Waldo Emerson was her mentor, encouraging her writing.

Although her early works were favorably reviewed, her writing did not acquire the finely honed passion for which she was noted until 1881. Until then a casual Jew, Lazarus was enraged by the first Great Russian pogrom which began that year. "The Banner of the Jew," published in *Critic* in 1882, was a militant call to arms. She continued to plead her cause in "The Dance of Death," a play about fourteenth century Jewish heroism, and in her book "Song of the Semite." She helped found New York's Hebrew Technical Institute, and advocated Zionism.

In 1883, Lazarus donated "The New Colossus" for an auction to raise money for the Statue of Liberty fund.

Lessing: A Moral Quest

Doris Lessing (1919-   ) has used her first hand observations of the cruelties of racism in Rhodesia, and her experience of the tensions between men and women, as the raw materials of her forceful fiction.

Born in Persia of British parents, she grew up on a 3,000-acre farm in Rhodesia. Her childhood, she says, was "hellishly lonely," and her inner life fostered a spirited independence. She dropped out of school at fourteen and studied the classics on her own.

She moved to London in 1949, bringing with her the manuscript of *The Grass is Singing,* a powerful novel set in South Africa. Published the following year, it was an immediate success. *Children of Violence,* a series of five novels, followed. These books chronicle the life of the fictional heroine, Martha Quest, as she grows to maturity, and painful understanding, in southern Africa.

The Golden Notebook (1962), Lessing's masterpiece, leaves the African material behind to describe the experiences and feelings of a creative woman living in London. Using the device of fictional diaries, Lessing records the many levels of her heroine's life and, with a cool, realistic eye, describes her conflicting emotions; shattered hopes, and final stoic acceptance of the fragmentation of modern life. In part, the book reflects Lessing's own disillusionment with Communist political activity. Critics have called *The Golden Notebook* a monument of twentieth century literature.

Lowell: The Eccentric Brahmin
Until she was thirty-five, **Amy Lowell** (1874-1925) was only another Boston Brahmin.

She was a descendant of the patrician Lowell dynasty, and while she was a mediocre student, given to chronic obesity, her childhood was surrounded by the books and learning of the scholarly Lowells. By 1900 both her parents were dead. Her first poem was published in the *Atlantic* in 1910, and her first book of verse, *A Dome of Many-Coloured Glass*, appeared two years later. The critics were unimpressed, but she was committed to a lifelong dream of becoming a writer.

In 1913, a trip to England, where she met Ezra Pound, made a profound impact on her work. Later, her preference was for the poetry of Carl Sandburg, Vachel Lindsay, and Edgar Lee Masters. Her writing flourished and appeared in the leading literary magazines of the day. Several books of poetry were published between 1915 and 1921. Her most famous poem, "Patterns," was included in *Men, Women, and Ghosts* (1916).

Lowell's best writing was in her criticism, particularly a two-volume biography of John Keats, published in 1925. Her reputation as a scholar was as solid as was her notoriety. A beloved eccentric, she insisted that all the mirrors in her house be covered, smoked large, black cigars, and punctuated her intellectual and refined conversation with some well placed epithets.

Her influence on poetry was greater than her poems themselves. At her death Robert Frost said, "How often I have heard it in the voice and seen it in the eyes of this generation that Amy Lowell had lodged poetry with them to stay."

McCarthy: Iconoclast and Wit
Mary McCarthy (1912-   ) a scathing wit and iconoclast, had a childhood that was nothing to laugh about.

Born in Seattle, Washington, she was an orphan at age seven. She and her three brothers (one of whom is actor Kevin McCarthy) lived with her great aunt and the latter's husband, who had, as she later wrote, "a positive gift for turning everything sour and ugly." Her impressions of those years are movingly recounted in *Memories of a Catholic Girlhood*, published in 1957. She graduated Phi Beta Kappa from Vassar.

Her capacity for total recall makes her fiction vivid, as does her highly stylized writing. "What I really do," she once said, "is to take real plums and put them into an imaginary cake." Satiric impatience with dishonesty characterizes her fiction, particularly *The Groves of Academe* (1952) and *The Group* (1963) Her nonfiction includes *Venice Observed* (1956); *The Stones of Florence* (1959) *Vietnam* (1967); and *Hanoi* (1968).

She has been awarded two Guggenheim fellowships and is a member of the National Institute of Arts and Letters.

McCullers: The Lonely Hunter
Carson McCullers (1917-1967) wrote novels that, like her life, are gothic in their pain.

She was born in Columbus, Georgia, and the South was the setting for most of her fiction. At seventeen she went to New York, bound for Julliard and a career in music.

In 1937 she married Reeves McCullers and for two years they lived in North Carolina. Her first novel, *The Heart Is a Lonely Hunter* (1940), was written there She was only twenty-three and it was an instant success.

Her personal handicaps were awesome — long periods of paralysis resulting from several strokes, and an aching sense of isolation. Her husband had his own demons. She divorced and remarried him, living with his alcoholism and drug addiction. He committed suicide in 1953.

Reflections in a Golden Eye (1941) was an enormous success. Her most famous book was *Member of the Wedding* (1946). For her dramatic version of *Wedding* she won the New York Drama Critics Circle award.

McCullers' fiction has been called neurotic, intense, compassionate, tough-minded, touching. She was reluctant to say it was also autobiographical. "It seems to me that writing," she once said, "or any art, is not dependent on an act of will but is created spontaneously from some objective source the author can only shape, control, and form."

Millay: Poetic Wit

What F. Scott Fitzgerald was to the prose of the 1920s, **Edna St. Vincent Millay** (1892-1950) was to poetry.

Her voluble verse and her sophisticated wit are best remembered in these lines: "My candle burns at both ends/It will not last the night/But ah, my foes, and oh, my friends/It gives a lovely light."

Born in Maine, she and her two sisters were brought up by her mother following her father's death. Her mother persuaded her to enter her poem, *Renascence,* in a contest. Although she did not win, the poem attracted a patron, who sent her to Vassar.

Millay lived in Greenwich Village, New York, during its golden days, writing under the pseudonym "Nancy Boyd." She published, *A Few Figs from Thistles* and *Second April* in 1921. In 1923, she won the Pulitzer Prize for *The Harp Weaver and Other Poems.* That year she married Eugen Jan Boissevain, who became her protector, mentor, and secretary.

A superb sonneteer, she was that rarity in American literature, a successful poet of immense popularity. As she matured, so did her writing and her interests. In 1927 she turned over the proceeds from "Justice Denied in Massachusetts" to the defense of Sacco and Venzetti.

Her later books were expressions of social conscience: *There Are No Islands Any More* (1940); *Make Bright the Arrows* (1940); and *The Murder of Lidice* (1942).

Moore: Poetry's MVP

The image of **Marianne Moore** (1887-1972) in later life is that of a small, elfin woman, wearing a black tri-cornered hat over her white, wispy hair, slugging it out verbally with Muhammed Ali.

Possibly the most celebrated poet in twentieth century America, Moore seems to have won as many awards as she wrote poems. Among her laurels were the Pulitzer Prize (1952); the Bollingen Prize (1952); the Gold Medal of the National Institute of Arts and Letters (1953); the Boston Arts Festival Poetry Award (1958); and many others.

Moore was born in St. Louis, Missouri, and moved with her mother and brother to Carlisle, Pennsylvania, when her father died in 1894. She graduated from Bryn Mawr College, where she majored in biology and histology; the precision of which was to be invaluable in her later writing.

T. S. Eliot transformed her from teacher to poet when he published some of her poems in the imagist journal, the *Egoist,* in London. *Poems* (1921), her first book of verse, was published by friends in London and appeared in the United States, in 1924, as *Observations.*

Marianne Moore at 81 tossed out the first ball of the New York Yankees' 1968 season.

Moore joined the staff of *Dial*, a prestigious literary journal, and edited it until its demise in 1929. That year she and her mother moved to Brooklyn, where she became a fixture and an avid Dodger fan.

Parker: The Ultimate Wit

Dorothy Parker (1893-1976), poet, critic, terminal wit, gave black humor a good name.

As a founding member of the famous Algonquin Round Table, she had a quotability based on bitchiness you love to hate. When she heard of the death of President Calvin Coolidge, she allegedly remarked, "How can they tell?" In fact, so much of her energy was dissipated in conversation that her reputation as raconteur surpassed that of writer.

She was born in New Jersey and attended the Blessed Sacrament Convent School in New York City. She worked for *Vogue* from 1916 to 1917, when she married Edwin Pond Parker. Dorothy Parker became editor and drama critic for *Vanity Fair*. The thanks she got for her vituperative reviews was the pink slip (Katherine Hepburn's range of emotions as an actress, Parker wrote, ran "the gamut from a to b.") She then wrote a popular column for *The New Yorker* called "Constant Reader," another outlet for her satirical social comment.

Parker's first volume of verse, *Enough*

Dorothy Parker originated the quip about men not making passes at women in glasses.

Rope (1927), a best-seller, included this gloomy quip: "Guns aren't lawful;/Nooses give;/Gas smells awful;/You might as well live." She divorced Parker in 1928 and the following year won the O. Henry Prize for her story, "Big Blonde." Her first book of short stories, *Lament for the Living* was published in 1930.

In 1933 she married film actor Alan Campbell (he died in 1963) and, while living with him in Hollywood, wrote several screen plays.

Parker paid willingly for her political outspokenness. After her appearance before the House Un-American Activities Committee in 1951, her literary output was slight. At her death she left most of her estate to Martin Luther King, Jr. and the NAACP.

Plath: Dying Right

"Dying/Is an art, like everything else/I do it exceptionally well." Dying was the thread with which **Sylvia Plath** (1932-1963) strung together the events in her life until at the age of 31, she finally got it right.

She was born in Boston, where her father was a professor of biology at Boston University. His death, when Sylvia was eight, was a severe blow to his daughter. Writing was an early-discovered talent, and she won newspaper sponsored contests for her short stories. By age eighteen she had work published in *Seventeen*. A brilliant student at Smith College, she still found time to write for *Mademoiselle* and *Harper's*, but these early successes did nothing to alleviate her depression. At Smith, she suffered a nervous breakdown and attempted suicide. Shock treatments and other therapy enabled her to return to Smith, where she was graduated *summa cum laude*.

In 1956 Plath went to England on a Fulbright Fellowship, where she met and married poet Ted Hughes. After two years in the United States, where she taught and wrote, they returned to England to live. Her first book, *The Colossus*, was published in 1960, the year of her daughter's birth. Her son was born two years later. By then she and Hughes had separated. She was only able to write by getting up before dawn and the awakening of her children.

Sylvia Plath told poignantly of her breakdown and suicide attempt in *The Bell Jar*.

Plath's other books of poetry included *Ariel* (1968); *Crossing the Water* (1971); and *Winter Trees* (1972), all published posthumously. On her final emotional decline she was able to write her finest book, *The Bell Jar* (1963), an autobiographical novel based on her breakdown. She committed suicide one month after its publication.

Porter: The Sublime Perfectionist

Katherine Anne Porter (1890-   ) loves writing and physical activity, passions which reflect the interests of two of her ancestors, O. Henry (Sidney Porter) and Daniel Boone.

Throughout her life, her only rest from writing has been outdoor sports — swimming, sailing, and horseback riding. As a writer of short stories, she is unsurpassed in her craft. A painstaking writer, her great reputation has been the result of a relatively small output.

Porter was born in Indian Creek, Texas, and was educated at southern convent schools. In 1906 she married, divorcing three years later. She became a newspaper writer in Chicago, and returned to Texas in 1914, working briefly as a singer. To support herself she was a hack writer, editor, and scriptwriter in California, Colorado, and New York. Her first volume of stories, *Flowering*

Judas (1930), established her reputation and earned her a Guggenheim fellowship but did not fill the coffers. Subsequent books of stories were also critical successes but did not sell well: *Hacienda, a Story of Mexico* (1934); *Noon Wine* (1937); and *Pale Horse, Pale Rider* (1939).

She married Albert Russel Erskine, an English professor, in 1938. They divorced in 1942, and she moved to New York.

Porter's only full-length novel, published in 1962, was *Ship of Fools,* a huge best seller and later a film. She won the Pulitzer Prize and the National Book Award for *Collected Short Stories* (1965).

Radcliffe: Gothic Genius

Anne Radcliffe (1764-1823) had a genius for scaring people half to death, and her readers loved it. Her Gothic horror stories had an enormous influence on Romantic literature.

She was born in London and, as an asthmatic child, spent much of her youth fantasizing about the supernatural. She was married at twenty-three to William Radcliffe, a lawyer, who became editor of the *English Chronicle*. Childless, she had time to develop her writing.

Her first book, *The Castles of Athlin and Dunbayne,* appeared anonymously in 1789, and *A Sicilian Romance,* the following year. *The Romance of the Forest* (1791) and *The Mysteries of Udolpho* (1794) brought her worldwide fame.

In her novels she created terrifying tension between elegance and evil. In *The Italian* (1796), her last novel, she perfected the romantic villain who, like Quasimodo, was repellent and tragic at the same time. With the exception of a collection of poems in 1815, she never published again. *Gaston de Blondeville,* written in 1802, was published posthumously.

Sand: Novelist in Pants

George Sand, (1804-1876) the most successful woman writer of the nineteenth century, always wrote about the "Grand Passion," one that seems to have eluded her all her life.

She was born Armandine Aurore Lucille Dupin in Paris, to a father of

George Sand scandalized the world with her trousers, cigars, and love affairs.

royal ancestry. When she was four, he died, and she lived unhappily caught in the conflicts between her mother and grandmother. After three years in a convent school, she went to Nohant to live with her grandmother. There she developed a love of nature and her own free spirit, which she indulged by wearing men's clothing.

She was married at nineteen to Casimir Dudevant, with whom she had two children but little happiness. Her frustration became intolerable and, at twenty-seven, she left her family to live in Paris. She fell in love with writer Jules Sandeau, with whom she wrote under the pen name, "J. Sand." She published her first novel, *Indiana* (1832), under the pseudonym "George Sand."

Never able to form a lasting romantic relationship, she had a series of lovers, including French poet Alfred de Musset, and, for nine years, composer Frederic Chopin. Most of her later life was spent in Nohant, where she found in nature the fulfillment she could not find in men.

Sand's novels chronicled the fluctuating state of her romantic mind. Her best books were produced in Nohant: *"La Mare au Diable"* (1846); *"La Petite Fadette* (1849); and *"Françoise le Champi"* (1850). They are the quintessence of the pastoral novel, favoring a naive belief in the goodness of humanity to the more pragmatic, post-Romantic realism. Politically, she supported and wrote about socialist and nationalist causes. Although she suffered a lifetime of periodic gloom, she was at heart an optimist: "I put up with life," she wrote, "because I love it."

Sappho: The Erotic Muse

Although relatively little is known about **Sappho** (c.625-570 B.C.) her reputation as a poetess is immortal. Plato called her the "Tenth Muse."

Her work was collected into nine books in the third century B.C., but only fragments have survived. Much of her work was destroyed by the Christians, who considered her poetry obscene.

She is said to have been born on the Greek Island of Lesbos and was a contemporary of Aesop, Solon, and King Croesus. She married Cercylas, by whom she had a daughter.

Sappho's poetry was a departure from that of her time. She wrote of love and passion, while other poets extolled their gods and heroes. Much of her work is considered homosexual in theme. She headed a school for aristocratic girls, and her poetry reveals her erotic attraction to them.

For all its controversy, her writing was simple, graceful, and skillful. She invented a 21-string lyre on which she accompanied herself for the poems she

Heroine of modern lesbians, Sappho revealed in verse erotic feelings for her girl students.

sang. She also invented the Sapphic stanza — three long lines and one short one — which was imitated by Horace and Catullus.

Her poetry about love, children, and death was eloquent: "We know this much/Death is an evil/We have the gods'/Word for it; they too/Would die if death/Were a good thing."

Sexton: Bloodletting poet

The poetry of **Anne Sexton** (1928-1974) is carefully worded bloodletting from a lifetime of emotional tension.

Born Anne Harvey, in Newton, Massachusetts, she had a depressing childhood. Her mistrust of people caused her to escape into her fantasies. Dolls gave her no pleasure because they symbolized people. Her cynicism about her childhood surfaced, in 1971, with "Transformations," a grim retelling of Grimm's fairy tales. Her Cinderella and the Prince live happily ever after "like two dolls in a museum case/ . . . their darling smiles pasted on for eternity/Regular Bobbsey Twins."

Anne eloped with Alfred Sexton when she was nineteen. After his return in

Anne Sexton laid bare in her poetry the intense emotions that led to her suicide.

1954 from Korea, where he served with the Navy, they started a family. With the birth of her second child Anne suffered a nervous breakdown and severe depression. Her poetry chronicled her emotional maze and, beginning in 1958, her work appeared in *Harpers, Partisan Review,* and the *New Yorker*. It has been criticized as "soap opera," but the raw feeling, laced with bitter irony and dark images of despairing strength, raise it above melodrama.

Her brilliant verse appeared in such collections as *All My Pretty Ones* (1962).

In 1967 she won the Pulitzer Prize for *Live or Die*. Her emotional instability eclipsed her need to write. After a bitter divorce and more bouts of depression, Sexton committed suicide.

Stein: The Collector

Gertrude Stein (1874-1946) may not have produced any comprehensible writing, but her importance as an artistic and literary tastemaker cannot be overestimated.

Stein was born in Allegheny, Pennsylvania, the youngest of seven children of wealthy German-Jewish parents. Stein's family lived in Europe when she was a young child, but later moved to California, where they lived from 1879 to 1892. The following year she entered Harvard Annex, soon to be Radcliffe College, where she majored in psychology and was indelibly influenced by William James. His intellectual bequest to her was a devotion to empiricism and stream-of-consciousness in writing. After graduation she entered Johns Hopkins University Medical School, quitting in her fourth year to join her brother Leo in Italy. They settled in Paris in 1903.

Financially independent because of legacies from their parents, they put together a priceless collection of paintings by Cézanne, Renoir, Daumier, Manet, Gauguin, and Braque. They particularly encouraged the work of Matisse and Picasso. At thirty-two, Gertrude had the most important salon in Paris, where the paintings, and Gertrude (called "the great Jewish Buddha"), were the main attractions.

Stein tried to apply the techniques of abstract painting to her prolific writing. She put words (rather than meaning) to

Gertrude Stein, "the great Jewish Buddha," collected priceless paintings and gifted writers.

paper the way an artist puts colors to canvas. Her writing was unintelligible. But her influence upon writers was enormous. After World War I, Paris was filled with American writers, and it was Stein who named them "the lost generation." She collected writers the way she had collected paintings: Sherwood Anderson, F. Scott Fitzgerald, Ezra Pound, and particularly Ernest Hemingway were her favorites.

Her first commercial success was "The Autobiography of Alice B. Toklas" (1933), in which Stein wrote cleverly of her relationship with Toklas; one that had begun in 1907 and continued until Stein's death. Toklas was proofreader, screener of visitors, confidante and, finally, nurse. Stein's dying words were typically cunning: "What is the answer?" she asked. When no one responded she added, "In that case, what is the question?"

Stowe: Uncle Tom's Creator

When **Harriet Beecher Stowe** (1811-1896)

met Abraham Lincoln, in 1862, the President is said to have remarked, "So this is the little lady who started our big war." Although such a compliment might have offended her modesty, the reaction to her book, *Uncle Tom's Cabin,* did not. Harriet believed that life carried within it an obligation to conspicuously right wrongs, and the book, an anti-slavery melodrama, was justification for her life.

Harriet was born in Litchfield, Connecticut, one of eight children in the remarkable Beecher family. Her father was a Calvinist who later became president of the Lane Theological Seminary in Cincinnati. Her brothers were clergymen who spoke vehemently against slavery; Henry Ward Beecher was the country's leading abolitionist. Catharine, her sister, ran the Hartford Seminary for Girls. Harriet's mother died when she was four, leaving her with the influence of her father's rigid morality, high expectations, and spells of depression.

In 1834 she married a widower, Calvin Ellis Stowe, a professor of Biblical literature with a meager income. In seven years she gave birth to five children. With Calvin's encouragement, she began to write to help the family's finances. In 1843 a collection of her stories was published. Her husband accepted a professorship at Bowdoin College in Maine, and there she produced two more children and ran a school.

It was only as a writer, however, that she felt she was "the instrument of God." In a spasm of moral fervor she wrote *Uncle Tom's Cabin*, in forty installments, for the anti-slavery newspaper, *National Era*. Published in book form in 1852, it was an unprecedented success, selling 300,000 copies in the first year alone, and contributed directly to the polarization of North and South which led to the Civil War.

Undset: Instinctive Writer

Sigrid Undset (1882-1949), the Norwegian novelist who had won the Nobel Prize in 1928, has been called "an instinctive writer," a term that implies an insufficiency of life experiences to explain the depth and variety of her characters. It is the term that is insufficient.

Undset has described herself as being a maverick from childhood, when she attended the first coeducational school in Norway and selected playmates with backgrounds different from her own. Her father, an archeologist, died when she was eleven, leaving his wife with three children to support. Undset turned down an opportunity to go to university because she had a horror of becoming a teacher. Instead, she worked in an engineering office from the age of sixteen, staying in what she thought to be a "temporary" position for ten years. Believing herself to be an "immensely important person," she worked up to eighteen hours a day and wrote two books.

In 1911 she married A. C. Starsvad, a Norwegian painter with three children by a former marriage. Undset had three more children by Starsvad before divorcing him in 1925.

Her knowledge of history and her extraordinary talent as a writer melded in her masterpiece, *Kristin Lavransdatter,* a triology: *The Bridal Wreath* (1920); *The Mistress of Husaby* (1925); and *The Cross* (1927). Set in the Middle Ages, it is an objective compassionate account of a woman's development as a person. It is Undset's historical novels that make her a great writer. The rather tedious and didactic work that followed her conversion to Roman Catholicism in 1924 was not as highly praised.

Soon after the Nazi invasion of Norway, Undset was forced to flee to Sweden because of her political outspokenness and then went to the United States. After the war she returned to her medieval log house in Norway, where she spent the rest of her life. In 1947 King Haakon VII awarded her the Grand Cross of St. Olaf, an honor usually given only to royalty.

Wharton: Aristocracy's Critic

If there is one role that fits a member of the genealogical aristocracy, it is that of social critic. **Edith Newbold Jones** (1862-1937) was eminently qualified.

Born in New York City, a descendant of early settlers of the American colonies, she was privately educated, and raised with the formidable formality of the old American upper class.

At twenty-three she married, suitably, a wealthy Bostonian, Edward Robbins Wharton, who retired from the banking business at thirty-six. His chief flaw was that, like most aristocrats of the day, he had too much leisure time. He shared with his wife one side of her character — a love of travel and society. But Edith's other side was emerging, and she began to write stories that appeared in magazines. Her first commercially successful book was *The Decoration of Houses* (1897). In the late 20s she suffered a nervous breakdown, and her doctor suggested that, as therapy, she write novels.

Wharton reached artistic maturity and discipline when she was forty. Her first novel, *The Decision* (1902), was followed with more than a book a year for the remainder of her life.

Her novels dealt with the fragility of formality, the vulgarity of the nouveau riche, and the shallowness of people of manners; but her most famous novel had nothing to do with privilege. *Ethan Frome* (1911) was a slim volume about ordinary people trapped by ordinary emotions in bleak New England. Her finest novel, for which she won the Pulitzer Prize, was *The Age of Innocence* (1920). In that prizewinning novel, she impaled priggishness and pretension with deadly accuracy, at the same time recording the colors, the flavor, the smells of New York and Newport society.

Wheatley: Slave to Poet

Phillis Wheatley's (1753-1784) life is of greater interest than her poetry. Her life was an extraordinary combination of timing, luck, and recognition followed by oblivion.

She was born in Africa and brought to the United States on a slave ship. Her exact age is unknown — it was assumed, because her baby teeth were falling out, that she was seven or eight. John Wheatley, a prosperous Boston tailor, bought her to be the personal servant of his wife.

The Wheatley family was kind to Phillis and gave her free run of the house and its library. Within eighteen months she had learned English and was studying the Latin classics. Her poetry, which she began writing at thirteen, showed the influence of neoclassical poets, particularly Alexander Pope.

Wheatley was a source of curiosity in eighteenth century Boston. Her writing, her wit, and intelligence were admired by notables, such as Thomas Jefferson. In 1773, she was sent to England for her health, where she was lionized. Plans to have her presented at court were afoot when she had to return abruptly to the United States because Mrs. Wheatley was dying.

She married John Peters, a free black. They had three children, two of whom died, and John abandoned his wife and their remaining child. Phillis worked in a lodging house and died penniless. Her only book, *Poems on Various Subjects, Religious and Moral,* was published in England in 1773.

Woolf: The Haunted Genius

Virginia Woolf (1882-1941) embodied the best that literature and learning could produce in the early 1900s.

She was born in London, the daughter of Sir Leslie Stephen, editor of the *Dictionary of National Biography*. The death of her mother, when Virginia was thirteen, was a blow from which she never recovered. But her extraordinary mind was developed by her father and his friends from early childhood. To fill her loneliness, Virginia studied in her father's vast library and talked with his friends — Thomas Hardy, Robert Louis Stevenson, and John Ruskin among others. She was twenty-two when he died, and eight years later she married Leonard Woolf, a brilliant writer and economist.

In 1917 the Woolfs began the Hogarth Press, using an old handpress. They published the works of unknown writers whose work they admired — Katherine Mansfield, *(Prelude);* T. S. Eliot,*(Poems);* and E. M. Forster, *(The Story of the Siren)* among them. Hogarth also published Virginia's *Kew Gardens.*

Virginia's writing synthesized the intellectual pulses of her time. Her novels show the influence of James Joyce, Marcel Proust, William James, and Sigmund Freud. Much of that influence she received first hand. The "Bloomsbury

Such notables as Thomas Jefferson admired the talents of black poet Phillis Wheatley.

group," that took its name from the Woolf's London neighborhood, included many of the leading artists and intellectuals of the early twentieth century. That she had time for those gatherings is amazing in view of the amount of time she spent writing. Her collected letters fill six volumes and she wrote over fifteen books, as well as many essays. Woolf's richest output was during the 1920s. She earned her reputation as one of the world's finest novelists with *Jacob's Room* (1922); *Mrs. Dalloway* (1925); *To the Lighthouse* (1927); and *The Waves* (1931).

Woolf's writing, which was intricate, sensual, brilliant in detail, and ingenious in the bending of time, took more out of her than it gave. Her life was clouded by the threat of madness, which she struggled to keep confined. In a last letter to her husband in 1941 she wrote, "I feel that I am going mad again. I feel we can't go through another of those terrible times. And I shan't recover this time. I begin to hear voices . . ." She stilled the voices by drowning herself.

Mediawomen

THE FEMALE JOURNALIST — FROM SOCIETY TEA TO LOCKER ROOM

Mary Richards, alter ego of Mary Tyler Moore, went to work in 1970 at television station WJM in a position only one step above the secretarial pool. By the time "The Mary Tyler Moore Show" signed off the air seven years later, she was producer of the station's evening news. If the evening news show was the perennial loser in the ratings war, it was hardly the fault of its bright, energetic producer.

The rise of Mary Richards was more than a Hollywood scriptwriter's fantasy. The life stories of many of the nation's top journalists follow a similar plot:

Helen Thomas, head of UPI's White House bureau, got her start as a seventeen-dollar-a-week copy girl.

ABC anchorperson Barbara Walters joined NBC as a secretary in 1958. Six years later she was co-hosting "Today."

Washington Post publisher Katharine Graham took another route to the top. She was daughter and wife of two *Post* publishers before taking over the helm herself.

Like most early American businesses, the first newspapers were operated close to home. Women served their apprenticeships between cleaning house and caring for their families. They frequently ran the print shop while their husbands sniffed out news at the local tavern or coffee house.

Widows often continued the newspapers started by their late husbands. Elizabeth Timothy became America's first woman publisher in 1738 when she took over Charleston's *South-Carolina Gazette* upon the death of her husband. According to business partner Benjamin Franklin, she did a better job of running the paper than her husband had.

The War of Independence brought a huge upswing in the popularity of the native press.

Ambitious printers seeking industrious, low-priced labor turned to the emerging class of young, single women. With their small, deft fingers, women could pick up type faster than men could. And, unlike their male counterparts, they were seldom caught drinking on the job.

By 1886, there were about five hundred women in newspaper editing jobs across the country. Women were beginning their

The indominatable "Nellie Bly" helped usher in a bright new era for women journalists.

assault on the newsrooms of the Eastern city dailies. In 1888, two hundred women worked on newspapers in New York City alone.

But the editorial departments and composing rooms were no more immune to discrimination against women than the world at large. Even William Allen White, of Kansas, the crusading editor of the *Emporia Gazette,* declared, "In our office, which was free of the female taint, we gossip bitterly and salaciously about the foreman and the printer girls of the other shop. Perhaps all this was the instinctive fear of a tide of feminism."

Who knows how the stouthearted band of late nineteenth century newswomen would have fared if Elizabeth Cochrane Seaman had failed to make it around the world in less than eighty days. But Seaman, a *New York World* reporter better known as "Nellie Bly," beat the record set by Jules Verne's Phileas Fogg by eight days — and helped usher in a new era for women in journalism. Though Seaman's escapade hardly opened the floodgate, more women began to move into reporting and editing positions.

A newspaper office was hardly considered a proper environment for a young lady. The *Los Angeles Herald* city room, as described by Adela Rogers St. Johns in 1914, was typical: "Our city room was a

Barbara Walters became a news story herself in 1976 by signing a $5 million ABC contract.

have developed an uncompromising detachment and a bold independence of thought which often put the men to shame.''

Female journalists have made particularly great inroads into the electronic media, with more women filling on-camera jobs today than ever before. (Yet women still constitute only 13 percent of all on-camera reporters on the network level.) A significant first was scored in 1976 when Barbara Walters became the first permanent anchorwoman of an evening network newscast. Walters was teamed with Harry Reasoner on the ''ABC Evening News'' for the first time on October 4, 1976. But as PBS commentator Lynn Sherr sighs, ''Think of the possibility of two women anchors of network news broadcasts, and you'll understand we're still in the ice age.''

Even more than journalists in other specialties, female sports reporters have had to contend with a strong measure of hostility from male colleagues, players, and coaches. Following a heated National Organization for Women (NOW) campaign against ABC and its all-male sports staff, Ellie Riger was hired in 1972 as television's first female sports producer. Riger has since won an Emmy for her coverage of the 1976 Innsbruck Winter Olympics and has produced several specials on women in sports.

On the technical side of broadcasting introduction of the lighter, portable film camera — dubbed ''microcam'' — is expected to open new opportunities for women in jobs from which they were often excluded.

Women's new found militancy has made itself felt in the executive suites of all three commercial networks. Early in 1977, an out-of-court agreement was being hammered out between NBC and a group of past and present women employees who had filed a class action suit charging sex discrimination.

Some women who have persevered to make it to the top of the journalism profession include:

Bonfils: "Annie Laurie"
When San Francisco was stricken with earthquake and fire in 1906, publisher William Randolph Hearst sent his star re-

fire trap. A test tube for breeding tuberculosis germs. A dust bowl. A wastebasket. An anteroom to the psycho ward.''

A few superstars like ''sob sister'' St. Johns, columnist Dorothy Thompson, and foreign correspondent Marguerite Higgins reported on the great events of their eras, from political turmoil and global war to murder trials and prize fights. But many women reporters went to the women's department to write wedding announcements and recipe columns until retirement. They received salaries considerably below those paid male reporters.

Barriers Removed in Sixties
It was not until the mid-1960s that female reporters saw many of the most formidable barriers removed. They began to receive assignments and pay comparable to those of their male co-workers. Most of the all-male journalism societies started opening their doors to women. Female sports writers defied the taboo that had forbidden them from following male athletes into their locker rooms for interviews.

Nevertheless women reporters have always been the outsiders, notes Tim Crouse in *The Boys on the Bus,* a book about covering the 1972 presidential campaign. ''Having never been allowed to join the cozy, clubby world of the men, they

porter a one-word telegram: "Go!" **Winifred Black Bonfils** (1863-1936), better known to newspaper readers as "Annie Laurie," took it from there.

Bonfils' career began in San Francisco, where she journeyed in 1890 searching for a wayward younger brother. She got a job on the *San Francisco Examiner* and quickly emerged as William Randolph Hearst's answer to Joseph Pulitzer's "Nelly Bly."

Taking her cue from Bly, Bonfils faked fainting on a street and was hauled by horse cart to a city hospital. She exposed the bad treatment she had received; her article spurred local reforms.

In 1892, Bonfils won an exclusive interview with President Benjamin Harrison by hiding beneath a table on his campaign train.

Hearst brought her to New York City in 1895 to work on his recently purchased *New York Journal*. She was unhappy and returned West a year later. Her greatest scoop came in 1900 when she slipped through police lines disguised as a man to report on the Galveston, Texas, storm and tidal wave that killed more than seven thousand people.

Despite failing eyesight, Bonfils remained a reporter until the end of her seventy-two years. Seven months before her death, she told readers of her recent airplane flight over Mt. Shasta.

Bourke-White: Life through a Lens

The photo essay — a series of photographs that tell a story better than words — was the invention of **Margaret Bourke-White** (1906-1971).

Bourke-White took up a camera — a second-hand reflex — to pay her way through Cornell University. She was a member of the original staff of *Life* and took the photo of Fort Peck Dam, Montana, which appeared on the cover of its first issue.

Bourke-White was noted for the stark realism of her pictures of the Great Depression and World War II. Her camera captured both the poor and the powerful, including Franklin D. Roosevelt, Josef Stalin, Winston Churchill, and Mahatma Gandhi. During the Second World War, she was aboard a ship that was torpedoed off the coast of North Africa.

In all, Bourke-White snapped photos in thirty-four countries. Her 1963 autobiography, *Portrait of Myself,* described her battle against Parkinson's disease, of which she finally died.

Brown: The Cosmo Look

Helen Gurley Brown (1922-   ) took over moribund *Cosmopolitan* in 1965 and quickly made it a winner. Like the "Cosmo girl" to whom she directed the magazine, Brown was a single career woman until she was thirty-seven.

Her 1962 best seller, *Sex and the Single Girl,* was written on her husband's suggestion after he came across some of her "delightful" letters to a former boyfriend. The book, which offered such off-beat advice as attending Alcoholics Anonymous meetings to meet men, catapulted her to national prominence.

Dubbed the "iron butterfly" by *Cosmopolitan* staffers, Brown claims she works a twelve-hour day, seven days a week. But contrary to the image her magazine sometimes seems to project, Brown is a staunch defender of marital fidelity. She once told a television interviewer she would "kill" her husband if she found him playing around.

Brown counters charges that her magazine encourages women to be manipulative by declaring, "It's fabulous to make a man feel good . . . I'm against slavery, but I am all out for total flattery."

Cosmopolitan editor Helen Gurley Brown asserts, "It's fabulous to make a man feel good."

Child: The French Chef

"Never apologize," is the cardinal cooking rule of **Julia Child** (1912-   ), America's beloved French chef.

Child began studying French cuisine at the famed Cordon Bleu school while her diplomat-husband was stationed in Paris. The couple met during World War II, when both worked for the Office of Strategic Services in Ceylon.

An apt cooking student, Child collaborated on *Mastering the Art of French Cooking* in 1961. The book has sold more than 1,250,000 copies.

One year later, Child's televised cooking classes went on the air, originating from WGBH-TV in Boston. Her mouth-watering recipes and easy kitchen manner quickly endeared her to viewers. Child was not above picking up and dusting off a cutlet that fell on the floor. "After all," she reminded her audience, "you're alone in the kitchen and no one can see you."

Of all the praise Child has won for her culinary talents, perhaps her favorite was a sonnet written by her husband for her forty-ninth birthday: "Julia, Julia, cook and nifty wench/whose unsurpassed quenelles and hot soufflés/whose English, Norse and German, and whose French/are all beyond my piteous powers to praise/Whose sweetly rounded bottom and whose legs/whose gracious face, whose nature temperate/are only equalled by her scrambled eggs."

Cooney: TV for Youngsters

The Cookie Monster and the rest of the "Sesame Street" gang were brought to us by **Joan Ganz Cooney** (1929-   ) of Children's Television Workshop.

Cooney came to New York in 1953 after a stint as a reporter for *The Arizona Republic* in Phoenix. After some publicity work for NBC and the U.S. Steel Hour, she became a producer of public affairs documentaries for the city's educational television station. In 1966, Cooney won an Emmy for her three-hour documentary, "Poverty, Anti-Poverty and the Poor."

Out of a chance cocktail party conversation, Cooney hit upon the idea of "a wall-less nationwide nursery school" to help less privileged youngsters catch up on their reading and math skills. Out of that

French chef Julia Child counsels television viewers to "never apologize" for kitchen gaffes.

idea, Children's Television Workshop was born in 1968, with Cooney as its first executive director.

"Sesame Street" premiered the next year to rave reviews. It was the first educational program to equal commercial television in ratings. Cooney modeled the show after the bright, fast-paced commercials that children so readily memorize and mimic. "We wanted it to jump, move and sound like 1970," she recalled.

The workshop's second series, "The Electric Company," made its debut in 1971.

Copley: She Balanced the Books

There is little of the flamboyant William Randolph Hearst or Rupert Murdoch in **Helen Kinney Copley** (1922-   ), who became head of the Copley Press in 1973 upon the death of her husband.

Once so frightened of public speaking that she took a year of speech lessons, Copley had been her husband's private secretary until their 1965 marriage. He left her saddled with a heavy estate tax burden ($16 million) and the Copley chain of newspapers, some of which were in the red.

Copley wasted no time in balancing the chain's books. She started with staff layoffs, undertook a corporate reorganization, and sold off several newspapers and other properties.

Having won a reputation as a shrewd business executive, Copley set about broadening the editorial scope of the staunchley conservative publishing chain. Under her direction, the *San Diego Union*, the group's flagship paper, and the afternoon *San Diego Tribune* have ventured into the once forbidden areas of women's and minority rights. She also lifted the ban on letters to the editor critical of the paper.

Curtis: Timeswoman

Charlotte Curtis (1929-   ) was acknowledged to be one of *The New York Times'* "most powerful men" even before she became editor of its influential Op-Ed page.

Curtis joined the *Times* in 1950 as its society editor, quickly becoming known — and feared — for her frequently biting attacks on the Beautiful People. She derided the black-tie audience at the opening of New York City's new Metropolitan Opera House in 1966 as a "mob of moguls and overachievers."

But Curtis insisted the tidbits that spiced her columns came right from the mouths of the moguls and overachievers themselves. "The lady who told me that they built their marble terrace because it's cold on the dog's stomach was perfectly happy to see herself quoted to that effect," Curtis declared.

Apart from her tongue-in-cheek society reporting, Curtis was credited with upgrading the *Times'* family/style section, filling its pages with important feature stories about women's — and men's — changing life-styles.

Curtis was the surprise choice to succeed Harrison Salisbury as editor of the Op-Ed page, a forum for *Times* columnists and outside contributors, in 1973.

Frederick: TV Pioneer

"Stay away from radio. It doesn't like women," commentator H.R. Baukhage advised his scriptwriter in 1938. But **Pauline Frederick** didn't listen. Soon she was doing radio interviews for NBC.

Frederick became one of television's pioneer reporters when she signed on with ABC in 1946. In 1948, she was the first female network reporter to cover the polit-

ical conventions. But she had to do double duty; not only did she interview Bess Truman and Frances Dewey, she also had to apply their television make-up.

Returning to NBC in 1953, Frederick began working the United Nations beat that made her famous. "She represents no nation but speaks for the world of concerned citizens," read the honorary Doctorate of Humane Letters she received from Manhattan College in 1971.

Frederick remained with NBC until her retirement in 1974. She is currently a commentator for National Public Radio.

Fuller: Foreign Correspondent

"Piquant, vivid, terse, bold, luminous" — these were the words Edgar Allen Poe used to describe the writing of **Sarah Margaret Fuller** (1810-1850). *New York Tribune* editor Horace Greeley proclaimed the transcendentalist writer "the most remarkable and in some respects the greatest woman whom America has yet produced."

So impressed was Greeley with Fuller that he made her the *Tribune's* literary critic in 1844.

In 1845, Fuller produced *Woman in the*

Foreign correspondent Sarah Margaret Fuller became embroiled in Italian civil strife.

Nineteenth Century, a feminist work that had a considerable impact on the 1848 women's rights convention in Seneca Falls.

Fuller became America's first woman foreign correspondent in 1846 when she set sail for Europe. She met Wordsworth and Mazzini in London, Sand and Chopin in Paris. But she was most intrigued by Italy and the cause of Italian freedom — especially after a chance meeting with Giovanni Angelo, the marchese d'Ossoli, a liberal nobleman ten years her junior. They became lovers, and she gave birth to their son in 1848.

When the French laid siege to the young Roman Republic five months later, Fuller ran an emergency hospital and carried supplies to Ossoli and his compatriots at the front. After their cause was lost, Fuller, Ossoli, and their son sailed for the United States. But they never reached their destination. Their ship ran aground off New York's Fire Island and their bodies were never found.

Graham: Press Baroness

Washington Post publisher **Katharine Graham** (1917-   ) has made some powerful enemies: Spiro Agnew, John Mitchell, Richard Nixon. But her admirers are more numerous. In a 1977 poll of business and political leaders conducted by *U.S. News and World Report* — a rival to her own *Newsweek* — Graham was voted the "top leader and shaper of national life" among women.

Graham's journalism career dates back to 1938, when she took a job on the *San Francisco News* covering the waterfront beat. But she came to her current post by way of birth, marriage, and widowhood. Her father, former World Bank head Eugene Meyer, sold the *Post* to Graham and her husband, Philip, for one dollar in 1948. Philip's suicide in 1963 thrust Graham into the presidency of the Washington Post Company.

Since then, Graham has molded the loosely structured, family-held operation into a publicly owned, highly profitable corporation. As the capital's leading newspaper, the *Washington Post* is must reading for government officials, members of Congress, and foreign diplomats.

Graham stood firm against White

The *Washington Post*'s Ben Bradlee and Katherine Graham rejoice after Pentagon Papers ruling.

House pressure on two notable occasions. The first came in 1971, when the *Post* and *The New York Times* printed the controversial Pentagon Papers. In a victory for freedom of the press, the newspapers' action was upheld by the U.S. Supreme Court.

Graham is probably best known for her unwavering support of her staff's reports on the Watergate scandal from 1972 to 1974.

Higgins: Korean Crusade

Marguerite Higgins (1920-1966) always packed her lipstick and toothbrush when she went off to cover a war. But she was just as tough as her male colleagues.

Higgins was based in Korea for the *New York Herald-Tribune* when Seoul fell to the Communists in June 1950. When she was evacuated against her will to Tokyo, she appealed to General Douglas MacArthur. "I am not working in Korea as a woman. I am there as a war correspondent," she declared. MacArthur agreed, and she returned to Korea at his side, obtaining an exclusive interview with the U.S. commander in the process.

Higgins saw the first American soldier killed in Korea and refused to leave when the *Herald* sent a man to take her place. The two vied for news space throughout the war.

Dressed in army fatigues, Higgins good-humoredly shared hardships with the soldiers and male reporters. One of her colleagues remarked, "Maggie wears mud like other women wear make-up." She shared a Pulitzer Prize for her work in Korea.

A decade later, Higgins went to South Vietnam to report on the growing U.S. presence there. She contracted an infection from which she slowly died.

McBride: Talk Show Pioneer

A pioneer of the modern talk show was homey radio host **Mary Margaret McBride** (1899-1976).

McBride began her radio career in 1934 in the guise of a folksy grandmother. But the thirty-five-year-old refused to keep up the pretense and soon unmasked herself. "Look, I'm not a grandma, nor a mother, nor am I married," she confessed. "Why don't I just be myself?"

She interviewed guests ranging from Eleanor Roosevelt to fan dancer Sally Rand on her forty-five-minute program, which became an early afternoon fixture on nationwide radio. She entertained listeners with stories of her Missouri childhood and such escapades as smuggling her pet goat into the country aboard a luxury liner.

On the fifteenth anniversary of her radio debut, some seventy-five thousand fans packed New York's Yankee Stadium to pay her tribute.

McGrory: Her Own Legwork

Pulitzer Prize-winning columnist **Mary McGrory** (1918-   ) still agonizes over each story as she did when she was a cub reporter. Unlike most nationally prominent pundits, she continues to do much of her own legwork.

The liberal-oriented *Washington Star* writer rose to fame during the administration of fellow Bostonian John F. Kennedy. She has served as unofficial adviser to such presidential hopefuls as Senators Eugene McCarthy, Robert Kennedy, and George McGovern.

By choice, McGrory stays out of the limelight. "I want to be read," she says, "But I don't want to be a personality."

McGrory has fought long and hard to win the respect of her male colleagues. Early in her career, *The New York Times'* James Reston supposedly offered her a job in his paper's Washington bureau — if she would answer the switchboard part-time.

Even the most chauvinistic men on the press bus now consider her their equal.

Mackin: Compulsive Worker

"I'm a compulsive worker," admits NBC's **Catherine "Cassie" Mackin** (1939-   ). Mackin's demanding schedule includes weekdays on Capitol Hill as her network's congressional reporter and weekends in New York hosting the Sunday evening news.

Mackin got her start in journalism on the *News American* in her native Baltimore. She first came to the nation's attention in 1972 as the only woman network floor reporter at the national political conventions. Wearing the Martian-like headgear with which floor reporters keep in touch with their anchor booths, the nimble Mackin proved herself the equal in knowledge and stamina to her more experienced male colleagues.

Later that summer, Mackin ran afoul of the Nixon White House when she became the first reporter to charge that the president was deliberately distorting the record of his Democratic opponent, Senator George McGovern. As Tim Crouse noted in *The Boys on the Bus,* "Perhaps it was no coincidence that it was a woman who went for Nixon's jugular. She had neither the opportunity nor the desire to travel with the all-male (journalism) pack; therefore, she was not infected with the pack's chronic defensiveness and defeatism . . . She could still call a spade a spade."

Paddleford: How America Eats

Buffalo, muskrat, snake, and 100-year-old eggs were all in a day's dining for food editor **Clementine Paddleford** (1900-1968).

Paddleford learned to cook in the kitchen of her family's Kansas farmhouse. She especially liked baking "because it smelled so good and looked the most important."

Writing six columns a week for the *New York Herald Tribune* and a Sunday syndicated feature called "How America Eats," Paddleford became noted for making food sound as succulent as it tasted. One of her most evocative descriptions was of a soufflé: "With a rapturous, half-hushed sigh . . . it settled softly to melt and vanish in a moment like smoke or a dream."

Paddleford visited every state and many

foreign lands looking for interesting new foods to describe to her readers. Returning from a hectic eating and drinking tour of France in 1946, she sighed, "It'll be good to be home again where ice water flows like champagne."

Patterson: Eccentric Editor

Eleanor Medill "Cissy" Patterson (1884-1948) refused to closet herself in the executive suite of the *Washington Herald*. Instead, the eccentric editor — who frequently arrived for work in evening gown or riding habit — donned disguises to pursue the hottest stories herself.

Patterson did not begin her journalism career until she was forty-five. Her grandfather was an owner of the *Chicago Tribune*, of which her father and cousin were later editors and publishers. Her brother published the New York *Daily News*.

After her second marriage ended in divorce, Patterson convinced her friend William Randolph Hearst to let her edit the financially troubled *Herald*. Within a few years, she doubled the paper's circulation.

Patterson was famed for her mercurial personality. After losing a lengthy battle for some comic strips to *Washington Post* publisher Eugene Meyer, Patterson sent him a pound of flesh — actually a pound of raw red meat.

She eventually bought both the morning *Herald* and the evening *Washington Times* from Hearst.

Pauley:Today's Woman

"Imagine being twenty-five and single and coming to New York with this kind of job," said **Jane Pauley** (1950-) after being picked in 1976 to succeed Barbara Walters on NBC's "Today." "The sum total sounds like lonely."

Only four years before, Pauley had "lucked into" her first television job as a newscaster on Indianapolis's WISH-TV. Two years later, she was spirited away to Chicago's WMAQ to become that city's first evening news anchorwoman. Chicagoans' response was not universally enthusiastic; one critic reduced her to tears by suggesting she had "the IQ of a cantaloupe."

Pauley proved him wrong. When Walters announced she was leaving "Today"

to anchor the ABC Evening News, Pauley nosed out such television veterans as Betty Furness and Catherine Mackin for the $125,000-plus "Today" job. That's a far cry from the $13,500 she made in Indianapolis.

Pauley shares "Today's" "women's stories" of food and fashion with co-host Tom Brokaw. "Why not?" she asks. "I can't cook to save my life."

Porter: Top Financial Writer

Ask for the name of the nation's best known financial columnist, and the answer will invariably be **Sylvia Porter** (1913-).

Porter switched her college major from English to economics when her widowed mother lost her thirty-thousand-dollar nest-egg in the 1929 stock market crash. She wanted to find out how all that money could have simply disappeared.

Just nineteen and fresh out of college, Porter applied for a writing job with the Associated Press. "We have never hired a woman in the financial department, and we never will," she was told.

Undaunted, Porter worked for an investment counselor and wrote a magazine column on the bond market. In 1935, she landed a job in the *New York Post*'s financial department. In fact, she *was* the department, hired on the same day an economy move wiped out the rest of the finance-reporting staff. She agreed to do the work of all the terminated employees.

Until 1942, she wrote under the by-line "S.F. Porter," and most readers assumed she was a man.

Porter's clear, consumer-oriented columns have won her a worldwide readership of more than forty million.

President Lyndon Johnson asked Porter to head the Export-Import Bank in 1965. She refused, preferring to continue explaining financial "bafflegab" to her readers.

Royall: First Muckraker

Anne Newport Royall (1769-1854) supposedly got her biggest scoop when she came upon President John Quincy Adams swimming naked in the Potomac. She promptly sat her wiry body atop the chief executive's discarded clothing, refusing to arise until he granted her an exclusive interview.

At least that is the Washington legend.

Although the story loses some credibility because the two were mutual admirers, it attests to Royall's remarkable tenacity.

Royall was left penniless at age fifty-four when her late husband's relatives voided his will and declared her an adulteress. To keep herself out of the poor house, she embarked upon a career that caused her to be dubbed America's first muckraking journalist.

Settling in Washington in 1830 to fight the government for her husband's Revolutionary War pension, Royall began publishing *Paul Pry,* a weekly specializing in political exposés and gossip. Woe to he who refused to buy a copy of the newspaper that Royall herself peddled through the halls of Congress. The stingy legislator was likely to find himself the page-one target of *Paul Pry*'s next edition.

Paul Pry was succeeded in 1836 by *The Huntress,* which Royall continued to publish into her eighty-fifth year.

In 1829, Royall barely escaped a public dunking after being judged a "common scold" for verbally abusing a Presbyterian congregation. Because of her age — and highly placed friends like Secretary of War John Eaton — her sentence was reduced to a ten dollar fine.

St. Johns: Star Reporter

Wrote **Adela Rogers St. Johns** (1894-   ) in her autobiography, "I was one of the first women reporters; maybe as an all-around police beat, sports, sin and society reporter, the first in the world." And she was all that by the time she was eighteen.

From her start as a seven-dollar-a-week writer for the *Los Angeles Herald,* St. Johns quickly rose to by-line status. On an early assignment to investigate corruption by charitable organizations, she dressed as a pauper and tried in vain to find food, work, and shelter.

St. Johns became William Randolph Hearst's star reporter and covered the biggest stories of the century: the Lindbergh kidnapping and Bruno Hauptmann trial, the romance of England's Edward VIII and Wallis Simpson, the Dempsey-Tunney "long-count" fight, and the assassination of "Kingfish" Huey Long. One of her biggest scoops came at the 1940 Democratic National Convention, when she reported that "spontaneous" demon-

Adela Rogers St. Johns: "An all-around police beat, sports, sin, and society reporter."

strations of enthusiasm were electronically engineered by a city boss for radio audiences.

In 1970, St. Johns received the Medal of Freedom for her "devotion to the idea that a democracy cannot survive without a free press."

Sanders: She Broke the Ice

Marlene Sanders (1931-   ) became the first woman to anchor a network television news show, filling in for a sick colleague in 1964. "I broke the ice and the networks didn't collapse," she remarked some years later.

Sanders' career began with a lowly slot on the staff of "Mike Wallace Interviews" on New York's WNEW-TV. She was the first female broadcaster to be sent to Vietnam.

In January 1976, Sanders was named vice president and director of television documentaries for ABC News. She is patient but optimistic about the future of women in television journalism. "Women have only just been admitted to the system," she explains. "Five years from now more of us will be ready for top jobs. It takes time."

Schiff: New York Publisher

The nation's oldest newspaper with a continuous line of daily publication is the *New York Post,* started by Alexander Hamilton in 1801 to propagandize against political rival Thomas Jefferson. "Naturally, I would have been on Jefferson's side," commented **Dorothy Schiff** (1903-), owner of the *New York Post* from 1939 to 1976.

Under Schiff, the *Post* gained a reputation for being politically liberal on the editorial page and increasingly middle-of-the-road in columns and news coverage. Although the *Post* has been the city's only evening paper since 1967, its circulation fell from 700,000 to less than 500,000 by 1977. Rumors of its demise or sale had surfaced periodically for several years prior to Schiff's announcement on Nov. 19, 1976 that she was selling the *Post* to Australian publisher Rupert Murdoch.

Schiff had made news earlier that year with the intimation in Jeffrey Potter's *Men, Money and Magic: The Story of Dorothy Schiff* that she had a secret personal relationship with President Franklin Roosevelt.

Scripps: Generous Benefactor

Ellen Browning Scripps (1836-1932), noted *The New York Times* upon her death, "gave a new glory to American womanhood by a life that added the best of the new to the best of the old."

Scripps answered the call for assistance from her older brother, James, when he sought to establish the *Evening News* in Detroit in 1873. There she kept the books, edited copy, corrected proofs, and prepared a front-page column of miscellany, "Matters and Things," which was intended to attract a broad range of readers — including women — to the paper. When her half-brother, E.W., eighteen years her junior, struck out on his own with the *Cleveland Penny Press* in 1878, Ellen Scripps backed him with money, articles, and her "Matters and Things," known familiarly in Cleveland as "Miss Ellen's Miscellany." Those columns were the beginning of Newspaper Enterprise Association, the newspaper feature service founded in 1902.

By backing E.W. in the many enterprises that grew into the Scripps-Howard newspaper group, she backed a winner. The daughter of a London bookbinder

turned American prairie farmer died a multimillionaire.

Scripps was as generous to worthy causes and institutions as she was to her brothers. Among her benefactions were the Marine Biological Association (now Scripps Institution of Oceanography), San Diego; Scripps Memorial Hospital (now Scripps Clinic and Research Foundation), La Jolla; Knox College, her alma mater; the San Diego Zoo; and her greatest gift, Scripps College in Claremont, California.

Seaman: "Nellie Bly"

Dauntless but demure **Elizabeth Cochrane Seaman** (1865?-1922), known to newspaper readers as "Nellie Bly," raced around the globe in seventy-two days, six hours, and eleven minutes. She became the nation's darling for it.

Indignation got Seaman her first reporting job. She wrote a letter to the *Pittsburgh Dispatch* lambasting an editorial — "What Girls Are Good For" — which claimed women were good for little more than housework. The paper's editor was so impressed with Seaman's writing that he changed his mind about working women — at least in her case — and put her on the payroll.

Seaman left the *Dispatch* in 1887 for Joseph Pulitzer's fast growing *New York World*. For her first story, she got herself committed to an insane asylum and wrote about the poor treatment given its patients. She went on to masquerade as a sweatshop worker, a petty thief, and a ballet corps dancer. But her coup came in late 1890 when she convinced Pulitzer to let her challenge the travel record set by Phileas Fogg in Jules Verne's *Around the World in Eighty Days.* Pulitzer wanted to send a man instead, but the persistent Seaman vowed she would quit her job and race Pulitzer's entry if she were not given the assignment.

Front pages were filled with accounts of Seaman's adventures. Upon her triumphal return to New York, she was greeted with a Broadway parade and a cannon salute. Everything from popular songs to race horses bore her name.

The rest of Seaman's life proved anticlimactic. She married a man fifty years her senior, and lost most of his money trying to run his businesses after his death. Late in life, she made a comeback attempt at writing for the *New York Journal,* but the times had changed and Seaman's style had not.

Smith: Attacked Corruption

Crusading Southern newspaper owner-editor **Hazel Brannon Smith** (1914-   ) became in 1964 the first woman to win a Pulitzer Prize for editorial writing. Smith acquired the first of her four Mississippi papers, the weekly *Durant News,* in 1935, the year she graduated from college. She turned it from a financial liability to an asset within four years.

She was threatened with financial ruin in 1953 when she denounced a local sheriff as "not fit to occupy office" for shooting a young black man without provocation. An all-male, all-white jury fined her ten thousand dollars for libel, but the decision was reversed by the state supreme court.

Her troubles were far from over. The White Citizens Council began pressuring her advertisers to boycott her newspapers and her subscribers to cancel their subscriptions. Crosses were burned on her lawn, her husband lost his job as administrator of the county hospital, her paper went $100,000 into debt, and her offices were firebombed.

It was in the year of the bombing that she was awarded the Pulitzer for "the whole volume of her work . . . including attacks on corruption." As racial passions moderated in the late 1960s, advertisers and subscribers began returning to her papers.

Tarbell: Knocked Rocky

Ida Minerva Tarbell (1857-1944), said newspapers of her era, did "more to dethrone Rockefeller in public esteem than all the preachers in the land."

In her exhaustively researched articles for *McClure's,* Tarbell described in careful detail how John D. Rockefeller acquired huge holdings, drove out competitors with unscrupulous tactics, and obtained an oil monopoly. The articles, later published in book form as *The History of the Standard Oil Company* (1904), enraged the public and led the federal government to lodge more than twenty antitrust suits against Standard Oil. On May 15, 1911, the Supreme Court confirmed Tarbell's well-documented conclusions by ruling the company a monopoly in restraint of trade.

Tarbell left *McClure's* in 1906 to found the *American Magazine.* She was its associate editor until 1915. Her major effort for the magazine was a series attacking the high protective tariff. President Woodrow Wilson said of those articles, "She has written more good sense, good plain common sense, about the tariff than any man I know of."

Thomas: White House Watcher

The person most likely to have been on the receiving end of Martha Mitchell's midnight phone calls was United Press International's **Helen Thomas** (1920-   ).

Thomas's career began in 1942 as a seventeen-dollar-a-week copy girl for the *Washington Daily News.* Her UPI beat has long been the White House, where she has covered everything from the most earthshaking pronouncements of heads of state to the death of Caroline Kennedy's pet hamster. (Thomas aroused the ire of Kennedy Press Secretary Pierre Salinger by telephoning him at 3 a.m. to inquire about the animal's health.)

Thomas was one of the few reporters who took the wife of former Attorney General John Mitchell seriously. It was Thomas who received Martha Mitchell's famous call describing how she was subdued and tranquilized shortly after the Watergate break-in.

Thomas is chief of UPI's White House Bureau, the first woman to hold that post.

Thomas's engagement to her long-time Associated Press rival, Douglas Cornell, was announced at a surprise 1971 shower by Pat Nixon. "They say the best marriages are made in heaven, but the best press marriages are made at the White House," commented then-President Richard Nixon.

Thompson: Influential Columnist

"She and Eleanor Roosevelt are undoubtedly the most influential women in the U.S.," declared a 1939 *Time* cover story on columnist **Dorothy Thompson** (1894-1961).

Through a chance meeting with a journalist aboard a ship bound for Europe in 1921, Thompson became foreign correspondent for the *Philadelphia Public Ledger* and the *New York Evening*

The highly opinionated Dorothy Thompson was credited with an uncanny nose for news.

Post. In 1936, she became a political commentator for the *New York Herald Tribune,* writing a thrice-weekly column called "On the Record." After 1941, the column was syndicated and appeared in 166 newspapers with an estimated readership of 7.5 million. She also broadcast a weekly radio show to 5 million listeners and wrote a montly column for *Ladies Home Journal.*

Thompson gained a reputation for her extraordinary news sense. Reporters seeing her arrive in town at noon came to expect that a major news event would happen no later than 1 p.m.

Thompson interviewed Adolf Hitler at the beginning of his rise to power, writing, "He is inconsequent and voluble . . . ill-poised, insecure. He is the very prototype of the Little Man." Hitler expelled her from Germany when he came to power in 1934.

Walters: $5 Million Woman

Barbara Walters (1931-) became a news story in 1976 when she accepted ABC's $5 million offer to make her television's first female co-anchor.

The new job ended Walters' fifteen-year association with NBC's "Today," which she joined in 1961 as a writer and occasional feature reporter. After watching a string of thirty-two glamorous "Today girls" serve brief stints on the show, Walters wished she had the courage to suggest to its producers, "Hey, fellas, look at me. I'm right here. How about me?"

She got her chance in 1964. It was clear from the start that Walters was a different breed from her predecessors; nobody ever called her the "Today girl."

Walters gained a reputation as an aggressive interviewer. She queried Mamie Eisenhower about her drinking habits and Lady Bird Johnson about her late husband's reputation as a lady's man. Walters once confronted Dr. Edgar Berman, author of the statement that women are unfit to be president because of their "raging hormonal imbalances," on the air. Her questions were rational, Walters coolly informed Berman, because, "It's not my time of the month."

At ABC, Walters has reportedly clashed with co-anchor Harry Reasoner about how the news should be presented. She believes the era of the "all-knowing, all-seeing anchorman" is past and opts for a more casual, flexible news format. Said ABC's chief news writer, "She'll sometimes take a piece of copy and say, 'Wait a minute — I don't understand this. And if I don't understand it, the viewer can't understand it, either.' "

OVER THE BACK-FENCE

Gossip — or talking about people — has recently become legitimate news. Even the most staid newspapers titillate readers with the latest on Liz's new husband, Cher's new baby, or Jackie's new life. Though the prim and proper *New York Times* has yet to print a comic page, it has launched a gossipy new magazine, *Us,* patterned after the highly successful *People.*

Now that gossip has gained a measure of respectability, men may start claiming it as their own. But for most of recorded history, men seem to have perpetrated the myth that gossiping is solely the passion of women. Even the word "gossip" — derived from the Old English godsibb, for godparent — early came to mean the women friends of a mother-to-be who whiled away the waiting hours with small talk. By the eighteenth century, the term was associated with any flighty, loose-tongued woman.

Gossip took on a new dimension when it moved from the back fence to the newspaper page. Benjamin Franklin is credited with introducing the gossip column to Colonial America in his *Pennsylvania Gazette*.

"The First To Tell"

Once the stars and would-be stars began thronging to Hollywood in the 1920s, gossip columnists were not far behind. The gossip queens of Hollywood's golden era were **Louella Parsons** and **Hedda Hopper.**

Parsons became the nation's first movie columnist in 1914, writing for the *Chicago Record-Herald*. She moved on to work in the New York literary stable of publisher William Randolph Hearst until she was told in 1925 that she was dying of tuberculosis. Vowing to spend her last six months happily, she took off for Hollywood.

Parsons' death failed to arrive on schedule, and she stayed on as Hearst's Hollywood columnist. In 1934, she became a radio personality with the launching of her "Hollywood Hotel," featuring stars plugging their latest films.

Parsons frequently dubbed herself, "the first to know and the first to tell it, too."

Hollywood's Mad Hatter

If a star had to appear on the gossip page,

A one-time actress, Hedda Hopper gained fame with her Hollywood gossip and crazy hats.

he or she probably preferred to find his or her name in Hedda Hopper's column rather than that of her less accurate, more vituperative rival, Parsons.

Hopper was a former actress, having made her Broadway debut in 1909 in *The Motor Girl*. She appeared in scores of silent films, beginning with *Virtuous Wives* in 1915. After trying her hand at real estate and fashion show commentary, she went on the air with a Hollywood gossip show in 1936. Two years later she launched her syndicated newspaper column, dangling participles and mixing metaphors all along the way.

Hopper, whose trademark was an exotic hat, said her proudest achievement was scooping her competitors on the breakup of the Elizabeth Taylor-Eddie Fisher marriage. In her autobiography, *The Whole Truth And Nothing But* (1963), Hopper continued her life-long feud with Parsons. She claimed that Parsons' doctor-husband had a tie-in with testing laboratories. "This private line into the womb could give her news that a star was pregnant before the girl herself knew it," Hopper said.

The Reigning Queen

No columnist since Parsons and Hopper has stricken the same terror into the hearts of showfolks. But blonde dynamo **Rona Barrett** — known in less polite company as "Rona Rat" — has come closer than any other Hollywood gossip to matching their reputation.

"When God made Rona, one piece was missing — a conscience," declared one of her enemies. Ryan O'Neal once allegedly mailed her a tarantula. Frank Sinatra — "a miserable man who has never known how to live with success," according to Barrett — has frequently called her "an ugly broad" in his nightclub act.

Like her illustrious predecessors, Barrett does not confine her tale-telling to one medium. She has made syndicated TV spots, written a gossipy autobiography, published fan magazines, and appeared as "worldwide entertainment and arts editor" on ABC's "Good Morning America."

A formerly "crippled, plain, fat kid" from New York, Barrett got her start as president of Eddie Fisher and Steve Lawrence fan clubs. Today she attempts to put more distance between herself and the entertainers she reports on. "I'm not friends with the stars," says Barrett, "because if I were I couldn't tell the truth about them."

Gotham Gossips

By virtue of being the nation's largest and, perhaps, most exciting city, New York attracks more than its share of gossip makers and columnists. One of the wittiest is Aileen Mehle, better known to her *New York Daily News* readers as **"Suzy Knickerbocker."**

Mehle describes herself as "the champion of the over-privileged." Though she occasionally stoops to include news of show people in her columns, her favorite subjects are diplomats, royalty, and other Jet Setters. "No matter what I say about them," says Mehle, "it can never be as bad as what they say about themselves."

A relative newcomer to the New York gossip beat is Southern-bred **Liz Smith**, also of the *Daily News*.

After a September 1976 Smith column told of troubles in NBC's upper echelons, buttons reading "I Didn't Talk to Liz Smith" appeared on the lapels of NBC executives. Buttons to the contrary, Smith claims she relies for most of her material on "New York's truthsayers — they have no axe to grind but they know something and just have to tell it."

New Gossip Capital

With Watergate and the dwindling awe of the press's treatment of public officials, Washington, D.C., has become the nation's capital of gossip as well as government.

A not-to-new member of the Washington scene is society columnist **Betty Beale**, who angrily resents being called a gossip. "The political columnists are the real gossip columnists in this town," she claims. "They get themselves all steamed up at the press bar and they go off half-cocked on some phony premise."

During the Kennedy years, the frolics that ended in midnight swimming pool dunkings of fully clothed politicians were Beale exclusives.

Gossip sometimes leads to the uncovering of important news stories, as when the *Washington Post's* **Maxine Cheshire** became curious about the lavish parties being thrown by Korean operative Tongsun Park. After more than five years

of investigation, Cheshire uncovered disturbing links between the Korean CIA and members of the U.S. House of Representatives. The *Post* nominated Cheshire's work for a Pulitzer Prize. But perhaps a greater tribute was Park's own response. At a private club founded by Park and his friends, a miniature shark was named Maxine.

Another *Post* reporter, **Sally Quinn**, is famed for her interviews with a gossipy flavor. In 1976, for example, she wrote a lengthy story on a young socialite rumored to be having an affair with Senator Edward Kennedy.

Said Henry Kissinger during his tenure as secretary of state, "After Maxine Cheshire has interviewed you and written an article about you, you want to kill her. After Sally Quinn has interviewed you and written an article about you, you want to kill yourself."

Among the latest additons to the capital gossip scene is "The Ear," a column begun in 1975 and written by *Washington Star* staffers **Diana McLellan** and **Louise Lague.** The daily update on the naughty doings of Washington bigwigs is credited with turning the once dowdy *Star* into a "must-read" paper.

McLellan and Lague claim they have spies everywhere, from the administration's inner sanctums to the news desk of the OP (Ear shorthand for *Washington Post* or "Other Paper").

When McLellan cites her recipe for Ear, she might just as well be describing the success formula of every popular gossip column, magazine, or television show: "A dash of wit. A touch of sex. A hint of corruption. And a little bit of dirt."

MS. LONELYHEARTS AND HER DAUGHTERS

Ann Landers admits that until she started writing her advice column, "I thought only a nut would write to a newspaper for help." But after receiving an average of one thousand letters a day since her column began in 1955, Landers has changed her mind.

Advice columns — once labeled "advice to the lovelorn" — have helped readers cope with problems of mind and heart since the earliest publications for female audiences. However, readership of these columns has never been limited to women only.

An early edition of London's *The Ladies Mercury,* launched in 1693, featured a heart-wrenching letter from a young man who had taken a mistress after catching his wife in bed with another man. To the man's inquiry as to whether his wife's adultery justified his own extracurricular activities, the editor responded in the negative "for the Pulpit Law pronounces it both ways Whoredom."

The advice column was officially born near the end of the Spanish-American War in the *New York Evening Journal*'s "Hen Coop," the office shared by Marie Manning and two other women reporters. The *Journal* had received three letters from readers seeking help with tragic personal problems, and Manning proposed a new column be created to handle such inquiries. July 28, 1898, marked the debut of "Letters from the Lovelorn," written by Manning under the pseudonym **"Beatrice Fairfax."**

"Dry your eyes, roll up your sleeves, and *dig for a practical solution,"* became Manning's standard advice. Though she had to invent some of her first queries, her mail soon ran as high as fourteen hundred letters a day.

According to Manning, the questions

"Be strong" was the advice Elizabeth Meriwether Gilmer gave her readers — and herself.

most frequently posed by her early correspondents included: "Should the young man get down on his knees while proposing? Should he get the consent of the girl's parents first? . . . What should they do about a chaperon when they went out on a bicycle built for two?"

Following a hiatus beginning in 1905 for marriage, motherhood, and suffrage work, Manning resumed giving advice in 1929. She found that her readers' typical problems were no longer the heartaches of young love, but "the forays of the love pirate, the ennui of the restless wife, and the problems of the children of divorced parents."

Manning's favorite advice columnist was her rival, Elizabeth Meriwether Gilmer, better known as **Dorothy Dix.** Gilmer gained her fame as a "sob sister" on the *New York Journal,* covering murder trials, vice raids, and human interest stories. But she much preferred writing her "Dorothy Dix Talks" column, which offered questions and answers two days a week and sermonettes the other three.

Gilmer's private life was as tragic as that of any of her writers. Her husband fell victim to an incurable mental disease soon after their marriage. He got progressively worse until his death thirty-five years later.

"I never once thought of divorce," said Gilmer. "I could not say to others 'Be strong' if I did not myself have strength to endure."

But nobody past or present has dished out advice like the Friedman twins, better known as Ann Landers and **Abigail Van Buren.** The similarities between the two began with their shared birth date and similar names. (Officially, Ann is Esther Pauline while Abby is Pauline Esther.) They looked alike and dressed alike. Both started giving advice before they entered their teens. "When they told me babies came from between the mother's legs — why, I fell off the curb. They always knew everything first," recalled one childhood chum.

The sisters were even married in a double ceremony in 1939. Van Buren is still married, while Landers made headlines when she and her husband were divorced in 1975.

Landers took over the *Chicago Sun-*

Times' advice column from its original Ann Landers, Ruth Crowley, in 1955. Van Buren's column started in the *San Francisco Chronicle* one year later. Both are now syndicated worldwide.

Despite rumors to the contrary, the sisters remain close. "When we are together we still sleep curled up in each other's arms like we always did," Van Buren recently confided. But she advises parents of twins to help them develop their own identities — and not to dress them alike. "Break up the vaudeville act," she counsels. "It may be good for the parents' ego, but for the sisters it means double trouble."

Both Landers and Van Buren pride themselves on the many clergymen, physicians, psychologists, and attorneys whose expertise they seek.

One advice giver who relies on nobody's word but her own is Miriam Blue, a cleaning lady who doubles as "family relations expert" at St. Louis radio station KMOX. The sixtyish **"Miss Blue"** owes her recently won fame to a KMOX disc jockey, who enticed her away from her broom to chat with his 100,000 listeners.

She now makes two radio appearances a week, dispensing advice that reflects her "live and let live" philosophy. To a wife who complained of tell-tale make-up on her husband's collar, Miss Blue suggested that he might have been wearing the cosmetics himself. "Give him the benefit of the doubt," she urged.

Miss Blue claims she has no intention of giving up her cleaning duties to devote full time to dispensing advice. After all, she says, fame is fleeting.

Abigail Van Buren advises parents of twins to "break up the vaudeville act."

But Van Buren and her identical twin, Ann Landers, are still the closest friends.

FEMALES IN THE FUNNIES

Lucy Van Pelt: Leading Loudmouth

Lucy Van Pelt, as *Peanuts* creator Charles Schulz once remarked, "is the dominant one in every family, the little girl who has no doubts about who is going to run the show."

Lucy's own words show no lack of self-confidence. "I believe in ME! I'm my OWN cause!" she announces.

Lucy's most frequent victim is poor, trusting Charlie Brown, who each fall gives her another chance to hold the football for his first kickoff of the season. And each year, Lucy pulls the ball away just as Charlie prepares to kick, sending him tumbling on his round bald head.

Lucy's one soft spot is her love for Schroeder, whose affections are directed toward Beethoven and his piano. She is vulnerable in another way to the kisses of the beagle Snoopy — she gags, screaming, "Help! I've been kissed by a dog."

Joanie Caucus: Liberated Woman

Joanie Caucus's dissatisfaction with suburban motherhood came to a head when her husband put his arm around her and announced, "My wife, I think I'll keep her." She immediately packed her bags and applied to law school. *Doonesbury* creator Garry Trudeau enrolled her in law school at the University of California at Berkeley after its students sent him an application in her name.

"I've received so much mail addressed to Joanie," Trudeau says, "that my mother thinks I'm living with her."

Joanie's love life has caused two crises in the newspaper world, the first when she learned early in 1976 that the love of her life was gay. The second came several months later, when *Doonesbury* readers found Joanie in bed with a man to whom she was not married. A number of newspapers across the country refused to print either of the episodes.

Orphan Annie: Ageless Chatterbox
Created in 1924 by Harold Gray, the plucky, pupil-less **Little Orphan Annie** never aged a day past eleven. After some early misadventures with overbearing guardians and misbehaving children, Annie and her dog, Sandy, joined forces

Orphan Annie: "Who's that little chatterbox? The one with the pretty auburn locks?"

with Daddy Warbucks, the world's wealthiest soldier of fortune.

The tousle-headed moppet, whose most frequent expression was "Leapin' Lizards," was a favorite of President Herbert Hoover, who shared her creator's conservative political philosophy. Auto maker Henry Ford took such an interest in one cliff-hanging episode that he wired Gray: "Please do all you can to find Sandy. We are all interested."

Mary Worth: Rags to Riches
The genteel, modish **Mary Worth** of today's comic pages has risen far in society since 1932 when, as destitute Apple Mary, she struggled to support herself and her crippled grandson by selling apples on street corners.

Like many Americans, Mary's fortunes turned upward with the onset of World War II. Her late husband's worthless securities regained value, providing Mary with leisure time to dispense grandmotherly advice to a succession of young actresses, models, and businesswomen.

Brenda Starr: Daring Reporter
"Brenda's always been women's lib," says Dale Messick of her flaming-haired, perennially twenty-three-old creation. From her first appearance in 1940 as top woman reporter for *The Flash*, **Brenda Starr** has demanded tough assignments equal to those given the paper's male reporters.

Modeled after Rita Hayworth, Brenda was to have been a Wild West outlaw until Messick decided she wanted to draw modern costumes. Brenda was unlucky in love until 1976, when she married the mysterious, one-eyed Basil St. John, who had courted her for years with black orchids.

To hints early in 1977 that impending motherhood would slow her down, Brenda's response was a characteristic "Wanna bet?"

Hollyhock: Librarians' Favorite
Many librarians who once disapproved of the comics are devotees of **Hollyhock**, the book-toting companion of Priscilla Nutchell.

According to *Priscilla's Pop* creator Al Vermeer, Hollyhock was born in a doodle during a long telephone conversation. "She's bailed me out of many a dry spell, what with her devotion to Priscilla and an ever greater love for the public library.''

Broom-Hilda: Hapless Witch
The green-complexioned, cigar-chomping witch **Broom-Hilda**, created by Russell Meyers in 1970, more often amuses than terrifies. Her magic tricks are rarely successful; an infrequent triumph at producing lightning or flying through the air without mishap is cause for rejoicing.

She gets little respect from her cohorts, a shaggy troll named Irwin and Gaylord, a bespectacled buzzard. Even her junk mail is addressed to ''Ugly Occupant.''

Betty Boop: Comic Mae West
The French doll look of the 1930s was epitomized by the flirtatious **Betty Boop,** who moved from animated cartoons to the Sunday comic sections in 1935.

Betty's face was modeled after that of singer Helen Kane, who countered by mounting an unsuccessful lawsuit against Max Fleischer, Betty's creator. Mae West was the inspiration for Betty's luscious curves.

On the screen, Betty incessantly batted her long eyelashes and blew kisses to the audience. The comic-strip Betty, a Hollywood actress with a dominating Aunt Tillie, behaved with a bit more decorum.

Betty's last cartoon, provocatively entitled *Yip, Yip, Yippie,* was released in 1939. In recent years, Betty has been rediscovered by youthful audiences at ''underground'' movie houses.

Daisy Mae: She Got Her Man
Long before the sexual revolution of the 1960s, **Daisy Mae** defied courtship tradition by her ardent pursuit of the reluctant Li'l Abner.

The blond, buxom Daisy Mae chased her hillbilly sweetheart for seventeen years before they were wed by Marryin' Sam in 1952. The important event merited a *Life* magazine cover story by the strip's creator, Al Capp.

Thanks to Daisy Mae, Sadie Hawkins Day, on which the women of Dogpatch can propose to any ''feller'' they can catch, has become a tradition at hundreds of high schools and colleges.

Wonder Woman: Amazon Superstar
Scantily attired in a star-spangled costume, **Wonder Woman** burst onto the

Wonder Woman teaches her female followers that self-confidence is the key to strength.

scene in 1941 to help the United States wage World War II. The daughter of Hippolyte, the Queen of the Amazons, Wonder Woman conquered evil with the aid of a golden lasso, an invisible plane, and ''bracelets of submission.''

But she seldom killed her adversaries. If they were beyond redemption, an act of God conveniently took them off her hands.

''Wonder Woman proves that women are superior to men because they have love in addition to force,'' said her creator, William Moulton Marston, a psychologist, prison reformer, and inventor of the lie detector.

Wonder Woman has enjoyed a resurgence in recent years, largely because feminists see her as symbolic of feminine self-reliance and strength.

A Wonder Woman television series, starring former Miss U.S.A. Lynda Carter, premiered in 1976.

Winnie Winkle: Steno Who Made Good
From a humble beginning as secretary to Barnaby Bibbs, **Winnie Winkle** worked

her way to the top of the Bonnaz fashion empire.

She first appeared in 1920 as *Winnie Winkle, the Bread Winner,* working to support her aging father and mother. Two years later, she introduced her Sunday readers to an adopted brother, Perry, who shared top billing with her for the next quarter century.

After a long string of boyfriends, Winnie married Will Wright in 1936. But after the birth of twins Wendy and Billy, ennui began to set in; Wright was sent off to war in 1941 and mysteriously disappeared. Winnie, the comics' first widowed heroine, has managed to elude matrimony ever since.

Maggie: Rolling Pin Aristocrat

The classic American couple, as represented in the media from the funny page to the television situation comedy, consists of a shrill, domineering woman and her meek, henpecked spouse.

An early such twosome was the parvenu **Maggie** and Jiggs of George McManus' 1913 creation, *Bringing Up Father.* Despite her high-society pretensions and couturier gowns, Maggie still made use of a rolling pin to keep her husband in line. The henpecked Jiggs, an immigrant who made good, plotted reunions at Dinty Moore's with his ribald, working-class cohorts, with whom Maggie no longer allowed him to associate.

Blondie: Brains and Beauty

Many comic fans doubted the 1933 marriage of Dagwood Bumstead to flapper **Blondie Boopadoop** would stand the test of time, especially after Dagwood's billionaire father cut off his allowance in disapproval.

But the young couple rose to the occasion. Dagwood, who barely reached Blondie's armpits during their courtship, literally grew. Blondie acquired a level head, becoming the sweetly dominating force in a family which expanded to include son Alexander in 1934 and daughter Cookie in 1941. During Blondie's first pregnancy, more than four hundred thousand persons wrote in suggesting names for the expected baby.

The strip, created by the late Murat "Chic" Young in 1930, has been syndicated on all continents and translated into

seventeen languages. In Latin countries, Blondie is "Pepita" and Dagwood, "Lorenzo." And, despite her weakness for a new hat, Blondie was pressed into service by the Dutch Government in 1947 to illustrate an anti-inflation campaign.

Lois Lane: Superman's Sidekick

Lois Lane's single-minded pursuit of Superman has won her fame second only to that of the Man of Steel himself. And, thanks to her success, almost every other comics superhero has got an admiring woman not far from his side.

When the comic book premiered in 1938, Lois had few ethics and a massive ego. She has since mellowed, softening the viciousness of her verbal attacks upon *Daily Planet* colleague Clark Kent, Superman's alter ego. In fact, 1975 found Lois stirring a love potion into Clark's Beef Bourguignon, which led to some after-dinner necking in front of the television.

Hurricane Hattie: Cigar-smoking Imp

Feminists who object to the naming of violent storms for women may take small comfort from the fact that the pint-sized bane of *Born Loser* Brutus P. Thornapple's existence is named for a hurricane.

Hurricane Hattie O'Hara, the 1975 creation of cartoonist Art Sansom, smokes cigars and walks her pet skunk, Taboo, on a leash. And she has a gift for the impertinent, as when she informs her parents, "I know where babies come from. . . . It's the birds and the bees I don't know anything about!"

Every "born loser" dreads the appearance of a Hurricane Hattie in his neighborhood.

THAT'S TABOO, 'N' I'M HURRICANE HATTIE O'HARA, YOUR NEW NEIGHBOR.

ROMANCE, RECIPES, AND REBELLION,

What do *Good Housekeeping, womenSports,* and *True Confessions* have in common? Very little other than being monthly magazines aimed at a female audience. But in spite of differences in their editorial philosophies and target audiences, the three got together with thirty-two other women's magazines in July, 1976, to publicize the Equal Rights Amendment.

The ERA articles of 1976 were far different fare from most of the articles in the earliest women's magazines, which appeared nearly three centuries ago. Romance and gossip, fashion and haughty discussions of the social amenities were their chief fare, along with home remedies for everything from seasickness to lovesickness and recipes for the dining table and the dressing table.

The first such periodical was *The Ladies Mercury,* launched in 1693 by a London bookseller. The magazine specialized in personal advice to women — and sometimes men — on age-old problems, including affairs of the heart, and affairs of heartburn.

Probably the first such magazine edited by a woman was *The Female Tattler,* published in London for about a year beginning in 1709. Its editor was one "Mrs. Crankenthorpe," known in real life as Mary de la Riviere Manley. The periodical delighted in personal abuse and scandal, and a grand jury termed it a "nuisance" within a few months of its founding.

Across the sea, in Boston, the somewhat less rigid pattern that most subsequent women's magazines in the United States would follow was being set by Sarah Josepha Hale. A widowed mother of five, Hale started her *Ladies Magazine* in 1828 to help make ends meet. Though hers was not the young nation's first women's magazine, it was the first to last more than five years.

Louis A. Godey, publisher of a rival magazine in Philadelphia, was so impressed with Hale's product that he bought her out in 1836 and hired her to meld both magazines. Hale became "editress" — as she insisted upon being called — of a combined publication, *Godey's Lady's Book,* published in Philadelphia.

Women's increasing affluence and leisure time, combined with a drop in postage rates, created a flurry of women's magazine activity during the late nineteenth century. *Ladies' Home Journal* was founded in 1883, *Vogue* in 1892, and *McCall's* in 1876.

Good Housekeeping was founded in 1885 to promote the "interests of the higher life of the household." From the outset it was consumer-oriented and demanded accuracy of facts reported. Reader participation soon became a mainstay of the publication. The April 28, 1888 issue offered $25 each for "the best Buffalo Bug Extinguisher, the best Bed Bug Finisher, the best Moth Eradicator, and the best Fly and Flea Exterminator."

With woman's role beginning to extend beyond the household, *Good Housekeeping* followed suit and soon found itself promoting women's suffrage and running a regular column on "Women's Work and Wages." In 1911, the magazine published an article by the controversial Havelock Ellis on the then scandalous subject of sex education. An innovation of the magazine's early years was the establishment of the Good Housekeeping Experiment Station — now the Good Housekeeping Institute — which was founded in 1901. The station tested products and practices recommended to *Good Housekeeping* readers in articles and advertisements. Only items which endured through extensive investigation were permitted to carry the Good Housekeeping Seal and appear in advertisements. The station's guiding force from 1912 to 1930 was Dr. Harvey Wiley. As chief chemist for the U.S. Department of Agriculture, Wiley had led the fight against food adulteration that resulted in the 1906 Pure Food and Drug Act.

Longtime circulation leaders in the women's magazine field — *Family Circle* and *Woman's Day* — were born during the 1930s. Both magazines employed a method ideally suited for Depression-poor America for winning readers: Copies were given away free by supermarket chains. Though the magazines eventually bore a price, they continue to rely on supermarkets for their distribution.

Along with general interest magazines like *Life, Look,* and *The Saturday Evening Post,* women's magazines fell upon hard times in the late 1950s and 1960s. Other women's periodicals fought rising costs by reducing size, cutting back circulation, and modernizing their editorial content.

An outstanding example was *Cosmopolitan,* given new life in the mid-sixties by Helen Gurley Brown. Brown vigorously redirected the venerable general monthly toward the single working woman, taking a cue from the popularity of her *Sex and the Single Girl,* a best seller. Impudent but discreetly veiled sex discussion became a major ingredient in *"Cosmo's"* success formula.

Confession and romance publications — like *True Confessions* and *Modern Romances* — have been a staple item among women's magazines and also continued to flourish. Though cover headlines hint strongly of outrageous promiscuity and depravity, they are largely come-ons. Inside the magazines, the reader encounters conventional views of morality and sexual encounters and clearly drawn distinction between right and wrong in fairly innocuous articles.

Women's magazines came under fire from militant feminists in the late sixties and early seventies for perpetuating woman's image as little more than housekeeper or sex object. Though some of the criticism was unfair and tactics demanding change often extreme, militance served to raise the consciousness of many editors and writers. Among them was John Mack Carter, then editor of *Ladies' Home Journal* and now editor of *Good Housekeeping,* who was isolated in his office for ten hours by 200 women activists.

The appearance of *Ms.* magazine in 1972 ushered in a new era in the history of women's magazines.

Founders of the magazine announced in its first regular edition that *Ms.* was to be "a publication created and controlled by women that could be as serious, outrageous, satisfying, sad, funky, intimate, global, compassionate, and full of change as women's lives really are." *Ms.* is considered by some to have grown less strident over the years, perhaps due both to changing public attitudes toward women and the magazine's efforts to broaden its readership base. Illustrative of its new, mellower tone was its May 1977 cover story, "I am the mother of eight, a housewife, a feminist — and happy."

Other magazines that followed the lead of *Ms.* include *Working Woman, Essence,* and *womenSports.*

Another phenomenon of the 1970s is *Playgirl,* a distaff version of *Playboy, Penthouse* and similar "skin" magazines. Launched in 1973, the magazine features photographs of nude male athletes, actors, and other celebrities. Other magazines like *Cosmopolitan,* which pioneered the male centerfold with actor Burt Reynolds, and *Viva,* the brainchild of Penthouse publisher Bob Guccione, have turned away from male nudity after finding that women readers were not especially interested in it.

What kinds of magazines will women be reading a generation from now?

As more women enter business, government, and the professions, many will begin subscribing to magazines like the *Harvard Business Review* or the *Journal of the American Medical Association* along with such traditional women's magazines as *Good Housekeeping* or *Cosmopolitan.*

Venerable women's magazines will continue to modernize. New magazines will appear; one recent example of this trend is *Savvy,* a magazine for the executive woman, which premiered as a *New York* magazine insert in 1977.

The more society changes, the more women's magazines will change! It is possible to conjur women's magazine articles of the future offering a battery of new situations to ponder within traditionally strong editorial formats and concepts. *Good Housekeeping* may offer "1997's Most Admired Woman: The President of the United States." *Cosmopolitan* may suggest to its female readers, "Sixteen Ways to Seduce Your Secretary." *WomenSports* may feature "Women Finish One-Two-Three in Unisex Boston Marathon" and "Olga Korbut: Life Begins At Forty." Gloria Steinem's memoirs may be serialized in *Ms.,* and *True Confessions* may titillate its readers with, "I Spent Six Weeks On A Spaceship With An All-Male Crew."

Entertainers

MUSICAL WOMEN

Anderson: A Memorable Voice

Arturo Toscanini called hers "a voice such as one hears once in a hundred years." Finnish composer Jean Sibelius said to her, "Miss Anderson, the roof of my house is too low for you."

Marian Anderson (1902-   ), the first black to sing at the Metropolitan Opera, was introduced to music at an early age. Anderson was singing in the Union Baptist Church of her native Philadelphia at the age of six. Because of her extraordinary talent, members of her congregation raised money to pay for a year of lessons with Giuseppe Borghetti, the famed music teacher. He was so impressed by her voice that he gave her a second year of lessons, free. An operatic career for a black, let alone a woman, was unprecedented in the 1920s, but Anderson's close family encouraged her to pursue it anyway.

In 1925, she won a contest over three hundred competitors at Lewisohn Stadium, and appeared in concert there with the New York Philharmonic. She performed abroad and astounded audiences and critics with her vocal range and the richness of her voice. National recognition in America followed a tour under the management of impresario Sol Hurok.

Barred from Constitution Hall, Marian Anderson sang to 75,000 at the Lincoln Memorial on Easter 1943.

Everybody loved her, at least almost everybody. The Daughters of the American Revolution refused to give her use of their Constitution Hall in Washington, D.C., in 1939. A storm of protest erupted over the incident, and First Lady Eleanor Roosevelt resigned from the DAR. Anderson did perform in Washington, D.C. however, on Easter morning 1943 in front of the brooding statue of Abraham Lincoln at the Lincoln Memorial. More than seventy-five thousand people came to hear her sing.

Anderson's Metropolitan Opera debut did not occur until 1955, ten years before her retirement. She sang the role of Ulrica in Verdi's *Un Ballo in Maschera,* about which she said, "There was electricity in the air . . . I trembled . . . The audience applauded before I could sing a note."

Andrews Sisters: Patty, Maxine, Laverne

The Minnesota sisters of Greek-Norwegian parentage made their first hit with a Yiddish song. It all started when their mother urged them to sing so they would stop squabbling.

Laverne (1915-1967), **Maxine** (1918-   ) and **Patti** (1921-   ) began singing in 1927. For ten lean years, they kicked around professional show business. Then, in 1937, they recorded "Nice Work If You Can Get It." But it was the flip side song, "Bei Mir Bist du Schon," that became a hit. The song earned the Andrews Sisters a gold record and made them stars, but it did not make either them or the composers rich. The Andrews Sisters had been paid a flat fifty dollars for the recording. Composer Sholom Secunda and lyricist Jacob Jacobs had sold the rights to the song for thirty dollars. (Later, the sisters got a 5 percent royalty on each record sold.) Their other hit songs included "Three Litte Fishes," "Rum and Coca-Cola," "Apple Blossom Time," and "Beer Barrel Polka."

The Andrews Sisters could not read music, but their voices blended beautifully. Not so their personalities. The act broke up in the 1950s after several disappointing film performances. Laverne died of cancer in 1967, and Patti became a singer/comedienne. Maxine was dean of women at Lake Tahoe's Paradise College and later counseled drug addicts and de-

The frequently feuding Andrews Sisters were all smiles in this scene from *Hollywood Canteen*.

linquents. In 1974, the surviving sisters were reunited in a Broadway musical, *Over Here!*

Baez: Protest Singer

Joan Baez (1941-   ) is the queen of folk/protest music. The woman who introduced Bob Dylan, she also made the most successful female folk album, "Joan Baez" (1960), in the history of LPs.

At 10, Joan Baez became "obsessed with stopping people from blowing each other's brains out."

The daughter of a Mexican physicist father, she felt like a misfit in childhood. "The white kids looked down on me because I was part Mexican and the Mexican kids didn't like me because I couldn't speak Spanish," she later commented. "I've been obsessed with stopping people from blowing each other's brains out since I was ten," she says.

Baez attended Boston University but dropped out to perform in Boston and Cambridge coffee houses. She came to national attention at the 1959 Newport Rhode Island Folk Festival.

Baez has consistently kept her maverick identity alive. She marched and performed in civil rights demonstrations. In 1963, she refused to appear on ABC-TVs "Hootenanny" because it refused to hire the blacklisted Pete Seeger. A disciple of Gandhi, she was active in the anti-war protests of the 1960s. In 1965, she refused to pay taxes that would support the Vietnam War, and she founded the Institute for the Study of Non-Violence. She married (and later divorced) draft resister David Harris, who spent much of their married life in jail. They have a son.

Baez's music and voice are still marvelous. With a nod to rock, she added electronic amplification to her arrangements.

Boulanger: Teacher Extraordinaire

In 1939, **Nadia Boulanger** (1887-   ), famed pianist and music teacher, became the first woman to conduct the Boston

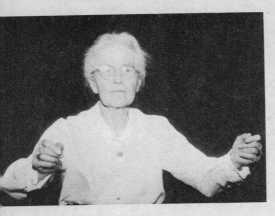

A critic praised Nadia Boulanger's musicianship as "at the same time so gentle and so firm."

Symphony. Her reaction to the event was characteristic: "I've been a woman for a little more than fifty years and I've gotten over my initial astonishment." She was also the first woman to conduct the Royal Philharmonic and the Philadelphia Orchestra. But, as kudos, she'd probably prefer Aaron Copland's assessment of his former teacher: "Nadia Boulanger knew everything there was to know about music."

Her father was a singing teacher, and music filled her house when she was small. She attended the Conservatoire National in Paris, and taught piano and composed music. In 1908, she won second prize at the prestigious Grand Prix de Rome musi-cal competition. Her sister, Lili, won first place five years later. After Lili's death in 1918, Boulanger devoted her time to teaching, first at the Conservatoire National and later at the Conservatoire Americain de Fontainebleau.

An exacting but inspiring teacher, she instructed every major U.S. post World War II composer.

Caldwell: Comic Opera

If opera ever becomes as popular as popcorn in the U.S., it will be because of **Sarah Caldwell** (1928-   ), director-conductor of the Opera Company of Boston. Caldwell is not only a supremely gifted musician, she is also down to earth, personally and professionally. She'd rather die than be boring. When the Boston strangler was terrorizing that city, Caldwell said, "Wouldn't it be wonderful if they'd catch the strangler at the opera."

Caldwell was an overachiever by the age of four. She was a mathematics and music prodigy. At ten, she gave violin recitals, and was a hit on her block because of the fireworks she staged each Fourth of July at her Maryville, Missouri, home.

Caldwell has the knack for turning "no" into "yes." *Time* wrote that Boston "did not really want its own opera." But with only five thousand dollars, Sarah founded the now great Opera Company of Boston in 1957. Many people think opera is boring. Not in Boston. For a circus scene in *The Bartered Bride,* Sarah hired clown

The indefatigable Sarah Caldwell sees her job as keeping opera from becoming "a crashing bore."

Emmett Kelly. For *Daughter of the Regiment,* Sarah cast Berverly Sills and, as insurance, had her slice potatoes to tempo, assisted by a brandy-toting Saint Bernard.

Caldwell's offbeat style persists offstage, too. She has been known to sleep in theater aisles rolled up in a curtain. Quick thinking and disdainful of fashion (at 5'3", she weighs 300 pounds), she transformed another curtain into a dress for a performance. Her accessories include huge wristwatches and sneakers, and she's lost so many purses she now carries her money around in a paper bag.

But Caldwell is no joke. She is highly esteemed as a director and conductor. At the opera, she has a say in casting, lighting, stage design, and fund raising. Her tenacity has kept the opera alive.

Caldwell has boundless energy, often rehearsing her musicians up to eighteen hours a day. In 1975, she was the second woman to conduct the New York Philharmonic. The concert was devoted entirely to the works of female composers.

Carr: America's First Chicana
Vicki Carr (1941-   ), born Florencia Bisenta de Casillas Martinez Cardona, likes to remind herself (and others) of her roots. "Look at me," she says to herself periodically, "a little Chicana from the Mexican-American neighborhood of L.A."

Carr first sang professionally as "Carlita" with Pepe Callahan's Mexican-Irish band when she was eighteen. She was a star at the Coconut Grove five years later and has since appeared on every major television variety show. In 1972, she was named "Singer of the Year" by the American Guild of Variety Artists.

Carr seems to spend as much time on education and health causes as she does on her singing career. Her concern about health began when her own, and her career, was threatened by an allergic reaction to tobacco smoke during a nightclub engagement. Although not a smoker, she temporarily lost her voice. She has since begun a campaign for legislation to ban smoking in public places. In 1974, she became national chairman for the American Lung Association.

Carr established the Vicki Carr

When Vicki Carr asked then-President Ford his favorite Mexican dish, he responded, "You!".

Scholarship Foundation for Mexican-American students in 1971. In less than five years, the foundation gave fifty thousand dollars in grants to more than fifty students. The students are, she says, "my own family." As a singer, her greatest hit to date is "It Must Be Him," which received a Grammy nomination in 1968.

Callas: Temperamental Diva
In her vocal prime, **Maria Callas** (1923-   ) was the world's most celebrated diva. She was a thin superstar with a volcanic temper. She also had a stunning collection of jewels and one of the world's wealthiest lovers — Aristotle Onassis. But more than that, she had the voice. Callas' versatile soprano was flawed by occasional brassiness, and chancy pitch, but no voice could match hers for an impact. Her acting ability and slenderness were unprecedented in the opera world. It wasn't always so.

Callas was born Maria Kalogeropoulos of Greek immigrant parents in New York City. She went to Greece and studied at Athens' Royal Conservatory during World War II and the Greek civil war. A fellow music student later described Callas' debut: "She was tall, very fat, and wore heavy glasses . . . Her whole bearing was awkward . . . not knowing what to do with her hands, she sat there quietly biting her nails while waiting her turn."

In 1947, she appeared in *La Gioconda* in Verona. There she met Giovanni Meneghini, a man whose wealth and experience transformed her into a glamorous star. While married to him, she began her liaison with Onassis. "She repaid my love by stabbing me in the back," Meneghini pouted. The Onassis affair ended when he met Jacqueline Kennedy. "First I lost weight, then I lost my voice, and now I've lost Onassis," Callas complained.

Callas was among the last of the temperamental prima donnas. Her feuds with rivals and managers — including a 1958 clash with Metropolitan Opera Director Rudolph Bing — were legendary.

Although she hasn't performed much since 1960, she has that sense of timing only the great stars have — she left her audiences asking for more.

Carpenter: Just Beginning

Karen Carpenter (1950-   ) has given sibling rivalry, cleanliness, and musicianship a good name. She is the female half of The Carpenters; her brother Richard is the other half. Her father, a big band buff, inspired their music. Richard studied classical piano at Yale while playing jazz piano in local clubs. Karen took up drumming with her high school marching band.

In 1966, with a tuba and bass-playing friend, they won the Hollywood Bowl Battle of the Bands. Although disco and rock music was far more profitable than the Carpenters' soft rock sound, they persisted. They experimented with layers of vocal and instrumental tracks to achieve seamless harmony. They made the charts for the first time in 1970 with their recording of the Beatles' "Ticket to Ride." A string of hits, including "Close to You" and "We've Only Just Begun," followed.

The Carpenters, like the Waltons, were a family whose time had come. Internationally, they have sold over 25 million singles and albums, and they've won three Grammies. More, no doubt, to come.

Carter: Country Music Pro

Maybelle Carter (1909-   ), one of country music's first commercially successful performers, is still going strong after nearly half a century in show business.

Carter grew up playing guitar and banjo in the Virginia mountains. Along with cousin Sara and Sara's husband A. P., she began singing in schoolhouses for fifteen cents a head. In 1927, the Carter Family auditioned for RCA Victor and began their recording career.

Over the next twelve years, the three recorded some 250 songs — Maybelle and Sara arranged the music and A. P. received the credit. The songs they performed — which included "Keep on the Sunny Side," "Wabash Cannonball," and "Will the Circle Be Unbroken" — later gained additional exposure when recorded by Joan Baez and others.

Maybelle devised the "church lick" guitar style still used by many country performers.

Sara and A. P. divorced in the mid 1930s, and both retired from performing in 1943. Maybelle then teamed up with daughters Helen, Anita, and June.

In 1950, they began a seventeen-year stint at the capital of country music, Nashville's Grand Ole Opry. Said Opry Manager E. W. (Bud) Wendel in 1973, "Every country music performer owes something to the Carter Family. Their influence is so great it can't be fully measured."

Carter and daughter June helped country star Johnny Cash kick his pill habit. Afterward, he married June. And he asked both women to join him in his command White House performance.

Cher: "Got You Babe"

Television's most carefully costumed musical performer, **Cher Bono** (1946-   ) is the first to admit that it's her style, not her voice, that turns people on.

Cherlyn LaPiere was born in California, an amalgam of Cherokee Indian, Armenian, French, and Turkish bloodlines. She dropped out of high school to study acting and eloped with Sonny Bono when she was eighteen. Sonny, an aspiring songwriter, and Cher performed as "Caesar and Cleo" on the club circuit. In 1965, they reverted to their own names and clicked with "Baby Don't Go," which they recorded thanks to a $168 loan. They were a smash with "I Got You, Babe," which sold three million copies.

Kids loved them. The Bonos wore

bell-bottoms and furry jackets; they were thrown out of the best places because of their unsuitable attire. But their popularity waned when the hard acid rock sound came into vogue. Fans were also not crazy about the Bonos' anti-drug stand, and no one liked their film, *Chastity* (also the name of their daughter, born in 1970), which was panned as trite. Then, they hit on a formula that was terrific for night-clubs and television but led to the death of their marriage: the art of putdown.

CBS caught their act on "The Merv Griffin Show" and gave them a summer replacement slot. Ratings were so good that they were moved to prime time in the regular season. But the ratings at home plummeted, and the couple split professionally and legally. Their solo television shows were not winners, so in 1976 they teamed up again for television. Cher, in the meantime, had married rock musician Gregg Allman and had a son with him, but their marital status also seemed unsteady.

Collins: Real McCoy

Judy Collins (1939-   ) is one of those miraculous artists whose voice and music will be remembered long after the glow of shinier stars has faded. Everyone in the music business calls every one else in the

Silver voiced folksinger Judy Collins predicts she'll reach her prime in her fifties.

business an artist. Collins is the real McCoy.

She was born in Denver, Colorado, the daughter of Chuck Collins, a well-known (and blind) radio personality. She is a musician to her toes. At six, she began studying classical piano with Antonia Brico (about whom she later made an Academy Award-nominated documentary), and practiced up to eight hours a day.

By sixteen, Collins realized she ought to have played more outdoors. "I decided that playing and screaming in the alleys had a place, too," she said. By nineteen, she had digressed to folk music, landing a singing job for one hundred dollars a week and "all the beer I could drink." Her first album, *Maid of Constant Sorrow*, was traditional folk music.

There is very little Collins does not take seriously and she naturally turned to songs of social comment. Like Joan Baez, Collins became a political activist. "We all felt a degree of responsibility that went way beyond the role of musician," she said. Although her owns songs, such as "My Father," and "Born to the Breed" are more personal than ever, her recent recording of "Bread and Roses" shows she's still reading the newspapers.

Fitzgerald: First Lady of Song

Ella Fitzgerald (1918-   ) is the best jazz singer there is. And she has dignity to match her phenomenal musicianship and voice.

Fitzgerald's childhood was spent in an orphanage in Yonkers, New York. Her terror on stage, which persists to this day, got her into singing. She had entered a Harlem amateur dance contest, and because of her shaking knees, could not maneuver. She sang instead. "When I won the contest, I was trying to sing like Connie Boswell," she recalls. "I stole everything I ever heard, but mostly I stole from the horns." Ella has always soaked up the horns, and every other instrument, which accounts for her flawless technique in "scat," the use of the voice as an instrument of the band.

Fitzgerald was discovered by bandleader Chick Webb in 1934. She sang with Webb's band and collaborated with him on her huge 1938 hit, "A-Tisket, A-Tasket."

According to Ella Fitzgerald, "The only thing better than singing is more singing."

Ella's rank as the First Lady of Song is corroborated by Frank Sinatra and Bing Crosby. Her particular brand of magic is the deeper meaning she gives to a song when her perfect voice combines the music and lyrics. She can sing anything, and has survived every fad in pop music. And her enthusiasm shows.

Flack: "Killing Me Softly"
Roberta Flack (1940-   ) has had a devoted flock since 1967, when the owner of Mr. Henry's Pub in Washington, D.C., set up a special room to showcase her.

But Flack takes nothing for granted, and from childhood on has always been a pro. Born in Ashville, North Carolina, she began studying voice and piano as a child. At thirteen, she won second prize in a statewide singing contest for black students in Virginia. Like most black singers, she did a good bit of singing in church. She also did a lot of eating. In high school, she weighed over two hundred pounds (long since lost). "All I did was play the piano and eat all day," she says, "and I did them at the same time." She must have spent some time studying, too, because she graduated from high school at fifteen and went to Howard University in Washington, D.C. There she majored in voice and music education because, although she longed for a career in music, she knew she'd have to pay the rent.

Her first teaching job, for twenty-eight hundred dollars annually, was in Farmville, N.C. One year later, she was in Washington, teaching by day and singing in clubs at night. That's when she switched from classical to popular music. Jazz pianist Les McCann, an early fan, helped her land a recording contract for her first album, *First Take*. In 1971, she replaced eighteen-time winner Ella Fitzgerald as *Downbeat's* Female Vocalist of the Year. "The First Time Ever I Saw Your Face" was the hit that brought her national attention.

Franklin: Lady Soul
Even if you got no religion, when you hear **Aretha "Lady Soul" Franklin** (1942-   ), it's hard not to be a believer. Franklin got gospel with her mother's milk. Her father, Reverend C. L. Franklin, was minister to twenty-five hundred souls at Detroit's New Bethel Baptist Church. Franklin sang in the choir and later toured as a gospel singer with his evangelical troupe. By the time she was twenty, Franklin had married and produced three children.

It wasn't until 1967 that she made her

Aretha Franklin after winning her fifth Grammy in 1972 as best female "R & B" performer.

brand of soul a best seller. "I Never Loved a Man (The Way I Love You)" was infectious in its power, drive, and intensity. "If a song's about something I've experienced or that could've happened to me," she says, "it's good. . . . Because that's what soul's all about." "Her impact goes beyond technique," *Time* echoed. "It is her fierce, gritty conviction." Franklin was named number one vocalist by *Billboard* in 1967 and won two Grammies in 1968.

Holiday: Lady Sang the Blues

Billie Holiday (1915-1959) was the best blues singer of her time. She was probably also more entitled to sing the blues than anyone else. Holiday was the illegitimate daughter of a thirteen-year-old girl and her fifteen-year-old boyfriend. Born Eleanora Fagan, she took her father's name (Holiday) and that of her favorite film star (Billie Dove).

Just about every detail of Holiday's life is depressing. She grew up desperately poor, earning money at the age of six by scrubbing the white front steps characteristic of Baltimore houses. She also ran errands for the women of a local brothel in exchange for listening to Louis Armstrong and Bessie Smith records. At ten, she was nearly raped by a boarder in her mother's rooming house. The roomer was sent to jail for five years. Billie was sent to a Catholic reform school. There, as punishment for some now forgotten infraction, Holiday was locked up in a room with the body of a girl who had recently died.

Holiday's first singing job was in a Harlem bar, where she earned the nickname "Lady." Her wage was the money thrown on the floor. Holiday's singing, like Piaf's and Garland's, was a mirror of despair. Her phrasing in a small but poignant voice was spellbinding. The blues lyrics she sang echoed the tragedy of her life. Benny Goodman and Artie Shaw recognized her talents, and she made many recordings with them.

Bad luck and lousy timing continued to haunt her. It was hard for a black woman to get served in a restaurant or find a bathroom. New York City's Lincoln Hotel forced her to use the service entrance. Her husband, Jimmy Morris, got her hooked

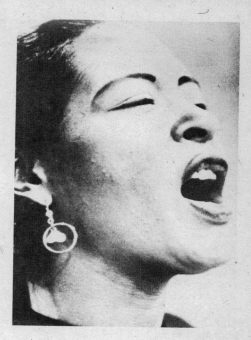

Billie Holiday's poignant blues singing mirrored the misery of her life.

on heroin, and she did one year in a drug rehabilitation center. Because of her record, she could not get a New York cabaret license, without which she could perform nowhere that liquor was served. Even so, ten days after her release she made a triumphant appearance to an overflow audience at Carnegie Hall. Holiday also wrote music. Her lyrics casually announced the facts of her agony as in "Gloomy Sunday": "Angels have no thought of ever returning you/Would they be angry if I thought of joining you?" Her strongly anti-drug biography, *Lady Sings the Blues*, written by William Duffy, was published in 1956. When she died three years later, critic Ralph Gleason wrote, "It's sad beyond words that she never knew how many people loved her."

Horne: Beautiful Singer

When **Lena Horne** (1917-   ) sings, it doesn't seem possible that she's old enough to be a grandmother. At sixty, she is one of the world's most beautiful women — her singing voice and her warm and elegant presence is at its most glowing.

Horne was born in Brooklyn, New York. Her parents were divorced when she was three. After a few fragmented years living with relatives in the South, she made her professional debut in the chorus line of Harlem's Cotton Club at age sixteen. She was the first black woman ever signed to a long-term Hollywood contract and the first black singer with a big league (Charlie Barnet) band. Her films include *Cabin in the Sky* and *Ziegfeld Follies*.

Horne's forty-four years in show business have been highly successful. Her career has been punctuated by such hits as "The Man I Love" in the forties and "It's Not Easy Being Green" for "Sesame Street" in the 1970s. She has toured the world several times, appeared on Broadway in *Jamaica* (1957), and has done several television specials. In recent years, she has been a civil rights activist.

Jackson: Gospel is Hope

Mahalia Jackson (1911-1972) was the first singer to make gospel singing profitable. Until she came along, gospel music was seldom heard outside black churches.

Jackson was the daughter of a part-time preacher and grew up in New Orleans. She was not permitted to listen to anything but gospel, which partly explains why she never sang anything else. "Gospel singing is a heart feeling," she once said. "It's also got His love, and that's what I've got to sing if I'm going to sing at all."

Professional singing wasn't to come until she was in her twenties. After graduation from elementary school, she got a job as a laundress and maid. At sixteen she moved to Chicago, where she worked as a hotel maid and in a factory while attending beautician school. Jackson opened a beauty shop, then a flower shop, then bought some real estate.

She began singing with a gospel group in her Chicago church and made her first record, "God Gonna Separate the Wheat from the Tares," in 1934. Her first million-seller was "Move Up a Little Higher" in 1945. The fervor of her singing caught on, and her first Carnegie Hall concert (1950) was a sellout. A *New York Herald Tribune* critic wrote, "Her voice . . . is ideally suited to . . . the gospel singer's specialized art — the falsetto

highs and the rumbling lows . . . the gentle whispered calms and the strident, shouting climaxes."

Joplin: Bourbon and Blues

The explosive Janis Joplin (1943-1970) was the only woman to rival such male rock stars as the Rolling Stones and Beatles in fan appeal.

Joplin spent a stifling childhood in Port Arthur, Texas. A loner, she spent her high school years reading poetry and listening to the folk and blues music of Leadbelly, Bessie Smith, and Odetta.

When she was riding high, she said of her Texas classmates, "It makes me happy to know I'm making it and they're back there, plumbers just like they were."

She drifted from Austin, Texas, to San Francisco, occasionally enrolling in college or picking up a job as a keypunch operator. In 1966, she became lead vocalist of Big Brother and the Holding Company. Her rendition of "Love is Like a Ball and Chain" at the Monterey Festival in August of 1967 drew gasps and raves. Her performance was erotic, her blues filled with passionate, angry agony.

Cashbox once described Joplin as "a kind of mixture of Leadbelly, a steam engine, Calamity Jane, Bessie Smith, an oil derrick, and rot gut bourbon funneled into

Janis Joplin said she did not intend to live to be 70 "sitting in some goddam chair watching TV."

the twentieth century somewhere between El Paso and San Francisco.''

Joplin on stage was a figure of constant motion and unequalled intensity, wringing every last fragment of feeling from her songs. Some said she ravaged a song to death.

Joplin had once observed that ''audiences like their blues singers to be miserable.'' She did not disappoint them — she embraced what she termed ''good old luscious sin'': sex, alcohol, and drugs.

By 1970, she was dead of a heroin overdose; her liver was so deteriorated that any combination of alcohol and drugs could have killed her at any time.

King: Tapestry of Success

If you asked **Carole** (née Klein) **King** (1942-   ) what she does for a living, she'd probably answer, ''I'm a songwriter.'' Wearing that hat, she is one of the most gifted talents in the recording industry. But she's also a well-known singer, winner of a Grammy as 1971's best female vocalist.

King was born in Sheepshead Bay, Brooklyn. She went to Queens College, where her classmates included Paul Simon and Neil Diamond. At twenty, she dropped out of college to marry lyricist Gerry Goffin. Through an introduction by Neil Sedaka, a childhood friend, King and Goffin became a songwriting team for Don Kirschner in New York's Brill Building, a well-known proving ground for songs. The list of their hits, always for other singers, is awesome: ''Will You Still Love Me Tomorrow,'' ''Locomotion,'' ''Hi-de-Ho,'' ''Natural Woman,'' ''Wasn't Born to Follow,'' ''Go Away Little Girl,'' and ''Chains,'' among them.

But Dorothy Parker's adage of marriage being for better or worse but not for lunch applied to the Goffins. They split up and King took her two daughters to California to begin a solo career. She sang briefly with The City, through which she met James Taylor, who encouraged her independence. Her second album, *Tapestry*, has to date sold over thirteen million copies, making it the second best seller in recording history. That was in 1971, the year she won four Grammies: best popular vocalist, album of the year (*Tapestry*), record of the year (''It's Too Late'')

and song of the year (''You've Got a Friend'').

Lee: Top Professional

Peggy Lee (1920-   ) has been one of the top jazz singers in show business for more than thirty years because she *works* at it. From the spotlight aimed at her hair to the musical arrangements to her gestures, Lee rehearses every detail of her act. ''We treat our show as a performance, rather than an evening of music,'' she has said. ''It has to be exciting. A woman always has to create all the excitement and romance and mystery she can.''

Her sultry, husky singing voice was a deliberate creation. While singing at the Doll House in California years ago, she discovered that she could quiet the audience by singing *sotto voce*.

She was born Norma Dolores Engstrom in North Dakota. After working in Hollywood as a waitress and boardwalk carnival barker, she got a job singing on a Fargo, North Dakota, radio station. In Minneapolis, she broke into the big time with Will Osborne's big band. Her first huge success was ''Why Don't You Do Right?'' with Benny Goodman's band.

Lee appeared in several films, and was nominated for an Academy Award for her role as the melancholy, alcoholic blues singer in *Pete Kelly's Blues* (1955).

She is also a composer. Lee wrote the music for the theme of the 1954 Joan Crawford film *Johnny Guitar*. Her hit songs include ''Golden Earrings,'' ''You Was Right, Baby,'' and ''It's a Good Day.''

Lind: Swedish Nightingale

When **Jenny Lind** (1820-1887) made her debut at age eighteen at the Stockholm Opera House, she sang in a voice modeled ''after no one's method. Only, as far as I am able, after that of the birds,'' she said. She became known as ''the Swedish Nightingale.''

At her peak, Lind earned $3 million in a year. She had joined forces with circus promoter P. T. Barnum for a concert tour of the United States. A shrewd businesswoman, she got one thousand dollars a performance, plus a share of the profits. Lind was as generous as she was practical. She gave ten thousand dollars in receipts from her first American concert to charity.

"Swedish Nightingale" Jenny Lind said she sang after no one's method—except that of the birds.

Coal miner's daughter Loretta Lynn today is a multi-millionaire who owns an entire town.

In 1852, she married her accompanist, Otto Goldschmidt, and formed her own company. As the troupe sailed down the Mississippi, they stopped at a town, announced a concert, sold tickets, and an hour after the performance, were on their way to the next stop.

Lind's admirers were legion, particularly for her performance of Amina in *La Sonnambula*. The House of Commons in London lacked a quorum on three occasions because its members were listening to her sing.

Lynn: From Rags to Riches

Loretta Lynn (1932-   ) has become the top country female performer in spite of her incredible, and endearing, naiveté. At thirteen, she was afraid to ride home with Mooney Lynn, her future husband, because "I'd never seen a car before."

The daughter of a coal miner, she grew up in a tar paper shack. The walls of the house were papered with pages from movie magazines. (Lynn was named after actress Loretta Young.)

Lynn married Mooney, over her parents' objections, at age fourteen, and the couple moved to Washington State. By the time she was eighteen, she had four children, and was taking in washing and picking strawberries to earn money.

Mooney once boasted that his wife could sing better than anyone except Kitty Wells, the reigning country music star. Members of a local country band heard the boast and hired her to sing with them on radio station KPUG in Bellingham, Washington. She was a hit.

Her first recorded song, "And Now I'm a Honky Tonk Girl," climbed to the top of the charts. In 1962, she got a fifteen dollars a week job at the Grand Ole Opry. A year later, she signed a lifetime recording contract that has made her a multimillionaire. Today, she owns song publishing companies, a chain of Western wear stores, a Nashville talent agency, a rodeo, and a town (Hurricane Mills, Tennessee).

Lynn's greatest hits are "Wine, Women and Song," "Blue Kentucky Girl," "Dear Uncle Sam," and "Don't Come Home a-Drinkin' with Lovin' on Your Mind."

Merman: Songwriter's Dream

"If you write for Merman," Irving Berlin once advised, "the lyrics better be good — because everyone's going to hear them." He called her "a songwriter's dream" because she sings songs exactly as written.

Ethel Merman (1909-   ), the brassy-voiced star of musical comedy, has chalked up more than six thousand performances in fourteen Broadway hits during her forty-seven-year show business career. She has appeared in ten films.

"I can never remember being afraid of an audience," she once said. "If the audience could do better, they'd be up here on stage and I'd be out there watching them."

Born Ethel Zimmerman, she was always confident of success. She worked as a secretary while singing in clubs and vaudeville — she can still type sixty words a minute.

Merman became a star with her 1930 Broadway debut in *Girl Crazy*. The song that did it, "I've Got Rhythm," was written by George Gershwin. "Don't ever let anyone give you a singing lesson," he told her. "It'll ruin you."

Her best known musicals are *Anything Goes, Gypsy, Call Me Madam,* and *Annie Get Your Gun.*

Bette Midler, "The Divine Miss M," climbed quickly from bathhouse to Broadway.

Midler: Truly Tacky

Bette Midler (1945-   ) prides herself on being "the last of the truly tacky women." She is different. Named after Bette Davis, she was one of the few Jews in Hawaii, where she grew up.

Her road to stardom began in a Hawaiian pineapple cannery. She landed a bit part in the 1965 film *Hawaii* and earned enough money to go to Los Angeles and then New York. After stints at typing and being a salesgirl, she got into the chorus of *Fiddler on the Roof.* Three years later, when she left the show, she was playing Tzeitel, one of the leads.

Midler's breakthrough into the big time was at the Continental Baths, a New York bathhouse whose toweled clientele was mostly homosexual. With the ingenious arrangements and accompaniment of her then musical director, Barry Manilow, she developed her camp singing style. Her music is mostly satirical nostalgia, such as "Boogie Woogie Bugle Boy" (à la the Andrews Sisters), "Leader of the Pack" (Shangri-las), and "Chapel of Love" (the Dixie Cups). That $50-a-night gig at the Continental Baths catapulted her into a sellout Philharmonic Hall concert in 1973 and a million-seller album, *The Divine Miss M.* She has had two one-woman Broadway shows.

Mitchell: Personal Poet

Joni Mitchell (1943-   ) has single-handedly, with her subtle melodies and art work, done more to beautify the record business than almost anyone else. She was born Roberta Joan Anderson and studied art in Canada at Calgary's Alberta College of Arts. Many of her paintings decorate her albums.

But folk singing soon took precedence. At nineteen, she married Chuck Mitchell, a cabaret performer. They toured together briefly before splitting up. Joni Mitchell went to New York, where she first succeeded as a songwriter.

Judy Collins' interpretation of Mitchell's "Clouds" in 1968 gave her career the boost it needed. That year Mitchell recorded her first album, *Songs to a Seagull.* Because her intensely personal, poetic lyrics can stand without music, the subtle melodies make each song greater than the sum of its parts. She describes songwriting as "going into a trance." The most important thing," she told *Time,* "is to write in your own blood. I bare intimate feelings because people feel."

Parton: Glitter Folk

Dolly Parton (1946-   ) knows perfectly well how she looks in her explosive blond wig, four-inch high heels, tight sequined

Dolly Parton, who grew up in a two-room mountain shack, sang on local radio from the time she was 11.

dresses, and fistfuls of diamonds. "Lots of women buy just as many wigs and makeup things as I do," she says. "They just don't wear them all at the same time."

Parton, country music's first woman to make it as both a singer and songwriter, is entitled to the fun she has dressing up. She was the fourth of twelve children raised in a two-room Tennessee shack.

Parton began writing songs at age five; her mother wrote them down for her. (Parton has been known to write as many as twenty songs a day.)

After high school graduation, Parton headed for Nashville, where, for one three-week stretch, she survived on hot dog relish and mustard. In 1967, country and western singer Porter Wagoner asked her to join his road show and later helped her land a lucrative recording contract with RCA. In 1974, she struck out on her own with a group called The Travelin' Family Band.

Parton's songs often deal with doom and the supernatural. According to *Newsweek*, she has produced "some of the most haunting and inventive lyrics in Nashville."

Tiny Parton — she's an even five feet tall — is married to asphalt-paving executive Carl Dean. They live with several of her brothers and sisters in a twenty-three-room Tennessee mountainside house.

Piaf: Little Sparrow

Edith Piaf (1915-1963) was to France what Billie Holiday was to the United States, a woman with a right to sing the blues.

Piaf was born Edith Gassion on a Paris sidewalk, daughter of a cabaret singer and a street acrobat. As a child she was blinded for three years by meningitis. She began singing on street corners for pennies. As an adolescent she had an affair with a legionnaire who left her. The child she had by him was stillborn.

Impresario Louis Leplée established her as a cabaret singer and nicknamed her Piaf, "little sparrow." A tiny woman who nearly disappeared in the black dress she always wore, Piaf became an international figure.

In 1947, she met her great love, world middleweight boxing champion Marcel Cerdan. His death in an air crash two years later was the beginning of a dizzying succession of troubles. The remainder of her life was punctuated by suicide attempts, alcohol, drugs, hepatic comas, jaundice, ulcers, four auto accidents, and seven operations.

In her last year, she married Theo Sarapo, a singer-hairdresser half her age.

Despite alcoholism, illness, and attempted suicides, Edith Piaf sang that she regretted nothing.

Singing was her safety valve. Her most popular song was "Non, je ne regrette rien" (I don't regret anything).

Previn: Very Fine Madness

The very fine madness of **Dory Previn** (1929-   ) has produced some very fine songs. They have documented her retreat from psychic paralysis, which peaked in 1969 when her husband, Andre Previn, left her for actress Mia Farrow. They chronicle her breakdowns and institutionalizations, the pills, and "screaming in my car in a twenty mile zone."

Previn got her start in show business as a chorus girl, summer stock actress, and model. She performed in nightclubs, writing new lyrics to current hits to distract audiences from her "vocal difficulties."

MGM producer Arthur Freed heard her and hired her to work on the film version of Jack Kerouac's *The Subterraneans*. One of the musicians featured in the film was Andre Previn.

After her marriage, Previn wrote television scripts and lyrics to movie themes, three of which were nominated for Academy Awards.

When the marriage broke up, a psychiatrist suggested she write free form verse. They became the songs of her album, *On My Way to Where,* which *Stereo Review* called one of the best albums of 1970. Her second album, *Mythical Kings and Iguanas,* was named one of the best albums of the decade by the *New York Times*.

Previn has exorcised most of her demons. She's able to travel now — once she was pulled screaming from a plane.

Price: The Perfect Aida

A benefactor saved **Leontyne Price** (1927-   ) from having to ". . . get me one of those slick dresses and sing in nightclubs." One of the first blacks to sing at the Metropolitan Opera, Price was born in Mississippi. The benefactor financed Price's training at New York's Juilliard School of Music.

She first attracted critical acclaim in 1952 when she starred on Broadway in *Porgy and Bess*. The *Washington Post* critic said, "Price will no doubt spend a long time in the role of Bess. But when she is available for other music, she will have a

dramatic career." Price toured the world in *Porgy* under State Department auspices from 1952 to 1954.

In 1955, she appeared in a series of television opera broadcasts, beginning with *Tosca*. In 1958, she sang *Aida* with the Vienna State Opera. She was hailed as "the perfect Aida, at last."

Price made her Met debut in 1961 as Leonora in *Il Trovatore*. She expressed surprise at receiving a rare forty-two-minute ovation. One critic called her performance "one of the great moments of opera in recent years."

The soprano has called her life "lonely," and once remarked, "Singing is the only important thing."

Reddy: "I Am Woman"

Helen Reddy (1942-   ) says she is not a feminist, but "a singer who has had my woman's consciousness raised." Nevertheless, her Grammy-winning song, "I Am Woman" became the anthem of the women's movement of 1972 and made Reddy a star.

Reddy is a straightforward person who readily admits that her husband, Jeff Wald, had a lot to do with her success and their millions.

The daughter of a popular Australian soap opera actress, Reddy, worked in vaudeville as a child. In 1966, she won a trip to New York in a "Bandstand International" contest. She also won an audition with Mercury Records that never materialized. When she was down to her last twelve dollars, some friends threw a party to raise money so she could stay in the States. Talent agent Wald crashed the party. He became her husband a few weeks later.

After a four-year push, during which the Walds moved to California, Reddy appeared on the "Tonight Show" in 1970. She was signed to a recording contract. Her first hit, "I Don't Know How to Love Him," was on the charts for twenty-two weeks.

Reddy was Flip Wilson's television summertime replacement in 1973. She made her film debut in *Airport 1975*.

When Reddy, now a naturalized American citizen, received her Grammy Award in 1973, she thanked her husband "because he makes my success possible."

She also thanked God "because She makes everything possible."

Ronstadt: Torchy Rock Queen

You certainly could say that **Linda Ronstadt** (1946-   ) has made it. She is the first female performer to have had four consecutive million-selling albums: *Heart Like a Wheel, Prisoner in Disguise, Hasten Down the Wind,* and *Linda Ronstadt, Greatest Hits.* In 1976, she won the Best Female Pop Vocalist Grammy Award. *Time* proclaimed her the queen of "torchy rock."

The theme of Buffy Sainte-Marie's songs has changed from anger to celebration.

Accepting her 1976 Grammy, Linda Ronstadt claimed it should have gone to friend Emmy Lou Harris.

Linda discovered radio at the age of five and decided to become a singer. When she went to school in her native Tuscon, Arizona, she "thought that it didn't make any difference if I learned to add, because I wouldn't have to when I was a singer."

At eighteen, she went to Los Angeles and formed the Stone Poneys with two other musicians. After three albums she became a solo, paying her dues on road tours. Her music has been especially influenced by the Eagles and Dolly Parton.

Sainte-Marie: Indian Folk Singer

When **Buffy Sainte-Marie** (1941-   ) was a child, she wanted to be a blonde so she would blend better with her Massachusetts classmates. Instead, the shy, dark little girl became an eloquent voice of her generation and her Indian people.

Sainte-Marie was born on a Cree Indian Reservation in Saskatchewan. Orphaned in childhood, she was adopted by a Massachusetts couple.

Her songs of social conscience made her a celebrity in the 1960s; her anti-war "Universal Soldier" was banned from the airwaves for two years. But her most famous piece is a melting love song called "Until It's Time for You to Go," which has been recorded by such singers as Glen Campbell and Roberta Flack.

Today, Sainte-Marie seems to have run out of bile. "Those angry songs just made people clap," she said in 1975, "nobody ever did anything about the Indians." Now her songs are about celebration, but she is still committed to her cause. She has started a scholarship fund to send Indians to law school, and she provides support to Indian handicraft, theater, and education projects through her North American Women's Association.

Schumann: Piano Prodigy

Clara Wieck Schumann (1819-1896) was a child prodigy; she gave her first concert at the age of nine. Her father taught piano and among his students was the young Robert Schumann, already one of Germany's foremost composers. Despite her father's objections, Clara and Robert were married in 1840.

She continued her musical career after marriage and also found time to give birth to and raise seven children. Her talent was such that her husband said she was the only pianist in Germany who did justice to his work.

But her success clouded their marriage. After one of her performances at court, Robert was asked, "Are you musical, too?" He drank heavily, lost his sanity, and died in 1856. Clara abandoned her own composing (she had written twenty-three works) to publicize her husband's work throughout Europe.

Shore: Loved by All

Everyone knows that mmmmmmWAH is **Dinah Shore** (1917-   ) throwing a kiss. She is one of those improbable people whom nobody seems to hate, a reputation she manages with charm and wit.

Shore was born in Nashville with the name Frances Rose Shore. At age two, she contracted polio, which crippled her right leg and foot. Her strength was restored by swimming, tennis, and massage.

At Vanderbilt University, Shore was president of her sorority and head of the women's government. She majored in sociology. After graduation, she went to New York and adopted her first name from the popular song "Dinah."

Shore (along with Frank Sinatra) was a singer on Martin Block's WNEW program. In 1939, she got her big break by getting a singing job with the Leo Reisman Orchestra.

In 1940, Shore was named "New Star of Radio" by a *World Telegram*-Scripps-Howard Poll. Her sentimental hits included "Yes, My Darling Daughter," "Blues in the Night," "Shoo Fly Pie," and "Anniversary Song."

Shore appeared in several uninspired films. "I bombed as a movie star," she once said. "I failed for a lot of reasons. The most important was that I'm not particularly photogenic." But the millions of people who watched the kissing-sweet

singer on her long-running television variety show didn't agree. In 1963, after twelve years with the show, she left television "to think a little." That was a year after her divorce from actor George Montgomery, to whom she had been married for nineteen years. In 1970, she became the host of a successful daytime television talk show.

Shore may be everyone's sugarplum, but she's nobody's Shirley McDimple. During her highly publicized romance with actor Burt Reynolds, she was asked to comment on a nude photograph of him in *Cosmopolitan*. "It doesn't do him justice," she said with a grin.

Sills: Bubbles

Beverly Sills (1929-   ) is a thoroughbred. She has one of the finest soprano voices of this century. She is the indomitable survivor of a cancer operation and mother of a retarded son and deaf daughter.

Little Belle Silverman's road to superstardom was as convoluted and unpredictable as the fun house at Coney Island. At three, "Bubbles" performed on a weekly radio show called "Uncle Bob's Rainbow Hour." By the time she was sev-

Beverly Sills is not just talented. She's also funny, intelligent, and palpably human.

en, she knew twenty-three arias. Belle also sang the Rinso White bird call, one of the first singing commercials.

Beverly Sills made her operatic debut at seventeen, singing *Carmen* with the Philadelphia Civic Opera. The coloratura soprano toured at an exhausting pace in operettas and operas.

She auditioned seven times before she was finally accepted by the New York City Opera (1955). In 1956, she received sublime notices for her creation of the title role of the American folk opera *The Ballad of Baby Doe*.

Sills married Peter Greenough in 1956 and retired for a time to help her daughter master such tasks as blowing out a candle. (That simple act takes weeks for deaf persons to learn.) Of her children's handicaps, she once said, "I felt if I could survive my grief, I could survive anything."

Simon: From a Famous Family

The poor little rich girl of rock music, **Carly Simon** (1945-   ), sprang from the Simon and Schuster publishing family.

Her first music teacher was folksinger Pete Seeger "in a little school in Greenwich Village, singing radical folk songs about roosters singing cock-a-doodle-doo," she recalled.

Simon attended Sarah Lawrence College, performing folk music with sister Lucy as, appropriately, the Simon Sisters.

The act broke up when Lucy married, and Carly decided to go it alone. She began working on her first album in 1966, but it was not released until 1971. Among her difficulties was her producer's feeling that the Simon wealth had deprived her of a singer's necessary quota of suffering.

When the album finally hit the stands, it demonstrated Simon's great versatility; it included hard rock, ballads, blues, country, folk, and jug band music.

Her first hit single, "That's The Way I Always Heard It Should Be," is the lament of a young woman questioning the traditional ideal of marital bliss. Her other hits include, "You're So Vain" and "Anticipation."

Simon married fellow rock singer James Taylor in 1972.

Slick: Colorful Extrovert

Grace Slick (1939-   ) is a refugee from the Haight-Ashbury mini-era of acid rock, marijuana gardens, and doing your own political thing.

Although she claims a middle class Chicago upbringing (she attended Finch College), there is little that is ordinary about her. After working as a fashion model and considering a movie career, she formed a group called the Great Society with her husband, Gerald Slick. When the group split up and the Jefferson Airplane needed a lead singer, Grace Slick took the mike. She wrote a number of the group's songs, including "White Rabbit."

Slick claims that her only material needs are a toilet and a bed, but she enjoys expensive champagne and fast cars. (She once paid cash for an Aston-Martin car.) She married Paul Kantner and had a daughter, called China. They have since split up.

Slick is an unexpectedly strict parent. "You've got to say no to kids," she says, "otherwise they'll turn into spoiled brats." She is also a closet John Denver fan. "But he looks like my five-year-old daughter. That's okay for her, but weird for a thirty-year-old man."

The singer's colorful personality livens up whatever stage or room she occupies. "I'll be seventy-five and hanging around bars yucking it up," she predicts. "I probably won't get picked up as much, but I'll be there."

Smith: Blues Queen

The blues songs of **Bessie Smith** (1894?-1937) are legendary. "Nobody Knows You When You're Down and Out" was only one of the songs that got her billing as the Queen of the Blues in the 1920s.

Smith began her career singing for coins on Chattanooga street corners. At thirteen, she was discovered in a minstrel show by Gertrude "Ma" Rainey, one of the first great blues singers.

Her rich, powerful, emotional vocal style were considered excessive by three recording companies. She also lost points when, during a test recording, she stopped the band and announced she had to spit.

It was that kind of earthiness that appealed to her fans. On stage, she was magnificent, graceful despite her six-foot, two-hundred-pound frame.

It is no accident when a great singer also turns out to be a first-rate actress. Smith proved that in her appearance singing the title song in the film *St. Louis Blues* (1939).

Smith hit hard times in mid-life. Her seven-year marriage to a former policeman (later her manager) broke up in 1930. Her drinking habit, begun in childhood, began to dominate her life. The Great Depression brought a decline in record sales. Radio, which was growing up, felt it could do without black performers.

Bessie died in an automobile crash in Mississippi. Her musical legacy is incalculable — Billie Holiday and Mahalia Jackson, among other singers, claim that Smith was the greatest influence on them.

Smith: Radio's First Lady

Everything about **Kate Smith** (1909-   ) is generous. She has the biggest, clearest voice that ever graced a radio program. During World War II, she sold more than

$600 million in war bonds, more than anyone else.

Smith is one of those rare popular singers who sing utterly straight. Her heartiness and laugh are as ample as her figure. "Being fat didn't worry me in the least," she once said. "It was the problem of making people realize its unimportance which floored me temporarily." She went to New York in 1926, hoping to become an actress. She got a role in the musical *Honeymoon Lane* and a series of Broadway shows. But Smith was seldom cast in a singing role — only in comic "fat girl" parts.

Her fortunes improved in 1930 when she was discovered by Columbia Records executive Ted Collins.

Smith made her radio debut in 1931 and became known as "the First Lady of Radio." Her radio trademarks were her cheery "Hello, everybody," and "Thanks for listenin'." Smith's theme song was

Grammys and Gold Records

It's all very well and good for critics to praise your albums, but let's face it, the true index of success is measured in awards and sales. The highest award in the recording industry is presented by the National Academy of Recording Arts and Sciences (NARAS). Beginning in 1958, the academy has awarded a Grammy, a gold Victrola statue, in several dozen categories.

Women have not fared well in the past twenty years. Of the eighteen Record of the Year awards, the top honor, handed out since 1958, only four have been won by female singers. Women *shared* the award with men four times. Astrud Gilberto shared it with Stan Getz in 1964, with her recording of "Girl from Ipanema." The women in the Fifth Dimension shared it with the men for "Up, Up and Away" in 1967, and again in 1969 for "Aquarius/Let the Sunshine In."

Carole King won it all by herself in 1971 with "It's Too Late." The next year, Roberta Flack won with "The First Time Ever I Saw Your Face" and in 1973 for "Killing Me Softly." Olivia Newton-John won in 1974 with "I Honestly Love You."

The Gold Record Awards, given for recordings that sell one million copies, reflect an even slower advance of women into top popularity—as measured by sales.

These awards, which the Recording Industry Association of America has been making since 1958, show some contrast, but not much, between how women did in 1969, for example, and in 1975.

In 1969, men won eighty-one Gold Records while women registered only four; combined forces won ten.

In 1975, the men garnered ninety-one, the women twenty-three; men and women together shared in ten. The women were still way behind, but not by so wide a margin.

Popular Favorite Songs by Women

On *Variety's* Golden 100 list of all-time popular songs, the words of four were written by Dorothy Fields, one of the top lyric writers in the legendary Tin Pan Alley. The songs were: "Exactly Like You"; "I Can't Give You Anything But Love, Baby"; "I'm in the Mood for Love"; and "On the Sunny Side of the Street."

Here are some other surprises:

SONG	COMPOSER
"Happy Birthday To You"	Mildred J. Hill
"Annie Laurie"	Lady John Scott
"America, the Beautiful"	Katharine Lee Bates (words only)
"Chopsticks"	Euphemia Allen
"I Love You Truly"	Carrie Jacobs Bond
"A Perfect Day"	
"Shine On, Harvest Moon"	Nora Bayes-Norworth
"Sweet Rosie O'Grady"	Maude Nugent
"Waltzing Matilda"	Marie Cowan
"In the Gloaming"	Annie Fortescue Harrison

According to the *Guinness Book of World Records,* "Happy Birthday to You" is one of the three most frequently sung songs of all times. On March 8, 1969, it became the first song sung in space when performed by the astronauts of Apollo IX for Christopher Kraft, director of space operations for NASA.

"When the Moon Comes over the Mountain."

Irving Berlin gave her exclusive rights to sing "God Bless America" over the airwaves in 1938.

"The Kate Smith Hour" ran on television from 1950 to 1956.

The Supremes: Motown Success Story

Ross, Diana (1944-   )
Ballard, Florence (1944-1976)
Wilson, Mary (1943-   )

The Supremes — **Diana Ross, Florence Ballard,** and **Mary Wilson** — grew up in a Detroit housing project, which featured "the three R's: rats, roaches, and rhythm and blues."

They began singing together at a local community center, billing themselves as the Primettes and earning fifteen dollars a week. Motown signed them in 1961 and groomed them to be the highly polished Supremes. For three years, they were taught how to sit, speak, shake hands, and climb onto a piano. In 1964, their song, "Where Did Our Love Go," rocketed to the top of the charts, and they had a record in the Top Ten each year for the next decade.

Television appearances and nightclub dates followed. By 1965, they were each

Singing was a ticket out of the Detroit ghetto for two of the three original Supremes.

making $250,000 a year, but stardom had its drawbacks. Motown worked them hard and chaperoned them strictly. "When the Supremes hit so fast," Ross says, "it got out of our hands. We became a piece of luggage, basically on automatic, always giving the same responses."

Ballard had a falling-out with Motown and left to become a single act. She died on welfare in 1975. She was replaced by Cindy Birdsong. Ross left in 1970 and was replaced by Jean Terrell. Ross starred in a 1971 television special, and made her film debut as Billie Holiday in *Lady Sings the Blues*. She received Academy Award nominations for *Lady* (1972) and for *Mahogony* (1975).

Wilson is still singing with the Supremes.

Trapp: The Sound of Music

The early life of **Maria Trapp** (1905-) is familiar to fans of *The Sound of Music*. She said of the popular musical, "It really happened that way."

She was born aboard a train as her mother hurried to the hospital. She was orphaned at age six, and became the ward of a left-leaning anti-Catholic.

As if to make amends, she converted to Catholicism at eighteen and decided to become a nun. Because of her independent, tomboyish nature and lack of formal religious training, she became the black sheep of the convent.

Nine months before she was to take her vows, she was assigned to work as governess for the family of Baron Georg von Trapp, a World War I hero. She was torn when the widowed baron proposed marriage but wed him with her mother superior's blessing in 1927.

The family lost its wealth in the worldwide depression of the 1930s: their home was turned into a hostel for traveling students and clergy.

One of their guests, Rev. Franz Wasner, heard the family singing together and appointed himself their manager. At the urging of Wasner and singer Lotte Lehmann, they entered the 1936 Salzberg Festival, where they won top honors.

They fled Austria after the 1938 Nazi takeover. An American concert tour ended abruptly when a promoter discovered Maria was pregnant with her third child. But with the help of friends, they

Maria Trapp donated most of her proceeds from *The Sound of Music* to foreign missionary work.

made a successful appearance at New York City's Town Hall.

The baron died in 1947, the same year the remaining family members became American citizens. The chorus broke up in 1955, and Maria devoted her time to her memoirs and missionary work.

Tucker: Red Hot Mama

Sophie Tucker (1884-1966), the "Last of the Red Hot Mamas," was born "on the road" in Russia. Her mother was on her way to join Tucker's father in America where he had fled to avoid military service.

Although her family name was Kalish, Tucker grew up as Sophie Abuza. Her father, fearful of being apprehended by Soviet authorities, had taken the identity of a deceased Italian friend.

Her father owned a restaurant in Hartford, Connecticut where Sophie occasionally sang. But she was forbidden to enter show business. On the pretext of taking a vacation, Tucker set off for New York in 1906 to become a singer.

Tucker sang for her suppers. She won a part in an amateur show and was required to wear blackface because the theater

Sophie Tucker, "Last of the Red Hot Mamas," was the first woman president of the actors' union.

manager thought her "too big and ugly."

She sang between the acts in a Ziegfeld Follies production, but was fired because the stars resented her eager reception. So she joined the Morris vaudeville circuit.

Tucker's nickname stemmed from her choice of *double entendre* hot numbers. They dealt with sex, she said, not vice.

During World War I she popularized the song "Mother (The Word that Means the World to Me)." She toured Europe where crowds raved over her "My Yiddesha Mama." Not so Hitler, who had her hit recordings of the song destroyed.

Tucker's films were not successful because they did not capture the essential Sophie. But when she sang "Some of These Days," she was in her prime.

Vaughan: The Divine One

In 1959, at Chicago's Blue Note, **Sarah Vaughan** (1924-   ) sang a set that made her fans, who call her "the Divine One," melt. At the end of the set she said to her spellbound audience, "You'll have to excuse me. I'm not in very good voice because of a terrible cold." She wasn't fishing for more applause; she was simply being characteristically dignified.

But Vaughan, who was born in Newark, New Jersey, can be very intimate indeed with a song. As jazz critic Leonard Feather once wrote, "Miss Vaughan . . . brought to jazz an unprecedented combination of attractive characteristics; a rich,

beautifully controlled tone and vibrato; an ear for the chord structure of songs . . . and a coy, sometimes archly naive quality alternating with a sense of great sophistication."

Vaughan got her start by winning a talent contest at Harlem's Apollo Theater in 1942. She was vocalist with the bands of Earl Hines and Billy Eckstine. She had her first runaway hit, "It's Magic," in 1950.

Wynette: Country's Total Woman

Tammy Wynette (1942-   ) is the Total Woman of country and western music. Her recording of "Stand By Your Man" is the biggest selling single by a woman in the history of country and western music. Wynette believes the song's success is due to its anti-feminist stance. "It sold a million," she explains, "so I guess the men bought it because they hoped their women would feel that way. And the women must have felt that way, too, because women buy most of the records."

Tammy born Wynette Pugh in Missis-

Tammy Wynette, who tells listeners to "Stand By Your Man," is three times "D-I-V-O-R-C-E"d.

sippi, was a cotton picker and beautician. As a twice-divorced mother (she has four daughters), she went to Nashville to crack the country market with her singing and songs. After she received numerous rejections by recording companies, producer Bill Sherrill decided to work with her. The professional chemistry worked. Her first hit, "Your Good Girl's Gonna Go Bad," was followed by fifteen consecutive chart-topping singles.

Wynette's songs are frequently laments of long-suffering housewives, such as "D-I-V-O-R-C-E" and "Don't Liberate Me."

THE DANCERS

Baker: The Toast of Paris
Josephine Baker (1906-1975) ranks with Benjamin Franklin as one of the United States' most elegant exports to France. In her salad days, she was the toast of Paris' *haute monde*. Her costume consisted of only a well-placed feather or decorous bunch of bananas. She used to tell her many male admirers, "Don't give me a diamond bracelet — I have a couple of dozen."

She had come a long way from St. Louis, her hometown. She had to drop out of school at the age of eight to help support her family by working as a domestic. As a teenager, she danced in vaudeville houses and was in the chorus line on Broadway in *Shuffle Along* (1923). In 1925, she introduced Le Jazz Hot to Paris in La Revue Nègre and became the headliner at the Folies Bergère. Her own club, Chez Josephine, opened in 1926.

Baker had style. She decorated her face with spit curls and blood red lipstick, and adorned her fabulous body with plumes and pearls. When she strolled the Champs-Elysées, she was often accompanied by leashed leopards.

During World War II, Baker worked for the French underground and subsequently received the Croix de Guerre.

Baker was married four times, first at age fourteen to an American, later to an Italian count, a French aviator, and a French-Jewish bandleader. Her adopted children were an international dozen whom she called her "rainbow tribe."

Josephine Baker, the toast of Paris, received love letters and marriage proposals by the thousands.

Castle: One-Step to Success
Dancing to the strains of "Too Much Mustard" in a Paris café, **Irene Castle** (1894-1969) and her husband Vernon became the toasts of two continents in 1911.

Couples everywhere were soon copying the dances of the former English actor and the New Rochelle doctor's daughter. "We made dancing look like the fun it was," Irene once said.

They earned thirty-one thousand dollars a week in 1914, operating a chain of ballrooms that offered instruction in such Castle steps as the Maxixe, the One-Step, and the quiet, dignified Castle Walk.

Admirers imitated the Castles' style as well as their dances. When Irene bobbed her hair, one million American women did the same.

They starred in silent films, sponsored a massive Madison Square Garden dance tournament, and danced the Castle Walk down the aisle at Chicago's first "tango wedding."

The fun came to an end in 1918, when Vernon, a Royal Flying Corps officer, was killed in a Ft. Worth, Texas, crash while training U.S. aviators for World War I.

Irene remained a popular figure, appearing in additional films and in vaudeville during the 1920s. An "Irene Castle Day" was declared at the 1939 New York World's Fair, and she created the "New York World's Fair Hop" to celebrate the occasion.

Charisse: Long-Legged Beauty

If there were a category in the Guinness Book of Records for the world's longest, loveliest legs, the winner might be **Cyd Charisse** (1923-   ). Born Tula Ellice Finkela, she took the name Cyd from her baby brother's efforts to say "sister." She got her last name from her ballet teacher, Nico Charisse, to whom she was married from 1939 to 1947.

Charisse began dancing to counteract the effects of a childhood bout with polio. She later danced with the Ballet Russe and, at the outbreak of World War II, began her Hollywood film career. Her first starring role, opposite Gene Kelly, was "Singing in the Rain" in 1952.

Charisse married singer Tony Martin in 1948, and they are currently appearing in a nightclub act. She still attends daily ninety-minute dance classes.

Fred Astaire considers Charisse to be the best dancing partner of his career.

De Mille: Choreography Is Hell

Agnes De Mille (1905-   ) found her childhood a mixed blessing. Her father and grandfather were playwrights and her uncle was film producer Cecil B. De Mille. She has described herself as "a spoiled, wealthy girl who learned with difficulty to become a worker."

In her career as a dancer and choreographer, De Mille has worked as hard as anyone. A film of Anna Pavlova inspired her to dance, but her family thought that dancing lacked respectability. She was finally permitted to study at the age of fourteen when her sister was given dancing lessons to correct fallen arches. Not only was she rather old to begin, but she lacked the tall, slender body of a dancer.

After years of grueling study she gained prominence as a choreographer, not a dancer. The Ballet Russe de Monte Carlo produced her *Rodeo,* with De Mille dancing the lead. Her other choreography credits include the hit musicals *Oklahoma, Carousel, Brigadoon,* and *Gentlemen Prefer Blondes.* She also choreogaphed the ballet *Fall River Legend,* based on the story of accused ax murderer Lizzie Borden.

Of her craft, De Mille has said, "This whole business of choreography is hell, sheer torture."

Duncan: Dancing Rebel

Isadora Duncan (1878-1927) was to dance what Sarah Bernhardt was to theater. She created and received more shocks in her life than the San Andreas Fault, and made a legend out of her gargantuan appetites and illusions.

At seventeen, Duncan appeared in a New York production of *A Midsummer Night's Dream* but was fired. She moved to Europe, where she developed her theories of dance, causing a stir by discarding traditional costumes and dancing barefoot in a toga. Her disjointed choreography involved frieze-like poses con-

Isadora Duncan attributed her hedonism to her mother's champagne and oyster diet before her birth.

nected by little steps with her head flung back and her arms trailing.

Duncan's track record professionally and personally was spasmodic. At her first Paris concert, the impresario absconded with the funds, the unpaid musicians close behind. Loie Fuller took her on a European tour, but Duncan ran off with a handsome Hungarian actor. In 1904, she opened a dance school in Berlin that folded within a year. She was well received in pre-revolutionary Russia, where she danced with Nijinsky and influenced the style of choreographer Michel Fokine.

Duncan's first child was by set designer Gordon Craig in 1906. Four years later, she had a son by Eugene Singer, millionaire son of the sewing machine's inventor. They lived opulently but parted when Singer found her making love to another man. In years to come, he often helped her out of financial crunches. Duncan's energy, spirit and imagination were shattered with the deaths of her children, who drowned when an automobile in which they were sitting slid into the Seine.

In 1921, she returned to the Soviet Union, where she married poet Sergei Esenin, fifteen years her junior. Touring the United States later, she was criticized for her feminist and Bolshevik views, and was banned in Boston for baring a breast. The marriage to Esenin was a disaster. Duncan left him, and he committed suicide a year later, slashing his wrist and writing her name in blood.

In middle age, Duncan became an alcoholic. Deserted by friends and family, she earned the critics' derision by her undisciplined performances. She died when a long scarf she was wearing caught in the wheel of a car, breaking her neck. More than ten thousand people attended her funeral.

Dunham: Black Culture Pioneer

Katherine Dunham (1912-   ), a pioneer in bringing black culture to the American stage, knows her craft inside out.

Dunham studied anthropology at the University of Chicago (where she is a member of the Women's Honorary Scientific Fraternity). On a graduate fellowship, she spent two years in the West Indies studying tribal dances. Living among the natives, she slept in a hut, rode a mule, ate spicy stews, and learned the secret dances of the independent and hostile Maroons of Jamaica.

Dunham dropped anthropology in 1939 to devote all her time to dance. Her dance companies — the Tropical Revue and, later, the Katherine Dunham Dance Company — performed exotic dances of both urban and tribal blacks. She also appeared in several musical comedies and in the film *Star Spangled Rhythm*. In 1945, she opened the Katherine Dunham School of Cultural Arts.

Her company toured the nation in the days when segregation was still common. Dunham once told an audience that had just given her a standing ovation, "I shall not appear here again until people like me can sit with people like you."

When the Twist became a dance craze in the 1960s, Dunham said, "We've been doing it for years. Only we called it the Florida Swamp Shimmy."

Farrell: Prima Ballerina

"Mostly I dance in order to be happy," says **Suzanne Farrell** (1943-   ). That satisfies people on both sides of the New York City Ballet's stage. Farrell, a prima ballerina and protogée of George Balanchine, has been a featured dancer with the company since 1962.

Born Roberta Sue Ficker, Farrell got a lot of support from her mother. When an opportunity arose for an audition with the New York City Ballet, Mrs. Ficker moved with her two daughters from Cincinnati to a New York hotel. There was sleeping space only for two; so Mrs. Ficker became a night nurse in order to be able to sleep while her daughters were at classes.

Farrell's magic as a dancer goes beyond technique; she is a superb actress. When developing her role in *A Midsummer Night's Dream,* she bought a cat so she could learn to talk to animals. (The role required her to pantomime a conversation with a donkey.) But she drew the line on research with a romantic role in *Meditation.* "I know nothing about love," she said, "but I was darned if I would go out and get a lover just so I could find out." All the same, she was a sensation as Don Quixote's dream woman, Dulcinea, in a full-length role created for her by Balanchine in 1965.

Farrell married a company soloist, Paul Mejia, in 1969; the two left Balanchine that year, ostensibly because of rivalry between the two men. Farrell rejoined the New York City Ballet in 1974.

Fonteyn: A Living Legend

The career of **Margot Fonteyn** (1919-   ) spans nearly half a century, and critics still apply such superlatives as "lyric" to her dancing.

She was born Margaret Hookham ("Who could dance with a name like Hookham?" she once said.), daughter of a British engineer and a Brazilian coffee heiress.

Fonteyn made her professional debut at fourteen with the Vic Wells Ballet (later called the Royal Ballet). At sixteen, she replaced retiring prima ballerina Alicia Markova in *Les Rendezvous*. One critic wrote that she displayed "some of that intoxicating quality always associated with great dancers."

When she was 17, she met Roberto Arias, a Panamanian student at Cambridge. They were married fourteen years later. In 1964, Arias was permanently paralyzed by a shot fired during Panama's presidential campaign. She is credited with saving Arias' life and restoring his will to live. She was jailed briefly in 1959 for her participation in a Panamanian coup attempt.

The ageless Margot Fonteyn was the first ballerina named Dame Commander of the British Empire.

Fonteyn was the first ballerina to be named dame commander of the British Empire, the equivalent of knighthood.

Fonteyn is probably most famous for her dance partnership with Rudolph Nureyev, of whom she said, "Nureyev brought me a second career like an Indian summer."

Gregory: Goddess of Dance

Rudolph Nureyev called her "America's prima ballerina assoluta." *Dance Magazine* says she is "a neo-classical goddess of the dance." So when the American Ballet Theater's **Cynthia Gregory** (1946-   ) decided to retire in 1976 "for personal reasons," shortly after her greatest success in Nureyev's *Raymonda,* the dance world was stunned.

People speculated that the real reason was her crumbling marriage, or her rigid dance schedule, or her being upstaged by foreign imports such as Michel Baryshnikov and Natalia Makarova, or the absence of a "perfect partner." Gregory claimed that she needed some time for growing up. In any case, when she returned less than a year later, she scored a triumph and made headlines.

Gregory's dancing career has overcome numerous difficulties. She had to audition three times to get into the American Ballet Theatre. Her height (*en point,* she is 6' 1") makes it difficult to find partners.

Cool and self-assured on stage, the private Gregory has been described as shy, uncertain, and self-critical. "I suppose that a dancer with a face like mine, my height, my technique, seems aloof," she once said. "I wish my fans knew how vulnerable I am."

Graham: Modern Dance Pioneer

More than any other dancer or choreographer, **Martha Graham** (1894-   ) has had a profound influence on modern dance. Graham's volatility was noted by dancer Ruth St. Denis, who said of her, "She danced like a young tornado."

Graham began her professional career at the Denishawn school and later became featured dancer in the Greenwich Village Follies. In 1924, she was a founder of the dance department at Rochester's Eastman School of Music. She made her debut as a choreographer in 1926. *Revolt,* which she staged the following year, was an avant

Modern dance pioneer Martha Graham wants audiences to feel "intensely alive."

the richest woman in the world," says *New York Times* critic Clive Barnes, "but sure as hell she is the richest woman who has ever taken an interest in ballet." Harkness' interest in ballet (and in music) began early in her life. She danced in *Aida* in her St. Louis debut and studied musical composition with Nadia Boulanger.

Ten years after her husband's death in 1954, she harnessed her fortune, and her total dedication, to form the Harkness Ballet. Her mission is to create a uniquely American style of ballet that combines adagio, jazz, and Spanish, Hindu, and ethnic forms with traditional ballet. The composer of *Music With a Heartbeat* (1957), she frequently writes scores for her dancers.

Harkness, who gets up at daybreak to take dance lessons and practice yoga, has little time or patience for the perquisites of wealth. Moreover, "I don't really like rich people," she says. "They're bored . . . and boring."

garde dance of social protest, the first to appear on the American stage. Critics called it ugly, stark, and obscure.

Graham has had to fight adjectives like that all her life. Her dancers' movements are angular and taut, they defy the normal limits of the human body. Graham's dancers have the toughest training in dance, and the results show. "I want to make people feel intensely alive," she says. "I'd rather have them against me than indifferent."

Believing we need to hear "ancestral footsteps," Graham uses themes from history, mythology, and the Bible. *Night Journey* (1947) is based on the Greek dramatic character Jocasta, who discovers she has married her son, Oedipus. *Cave of the Heart* (1946) deals with the Medea legend and woman's tendency to destroy herself and her loved ones.

Graham stopped dancing in 1969 to concentrate on choreography and directing her dance company and school.

Harkness: Dancing Debutante

Rebekah Harkness (1915-   ) is a serious artist who refuses to be thought of as a privileged debutante. The heiress to a Standard Oil fortune ". . . is certainly not

Jamison: Blazing Beauty

Judith Jamison (1944-   ) took up dancing to give her lanky body poise and improve her stage presence as a singer, which is what the daughter of a sheet metal worker wanted to be. Thanks to her change of heart, and to Agnes De Mille, she became the dancer of whom *Newsweek* critic Hubert Saal wrote, "In motion, she blazes with a fearful intensity, hurtling through the air like a spear plunged into the heart of space."

Black, beautiful, and tall (5' 10''), Jamison took a master dance class with De Mille in Philadelphia. De Mille asked her to audition for her new ballet, *The Four Marys* and gave her the part. While waiting for more dance jobs, she operated the log flume ride at the 1964 New York World's Fair.

Jamison auditioned for the Harry Belafonte Show in 1965. She didn't make it, but she impressed onlooker Alvin Ailey, who hired her for his predominantly black modern dance troupe. She has become its premiere dancer. Ailey created the long solo, "Cry," a montage of black womanhood, for her in 1971.

Dance Magazine gave her its annual merit award of the year in 1972. The same year, she was named adviser to the National Council on the Arts by President Richard Nixon.

Keeler: Classic Tapper

At a testimonial to her former director-choreographer Busby Berkeley, **Ruby Keeler** (1909-   ) said, "I couldn't act. I had that terrible singing voice. And now I can see I wasn't the greatest tap dancer in the world either." If not she faked it very, very well in her first film appearance, *Forty-Second Street,* a classic tap dance film.

When Keeler started dancing, the only place she could get work was in speakeasies. She was then thirteen. Florenz Ziegfeld spotted her in a chorus line and gave her the lead in a touring company bound for Broadway. She got married instead — to Al Jolson — and moved to Hollywood.

Keeler was frequently paired in films with Dick Powell, and she starred in *Gold Diggers of 1933* and *Flirtation Walk.* She divorced Jolson in 1940. In 1941, she made her last film, *Sweetheart of the Campus.*

She retired when she remarried, but returned to the stage after her husband's death to star in the successful Broadway revival of Berkeley's *No, No, Nanette.*

LeClerq: Ballet Great

Until her career was ended by polio in 1956, **Tanaquil LeClerq** (1929-   ) was considered one of the world's great prima ballerinas.

LeClerq was born in Paris of American parents. She was raised in New York City, where she began studying ballet at seven with Michael Mordkin, then the most distinguished teacher in America. At twelve, she dropped out of school, studying with private tutors so she could devote all her time to dance.

LeClerq won a scholarship to the School of American Ballet, run by George Balanchine and Lincoln Kirstein, in 1940. When they formed their Ballet Society in 1946 (it became the New York City Ballet in 1948), she was the prima ballerina. She married Balanchine in 1952; they were divorced in 1969.

Said to have had the longest legs on the dance stage, LeClerq has not lost the spirit that made her a superlative dancer. Today, she is a brilliant teacher and coach.

Gypsy Rose Lee 'took it off'' for a variety of causes, including War Bonds and the Red Cross.

Lee: Chic Peeler

Gypsy Rose Lee (1914-1970) was a thinking man's stripper, a chic peeler, a lively writer, and woman of wit and charm.

The facts of her life were chronicled in her autobiography *Gypsy,* and in the play and film based on the book. She was born Rose Louise Hovick and co-starred with her sister, actress June Havoc, in a children's act. Lee was the fat one with the uneven teeth. At fifteen, Lee learned the art of striptease from "Tessie the Tassel Twirler," and became a featured performer at Minsky's in New York City and assorted other burlesque houses.

Writer Damon Runyan became a friend and introduced her to his bookish crowd. H. L. Mencken coined a word for her profession to give it middle-American respectability: "Ecdysiast" (from the Greek word meaning "getting out" and the zoological term for "molting"). Lee "took it off" for a number of causes, among them the Newspaper Guild, the Spanish Loyalists, War Bonds, and the Red Cross. She later appeared on the legitimate stage and in films.

Lee began writing when Walter Winchell asked her to do a guest column. She wrote several mysteries. In later life, she hosted a television talk show on which she said, "I've got everything I always had. Only it's six inches lower."

Makarova: Russian Prima Ballerina
The last day of the Kirov Ballet's 1970 London season, **Natalia Makarova** (1941-   ) slipped out to do a little shopping. She never went back. That evening, the British Home Office announced that she had been granted asylum.

Makarova, a spirited and occasionally temperamental star, left her mother and two ex-husbands in Russia. She had joined the Kirov when Rudolph Nureyev was with it, and she had made an early debut as prima ballerina to counteract the publicity created by his defection.

Of her own defection, Makarova has said, "I wanted to be free, free to dance as I please, free to develop my art." She has since appeared with the world's leading ballet companies, including the Royal Ballet and the American Ballet Theater (ABT). At her New York ABT debut, she fell during a curtain call. Said *Time,* "It was like a man who had scaled Mt. Everest slipping in his shower."

Montez: Dancing Toy
Lola Montez (1818-1861) was born Marie Delores Eliza Rosanna Gilbert in Ireland. When her early marriage to a British Army officer ended in divorce, she took the name Lola Montez, invented a line of Spanish ancestors, and became a dancer. The critics called her performance "suggestive, lewd and immoral," adjectives

Lola Montez is thought to be the first woman photographed smoking a cigarette.

she encouraged throughout her career.

Montez was not well received in London, but Paris, Berlin, and Warsaw audiences loved her. So did composer Franz Liszt, who took her to Paris, where she became a favorite of the avant-garde set surrounding writer George Sand.

In Munich, she gave a command performance for King Ludwig of Bavaria. She became his mistress, and he gave her a castle and the title of countess. She was blamed for the collapse of his regime in 1848, when crowds marched in the streets shouting "down with the whore." Ludwig abdicated and Montez fled. She also later fled from England following her marriage to a man whose aunt accused her of bigamy. (Montez was acquitted when her first husband's death was revealed.)

Montez's third marriage was to Patrick Purdy Hall, co-owner of a San Francisco newspaper, whom she met during a U.S. tour. He became her manager and best press agent, running stories about her sordid past. She divorced Hall and settled in northern California. Later she toured the United States and England giving religious lectures as a professed redeemed sinner. While in New York, she became ill; an alleged former school chum offered to take Montez home. After deeding all her possessions to the woman, Montez was moved to a tenement in Hell's Kitchen, where she died.

Pavlova: The Dying Swan
Anna Pavlova (1881-1931) is probably the most famous name in the history of ballet.

Pavlova decided to become a ballerina at the age of eight after seeing a performance of *Sleeping Beauty*. At ten, she was one of seven or eight children out of one hundred applicants to be admitted to the Russian Imperial Ballet School. She joined the Imperial Ballet at seventeen and by twenty-four was prima ballerina.

Pavlova left the company to perform with Vaslav Nijinsky in the Ballet Russe of Sergei Diaghilev. In 1909, she formed her own company and toured the Americas, the Orient, India, Egypt, and South Africa. During her career she logged more than 350,000 miles touring the world.

She was a tireless performer and as demanding of her troupe as herself. Her

Anna Pavlova demonstrated her sensitivity and delicacy of movement as "The Swan."

dancers were often forced to practice until their toes bled. During a performance in Havana, Pavlova fainted three times offstage, although her dancing was so good that the audience was unaware of her difficulty.

Pavlova had only one choreographic work to her credit, *Autumn Leaves* (1918). She was not an innovative dancer, nor did she possess flawless technique. But she did have sensitivity and delicacy of movement, epitomized in *The Dying Swan*, her most famous role.

In 1920, she founded a home in Paris for refugees from the Russian Revolution. She died from pneumonia contracted while helping the injured in a British trainwreck. (She was among the passengers.)

Powell: Top Tap Dancer

Eleanor Powell (1912-   ) was crowned the world's greatest female tap dancer by the Dancing Masters of America in the same year she starred in the film *Broadway Melody of 1937*.

Powell was carefully groomed for her movie career. At thirteen, she had been discovered on an Atlantic City beach. She appeared on Broadway for several years and was then signed to a film contract by MGM. Voice teachers, orthodontists, and other beautifiers prepared her for film debut. At her peak she earned $125,000 per film and cut several records tapping out dance routines to musical accompaniment.

In 1943, she married actor Glen Ford

and retired when she became pregnant. "I'm an old fashioned mother," she said. "I didn't consider that I had a choice." Her son, Peter, encouraged her to end her retirement. In 1961, she put together a successful nightclub act. She later became an associate preacher of a religious faith that advocated "love a-go-go."

Rand: Feathers and Fans

Chicago's 1933-34 Century of Progress exposition was a lively place. It featured America's original muscle dancer, Fahreda "Little Egypt" Mahzar, as Queen of the Midway.

And it marked the debut of a new dancing phenomenon in the person of **Sally Rand** (1904-   ).

Rand was born Helen Beck in the Ozarks. She took her surname from a handy Rand-McNally Atlas.

She left home at thirteen to become a cigarette girl in a Kansas City club, and later won bit parts in movies and vaudeville shows. Stranded in depression-era Chicago when the play in which she was performing folded, she mysteriously splurged a week's salary on a white horse and trailer.

The mystery was solved on the exposition's opening night, when Rand appeared, masquerading as Lady Godiva. Her picture made every newspaper in town. She quickly received a job at the exposition's Streets of Paris concession.

Wearing only ostrich feathers, Rand performed her sensuously slow fan dance to Debussy's *Clair de Lune*. Her act alone pulled in enough money to guarantee the entire fair's financial success.

Rand continued to present the same act at fairs and carnivals for more than thirty years, maintaining her 36-24-37 figure into senior citizenry. She came out of semi-retirement in 1965 to host the hit Broadway revue *This Was Burlesque*.

Rogers: Dancing Actress

Ginger Rogers (1911-   ), with Fred Astaire, was part of the most famous dance team in history.

Rogers was born Virginia Katherine McMath. Her parents were divorced shortly after her birth. In a gruesome custody battle, Rogers was twice kidnapped by her father, but the courts settled the dispute by awarding custody to her

The Rockettes

The statistics about the world's most famous kick line are boggling: In more than seventy-one thousand performances, more than 60 million people have seen their precision dances.

The troupe was the brainstorm of Russell Markert in 1925. They were then called the "Missouri Rockets," numbered sixteen, and first performed at St. Louis' Missouri Theater. When Radio City Music Hall opened in New York in 1932, the company became a fixture and got its current name. The original Rockettes worked sixteen hours a day, seven days a week.

Today, the thirty-nine dancers (only thirty perform at a time) get every fourth week off. They are about 2½ inches taller than the original group, ranging in height from 5'5½" to 5'8½". On stage, they appear to be the same height because the shorter women are put at the ends of the line, the tallest women in the middle. Other requirements are that they be pretty, have good legs and dance training, and be white. (For uniformity, it's said, no blacks are hired and no Rockette can have a suntan.)

The Rockettes stay with the company for an average of 4½ years. Some leave for Broadway, but most have no higher theatrical ambitions. Once a dancer leaves, she is not re-hired. "I'm not running a transient hotel," Markert once said.

mother, who was a reporter for the *Ft. Worth Record* and business manager for the Ft. Worth Symphony. Although she had hoped her child would be a painter, she quit both jobs to become her daughter's manager after Rogers won the Texas State Charleston Contest in 1925.

After four years in clubs and vaudeville, Rogers made it to Broadway. Her first film role was in *Young Man in Manhattan*. At twenty-two, she landed her first major role, opposite Fred Astaire, in *Flying Down to Rio* (1933). The gossip mill had it that the two dancers bickered, but apparently that wasn't so. Astaire choreographed their routines and Rogers worked hard to dance as well as her partner. *Top Hat* (1955) is considered their best film. In 1945, she was the highest paid performer in Hollywood and had the eighth highest individual income in the United States with a salary of $292,159.

Astaire eventually danced with younger leading ladies and Rogers appeared in more dramatic roles. She has made over seventy films, and in 1940 won the Best Actress Academy Award for *Kitty Foyle*.

Rogers has had a series of marriages and retirements. She starred in the Broadway musical *Hello Dolly* in 1965.

Tallchief: Firebird

When **Maria Tallchief** (1925-   ) divorced George Balanchine, she said the reason was that she wanted children and he did not. "Anyone can have children," he allegedly told her, "few can dance."

Few could dance as brilliantly as Tallchief, the daughter of a full-blooded Osage and his Scotch-Irish wife. She was born on an Oklahoma Indian reservation, and when oil was discovered on her father's land, her family was able to give her costly piano and dance lessons.

Tallchief joined the Ballet Russe de Monte Carlo in 1942, shortly after her high school graduation. In 1946, she married choreographer Balanchine and with him formed the New York City Ballet. She considered him the major influence on her career. Tallchief's most famous role was in the Stravinsky-Diaghilev-Balanchine *Firebird,* and, so far, hers is the definitive interpretation.

She retired from performing in 1967 to teach.

Tharp: Versatile Choreographer

That **Twyla Tharp** (1941-) is unorthodox can be seen in the facets of her life. She was named after a hog-calling princess named Twila. An art major in college, Tharp has studied piano, violin, viola, and drums. She is also one of America's most versatile and prolific choreographers.

A latecomer to dance, she debuted with the Paul Taylor Dance Company in 1965, and in the same year, in 1965, formed her own troupe. She uses pop and jazz music to underscore her choreography, which is a blend of ballet and modern dance. *Tank Dive,* her first work, was performed to Petulia Clark's recording of "Downtown."

In 1975, she achieved widespread notice with *Deuce Coupe,* presented by the Joffrey Ballet. (It used the music of the Beach Boys.) In it, a ballerina performs classical steps while other dancers frug, jerk, and bugaloo. In 1976, she put on ice skates (she was a novice) to choreograph a dance for Olympic gold medalist John Curry.

Tharp ascribes her versatility to boredom. "You can keep on chewing gum for ten hours, but after about a minute and a half you've got all the good out of it," Tharp once said.

FUNNY LADIES

Allen: No Dummy

For more than thirty years, the funniest thing about George Burns was his wife, **Gracie Allen** (1905-1964). That lady could make a door funny. "The trick is to do what Gracie Allen did — " Carol Channing once observed, "make implausible things plausible." Like her given name — Grace Ethel Cecile Rosalie Allen. "I'm not sure of the order," Allen said, "but together they should spell 'Grace.'" Like searching for an imaginary lost brother, which Allen did as a publicity stunt that was so successful that her real brother had to go into hiding.

Allen was a vaudeville trooper from the age of three but later opted for a secretarial career. At age seventeen, she met an aspiring comedian, George Burns, and they formed a team. Allen's wonderfully ludicrous questions soon reduced Burns to straight man. He married her three years after the act began.

The Burns-Allen combination was enormously popular, and for years was a radio hit. Allen ran for president in 1940 against Franklin Roosevelt (Democrat) and Wendell Wilkie (Republican), as a candidate "for the same old party, George Burns." In the 1950s they did a television series, ending with Allen's retirement in 1958. It is still on television in reruns.

Brice: Made 'em Laugh

Fanny Brice (née Borach) (1891-1951) could make 'em laugh or make 'em cry — either way, it didn't hurt. "You have to have a softness about you," she once said, "because if you do comedy and you are harsh, there is something offensive about it."

When Brice worked as a package wrapper in a department store, she made up a story about a blind father and her starving family, reducing her co-workers to sobbing hulks. "I had them all crying," she said, "and I loved it."

She loved performing from childhood on, and began by appearing with neighborhood newsboys in backyards and poolrooms. She dropped out of school at age thirteen when she won an amateur contest singing "When You Know You're Not Forgotten by the Girl You Can't Forget."

Her first theatrical credit was a personal flop. George M. Cohan hired her for the chorus line of his *Talk of New York* and fired her because she couldn't dance. In *A*

Fanny Brice with a real pet monkey — not Baby Snooks' decorated baby brother — in 1921.

Royal Slave, she played an alligator. Her big break came when Florenz Ziegfeld heard her sing Irving Berlin's song "Sadie Salome" with a Yiddish accent. He signed her for the Ziegfeld Follies of 1910.

Brice made 'em laugh along with W. C. Fields, Eddie Cantor, and Will Rogers for over ten years. She made 'em cry with a ballad, "My Man," which became her trademark, particularly since her celebrated, unhappy marriage to Nicky Arnstein was common knowledge.

Brice's most memorable character was Baby Snooks, a character she created for radio in 1936. In one bit, Snooks pasted patches of mink carved from her mother's mink coat all over her baby brother, Robespierre, and tried to sell him as a pet monkey. Brice played Snooks until her death in 1951. She also appeared in films — *My Man* (1929), *The Great Ziegfeld* (1936), and *Everybody Sing* (1938).

Carol Burnett received a congratulatory kiss from producer-husband Joe Hamilton at the 1975 Emmys.

Burnett: Comic Cinderella

Carol Burnett (1934-   ), complete with overbite, scoop laugh, and body English is everybody's favorite. Judging by her longevity as a television star, she may be the best thing to have happened to television audiences since electricity. After ten years, hers is the longest running variety show starring a woman in TV history.

Where she got her humor is a small mystery, since her childhood, which she claims was loving, was not particularly funny. Both her parents were alcoholics, and she lived across the hall from them with her grandmother in a one-room apartment featuring a closet rack in the shower and a Murphy bed.

Burnett wanted to be a journalist — until she got her first laugh in a Hollywood High School play. "I was in heaven," she recalls. She went to UCLA as a drama student. Her appearance in *Annie Get Your Gun* impressed someone in the audience: an anonymous benefactor who gave her one thousand dollars to get started in show business. There was one condition — that she help other theatrical fledglings.

Burnett kept the bargain. She went to New York and worked as a hatcheck girl and performed in industrial shows. To showcase her talents and those of friends, she organized the Rehearsal Club Revue

of 1955. The revue led to an agent and a job as the girlfriend of a ventriloquist's dummy. In 1957, she was a hit in a nightclub show and on television with the song "I Made a Fool of Myself over John Foster Dulles." (Dulles was President Eisenhower's secretary of state.) The song got her on "The Jack Parr Show" and led to a job as a regular on "The Garry Moore Show" in 1959. Critics called her the "first lady of television," a title she still holds.

The Cinderella aspect of Burnett's rapid stardom does not apply to the star, who is no princess. She has a delicious lack of illusions. "To succeed in movies," she once said, "you have to look like Marilyn Monroe or Tony Curtis. Unfortunately, I look more like Tony Curtis." She claims an inability to tell a joke. "But people identify. Everybody's had spinach on a tooth."

Coca: Perennial Pixie

Okay, every critic alive says that every comedienne alive has a rubber face. But **Imogene Coca** (1908-   ) really does. She is a bona fide clown.

At fourteen, when her parents gave her the choice between high school or the stage ("I was one of those horrible little children who sing with no voice"), it was no contest. Her comic talents were discovered by Leonard Sillman, producer of

Top television clowns of the fifties were Sid Caesar and rubber-faced Imogene Coca.

Astride a pearl laden broomstick, Phyllis Diller celebrated Halloween on a New York rooftop.

New Faces (1934). He moved her up from the chorus line to a featured pantomime spot.

Coca developed a successful nightclub act during the early 1940s, but television made her famous. She co-starred with Sid Caeser on his weekly "Your Show of Shows." *Life* called her humor "a matter of subtle and almost imperceptible shadings." She won an Emmy from the Academy of Television Arts and Sciences in 1951 for "best actress." She also appeared on a television sitcom, "Grindel."

Diller: Gilded Chicken

When **Phyllis Diller** (1917-   ) is on stage, you notice. A likely getup is a mini-tent dress, heavy with rhinestones and sequins, gold high-heeled ankle boots, black satin opera-length gloves, and a two-foot-long cigarette holder. Her blonde hair looks like feathers. All angles and sharp edges, she looks like a gilded chicken.

It's all by design because Diller leaves nothing to chance, and certainly not her laughs. Of her 1965 split from her husband, Sherwood Anderson Diller ("Fang"), she said, "Fang applied to the ASPCA for a divorce. Claims he married a dog." She was a housewife until her professional debut at San Francisco's Purple Onion when she was thirty-seven, but she says, "I buried a lot of my ironing in the back yard."

Diller has no trouble with self-esteem. When she underwent plastic surgery for her face and figure, she talked about it. "You look in the mirror each morning and get the first message of the day," she once said. "I don't have to decode it now."

Fields: One Liner

Totie Fields (1931-   ) comes from the Borscht Belt school of comedy. Her raucous laugh and good-natured self-deprecation are spun out in loud one-liners. Fields used to be a very heavy woman. But she didn't have a weight problem, she said, she had a height problem. For her weight, she should have been a foot taller. Field's bulk was her bread and butter as a comic, the foil for jokes about her problems with snap-crotch body shirts.

Field's problem today is that she's thin, but how she got that way is no laughing matter. In 1976, she contracted phlebitis and one of her legs had to be amputated. But her sense of humor has saved her from morbidity. "The minute I put the rings on," she announced at her first public appearance after surgery, "I knew I was well. I don't care if I lost a leg, I've got my fingers." Fields has mastered the use of an artificial leg and has prepared a new Las Vegas act.

Meara: Funny Redhead
Anne Meara (1929-   ) has made a career out of being an Irish Catholic. She's been to so many wakes, she says, that "every time I see a carnation, I cry." A convert to Judaism, she says her mother-in-law once tried to teach her Yiddish from the back of a matzoh box. She calls her husband, Jerry Stiller, with whom she does a comedy act, "Hershey Horowitz".

She met Stiller at an open audition. They've been married since 1954, and formed the Stiller and Meara act to supplement their acting earnings. A six-show per year contract with Ed Sullivan established them as a comedy team. They have also performed in plays — *Prisoner of Second Avenue* and *Last of the Red Hot Lovers*. Meara has had roles in *Lovers and Other Strangers,* and *The Out-of-Towners*. Currently she is playing a leading role on television's "Rhoda."

May: Talent for Barbs
Of all the comedians spawned in Chicago's Second City, the most famous are Mike Nichols and **Elaine May** (1932-   ). May had met Nichols at the University of Chicago, where she was a student without portfolio. (She was never formally admitted.) "People had told me I should meet Elaine," Nichols later recalled. "It was said that she and I had the cruelest tongues on campus."

May, the daughter of a Yiddish theater actor, and Nichols had a caustic chemistry that impaled the establishment and pretense. In order to keep their routines fresh, the skits were never written down. Most of their material was improvised, including their Broadway two-person show, *An Evening with Mike Nichols and Elaine May* (1960-61).

The Nichols-May act broke up in 1961 at her insistence. "I told Mike there was no way we could top ourselves. At least

not together." Separately, they have become successful directors. May's credits include the films *A New Leaf,* which she wrote and starred in, and *The Heartbreak Kid.*

Mabley: Dirty Old Lady
Jackie "Moms" Mabley (1894-1975) could get a laugh before she even opened her toothless mouth. She looked like a ragpicker who had wandered through the stage door by mistake — bug-eyed, with a jutting chin, oversize boots, argyle socks, and an egg-stained sweater. The craggy, crazy, endearing hag was a role she created in the 1920s. "I'm a dirty old lady," she liked to say.

Mabley was born Louella May in North Carolina's Blue Ridge Mountains. At sixteen, when she left home, she was already a mother: she took her stage name from Jack Mabley, an ex-boy friend. "He took a lot off me," she said, "and the least I could do was take his name." While performing in Dallas, she was discovered by a black comedy team, Butterbeans and Suzy. They found her an agent, and her weekly salary quickly increased from fourteen dollars to ninety dollars. She toured the South on the black vaudeville circuit, played a few bit parts in films, and became

Moms Mabley had an interracial philosophy: "God created all men equal, ain't that enough?".

a headliner at Harlem's Apollo Theater. There she "mothered" the likes of Louis Armstrong, Duke Ellington, Count Basie, and Cab Calloway — hence, the nickname.

In 1967, Moms appeared on television's first all-black variety show, produced by Harry Belafonte. In 1974, she starred in *Amazing Grace*.

Moms loved to joke about sex. "The only thing an old man can do for me," she said, "is bring me a message from a younger man." It was easy, she said, to attract younger men: "All you have to do is knock on their door and ask them, 'Say, doll, do you have change for a hundred dollar bill?'"

Livingstone: Benny's Mrs.

Mary Livingstone (1908-   ) became a comedienne in self-defense. She got tired of sitting around hotel rooms when she went on the road with her husband, Jack Benny. Livingstone was born Sadie Marks, the daughter of a Vancouver, B.C., synagogue president. The Marks family frequently entertained vaudeville performers who were appearing in town. When Livingstone was thirteen, the Marx Brothers came to visit with Jack Benny in tow.

Benny and Livingstone married in 1927. She joined Benny's act as the target of Benny's jokes. On her first appearance on his radio show, she was billed as "Mary Livingstone from Plainfield, New Jersey, reading a poem." Livingstone continued with Benny on radio and television until 1958 when, pleading stage fright, she retired.

Pearl: Homespun Humor

Sarah Ophelia Colley, the refined finishing school graduate, didn't get a laugh until she bought a wide-brimmed straw hat for $1.98 and changed her name to **Minnie Pearl** (1912-   ). Pearl has been a regular on the Grand Ole Opry since 1940. Her trademark greeting, "How-dee", is also frequently heard on television, at fairs, and on the radio circuit.

Her downhome humor is spun around the people of "Grinder's Switch," especially her Uncle Nabob. She also likes to joke about "ketchin fellers," and particularly about her husband, a retired pilot who flies her to performances.

The Grand Ole Opry's Minnie Pearl decked out in trademark $1.98 wide-brimmed straw hat.

Pearl has written a country cookbook and started a nationwide chain of fried chicken restaurants.

Raye: GI's Favorite

Martha Raye (née Margi Yvonne Reed) (1916-   ) has spent a good portion of her career looking for a war, to the eternal gratitude of hundreds of thousands of American G.I.s "The queen of buffoons" — so said the *New York Herald Tribune* — got her first acting job in vaudeville.

Raye became famous for a song, "Mr. Paganini," in the 1936 Bing Crosby film *Rhythm on the Range*.

The woman who won a contest for having legs as good as Marlene Dietrich's became even more famous for her tireless entertainment of troops during three wars. An honorary lieutenant colonel, she was the only woman authorized to wear the uniform of the Green Berets during the Vietnam War by special order of President Lyndon Johnson. Between 1965 and 1972, she spent at least four months a year entertaining in Vietnam. At a small field hospital near Soctrang, while nursing wounded soldiers for thirteen hours, she caught a bullet in the rib cage. ("I've had worse hangovers," she joked.)

Once the war ended, Raye had a tough time getting work. "It was hard to get a guest shot or do any TV shows," she has said. "People would say, 'Oh, she's a warmonger.' Which is ridiculous . . . I was just helping the men who were there. They didn't want a war any more than anyone else in the world."

The clown, who can also dance, appeared on Broadway in *No, No Nanette* in 1972 and in 1976 replaced Nancy Walker on NBC's "McMillan."

Rivers: Her Own Buddy

Joan Rivers (1935-   ) is the comedienne you love to quote. On being shy, fat, and lonely as a kid: "I was my own buddy in camp." On giving birth: "I want a Jewish delivery — to be knocked out in the delivery room and wake up at the hairdresser's."

Egghead Rivers, who was born Joan Molnsky, won English honors and a Phi Beta Kappa key at the age of nineteen. She became fashion coordinator of a New York department store but switched to comedy writing. Rivers was a secretary by day and by night performed, free, at nightclubs for comic hopefuls. Rivers paid her professional dues working in second string clubs, resorts, and strip joints. For a time she toured the Pacific in a USO tour with the team "Jim, Jake and Joan." Then she started writing material for Bob Newhart, Phil Foster, and Phyllis Diller.

As Joan Rivers, very funny lady, she made her "Tonight Show" debut in 1965 and went on to top nightclubs and television shows. In 1968, she had her own syndicated morning talk show, "That Show."

As "the victim who strikes back," she used humor to cope with a world that was "sad and tough." Rivers' memories of her childhood as a shy, overweight youngster who spent Saturday nights alone is the genesis of her jokes. She's still writing. Her book, *Having a Baby Can Be a Scream,* was a best seller, and she has completed the script for a film that she will direct.

Tomlin: One Dinga-Ling

Lily Tomlin's (1936-   ) career is a divine comedy in which she plays all the parts. All of her characters are recognizable types whose mannerisms are enlarged to become caricatures. Ernestine, the tele-

phone operator who redundantly asks, "Is this the party to whom I am speaking?", can destroy your life by pulling your plug. Edith Ann, the runny-nosed prepubescent philosopher, makes you want to enlarge the hole between her front teeth. The Very Refined Lady is so tasteful she's distasteful.

Many of Tomlin's characters were developed for her stint on the television program, "Rowan and Martin's Laugh-In." And most of them were gleaned from her years as a starving actress in New York, beginning in 1962. Her artistic concentration is epic. It took her four days in a Burbank supermarket to develop Dot, the check-out lady. Her debut as a dramatic actress in the film *Nashville* earned her an Oscar nomination for best supporting actress. She co-starred with Art Carney in the film *The Late Show.* And her reviews for her one-woman Broadway show in 1977 were rapturous.

Tomlin's personal needs are simple. The actress who once worked as a tem-

Lily Tomlin played a whacko looking for her kidnapped cat in the film, *The Late Show.*

Self-Deprecatory Humor

According to a study by Joan Levine of Temple University, funnywomen are more apt to poke fun at themselves than are male comics — 53 percent more apt. Levine studied the monologues of four female and four male comics: Phyllis Diller, Totie Fields, Lily Tomlin, Moms Mabley, George Carlin, Robert Klein, Bill Cosby and David Steinberg. She showed that women razzed themselves in 64 percent of their jokes, while men victimized themselves 11 percent of the time.

"You can say the nastiest things about yourself," Phyllis Diller has said, "without offending anyone." A Dillerism: In discussing her Living Bra, she claimed "it died of starvation."

Levine concluded that "comediennes are echoing the values of their social milieu in order to attract and keep a mass audience." So, apparently, are comedians when they knock women. More than 15 percent of men's barbs are aimed at women, while women reciprocate only 7 percent of the time. Henny Youngman became king of the wife jokes thirty years ago when he said, "Take my wife . . . please." But the wives of the joke kings struck back in a 1975 *Esquire* article.

Sadie Youngman said she laughs harder at her husband's jokes than anyone. Then she added, "My husband's on a diet — coconuts and bananas. He hasn't lost any weight but he can climb a tree."

Patti (Mrs. Pat) Cooper says of her husband, "I laugh at everything he does. That's probably why, in twelve years of marriage, we only have one child."

Roxane (Mrs. Jack) Carter admits to some anxiety at being the wife of a comic. "We're very close," she says, "but after two years of marriage he still calls me occupant." Then she added the best husband joke of all: "There's a new monster movie where the creature eats only the brains of comedians. He starves to death."

---

porary secretary, scorching her only suit every morning and sleeping in a footlocker every night, told *Ms.* that what she wanted, when she became famous, was: "To get up in the morning and have something to wear. To have a hairdo I could take care of easily and hands that were well groomed. To have something to eat in the house when I wanted it."

THE WOMEN UNDER THE BIG TOP

Bailey: Circus Owner

History's only female circus owner was the beloved **Mollie Bailey** (1841-1918).

Against her parents' wishes, she slipped out of the house to attend a traveling circus, and immediately fell in love with James Bailey, a musician in the show. The two eloped in 1858. Mollie Bailey was disowned by her father.

Before leaving town, she helped herself to a horse and wagon from the family plantation. The animal was the foundation of a circus that would eventually include an elephant, a camel, tightrope walkers, acrobats, and clowns.

When the Civil War broke out, Mollie accompanied her soldier husband to Confederate ranks, working as a nurse.

Disguised as an old lady selling cookies, she made dangerous journeys through enemy territory to get badly-needed quinine for the troops; often she brought back valuable information about Union plans.

After the war, the Baileys hit the road again with a Houston-based circus called "A Texas Show for Texas People." It took seven wagons to transport the one-ring circus's animal acts.

Once the company was surrounded by Indians while camped between towns. Mollie boldly beat upon a drum and scared off the aggressors. The Indian chief, who later became a friend, told her they thought the noise came from cannons fired from some distance.

When her husband fell ill in 1885, Mollie took complete charge of the circus, renaming it "Mollie Bailey's Show."

Bump: Tiny Superstar

One of the legendary circus figures was the tiny (32 inch-29-pound), but perfectly formed, **Mercy Bump** (1841-1919), better known to thousands of Big Top fans as Mrs. Tom Thumb. The daughter of average-sized parents, she had four six-foot tall brothers who took turns carrying her to school. A good student, with a particular interest in music and poetry, she became a third-grade teacher at sixteen.

However, the classroom was too quiet for Bump's taste. She teamed up with P. T. Barnum, who outfitted her in stylish new clothes and introduced her to New York Society.

Bump married the likewise diminutive Tom Thumb in an elegant 1863 wedding at

Tom Thumb and Mercy Bump at their 1863 wedding that pushed Civil War news off the front pages.

Grace Church, attended by governors and members of Congress. Accounts of the marriage pushed Civil War bulletins off the front pages. First Lady Mary Todd Lincoln sent the couple Chinese firescreens inlaid with gold, silver, and mother of pearl.

During a tour of the U.S. in 1883, the Thumbs narrowly escaped serious injury in a fire at Milwaukee's Newhall House. Tom never recovered from the shock of the tragedy, and died the next year. A spendthrift, he left Bump virtually penniless.

Undaunted, Bump resumed her circus career and later married "Count" Primo Magri, with whom she formed a midget opera company.

Leitzel: Center Ring Aerialist

One of the most beloved circus performers, aerialist **Lillian Leitzel** (1892-1931) commanded the center ring from the beginning of her career. She was the only circus star to merit her own private car on the company train, and candy salesmen were barred from hawking their wares during her performance.

Leitzel's solo turn began with her graceful ascent of a rope to a height of 50 feet. Grasping a pair of Roman rings, she did handstands to the strains of the "William Tell Overture." When the band commenced the "Flight of the Bumblebee," Leitzel performed her most difficult feat — one-arm "planges" — in which she rapidly threw her body over her own shoulder many times in succession. Each plange dislocated her shoulder, but her powerful muscles snapped it back into place immediately. On one occasion Leitzel performed 239 such rotations without a pause. She was famed for never using a net.

Married three times, the fiery Leitzel chopped off one of the fingers of her second husband, sideshow manager Clyde Ingalls, with a butcher knife during a marital spat.

Although quick-tempered, Leitzel was friendly and generous. She was adored by the circus children, to whom she taught reading, writing, music, and poetry, in addition to the trapeze.

As a favor to struggling booking agent Frank McClosky, Leitzel accepted an offer to appear in a Copenhagen nightclub. During the performance, one of her rings crystallized and broke. She plunged head first twenty-nine feet to the ground.

Two days later the circus world mourned her death.

Oakley: Sharpshooter

Wyatt Earp may have been "the fastest gun in the West," but **Annie Oakley** (1860-1926) certainly was a close second. Born Phoebe Ann Moses in Darke County, Ohio, "The Girl of the Western Plains" shot game as a child to pay off the mortgage on the family farm.

Her rise to fame began when she outgunned celebrated marksman Frank Butler in a shooting match. The opponents fell in love and were married. Butler taught his bride how to read, and worked with her on developing an act. They joined Buffalo Bill's Wild West Show as a team in 1885.

Oakley could split a playing card held edge on at thirty paces. She shot flames off a revolving wheel of candles, glass balls while lying on the back of a galloping horse, and knocked ashes off cigarettes held in trembling mouths.

She once performed the latter trick with the then Crown Prince of Germany, Wilhelm, as a target. During World War I, when he was the hated Kaiser, she said, "I wish I'd missed that day."

Said humorist Will Rogers on her death; "Annie Oakley was a greater character than she was a rifle shot . . . her thoughtful consideration of others will live as a mark for any woman to shoot at."

Stark: She Loved Cats

The first woman tiger-tamer, **Mabel Stark** (1892-   ) believed kindness and patience to be of supreme importance in training animals.

The daring blonde worked with as many as sixteen tigers at once. She taught her mammoth cats to wrestle with her, and sent shivers up spines when she climaxed her performances by putting her head in the mouth of a full-grown Bengal tiger.

Despite her faith in tender, loving care, Stark was attacked many times by her playful tigers. Performing during torrential rains in 1928, she slipped in the mud and two of her oversized pets pounced. Before she was rescued, they had gnawed a hole in her neck near the jugular vein, another

Annie Oakley could shoot the head off a running quail by the time she was 12.

in her shoulder, torn a deltoid muscle, and mangled one of her legs. It took doctors four hours to sew her together. Plastic surgery, X-ray and radium treatments were required to restore her beauty. But Stark was back in the cage two months later.

The fearless lady continued showing tigers until she was well into her seventies.

Williams: A Born Ham

Peggy Williams (1948-   ), who describes herself as "a born ham" was the first female clown hired by today's Ringling Brothers and Barnum & Bailey Circus. A speech pathology major in college, she became a pantomime afficionado after learning to use her hands and face to communicate with deaf children.

Williams is far from the most glamorous woman in the center ring. Her chalk-white face, cherry-red nose, and painted-on mile-wide mouth are meant to win laughs, not wolf whistles. Her clown makeup takes 45 minutes to apply.

Each circus clown has a specialty. Williams' is illusion tricks, making people and/or objects appear to vanish. "Physical jokes, like falling over backwards," she says, "aren't my style." In fact, she once broke a foot while attempting a cartwheel.

Stars

HEROINES OF THE SILVER SCREEN

Who is that woman on the silver screen? She is not just the creation of the screen-writer who wrote her lines, the director who interpreted them, and the actress who brought them to life. The film heroine is an extension of us all, mirroring many of the looks, traits, and values we as a society deem important. She, in turn, helps to reinforce those qualities among her viewing public. Hence, flashbacks from film history can illustrate how woman's position in American life has changed over the last sixty years — and how it has remained the same.

America's Sweethearts

The first female screen stars were the curly-locked Lillian and Dorothy Gish and Mary Pickford — young, meek, uncomplaining, and, most of all, childlike. Their films expressed the personal puritanism of their director, D. W. Griffith: the pure and moral were ultimately rewarded, while the ambitious or lustful doomed themselves to an unhappy ending.

   Orphans of the Storm (1921), the last film the Gishes made with Griffith, is representative of the genre. The two play country-bred stepsisters en route to Paris during the French Revolution. One is abducted by a lustful marquis who wants to end her virginal purity. After escaping a host of dangers from rape to the guillotine, the two stepsisters are reunited in a well-deserved happy ending.

   Though women were demanding the vote and other grown-up privileges outside the theater, audiences inside were captivated by "America's Sweetheart," the eternally youthful Pickford. In a *Photoplay* poll, her fans said they wanted to see Pickford play such roles as Heidi and Anne (from *Anne of Green Gables*) rather than parts more appropriate for a woman of her thirty-two years.

The Flapper: Jazzy But Virtuous

Though Pickford remained popular well into the twenties, a new woman emerged who was more attuned to the changing times. She was the flapper, a giddy young pseudosophisticate out for a good time. For all the flapper's seeming flaunting of inhibition, she never strayed too far from the moral code. Though she often

Purity and goodness triumphed in D.W. Griffith's films starring Lillian and Dorothy Gish.

worked — typically in a low-status job like salesclerk — the flapper was ready and willing to abandon her career at the pop of The Question.

   Jazz babies Clara Bow and Joan Crawford were two of Hollywood's leading flappers. In *It* (1927), Bow is a playful shopgirl who sets her cap for her boss; her good-natured gold digging succeeds because she has the elusive "it."

   Hollywood did not take long to realize that sex sells movies. The heavy petting, orgiastic parties, and even occasional nudity in some films of the early twenties would have earned them an "R" rating — if not an "X" — by current standards. The public got so outraged that filmmakers organized the Motion Picture Producers and Distributors of America in order to censor themselves before sterner critics took on the task. Initially, the MPPDA under "Czar" Will Hays was relatively ineffectual; screen depravity abated only slightly though the forces of good now had to triumph in the final reel.

Enigmas and Wisecrackers

Women grew up in the films of the late twenties and thirties.

A young Joan Crawford played the quintessential flapper in *Our Dancing Daughters*.

Moviegoers became enamored of all things foreign, and the exotic and aloof Greta Garbo and Marlene Dietrich became stars. Both were mysterious, alluring, and curiously masculine. They operated outside the prescribed social code — and usually had to suffer for it. In *Anna Karenina* (1935), for example, Garbo is forsaken by the man for whom she abandoned her family and throws herself beneath a train.

At the same time, films glorified the platinum blond bombshell and her repertoire of repartee. Mae West and Jean Harlow wisecracked their way onto the screen, their vulgarity tempered by their wit. "I used to be Snow White, but I drifted," West cracked. More often than not, tart blondes got what they wanted, usually a man or his money.

The Career Woman

The fallen women inhabiting the movie screen did little to hush the cry for film censorship. The Legion of Decency was established in 1934 to impose a new, stiffer Production Code drawn up by Catholic churchmen. As a result, women were forced out of the bedroom and into the workplace. A procession of female reporters, detectives, private secretaries, spies, and actresses paraded across the screen, portrayed by more down-to-earth types like Katharine Hepburn, Jean Arthur, and Bette Davis. They were at times very strong, intelligent, honest, and secure. Still, they posed little threat to the male-dominated scheme of things. Most were just biding their time until they would be swept off their feet by an honorably intentioned man, often a boss or colleague. Women who resisted turning housewife were usually treated harshly; one who escaped the pattern was Hepburn's Tess Harding in *Woman of the Year* (1942). Though she married newsman Sam Craig, played by Spencer Tracy, Harding retained an identity of her own beyond that of her husband.

The World War II years marked a high point for films for and about women, due largely to the fact that male moviegoers — as well as many actors — were otherwise engaged. Women on the screen, like their real-life counterparts in the audience, coped courageously with the "maleless" society.

Whereas men have always been allowed to be pals on screen, women were destined to be rivals once the Gish sisters faded

Katherine Hepburn's Tess Harding did not retreat to kitchen and nursery after marriage.

from glory. The forties proved an exception to this rule, as women joined forces against wartime loneliness and deprivation. In *Tender Comrade* (1943), Ginger Rogers played a young mother comforted by her three female housemates when she received notice that her husband had died in battle.

The film counterparts of Rosie the Riveter didn't burst into tears at the sight of a loose bolt, and the woman of the forties was more apt to be capable than helpless, brave than childish. Claudette Colbert was a welder in *Since You Went Away* (1944), Lana Turner was a war correspondent in *Somewhere I'll Find You* (1942), and Rosalind Russell was an executive in *Take a Letter, Darling* (1942).

In place of the thirties' mystery woman, the later forties had the sexy, independent, knowing woman, often played by Lauren Bacall as in *To Have and Have Not* (1944). These characters were of the tough-but-tender school, allowed to fall in love without falling apart.

Pinup as Film Star
Johnny came marching home after four years of ogling pinup photos of Betty Grable's legs and Lana Turner's well-filled-out sweater. G.I. barracks decor was transferred to the screen via glamor girls like Rita Hayworth, warbling "Put the

Blame on Mame" in *Gilda* (1946). Movie audiences finally got a look at Jane Russell's endowments when *The Outlaw* was

In *How To Marry A Millionaire*, woman's lot was to snare Mr. Right — or at least Mr. Rich.

released in 1946 after a three-year battle with the censors.

Meanwhile, the liberated career woman was relegated to the back lot. A woman's career became that of catching a husband, as exemplified by Marilyn Monroe, Lauren Bacall, and Betty Grable in *How to Marry a Millionaire* (1953). (The story, however, was first filmed in 1928.) Other working women were either neurotic beyond belief, as was the case with Bette Davis in *The Star* (1952), or soon to capitulate to marriage and true happiness, like Joan Crawford in *Torch Song* (1953) or *Johnny Guitar* (1954).

Once wed, a woman was either doting and devoted, like June Allyson in *Woman's World* (1954), or Elizabeth Taylor in *The Last Time I Saw Paris* (1955), or destructive and dowdy, as was Shirley Booth in *Come Back, Little Sheba* (1952). When wartime brides began to realize that marital bliss was sometimes elusive, Hollywood offered *Tea and Sympathy* (1956). The divorced woman was portrayed with greater sensitivity. Typical were Bacall in *Written on the Wind* (1956) and Deborah Kerr in *From Here to Eternity* (1953).

The Villainess

Perhaps feeling threatened by any kind of female aggressiveness, Hollywood has often made much of the heartless, unredeemable woman who usually gets her comeuppance in the final reel. Bette Davis played such a character in *Of Human Bondage* (1934). A no-account waitress-whore, she was bent on destroying a medical student who had somehow fallen in love with her. She got what was coming to her: an early death.

Davis was just as evil fifteen years later, shooting an old man who would have stopped her from running away with her lover in *Beyond the Forest* (1949). Equally nefarious was Barbara Stanwyck in *Double Indemnity* (1944), prodding insurance salesman Fred MacMurray to help her murder her husband and collect his insurance.

If women were victimizers, they were also victims. A popular postwar type was the woman stalked by an unknown killer, as was Stanwyck in *Sorry, Wrong Number* (1948), or mentally disturbed, like Olivia

de Havilland in *The Snake Pit* (1947), or prey to a murderous husband, á la Ingrid Bergman in *Notorious* (1946). A few years before, Ginger Rogers took her mental disorders to a psychiatrist in *Lady in the Dark* (1941). His diagnosis: "You've had to prove you were superior to all men; you had to dominate them." Was Hollywood trying to tell us something?

Does She . . . or Doesn't She?

Innocence was the trademark of the fifties' screen heroine. Even sex goddess Marilyn Monroe spoke in a whisper-soft, little-girl voice; men wanted to protect her as much as seduce her. Though unchaste, Brigitte Bardot was ever kittenish. Elsewhere on the screen, women continued to save it for marriage. The most tenacious clingers to virginity included Debbie Reynolds in *Tammy* (1957), Sandra Dee in *Gidget* (1959), and Doris Day in *Teacher's Pet* (1958). Their brand of youthful innocence was perpetuated in the sixties with the Beach Party films, such as *Beach Blanket Bingo* (1965), *Bikini Beach* (1964), and *How to Stuff a Wild Bikini* (1966).

But the Pill had made the virginal miss of the fifties an anachronism, to be replaced by the more swinging Shirley MacLaine in *The Apartment* (1960) and Audrey Hepburn in *Breakfast at Tiffany's* (1961). Nymphets like Sue Lyon in *Lolita*

Audrey Hepburn's Holly Golightly demonstrated that film Puritanism was on the wane.

(1962) and Ewa Aulin in *Candy* (1968) came of age sexually while still in their teens.

Britain produced two heroines who seemed uniquely of the sixties. *Darling* (1965) starred Julie Christie as a female Alfie, a mod *bon vivant* who lived for kicks. Lynn Redgrave's *Georgy Girl* (1966) was a social misfit who wanted to conform. Though especially appealing to young audiences, neither character advanced the image of women in film. Like Anne Bancroft's middle-aged Mrs. Robinson in *The Graduate* (1967), they were not permitted to mature out of emotional adolescence. Women's liberation on the screen pertained only to matters sexual; soon every film aimed at a postpubescent audience was expected to include at least one nude scene — and the nude was female. Men rarely shed more than their shirts until Alan Bates and Oliver Reed wrestled nude in *Women in Love* (1969).

By the seventies, Hollywood seemed to have declared women obsolete. Oscar-winning "best pictures" like *Patton* (1970), *The French Connection* (1971), *The Godfather* (1972), and *The Sting* (1973) employed women merely for decoration — if at all.

According to Screen Actors Guild President Kathleen Nolan, 73 percent of featured and supporting roles in films currently go to men. The number of women whose names carry any weight at the box office has dwindled to fewer than five; Barbra Streisand, Liza Minnelli, Diana Ross, and Tatum O'Neal are the only women considered "bankable" by most filmmakers.

Some blame woman's sorry lot on television. Common logic has it that a woman controls the TV knob (except on Sunday afternoon and Monday night), while the man determines which movie a couple will see. Interpersonal dramas — the stuff of which women's pictures were made — more appropriately belong on the small, intimate television tube, they argue. The costlier, more panoramic film epics — the male-dominated Western, war, and disaster movies, for example — are better suited to the larger-than-life-sized screen.

Indeed, some of the better dramatic images of women have been those presented in television series and specials. *"That*

Girl", *"The Mary Tyler Moore Show"*, *"One Day at a Time"*, and specials on Eleanor Roosevelt, Babe Didrikson Zaharias, and Amelia Earheart are but a few examples. Many of today's top female actresses in television — Lucille Ball, Mary Tyler Moore, and Jean Stapleton, for example — acquired the bulk of their fame through television.

The decline of the big studios and resulting breakdown of the "star system" also come in for some of the blame. For all their faults, the studios kept their contract players working. Filmdom's best actresses seldom sat out two or three years just waiting for a decent role to come along as they do today.

It goes without saying that movies are like every other business in their domination by men. Hollywood's top executives have more often than not gained power by appealing to mass tastes and values — not by sticking their necks out for an unpopular cause like women's liberation. But, ironically, part of women's current problem with films has been blamed on the women's movement. "We're in a period of transition," says Jane Fonda. "The fifties and sixties stereotype woman's role is no longer plausible. The people who finance films aren't sure what women's films might make money because the new image of women isn't clear."

But the seventies have not been entirely bleak. Were Academy Awards given for the films best depicting women, some of the recent winners might include:

1970: *Diary of a Mad Housewife*. Carrie Snodgrass stars as a woman rebelling against her overbearing husband — and, later, against an equally obnoxious lover.

1971: *Klute*. Jane Fonda brings sensitivity to her portrayal of a high-class call girl, successfully sidestepping both the "evil woman" and "hooker with a heart of gold" stereotypes.

1972: *A Touch of Class*. Glenda Jackson proves life can go on — even after a woman breaks off an affair with her married lover.

1973: *Sounder* and *Lady Sings the Blues*. The screen's first honest images of black women are presented by Cicely Tyson and Diana Ross.

1974: *Alice Doesn't Live Here Anymore*. Ellen Burstyn, as a widowed

Ellen Burstyn played a widowed mother making it on her own in *Alice Doesn't Live Here Anymore*.

housewife, comes of age at thirty-five.

1975: *Hester Street*. A Jewish immigrant version of Alice achieves a measure of independence in turn-of-the-century New York City. An added plus is the film's female director, Joan Micklin Silver.

1976: *A Star Is Born*. For all her much criticized posturing, Barbra Streisand proves an ambitious woman can make it to the top. She refuses to let the talented but tormented man she loves "trash" her life.

The rest of the decade promises to be brighter for women on the screen. Actresses are speaking out more vociferously for rewarding roles. A new generation of aspiring stars — Sissy Spacek, Shelly Duvall, and Diane Keaton — are winning admirers.

The number of women working on the other side of the camera — as producers, directors, screenwriters, and so on — is up. Plans are underway to bring to the screen some of the best-selling recent novels by and about women, including *Fear of Flying, Looking for Mr. Goodbar*, and *Memoirs of an Ex-Prom Queen*.

But women can progress on screen only as far as audiences will let them, as measured by Hollywood in cold, hard cash. If the new women's films fall flat at the box office, we will have ourselves to blame for another male-dominated decade of soldiers, shoot-outs, and sharks.

THE NAMES ON THE MARQUEE

Ann-Margret: "Bye, Bye, Birdie"

Ann-Margret (1941-   ) isn't the best dancer in the world. Nor is she best singer or actress. But she is a presence, a naive, sultry entertainer who is rarely ignored.

Ann-Margret Olsson was born in Sweden. Her father, an electrician, came to the United States shortly after her birth. Ann-Margret and her mother immigrated to Illinois five years later.

Ann-Margret won a runner-up spot on the Ted Mack Original Amateur Hour when she was sixteen. The summer after her freshman year at Northwestern University she headed for Las Vegas with three other students. When their money ran out, they went to Los Angeles to get bookings and carfare home. Ann-Margret was discovered by George Burns in Vegas, which led to a recording contract and a part in the film *State Fair* (1962). Her slow sizzle when she sang "Bachelor in Paradise" at the 1962 Academy Awards made her a hot item in the film world.

Ann-Margret's second film, *Bye, Bye, Birdie* garnered cordial reviews. In the three following years she made about a dozen films, none of which were particularly noteworthy. Roger Smith, a former television star, became her manager and turned her career around after they married in 1967. She made a series of lavish, critically acclaimed specials for CBS and broke attendance records at hotels shows in Las Vegas and Miami.

In 1971 Ann-Margret, directed by Mike Nichols, gave an Academy-Award-nominated performance in the film *Carnal Knowledge*. Critics were also dazzled by her performance in *Tommy,* a filmed rock opera, released in 1975.

Arthur: Gorgeous Comic

Jean Arthur (1905-   ) in her prime was a dish — bright eyes, a mouth with a perpetually bemused curve, and terrific legs. With voice pitched low and an occasional crack in it, she often sounded like a knowing child.

Born Gladys Greene in New York City, she was a model and, beginning in 1924, a film actress. After several years in films and Broadway plays she found her comic type in the film *The Whole Town's Talking* (1935). She played essentially the same role in most of her films — the witty, spunky, lovesick girlfriend-wife. Arthur was a stenographer in *Easy Living* (1937), a salesgirl in *The Devil and Miss Jones* (1941). *Mr. Deeds Goes to Town* (1936) was probably her most famous film.

In 1943 she made *The More the Merrier* and was nominated for an Oscar. Her contract with Columbia Pictures ended the following year, after which she made few films. *Shane* in 1954 was a notable, dramatic exception.

Bacall: Tough, Seductive, and Beautiful

In her debut film *To Have and Have Not* (1944) opposite Humphrey Bogart, the husky-voiced **Lauren Bacall** (1924-   ) gave her leading man a riveting gaze through arched eyebrows that became her trademark. That look upward, she later said in an interview, was not intended to be sexual. She held her head low, she said, to conceal the fact that she was trembling from terror and that was the only way to hold still.

Born Betty Pepske in New York, she had a rich-to-richer rise to stardom. After attending the American Academy of Dramatic Arts, she became a model. Director Howard Hawks saw her on the cover of *Harper's Bazaar* and signed her to a seven-year contract.

The chemistry of Bacall-Bogart was

The Lauren Bacall-Humphrey Bogart combination was dynamite both on screen and off.

money at the box office and an inevitable off-screen item. They married in 1945 and made three successive films — *The Big Sleep* (1946), *Dark Passage* (1947), and *Key Largo* (1948). The gutsiness of the women she played applied privately as well — Warner Brothers suspended her twelve times because of casting quarrels, and she bought out her contract in 1950.

Her finesse with comedy was abundant in *How to Marry a Millionaire* (1953) and *Designing Woman* (1957). Bogart died during the filming of the latter picture and her films after that were middling.

Not so her Broadway roles. She was an enormous hit in *Cactus Flower* (1967) and *Applause* (1970).

Ball: Love that Lucy

Although **Lucille Ball** (1911-   ) has made more than seventy movies, it is the Lucy of television that is known all over the world. The carrot redhead with an enormous smile and laugh is one of the wealthiest and most enduring stars in media history.

Ball was born in Jamestown, New York, and began her career in New York City at fifteen. After a stint at modeling under the name of Diane Belmont, she got a part in *Roman Scandals* (1933). Her first good film role was in *Stage Door* (1937).

Carrot-top Lucille Ball is among the wealthiest and most enduring stars in media history.

Ball married Dezi Arnaz in 1940. In 1950 they formed Desilu Productions and the following year brought their comedy series, "I Love Lucy," to television. Reruns of the program are still running, showing Mrs. Ricki Ricardo as the bubble-brained wife of the Cuban drummer.

Ball did a Broadway musical, *Wildcat*, in 1961, following her divorce from Arnaz. Her latest film, *Mame*, was released in 1974.

Bankhead: A Real Presence

More people remember **Tallulah Bankhead** (1902-1968) for her presence than her performances. Everyone older than forty knows, for instance, that she called people "dahling" because she was rotten at remembering names. They know that Bette Davis imitated her, or that she imitated Bette Davis. They know also that she had a deep, seductive voice, a searing sense of humor, and that she had a habit of taking off her clothes in public.

Bankhead was a first-rate actress — she won the New York Drama Critics' Circle Award for her performance in Lillian Hellman's *The Little Foxes* in 1939. She won it again in 1942 for *The Skin of Our Teeth*.

Although much else she did profession-ally was mostly mediocre, Bankhead gave memorable performances on stage in *A Streetcar Named Desire*, *Private Lives*, and *The Milk Train Doesn't Stop Here Anymore*.

Bankhead was especially quotable. The daughter of a U.S. senator from Alabama, the first thing she did when she came to New York in search of glory was to move into the Algonquin Hotel and hire a maid. Because of her wit and brilliance, she became, along with Dorothy Parker and Alexander Woollcott, a member of the Algonquin "Round Table." Impatient with the progression of her theatrical career — she had only minor roles — she moved to London in 1923. She starred in several plays and lingered there for eight years.

Foxes made her a star in the United States. Her personality made her a force, and she played herself for many years on radio. She could outtalk, outsmoke (four packs of cigarettes a day), outdrink anybody.

Bara: The Vamp

Theda Bara (1890-1955) used to shiver your grandfather's timbers. She was the embodiment of female sexuality run amok. Although she made all of her films (silent) in only four years, (1915-19), the "vamp" was notorious for her roles as an insatiable tease.

Theodosia Goodman, an Ohio tailor's daughter, was transformed into Arab seductress Theda Bara.

Still kittenish at 40, Brigitte Bardot claims she won't grow old until she first grows up.

Theda Bara was a product of publicity hype. William Fox remodeled Theodosia Goodman from Cincinnati into Theda Bara (an anagram of the words "Arab Death"). In her first film she was a star and said: "Kiss me, my fool." *Salome* (1918) and *Kathleen Mavourneen* (1919) followed.

For six years she tried to become a successful Broadway actress, but the publicity that rocketed her to stardom soon turned into overkill. She retired after an unsuccessful attempt at a film comeback.

Bardot: French Sex Kitten

You know who **Brigitte Bardot** (1934-   ) is. She's the forty-three-year-old French movie star who looks as marvelous today as she did twenty years ago. Throughout her film career she has played pouty, well-endowed, playful ingenues.

Bardot was a top model when, in 1950, a magazine cover photo brought her to the attention of film director Roger Vadim. Vadim, whom she married in 1952, is generally credited with her development as an actress.

After several small film parts, Bardot created a stir in *La Lumière de Face* (The Light Across the Street) in 1955. *And God Created Woman*, written and directed by Vadim (1956), marked the end of their marriage and made Bardot a box-office bonanza around the world.

In 1959 she proclaimed what seems to be her current ambition: "I am now spending my life trying to erase the Bardot legend."

Barrymore: Theatrical Royalty

"We became actors not because we wanted to go on the stage, but because it was the thing we could do best." So said **Ethel Barrymore** (1879-1959) of her acting career and that of her two famous brothers, Lionel and John. If ever there was a theatrical royal family, the Barrymores were it, but, unlike royalty, talent graced each generation.

Ethel May Barrymore was born in Philadelphia, the daughter of two actors, Maurice and Georgiana Drew Barrymore. She made her stage debut at fourteen in a New York production of *The Rivals*.

Known for her imperious beauty, her elegant, husky voice (one critic called her Ethel Barrytone), and her command of the stage, she was the first lady of American theater for forty years. Her most famous Broadway role was Miss Moffet in *The Corn Is Green* (1942).

Barrymore starred in several silent and talking movies. In 1932 she appeared with her brothers in *Rasputin and the Empress,* and her performance in *None But the Lonely Heart* in 1944 won her an Academy Award.

Bergman: A Private Life

In the 1950s Ed Sullivan, host of a television variety show, in a spasm of bad taste, asked the studio audience (and presumably the nation) whether or not **Ingrid Bergman** (1915-   ) should be a guest on his program. The Swedish film star had outraged American sensibilities by having the audacity to demand a private life. She had left her husband for another man.

That brouhaha did little to hamper the talent, beauty, and award-winning performances Bergman has given over the years. Born in Sweden, she attended the School of the Royal Dramatic Theatre in Stockholm. In 1935 she made her first film debut in Sweden and was a star within three years. Married to Petter Lindstrom, she made *Intermezzo* in 1938, a few months before the birth of her daughter, Pia. David O. Selznick signed her to make

Top Money-Making Women of the Movies

The Motion Picture Almanac conducts an annual poll of exhibitors in the United States to determine the top 10 money-making stars of the year. The leading female film star and her ranking (in parentheses) for each year follow:

1932—Marie Dressler (1)
1933—Marie Dressler (1)
1934—Janet Gaynor (3)
1935—Shirley Temple (1)
1936—Shirley Temple (1)
1937—Shirley Temple (1)
1938—Shirley Temple (1)
1939—Shirley Temple (5)
1940—Bette Davis (9)
1941—Bette Davis (8)
1942—Betty Grable (8)
1943—Betty Grable (1)
1944—Betty Grable (4)
1945—Greer Garson (3)
1946—Ingrid Bergman (2)
1947—Betty Grable (2)
1948—Betty Grable (2)
1949—Betty Grable (7)
1950—Betty Grable (4)
1951—Betty Grable (3)
1952—Doris Day (7)
1953—Marilyn Monroe (6)

1954—Marilyn Monroe (5)
1955—Grace Kelly (2)
1956—Marilyn Monroe (8)
1957—none
1958—Elizabeth Taylor (2)
1959—Doris Day (4)
1960—Doris Day (1)
1961—Elizabeth Taylor (1)
1962—Doris Day (1)
1963—Doris Day (1)
1964—Doris Day (1)
1965—Doris Day (3)
1966—Julie Andrews (1)
1967—Julie Andrews (1)
1968—Julie Andrews (3)
1969—Katherine Hepburn (9)
1970—Barbra Streisand (9)
1971—Ali MacGraw (8)
1972—Barbra Streisand (5)
1973—Barbra Streisand (6)
1974—Barbra Streisand (4)

the English version the following year, and the film was an enormous success.

In 1945 she won the Best Actress Academy Award for her performance in *Gaslight*, and in 1946 she was the top female Hollywood money earner.

Ingrid Bergman survived public ostracism to emerge a more highly acclaimed actress than before.

In 1946 she played Joan of Arc in Maxwell Anderson's play, *Joan of Lorraine*, for which she won a Tony. The film version, in which she also starred, was less successful.

Bergman met Italian film producer Roberto Rossellini and starred in one of his films (*Stromboli*) in 1949. The birth of a son preceded their marriage by two months and that's what upset the American public and kept her away from the United States for eight years.

Bergman and Rossellini split up and in 1957, she made the film *Anastasia*, for which she won the New York Film Critics' Award and her second Oscar. She came back to the United States and made several more films, and in 1959 appeared in *The Turn of the Screw* on NBC television (she won an 'Emmy').

Bergman won a best supporting actress Oscar for *Murder on the Orient Express* (1974).

Bow: The "It" Girl

Clara Bow (1905-1965) was queen of the

Publicity agents claimed Clara Bow dripped with the personal magnetism known as "It."

young flapper generation. She was the "It" girl of the twenties because she had "it." In assorted, sordid 1970's biographies, you can read all about her alleged sexual appetites, but in the 1920s she had two things going for her: movies without sound tracks and a kewpie-doll sex appeal.

Bow was born in Brooklyn and, thanks to a beauty contest, went to Hollywood when she was a teen-ager. Her big film break came in 1927 and the title of the movie was *It*. She made about thirty movies in the 1920s, including *The Plastic Age* (1926), *Rough House Rosie* (1927), and *Dangerous Curves* (1929).

Bow's Brooklyn accent and the advent of recorded sound ended her career.

Christie: British Mod
Julie Christie (1941-   ) became famous

Mod Julie Christie loved 'em and left 'em with Academy Award winning style in *Darling*.

as the apotheosis of British mod in *Darling* (1965), and won an Academy Award for it. Born in India of British parents, she was educated in England and studied art in Paris. From 1957 to 1960 she was with the Frinton-on-the-Sea Repertory Company in England. Her film debut was *Crooks Anonymous* in 1962.

After *Darling*, critics were unimpressed with most of her films — *Doctor Zhivago* (1966), *Far From the Madding Crowd* (1967), and *Petulia* (1968). They liked her in *The Go-Between* (1971), a film that won the Cannes Grand Prix. *McCabe and Mrs. Miller* (1972) and *Shampoo* (1973) were box-office successes.

Colbert: French Comedienne
Claudette Colbert (1905-   ) was one of Hollywood's most popular leading ladies and, during the 1940s, its highest paid star. Playing the gamut of Hollywood's concepts of woman, she was at her best in comedy.

Born in France, she moved to New York when she was six and made her stage debut in 1923 in *The Wild Wescotts*. Her first big film role was in *The Smiling Lieutenant* (1931). In 1932 she exhibited a lot of sex appeal in Cecil B. DeMille's *The Sign of the Cross*. Her blockbuster was *It Happened One Night* (1934) opposite Clark Gable, for which she won an Academy Award.

Colbert's last big film success was *The Egg and I* (1947). Her stage success continued. She starred in Broadway's *The Marriage-Go-Round* (1958), which ran for 450 performances, and in *The Irregular Verb to Love* (1963).

Crawford: Love to Hate Her
Joan Crawford (1906-1977) was the movie star you often loved to hate. A star who made it from silents into talkies, she was the epitome of the glamorous, Hollywood Star. Her films chronicle her hard work and ambition as much as her talent, which did not really flourish until she had been in films for nearly twenty years.

The story of Crawford's life reads like a grade-B movie. Born in San Antonio, her name was Lucille LeSueur. Her parents were separated before she was born and her mother married a vaudeville theater manager They divorced in 1915, but by then Crawford was hooked — on dancing.

Durable Joan Crawford aged on screen from flapper to career girl to tormented older woman.

Bette Davis was the prototypical liberated woman 30 years before it became fashionable.

She won an amateur dance contest and danced in a Chicago cafe. A stint in the chorus line of a Broadway show — *Innocent Eyes* — led to her screen debut as Norma Shearer's stand-in in *Lady of the Night* (1925).

Crawford became a symbol of the jazz age in *Our Dancing Daughters* (1928), in which she played a flapper. Her first talkie was *Hollywood Revue of 1929* and her first dramatic role was in *Paid* the following year.

Like Bette Davis, Crawford hounded her studio (MGM) for substantial parts. It was those parts that always pulled her out of a box-office slump: *The Women* (1939), *A Woman's Face* (1941), and *Mildred Pierce* (1945), for which she won an Oscar.

Her career began to fade in the 1950s and artistically hit rock bottom in a horror film, *Whatever Happened to Baby Jane* in 1962, although the film was a box-office bonanza. Before and after the death of her husband Alfred Nu Steele, chairman of the board of the Pepsi Cola Company, she used her considerable energies to promote the product. "The need to work is always there, bugging me," she said.

Davis: Hollywood's Jezebel

In her nearly eighty films over fifty years, **Bette Davis** (1908-   ) was the flinty, acid-tongued dame who could speak words as though she were spitting nails. Her toe-to-toe combat in the front offices of Hollywood film companies made her a force to be reckoned with as well.

Davis was born in Lowell, Massachusetts, as Ruth Elizabeth Davis. She began acting in summer-stock productions with the Provincetown Players and made her first film *Bad Sister* (1931), playing the good sister. Her performance went unnoticed.

Not a classic beauty, she was the classic, electrifying bitch in *Of Human Bondage* (1934), which established her as a heavyweight. She won her first Oscar for *Dangerous* (1935), and has received ten Oscar nominations and two Best Actress awards from the film industry.

Davis' confrontations with the front office of Warner Brothers led to sixteen suspensions without pay. "I did have the courage," she said recently, "and it made my career what it became.

In 1938 she played a southern scorpion in *Jezebel*, for which she won her second Oscar. Her most memorable films in the 1940s were *The Letter, Little Foxes*, and *Watch on the Rhine*. Possibly her best film was *All About Eve* (1950).

She appeared on Broadway in *The Night of the Iguana* (1961) and took out trade advertisements announcing her availability for films, Her most recent films have included such chillers as *Whatever Happened to Baby Jane?* (1962) and *Hush, Hush Sweet Charlotte* (1965). In 1977 she won the American Film Institute Life Achievement Award.

Female Academy Award Winners

1927-28 *Actress:* Janet Gaynor, Seventh Heaven

1928-29 *Actress:* Mary Pickford, Coquette

1929-30 *Actress:* Norma Shearer, The Divorcee

1930-31 *Actress:* Marie Dressler, Min and Bill

1931-32 *Actress:* Helen Hayes, Sin of Madelon Claudet

1932-33 *Actress:* Katharine Hepburn, Morning Glory

1934 *Actress:* Claudette Colbert, It Happened One Night

1935 *Actress:* Bette Davis, Dangerous

1936 *Actress:* Luise Rainer, The Great Ziegfeld

1937 *Actress:* Luise Rainer, The Good Earth

1938 *Actress:* Bette Davis, Jezebel

1939 *Actress:* Vivien Leigh, Gone With the Wind

1940 *Actress:* Ginger Rogers, Kitty Foyle

1941 *Actress:* Joan Fontaine, Suspicion

1942 *Actress:* Greer Garson, Mrs. Miniver

1943 *Actress:* Jennifer Jones, The Song of Bernadette

1944 *Actress:* Ingrid Bergman, Gaslight

1945 *Actress:* Joan Crawford, Mildred Pierce

1946 *Actress:* Olivia de Havilland, To Each His Own

1947 *Actress:* Loretta Young, The Farmer's Daughter

1948 *Actress:* Jane Wyman, Johnny Belinda

1949 *Actress:* Olivia de Havilland, The Heiress

1950 *Actress:* Judy Holliday, Born Yesterday.

1951 *Actress:* Vivien Leigh, A Streetcar Named Desire

1952 *Actress:* Shirley Booth, Come Back, Little Sheba

1953 *Actress:* Audrey Hepburn, Roman Holiday

1954 *Actress:* Grace Kelly, The Country Girl

1955 *Actress:* Anna Magnani, The Rose Tattoo

1956 *Actress:* Ingrid Bergman, Anastasia

1957 *Actress:* Joanne Woodward, The Three Faces of Eve

1958 *Actress:* Susan Hayward, I Want to Live

1959 *Actress:* Simone Signoret, Room at the Top

1960 *Actress:* Elizabeth Taylor, Butterfield 8

1961 *Actress:* Sophia Loren, Two Women

1962 *Actress:* Anne Bancroft, The Miracle Worker

1963 *Actress:* Patricia Neal, Hud

1964 *Actress:* Julie Andrews, Mary Poppins

1965 *Actress:* Julie Christie, Darling

1966 *Actress:* Elizabeth Taylor, Who's Afraid of Virginia Woolf?

1967 *Actress:* Katharine Hepburn, Guess Who's Coming to Dinner

1968 *Actress:* (tie) Katharine Hepburn, The Lion in Winter; Barbra Streisand, Funny Girl

1969 *Actress:* Maggie Smith, The Prime of Miss Jean Brodie

1970 *Actress:* Glenda Jackson, Women in Love

1971 *Actress:* Jane Fonda, Klute

1972 *Actress:* Liza Minnelli, Cabaret

1973 *Actress:* Glenda Jackson, A Touch of Class

1974 *Actress:* Ellen Burstyn, Alice Doesn't Live Here Anymore

1975 *Actress:* Louise Fletcher, One Flew Over the Cuckoo's Nest

1976 *Actress:* Faye Dunaway, Network

Doris Day might have changed image by accepting the proffered role of *The Graduate*'s Mrs. Robinson.

Day: Squeaky Clean

Doris Day (1924-   ) has always been everyone's favorite virgin. Even when romping with Rock Hudson in such films as *Pillow Talk* (1959), she was virtue incarnate. Her squeaky cleanliness made her one of the top ten box-office draws from 1959 to 1966.

Day (née Kappelhoff) started singing on Cincinnati radio stations in the early 1940s and became lead singer for several big bands (Bob Crosby, Les Brown) of the swing era. After testing for Warner Brothers she made some middling musicals which required a lot of smiling. She finally got a dramatic role in *Young Man with a Horn* (1950). Day also played dramatic roles in *Love Me or Leave Me* (1955) and *Midnight Lace* (1960).

Although most of her roles have been cloying Pollyannas, some have been self-assured, though mutable, career women. In *Teacher's Pet* (1958) and *Lover Come Back* (1962), she played women who were vulnerable, not always perfect or right.

De Havilland: "The Heiress"

Although **Olivia de Havilland** (1916-   ) was not a Hollywood superstar in the 1930s and 1940s, she was a working star, one whose acting capabilities kept her employed steadily from the age of eighteen.

Born in Tokyo of British parents, she moved to California when she was three.

In 1934 she appeared in *A Midsummer Night's Dream* at the Hollywood Bowl and made the film version at Warner Brothers. She made eight films with Errol Flynn, beginning with *Captain Blood* in 1935 and later in *Robin Hood* (1938).

She played the saintly Melanie in *Gone with the Wind* (1939), and was nominated for an Oscar for *Hold Back the Dawn* in 1941 (she lost to her sister Joan Fontaine). De Havilland won her first Oscar for *To Each His Own* (1946). She made *The Snake Pit,* in 1947, an unprecedented film about a mental institution. Her second Oscar was for *The Heiress* (1949). In 1962 she made a horror film — *Hush, Hush Sweet Charlotte*.

Dietrich: World-weary Beauty

The fascination of **Marlene Dietrich** (1901-   ) today is exactly what it was almost fifty years ago when she began making films: she is beautiful, aloof, sophisticated, demanding, generous, world weary.

Born in Germany, she made several films there before the American public saw her in *The Blue Angel* in 1930, directed by her mentor, Josef von Sternberg. Her films were banned in Germany because she refused to return there under Hitler's orders.

Desire (1936) was a romantic comedy,

Life imitated art when *The Blue Angel*'s Marlene Dietrich became a cabaret singer in later life.

and was followed by other films that were not popular. *Destry Rides Again* (1939) established her as a major star. In the film she was sexy, playful, accessible. She made few films in the 1950s. Possibly her best role was her last — *Judgment at Nuremberg* (1961).

Dietrich, the cabaret singer, is as famous as the star, and in her suggestive, ennui-filled voice has sung in clubs all over the world. She won the U.S. Medal of Freedom and the French Legion of Honor for her front-line entertaining during World War II.

Dunaway: Clyde's Bonnie

Faye Dunaway (1941-   ) had played on Broadway and off Broadway (*A Man for All Season's* and *Hogan's Goat*) when she shot her way to stardom in the film *Bonnie and Clyde,* which won her a nomination for an Academy Award in 1966.

Dunaway's road to success was a steady progression because her gifts of talent and steely determination were recognized. While a student at Boston University, she played the lead in Arthur Miller's *The Crucible,* directed by Broadway director Lloyd Richards who recommended her for the Repertory Theatre of Lincoln Center in New York. She was fresh out of college when she made her Broadway debut in *Seasons. Bonnie and Clyde* was her third film.

Her subsequent films were unspectacular and were separated by stage and television appearances. Two films did, however, showcase her superb skills: Roman Polanski's *Chinatown* and *Network* (1976), for which she won the Best Actress Oscar.

Fawcett-Majors: Poster Girl

The only person with a face more familiar than **Farrah Fawcett-Majors** (1946-   ) may be George Washington, and that's questionable. With only one television series (Charlie's Angels) under her belt, her face and flawless body glow with innocent expectation on what is probably the hottest selling poster of all time.

Fawcett-Majors has made enough commercials to make her recognizable in the Sahara desert.

The hyphenated name is her only nod to women's lib. Her contracts stipulate that she be sprung at 6 P.M. so she can be home in time to fix dinner for her "Six Million Dollar" husband, Lee Majors.

The Texas daughter of an oil contractor has made a handful of forgettable films, and is admittedly not overly endowed with acting talent. She's sanguine about Hollywood and stardom. "I'd like to do a movie, but if not, it's not the end of the world," she has said.

Fonda: Activist Actress

Most people have only one life. **Jane Fonda** (1937-   ) owing to her inability to keep a low profile, seems to have had several. The daughter of actor Henry Fonda, she started life among the privileged. Educated at Vassar College and New York's Actors Studio, she starred with her father in an Omaha production of *The Country Girl* in 1955. In 1960, family friend Joshua Logan gave her a big part in her first film, *Tall Story,* which he directed. That film and her next, *A Walk on the Wild Side* (1961) were critically praised. Not so *In the Cool of the Day,* for which the Harvard Lampoon gave her the worst actress award for 1963.

Then Fonda emerged as a sexpot around the time she married French film director Roger Vadim after making *La Ronde* with him in France. She was a

Klute sealed Jane Fonda's reputation as one of the nation's most talented young actresses.

reincarnation of Brigitte Bardot in his *Barbarella*.

Fonda again emerged as a serious actress in 1969 with her brilliant performance as a Depression marathon dancer in *They Shoot Horses, Don't They?*, for which she won the New York Film Critics' Best Actress Award.

As her ability as an actress coalesced and her marriage to Vadim crumbled, Fonda became a political activist. She was outspoken — often strident — as an antiwar critic and civil rights exponent. She was also by 1972 an Academy Award-winning actress for her role in *Klute*. Critic Pauline Kael said, "There isn't another young actress in American films who can touch her."

Today, although she still has her causes — she is currently married to former antiwar activist and once Senate hopeful Tom Hayden — the stridency has gone. Her 1977 film, *Fun with Dick and Jane*, is a romantic comedy about a couple of cute crooks. In *Julia*, her latest film, she portrays Lillian Hellman in an episode from Hellman's book *Pentimento*.

Fonda admits that she's a better actress than she used to be, and her new calm may account for ripe performances. "If you view things in a broader sense," she says, "you bring so much more to it."

Garbo: Reclusive Star

Greta Garbo (1905-   ) in her youth was the prototype of the Beautiful Face. Other faces have certainly been a treat to look upon, but looking at Garbo provoked a kind of awe that, by comparison, renders the Mona Lisa redundant.

Garbo was not only beautiful, she was also elusive. "I van to be let alone" is a lifelong credo that has made journalists and fans maniacally curious.

Although Garbo made few films in her career, she played some of the best roles for women: *Anna Christie* (1930), *Mata Hari* (1931), *Grand Hotel* (1932), and *Queen Christina* (1933).

Born Greta Gustafson in Sweden, she made her first American film, *The Torrent,* in 1926. The quintessential tragic figure she played on film was perfected in *Anna Karenina* (1935) and *Camille* (1936). Stories of miserable love affairs were her specialty in the 1930s, and she played them all with sob-inducing flair. *Ninotchka* (1939) was a hugely successful comedy and proof of her range as an actress.

At thirty-six Garbo dropped out of films at the height of her career, ensuring the public's unblemished memory of her beauty and artistry in her twenty-four films.

Greta Garbo supposedly repeated her *Flesh and the Devil* love scenes with John Gilbert off screen.

Emmy Awards

Best Actress category begun with 1950 awards; drama (*) and comedy (§) categories first divided with 1952 awards.

Beginning with 1953 awards, actresses were awarded for their roles in continuing series. The series is given after their names, in parentheses. When not specified */§, only one award was given in a Best Actress in a Series category.

1950
Gertrude Berg
1951
Imogene Coca
1952
*Helen Hayes
§Lucille Ball
1953
Eve Arden (Our Miss Brooks)
1954
Loretta Young (The Loretta Young
   Show)
1955
Lucille Ball (I Love Lucy)
1956
*Loretta Young (The Loretta Young
   Show)
§Nanette Fabray (Caesar's Hour)
1957
Jane Wyatt (Father Knows Best)
1958-59
*Loretta Young (The Loretta Young
   Show)
§Jane Wyatt (Father Knows Best)
1959-60
Jane Wyatt (Father Knows Best)
1960-61
Barbara Stanwyck (The Barbara
   Stanwyck Show)
1961-62
Shirley Booth (Hazel)
1962-63
Shirley Booth (Hazel)
1963-64
Mary Tyler Moore (The Dick Van Dyck
   Show)
1964-65
(No award made to an actress in a
   series role.)

1965-66
*Barbara Stanwyck (The Big Valley)
§Mary Tyler Moore (The Dick Van Dyck
   Show)
1966-67
*Barbara Bain (Mission: Impossible)
§Lucille Ball (The Lucy Show)
1967-68
*Barbara Bain (Mission: Impossible)
§Lucille Ball (The Lucy Show)
1968-69
*Barbara Bain (Mission: Impossible)
§Hope Lange (The Ghost and Mrs.
   Muir)
1969-1970
*Susan Hampshire (The Forsyte Saga)
§Hope Lange (The Ghost and Mrs.
   Muir)
1970-71
*Susan Hampshire (The First
   Churchills)
§Jean Stapleton (All in the Family)
1971-72
*Glenda Jackson (Elizabeth R)
§Jean Stapleton (All in the Family)
1972-73
*Michael Learned (The Waltons)
§Mary Tyler Moore (The Mary Tyler
   Moore Show)
1973-74
*Michael Learned (The Waltons)
§Mary Tyler Moore (The Mary Tyler
   Moore Show)
1974-75
*Jean Marsh (Upstairs, Downstairs)
§Valerie Harper (Rhoda)
1975-76
*Michael Learned (The Waltons)
§Mary Tyler Moore (The Mary Tyler
   Moore Show)

Gardner: Passionate and Beautiful

Ava Gardner (1922-   ) was a product of the Hollywood studio factory that manufactured starlets like gumdrops. After the North Carolina beauty's first screen test, an MGM executive allegedly said, "She can't act; she didn't talk; she's sensational."

Her career and private life have been highly publicized. As a contract star she had to do what the movies handed her, which did nothing to improve her acting ability. What got attention for her was her marriage to Mickey Rooney, then at the top of his career. That marriage lasted a little over a year, as did her next marriage to Artie Shaw. Gardner's popularity gained momentum, mainly because publicity departments ground out pictures of her as sultry, glamorous, a bit wicked.

Gardner's acting talent was showcased in *Showboat* (1951), *The Snows of Kilimanjaro* (1952), and *The Barefoot Contessa* (1954), films in which she was vastly more than just another pretty face. She received her only Academy Award nomination for *Mogambo* (1953), and was box-office dynamite. Her stormy and highly visible romance and marriage to Frank Sinatra in 1951 ended in divorce in 1957.

Gardner's performances in *On the Beach* (1959) and *Seven Days in May* (1964) finally got her the kind of critical praise she deserved, possibly because the roles were gritty and good. Her finest performance may have been in *The Night of the Iguana* (1964), in which she plays a bawdy, passionate woman of ebbing beauty with venom and understanding.

Judy Garland won her life's wistful theme song, "Somewhere Over The Rainbow," in *The Wizard of Oz*.

Garland: Everybody's Dorothy

When **Judy Garland** (1922-1969) sang "You Made Me Love You" in *Broadway Melody of 1938*, it was impossible to believe that the mature, succulent voice belonged to a fourteen-year-old. The following year the voice and the actress captivated everyone who saw *The Wizard of Oz*.

There are no surprises in the facts of Garland's life because she loved to talk about them. Judy (née Gumm) Garland was born in Grand Rapids, Minnesota, the daughter of vaudevillians. She and her two older sisters were billed as the Gumm Sisters. When the act broke up, Garland continued to sing on her own.

When she landed the role of Dorothy in *Oz*, she was already a veteran of several films. She received an Academy Award for the role. She starred in several film musical comedies in the 1940s — *Babes in Arms, Strike Up the Band, For Me and My Gal*, and *Meet Me in St. Louis*. By the end of the decade she had acquired a reputation for unreliability, because of her alleged dependence on pills that had been prescribed at the insistence of studio chiefs to control her weight. She abandoned or was fired from several pictures. In 1954 she made *A Star is Born*, which

is considered her best dramatic performance. In 1961 she received an Oscar nomination for *Judgment at Nuremberg*. Her last film was *I Could Go on Singing*.

Garland died from an overdose of sleeping pills in 1969, leaving one million dollars in debts. Despite her demons (if not because of them), she was still a draw even in death — twenty thousand people mobbed her funeral.

Gish: Silent Movie Queen

Lillian Gish (1869-   ) queen of the silent silver screen, drew critical praise throughout her film career. With D. W. Griffith's direction, she was the fragile, virginal epitome of virtue in *Birth of a Nation* (1915), *Intolerance* (1916), and *Broken Blossoms* (1918).

Born in Ohio, she grew up in New York City with her sister, Dorothy, also a Griffith protégé: Gish's appearance was a throwback to the later Victorian era. She played either good girls who were rewarded, as in *Orphans of the Storm* (1922), or bad girls who repented, as in *Way Down East* (1920). The kind of purity she portrayed in the decade had lost its appeal by the 1920s. She won an honorary Academy Award in 1971.

Though limited in her early films, her

stage roles were more varied, ranging from Marguerite Gautier in *Camille* to the nurse in *Romeo and Juliet* (1965). She is currently at work on a film directed by Robert Altman.

Grable: Lovely Legs

World War II GIs loved **Betty Grable** (1916-1973) because of her legs. Three million photographs of her scattered around the world at assorted war fronts made her their favorite pinup.

"My legs made me," Grable said, admitting also that she had little voice and below-average dancing skills. All the same, she was one of Hollywood's most popular musical-comedy actresses in the 1940s. Her forty-plus films grossed millions of dollars, her characters were fun, and she took war-weary minds off their troubles.

Grable was born in St. Louis and honed for Hollywood by her mother, who provided dancing and saxophone lessons. "It's good she pushed me," Grable said, "because I'm basically a lazy person." Her films included *Tin Pan Alley* (1940), *Four Jills in a Jeep* (1944), and *Follow the Fleet* (1936).

Harlow: Star with Sass

Jean Harlow (1911-1937). She was a star with sass. She was tough, flamboyant, and had a sense of humor that, in her prime, was (tragically) seldom reported in the media.

Harlow was born in Kansas City, Missouri, and married a wealthy young businessman when she was sixteen. They moved to Beverly Hills, and she began in minor film roles. She was an immediate sensation when she starred in *Hell's Angels* (1930).

It was her style rather than her acting ability that brought Harlow success. With bleached platinum blond hair and a lusty, slim body, she portrayed three-dimensional women who liked sex at a time when the subject was roses.

In 1933 she made *Red Dust* with Clark Gable, who was a lifelong friend. She made *Dinner at Eight* the same year to rapturous reviews. *Bombshell* (1933) is considered her best film, in which she gleefully satirized her sex-driven image. *Saratoga Trunk* (1937) was her last film, and she died, reportedly of uremic poison-

"Blonde Bombshell" Jean Harlow was Hollywood's leading sex goddess of the 1930s.

ing, before the shooting was completed. She was twenty-six.

Harris: Riveting Performer

A noted drama teacher once said that there are some actors with whom you simply cannot share a stage because you will be ignored as though invisible. **Julie Harris** (1925-   ) is such an actress, a tiny woman with a presence so riveting that you look at no one but her. In her thirty years on the Broadway stage she has won five Tonys and appeared in twenty-six plays.

Harris was born in Gross Pointe, Michigan. She studied at the Yale University School of the Theatre and New York's Actors Studio. Her Broadway debut was in a short-lived play, *It's a Gift*. In 1948 critic Richard Watts wrote of her performance in *Sundown Beach* (1948) that she was going to be "one of *the* important actresses of her time."

Her portrayal of Frankie Adams in *The Member of the Wedding* (1950) fulfilled Watts' expectations. She repeated the performance in the film version.

Women and Television

If you thought Farrah Fawcett-Majors and the other Charlie's Angels only appealed to male television audiences, guess again. According to the Nielsen Television Index, a higher percentage of women than men in Nielsen households watched the three female detectives fight crime during the last three months of 1976. Some 21.2 percent of women in homes surveyed by the A.C. Nielsen Company viewed the show, as compared with 18.4 percent of men in such households.

Nielsen found that the shows attracting the highest percentages of female viewers during October through December, 1976 were, in descending order: Big Event Part 1, Happy Days, NBC Monday Night Movies, Laverne and Shirley, Charlie's Angels, All In The Family, M*A*S*H, The Waltons, Little House on the Prairie, Bionic Woman, ABC Friday Night Movie, One Day At A Time, Baretta, Alice, and Rich Man, Poor Man — Book 2.

Though most of the same shows rated high among male viewers, men did not include The Waltons, Little House on the Prairie, Bionic Woman, Alice, or Rich Man, Poor Man in their top fifteen.

NFL Monday Night Football, and 60 Minutes ranked second and third in popularity among male viewers, but did not make the list of women's favorites.

Women, in general, watch more television that men, says Nielsen. In 1976, women over age 18 spent an average of 32 hours and 47 minutes each week in front of the TV set as compared with 28 hours and 41 minutes weekly for the population as a whole.

Harris has always played to the limits of her artistry, which seems unlimited. She played Sally Bowles in *I Am a Camera* (1951), Joan of Arc in *The Lark* (1955), and Emily Dickinson in her one-woman show, *The Belle of Amherst* (1977).

Harris' films include *East of Eden* (1955), *Requiem for a Heavyweight* (1962), *Harper* (1966), and *Reflections in a Golden Eye* (1967).

Hayes: Theater's First Lady

Helen Hayes (1900-   ) is "First Lady of the American Theater" and has a Broadway theater named after her. She made her stage debut at the age of five in her native Washington, D.C., her Broadway debut at the age of nine, and her first film at ten. Having grown up in theaters and films, she has seldom left them.

Her career is marked as much by achievement as by longevity. She won an Oscar for *The Sin of Madelon Claudet* (1931), the Drama League of New York Medal for her tour de force performance in *Victoria Regina* (1935). Hayes won a Tony for *Time Remembered* in 1958. She won a second Oscar for *Airport* (1971).

Helen Hayes said dance lessons she took to correct pigeon toes started her on a stage career.

Hayes's range as an actress is obvious from the variety of plays in which she has appeared, including *The Glass Menagerie* (1948), *A Touch of the Poet* (1958), and *What Every Woman Knows* (1926, 1954).

Hayward: "I'll Cry Tomorrow"
Susan Hayward (1918-1975) was an actress who dignified any movie she was in, even the flops, of which there were many.

Born Edyth Marriner in a Brooklyn slum, she was a model whose photograph came to the attention of Hollywood producers. Her first film role was a bit part in *Girls on Probation* (1938). *The Hairy Ape* (1944) established her as a star.

During her career she played an alcoholic in *Smash Up, the Story of a Woman* (1947), a southern belle in *Tap Roots* (1948), and Bathsheba in *David and Bathsheba* (1951). When she made *With a Song in My Heart* (1952) her box-office standing was at its peak. She won her first Oscar for *I'll Cry Tomorrow* (1955).

Hayward was small, with mahogany-colored hair, and a husky voice. Her best-known role was that of Barbara Graham in *I Want to Live:* (1958), in which she played the murderess facing execution. She won her second Academy Award for this role.

Hepburn: Upper-class Charm
Brussels-born **Audrey Hepburn** (1929-) has had a refined image almost from the beginning of her career. At twenty-two she starred in the Broadway play *Gigi*. At twenty-four she won an Academy Award for the film *Roman Holiday*.

Hepburn's enduring charm is that she has always seemed proper without being stiff, spunky without being spoiled. Her reed-slim, high-fashion face and figure, and her breathy, upper-class accents (she was raised in Holland and Britain) have contributed to her appeal. She made audiences and leading men William Holden and Humphrey Bogart melt in *Sabrina* (1954). In fact, she's had that effect in almost all her films, including *Funny Face* (1957), *Charade* (1963), and especially *Breakfast at Tiffany's* (1961).

Her most recent film is *Robin and Marian* (1975).

Hepburn: A Strong Individualist
Katharine Hepburn (1909-) is probably the most respected actress to emerge from Hollywood because she has never confused her movie-star image with her strong individualism. The highly charged and well-bred woman has always done exactly what she wanted, and has never been accused of reticence or vulgarity. The only actor or actress to be nominated for eleven Academy Awards, her box-office fortunes have run the gamut from A to Z, but her ego has never flagged.

Hepburn's ironclad sense of worth and work began in her native Hartford, Connecticut, where her physician father and feminist mother imbued her with the sense to break rules that are stupid. She was educated at Bryn Mawr and took her stiff upper-class voice to Hollywood where she wore oxfords and trousers and no makeup, in an era when carefully applied allure was an actress's stock in trade. She was practically typecast as Jo in *Little Women* (1933).

Hepburn's first film was *A Bill of Divorcement* (1932). She nearly stole the movie from John Barrymore.

Her sharp manner may have contributed to her reputation as box-office poison in the 1930s, but she refused to let up on her insistence for good roles.

She starred in *Philadelphia Story* on Broadway in 1939, having the presence of

"Kate Hepburn: "I have angular features and an angular personality that sometimes jabs. . .""

mind to buy up the movie rights. The film version won an Academy Award nomination for her as well as the New York Film Critics' Award. She also co-owned the screenplay for *Woman of the Year* (1942), the first of several very successful films with Spencer Tracy. Their other films included *State of the Union* (1948), *Adam's Rib* (1949), and *Pat and Mike* (1952). Their final film, completed shortly before Tracy's death, was *Guess Who's Coming to Dinner* (1967).

Hepburn's Oscars were for *Morning Glory* (1933), *Guess Who's Coming to Dinner*, and *The Lion in Winter* (1968). She is the only actress to win the Best Actress Award three times.

Holliday: Not So Dumb Blonde

Judy Holliday (1922-1965) was just about the funniest film actress of her time, and the public was robbed when she died at the age of 42.

Born in New York City, she made her first film, *Winged Victory*, in 1944. Despite an IQ of 172, Holliday was frequently cast as a dumb blonde in such films as *Adam's Rib* (1949). But she was dumb like a fox in *Born Yesterday* (1950), and won an Oscar. She had played the Broadway version first, and repeated the sequence for *Bells Are Ringing* (1960).

Holliday had a mastectomy at thirty-seven and did one more Broadway show, *Hot Spot* (1963), before her death from cancer.

Jackson: A Touch of Class

Critic Stanley Kauffman once wrote of **Glenda Jackson** (1938-   ), "She is not an actress in order to be loved but in order to act."

Born in England, she joined the Royal Shakespeare Company in 1964 and was singled out for her performance of Charlotte Corday in *Marat/Sade* in England and New York in 1964. The play established Jackson as a serious actress. For *Women in Love* (1969), she won the New York Film Critics' and Academy Awards. Critics also praised the films *Sunday Bloody Sunday* (1971) and *A Touch of Class* (1973).

The tall, angular actress has a range that rivals the best of British theater. The embodiment of her talent for wit, romance, and brittle genius was the role of Queen

Compared to Glenda Jackson, said one critic, every American actor needs more drama schooling.

Elizabeth I in the BBC production of "Elizabeth R" a tour de force performance. Her latest film is *Nasty Habits* (1977).

Kelly: Her Serene Highness

Grace Kelly (1928-   ) became Her Serene Highness of Monaco more than twenty years ago, but she remains a matter of curiosity to her movie fans.

Born into Philadelphia society, Kelly was a model during her student days at

Grace Kelly met her prince while filming *To Catch A Thief* on location in southern France.

New York's American Academy of Dramatic Arts. She made her Broadway debut in 1949, and landed her first big film role, opposite Gary Cooper, in *High Noon* (1952). In 1955 she won an Academy Award for *The Country Girl,* and the following year was somewhat typecast in *High Society.*

Her marriage to Prince Rainier III in 1956 ended her film career.

Kerr: Well-bred English Lady

It took a long time for **Deborah Kerr** (1921-   ) to show she was more than just another long-suffering brick of a British lady in films. Her stage debut was as a member of the Sadler's Wells *corps de ballet* in 1938. Kerr's big film break was *Major Barbara* in 1941, and she starred in a string of films in which she was perfectly prim.

Black Narcissus (1947) got her credit for being the heavyweight actress she is, and she won the New York Film Critics' Award for it. But she continued to play the long-suffering heroine in such films as *The Hucksters* (1947), *If Winter Comes* (1947), *King Solomon's Mines* (1950), and *Quo Vadis* (1951).

She fought for the role of the promiscuous army wife in *From Here to Eternity* (1953), for which she received an Oscar nomination. She made her Broadway debut to great praise in *Tea and Sympathy* (1956), and became a Hollywood hit in the film version of the play in 1956. She was brilliant in *The Night of the Iguana* (1964) as a neurotic spinster. *The King and I* (1956) was probably her most popular film.

Leigh: Scarlett O'Hara

Vivien Leigh (1913-1967) made a lot of famous Hollywood stars unhappy when she landed the role of Scarlett O'Hara in *Gone With the Wind* after a talent hunt that rivaled a political convention. That was in 1939, and she won an Oscar for the film.

Born in India of British parents, she was already an established star in the English theater. She was as successful on stage, as in films and managed to have a tandem theater-film career.

She was married to Laurence Olivier when she played Juliet to his Romeo on Broadway, and Emma to his Alexander Lord Horatio Nelson in the film *That Hamilton Woman* (1941). She toured with him in the Old Vic, England's venerable repertory company. A 1949 London production of *Streetcar Named Desire* led to the role of Blanche DuBois in the 1951 film. She won another Oscar for this film.

Divorced from Olivier in 1960, she made her last film, *Ship of Fools,* in 1965.

Lombard: Gable's True Love

If **Carole Lombard** (1908-1942) could see what has happened to her in books and films since her death in an airplane crash, she would come back and grind grapefruits in a few faces. Lombard was capable of anything, was never known for moderation, and certainly wouldn't stand for inaccuracy.

Born Jane Peters in Fort Wayne, Indiana, she had a spell-binding face, pale blond hair, and a flawless figure. She also had an outrageous sense of humor, often black, and endless capacity for fun.

Lombard started in films with Mack Sennett in 1927 in *The Girl From Everywhere.* In 1934 she became a star and first-rate comedienne in *We're Not Dressing.* In 1937 she was Hollywood's top money-maker.

After her marriage to Clark Gable in 1939, she limited her film appearances. *To*

Extensive surgery restored Carole Lombard's face after a disfiguring car crash early in her career.

Child waif turned superstar, Sophia Loren is thought by many the world's most beautiful woman.

Be or Not To Be (1942) was completed two weeks before her death.

Loren: Sensuous Italian Beauty
The wealth and international fame Italian actress **Sophia Loren** (1934-   ) enjoys today are a far cry from her early years. Loren, an illegitimate child, was born in an Italian charity hospital. In wartime Italy, poverty and breadlines made up her social milieu. Loren remembers those days vividly. "Compared to pain," she said, "money is never real."

After entering a beauty contest at fifteen, she came to the attention of film producer Carlo Ponti. He changed her professional name (and later married her), and guided what has become a spectacular film career.

Loren's talent for comedy and depressing dramatic roles have provided counterpoint to her credits. She was hilarious in *Marriage Italian Style* (1964) and *Yesterday, Today and Tomorrow* (1963), and electric in *Two Women* (1961), for which she won an Academy Award as Best Actress.

She still makes an occasional movie ("If I stopped [working] right now I would feel a little like my arm was cut off"), but prefers spending most of her time with her husband and two sons.

Loy: The Thin Man's Lady
Myrna Loy (1905-   ) made more than sixty movies before she became a star.

as a dancer in a Grauman's Chinese Theatre chorus line. *The Animal Kingdom* made her famous in 1942, and after that she appeared opposite a number of superstars, including Clark Gable.

She always was the dutiful wife, especially in *The Thin Man* as Nora Charles (1934). She was the perfect (and, at last, perfectly believable) wife and mother in *The Best Years of Our Lives* (1946), and hilarious in *Cheaper by the Dozen* (1950).

Offscreen, Loy has shown an active social conscience. During the McCarthy era she was one of a handful of actors to protest treatment of actors by the House Committee on Un-American Activities.

Of the golden era of Hollywood, during which she was one of its most successful stars, she later said "When you think of those years now with all that . . . sweetness and light, you must admit it wasn't all that. Quite, quite horrible."

MacDonald: Romantic Soprano
Jeanette MacDonald (1907-55) of the perpendicular eyebrows, rosebud lips, and sparrow voice never got beyond her persona as Nelson Eddy's sugary soprano. However, she was just what filmgoers of the 1930s wanted, and MacDonald had a slavishly loyal following at the box office.

Born in Philadelphia, she sang and danced in a series of Broadway musicals in the 1920s. In 1929 she was Maurice Chevalier's leading lady in the film *The Love Parade*, making her a star first time out.

The first of her eight pictures with baritone Eddy was *Naughty Marietta* (1935), and the mix between the stars and their saccharine romantic stories spelled "gold mine" for MGM.

San Francisco (1936), starring MacDonald opposite Clark Gable, was one of the most popular films of the 1930s. One of the few times she was allowed to shuck her cloying image and showcase her talent as a comedienne was in *Broadway Serenade* (1939). She was at her funny best in *Cairo* (1942).

After an abortive attempt at grand opera she made a few more films, the last of which was *The Sun Comes Up* in 1949.

MacLaine: Happy Hoofer
Shirley MacLaine (1934-   ) on film and

stage has grown up from America's happiest hooker to smash hoofer. Offstage she has had a thing or two to say and write about the state of the world. Privately, she has hung out with Frank Sinatra and New York City's intellectual elite.

Shirley MacLean Beaty (she's Warren Beatty's sister) was born in Richmond, Virginia, and began studying ballet when she was two. Her first Broadway musical was *Me and Juliet* (1953) as a dancer in the chorus. Her next musical was *Pajama Game,* in which she understudied Carol Haney, the leading dancer. She replaced an injured Haney, was spotted by a Hollywood producer, and was signed for her film debut in *The Trouble with Harry* (1954).

MacLaine was decorative and funny in several subsequent films, but was taken very seriously for her heartbreaking Ginny Moorehead in *Some Came Running* (1959). She was nominated for an Academy Award for the role. MacLaine was hilarious in *Ask Any Girl* (1959).

She has, she claims, played hookers in fourteen films, including *Irma La Douce* (1963) and *Sweet Charity* (1968).

In the 1970s MacLaine dropped out of films and opted for politics, working in Senator George McGovern's 1972 campaign. She led the first women's delegation to China, and has written two best

sellers — *Don't Fall Off the Mountain* and *You Can Get There From Here*.

Mercouri: Never on Sunday

Melina Mercouri (1925-   ), studied classical theater for years in Greece and has appeared in more than a hundred plays, but it was her debut in an American film, *Never on Sunday* (1960), her first comedy, for which she is best known.

Born into one of Greece's most distinguished families, she spent a lot of her privileged youth being thrown out of schools. She also spent a lot of time with writers and politicians who visited her home.

Mercouri married at seventeen, but was soon separated. She enrolled in the National Theater Academy. She appeared in numerous plays to critical enthusiasm.

Her film career begain in 1954 when she started in *Stella,* a movie made in Greece. In 1956 she met American director Jules Dassin (whom she later married), and starred in several of his films, including *Never on Sunday* and *Topkapi.* In 1967 she starred in the Broadway versions of *Sunday* and *Ilya, Darling.* Her most recent film is *Nasty Habits* (1977).

Offscreen, Mercouri has been active in Greek politics. She was an outspoken critic of the military junta in 1967, and lost her Greek passport. After the junta collapsed in 1974, she ran for Parliament and lost by only ninety-two votes.

Minnelli: With a "Z"

When **Liza Minnelli** (1946-   ) made her Broadway debut at nineteen in *Flora, the Red Menace,* she won a Tony. When she made her second film, *The Sterile Cuckoo* (1969), she was nominated for an Academy Award. She got the Oscar in 1972 for *Cabaret.* She won an Emmy for her television special, "Liza with a Z."

Minnelli has gotten her impressive career together in spite of a chaotic youth. During her childhood she attended about twenty schools in California and Europe. As the daughter of the late Judy Garland and film director Vincente Minnelli, she gives credit for her early success to Garland. "It was simply my mother's name, plus the curiosity factor."

Today, it is hard to imagine how Minnelli can top herself, having collected

"Sure I'd play a hooker again," says Shirley MacLaine. "If she got to be Secretary of State."

Marilyn Monroe said she began play acting to escape the reality of her luckless childhood.

armloads of awards in every medium of the profession. But she's philosophical about it. "Listen," she says, "I know show biz ain't all singin' and dancin'."

Monroe: Original Sex Symbol

Fifteen years after her death, the public is still fascinated with **Marilyn Monroe** (1927-62). Everybody but her garbage collector has written a book about her.

Everyone knows she was born Norma Jean Baker, was raised in orphanages, and was married at fourteen. Monroe married again to Joe DiMaggio, married again to Arthur Miller, wanted babies, brought home strays, went to bed a lot, couldn't tell time.

A lot of people have speculated that she was/was not a great actress and comedienne. She was without a doubt the last of the great big studio movie queens and for whatever reason, she always got a response from her audience.

Monroe's first noteworthy role was in *The Asphalt Jungle* (1950), followed by *All About Eve* (1950). Her most ethereal, heart-stopping role was in *Bus Stop* (1956). The ultimate of her sexpot roles came in *Gentlemen Prefer Blondes* (1953).

Her best films were made toward the end of her life — *Some Like It Hot* (1959) and *The Misfits* (1961).

She died in 1962 from an overdose of barbiturates. That year she had told a *Life* interviewer, "I never understood it — the sex symbol — I always thought symbols were things you clash together. That's the trouble, a sex symbol becomes a thing — I just hate to be a thing."

Moore: Newsroom Sweetheart

Mary Tyler Moore (1937-   ) is contemporary America's sweetheart. When her television series, "The Mary Tyler Moore Show" aired its final segment in 1977, magazine-cover stories mourned its passing and America sat home to tearfully watch that last Saturday-night episode. Her appeal was best explained by former co-star, Valerie Harper: "She likes a great big glass of cold milk . . . to wash down her birth-control pill."

Moore was born in Brooklyn and grew up in Los Angeles. After several minor television roles she was signed as Laura Petrie on "The Dick Van Dyke Show" from 1961 to 1966. She returned to New York to play Holly Golightly in the Broadway musical *Breakfast at Tiffany's*, but it never opened. She then made some films, *Thoroughly Modern Millie* (1967), *What's So Bad About Feeling Good?* (1968), and *Change of Habit* (1969). The best that can be said of her movies is that she was pert.

Moore is a tough, disciplined performer who knows exactly what she does best. "I'm not an actress who can create a character," she says. "I play me."

Moore is married to her producer, Grant Tinker. Their production company, MTM Enterprises, has her name but his muscle.

Moreau: French Earthiness

It took many years for **Jeanne Moreau** (1928-   ) to evolve from a sexy, artistically limited French starlet to the great actress she is today.

Born in Paris, Moreau got her training with the Comédie Française, France's most respected repertory company. She made her film debut in *Last Love* (1949), the first of many movies in which she played sexually aware, if not liberated, characters. Not until the film *Elevator to the Scaffold* in 1958 were her screen possibilities fully revealed.

The quality of her vehicles improved, but she played essentially the same roles, using her softly erotic, full features to their suggestive limits.

The erotic woman gained a trace of menace in *Jules et Jim* (1962) for which she received international rave reviews.

Moreau is working at full capacity with the release of her latest film, *Lumière* (1977), which she directed and wrote.

Neal: A Splendid Recovery

Patricia Neal (1926-   ) of the well-modulated voice began making films in 1949, but didn't find her film niche until 1963 when she made *Hud*.

The Kentucky-born actress was, however, very successful on Broadway from the beginning. After studying drama at Northwestern University, she made her Broadway debut in *Seven Mirrors* (1945). The following year she played a leading role in Lillian Hellman's *Another Part of the Forest*, and won five awards, one of them a Tony.

Her first film, *John Loves Mary* (1949), was a critical disaster. Her next films, *The Fountainhead* (1949) and *Bright Leaf* (1950) fared no better.

The Hasty Heart (1950) got kinder reviews, but most of her 1950s' films were unworthy of her talent. In 1952 she returned to Broadway in *The Children's Hour* where the love affair with reviewers resumed. With *Hud*, Neal came into her own on the screen, and won an Oscar for it.

In 1965 she suffered a series of strokes that totally incapacitated and nearly killed her. With the drive and encouragement of her husband, writer Roald Dahl, she recovered. In 1968 she made *The Subject Was Roses* and won a second Oscar.

Pickford: America's Sweetheart

"America's Sweetheart" **Mary Pickford** (1893-   ) tickled the fancy of millions of silent filmgoers from 1912 to 1928. People loved her for her blond curls, her baby face, and her virginity and innocence. Then Pickford made a mistake. She grew up, and it finished her movie career.

Born in Canada, she began her stage career at five, and became a superstar in the film *A Poor Little Rich Girl* (1917), in which she played a child.

Her personal wardrobe consisted of ma-

Despite her childlike image, Mary Pickford earned a womanly salary of $350,000 a year by 1917.

ture, stylish clothes to be worn at home, and girlish frills for public appearances. Other ingenue films were *Rebecca of Sunnybrook Farm* and *Daddy Long Legs*.

At thirty-seven she cut off her curls and played leading roles in *The Taming of the Shrew* and *Coquette* (for which she won an Oscar), her first "talkies." Audiences were not receptive, and she retired from films in 1929.

A founder of United Artists, she was married to Douglas Fairbanks and later to Charles 'Buddy" Rogers.

Reynolds: Adorable Ingenue

During the 1950s **Debbie Reynolds** (1932-   ) was eternally typecast as the All-American girl next door and it nearly finished her career.

Born in Texas and raised in California, she won the Miss Burbank title and got a screen test from Warner Brothers. After a few bit parts she transferred to MGM and appeared in *Three Little Words* (1950) as the "boop boop a doop" girl. Her best role was in *Singin' in the Rain* (1951).

Reynolds' considerable comic skills emerged in *The Tender Trap* (1955). She played a straight dramatic role in *The Catered Affair* with skill, but returned to cute roles in *Bundle of Joy* (1956) with her then-husband, Eddie Fisher.

Reynolds again played an adorable ingenue in *Tammy and the Bachelor* (1957).

It Started with a Kiss (1959) had humor with more bite; *The Rat Race* (1960) was no humor, all bite, and a dramatic departure for Reynolds. That was about the time that Fisher left Reynolds for Elizabeth Taylor. Reynolds married Harry Karl (they have since divorced). Her most memorable film in the 1960s was *The Unsinkable Molly Brown* (1964). She scored a personal triumph on Broadway in *Irene* (1973).

Currently she is dazzling audiences in her nightclub act in Las Vegas and elsewhere.

Russell: Auntie Mame

Toward the end of her career, **Rosalind Russell** (1911-1976) mused, "I'll match my flops with anybody's. But I wouldn't have missed them. Flops are a part of life's menu and I'm never a girl to miss out on any of the courses."

At the end of the first act of the play, *Auntie Mame*, Russell said these lines which typified her attitude toward life, "Life is a banquet, and most of you poor sons-of-bitches are starving to death!"

Rosalind Russell was Auntie Mame, and her spectacular career and full life were characterized by wit, guts, and style. So, too, were the twenty-three career girls she played in films over the years.

Born in Waterbury, Connecticut, she made her film debut in *Evelyn Prentice* in

In later life, "Roz" Russell maintained high spirits despite agonizing arthritis and cancer.

1934 after several years in stock and on Broadway. She perfected the comic-bitchy professional woman in *His Girl Friday* (1940) and *Take a Letter, Darling* (1942).

Russell did the play *Auntie Mame* in 1956 and the film in 1958. Her finest dramatic role was in *Picnic* (1956).

Shearer: First Lady of Silent Screen

By 1927 **Norma Shearer** (1904-   ) had made several silent movies, such as *He Who Gets Slapped,* but her career was in its infancy. That was the year she married Irving Thalberg, the boy wonder of Hollywood, and everything changed.

Marrying MGM's production chief virtually guaranteed Shearer her choice of roles. She was sophisticated and elegant in *Their Own Desire* (1930), and won an Oscar for *The Divorcee* (1930). After *Smilin' Through* (1933) she was called "The First Lady of the Screen." In 1936 she starred in one of Thalberg's "prestige" productions, *Romeo and Juliet,* whose chief merit was that it brought Shakespeare to the masses.

Thalberg died in 1936, and Shearer did six more films, including *Marie Antoinette*.

Stanwyck: Tough Women

The tough, aggressive women **Barbara Stanwyck** (1907-   ) portrayed were played with a conviction that came from experience. Born in Brooklyn, Stanwyck was orphaned at four and was raised by her older sister and assorted relatives.

She began as a dancer in speakeasies, then on Broadway. Her first film was *Broadway Nights* in 1927. Her hardbitten, sensuous appearance made her typecasting inevitable in such films as *Illicit* and *Ten Cents a Dance*. By 1932 and *Forbidden,* she was a critic's delight and a big box-office draw. In 1937, she made *Stella Dallas,* a tear-jerker and classic "woman's" movie. In 1944 she was the highest paid woman in the United States.

Stanwyck was good at comedy in *The Mad Miss Minton* (1938). But her peak performance was in *Double Indemnity* (1944), for which she was nominated for an Oscar. Her fourth Oscar nomination (she never won one) was for her 1948 film, *Sorry, Wrong Number*.

On Barbra Streisand's mantle sit an Emmy, Grammy, Tony, and Oscars for best actress and best song.

Stanwyck won an Emmy for her television series, "The Big Valley," which ran from 1965 to 1969.

Streisand: Superstar

Barbra Streisand (1942-   ) has displayed the delicacy of a Sherman tank since she began her career in a smoky club in Greenwich Village when she grabbed the mike as though it were a weapon, and snarled her way through a song. Her success has been stunning, and while she may not evoke warmth, no one can deny that her talent is one in a million.

Streisand left her native Brooklyn immediately upon graduation from Erasmus Hall High School with a 93 percent average. Her Village appearance, an off-Broadway one-nighter, and several television appearances brought her to the attention of Broadway producer David Merrick. He signed her for the role of Miss Marmelstein in *I Can Get It for You Wholesale* (1962).

From there she went on to star in the play and film versions of *Funny Girl* (1964), for which she won an Oscar. She starred in the film version of *Hello Dolly!*, released in 1970, the year she won a Tony for "star of the decade" for her work in the theater.

Her latest film is *A Star Is Born* (1976).

Swanson: Eternal Beauty

Gloria Swanson (1898-   ) seems to be eternal. The still stunning actress began in silent films in 1913. "Since there is no more live television," she said recently, "it's getting harder to prove you're not dead."

Swanson was Hollywood's leading glamour girl and box-office draw from 1918 to 1926. The Chicago-born, sultry beauty starred in several Cecil B. DeMille productions, including *Male and Female* (1919). She formed her own production company and was in the phenomenally successful *Sadie Thompson* in 1927.

Swanson continued to appear, although less frequently, in films in the 1930s and 1940s, but it was *Sunset Boulevard* (1950) that was her best picture to date. Her performance as an ebbing, insane film star was universally applauded and won her an Academy Award nomination, her third.

Taylor: Diamond Liz

Living well is the best revenge or, as **Elizabeth Taylor** (1932-   ) once put it, "Success is a great deodorant." Taylor has been the object of more press coverage than just about anyone, much of it nasty. But she is just plain unsinkable.

Born in England, she began her film career at the age of ten in a bit part in *There's One Born Every Minute* (1942). She was known then for her spectacular

Elizabeth Taylor proved *The Harvard Lampoon* wrong with films like *Cat On A Hot Tin Roof*.

beauty, an asset that helped establish her as a major star in *National Velvet* (1945).

Taylor played Amy in *Little Women* (1949) and, at eighteen, played her first romantic lead in *Conspirator*. The Harvard Lampoon, echoing popular critical sentiment, gave her an award "for so gallantly persisting in her career despite a total inability to act."

Then there were all those marriages to Nicky and Michael and Mike and Eddie and Richard and Richard and John Warner, her current husband. Every one of them was a celebrity of sorts which didn't hurt her box-office receipts.

Seldom has Taylor been subtle, from her violet eyes to her two-knuckle diamonds, to her appetite, to her humor. She eventually proved the Harvard Lampoon wrong by turning in two Academy Award winning performances: *Butterfield 8* (1960) and *Who's Afraid of Virginia Woolf?* (1966).

Turner: America's Sweater Girl

The story of how **Lana Turner** (1920-   ) got her start in films sounds like something out of a Hollywood movie. At fifteen she was discovered at a drugstore across the street from her high school. She was taken to director Mervyn LeRoy who signed her for a small but memorable part in *They Won't Forget* (1937). The part folks remembered was the sweater and skirt she wore in the film, and she was thereafter touted by publicity agents as America's "Sweater Girl."

After her appearances in *We Who Are Young* in 1940, she was taken seriously as an actress, as least seriously enough to put her in major productions. *Ziegfield Girl* (1941), *Dr. Jekyll and Mr. Hyde,* and *The Postman Always Rings Twice* (1945) were some of her best films in the 1940s.

Her popularity declined as she grew older and her television series, "The Survivors," bombed.

Tyson: Star from Harlem

Cicely Tyson (1939-   ) drew triumphant critical acclaim for her magnificent performance in the title role of the 1974 television special "The Autobiography of Miss Jane Pittman." Of her performance, critic Rex Reed wrote "It is one of the most brilliant performances I have ever seen."

Tyson brought to her role a childhood background of poverty in East Harlem, New York, great beauty, and an obsessive desire to be successful. She was in the off-Broadway production of *The Blacks* in 1961 and on Broadway in *Tiger, Tiger, Burning Bright* in 1962.

In 1963 she became the first black actress to have a role in a television series, "East Side/West Side." Her first important film role was in *Twelve Angry Men* (1957). One of her best films to date is *The Heart Is a Lonely Hunter* (1968). She won an Academy Award nomination and rapturous reviews for her leading role in *Sounder* (1972), and an Emmy for "Pittman."

Ullman: Bergman Protégée

Liv Ullmann (1930-   ) is the heir to Ingrid Bergman's reputation as the young, earthy, understanding European lover.

Born in Tokyo of Norwegian parents, she developed into one of the most respected actresses under the guiding hand of Swedish filmmaker Ingmar Bergman. Her first film with him was *Persona* (1966), in which she gave a glowing performance of controlled passion. Other films with Bergman, with whom she had a long affair, were *Shame* (1968), *The Passion of Anna* (1969), and the award-winning *Cries and Whispers* (1972). For *Cries* she won an Oscar nomination and the New York Film Critics' Award. Probably her most famous film with Bergman is *Scenes From a Marriage* (1974).

Ullmann made a stab at Hollywood in such films as *Lost Horizon* (1973) and *40 Carats* (1973).

She was a smashing success in her New York theater debut as Nora in *A Doll's House* in 1975, and later in the title role in *Anna Christie* (1977).

West: Sexy Comic

Mae West (1892-   ) of the half-mast eyelids, come hither voice, and no-nonsense seductiveness is a living institution. Her aggressive sexuality and comic genius established her as a diamond-studded star decades ago.

She was born in Brooklyn and arrived in Hollywood in 1932. Her first film was *Night After Night* (1932), followed by *She Done Him Wrong* (1933) and *I'm No Angel* (1933), both of which she wrote.

West could make the telephone directory sound like a proposition. But some of her lines were hysterically lacking in subtlety, such as "Are you packin' a rod or are you just glad to see me?"

Her best writing was a play in which she also starred — *Diamond Lil* — that opened in Brooklyn in 1928. For her role in the Broadway play *Sex*, she served eight days in jail for "indecency." The title was the most suggestive thing about the play.

Mae West perpetuates her savvy moll image. "I was the first liberated woman, y'know," she said in a recent interview. "No guy was gonna get the best of me, that's what I wrote all my scripts about."

Winters: Outspoken Actress

You either love or hate **Shelley Winters** (1922-   ) but you can't ignore her. The loud, outspoken, supremely gifted actress has had a lion's share of unqualified film successes and embarrassing bombs.

She was born Shirley Schrift in St. Louis and grew up in Brooklyn. Her first important Broadway plays were *The Night Before Christmas* and *Rosalinda* (1942). The latter got her a contract with Columbia Pictures, for which she made *Knickerbocker Holiday* (1944).

By 1948 and *A Double Life,* Winters was usually cast as a tawdry, stupid victim of men. Her finest variation of this theme was *A Place in the Sun* (1951), for which she was nominated for an Oscar. She won the Academy Award for Best Supporting Actress in *The Diary of Anne Frank* (1958), and won another Oscar nomination for *A Patch of Blue* (1964).

Wood: Child Star Who Grew Up

Everyone over forty remembers little **Natalie Wood** (1938-   ), the sulky-sweet child star of *Miracle on 34th Street*. Unlike many other screen kids, Wood grew up — wow, did she grow up — into the stripping *Gypsy* of 1962.

She was born Natasha Gurdin in California, daughter of Russian immigrants. Her mother was a ballerina, and mother and child got bit parts in *Happy Land* when Natalie was four. She threatened to upstage co-star Orson Welles in *Tomorrow Is Forever* (1946).

Wood made a bunch of movies in the 1940s and 1950s, and finally broke into adult roles in *Rebel Without a Cause* opposite the legendary James Dean in 1955. She won the title role of *Marjorie Morningstar* over one-hundred competitors. Her first important reviews came for *Splendor in the Grass* and *West Side Story,* both released in 1961. Her most recent film, *Bob and Carol and Ted and Alice* (1969), was a box-office bonanza.

Woodward: Character Counts

Unlike her husband, Paul Newman, **Joanne Woodward** (1931-   ) has never been a screen idol, but she's a first-rate actress. Whatever role she has played, Woodward has remained unique — her overriding concern has centered on the character rather than the glamour of her roles on the screen.

Born in Georgia, she attended Louisiana State University and studied acting in New York at the Actors Studio. Her first job on Broadway was as an understudy in *Picnic* (1953), where she met Newman.

Woodward's big Hollywood splash came in *The Three Faces of Eve* (1957), for which she won an Academy Award. Curiously, after *From the Terrace,* re-

Fame came to Joanne Woodward via a role nobody else wanted in *The Three Faces of Eve*.

leased in 1960, she didn't get a really good role until *A Fine Madness* (1966).

Her finest film performance, under her husband's direction, was *Rachel Rachel,* for which she won the New York Film Critics' Award. Newman also directed her — and their daughter — in *The Effect of Gamma Rays on the Man-in-the-Moon Marigolds* (1972).

Wyman: Doe-eyed Charmer

These days **Jane Wyman** (1914-   ) is best known as the ex-Mrs. Ronald Reagan. But in her heyday she was the heart-shaped-face-with-doe-eyes charmer in dozens of films. Although many of them were so-called "women's pictures," filled with tears and pathos, she also gave first-rate performances in numerous substantial films.

Wyman was born in Missouri and was taken to Hollywood by her mother when she was eight. But Hollywood wasn't interested yet.

In 1935 she started singing on radio programs. The following year she signed her first studio contract with Warner Brothers and began making films as a comedienne.

Critics became very interested in Wyman with the release of *The Lost Weekend* (1945). In 1946 she earned an Oscar nomination for *The Yearling.* She won the Oscar in 1948 for *Johnny Belinda.* Her performance in *The Glass Menagerie* (1950) was very well received.

Her most recent film, *How to Commit Marriage,* was released in 1961.

Young: "Beautiful Hack"

It's almost unbelieveable that anyone can look so everlastingly, breathlessly beautiful as **Loretta Young** (1912-   ) still does. Over the years she made close to one hundred films, most of them worthy of her reputation as "Hollywood's beautiful hack."

Born Gretchen Young in Salt Lake City, she made her film debut at fifteen in *Naughty But Nice.* In the 1930s she played the smiling martyr endlessly, but finally made a comedy, *Ladies in Love,* in 1937.

The peak of her career was *The Farmer's Daughter* (1947), for which she won an Oscar. She was nominated for an Oscar for *Come to the Stable* (1948).

"The Loretta Young Show" was one of the most popular television programs from 1953 to 1961.

NINE CINEMA HEART THROBS

Women don't just go to films to see actresses, of course. Here are nine of the greatest sheiks, swashbucklers, and con artists in cinema history.

Rudolph Valentino (1882-1926), an Italian navy dropout, was type cast as passionate Arabs and Latins in popular epics like *The Sheik* (1921), *Blood and Sand* (1922), and *The Young Rajah* (1922). Upon his death in New York City, rioting broke out in the crowd waiting to file past his casket and more than one hundred police reinforcements were required to calm things down. Excerpts from Valentino's diary published after his death indicate the screen's great lover might have been homosexual.

Douglas Fairbanks (1883-1939) and Mary Pickford were the idols of the nation by the time of their 1920 marriage. Heretofore an all-American boy, Fairbanks then acquired a moustache and a sophisticated new image. He swashbuckled his way through a number of costume extravaganzas, among them *The Mark of Zorro* (1920), *The Three Musketeers* (1921), and *Robin Hood* (1922). His dashing days were over by the time films began to talk.

John Barrymore (1882-1942), "The Great Profile," gained a reputation as one of Hollywood's greatest lovers as much for his off camera exploits as for his considerable dramatic talents. The height of his screen popularity came in the 1920s, when he starred in such classics as *Beau Brummel* (1924) and *Don Juan* (1926). Barrymore's dissipated lifestyle helped bring about his fall; the drunken former matinee idol he portrayed in *Dinner At Eight* (1933) was much like Barrymore, himself.

When the advent of the talkies doomed the careers of many silent screen lovers, Hollywood turned to **Clark Gable** (1901-1960), a former factory worker, oil well driller, and bit part actor. Undisputed stardom came to Gable with *It Happened One Night* (1934). One scene from the film revealed that Gable did not wear an undershirt, and he was blamed for their subsequent decline in sales. Gable was a bit

One of the first matinee idols was Rudolph Valentino, shown here with co-star Vilma Banky.

too overpowering for *Gone With The Wind* co-star Vivian Leigh; she said his false teeth and bad breath made their embraces less than memorable.

Mae West spied a young hopeful named **Cary Grant** (1904-   ) on a Hollywood set in 1933. If that "tall, dark, and handsome" man could talk, said West, she wanted him for her next film, *She Done Him Wrong* (1933). She got her wish, and Grant became the lucky recipient of her invitation to "come up and see me sometime." Now retired, Grant was for more than three decades one of Hollywood's handsomest and most debonair leading men.

Watching **Marlon Brando** (1924-   ) slouch and mumble his way through *A Streetcar Named Desire* in 1951 or *The Godfather* twenty-one years later, one would hardly class him as a screen idol in the traditional mold. Brando won fame by becoming the anti-hero, and in the process revolutionized American film acting. The role of mafioso Don Corleone revitalized Brando's sagging career and won him a second Oscar in 1972. But he turned down the award to protest Hollywood's treatment of American Indians. He was nominated for a less coveted award in 1977, The Diet Workshop's "Famous Fatty of the Year."

Paul Newman (1925-   ) is a fighter, just like the boxer he played in his first film, *Somebody Up There Likes Me* (1957). "I was proud as hell to be No. 19 on Nixon's enemy list," he says. Newman's athletic exploits are not limited to the film set. He took up amateur auto racing after portraying a driver in *Winning* (1968), and in 1976 won his first national-class championship meet. Newman's much admired baby blue eyes are color blind.

Steve McQueen (1930-   ) came to Hollywood via reform school, the Marines and New York's Actors' Studio. Television's *Wanted: Dead or Alive,* in which he played an old West bounty hunter, propelled him to national fame in 1958. Whether on the right or wrong side of the law, McQueen's characters are coolly heroic. The actor adds to his aura of bravery by being one of the few Hollywood stars to do most of his own stunt work.

Robert Redford (1937-   ) took up acting only after turning in his college baseball scholarship and bumming around Europe trying to become an artist. He decided early in his screen career to play only characters with whom he felt comfortable, "intrinsically American guys with their roots solidly in the American scene or tradition." An outdoorsman, Redford has devoted much of his time recently to crusading for a cleaner environment. He produced the 1976 blockbuster, *All The President's Men*.

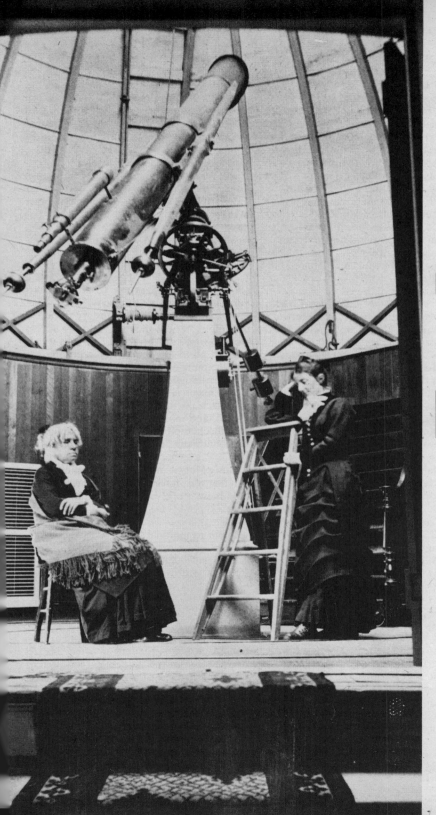

Explorers

EXPLORERS AND SCIENTISTS

Adamson: Listens to Lions

Austrian-born **Joy Adamson** (1910-   ) is the author of *Born Free,* which became an international bestseller, a movie, a song, and a television series. She and her husband George, a retired game warden, who are now separated, devoted themselves to rehabilitating wild animals born or raised in captivity for a return to life in Kenya.

Stars of *Born Free* were the lioness Elsa and her cubs. The Adamsons adopted Elsa in 1956. She was the cub of a lioness George had killed in self-defense. Eventually the Adamsons released Elsa into the wild near her birthplace. There she throve, mated, and bore three cubs.

Joy Adamson holidayed in Kenya in 1937 and "immediately fell in love" with the place. In addition to her wildlife work and her writing, she is both an accomplished artist and a classical pianist.

Her books have often been illustrated with her own paintings and photographs. More than thirteen million people around the world have bought Adamson's trilogy of books on Elsa: *Born Free, Living Free,* and *Forever Free*.

"I'm not a dreamer," Joy Adamson has said. "I think George and I proved that with Elsa. Since we humans have the better brain, isn't it our responsibility to protect our fellow creatures from, oddly enough, ourselves?"

Apgar: Baby's Friend

Virtually every infant delivered by a physician today is seen first through the eyes of **Dr. Virginia Apgar** (1909-1974). She devised the classic Apgar Score to evaluate the health of newborns. The test forces physicians to evaluate five critical points of health: Activity, Pulse, Grimace, Appearance, Respiration.

She created the test when she was a young anesthesiologist, after noting that newborn babies were usually wrapped in a blanket and put aside to be checked out later. Too often, "later" was too late, especially for babies who could have benefited from immediate special treatment. Apgar was modest about the test.

She was the first woman to receive a surgical internship at the Columbia University College of Physicians and Surgeons. She later gave up surgery for anesthesiology, a field she felt was more accessible to women. "Women," she observed, "won't go to a woman surgeon. Only the Lord can answer that one."

After assisting with some 17,000 births, Apgar began a second career, receiving, in 1959, a M.A. in public health from Johns Hopkins. She went to work as head of the division of congenital malformations of the National Foundation-March of Dimes. In 1967 she was named vice president and director of basic research, and in 1973 the Foundation named her senior vice president in charge of medical affairs.

Joy Adamson believes we must protect our fellow creatures from ourselves.

Baker: Public Health Pioneer

As a medical inspector for the New York City Health Department in 1901, **Sara Josephine Baker** (1873-1945) was ordered to seek out sick babies among Negro and Irish families in New York City's "Hell's Kitchen" area. The experience spurred her into an attack on New York's dreadful infant mortality, which sometimes reached 1,500 per week. Summer was the worst time.

In 1908, with a team of thirty trained nurses, Baker moved into a neighborhood of Italian immigrants and taught the mothers simple child care principles, such as bathing, clothing, and breast feeding. By the end of that summer, infant deaths in the area had dropped by more than one thousand over the previous summer. This work led to the establishment of New York's Division of Child Hygiene, with Baker as director.

During World War I, Baker observed, "It's six times safer to be a soldier in the trenches of France than to be born a baby in the United States."

Baker became one of the first experts in child health and public health education, bringing information to the people who needed it most. She received her M.D. degree from the Women's Medical College of the New York Infirmary for Women and Children in 1898. In 1917 she earned a Doctorate of Public Health from New York University. It was the first such degree awarded to a woman.

Benedict: Leading Anthropologist

Ruth Benedict (1887-1948) was the leading American anthropologist of the mid-1940s. Educated at Vassar, from which she received her Bachelor's degree in 1909, Benedict didn't begin her career in anthropology until she was thirty-four years old. She had previously tried many of the roles traditionally assigned to women — teacher, social worker, housewife.

"So much of the trouble is because I am a woman," she wrote. "To me it seems a very terrible thing to be a woman." She suffered fits of depression during her early life, perhaps the result of her father's death at an early age and her mother's hysterical grief.

As an anthropologist, she set forth the revolutionary thesis that each culture in the world could be observed as a human personality and described in the same terms. She also believed in understanding the cultures of other nations, rather than judging them by the yardstick of our own. Her insights were embodied in *Patterns of Culture* (1934), still considered a basic introduction to anthropology.

During World War II Benedict worked in the Office of War Information. Soon after she wrote *The Chrysanthemum and the Sword: Patterns of Japanese Culture* (1946). That book led the Office of Naval Research to make a large grant to Columbia University for a program of "Research in Contemporary Cultures," with Benedict in charge. Having been passed over for high academic position at Columbia years before when she was a lecturer there, Benedict now headed the largest anthropological research program in the country. She died of a heart attack soon after.

Cori: Nobel Biochemist

Gerty Theresa Cori (1896-1957) was the first woman to win the Nobel Prize in Medicine. The biochemist shared the 1947 award with her husband, Dr. Carl F. Cori, and Dr. B.A. Houssay of Argentina. The Coris were cited for their studies on the human body's use of starches and sugars to sustain life.

Their chief discovery involved finding a new enzyme, called phosphorylase, which holds a crucial position in the process of converting animal starch to simple sugars which the body then converts to energy.

Cori was born in Prague and received her medical degree from the University of Prague in 1920. She and her husband moved to the United States in 1922 and became citizens in 1928. In 1931 she joined the faculty of Washington University in St. Louis, where she remained until her death at age 61.

Curie: Discovered Radioactivity

Perhaps the best known of all woman scientists is the Polish-born Marja Sklodowska (1867-1934), better known by her married name, **Marie Curie.**

Hers was a life of "firsts." In 1903, with her husband, Pierre, and Henri Becquerel, she was awarded the Nobel Prize for Physics for the discovery of radioactivity. In 1906 she became the first woman

Nobel prize winners Marie Curie and daughter Irene Joliot-Curie in their laboratory.

teacher at the Sorbonne in Paris. In 1911 she won the Nobel Prize for Chemistry for her discovery and isolation of pure radium. She thus became the first person to receive two Nobel Prizes. Her elder daughter, Irene Joliot-Curie, also won a Nobel Prize in 1935.

She was born in Warsaw, Poland. Her father was a teacher of mathematics and physics. She taught herself physics and chemistry in Paris, attended lectures at the Sorbonne, and corresponded with her father on problems relevant to chemistry and physics.

In 1896 she married Pierre Curie. He was killed in a street accident in 1906.

A devoted mother as well as a brilliant scientist, Curie insisted on personally attending to her daughters Irene and Eve, and wouldn't entrust anyone else with even their daily baths.

At age 64, Curie was still working, putting in twelve-hour days in her laboratory. She was so frail and delicate, recalled one of her students, it was almost "as if she could walk through walls."

Her hands had become scarred by thousands of hours of work with the radioactive substances she had discovered. In 1934 Marie Curie died of leukemia, caused by excessive exposure to radium.

Hamilton: Occupational Health
Armed with her medical diploma and the experience of working with Jane Addams at Chicago's Hull House, toxicologist **Alice Hamilton** (1869-1970) made a career of studying working people's ills. She was concerned about air and water pollution decades before such interests became popular.

She not only examined patients, but clambered into mines and trudged through industrial plants, learning more about them than most engineers. Her path through the field of occupational health was not strewn with flowers. One of the first industrialists she approached raged, "Do you mean to say if a man in my employ gets lead poisoning, I'm responsible?" But she quietly and persistently pushed state and federal governments to compel employers to provide proper safeguards for working people in industry.

In 1919, Harvard University made Hamilton an assistant professor of industrial medicine. They had never before admitted a woman to the faculty, but nobody else in the country knew enough about the subject to teach it.

Hodgkin: Insulin's Secrets
Most people would consider it an achievement simply to maintain sanity in a household composed of a husband and three children, and a sister and her brood of five.

But **Dorothy Hodgkin** (1910-   ) added to her family responsibilities an important scientific career that was capped by the 1965 Nobel Prize in Chemistry. She was only the third woman to receive the award. It was given for Hodgkin's determination of the structure of biochemical substances such as penicillin and vitamin B-12.

Until she went to Somerville College in Oxford in 1928, Hodgkin's chief interest had been archaeology. One of her most treasured achievements is the work she did on the mosaics of Byzantine churches in Transjordan. (She was born in Egypt; her father was an archaeologist.)

In 1969 Hodgkin announced that after years of painstaking X-ray analysis she had deciphered the three-dimensional structure of insulin.

Hopper: Computer Pioneer
Grace Murray Hopper (1906-   ) could be called the mother of electronic computer automatic programming. During World War II, Hopper had worked with Mark I, the cumbersome predecessor of today's computers.

From that original experience, Hopper helped pioneer the current methods of computer programming, and devised a "compiling system" that serves as an interface between human and machine.

"Nobody believed it could be done," Hopper has said. "Yet it was so obvious. Why start from scratch with every single program you write? Develop one that would do a lot of the basic work over and over again for you."

As a child, Hopper would take apart her mother's alarm clocks, "to see what made them tick . . . . You bring any gadget around, and I've simply got to find out how it works," she said.

She received her bachelor's in mathematics and physics, and a Phi Beta Kappa key in 1928 from Vassar. She then attended Yale where she received Master's and Ph.D. degrees in 1930 and 1934. In December 1943, Hopper was commissioned as a lieutenant in the Naval Reserve in which she eventually became a Commander.

Hypatia: Ancient Mathematician

Hypatia (c.370-415) was a popular teacher in ancient Alexandria; her home and her lecture room were frequented by the greatest scholars of the day.

Hypatia was considered by her scholarly peers to be something of an oracle. Enthusiastic students came from far and near to hear her lectures, which sparkled with mathematical ingenuity.

Her father was Theon, a distinguished professor of mathematics at the University of Alexandria, and her early life was spent in close contact with that scholarly institution. Later she traveled abroad, and in Athens, studied under Plutarch the Younger. Upon her return to Alexandria, the magistrates invited her to teach at the University.

She was killed during a religious conflict. A rumor was spread that Hypatia was blocking reconciliation between the Christians and the aristocrats. One day during Lent, Hypatia was pulled from her chariot, stripped naked, dragged to the church, and butchered by a group of fanatics.

Virginia Johnson: Scientific Sex

Were **Virginia Johnson** (1925-   ) and her colleague Dr. William H. Masters, guilty of dehumanizing sex or did the St. Louis researchers "put sex back into its natural context," as they claimed?

The controversy arises over the research for their book *Human Sexual Response,* a landmark study of human sexuality based on observations of nearly 700 men and women in some 10,000 sexual encounters.

Johnson and Masters were married in 1971. "I never quite came of age until I met him," Johnson said.

Without a college degree, Johnson was hired by Masters in 1956 as a research associate in a new program of sexual research he was developing. Masters had given up a $100,000-a-year practice in gynecology to go into the new field.

Johnson still has no college degree; her formal training in psychology was limited to a few courses. Her previous career had been as a singer with bandleader George Johnson — her third husband.

The famed sexual therapy program Johnson and Masters offer has reportedly helped thousands of couples find new sexual freedom and fulfillment.

Joliot-Curie: All in the Family

Irene Joliot-Curie (1897-1956) was part of the only family in which both parents, and later a daughter and her spouse won Nobel prizes.

Joliot-Curie and her husband, Frederic, won the Nobel Prize for Chemistry in 1935 for their discovery that radioactivity could be produced artificially. The discovery was one of the developments which led to the atomic bomb.

Aside from her brilliant scientific life, Joliot-Curie led a controversial political life, because of her Communist sympathies. In 1951, the French government dropped her from its Atomic Energy Commission, of which she was a founding member.

She took the name Joliot-Curie because her famous parents had no male heirs. She and her husband agreed that the combination of surnames should become their family name.

Joliot-Curie started her career as her mother's assistant at the Radium Institute of the University of Paris where she soon met her husband-to-be. She succeeded her mother as director of the Curie Laboratory of the Radium Institute in 1932. From June to September of 1946, she was France's first woman cabinet minister, Undersecretary for Scientific Research.

She died in 1956 from leukemia (as did her mother in 1934) apparently caused by overexposure to radioactive materials.

Kenny: Physiotherapy Pioneer
They said that her treatment of polio was "harmless, but of unproved value," but **Sister Elizabeth Kenny** (1886-1952) wasn't prepared to believe it wouldn't work.

Contrary to accepted teachings of the day, she obtained good results with polio victims by moving, massaging, manipulating, and "re-educating" the muscles of polio victims.

She started her program in her native Australia, and later gave treatments in Great Britain during World War I. In 1933, when polio outbreaks were frequent, she set up a clinic in Townsville, Australia. Physicians pooh-poohed Sister Kenny's treatment for years, but by 1939 the techniques were being made available in hospitals all over Australia.

In 1940 she came to the United States. After she gave a lecture at the University of Minnesota, that institution provided a few hundred dollars for equipment, and Sister Kenny set up shop at the University Medical School.

By 1941 the National Foundation for Infantile Paralysis (later the March of Dimes) endorsed Sister Kenny's work. The Elizabeth Kenny Institute was founded the following year to train nurses and physiotherapists in her techniques.

Lasker: Medical Philanthropist
It's just possible that the woman who has done the most for the health of humankind is not a scientist or a physician at all, but a philanthropist who has poured her funds and her energy into encouraging medical research against cancer, heart disease, mental illness, and other major killers and cripplers.

Mary Lasker and her second husband Albert D. Lasker, an advertising executive, established the Albert and Mary Lasker Foundation in 1942. Since her husband's death, Mary Lasker has devoted much of her time to the Foundation.

The Albert Lasker Awards have been given annually since 1944 to honor physicians and scientists for outstanding achievements in medical research and public health administration. Twenty-five of the Lasker Award Winners have gone on to win Nobel prizes.

Lasker is active in dozens of other health-oriented endeavors and has constantly encouraged Congress to increase funding for scientific research, and is a recipient of the Medical Freedom Award.

Leakey: Bones in Olduvai
Before **Mary Leakey** (1904-   ) and her late famed husband, Louis Leakey, began their work, it was thought that man first roamed the earth about 100,000 years ago.

In 1942, Mary Leakey discovered an important cache of late Stone Age hand axes. Six years later she found a 25-million-year-old skull of "Proconsul" on the island of Rusinga in Lake Victoria. Proconsul was an apelike creature, and the skull was the oldest of its kind.

In 1975, at Laetolil, Tanzania, where

Sister Elizabeth Kenny demonstrated her method of polio treatment to Minneapolis nurses.

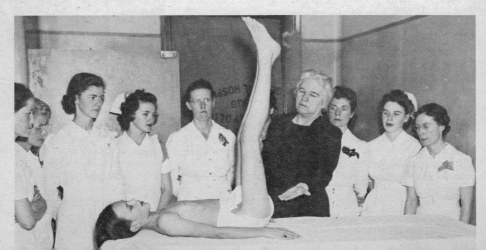

Archaeologists Mary and Louis Leakey displayed the fruit of their life-long labors, an ancient skull.

she went to search for fossils after her husband's death, Leakey found teeth and jaws of some eleven creatures, which helped push back the dates of the first true men to almost four million years ago. By the time of her husband's death, the date of early man had been pushed back to about one and a half million years ago.

She was born in London and educated in France. At age eleven she learned to love archeology while exploring the prehistoric caves of southern France.

Since her husband died in 1972, Leakey has lived in a one-room grass-roofed hut in Olduvai Gorge, Kenya.

Mayer: Physics Nobelist

The only woman besides Marie Curie to win the Nobel Prize for Physics, was **Maria Goeppert-Mayer** (1906-1972), who received the award with J. Hans D. Jensen of Heidelberg, Germany, in 1963. She was the first American woman to be so honored.

Mayer and Jensen were honored for their research on the structure of atomic nuclei and their theory of the onionlike layers of neutrons and protons held together by various complicated magnetic forces.

First received with skepticism, the concept is now a basic to physicists who are trying to understand more about the atom's nucleus.

When notified of her 1963 Nobel prize, Marie Goeppert-Mayer exclaimed, "It can't be true."

Both she and her husband, Joseph Mayer, were members of the National Academy of Sciences. She was a professor of Physics at the University of California, and wrote some 40 scientific articles and monographs.

Mead: Mother to the World

Time magazine has described **Margaret Mead** (1901-   ) as "something more

A young Margaret Mead posed with a friend, Fa-amotu, on Samoa in 1925.

than an anthropologist and something less than a national oracle." One of her colleagues once observed that "Margaret sees herself as the mother of us all."

They are both good descriptions of the woman who is anthropologist, psychologist, writer, lecturer, teacher, and more. She has devoted years to the study of primitive people on the islands of the Pacific.

Mead — often to the chagrin of her colleagues — has freely adapted and extrapolated her findings to the contemporary Western world. During World War II, for example, she wrote a book explaining to GIs how to get along with British girls in the light of cultural differences.

"People kept saying to me, 'How can you understand kids so well?'" Mead once said. And she answered, "If I can understand Stone Age savages, I can certainly understand kids in our society."

In order to carry out her research on primitive societies, Mead has mastered no fewer than seven primitive languages. Her far-flung work has included a 1925 study of girls on a Samoan island (*Coming of Age in Samoa*, 1928), a 1928-29 study of the Manus tribe of the Admiralty Islands of New Guinea (*Growing Up in New Guinea*, 1930), a 1930 study of an unnamed American Indian tribe (*The Changing Culture of an American Indian Tribe*, 1932).

Such studies have led Mead, as she has said, to see "what few people have ever seen — people who have moved from the Stone Age to the present in thirty years — kids who say, 'My father was a cannibal, but I am going to be a doctor.'"

Meitner: Woman Behind The Bomb

Had physicist **Lise Meitner** (1878-1968) remained in Hitler's Germany to continue her work on nuclear fission, the Axis powers might have beaten the West to the atomic bomb. But Meitner, an Austrian-born Jew, fled Germany for Sweden in 1938, taking with her the secret that might have won the war for the Nazis.

One of the first to split the atom, Meitner figured out the mathematical calculations necessary to perform the feat during her flight. But, she later recalled, "we were unaware what kind of powerful genie we were releasing from a bottle." Meitner frequently hoped that atomic energy would be used "for the benefit of mankind and not for its destruction."

"I could not help thinking," wrote Eleanor Roosevelt of Meitner, "that her courage was a challenge to every other woman in the world. . . ."

Mitchell: Lady Astronomer

The comet that **Maria Mitchell** (1818-1889) discovered from the roof of her Nantucket, Massachusetts home in 1847 was named for her.

In 1848 she became the first woman elected to the Academy of Arts and Sciences in Boston. No other woman was named to the Academy until 1943.

Lise Meitner, whose research contributed to the bomb, hoped the atom could be used peacefully.

Mitchell was a member of Vassar's first faculty. Her research there included reports on solar eclipses as well as changes she observed on the planetary surfaces of Jupiter and Saturn.

Mitchell was a professor who didn't believe in grades. "You cannot mark a human mind," she would say.

She was the founder, in 1873, of the Association for the Advancement of Women, a group of professional women who meet annually to discuss their work.

In 1922 a bust of Mitchell was placed in New York University's Hall of Fame.

Patrick: River Doctor

The life work of **Ruth Patrick** (1907-   ) has been diagnosing ailments in some of the largest bodies in the world — bodies of water.

Patrick is a limnologist, a specialist in analyzing and dealing with pollution in fresh-water rivers and streams.

In 1975, Patrick won the world's most remunerative science award, the $150,000 John and Alice Tyler Ecology Prize, administered by Pepperdine University of Los Angeles.

By 1975 Patrick had worked with more than 100 industries and agencies in studying more than 1,000 river sections throughout the world. She developed theories of fresh water aquatic life that are applied to environmental impact studies throughout the world.

She invented an instrument called the diatometer, which plots the growth of diatoms, or microscopic algae. They are an accurate barometer of the ecological health of fresh-water ecosystems.

Sabin: Medical Teacher

Florence Rena Sabin (1871-1953) was a physician who led a life of firsts. She was the first woman admitted to the Johns Hopkins Medical School (1896), its first female graduate four years later, and, in 1917, the first female teacher at a major American medical school.

In 1925, Sabin went to work full time on the staff of New York's Rockefeller Institute for Medical Research.

One of her major achievements was the discovery of keys to how the human lymphatic system works, moving its fluids throughout the body.

Florence Sabin began a second career at 73, campaigning to clean up Colorado.

Dr. Simon Flexner, head of medical research at the Rockefeller Institute called Sabin "one of the foremost scientists of all time."

In 1939 she retired to her native Colorado. In 1944, at age 73, she was named head of the Colorado Postwar Planning Committee's health committee. She began a campaign to clean up Colorado. Out of her efforts came a series of bills in 1947 which called for methods of combatting diseases spread by contaminated food, water, and sewage disposal.

When Colorado's governor Lee Knous was asked how he would get such programs through the Legislature, he replied: "I'll have the little old lady on my side. There isn't a man . . . who wants to tangle with her."

Every health measure passed.

Slye: Mouse Breeder

Maude Slye (1879-1954) bred a better mouse and the world beat a path to her laboratory door.

The Chicago pathologist won many awards for her work, including gold medals from the American Medical Association and the Radiological Society of America.

When Slye was a graduate student at the University of Chicago she got a pair of mice with an unusual neurological disease and began to interbreed them with other mice. Soon she was working with tens of thousands of mice and examining their hereditary characteristics, with a special attention to the possible genetic aspects of cancer.

At first the work was scoffed at by other researchers and physicians, but Slye proved that the tendency toward developing cancer was a regressive hereditary characteristic. In these mice, she found, a form of cancer could be bred out by successive matings with individuals whose genetic constitution was free of the disease.

So concerned was she over the welfare and purity of line of the mice in her laboratory that once, when she visited her sick mother in California, Slye rented a railroad boxcar and took the mice along.

Tabei: Conquered Everest

Junko Tabei (1940-   ) on May 16, 1975, became the first woman to reach the top of Mt. Everest.

Tabei was one of fifteen Japanese women mountaineers who had been chosen from hundreds of mountaineering clubs to make the trip to the 29,028-foot peak in Nepal.

It took a month of climbing, during which an avalanche injured ten women at 25,000 feet, before Tabei mounted the last few hundred feet to the top of Everest with a Sherpa guide.

"I was the only one to make it, but not because I was the best climber. Only because I was in the best physical condition," she said. "But even one climber reaching the top from a good team means that the whole group has succeeded in reaching the top."

In spite of her accomplishment, Tabei claims to be "just an ordinary housewife. I let my husband make all those important decisions. I only like climbing, not political things. When I reached the top I really didn't think there was anything extraordinary about being the first woman . . . I only thought . . . I'm glad I'm at the top. Then I descended."

Taussig: Heart Doctor

Helen Brooke Taussig (1898-   ) helped develop the "blue baby" operation with Dr. Alfred Blalock, a surgeon.

It was one of the pioneering operations on the human heart, performed on infants who were born with severe heart defects that caused their blood to circulate improperly. She found, specifically, that the defects involved were a leaky wall in the heart that needed to be closed, and an artery cloture in the vessel from the heart to the lungs.

Taussig helped Blalock develop the surgical techniques to correct these defects. It was one of the first widely successful operations to be performed on the heart of a living human being.

Taussig was born in Cambridge, Massachusetts, and studied at both Harvard and Boston University medical schools. In 1924, she switched to Johns Hopkins Medical School in Baltimore, and there she received her M.D. degree in 1927.

Originally Taussig had been denied an internship in medicine at John Hopkins because one woman in her class had already been accepted. So she turned to pediatrics.

She has received the President's Medal of Freedom, and the French Legion of Honor, among other awards. In 1965, she became the first woman to be named as president of the American Heart Association.

Wu: Physics Queen

Chien-Shiung Wu (1912-   ) helped destroy a law of nature, and in doing so earned the designation "queen of nuclear physics," from colleagues.

Her most celebrated experiment disproved the "law of parity" which stated that like nuclear particles always acted alike.

In fact, it was two Chinese scientists working in the United States (Drs. Tsung Dao Lee and Chen Ning Yang) who challenged the law of parity. But it was Wu who carred out the experiments that proved their challenge was correct.

"The traditional roles of wife and mother and the role of dedicated scientist are actually compatible," Wu says. "Isn't it more satisfying for a woman to have her own intellectual endeavor along with the responsibility of home and children?"

Wu was born in Shanghai and did undergraduate work at universities in China. She received her doctorate at the University of California. In 1944, she became a professor of physics at Columbia University. In 1954, Wu became an American citizen.

WOMEN ALOFT

Soaring all of twelve feet off the ground in 1910, **Blanche Stuart Scott** became the first woman to pilot an airplane. She flew from one end of the Fort Wayne, Indiana, Driving Park to the other. "In those days," she later recalled, "they didn't take you up in the air to teach you. They gave you a bit of preliminary ground training . . . You got in. They kissed you good-bye and trusted to luck you'd get back."

Ever since, women have risked danger and social opprobrium to soar into the skies.

Many women had to content themselves with being passengers on planes piloted by men. Like **Mrs. Hart O. Berg,** Wilbur Wright's first female passenger. Because the earliest planes had no cockpits, Berg had to tie a rope around her long skirt at the ankles to keep it from flying above her head.

Maude Campbell paid $180 in 1926 to become the first woman passenger on a commercial airplane. Her Salt Lake City to Los Angeles flight aboard an open-cockpit biplane took nearly seven hours. The plane, Campbell recalled, contained "just me, the pilot, and my parachute — they told me that if anything went wrong, to jump, count to ten, and pull the rip-cord." Campbell, now a great-grandmother, made a shorter flight — from California's Long Beach International Airport to Los Angeles Airport — aboard a plane of similar type and vintage in 1976.

But aviation has not always been kind to women — beginning with **Julie Clark,** the first woman to die in an air crash. Clark's biplane struck the limb of a tree and flipped over while she was circling the Illinois State Fair Grounds in 1912.

Besides braving the dangers of the skies, aspiring airwomen have had to convince men that they had what it took to be pilots. Blanche Stuart Scott commented shortly before her death in 1970 that she still saw little future for women in aviation because of discriminatory attitudes toward her sex.

Perhaps no women in the field of aviation suffered more sex discrimination than the thirteen original women astronauts, tagged by the press "Spacegals," "As-tronettes," and "Astrodolls." In a grueling series of tests, the women proved themselves more resistant than their male counterparts to everything from radiation and heart attack to loneliness and cold. And they consumed less precious oxygen and food than the men.

Nevertheless, the women were dropped from the space program in July 1961 without explanation. The hostile environment the thirteen faced was amply illustrated by the reaction of a NASA spokesman to their protests: "Talk of an American spacewoman makes me sick to my stomach."

Much has changed in the sixteen years since the women astronauts were sent packing.

More than one thousand women have applied for work on the space shuttle, which is scheduled to make its first flight in 1979. "Many women qualify, and we expect a good number to be accepted," said George W. S. Abbey, director of flight operations at the Lyndon B. Johnson Space Center in Houston.

Earhart: Daring Aviatrix

"Someone must always go first," declared **Amelia Earhart** (1898-1937). The daring "aviatrix" was not afraid to be that someone.

Earhart became a national heroine in 1928 as the first woman to cross the Atlan-

Courageous aviator Amelia Earhart disappeared on a 1937 flight around the world.

tic by airplane. She was only a passenger on that crossing, but four years later she repeated the flight solo. Plagued by a fire on her plane's exhaust manifold and a dwindling fuel supply, she sighted land in the nick of time and landed in an Irish cow pasture.

Earhart's last flight was to be a trip around the globe at the equator. She would have been the first person to accomplish that feat. But the flight was cut short on July 2, 1937, when Earhart and her navigator disappeared over the Pacific. From that day to this, many theories have been advanced regarding her disappearance. Some suggest that she had been on a spy mission for her friend, President Franklin D. Roosevelt.

Earhart was not only an aviator but a writer, settlement house worker, and feminist. "Women must try to do things as men have tried," she wrote. "When they fail, their failure must be but a challenge to others."

Cochran: Wings of Beauty

The luckless childhood of **Jacqueline Cochran** (1910-   ) gave little promise that she would have one successful career, let alone two.

Orphaned in infancy, Cochran grew up hungry, without even shoes or a doll. By the time she was eight, Cochran worked twelve-hour days in a Georgia cotton mill for six cents an hour. At the same time the ambitious child was learning to read. Then she got a job in a beauty shop. She moved on to bigger and better salons in Montgomery, Philadelphia, New York, and Miami Beach. In 1932, with three weeks' vacation stretching ahead of her, she decided to learn to fly. Within three days, she was flying solo. Recalled one of her early aviation friends, "We couldn't help rooting for Jackie. Here she was, a pretty blonde who hadn't even finished grammar school, but she buckled down over the heavy textbooks and mastered celestial navigation and Morse Code."

In 1941, Cochran piloted a bomber to England and trained British women for air transport service. It was said she would not allow herself to be photographed after the flight until she had changed from her flying slacks into a fresh dress. (Aviation lore also has it that Cochran once stayed

with a burning plane until she found her purse, which contained her lipstick.)

Returning to the United States, Cochran organized the Women's Airforce Service Pilots (WASPS), who flew about sixty million noncombat miles for the Army Air Force during World War II.

After the war, Cochran set about breaking one air speed record after another. In 1964, she set the women's world speed record of 1,429 miles per hour.

Her other career? Cochran ran her own cosmetics business under the trade name "Wings of Beauty."

Scott: She Loves Flying

"Flying has been nearly as exciting as a love affair," says British aviator **Sheila Scott** (1927-   ). "But far less dangerous."

It would take a supremely perilous love affair to outdo some of Scott's airborne exploits.

An aspiring actress, Scott caught what she calls "flying fever" in 1959. Six years later, she embarked on the longest consecutive solo flight in history, a 31,000-mile flight around the globe. The venture was initially plagued by equipment failure. Later, exhaustion, fever, and dysentery threatened to cut it short. But Scott triumphantly flew her Piper Commanche into London Airport on June 20, 1965, to complete the trip.

In 1971 Scott flew over the North Pole. She was the first person to make the equator-to-equator flight solo in a light aircraft. The National Aeronautics and Space Administration (NASA) monitored her physical and mental responses to the stress of the flight. According to an astronaut who worked with her, Scott "belongs in the company of Lindbergh and Earhart and Saint-Exupéry . . . Her contributions to aviation and to the preservation of the individual human spirit of exploration and adventure are almost unparelleled in our time."

Tereshkova: First Space Woman

"This is Seagull. I see the horizon. A light blue, a blue band. This is the earth. How beautiful it is. Everything goes fine."

With these words, **Valentina Tereshkova** (1937-   ) announced her launching as the first — and so far the only — woman in space. The Soviet cosmonaut was lifted

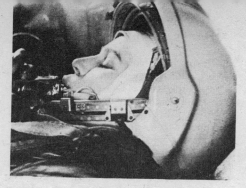

Returning to earth, Valentina Tereshkova said, "In space, too, our men will not feel lonely now."

into space on June 16, 1963. During her nearly three-day mission, she completed forty-eight orbits totalling 1,225,000 miles.

A former cotton mill worker, Tereshkova first went aloft as a parachute jumper. Unlike even some of the toughest paratroopers, she showed no apprehension at her first jump. Observers reported she just "sauntered" out into the open sky. By the time she entered the Soviet space program, Tereshkova had 126 jumps to her credit.

Tereshkova's space flight was virtually flawless, except for a brief interval when ground control lost radio contact because she took an unscheduled nap.

MOTHERS OF INVENTION

"You women may talk about your rights, but why don't you invent something?" inquired an old Vermont farmer of feminist Ada Bowles around the turn of the century. "Your horse's feed bag and the shade over his head were both invented by women," she tossed back.

"The old fellow was so taken aback that he was barely able to gasp 'Do tell'," Bowles recalled later.

Women have a long history of inventiveness, growing out of their desire to make life easier for themselves and their families.

Every schoolchild knows that Eli Whitney invented the cotton gin, which revolutionized cotton production and shaped the course of United States history. But the invention might never have come about had it not been for Catherine Littlefield Greene. A widow with five children, Greene had her hands full running a Georgia boarding house in 1792. With so much to do, she resented the time she had to spend separating cotton from its seeds before she could spin thread.

So she suggested to one boarder, a young tutor named Whitney, that he devise a machine to do the job for her. Whitney worked on the project, but was about to give up because the wooden teeth he was using to separate cotton seeds from lint were not strong enough. Greene suggested he substitute wire teeth, and the gin was completed ten days later.

Though Greene did not receive a joint patent for her contributions, she and her second husband became Whitney's partners in manufacturing the cotton gin.

Twelve-year-old Margaret Knight came up with the first of her twenty-seven known inventions in 1850 when she visited the textile mill where her elder brothers worked. She saw a shuttle fall out of a loom, injuring a worker with its steel tip. Knight promptly devised a stop-motion mechanism to prevent such accidents. Though the contrivance was put into use, she never patented it.

Dubbed a "woman Edison," Knight invented items ranging from a shoe-cutting machine to a device that folded square-bottom paper bags. Her last series of patents and assignments involved rotary engines and motors for automobiles. Knight's inventions never brought her much money; she left an estate valued at only $275.05 when she died.

Lydia Pinkham formally entered the ranks of inventive women in 1876 by marketing a home remedy that promised to cure ills ranging from sterility to kidney distress. She had long brewed a concoction of roots and seeds — plus a generous dose of alcohol as "solvent and preservative" — for her neighbors. After her husband went bankrupt, Pinkham turned the activity into a highly profitable business that grossed $300,000 a year by the time of her death in 1883. (Sales peaked at $3,800,000 in 1925.)

Believing "only a woman can understand a woman's ills," Pinkham encouraged customers to write her for help on their health problems. Most of her responses were sensible: balanced diet, adequate exercise, and cleanliness. The value of Pinkham's "Vegetable Compound" stemmed more from positive thinking than from any medicinal proper-

LYDIA E. PINKHAM'S VEGETABLE COMPOUND

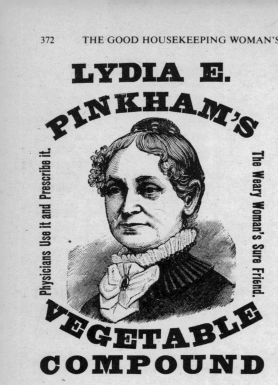

Physicians Use it and Prescribe it.

The Weary Woman's Sure Friend.

Lydia Pinkham claimed her tonic was "pleasant to the taste, efficacious, immediate and lasting."

ties of its ingredients. Its 18 percent alcohol content also might have helped temporarily ease its users' physical and emotional complaints.

Women have been responsible for many significant recent inventions: pneumatic tires, heating and ventilating systems for buildings, snow plows, digging machines, paving blocks — even the white line down the center of a road. But some of the following female inventions seem as humorous as they are practical:

• Perhaps prompted by the sloppy kisses of husband or father. May Evans Harrington invented a "mustache-guard for attachment to spoons or cups when used in the act of eating soup and other liquid food or drinking coffee." Harrington's device to raise the mustache above the contents of cup or spoon was patented in 1889.

• Credit for invention of the ice cream cone goes to an anonymous female companion of Charles E. Menches. The couple was attending the 1904 Louisiana Purchase Exposition in St. Louis, Missouri when Menches presented her with a bouquet of flowers and an ice cream

sandwich. The inventive young woman rolled up one layer of the sandwich to form a container for the flowers and the other into the first cone to hold ice cream.

• A rather grisly sleep-inducing collar was the 1885 invention of Fanny W. Paul. The device was designed to bring "quiet to the brain in persons suffering from wakefulness or insomnia" by applying pressure to the arteries and veins of the neck to control the flow of blood. From the sound of it, the sleep induced by Paul's invention could have proved permanent.

• Bertha Dlugi loved her birds but hated cleaning up after them. Instead of confining them to their cages, she invented in 1959 a parakeet diaper to be attached to feathers by strips of tape.

• The pie cutting guide invented by Clair and Mary Weaver in 1963 was hailed as a solution to dinner table arguments over who had the largest piece of pie. The Weavers' invention was capable of dividing a pie into four, five, or six equal pieces.

• When a diligent twelve-year-old has homework to be done, she dislikes wasting time in a dark car while her mother finishes shopping. Becky Schroeder did, and solved the problem by inventing a luminous writing board in 1974. Schroeder was one of the youngest recipients of a U.S. patent.

Some women inventors are well known in other fields: actresses Hedy Lamarr, Edie Adams, and Julie Newmar, for example.

• In 1942, Lamarr, along with composer George Antheil, received a patent for a secret torpedo control system. She was awarded the patent under her real name, Hedy Kiesler Markey.

• Adams was for many years seen in Muriel Cigar commercials purring, "Why don't you pick one up and smoke it sometime?" But she could do more than purr. Patents for ring-shaped cigarette and cigar holders were awarded to her in 1965 and 1966, under the names Edith A. Kovacs and Edith Adams Mills, respectively.

• Pantyhose designed to "make your derriere look like an apple instead of a ham sandwich" are the invention of dancer-actress Newmar. She received a patent for her pantyhose with an elastic back seam in 1976.

Reformers

THEY HAD A CAUSE

Mott: Quaker Reformer

When **Lucretia Coffin Mott** (1793-1880) was fifteen years old, in 1808, she learned that men teachers were paid more than twice as much as women teachers at her boarding school near Poughkeepsie, New York, and she became a feminist. In 1811, she married James Mott, a man who shared all his wife's convictions about the need to free women and slaves.

They had six children, and Lucretia Mott's time was filled with domestic duties. On a single day, she wrote, she did a large wash and "I hurried to get the ironing away before the people flocked in. Five came before dinner. I prepared mince for forty pies . . . picked over some lots of apples, stewed a quantity, chopped some more, and made apple pudding."

Then, in 1833, when household duties had lessened, Mott helped organize the American Anti-Slavery Society; because it did not at first admit women, she also formed a "women's auxiliary" — the Philadelphia Female Anti-Slavery Society. On one occasion, an angry anti-abolitionist mob headed toward her house intending to burn it down. While she waited quietly in her living room, expecting the worst, a friend of hers steered them in the wrong direction.

Mott was one of several American women chosen as delegates to the World Anti-Slavery Convention in London in 1840. When the delegation arrived in London, they found women were not allowed to participate. Outraged — and also amused by the irony of a convention that wanted to free slaves and shackle women — Mott and another feminist, Elizabeth Cady Stanton, sat in their hotel room reading Mary Wollstonecraft's *Vindication of the Rights of Women*.

They organized the Seneca Falls Convention, which met in New York on July 19, 1848, marking the official beginning of the women's rights movement in America. Since none of the women felt qualified to preside, James Mott took the chair. But his wife and Stanton dominated the assembly, and for the rest of her life Mott rarely missed a suffrage or feminist convention. In 1850, she wrote a carefully reasoned *Discourse on Women* in which she said women were considered inferior only because they had always labored under such severe oppression; thereby she linked the cause of women with the cause of slaves. In 1866, she was named first president of the American Equal Rights Association.

Although she always wore her white Quaker cap, shawl, and gray dress in public, Mott also railed against the more dogmatic parts of her religion. Her Quaker doctor once refused to treat Mott because he disagreed so strongly with her statements on women's rights. The press ridiculed her until after the Emancipation Proclamation. But others admired her bravery from the beginning. After hearing her speak, Henry David Thoreau remarked: "Her self-possession was something to see . . . Her subject was 'The Abuse of the Bible' and thence she straightway digressed to slavery and the degradation of women. It was a good speech." When her husband died in 1868, she replaced him as president of the Pennsylvania Peace Society.

Wright: Human Rights Advocate

Frances Wright (1795-1852), a well-educated, well-traveled Scot, defied the traditions of her day by traveling throughout America in 1828 and 1829 to talk about the evils of organized religion, which she considered a scourge on human happiness, and of the repression of women — two themes that earned her the wrath of clergymen and most respectable citizens.

But many working men, some slaves, and a few bold women responded to her cause. She had earlier, in 1825, tried to start a rural commune, called "Nashoba," near Memphis. She bought thirty slaves — promising them eventual emancipation — and tried to clear the land and grow crops. The project failed miserably, in part because neighbors were scandalized by the commune's approval of "free love." Wright eventually spent half of all her savings to transport the slaves to Haiti, where she freed them and also found homes and work for them.

Having learned her lesson, she took her causes to the urban areas, where she fared better than she had in the rural South. She received her best reception in New York City and decided to live there. When Walt

Whitman, who was ten years old at the time, was taken to one of her lectures by his admiring father, he recalled her as one of the few people who could "excite in me wholesale respect and love."

Wright began to publish a periodical called *Free Enquirer* with a longtime friend, Robert Dale Owen. Both in print and on the dais, she spoke out against capital punishment and for liberalized divorce laws, birth control, and free state boarding schools where children could learn industrial skills (but not religion). This last proposal sounded good to many workers, who blamed child labor for rising unemployment. Although she disagreed with the workers' spokesman, Thomas Skidmore, on most other issues, she soon became a central figure in the emerging labor movement, which became known as the Fanny Wright party.

Crandall: Quaker Abolitionist

In 1831, **Prudence Crandall** (1803-1890), a twenty-eight-year-old Quaker, battled the citizens of her home town of Canterbury, Connecticut, by insisting a black girl had the right to be educated in the all-white Canterbury Female Boarding School she operated on the town square. When Crandall accepted the black girl's application, outraged parents and financial backers threatened to pull their children and money out of the school. There were threats of physical harm as well, and, afraid for her students' safety, Crandall closed down the school temporarily. But within weeks, she announced it would reopen — as a school for black girls only.

This act made her cause célèbre. Grocers refused to supply the school with food, and the local Congregational church barred her pupils from services. Town officials threatened to arrest and whip the students for "vagrancy." The town council passed a "black law" forbidding any school to teach blacks from out of state. Crandall, who continued to run her school, was arrested and taken to the county jail, where abolitionist supporters let her spend one night, to draw attention to the case, before bailing her out. Whites broke the school windows, polluted its well with feces, tried to set it on fire, and launched a mob assault against it before she gave up the fight in September 1834.

Her bravery is credited with converting John Quincy Adams to the abolitionist cause. Already an old man, Adams introduced the first anti-slavery petitions in the House of Representatives and finally managed to defeat the rule that automatically tabled any discussion of slavery in Congress.

Crandall married an abolitionist and moved to Troy Grove township in Illinois, where she worked for women's rights, and then to Elk Falls, Kansas. She told an interviewer in 1886: "My whole life has been one of opposition. I never could find anyone near me to agree with me . . . (Even my husband) would not let me read the books that he himself read, but I did read them. I read all sides and searched for the truth . . ." The penitent Connecticut legislature voted her an annual pension of $400.

Grimké Sisters: They Spoke Out

Sarah Moore Grimké (1792-1873) and **Angelina Emily Grimké** (1805-1879), sisters from an upper-class, slave-owning Presbyterian family in Charleston, South Carolina, were also among the first women to speak out against slavery and for women's rights. Sarah, the elder (she was the sixth of fourteen children), was tutored at home in "young ladies" subjects, and protested being denied studies in Greek, philosophy, and law. She defied state laws and taught her slave maid to read.

In 1821, after her father had died, Sarah moved to Philadelphia and became a Quaker. When she returned home eight years later, she found her younger sister Angelina deeply disturbed over the immorality of slavery. Angelina returned with Sarah to Philadelphia, and also became a Quaker. They refused to live again in the South.

Angelina was the first of the sisters to become active in civil rights. She joined the Philadelphia Female Anti-Slavery Society and, in 1835, a letter she wrote against slavery was published in the *Liberator;* for the first time, the respectable Grimké name became linked publicly to abolition. Angelina began to write abolitionist pamphlets and moved to New York City to hold anti-slavery meetings in which she talked about "the blood, sweat and tears of my sisters in bond." Sarah Grimké stayed behind in Philadelphia until 1836, when she attempted to speak against slavery in a Quaker meeting and was publicly silenced and rebuked.

The Grimké sisters became the first women to speak to "mixed" audiences of men and women — and the strong objections to these appearances catapulted them into women's rights. They were also among the earliest Americans to dispute St. Paul's teachings on the inequality of women. In 1838, Sarah remarked in her *Letters on the Equality of the Sexes and the Condition of Women:* "The idea is inconceivable to me that Christian women can be engaged in doing God's work and yet cannot ask His blessing on their efforts except through the lips of a man."

In 1838, Angelina married Theodore Weld, an abolitionist who agreed that Angelina did not have to promise to obey him. He also renounced the customary legal rights of the husband to own and manage his wife's property. Sarah lived with the couple, and their work in abolition declined.

Dix: Prison Reformer

In March 1841, a Harvard divinity student asked thirty-nine-year-old **Dorothea Dix** (1802-1887) to teach a Sunday School

Sickly Dorothea Dix found new strength in fighting for the mentally ill.

class to women in the East Cambridge, Massachusetts jail. Dix, a former school teacher, had collapsed from emotional and physical exhaustion five years earlier; she had been unable to work ever since. Now she was about to find new energy.

When she visited the jail on Sunday, she found among the prisoners a number of women whose only crime was insanity. The mentally ill were kept in the basement with no heat, no lights, no ventilation. When the jailor tried to calm her by telling her "lunatics" were insensitive to cold, she became so outraged that she took the matter to the local court. Heat was provided eventually.

Dorothea Dix had found her calling. For eighteen months, at her own expense, she inspected five hundred jails, alms-houses, and houses of correction in Massachusetts. In January 1843, she appeared before the state legislature and read from her notebook stories of mentally ill confined "in cages, closets, cellars, stalls, pens" and "chained, naked, beaten with rods, and lashed into obedience." The legislators voted $200,000 to provide at Worcester a more humane facility for the mentally ill.

Between 1843 and 1847, Dix traveled thirty thousand miles across the United States investigating prison conditions and presented evidence to the state legislators, most of whom she shamed into action. Through her efforts, 110 asylums and hospitals were built in the next few years, and the public attitude toward the mentally ill began to improve slightly. With encouragement from the educator Horace Mann, she wrote a book on prison reform; penologists later adopted many of her suggestions, including prisoner education and separation of criminals according to the kinds of crimes they commit.

Howe: Abolitionist Poet

On April 23, 1843, **Julia Ward Howe** (1819-1910) married a man fanatically opposed to any woman's involvement in activity outside the home. Her husband, an ardent abolitionist, also would not permit women to speak at public meetings on slavery. She bore him six children and complied with his wishes, but from time to time they considered divorce.

After visiting a soldiers' camp near

Friends noted a new brightness in Julia Ward Howe's face after she took up women's rights.

women's clubs in New England and in 1868 met Lucy Stone, whose strength and fearlessness so impressed her that she again defied her husband and became involved in women's suffrage. Together, she and Stone founded the American Woman's Suffrage Association.

Howe became president of the American branch of the Women's International Peace Association and in 1872 went to London as a delegate for the Prison Reform Congress. She continued to write books of poetry, and was the first woman elected to the American Academy of Arts and Letters.

Through all of this, she remained married. Her husband reportedly adopted an attitude of detached amusement.

Willard: WCTU Activist

Frances Willard (1839-1898) was born in Monroe County, New York, and grew up on an isolated farm near Janesville, Wisconsin, where she often saw no one outside the family for months at a time. As a child, she liked to be called "Frank," yearned for an education, and resented the fact that her brother could vote while she could not. Voting was important to the family: her father was a member of the Wisconsin legislature. After much resistance, her father allowed her to go to the Methodist-affiliated North Western Female College in Evanston, Illinois.

In 1871, she became dean of women of Northwestern University, which had just merged with the Evanston College for

Washington, D.C., during the Civil War, Julia Ward Howe felt compelled to write a poem about her feelings. Afraid of her husband's reaction, she published the poem anonymously in the February 1862 issue of the *Atlantic Monthly*. It was "The Battle Hymn of the Republic." President Lincoln wept when he first heard it sung to the tune of "John Brown's Body." For Howe, the poem became a symbol of personal liberation as well as national inspiration.

She slowly received recognition for the poem and began to lecture on abolition in Unitarian churches. She started the first

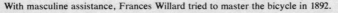

With masculine assistance, Frances Willard tried to master the bicycle in 1892.

Ladies. Her attempt to retain autonomy for the women's college was constantly threatened by Northwestern University President Charles Flower, her former fiancé. She finally resigned in exasperation and soon joined the Women's Christian Temperance Union (WCTU), an affiliation which was to bring her fame.

She became national secretary of the WCTU in 1874; her first public act was to kneel and pray in a Pittsburgh saloon. But, unlike many temperance workers of the day, she used the issue of alcohol as a way to unite women and gain women's rights. Her early pro-suffrage speeches at the WCTU convention were met with the reprimand: "We do not propose to trail our skirts through the mire of politics."

Willard was elected president of the national WCTU in 1879, and she began to convert it into a strong women's movement with midwestern, conservative roots. Under her leadership, it grew to 200,000 members. By 1880, the national convention finally endorsed women's suffrage "as a weapon for the protection of her home." Under Willard's guidance, the WCTU also organized pressure groups to work in areas like prison and labor reform, adult education for working women, the hiring of policewomen, and world peace. This work paved the way for other reform groups.

Winnemucca: Voice of the Paiute

Sarah Winnemucca (c.1844-1891), a Paiute Indian, volunteered in 1878 at the age of thirty-four to scout the hostile country of Idaho for the United States Army. Her motives were mixed: first, she wanted to help the army end an Indian war in which she believed her people would suffer; second, she wanted to rescue her father, who had been forced against his will to join the warring Bannock Indians. She traveled more than one hundred miles of unexplored territory into Oregon, where she found her father, helped him and his followers escape, and then returned to the army troops with valuable information. Later, she served as a guide, scout, and interpreter for General Oliver O. Howard.

Winnemucca was born in Humboldt Sink, in what is now Nevada, with the Indian name Thoc-me-tony, meaning "Shell Flower." She adopted the English name

Eloquent Sarah Winnemucca carried the cause of her Paiute Indians across the nation.

Sarah while living with a white family in Genoa, Nevada. She had known and liked whites since she was six years old when her grandfather, impressed with white people's ways, had taken her to live for a while with ranchers in the San Joaquin Valley.

Her enthusiasm for whites was diminished during the 1860s, when white settlers forced the Paiutes into a reservation at Pyramid Lake, north of Reno, where corrupt Indian agents abused them and murdered many of the women and children in retaliation for Indians' stealing some cattle.

In 1872, the Paiutes were moved again, this time to the Malheur Reservation in Oregon; when unscrupulous Indian agents took over, the Paiutes began to flee, some of them joining the Bannock Indians who were preparing for war. After the war, which the army won, the Paiutes and Bannocks were punished by being exiled to Yakima Reservation in Washington territory.

Winnemucca began to plead the Paiutes' cause, first in San Francisco and then in Washington, D.C. After hearing her, Secretary of the Interior Carl Schurz authorized the Paiutes' return to Oregon and promised them individual plots of land, but the Indian agent in Washington territory refused to let them go back.

Winnemucca began lecturing across America to get help for her people. Moved by her beauty and eloquence the whites called her "The Princess;" the Paiutes called her "Mother." She collected thousands of signatures requesting the government to grant land to the Paiutes; Congress passed the bill in 1884, but the secretary of the interior never acted on it.

Winnemucca, who had been through two unhappy marriages, was married a third time in 1881, to an army lieutenant; he died of tuberculosis in 1886. She opened a school for Paiute children near Lovelock, Nevada, and taught for three years even though she suffered severely from rheumatism and recurrent fevers.

Barrett: Champion of Unwed Mothers

One rainy evening in 1880, an unwed mother crept into the rectory of an Episcopalian church in the slums of Richmond, Virginia, holding her baby and begging for help. **Kate Waller Barrett** (1857-1925), the minister's twenty-three-year-old wife, vowed after hearing her story to help other unwed mothers as well. From Richmond, Barrett and her minister husband moved to a parish in Henderson, Kentucky, where both worked among local prostitutes. In 1886, they moved to Atlanta, where Barrett, who had seven children, went to medical school.

With her medical degree for support, she tried to open a home for unwed mothers in four different locations in Atlanta. In each case, she was forced out by hostile neighbors. Finally, she received the backing of the city council, and a $5,000 contribution from Charles N. Crittenton, a millionaire devoted to rescuing "fallen women." Barrett began spending all her time and energy on her home, which became part of the National Florence Crittenton Mission, and eventually supervised about fifty homes across the country.

Under her guidance, the Crittenton movement stopped trying to convert prostitutes and concentrated instead on the needs of young unmarried mothers. It encouraged mothers to keep their children, taught them about baby care, and trained them for jobs. When Charles Crittenton died in 1909, Barrett succeeded him as president of the flourishing mission.

Addams: Mistress of Hull House

Jane Addams (1860-1935) and a friend, Ellen Starr, rented a house on the corner of Polk and Halstead streets in Chicago, furnished it with good family pieces and European art, and, on a cool autumn evening in 1889, opened the front door and invited the neighborhood in. Hull House became a pioneer in American settlement work. Its volunteers established a day nursery and the city's first public playground, taught sewing and cooking, and held Saturday night dances.

The starving were fed, the unemployed were given work, and the neglected and beaten were given sanctuary. "Jane's idea," Ellen Starr wrote that first year, "is that [settlement work] is more for the benefit of the people who do it than for the other class . . . that one gets as much as she gives." At first, Addams paid all expenses from her own pocket.

Addams was born in Cedarville, Illinois, on September 6, 1860, the eighth of nine children. Her family was well off, and her father sent her to medical school. Surgery for a congenital spine defect weakened her health and forced her to drop classes. Her doctor sent her abroad: in England, she saw the poor eating off the street; in Germany, she saw brewery workers carrying on their backs huge wooden tanks filled with hot liquid that spilled over the sides, scalding their bodies. She lived four years in Baltimore, where she was relatively inactive and suffered from "nervous depression," and then returned to Europe in 1887.

In London's East End, she visited Toynbee Hall, a settlement started by a group of Oxford men who, influenced by British social critic John Ruskin and Leo Tolstoy, were trying to ease the suffering brought on by rapid industrialization. She decided to start a similar settlement in a crowded immigrant section of Chicago.

Her energy, diplomacy, warmth, and bravery made Hull House a leader in broad areas of social reform. Under Hull House pressure, Illinois passed its first factory inspection act, established the nation's first juvenile court, formulated child labor laws, streamlined welfare procedures, and initiated compulsory school attendance. When garbage collection deteriorated, Addams got herself appointed garbage inspector and followed the collector on his rounds each morning starting at six. When she forced the city to scrape

Said a friend, Jane Addams "like the sunlight shone alike on the just and unjust."

years of accumulated dirt from the streets, the death rate in her district dropped from third to seventh in the city.

In the early 1900s, Addams also became involved in women's rights, politics, and pacifism. "It is easy to kill a man. It is not easy to bring him forward in the paths of civilization," she said, and shocked many of her backers by opposing America's entry into World War I. Because of her enthusiasm for the labor movement, many of Chicago's wealthy citizens came to fear her as a dangerous radical.

During those years, she also wrote hundreds of articles and books, and she lectured around the country. Although she had a weak heart, she kept up her pace and, in 1931, was co-recipient of the Nobel Peace Prize, sharing it with educator Nicholas Murray Butler.

Wald: Angel of Henry Street

One morning in March of 1893, **Lillian Wald** (1867-1940) was called from her classroom in New York City's Woman's Medical College to tend a sick woman in a tenement house. Shocked by the living conditions she saw, Wald left school and began a lifetime career as a public health nurse. Convinced that the only way to improve community health care was to live in the neighborhood where care was needed, she and a friend, Mary Brewster, moved to the lower East Side, where new immigrants were concentrated. She received financial backing from Mrs. Solomon Loeb and banker Jacob H. Schiff

and, by 1895, had moved into larger quarters at 265 Henry Street, beginning the now-famous Henry Street Settlement.

Unlike Jane Addams at Hull House in Chicago, Wald always considered health care her first priority. By 1913, the Henry Street Visiting Nurses Service had ninety-two nurses who were making 200,000 home visits a year. From the be-

Nursing a sick woman in a New York tenement, Lillian Wald vowed to live and work in the slums.

ginning, Wald made sure the nurses services remained free of religious or political affiliation, and charged fees based on ability to pay. With Wald's encouragement, the city of New York established the first public school nursing program in the United States, Columbia University Teachers College began to offer courses in nursing and health, and the American Red Cross set up a program which evolved into the Town and Country Nursing Service.

Henry Street soon expanded its narrow medical focus. Although health remained its primary concern, it also offered scholarships to help children stay in school until they reached the age of sixteen, established parks and playgrounds, and worked for legislation to outlaw child labor.

Wald worked actively in her settlement house, in women's suffrage, and in the peace movement until the 1930s.

Nation: The Hatchet Lady
Carry Nation (1846-1911), who stood six feet tall and wore a flowing black robe, cape, and bonnet, terrorized the patrons of Kansas bars in the early 1900s by entering

Hatchet-wielding temperance crusader Carrie Nation posed on a European-bound steamship in 1904.

saloons, singing a temperance song, and then smashing their bottles, bar furniture, and risqué wall decorations with her hatchet. Considered insane by many, she was able nonetheless to make whole towns "go dry" with her performances. She received donations from prohibitionists all over the country, using the money to pay her fines and court costs and to support a home in Kansas City for wives and mothers of alcoholic men.

Nation was born in Kentucky to an itinerant father and a mother who later in life was committed to a mental hospital. When she was twenty years old, Nation married an alcoholic who died from his drinking within a year after the wedding. She taught school in Missouri and remarried in 1877; the second marriage, too, was unhappy and ended in divorce in 1901.

Certain she had found a divine mission in saloon-smashing, Nation traveled coast-to-coast giving lectures and selling miniature hatchets. She eventually went on the vaudeville circuit, and, as she traveled, she invaded bars along the way. In January 1910, she was beaten up by the woman owner of a Montana bar and never used her hatchet again. One year later, she collapsed on a stage in Arkansas; she died in six months, apparently of congenital syphilis.

Although Nation was a figure of ridicule to many, she publicized the cause of prohibition more widely than anyone had ever done, spurred the formation of temperance groups, and contributed to the eventual passage of the Eighteenth Amendment.

Balch: Struggled for World Peace
Emily Greene Balch (1867-1961) was a co-recipient of the 1946 Nobel Peace Prize (with YMCA leader John R. Mott) for her lifetime struggle to promote world peace. Born in Massachusetts, Balch graduated from Bryn Mawr College and began her career as a social worker with the Children's Aid Society in Boston. In 1892, she helped found Boston's Denison House Settlement and the Women's Trade Union League; she also helped draft the first minimum wage bill ever presented to a state legislature.

Later, she returned to college, studying economics at the Harvard University

Emily Balch never wavered in her dedication to world peace, though it cost her a job.

Annex (now Radcliffe). She taught at Wellesley College for several years but was dismissed during World War I for her pacifist ideas. In 1910, she published *Our Slavic Fellow Citizens,* considered a landmark exploration into immigrant problems.

In 1915, she was a delegate to the International Congress of Women, at The Hague, and co-founded with Jane Addams the Women's International League for Peace and Freedom. Balch worked on disarmament with the League of Nations and advocated creation of a women's international political party to promote peace.

In 1933, Balch began helping victims of fascism, especially Jews, and during World War II she helped the Japanese-Americans. In 1947, she urged President Truman to grant amnesty to conscientious objectors.

Henrietta Szold: Zionist

Henrietta Szold (1860-1945) was a teacher and writer in Baltimore and New York City before a 1910 trip to Palestine turned her to the cause of Zionism.

The eldest of eight girls of a Hungarian-born rabbi in Baltimore, Szold received from her father the attention and education usually given to a firstborn son. Fluent in German, French, and Hebrew as well as her native English, Szold spent her early life teaching school, organizing night school classes for Jewish immigrants to this country, and translating books for the Jewish Publication Society.

After an unhappy love affair in 1909, Szold took a trip abroad for six months and visited Palestine for the first time. Shocked by the disease and unhealthy conditions she saw there, she decided to devote her life to improving the health conditions of the people of Palestine.

She became the founding president of Hadassah, a women's organization dedicated to health work in Palestine. In 1913, it raised money for its first practical aid, the Hadassah Medical Unit, which was sent to Jerusalem to provide nursing to the poor. Today Hadassah maintains two modern, large hospitals in Jerusalem, both of which care for Arabs as well as Jews. Hadassah is the largest women's organization in the United States today with more than 350,000 members.

Szold traveled between Palestine and the United States, serving in administrative posts within the Zionist organization. In the early 1930s, she had planned to return to the United States from Palestine permanently. But Hitler's rise to power forced her to stay in Palestine to implement a plan that brought German-Jewish adolescents to Palestine to complete their education. The program, sponsored by Youth Aliyah in Palestine, was profoundly important, since many of the young people who were sent from Germany became the sole survivors of their families.

Parks: Symbol of the Bus Boycott

On December 1, 1955, **Rosa Parks** (1914-   ), a middle-aged black woman with her arms full of groceries, sat down in the first row of the "colored" section of a bus in Montgomery, Alabama. As the bus grew crowded, blacks began to relinquish their seats to whites. When two more white men got on, the bus driver told Rosa

Parks to stand up. She looked out the window and pretended not to hear. The driver stopped the bus, came over to her, and told her again to move. She continued looking out the window. Rosa Parks was arrested and became the symbol of a massive black revolt that resulted in a United States Supreme Court decision banning segregation on public transportation.

To protest her arrest, 98 percent of Montgomery's fifty thousand blacks refused to ride the bus. Black churches supported the boycott, and car pools were formed. Community meetings were held, and blacks demanded courteous treatment from drivers, seats on a first-come first-sit basis, and black drivers for buses serving black neighborhoods. In the morning, blacks walked to work; students hitchhiked; one man rode a mule; several drove horse-and-buggies. "A miracle has taken place," said Dr. Martin Luther King, Jr., who first came to national attention as a leader of the boycott.

On April 23, 1956, the United States Supreme Court affirmed that state and local laws requiring segregated buses were indeed unconstitutional.

Rosa Parks now lives in Detroit, where she works as a staff assistant to Congressman John Conyers, Jr.

Rosa Parks refused to give up her seat on a bus and gave birth to a civil rights "miracle."

Fannie Lou Hamer brought the concerns of Mississippi blacks to the 1968 Democratic convention.

Hamer: Civil Rights Activist

Fannie Lou Hamer (1917-1977) was born in Mississippi, the youngest of twenty children of Jim and Lou Ella Townsend, black sharecroppers on a Montgomery County plantation. As soon as she could walk, she worked in the cotton fields.

In 1945, she married another sharecropper. They adopted two children; one died of malnutrition. In 1962, Hamer attended her first civil rights rally at the local Ruleville Baptist Church. "I heard it was our right as human beings to register and vote," she said. "I never knew we could vote before. Nobody ever told us." That year she became a field worker for the Student Non-violent Coordinating Committee (SNCC), and, from then until her death in 1977, she worked to get southern black farmers to register to vote, join labor unions, and form agricultural cooperatives.

When Hamer joined SNCC, the owner of her plantation kicked her out of her family's shack. She was forty-five years old. "It was the best thing that could happen. They set me free," she said. "Now I can work for my people." During her SNCC work, she was beaten, arrested, and shot at, and she became one of the most influential, respected, and durable of the Deep South's black leaders. With her thunderous voice and homespun wisdom, she told Congressmen and northern audiences about the violence against civil rights workers in the South.

At the 1964 Democratic Convention, she appeared before a national television audience and described in forceful detail what life was like for Mississippi blacks. She also helped found the black-led Mississippi Freedom Democratic Party, which challenged the regular white-led party for Democratic convention seats. They failed in 1964 but won in 1972. Hamer worked to unite the black and white factions, and in 1976 a single integrated unit of delegates represented the Mississippi Democratic Party at the national convention.

Despite her national prominence, Hamer continued to live in a three-room house in Ruleville, Mississippi. "Why should I leave Mississippi?" she asked. "I go to the big city and with the kind of education they give us in Mississippi, I got problems. I'd wind up in a soup line there. That's why I want to change Mississippi. You don't run away from the problems, you just face them."

King: Leader in Her Own Right

Coretta Scott King (1927-   ) worked quietly beside her husband, the Reverend

An Atlanta memorial to her late husband has been a focus of Coretta King's recent work.

Dr. Martin Luther King, Jr., until after his murder in a Memphis motel in April 1968. Then she became a civil rights leader on her own. The day before her husband's funeral, she traveled from Atlanta back to Memphis to take his place at the head of forty thousand people who were marching on behalf of the city's striking garbage collectors — a strike which had brought Dr. King to the city in the first place.

Coretta King, a woman of dignity and charm, was born in Marion, Alabama. Her father ran a country store, and she walked five miles each morning to the one-room school serving black children in the area. Each morning, a yellow bus filled with white children would pass her on its way to a bigger, better school. King won a scholarship to Antioch College, where she studied education and music. She met her future husband while taking postgraduate courses at Boston's New England Conservatory of Music.

At six o'clock one December morning in 1955, Coretta King looked out of her darkened living room window, waiting for the first bus to roll down her street. When it passed before her, the usually full bus was empty, and she called joyfully to her husband to come look. The first day of the Montgomery bus boycott had begun, and it was a success. It was to last over a year, and out of it was born the civil rights movement and the Southern Christian Leadership Conference (SCLC). The Kings believed their struggle for civil rights was God's will. Both practiced nonviolence; Gandhi was their model.

Coretta King worked behind-the-scenes to help her husband organize sit-ins in segregated restaurants in Atlanta and Albany, Georgia; "freedom rides" on segregated buses all over the South; protest marches in Birmingham; and the 1963 March on Washington, where a quarter million people gathered at the Lincoln Memorial. She also organized more than thirty "freedom concerts" to raise money for the SCLC. "If I had married a lesser man . . . , I guess I would have ended up wearing the pants. But I didn't have to because he was a man I respected and he allowed me to be his co-worker," she said

As the Kings' civil rights activities increased, they and their four children received hundreds of threatening phone calls; their home was bombed and shot at. From the day that President John Kennedy was killed, the family believed that Dr. King would probably die the same way.

After his murder, Coretta King began speaking in public — first from her husband's old notes, then in her own words — and has called on American women to unite into a "solid block of women power to fight the three great evils of racism, poverty and war."

Carson: Nature's Child

Rachel Carson (1907-1964) finished *Silent Spring* when she was fifty-five years old, shortly before her death. The book described the devastating effect of pesticides like DDT, protested the violent disregard for nature's delicate balance, and helped give birth to the environmental protection movement. She worked four years on the manuscript; when it was completed, she went to her study, turned on a Beethoven violin concerto, and wept. "I had said I could never again listen happily to a thrush song if I had not done all I could. And the thoughts of all the birds and other creatures and all the loveliness that is in nature came to me with such a surge of happiness, now that I *had* done what I could," she said.

Carson was born in Pennsylvania's Allegheny Valley and grew up wanting to see the ocean. She studied marine zoology at Pennsylvania College for Women and Johns Hopkins University, and worked summers at the Marine Biological Laboratory in Woods Hole, Massachusetts. Later, she was staff biologist at the University of Maryland, aquatic biologist with the United States Bureau of Fisheries, and director of the United States Fish and Wildlife Service's publishing program. To help support her mother and two young nieces, she began to write.

Her first book, *Under the Sea Wind,* was published in 1941 and made little money; her second book, *The Sea Around Us,* published in 1956, won her the National Book Award and some financial freedom. She bought land on the Maine coast and built a house. Although by this time she suffered from severe sinus infection, a heart condition, an ulcer, inoperable cancer, and arthritic hands, she was

After finishing *Silent Spring,* Rachel Carson wept because she had done all she could.

determined to speak out against the pesticides being used in increasing quantities. Critics claimed she was a hysterical, silly woman, who romanticized nature. She replied that the balance of nature can no more be ignored than a man on the cliff's edge can ignore the law of gravity. *Silent Spring* was published in 1962. Carson died in Silver Spring, Maryland, on April 14, 1964. On December 31, 1972, the United States government banned all domestic uses of DDT.

Brownmiller: Against Our Will

In 1975, feminist **Susan Brownmiller** (1935-   ) published a controversial book exploring rape as an act of power rather than an act of sex. In *Against Our Will,* the most comprehensive study ever done on rape, Brownmiller said rape "is nothing more or less than a conscious process of intimidation by which *all men* keep *all women* in a state of fear." During her four years of research, Brownmiller concluded that the typical rapist, far from fitting the stereotypes of a deviant, troubled man, is instead "little more than an aggressive,

Susan Brownmiller's powerful study of rape brought feminist concerns to the forefront.

hostile youth" acting out the social mechanisms that men have always used to control their women.

The reason other men get upset about rape, she said, is because it violates their property rights. Brownmiller theorized that marriage has its historical roots in the fear of rape: once a woman "belongs" to a man, she need no longer fear the predatory demands of other men; her man, who has exclusive rights, will protect her.

Brownmiller's book became an important tool for feminists. As many as half a million women are attacked by rapists each year, 10 percent of the attacks are reported, and only 2 percent of the offenders are convicted and put in jail. Rape is the fastest rising violent crime reported; women had already established more than 150 rape crisis centers when *Against Our Will* appeared. The book's popularity exposed feminist concerns to more women and men than ever before.

Brownmiller is the only child of a New York City clothing salesman and his wife, a secretary. She studied government at

Cornell University, dropped out to become an actress, and worked as a researcher for *Newsweek*, a civil rights worker in Mississippi, a *Village Voice* staff writer, and a TV reporter before beginning her book.

Williams: She Campaigns For Peace

Betty Williams (1943-   ), a Catholic housewife from Ulster, began in 1976 a one-woman campaign against militant Catholics and Protestants, and for peace in Ireland. Williams' campaign began on the afternoon of August 10th, when she saw an IRA (Irish Republican Army) man shot through the heart by British troops as he was driving down a Belfast street in his car. The man had allegedly fired on the British patrol. The IRA man's car went out of control and careened onto the sidewalk, where it injured a woman and killed three of her children.

Williams, the daughter of a Presbyterian father and Catholic mother, decided she had seen enough killing in Northern Ireland. Within two days, she found one hundred other Catholic women willing to sign petitions and to march each week for peace. One of them, the dead children's aunt, Mairead Corrigan, who was a twenty-four-year-old secretary, became her staunchest ally. By the third week, sixty thousand women had joined the marches in Dublin, Cork, and Galway. In Belfast, twenty-five thousand Catholic and Protestant women marched into Shankill Road, an area off-limits to Catholics for the last six years.

The lives of Williams, her husband, and her two children have been threatened constantly, especially by the Catholic IRA, since she began to work for peace. The IRA feels she is weakening its militant cause. Another peace leader, Bridget McKenna, was shot in the face as she stood in the doorway of a shop. Williams said she was frightened but would not give up.

"The deaths of those children burst a dam inside of me," she said. "The violence must be stopped. If I thought my own son would take up a gun to kill, I would give him a cyanide pill. I would destroy what I gave birth to if he tried to take away the life of another . . . This peace movement is Northern Ireland's last chance . . . our children have lost the art of playing, and I would love to give it back to them.''

THE REVOLUTIONARIES

Luxemburg: German Revolutionary

Rosa Luxemburg (1871-1919) was one of the world's most able theorists of international socialism. She disagreed with Lenin's interpretation of "the dictatorship of the proletariat," believing that a true Marxist should use democracy rather than abolish it. She opposed terrorism in Russia and predicted, accurately, that if free discussion were suppressed, the young and idealistic Bolshevik government would evolve into a massive bureaucracy. Today, the Soviet Union still regards her views as a dangerous deviation.

Controversy arose in 1974 when West Germany honored Rosa Luxemburg on a postage stamp.

Luxemburg was born in Poland, became an underground revolutionary in her teens, and, at the age of eighteen, was forced to flee to Switzerland to avoid prison. She received a doctorate in political science from the University of Zurich in 1897 and one year later migrated to Berlin, where she worked in the German Social Democratic Party. In 1914, she formed with Clara Zetkin an extreme left-wing splinter group, the Spartacus League. In 1915, she was sent to prison for urging German soldiers to mutiny rather than fight their "brother" Socialists in other countries. From her prison cell, she smuggled articles on revolution to the outside world.

She was released in 1918 and drafted the political program adopted by the German Communist Party. On January 15, 1919, she and another left-wing revolutionary, Karl Liebknecht, were arrested on charges of instigating street fighting in Berlin. While being transported to prison, they were attacked and murdered by anti-Communist army officers.

Goldman: Articulate Anarchist

Emma Goldman (1869-1940), called the "mother of anarchy in America," was born in Kovno, Lithuania; before her death in Toronto, Canada, she was to advocate and practice a personal and political freedom considered audacious even in today's era of "liberation." Goldman left Russia with her sister in 1886 and found a job working for $2.50 a week in a clothing factory in Rochester, New York, an experience that quickly converted her into an anarchist. She moved to New York City three years later, where she ran the anarchist periodical *Mother Earth,* preached and practiced free love, and was arrested several times for her lectures on atheism, patriotism, and birth control.

During one of those lectures, she advised the women in her audience to keep their minds open and their wombs closed. She served one year in jail for telling unemployed men in New York City's Union Square that it was their "sacred right" to steal bread if they were starving.

She was a passionate and articulate rebel. Civil libertarian Roger Baldwin said hearing her was "the eye-opener of my life. Never before had I heard such social passion, such courageous exposure of basic evils, such electric power behind words, such a sweeping challenge to all values I had been taught to hold highest. From that day forward I was her admirer."

She formed many deep and lifelong friendships, including Russian immigrant and revolutionary Alexander Berkman, whom she met in New York City. Shortly after their meeting, he was sent to prison for fourteen years for attempting to kill steel magnate Henry Frick during a steelworkers' strike in Pittsburgh. They worked together again after his release. Both were arrested in June 1917 for urging men to avoid the draft. They were sent to

Disillusioned with the USSR, Emma Goldman declared, "You are still free in America."

prison for two years, and after their release both were deported to Russia.

Goldman had high hopes for the success of the Russian Revolution, but her ideals were crushed under Soviet bureaucracy, and she lashed out again, this time at Russian party elitism and the "triumph of the state."

Goldman loved the United States, and, when she was permitted to return for ninety days in 1934, she told her audiences: "You are still free in America . . . No spies enter your homes for incriminating documents. No legalized assassins shoot you down in the street." During the Spanish Civil War, she worked in London gathering financial and moral support to fight Franco.

Her friend Berkman, despondent and seriously ill, committed suicide in 1936, and she fought constant depression after that. When she died from a stroke in 1940, United States officials allowed her body to be returned to America. She was buried in Chicago, near the graves of striking workers murdered in Haymarket Square in 1886.

Kollontai: Free Love Exponent

Alexandra Kollontai (1872-1952), Russian-born daughter of a czarist general, rejected her privileged status in 1896, at the age of twenty-four, and began to work for revolution and women's rights. She left her husband when she found he did not share her feminist and left-wing ideas, and studied in Switzerland until the Russian Revolution was under way. The week before the Communists gained power in October 1917, she held Russia's first major women's conference.

She was an articulate and passionate exponent of unorthodox ideas on sex, marriage, and the family: she felt all three, as practiced, oppressed women. In her novel *Free Love,* Kollontai said she tried to "teach women not to put all their hearts and souls into the love of a man, but into the essential thing, creative work . . . If love begins to enslave her she must make herself free, she must step over all love tragedies, and go on her own way."

She joined the Bolsheviks in 1915 and two years later was elected to the Central Committee, where she was one of the nine members to vote with Lenin for armed insurrection. She served in the Bolshevik government as the first woman cabinet minister and first woman ambassador. In 1920, Kollontai became a leader of the Workers Opposition, a movement to protest the ways in which the revolution was moving from its original ideals.

Despite her dissent, from 1923 to 1945 Kollontai served in various diplomatic posts in Norway, Mexico, and Sweden. She received the Order of Lenin and was the only major opposition leader to survive the purges of the 1930s. In 1944, she negotiated the Soviet-Finnish armistice. During her final years, she served as adviser to the Ministry of Foreign Affairs. She died in 1952.

Flynn: "Rebel Girl"

Elizabeth Gurley Flynn (1890-1964) dropped out of her South Bronx, New York high school, became an organizer for the International Workers of the World, and was arrested for her Socialist speeches — all before she reached the age of sixteen. Her parents were both

Socialists. In 1912, when she was twenty-two, Flynn was a leader in the textile strike in Lawrence, Massachusetts, where women and children chanted "give us roses, bread and roses" and were brutally beaten by police and strike-breakers. Union organizer Joe Hill was writing about Flynn in his song "Rebel Girl" when he said: "To the working class, she's a precious pearl."

Flynn also organized nationwide defense committees for Joe Hill, labor agitator Tom Mooney, and Italian-born anarchists Nicola Sacco and Bartolomeo Vanzetti. She led iron-ore miners' strikes in the Midwest and West, and was one of the founders and a member of the board of the American Civil Liberties Union. The ACLU expelled her in 1940 for being a Communist; in 1976, twelve years after her death, it repealed the expulsion, saying it was "not consonant with the basic principles on which the ACLU was founded." Flynn served two years in prison for her Communist affiliations. In 1961, after her release, she was made national chairman of the United States

"Rebel Girl" Elizabeth Gurley Flynn was arrested for radical activities before she was 16.

Communist Party, the first woman to hold that post. She remained chairman until her death in Moscow in 1964.

Chiang: China Power

During the early 1960s, **Chiang Ch'ing** (1914?-   ) spearheaded a cultural revolution in China and became the most powerful woman in the world's most populous country. Under her watchful eye, the nation's singers, writers, and artists created only those works that would glorify the ideas of her husband, Mao Tse-tung, chairman of the Chinese Communist party until his death in 1976. During the cultural revolution, she dressed in army uniform, pulled back her hair under an army cap, and encouraged the Red Guards to destroy revisionist art and life styles that she felt had begun to compromise Mao's revolutionary principles. By the time the cultural revolution began to wane in 1969, Chiang had become a leader of the hardline Maoist faction in the ruling Politburo of the Chinese Communist party.

Chiang Ch'ing's real name is Ch'ing Yun, which means "Blue Cloud." She was born in a poor family in Shantung Province and at the age of nineteen married her first husband, a Communist organizer who reportedly turned her into a Marxist and feminist. Later, she changed her name to Lan Ping ("Blue Duckweed"), divorced her husband, and moved to Shanghai to become an actress. People who knew her at the time recalled her as "a pretty, primly dressed, unusually reticent girl of limited talents." After another marriage, she met Mao Tse-tung in 1939 at the Lu Hsun Art Academy in Yenan, where she was teaching dramatics and he had come to give a lecture. Mao was 43; she was twenty years younger. The encounter was, as the Chinese describe it, "like dried wood on a roaring fire"; Mao gave her the name Chiang Ch'ing ("Green River").

For the next twenty years, Chiang was a housewife, mother, and quiet companion to Mao. When the Revolution was won in 1949, she served in several posts but played no public role in the transformation of Chinese society. It was only with Mao's permission and support that she came out of her house to lead the Cultural

Once a leader of China's hardliners, Chiang Ch'ing today lives under virtual house arrest.

Revolution. By 1971, she was ranked third in the party hierarchy, directly under Mao and the late Premier Chou En-lai, and many believed Mao was preparing his wife as his successor. In 1971 and 1972, she also directed performances of the play *Red Detachment of Women* for the American table tennis team and for President and Mrs. Nixon.

After Mao's death, she struggled to retain control over the party, but failed and was attacked on wall posters as a vain and tyrannical woman who had betrayed the Chinese people. Although many have questioned her motives, none doubt that she is strong-willed, courageous, and dedicated passionately to Maoism. During a 1972 interview with Dr. Roxanne Witke, professor of Chinese history at the State University of New York, Chiang said that although Chinese women had played a large part in all the successive revolutionary struggles in China, their status is not equal to that of men in all aspects. Today she is sixty-two years old, in ill health, and lives under virtual house arrest.

VOLUNTEERS

American women are avid volunteers. In 1973, at least twenty-seven million women did volunteer work — from being "candy-stripers" in local hospitals to raising money for Easter Seals. Their free labor is worth about $18 billion a year. One of America's most publicized volunteers is Lillian Carter, mother of President Jimmy Carter, who at the age of sixty-seven joined the Peace Corps and worked for two years in India. The wives of American presidents are always active in volunteer work.

"Volunteerism" has in the past been an acceptable outlet for women's energy. In recent years, however, it has come under attack as a way of keeping women economically powerless and dependent on men. Many believe that women who have valuable services to offer should be paid for those services.

However, many middle-aged and older women have found that volunteer commitment can be a liberation of its own kind, and have used it as a first step to gain access to the world outside their homes. And many women have dedicated their time, energy, even their lives to causes that were too controversial to attract financial support.

For example: **Joanna Graham Bethune,** the wife of a rich man and one of America's first volunteers in organized charity, founded the Society for Relief of Poor Widows with Small Children in 1797, and in 1811 was instrumental in building one of the nation's first orphanages. She also opened the first Sunday schools in America, which taught reading and writing to illiterate immigrants who had to work the other six days.

— **Caroline Bayard Stevens Wittpenn,** daughter of a wealthy New Jersey family, battled in the 1890s for separate women's reformatories, removed children from almshouses, and established a system of juvenile courts in her state.

— In 1953, **Mary Church Terrell,** the daughter of ex-slave parents and founder of the National Association of Negro Women, headed a committee of Washington, D.C. citizens demanding enforcement of a seventy-five-year-old law forbidding discrimination in restaurants. The

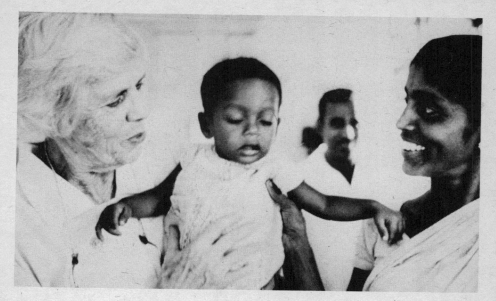

Lillian Carter, America's number one volunteer, during her Peace Corps days in India.

resulting battle went all the way to the United States Supreme Court, which ruled in her favor and paved the way for integration in the nation's capital.

— In Chicago, forty-seven-year-old **Gale Cincotta** organized a 1970s coalition to fight mortgage lenders whose policies were contributing to urban blight. She has become a national leader in neighborhood political action. She now heads two organizations that monitor the policies of Chicago real estate brokers, banks, and federal agencies. Cincotta leads sit-ins, testifies before Congress and in court, and in 1976 won passage of a federal law forbidding red-lining — the slum-creating practice by which banks refuse loans on a geographical basis.

VOLUNTEER ORGANIZATIONS

Nobody ever got rich doing volunteer work. At least, not in terms of dollars. But many women have found that donating their spare hours to helping others is rewarding in its own way. These suggestions might be helpful.

Don't take the first volunteer job that comes along. Find a position suited to your interests and skills.

Your local library's community information file may be a good place to begin the search. Investigate opportunities available with hospitals, schools, day care centers, religious and political organizations, women's groups, community centers, and cultural and health agencies.

The following national organizations can also steer you to some volunteer possibilities:

ACTION
806 Connecticut Avenue, NW
Washington, D.C. 20003
(ACTION is the federal agency that runs such programs as the Peace Corps, VISTA, and Foster Grandparents. Stipends are paid workers in some of these programs.)

American Cancer Society
777 Third Avenue
New York, New York 10017

American Civil Liberties Union
410 First Street
Washington, D.C. 20003

American Friends Service Committee
1501 Cherry Street
Philadelphia, Pennsylvania 19102

American Society for the Prevention of
    Cruelty to Animals
441 East 92nd Street
New York, New York 10028

Associated Councils of the Arts
1564 Broadway
New York, New York 10036

Association of the Junior Leagues of
    America
Waldorf Astoria
301 Park Avenue
New York, New York 10022

Call for Action
(Branches in 45 major cities; check
    phone book for listing.)

Catholic Social Services
(Check phone book for listing.)

Chinese Women's Association, Inc.
5432 152nd Street
Flushing, New York 11355

Church Women United
475 Riverside Drive
New York, New York 10027

Common Cause
2030 "M" Street, N.W.
Washington, D.C. 20036

Friends of the Earth
529 Commercial Street
San Francisco, California 94111

General Federation of Women's Clubs
1734 "N" Street, N.W.
Washington, D.C. 20036

Hadassah
50 West 58th Street
New York, New York 10019

National American Indian Women
    Association
3201 Shadybrook Drive
Midwest City, Oklahoma 73110

National Association for Retarded
    Children
420 Lexington Avenue
New York, New York 10017

National Association of the Deaf
814 Thayer Avenue
Silver Spring, Maryland 20910

National Center for Voluntary Action
1785 Massachusetts Avenue, N.W.
Washington, D.C. 20005

National Consumers League
1785 Massachusetts Avenue, N.W.
Washington, D.C. 20005

National Council of Negro Women
1346 Connecticut Avenue, N.W.
Washington, D.C. 20036

National Foundation, March of Dimes
1275 Mamaroneck Avenue
White Plains, New York 10605

National Society for the Prevention of
    Blindness
79 Madison Avenue
New York, New York 10016

National Women's Christian
    Temperance Union
425 13th Street, N.W.
Washington, D.C. 20004

Public Interest Research Group
2000 "P" Street, N.W.
Washington, D.C. 20036

United Cerebral Palsy Association
66 East 34th Street
New York, New York 10016

U.S. Committee for UNICEF
331 East 38th Street
New York, New York 10016

Women's International League for
    Peace and Freedom
120 Maryland Avenue, N.E.
Washington, D.C. 20002

Women's Lobby
1345 "G" Street, S.E.
Washington, D.C. 20003

Young Women's Christian Association
    of the U.S.A.
600 Lexington Avenue
New York, New York 10022

Spiritual Women

WOMEN IN THE CHURCH

"So God created man in his own image, in the image of God he created him; male and female he created them." — Genesis 1:27

With this first — and somewhat ambiguous — reference to sex in the Bible, the debate over woman's place in Western religion began. Were men alone cast in God's mold? Or were both men and women created to resemble a sex-neutral supreme being in spirit rather than body?

Woman's role in Biblical times was as a supportive but subservient adjunct to man. Wives the world over dutifully tended children and kept house while husbands received and interpreted the laws of their gods. Of course, a rare woman challenged her expected role: the inquisitive Eve, the brave Esther, the prophet Deborah.

Many ancient deities were undeniably female. The same voluptuous Great Mother goddess was revered by the Phrygians as Semele, by the Semites as Astarte, by the Sumerians as Ishtar, by the Egyptians as Isis, and by the Greeks as Demeter. Such goddesses sprang from the earliest human need to explain the natural cycle of birth, maturation, death, and renewal.

The coming of Jesus seemed to signal a more important role for women in religious life. "When we examine the relationship of Jesus to women," notes Rev. Eva Zabolai-Csekme of the Lutheran World Federation, "we realize that He at all times and all places regarded them as fully human beings just like anyone else."

Sister Elizabeth Carroll of the Catholic Sisters of Mercy agrees that Jesus defied convention to teach that "there are no distinctions between . . . male and female." But within fifty years of his crucifixion, she notes, a "strong strain of antifeminism" surfaced among his followers, and the position of women in the Church began to decline. Those "antifeminist" forces confirmed their power in the Church when the priesthood was limited to men.

From the end of the first century through the nineteenth century, women, with few exceptions, held second-class status in Western religion. During the Middle Ages, the Church gave tacit approval to the domination of women by their husbands and fathers. Women were taught by their priests to win male goodwill through increased piety and obedience.

From the fourth century on, some women opted for a more bearable or rewarding subservience by entering convents. Though dominated by penance and prayer, convent life sometimes afforded women the possibility of some education and an opportunity to exercise some authority in their own religious communities.

Devotion to Mary

Perhaps it was the ancient tradition of goddess worship that accounted for the continuing popularity of Mary, the mother of Jesus.

By the eleventh century, says Robert Biffault in *The Mothers,* "The Holy Virgin . . . had well replaced the male Trinity in the devotion of the people. God the Father was unapproachable and terrible. Christ had the stern office of a judge. The Queen of Heaven alone could show untrammelled mercy."

Woman's accepted role in religion was challenged in the legend of Pope Joan, who supposedly headed the church as John VIII from 855 to 858. She was believed by many Catholics to have been a real person until the story was unmasked as myth in 1601, when historians discovered that no Pope John VIII had ruled during that time period.

According to one story, the learned Joan disguised herself as a monk to follow her Benedictine lover to Athens. She moved on to Rome, where she became a cardinal and later pope. Some versions of the tale suggest that she was pregnant at the time of her election to the papacy and gave birth to her child during a procession through the Vatican. She was, according to legend, immediately dragged out of the city and stoned to death.

Joan's story is not without historical inspiration. It is thought to have stemmed from gossip that Marozia, an infamous tenth century Roman senator, and Theodora, her mother, secretly ruled the Church.

Religion also had to contend with an occasional real-life female rebel. In 1428,

England's Margery Backster was hauled before the bishop of Norwich on charges that she repudiated crucial Church doctrines and practices. She refused to attend religious festivals, go on pilgrimages, or fast when she was supposed to. She even denounced the religious hierarchy as persecutors of the people.

Two centuries later, the Massachusetts Bay Puritans were challenged by the independent-minded Anne Hutchinson. The so-called "American Jezebel" was persecuted not only because she questioned Puritan doctrine, but also because it was thought impudent for a woman to speak out against the male ministers of the community.

The male-dominated religious establishment received one of its first direct challenges in the 1850s when Antoinette Brown Blackwell sought to become the nation's first ordained female minister. Even her usually supportive family and friends discouraged Blackwell from taking up the cloth.

Encouraged only by the feminists of her day, Blackwell studied theology at Oberlin College and published a paper criticizing St. Paul's overused admonition, "Let your women keep silence in the churches." With her ordination into the Congregational ministry in 1853, woman's first victory in the continuing struggle for the pulpit was won.

The feminist awakening of the last decade has led women to re-think their traditional role in religion. Though their most publicized quarrel with the organized church has centered on the ordination of women to the clergy, they are also seeking to change other areas of religious law and liturgy.

Protestants: First Rules, Now Attitudes

So many strains of Protestantism exist that it is difficult to draw conclusions about the status of women in this branch of Christianity. Generally, the more theologically liberal sects such as the Methodists and Congregationalists have led the way in according their female members equal status.

In comparison with the older Jewish and Catholic faiths, Protestantism has usually been more accommodating to movements for change springing up from within its ranks. Hence, Protestant denominations were the first to open the clergy to women. Almost all Protestant sects now ordain women; as of May 1977, the United States had more than fifteen hundred Protestant clergywomen. The largest number of women ministers — six hundred in all — are affiliated with the Methodist church.

One of the last holdouts was the Episcopal church, whose General Convention voted by a slim margin in 1976 to admit women to the priesthood. The issue had threatened to tear the church apart after eleven women defied their religious superiors in 1974 by receiving unauthorized ordinations. The Episcopal church is not yet at peace. During Jacqueline Means' ordination in 1977 as the first officially sanctioned woman priest, one Episcopalian stood up to condemn the ceremony as "heresy" and "sacrilege." He then marched out of the church along with eleven followers.

Mormons — who consider themselves an independent faith but are usually classified as Protestants — have yet to give in to the ordination demands of their feminist members. The going has not been easy for the women, who have been denounced by their church president as "Pied Pipers of sin." The Mormon church has gone on record as opposing the Equal Rights Amendment as well as abortion and birth control.

Though their ranks are slowly but steadily growing, women in the Protestant ministry are still up against tradition. For many people, a minister continues to mean a middle-aged family man with a dutiful wife who sings in the choir.

Catholics: No "Natural Resemblance"

Of Western faiths, the rigidly structured, tradition-bound Catholic church is among the most resistant to change by feminist reformers. In January 1977, Pope Paul VI reaffirmed the church's stand that women cannot be priests because "Jesus Christ was a man and His representatives on earth must bear a natural resemblance to Him."

But the pope's statement did not silence debate on the issue of women priests. The push for admitting women to the priesthood has been especially strong in the

United States, where hundreds of women are seeking ordination. A prayer vigil and procession — the first organized demonstration against the pope's ruling — was held in eight U.S. cities on February 27, 1977.

Change is nonetheless afoot in the Catholic church. Inspired by Vatican II, nuns have updated their garb and lifestyles. In 1974, Sister Kathleen Cannon, chaplain at Connecticut's Albertus Magnus College, became the first woman preacher in the history of Catholicism. Cannon is allowed to preach the homily after the gospel in the Mass, a function traditionally reserved for priests or ordained ministers.

Under pressure from women's rights advocates, many metropolitan-area parishes have quietly begun to use altar girls at Mass. Though the Vatican has traditionally limited serving at Mass to boys and men, some Catholic bishops have looked the other way when churches extended the honor to girls. Other bishops are pressuring Rome to repeal the ban against altar girls, though they have so far met with no success.

Jews: Establishing New Traditions

Judaism has long held that woman's proper place is in the home, raising children in the faith and running the household while her husband studied the Torah and prayed. Many argue that the emphasis on woman's procreative role remains valid, largely because the number of practicing Jews has declined as a result of the Nazi holocaust, intermarriage, and the popularity of birth control among Jewish couples.

"Judaism has always put women on a pedestal," declares Michal Bernstein, one of Reformed Judaism's handful of female rabbis. "In the morning blessing, a man thanks God he's not a woman, because a woman does not have the obligation and honor of serving God . . . That is a copout. If our role in society has changed, our religious role must, too."

In Orthodox synagogues, women still sit apart from men. They are usually not counted in the minyan (the quorum of ten needed for a service) and are given no say in marriage ceremonies, divorces, and rituals celebrating the birth of their sons. Even in the less rigid Conservative

Trailblazers like Rabbi Sally Priesand are changing woman's age old place in religion.

synagogues, women seldom don the tallis (the prayer shawl) or carry the Torah.

But things are changing for Jewish women as they are for their Christian sisters. Beginning with Sally Priesand in 1972, Reformed Judaism has ordained several women rabbis. According to a 1976 Rabbinical Assembly poll, the number of Conservative congregations counting women in the minyan increased from 7 to 37 percent between 1973 and 1976. Even in some Orthodox synagogues, women are now allowed to read the Torah on special holidays,

Illustrative of woman's changing status are new or revised liturgies that give women a greater role in the traditional celebrations of their faith. The Bas-Mitzvah, the girls' coming of age celebration, is beginning to approach the boy's Bar Mitzvah in significance among many Jewish families. Several Haggadahs (Passover ritual books) offer women an expanded part in the ceremony marking the deliverance from Egypt. Ceremonies have recently been written to celebrate the birth of female children.

Not all women endorse feminist-inspired changes in religious practices that are centuries old. Remarked one Orthodox Jewish woman, "What I have is comfortable and the laws give me faith. I resent them trying to tear everything down."

For Women, God Lives

Despite all the controversy, recent surveys indicate that religion still plays a major part in the lives of most American women. One recent study of sixty-five thousand women found that nine out of ten believe in God. One woman in four classifies herself as "very religious," while 83 percent say they are at least "moderately religious."

According to a Gallup Poll, church attendance rose in 1976 for the first time in twenty years. The Gallup organization found that 46 percent of American women attend religious services during a typical week, as compared with 37 percent of American men.

Four out of every ten Americans — and nearly half of all Protestants — believe the Bible "is to be taken literally, word for word." And 34 percent of both sexes — nearly 50 million adult Americans — claim to have had a "born again" religious experience.

Do American women favor efforts to improve their status in religion? Responding affirmatively in the sixty-five thousand women study were 36 percent of Jewish women surveyed, 24 percent of Catholic women, and 12 percent of Protestant women. Some 66 percent of Catholic women favored women clergy, as did 86 percent of Jewish women and 82 percent of Episcopalians. All told, 72 percent of the women polled favor the idea of women in the pulpit. Only the Mormon women still voted no; only 25 percent believed women should be ordained.

Though most women continue to think of God as "He," a surprising 38 percent expressed the view that God is neither male nor female.

Commentators who pronounced God dead a decade ago obviously did not consult American women. It stands to reason that women's commitment to their faith may even increase as more religious opportunities are opened to them. As Episcopal laywoman Sarah Mallory noted at the ordination of priest Jacqueline Means,

"Now I've seen God's 'man' put together as he should be — male and female. Remember where it says in Genesis: 'He gave *them* dominion.' "

BIBLICAL WOMEN

Deborah: Prophet of Victory

Generals who question the wisdom of sending women into battle might do well to study the story of **Deborah.**

Though the wife of an obscure man, Deborah rose to great power through the wise counsel she gave to all who consulted her. She railed against the oppression of her people by the king of Canaan. Convinced the men of Israel had bungled their rebellion against the Canaanites, she summoned Barak, a military leader, and gave him a battle plan. But Barak feared Canaan's 900-chariot army, and refused to go into battle without Deborah at his side. She agreed to ride with his army, and prophesied victory.

Though Deborah's people lacked the military might of their adversaries, they had God on their side. A violent storm of sleet and hail disabled the Canaanite forces, but left the Israelites unscathed. Sisera, commander of the enemy army, fled to the tent of Jael, wife of Heber the Kenite, who was neutral in the conflict. Jael killed Sisera in his sleep, confirming Deborah's prophesy that "the Lord shall sell Sisera into the hand of a woman."

The triumphal Ode of Deborah, one of the earliest martial songs, was composed to celebrate Israel's victory over its oppressor.

Delilah: Enchanting Enemy

Samson may have been the strongest man in the ancient world. But his will was weak when it came to attractive women. Though he had vowed to wreak havoc on the Philistines, he became their captive after succumbing to the charms of the beautiful but treacherous **Delilah.**

Traditionally, Delilah is thought to have seduced Samson and betrayed him for 1,100 pieces of silver. But the Biblical story relates that it was only after their torrid love affair was well underway that the Philistine elders bribed her to learn the secret of Samson's great strength so they could end his raids against their towns.

Pressed for his secret, Samson told Delilah three lies about how he might be deprived of his strength. Each time, she tried the method he had told her, and each time he mocked her. Finally, the foolish man told her the truth: if his hair was cut, he would be as weak as other men. Of course, she tried this method too. Samson was turned over to the Philistines, who gouged out his eyes, and set him to grinding grain like an ox.

The Bible does not indicate that Delilah felt any remorse over betraying her lover. However, in his poem *Samson Agonistes* (1871), Milton depicted her visiting Samson in prison to seek forgiveness.

Esther: Savior of the Jews

The courage of **Esther,** the beautiful Queen of Persia, is still celebrated by Jews each March at their Purim festival.

According to the book of the Bible named for her, the orphaned Esther was descended from a noble Jewish family taken into captivity in Babylonia about 597 B.C. When King Ahasuerus of Persia sought a new wife, Esther's cousin and guardian, Mordecai, brought her to the royal palace. The king was instantly taken by her beauty, and made her his queen, without discovering she was Jewish.

Esther soon learned that the King's adviser, Haman, was plotting to have Mordecai hanged and to destroy the Jewish people. When Mordecai asked her to intervene with the king, she asked the Jews to fast with her and said, "Then I will go to the king, though it is against the law; and if I perish, I perish." She knew she risked her life by challenging her husband's favorite counsel.

Esther first lulled Haman with false friendship, while she prepared a trap. At a feast attended by Haman, Ahasuerus asked Esther what he could do for her. She accused Haman of plotting to kill her people and the king ordered Haman to be hanged on the same gallows he had prepared for Mordecai.

Eve: Fell To Temptation

Poor Eve! Were she around today, her inquisitive nature might make her an outstanding research chemist or investigative reporter. But her curiosity about the forbidden fruit of knowledge brought about

Many modern women believe that Eve — as well as her female descendants — got a bum deal.

her downfall — and that of generations of women who followed her.

The beautiful Eve was the first woman, fashioned by God from Adam's rib. The couple's carefree life in the Garden of Eden came to an abrupt end after Eve had a chat with the serpent. Once she learned that the tempting fruit held the knowledge of good and evil, Eve promptly took a bite, and persuaded Adam to do the same. When God found out they had disobeyed his edict, the two were cast out of paradise. He condemned Adam to a life of hard labor. Eve's punishments were the pain of childbirth and servitude to her husband.

From the nineteenth century on, scientists have challenged the Biblical version of the creation. The American psychologist Theodor Reik, however, questions the story from a different angle. In the *original* account of the Creation, Reik suggests, Eve preceded Adam.

Jezebel: Martyr To Her Faith?

Had the story of **Jezebel** been told by her own people, she might have emerged as a religious martyr, rather than as one of the Bible's wickedest women.

Raised in a kingdom to the north of Israel, Jezebel moved to Israel upon marrying its king, Ahab. She refused to convert to her husband's faith, and insisted the lewd cult of Baal be established in Israel. Ahab submitted to his wife's dictates, and condoned the slaughter of many Jewish holy men and the banishment of the rest. The prophets Elijah and Elisha remained, however, to carry on a continual propaganda campaign against her.

After Ahab died in battle, Jezebel's sons ruled Israel for about thirteen more years. Elisha announced the true king was a Jew named Jehu, who began a revolt that ended with the death of Jezebel's reigning son. Jehu ordered Jezebel thrown from a window to her death.

Lot's Wife: Turned To Salt
One of the best known women of the Old Testament bears no given name, and her story is told in just fifteen words. She is **Lot's Wife.**

The family of Lot lived comfortably in the evil city of Sodom. Mrs. Lot is assumed to have preferred pleasures of the flesh over purity of the spirit.

An angel of God warned Lot that fire and brimstone were to destroy Sodom, and its sister city of Gomorrah, for the wickedness of their people. The family fled. "But," the Bible recounts, "his wife looked back from behind him, and she became a pillar of salt."

Geologists have suggested that an ancient explosion might have dislodged a layer of rock salt lying beneath the Mountain of Sodom, literally causing fire and brimstone to rain upon the region. Regardless, the tale remains a graphic warning against turning back from one's faith; as Jesus later cautioned his followers, "Remember Lot's wife."

Mary: The Madonna
Some of the Western world's greatest pieces of music, literature, and art venerate **Mary,** the simple peasant girl who gave birth to the Christian savior, Jesus.

Mary was a serious, pious young woman of no more than twenty when the Angel Gabriel appeared to her, announcing that she had been chosen to bear the son of God. "Blessed art thou among women," he told her, a refrain that would be carried down through the centuries.

Unwed pregnancies were cause for social ostracism in Mary's Nazareth, yet she freely accepted God's will. Joseph, her betrothed, believed her story and took her in. After making the 90-mile journey by donkey from Nazareth to Bethlehem for the Roman census, Mary gave birth to her child in the stable of an inn. The virginity of Mary remains an issue of sharp debate among Christians; many Biblical scholars claim that mistranslation converted a common word for "young girl" into "virgin."

Warned that King Herod had decreed the death of all male infants. Mary traveled with her husband and son into Egypt. Later they returned to Nazareth, where Mary tended her son as he "increased in wisdom and stature, and in favor with God and man."

Mary appears in the Scriptures during Jesus's ministry, and was with him when he died on the cross. She is last mentioned praying with the apostles in Jerusalem, after the Ascension.

Mary Magdalene: Reformed Woman
"I've had so many men before, in very many ways," sings the **Mary Magdalene** character in the rock musical, *Jesus Christ Superstar.* All that changed once she met

Michaelangelo's *La Pieta* is one of the best known works of art venerating the Madonna.

Jesus, who revealed through her how even the most debased sinner can receive divine forgiveness.

The Bible tells of Jesus cleansing Mary of the seven devils, though whether they were symbols of her sins or a physical illness cannot be definitively stated. She accompanied Jesus during his ministry in Galilee, and stood alongside his mother at the Crucifixion.

Mary Magdalene was the first to see the resurrected Christ upon going with two other women to his tomb on Easter morning.

Ruth: "Whither Thou Goest . . ."

The Bible's most poignant story of human love is not that of man and woman, but that of a young widow for her elderly mother-in-law.

Ruth, a Moabite, married the son of foreigners who had been driven by famine from their native Bethlehem. After the death of Ruth's husband and his brother, her widowed mother-in-law, Naomi, prepared to return to her homeland. Ruth insisted, over Naomi's loving protests, upon accompanying her. "Entreat me not to leave thee," she said, "or to return from following after thee: for whither thou goest, I will go; and where thou lodgest, I will lodge: thy people shall be my people and thy God my God."

Ruth's devotion to her mother-in-law overcame Naomi's hostility to foreigners. She set about supporting herself and Naomi by gleaning the fields of Boaz, a wealthy kinsman of her late husband. Thanks in part to Naomi's matchmaking, Ruth and Boaz were married.

Sarah and Hagar: Mothers of Nations

The Bible's first miracle birth was that of Isaac to the aged **Sarah** and Abraham. Long barren, Sarah took up the nomadic life with her husband when she was nearing 65, upon God's promise to "make of thee a great nation."

After eleven years of wandering, God had yet to make good on his vow. Sarah lost hope that she would ever conceive, and offered her maid, **Hagar,** to Abraham so his line would continue. The child of Hagar and Abraham, Ishmael, is the legendary ancestor of the Arabs.

When Abraham was about 100 and Sarah nearing 90, Isaac was conceived.

When her son was a toddler, Sarah insisted that the overly proud Hagar and Ishmael be driven out of their household. God concurred, and Abraham banished the two into the desert, where God provided water for them.

But Sarah's trials were not yet over. When Isaac was thirteen, God insisted that the boy be delivered up to him as a human sacrifice to test Abraham's faith. When Abraham showed his willingness to give up even his beloved son for his religion, God relented and allowed the boy to live. From the line established by Sarah and Abraham sprang the House of Israel.

Salome: Demanded a Head

Salome, according to some stories, had an unusual way of showing her affections. Scorned by John the Baptist, the object of her infatuation, she demanded his head on a platter.

The New Testament, however, leaves more to the imagination. John became the enemy of Salome's family when he denounced her mother, Herodias, for divorcing Herod Philip and marrying his brother, Herod Antipas, governor of Galilee. Herodias wanted John killed, but her new husband feared the man and his popular following. After young Salome pleased her stepfather by dancing at his birthday feast, he promised her "whatsoever she would ask." At her mother's urging, Salome de-

Salome's treatment of John may suggest there is no wrath like that of a woman scorned.

manded John's head, and Herod Antipas reluctantly complied.

WOMEN OF FAITH

Cabrini: Cared for the Orphaned

Frances Xavier Cabrini (1850-1917), the first American citizen to achieve sainthood, established sixty-five orphanages in Italy, the United States, and Central and South America, and numerous hospitals in the United States.

This dynamic woman was frail during her youth. Born in Italy to older parents, she knew at an early age that she wanted to join a convent, but her poor health kept her from being admitted.

Instead she pursued an education and became, first a teacher, then an assistant in an orphanage called the House of Providence. After three years there, her spiritual adviser, Monsignor Don Serrati, allowed her and seven girls from the orphanage to take their vows.

By 1887, she was in charge of eight convent houses in Italy, and in 1888 she opened a free school and a nursery in Rome with the approval of the Vatican.

That same year, at the age of 38, she came to the United States, where, combining religious zeal with administrative skill, she founded and managed many more houses over the next 28 years.

Piety and administrative skill were united in the person of Saint Frances Xavier Cabrini.

Elizabeth Seton, founder of America's first Catholic schools, became a saint in 1975.

Seton: First American-born Saint

Elizabeth Ann Bayley Seton (1774-1821) is the newest and first American-born saint in the Roman Catholic religion.

Her background is unusual for a Catholic saint: She was born into a well-to-do Anglican family, was not a particularly religious girl, married, had five children, and was widowed — all before she turned to Catholicism.

Her young life was not particularly devout. She attended dances, had beaus, and in 1794 married William Magee Seton.

Their marriage was a loving one, but was plagued by bankruptcy and by William's ill health, which brought his death in 1803. While she was in Italy with her husband she was introduced to Catholicism through his business friends.

After a year of debating with herself, she converted to Catholicism, which alienated her from many family members and cost her badly-needed inheritances from her godmother and stepmother.

The alienation was as much for social as for religious reasons. In the United States in the eighteenth century, Catholics were usually "lower-class" immigrants and considered "public nuisances."

In 1808, Seton was asked to start a Catholic school in Baltimore to teach daughters of prominent Maryland families. After one year, she was able to realize a long held dream — to found a religious community modeled upon the Sisters of Charity. In 1809 she took her vows, became Mother Seton, and started her convent of the Sisters of Charity of St. Joseph on a farm in Emmitsburg, Maryland.

The Emmitsburg community grew rapidly, primarily as a school. Branches of the order were opened in New York City and Philadelphia.

Teresa of Avila: Reformer

When Teresa of Avila (1515-1582) joined the Carmelite Order in 1535, her fellow-nuns led a comfortable life; some even had personal servants. Her efforts to return the order to an austere and devout way of life was the first of many cloister reforms of the sixteenth century, and earned her sainthood.

Teresa had a pleasant childhood in Avila, Spain, under the guidance of two religious parents.

Although she was a devout nun within the Carmelite Order, it was not until she was forty-four that she started her reform work. She was moved by Christ's suffering when she saw a picture of him, covered with wounds, and she resolved to live the remainder of her own life in a suitably austere manner.

In 1556, she founded a small house for her reform movement, where the nuns lived in uncompromising poverty: habits of coarse brown serge, sandals of rope, abstinence from meat, and no furniture.

Her house won the admiration of the head of the Order, who supported her in her reform work. During the next fifteen years, Teresa opened sixteen more reformed convents in Spain.

Teresa was also one of the great Spanish mystics. In her book, *The Interior Castle,* she guides the reader through "abodes" of the human soul until she reaches the innermost chamber, which is the dwelling place of God.

Hutchinson: Puritan Rebel

Anne Marbury Hutchinson (1591-1643) was the first person to strongly challenge the rigidity of the Puritan religion of the Massachusetts Bay Colony. Although she was banished for her independence, she stands as a symbol of religious freedom and personal courage.

The daughter of an Anglican minister in England who was twice imprisoned for his religious beliefs, Anne learned early to stand up for her ideas. During her years as a young wife and mother of twelve, she became a disciple of Anglican minister John Cotton and his reinterpretation of the Puritan doctrine.

When Cotton was forced out of England for his views, she and her family followed him to Boston in 1634. There she established weekly meetings of women to discuss the latest sermons. She began to expound her own theological views, which emphasized a direct relation between God and believers through intuition rather than by observance of minister' rules and rigid adherence to formal doctrine. Her discussions were popular for a brief time and attracted many of Boston's religious leaders.

In 1637, however, her chief opponent, John Winthrop, was elected Governor of the colony, and Hutchinson was brought to trial for her views. Even John Cotton turned against her.

Banished from the colony, she moved first to Narragansett Bay, Rhode Island, and then, after she was widowed, moved to what is now Pelham Bay Park in the Bronx, New York. In 1643, she and all her children but one, were massacred by Indians.

Lee: Soul Shaker

"It is not I that speak," Shaker founder Ann Lee (1736-1784) told her followers. "It is Christ who dwells in me." They took her word for it, and considered her to be the second coming of Christ.

Lee led a troubled life before becoming a leader, in 1770, of England's small community of "Shakers," so named because they worshiped God by singing, dancing, speaking in tongues, and other ecstatic practices. Unschooled, she worked in a textile mill and was already a Shaking Quaker before her marriage to a blacksmith in 1762. The marriage was unhappy, and the four children she bore died in infancy. Convinced she was responsible for their deaths, Lee went without food and sleep. In her weakened condition, she had a religious vision which convinced her that celibacy was the route to salvation.

While serving time in jail for her beliefs, Lee had a second vision in 1774, which revealed to her that the Shakers would fare better in the New World. She resettled in New York along with seven of her followers.

She proselytized throughout New England and New York, her charismatic personality winning many converts to the faith. In addition to celibacy, Shakers opposed slavery and advocated equal rights and responsibilities for both sexes.

Shakers — known officially as the United Society of True Believers in Christ's Second Appearing — believed that they could perpetuate their numbers, despite their ban on "cohabitation of the sexes," by winning converts and adopting orphans. But by the early 1970s, the sect had dwindled to 20 aged members.

Eddy: Mind Healer

Some people view **Mary Baker Eddy** (1821-1910), founder of the Christian Science religion, as a female Elmer Gantry, publicly pretending to a devout religious life, but privately bent on making a fortune from her new religion.

It is true that when she died her estate was worth more than two-and-a-half million dollars, but it also seems apparent that her religion was an attempt to bring others the relief she had found by "mind healing."

From her birth to after her fortieth birthday, Eddy was plagued by almost constant physical and emotional illness. When she was growing up she suffered from chronic back trouble, which kept her from attending school regularly. At age twenty-two, Eddy married a family friend, but six months later, when she was six months pregnant, he died of yellow fever.

The events triggered severe emotional upset, and for the next nine years her family treated her hysteria and nervous symptoms by nursing her as an infant, rocking her like a baby to quiet her, and giving her morphine.

Eddy married again, but her numerous ailments continued until 1862, when she visited a Dr. Phineas P. Quimby in Portland, Maine. Dr. Quimby believed in healing through prayer.

The method seemed to work for Eddy, and she adopted his philosophy that disease could be cured by spiritual concentration. Three years later, she apparently cured herself of a back injury through prayer, and committed herself to proselytizing her belief in mind healing.

Her thinking appealed to many people, especially women, who found little relief for many illnesses, since 19th century doctors generally assumed that women were naturally sickly and should bear their disabilities without complaint.

In June 1875, the first public Christian Science Service was held, and that autumn, Eddy's first edition of *Science and Health* was published. In 1879, the Church of Christ (Scientist) was formally chartered. In 1908, the *Christian Science Monitor* was first published. By 1906, the federal religious census showed a membership of 85,717 Christian Scientists; by 1936, it had grown to 268,915 members. Today the membership of the church is not recorded, though there are some 2,300 churches.

In addition to being popular, the Christian Science religion proved very lucra-

When prayer cured her aching back, Mary Baker Eddy founded the Christian Science Church.

tive. Eddy charged $300 per person to train in mind healing, and made more than $100,000 in fees.

McPherson: Holy Roller
Another religious leader whose motives were often questioned was evangelist **Aimee Semple McPherson** (1890-1944), founder of the International Church of the Foursquare Gospel.

Canadian-born Aimee Elizabeth Kennedy was brought up working for the Salvation army under the tutelage of her mother, who was thought to have given McPherson her evangelistic fervor. At age seventeen, McPherson was converted at a Holy Roller pentecostal revival. She married the evangelist who had converted her, Robert James Semple.

Semple died two years later of typhoid fever. McPherson began preaching at revival meetings throughout the country, with her mother. A second marriage ended in divorce because her husband, Harold Stewart McPherson, could not accommodate himself to her itinerant preaching.

In the fall of 1918, McPherson and her mother settled in Los Angeles at their followers' request and built a temple that seated 5,300 people. She was soon preaching to the largest congregation in the world.

In 1926, at the height of her religious popularity and monetary success, McPherson disappeared. The real story is still a mystery, but on May 19, 1926 it was reported she had drowned. A month later, however, she reappeared in the Southwest, saying she had been kidnapped. It is believed that she had fallen in love with a radio operator, but because she had always preached against remarriage for divorced people, she felt she could not marry. Instead, she had run off with her lover.

Although she continued her revivals in this country and in Europe, her personal life became increasingly unhappy.

She died in 1944 in Oakland, California, of an overdose of sleeping pills. Her son succeeded her as president of the International Church of the Foursquare Gospel. When she died there were more than 400 branches of her church in the United States and Canada, almost 200 mission stations abroad and about 22,000 church members. The church continued to grow after her death.

Day: Social Reformer
Dorothy Day (1897-   ) converted to Catholicism when she was thirty. Six years later she co-founded the *Catholic Worker,* an influential monthly newspaper dedicated to social reconstruction.

Day had been a socialist reformer when, after much soul-searching, she joined the Catholic Church. With French-born Catholic Peter Maurin, she advocated "the green revolution," social reform based on communal farming and the establishment of houses of hospitality for the urban poor.

Day and Maurin espoused their ideas in the *Catholic Worker,* which had a circulation of 150,000 within three years. The newspaper took radical positions on many issues. During World War II, it was an organ for pacifism and the support of Catholic conscientious objectors.

A number of settlement houses were founded in connection with the newspaper. Day, like her co-workers, lived in the New York house in voluntary poverty. Her autobiography, *The Long Loneliness,* was published in 1952.

White: Seventh Day Adventist
A religious vision that revealed that the Christian Sabbath must be celebrated on a Saturday started **Ellen Gould Harmon White** (1827-1915) on the preaching trail that led to the founding of the Seventh Day Adventist Church in 1863.

White and her family were Methodists in Maine when they accepted the prediction of Baptist former-preacher William Miller that Christ's new *advent* on earth would occur "about 1843." When Miller's prediction failed, White gained a congregation by convincing many of his followers of her power and revelations.

White married another Adventist preacher, James Spring White, and the couple carried on their faith, which was formally organized in 1863. Although White never claimed to be a prophet, it was her interpretation of the Scriptures that largely determined the orthodoxy of the Seventh-Day Adventists, and her visions were unquestioningly accepted as principles of the church.

She preached about the importance of a healthy diet, probably a result of concern about her own tendency toward ill health, and she also opposed slavery.

After her husband's death in 1881, White continued to expand the influence of the Church. From 1903 on she lived near St. Helena, California. She died there in 1915, after suffering a fractured hip.

Today the Adventists have two-and-one-half million members in 185 countries, including 480,000 people in the United States.

Kuhlman: Faith Healer

One of the most revered faith healers in the United States was **Kathryn Kuhlman** (1907-1976), a Missouri-born evangelist.

Kuhlman had her first religious experience when she was thirteen and started preaching when she was fourteen. After two years of informal Bible study, she was ordained a minister by the Evangelical Church Alliance.

After a second religious experience in 1946, she began to talk more and more about the Holy Spirit. During one of her sermons, a woman in the congregation claimed to have been cured of a tumor. Following that initial "spontaneous cure," Kuhlman began to preach about

Faith healer Kathryn Kuhlman told followers, "Your faith in God cures you."

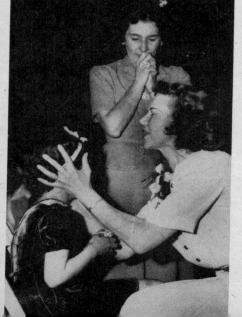

the Holy Spirit's power to cure. She took no personal credit for the cures.

Besides her preaching and healing, she was president of the Kathryn Kuhlman Foundation, a charitable organization devoted to missionary churches, drug rehabilitation, and the education of blind children.

Mother Theresa: Dedicated to the Poor

One of the most selfless and respected figures in the Roman Catholic Church today is **Mother Teresa of Calcutta** (1910-   ).

Born in what is now Yugoslavia, Mother Teresa said she knew by age twelve that her vocation was to help the poor. When she was eighteen, she joined the Sisters of Loretto, a community of Irish nuns who had a mission in Calcutta.

In 1946, she asked the Vatican for permission to leave the convent and live among the poor. Her request was granted, and she opened the first of several open-air schools in Calcutta. By 1950 the Missionaries of Charity had become an official religious community. In 1952 Mother Teresa opened the Nirmal Hriday Home for Dying Destitutes in a dormitory donated by the city of Calcutta. The community opened its first home outside of Calcutta in 1959, and today there are twenty-two houses in India and other countries.

Mother Teresa has been described as "charismatic" and "mesmerizing." British writer Malcolm Muggeridge believes an "actual miracle" happened when he was in her presence. While filming a program for the British Broadcasting Corporation, there was not enough light to shoot pictures inside one of Mother Teresa's homes. The cameraman tried anyway, and the resulting film came out in a particularly beautiful light, which the cameraman and Muggeridge, who was also on the scene, believe technically impossible.

Jungreis: Revivalist of Judaism

Judaism is not an evangelistic faith, nor one in which women have been encouraged to play a highly visible role. Nonetheless, Jewish revivalist **Esther Jungreis** (1938-   ) has won herself a reputation as her religion's Billy Graham.

Jungreis was born in Hungary, daughter of her town's chief rabbi.

She survived Bergen-Belsen and Auschwitz concentration camps, and later emigrated to America, in 1945. Ten years later she became a "rebbetzin" (rabbi's wife) by marrying Orthodox Rabbi Theodore Jungreis.

In 1973, she founded Hineni ("Here I am"), a Jewish revivalist organization whose membership now totals 17,000.

Unlike Graham and other Christian evangelists, Jungreis is not attempting to convert others to her faith. Instead, she is seeking to bring assimilated Jews back into the fold.

Jungreis has carried her message to such arenas as New York's Madison Square Garden and the Hollywood Palladium.

GODDESSES

Demeter: Mother Earth

Ancient Greeks explained the changing of seasons in terms of a bargain between **Demeter,** or Mother Earth, and Hades, god of the underworld.

Usually gay and generous, Demeter was devastated when Hades fell in love with her daughter, Persephone, and abducted her to the Land of the Dead. Out of anger and grief, Demeter halted the grass from growing and the trees from bearing fruit. Famine ravaged the land, and the chief god, Zeus, ordered Hades to release Persephone.

But the law forbade visitors from leaving the underworld after tasting its fruit, and Persephone had eaten several pomegranate seeds from Hades' garden. A compromise was arranged: Persephone would live with her mother nine months of the year, and with Hades the other three.

In gratitude for the return of her daughter, Demeter taught those who helped her the arts of agriculture, and had corn scattered throughout the world. Demeter's cult was centered at Eleusis, the seat of an ancient mystery religion that remained a powerful force until well into the Christian era. Her Roman counterpart was Ceres.

Juno: Guardian of Women

Like the Greek Hera, the Roman goddess **Juno** was queen of heaven. She was both sister and wife of the chief god, Jupiter, and the protector of women. As worship of her spread, she sometimes took on war-like aspects. According to Plutarch, she turned back the Gauls in 390 B.C. by the cackling of her sacred geese.

Each Roman woman had a personal Juno to whom she made sacrifices in exchange for help in performing her duties as wife and mother. The bride invoked Juno to protect her new home, the barren woman to make herself fertile, the woman in labor, to ease the pain of childbirth, the new mother, to guard the health of her child. On the first of March, Roman matrons brought special offerings to Juno's temple in a celebration called the *matronalia.*

Ishtar: Two-Faced Babylonian

Like many ancient goddesses, **Ishtar** of Babylonia had a dual identity; she was associated with war and death, as well as with love and fertility.

Ishtar took her grown son, Tammuz, as her lover. In some unexplained way, her love killed him. (This event was often symbolically reenacted by the sacrifice of a god-king or his stand-in.) Ishtar de-

Juno, depicted here by Natoire, was considered the special protector of Roman women.

Ishtar or Astarte symbolized the central mystery of life via her command over birth and death.

scended to the underworld to rescue Tammuz, and while she was gone, sexual desire vanished and the earth fell barren. Upon Ishtar's return to earth with her resurrected son, the earth became fruitful again.

Thus, Ishtar of the upper world was worshiped as a fertility goddess. But the underworld aspect, which she revealed while battling the forces of darkness for Tammuz, was warlike, bringing death and terror. In all her forms.

Known as Inanna of Sumeria, and Astarte of the Phoenicians, Ishtar was worshiped from about 3000 B.C. until after the birth of Christ. Her rites, at one time or another, were observed from Persia to the British Isles. She was the ancient world's leading rival to the Hebrew God, and Old Testament prophets condemned the image-making and ritual prostitution that were part of her worship.

Isis: Mother of Pharoahs
The most powerful goddess of ancient Egypt, **Isis,** formed the ruling triad of deities with her husband-brother Osiris, and their son Horus.

Another brother, Seth, grew jealous of Osiris's virtue and fame. He tore Osiris's body into fourteen pieces and scattered them around the earth. Isis and Horus, whom she had protected from Seth until he reached manhood, found all the pieces but the phallus. They reassembled them, and wrapped the body, mummy-fashion in rolls of cloth. Isis fanned the corpse with her wings and restored Osiris to life. He became ruler of the underworld, while Horus became king of the living. Because the living pharoah was considered a personification of Horus, Isis was looked upon as the mother of kings. She was revered as the source of all life, protector of the dead, and healer of the sick.

Sedna: Ugly Sea Goddess
Many goddesses are pictured as beautiful idealizations of womanhood. Not so the fearsome **Sedna,** Eskimo goddess of sea animals.

Sedna had only one eye; black hair grew where her right eye should have been. Tangled in her tresses were the foul-smelling sins of humans. She was so ugly that ordinary men would be stricken dead if they looked upon her.

Depictions of Isis suckling Horus strongly resemble later works of Madonna and Christ Child.

Most tales of Sedna's origin suggest she was thrown from a boat by her father. As she attempted to grasp hold of the vessel, he chopped off her fingers one by one. She sank to her new kingdom in the deep, and sea creatures grew from her severed fingers.

When angered by such acts as secret abortions and improper hunting, she experienced pain in the stumps of her limbs and retaliated by causing shortages of wild game. When famine threatened, Eskimo conjurers were advised to capture Sedna and raise her out of the water, releasing her only after she gave in to demands for food.

Hindu Goddesses

Hindu mythology is a panorama of gods and goddesses, interrelated, but each with specific roles. An ancient Hindu text credits a Great Mother, known as **Mahasakti**, with the origin of the great gods Brahma, Atman, and Siva. These gods, in turn, often manifest themselves as their wives and daughters. These manifestations are also called "skatis."

Siva, the destroyer, has many skatis. Among them is his wife, **Uma**, who is said to have once joined him in meditation in the mountains. She mischievously slipped behind him when he was engrossed in his thoughts and covered his eyes with her hands. Instantly, the sun went out and life began to fail. But, just as suddenly, Siva's forehead opened, and a third eye appeared, great and flaming with the brightness of a new sun. Overcome with the consequences of her play and awed by Siva's power, Uma begged his forgiveness, and he set the earth and heavens right again.

Another of Siva's skatis, **Parvati**, is depicted as a beautiful and intelligent woman who discusses love and metaphysics with him. Many sacred texts, called the "Tantras," are in the form of dialogues between Siva and Parvati. Siva sometimes gives Parvati the task of dancing the cosmic dance, and she then assumes the name **Ma Kali**, or black mother. Kali is both terrifying — brandishing a blood-stained knife and dripping human head — and comforting, wearing a necklace which symbolizes the weaker side of human personalities that she helps correct. Until the beginning of the nineteenth century, human sacrifices were offered to Kali. Even today she receives many animal sacrifices.

Buddhist Goddesses

Buddhists also worship skatis who dispense knowledge or compassion and often have a second, warrior-like personality.

Tara, the most honored Buddhist goddess, is personified as Supreme Wisdom and as the Mother of All Buddhas. She is said to have come from the tears of the sage, Avalokitesvra, and represents mercy. In the Orient, she is beloved as **Kuan-yin.** When depicted in white or green, she is gentle and loving; but she can also be menacing, when portrayed in red, yellow, or blue.

A militant Buddhist goddess is **Kunda,** who has anywhere from four to sixteen arms and an arsenal of weapons. According to her legend, Kunda helped the tree spirit kill a wicked queen in whose bed a new king of Bengal was murdered each night. Despite her military attire, Kunda is a kindly goddess. Her first pair of hands is depicted in a teaching pose; another symbolizes charity; others hold prayer beads and a gold lotus flower. She reserves her weapons for the wicked.

Kumari: Modern Goddess

Most gods and goddesses belong to an earlier period in human history. But modern Nepalese still worship **Kumari,** who is thought to be the Mother Goddess, Devi, in the body of a living girl. Kumari is kept secluded in her palace, visited frequently for advice on important matters. She emerges only once a year during Katmandu's Indra Jatra festival. Sitting in a chariot piled high with pillows to protect her from the slightest injury, Kumari grants the king the right to rule for another year, and he touches his head to her feet in humility.

But a Kumari's reign is short. As soon as she bleeds — either from injury or her first menstruation — she is replaced by another young girl. Her life afterward is likely to be unfortunate, because men are warned that bad luck or even death will befall them if they marry an ex-goddess. Most dedicate their lives to the gods, begging for food on streetcorners. Some have become prostitutes.

Sportswomen

WOMEN IN SPORTS

One of these crisp fall days, Dad is going to sit down for a long afternoon of football-watching and see Mom playing quarterback. Or he might watch her win the Boston Marathon. It could happen, you know. "The female body is better suited for endurance races — the 26.2-mile marathon and longer runs up to 100 miles — than a male," says marathon runner Dr. Joan Ullyot, an exercise expert from the University of California Medical Center in San Francisco.

The gap between men and women in setting sports records is narrowing. And the notion that a woman must be sporting but not a sports star is disappearing. The gains made by women in the sports world, most of them recent, have taken time — about 4,000 years.

In most ancient cultures, women's sports were severely limited or forbidden but not unknown. Egyptian murals dating back to 2050 B.C. depict women playing ball games. In ancient Egypt, gymnastics, exercises, wrestling, lifting, swimming, and ball games were open to both sexes. In China, Babylonia, Sumeria, and Assyria, however, physical activity for women was limited to dancing. In Persia, all physical activities by women were forbidden by religious edict.

Things were better in early Greece during Minoan and Mycenaen times (1400-1100 B.C.), when women participated equally with men in all areas of life. Their physical prowess was celebrated in period pottery, particularly the feats of three legendary heroines: *Cyrene,* who wrestled with a lion; *Atalanta,* who offered to marry the man who could out-distance her in a race (the losers would be hanged); *Penthesileia,* Queen of the Amazons, who had great skill in archery and horse-handling.

In Sparta (ninth to third century B.C.), everyone from seven to twenty went through the *agoge,* a rigid training in physical fitness. The state encouraged women to prepare their bodies for childbearing. Girls exercised publicly in the nude in such sports as running, jumping, throwing the javelin, lifting weights, and wrestling.

Athenian society, in 4th century B.C., ranked women as second-class citizens, although Socrates and his pupil, Plato, encouraged Spartan principles. Women were not permitted to participate in the Olympic games. Although historians date the Olympics to 1453 B.C., the first records of winners date from 776 B.C. Men competed in the nude and women were not permitted to watch. A woman caught in the stadium risked death by being thrown from a high mountain.

In retaliation, women held their own games in honor of Hera, wife of Zeus and Queen of heaven. The Heraea Games were sufficiently important to attract competitors from Asia Minor.

By the 128th Olympics, women were included in the competition. The winner of the chariot race in the Games was Belisiche, a Macedonian woman. A statue discovered at Delphi depicts three daughters of Hermesian who won foot and chariot races in the middle of the first century B.C. The Christian Romans banned the Olympic competitions as pagan in 392 A.D. The games were not revived until 1896.

During the Middle Ages, asceticism and scholasticism eliminated what little sports participation had existed for women — and, to a great extent, that for men as well. These concepts branded anything pleasurable as a sin, and permitted women to do little or nothing in the way of physical activity.

Some Early Sports Welcomed Women

One early sport that was equally accessible to members of both sexes was archery. All British monarchs, including Queen Elizabeth I and Queen Victoria, were trained in archery as a matter of course.

Stag hunting was imported into England with the Norman invasion in 1066. It became a popular royal sport. In the seventeenth and eighteenth centuries it was replaced by hare and fox hunting as royal stag herds were depleted.

In early American history, Puritanism excluded both men and women from pleasurable leisure activities. Nineteenth century Victorian ethics strictly limited the role of women to childbearing and housework. Women, it was observed by physician James MacGregor Allen in 1869, are "unfit for any great mental or

Tennis was introduced to the U.S. in 1874 by a woman — Mary Outerbridge of Staten Island.

physical labor,'' during their menstrual periods.

Croquet, in those days, was an acceptable female sport, but not roque — the same game, played on a clay court with smaller hoops. The American Roque League excludes women from its annual championships to this day.

By the 1870s, women began appearing as spectators at sporting events. But they weren't allowed to sell refreshments! An 1862 ban on hiring women as vendors is currently being pried from the New York City lawbooks.

During the 1880s, roller skating, bicycling, tennis, and golf became popular sports, and women began to participate in them.

Social strictures on women in sports persisted into the 20th century. Elaine Burton created a stir when she won the 100-yard-dash at the British Northern Counties Championship in 1919. She was the first woman to compete wearing shorts and spiked shoes. (She later became a member of Parliament.)

Margaret Curtis of Boston was a winner of the Women's Golf Championship four times under the most elaborate dresses,

petticoats, hats, and stockings. May Sutton, the first famous American woman tennis player, and twice a Wimbledon winner, won in spite of fashionable encumbrances.

Dress aside, the American woman who pioneered the liberation of women in sports was Eleanor Sears, a Bostonian who played "a man's game" in every sport that interested her. Sears was superb at golf, tennis, swimming, and riflery.

Women occasionally made headlines in untraditional sports. Annie Taylor went over Niagara Falls in a barrel in 1901. Annie Oakley was one of the sharpest shooters of all time.

Mt. Holyoke Female Seminary initiated calisthenics in 1832, replacing them with gymnastics in 1862. In the late 1800s, Wellesley and Smith Colleges offered crew and basketball for women.

Women were not allowed to take part in the modern Olympics until 1900 when six competed in tennis. Women were barred in 1904, but surfaced for archery in 1908, and swimming four years later. It was only in 1924 that women became a permanent part of the Olympics.

By 1920, 22 percent of American col-

19th century women managed to glide gracefully over the ice despite encumbering costumes.

biological destiny of women in the 1950s, for example, precluded her participation in "unfeminine sports." Not until the late 1960s and 1970s, for instance, were studies conducted and published that showed women could sustain as many injuries as men with no ill effects. A women's professional football team was occasion for coarse jokes in the 1950s — not today.

Women's Sports Expanded

The first meeting of the First National Institute on Girls' Sports was held in 1963 "to increase the depth of experience and expand opportunities for women in sports." The Commission on Intercollegiate Athletics for Women, which draws up guidelines for athletic events and sanctions competitions, was formed in 1966.

Increased acceptance of women on all levels of sports was closely connected to the demystification of menstruation. In 1962, G. J. Erdelyi surveyed 729 women athletes. He found that none was prevented by menstruation from competing. In fact, physical activity was found to alleviate certain side effects of menstruation, according to a 1962 report. A study of 24 Olympic women athletes by W. A. Pfeiffer in 1950 showed that these women had easier deliveries during childbirth than other women. Moreover, these women often improved their athletic performances after childbirth.

The biggest medical bugaboo was that pregnant women ought not to participate in sports, and that a woman's reproductive organs could be permanently harmed by strenuous sports. C. L. Thomas in 1931 demonstrated that the uterus is well protected. It floats like an egg in an air-free jar of water and is virtually jolt-proof. C. H. McCloy confirmed these findings in 1969 with a study of landing shock in jumping for women.

One ironic twist to the biological brouhaha was the introduction of femininity tests at the Olympics in 1968. These tests were designed to prove that one was actually a female, because some men were supposedly masquerading as women in the women's events and had unfair advantage. The test involves taking a smear from inside the mouth. A laboratory test looks for the existence of microscopic structures called Barr bodies, which occur only in

leges had some form of intercollegiate competition for women in sports. In 1923, national competition in track and field for women was introduced, with governing associations to formulate rules. The National Amateur Athletic Federation founded a women's division in 1923.

If one person can take credit for serious sports competition by women in the 1920s it is Mildred "Babe" Didrikson Zaharias. She attracted an enthusiastic press because she was an extraordinary and nearly unbeatable athlete. She was also a pro at publicity, clipping articles about herself while golfer Glenna Collett and track-and-field star Stella Walsh quietly piled up trophies.

Women did not make much sports headway during the 1930s, 1940s, and 1950s because the world had other things on its collective mind. The Depression made survival a priority over setting sports records, and World War II took care of most of the 1940s (the 1940 and 1944 Olympics were canceled).

In general, the percentage of women in newsworthy sports is a barometer of women's role in society as a whole. The

female cells. Russian Tamara Press, the Olympic gold medal winning shot-putter, and Austria's Erike Shinegger, women's world champion in downhill skiing, withdrew from competition after the introduction of the tests.

Men are physiologically stronger than women because they have more muscle tissue. In fact, according to some authorities, no amount of training will give women more muscle tissue than men. Men have proportionately larger lungs and hearts, as well as other physical advantages over women. However, some authorities also believe, now that women are being pushed harder by coaches, there will be some startling new records set by women. Between 1924 and 1972, the size of the man's lead in the Olympics' 400-meter freestyle swimming was cut from 16 percent to 7.3 percent.

Courts Promoting Women in Sports
Recent federal legislation has far-reaching implications for sports activities in 16,000 public school systems and 2,700 postsecondary institutions. The new rules require physical education classes to be

Modern women — and girls — are striking for equality in all segments of sports.

coeducational, except in contact sports and sex education. They do permit grouping of students by ability, and allow separate toilet and locker room facilities, provided the facilities are comparable. Schools that do not comply risk loss of federal funds.

Some other rulings have been significant. In one of them, the Supreme Court of the state of Washington ruled that a high school girl should be allowed to play on the boys' football team.

At Yale University in 1976, the women's rowing crew protested their lack of shower facilities by walking into the office of the physical education director wearing nothing but "Title IX" printed in blue ink on their chests — that's the section of the federal law that calls for equal locker room facilities, among other items, for women. The Yale women quickly won their case!

At last, too, women are achieving a modicum of equality at the big sports cash register. Thanks to tennis star Billie Jean King and others, women are beginning to get much larger prize purses.

On the collegiate level, in 1971 there were an estimated 200 women's athletic scholarships. Now, at least 350 colleges are offering from 5 to 60 scholarships each to women athletes. Women are being recruited by colleges and enduring the same kinds of pressures from scouts as their high school brothers.

TENNIS

Austin: Tennis Prodigy
The tennis credits of **Tracy Austin** (1962-   ) rate a Guinness Book of Records scrutiny: She began playing at the age of two, coached by Vic Braden. At age four she was a cover story subject for *World Tennis*.

Austin, a native of Rolling Hills, California, seems to do everything right. According to one coach, there are "no weaknesses in her game."

A straight-A high school student, Austin spends her summers traveling the tennis circuit with coach Robert Lansdorp. By 1977 she had qualified to play on the Virginia Slims Tour. Among her trophies is a victory over aging male pro Bobby Riggs.

"She's tough and she's very fast," sighed world ranked player Dianne Fromholtz in 1977 after losing in an upset to Austin. "I took her too lightly, thinking, 'how can anyone so young be so good?'"

Bueno: Brazilian Superstar

At age 14 **Maria Bueno** (1940-   ) was a heroine of her native Brazil, when she won her first national championship. In the early 1960s she was the undisputed female tennis superstar. Too much tennis destroyed the tendons in her right arm, and Bueno dropped out of competition (she played 110 games in seven hours at Wimbledon in 1967). During her career she won 585 tournaments.

After seven operations on her arm, Bueno is attempting a comeback. Because of fatter prizes, Bueno is now making money at tennis for the first time. Her game lacks the fire it once had, but she is still a favorite of the fans. In Brazil, where she lives between tours, one can write to her by simply putting her name on the envelope.

Casals: Tennis Feminist

Californian **Rosemary Casals** (1948-   ) gets crazy when the name of her granduncle, Pablo Casals, is brought up. "I've never met the man . . . If people know me I want it to be because of what I've done," she says. One of the world's best tennis players, the 5-feet-2 star has made a fortune on the tennis circuit, besides establishing herself as a tough, funny tennis feminist. Billie Jean King asked the fifteen-year-old Casals to be her doubles partner at the 1964 Forest Hills tournament. They proved to be a good team; together they have won two victories at Forest Hills, four at Wimbledon, and four at the U.S. Indoor Championships. When King took on Bobby Riggs in their 1973 battle of the sexes, Casals provided blistering TV commentary from the sidelines.

Casals' commitment to tennis is nearly total. "Tennis is my life," she told her high school teachers as she cut classes to play in tournaments. But Casals occasionally breaks training to smoke a cigar or drink an exotic concoction, such as gin and green chartreuse with a beer chaser.

Casals ranked fourth on the 1976's list of leading female tennis money winners.

Connolly: A Short Career

Maureen Connolly (1934-1969) was the first woman to win the tennis grand slam: the British, French, Australian, and U.S. championships.

Born in San Diego, Connolly was runner-up in the first tournament she entered, only months after she began taking lessons. At fifteen, she was the youngest U.S. Girls Champion ever and had won more than 50 championships. Standing 5-feet-4, Connolly was called "Little Mo" by the press. Her game was steady and accurate, with few fireworks.

Connolly's tennis career was cut short in 1954 when her leg was crushed in a horseback riding accident. She died of stomach cancer at age thirty-four.

Court: Aussie Star

At eight, **Margaret Smith Court** (1942-   ) joined the neighborhood boys in sneaking at night onto the courts of the local tennis club. They were hidden from the club warden's sight as long as they kept the ball in the front of the court. "It was my job to stand at the net and volley back every ball," Court remembered. "If anybody tells me today that I can volley well, I recall those moments I had to volley or get caught." She did get caught — by club owner Wally Rutter. He gave Court her first lesson, and started her on a career that is the winningest in women's tennis history.

In 1960, Court was the youngest person ever to win the Australian Senior Invitational. A decade later, she became the second woman ever to win the Grand Slam (U.S., British, French, and Australian Championships). When she left the tour for the birth of her third child in 1977, she had a record 66 tournament victories.

Court's success can be ascribed to her supreme fitness, the product of years of grueling exercise. On court, however, she is "a steam roller," as colleague Rosemary Casals put it. One of the few times Court lost her cool on the court was in her much publicized defeat by Bobby Riggs in 1973.

Unlike tennis feminists Casals and Billie Jean King, Court keeps a low profile, traveling on the tour with her husband and children. "The Courts are women's lib in action, and they don't even know it,"

King says. "She makes the money and he takes care of the kids."

Evert: "Always Good"

"What can one do?" despairs French tennis player Francoise Durr. "Billie Jean (King), she can be very good, then not so good. Evonne (Goolagong) can be good, then awful. But that Chris. Nobody has ever seen her bad. She is *always* good."

Christine Evert (1954-   ) is undisputedly the Number One woman tennis player in the world today. Applying unflappable concentration, she brings home trophy after trophy.

Evert was born in Ft. Lauderdale, Florida. Her father is manager and teaching pro at the Holiday Park Tennis Center. Like her siblings, Evert began playing tennis when she was six.

At sixteen Evert was the youngest player ever to represent the United States in the Wightman Cup Championship. The same year — 1971 — she was the youngest semi-finalist ever in the U.S. Open at Forest Hills.

Evert's game features a powerful, two-handed backhand. She has won Wimbledon twice (1974 and 1976), Forest Hills twice (1975 and 1976), and the French Open twice (1974 and 1975). In 1974 she lost only seven of 103 matches.

By 1976, her fourth year as a pro, Evert had earned more than $1 million and was voted *Sports Illustrated* Athlete of the Year, becoming the second woman ever to receive the award. (Billie Jean King was the first).

Gibson: Broke Color Barrier

Althea Gibson (1927-   ) was the first black to break the color barrier and play in the U.S. Nationals at Forest Hills. Born in Silva, North Carolina, she was raised in Harlem. Gibson says that as a youth she was "wild and arrogant," and was an habitual school truant.

She began piling up tennis trophies in the 1940s. In 1944 and 1945, she won the National Negro Girls' Championships. Gibson received an athletic scholarship to Florida A&M where she played on the men's softball team.

It took an editorial by former champion Alice Marble in *American Lawn Tennis Magazine* to get her to Forest Hills in

Chris Evert claims she has "a burning desire to win every time I step on the court."

Althea Gibson was the first black to play — and win — at the Forest Hills U.S. Championships.

1950. The next year she was the first black American to play at Wimbledon.

In 1956, Gibson won the French Open Doubles with Angela Buxton. She won the Forest Hills and Wimbledon crowns in 1957, and repeated the Forest Hills victory in 1958.

For a while Gibson toured with the Harlem Globetrotters, playing exhibition tennis and earned $100,000. But her sports prowess had peaked. She became a semiprofessional singer and for many years played pro golf with middling success.

Gibson became Director of the New Jersey State Athletic Commission in 1975.

Goolagong: Near the Top

Evonne Goolagong, (1951-   ), ranked second best women tennis player in the world, is givng Chris Evert a run for her money. The daughter of an impoverished Australian sheepherder, Goolagong was discovered by two tennis instructors for the Victor A. Edwards Tennis School. When Goolagong was thirteen, Edwards persuaded her parents to make him her guardian. She moved in with his family and began training.

At eighteen, Goolagong beat her countrywoman Margaret Court at Wimbledon. By 19, she had won the New Zealand, the Tasmanian, and the French Open championships and taken the Wimbledon title again. Since 1971, she has been three times a Wimbledon finalist, four times a Forest Hills finalist, and a three-time winner of the Australian Open.

"Eva has never had to work at her game," says Court. "You get the feeling that she just doesn't give a damn," says professional rival Virginia Wade, "and it throws you off." Says Goolagong, "Winning is just not everything."

In 1975 she earned nearly half a million dollars on the court circuit. Married to Roger Cawley, Goolagong had her first child in 1977.

Heldman: Does Everything

Billie Jean King may be the most publicized spokesperson for financial parity on the pro tennis circuit, but **Gladys Heldman** (1922-   ) did a lot of the spadework. Her list of accomplishments is stunning: she graduated Phi Beta Kappa from Stanford University in three years; took up tennis for the first time after mar-

rying and having two children; won 82 amateur trophies; played at Wimbledon and Forest Hills; founded and edited for 21 years *World Tennis* (which she sold to CBS in 1974 for a hefty profit); promoted the Virginia Slims tennis circuit (19 sponsors turned her down); and is a board member of 30 corporations.

Heldman, the daughter of a New York City judge, lives with her oil company executive husband in Texas. "Determination and heart are much more important than talent," she says.

Heldman's daughter, Julie, is a top U.S. tennis player.

Jacobs: Wore the Shorts

Helen Hull Jacobs (1908-   ) is the only woman who won the U.S. Championships at Forest Hills four years in a row (1932-1935). She was also the first woman to wear shorts in a major tennis tournament.

Jacobs won her first title in the 1924 National Junior Tennis Championship (and won in 1925 as well). From 1927 to 1938, she was a member of the American Wightman Cup team. In 1936 she won the Women's singles at Wimbledon.

Jacobs' game was not spectacular — even by 1930s standards. "But she had something else," wrote colleague Alice Marble, "more will to win, more drive and guts than anyone else. Plagued by sprains and injuries throughout her tennis career, Helen never gave up."

Jacobs probaly prefers to be remembered as a writer. After a stint in the navy (she retired with the rank of Commander) she wrote a series of children's books, three historical novels, and fourteen books on tennis.

King: "The Most Important"

Billie Jean King (1943-   ) has been called "probably the most important sports hero in the country." The woman who used to walk three and a half miles to school to strengthen her legs deserves the praise. She helped establish the women's professional tennis tour. She publishes *womenSports*. She has been an outspoken proponent of women in all sports. She has a long string of tournament victories to her credit. Viewers in thirty-six nations saw her beat Bobby Riggs in straight sets in their 1973 "Battle of the Sexes" match. "This is a culmination of nineteen years of

"I'm always thinking how I can make something a little bit better," says Billie Jean King.

tennis for me," she said afterward. "I've wanted to change the sport and tonight a lot of non-tennis people saw the sport for the first time."

Born in Long Beach, California, King abandoned softball for tennis, which she considered a "more ladylike" sport. She began playing tennis in earnest at age eleven. At sixteen she was ranked nineteenth in the United States. Alice Marble offered to coach King, and within a year King was ranked fourth.

In 1964 King quit college and spent three months working on her groundstrokes with Mervyn Rose in Australia. Then came her stunning string of victories. She won the Wimbledon singles title six times: in 1966, 1967, 1968, 1972, 1973, and 1975. She has won the doubles nine times.

In 1971 King became the first woman athlete to earn $100,000 in one year. The next year she was the first female named Athlete of the Year by *Sports Illustrated*. King was Associated Press Athlete of the Year in 1967 and 1973.

Lately, Billie Jean King has been devoting more time to her business interests and less to tennis. She remains a major force in the women's sports arena.

Lenglen: "Pavlova of Tennis"

Suzanne Lenglen (1899-1938) is credited with "transforming tennis from a participant into a spectator sport." The French-born star developed her almost unbeatable game by constant practice. As a child she could hit a handerkerchief target placed anywhere on the court.

Lenglen made her Wimbledon debut in 1919, winning the singles championship. From 1919 to 1923 she won all the French titles (singles, mixed doubles, doubles). She repeated the performance in 1925 and 1926 despite frail health — she suffered from asthma and jaundice.

In all, Lenglen was six times a Wimbledon singles winner; six times in doubles and three times in mixed doubles.

Called "The Pavlova of Tennis," Lenglen was a tempermental superstar known to leave a game rather than lose to an opponent. Though Britain's Queen Mary had made a special trip to the 1926 Wimbledon championship to watch her play, Lenglen deliberately arrived half an hour late for her match.

Lenglen retired in 1926, and, after some professional exhibitions, ran a coaching clinic in Paris. In 1974 she was voted the outstanding player in women's tennis history by a panel of tennis writers.

Marble: Refused to Quit

When Alice Marble (1913-   ) was fifteen, her brother brought home a tennis racket for her. He thought tennis was a more suitable sport for a girl than baseball, at which she excelled.

The daughter of a lumberman in Plumas County, California, Marble was so good at baseball that she was allowed to warm up with the San Francisco Seals, a top pro team. But she liked tennis more, and took an evening job at a soda fountain to earn money to buy tennis balls.

In 1931 she won the California Juniors. Two years later, at nineteen, she played against Britain in the Wightman Cup. In 1934, she collapsed and was told she had tuberculosis and that she would never play again. Two years later she was back on the courts; her recovery was speeded by an encouraging letter from actress Carole Lombard.

Marble won the U.S. singles title at Forest Hills in 1936, and again in 1938, 1939, and 1940. She won the women's singles at Wimbledon in 1938, and in 1939, the singles, doubles, and mixed doubles.

In 1939 she was Associated Press Athlete of the Year, and in 1949 became a professional radio sports announcer and supper club singer.

Moody: Little Miss Poker Face

Helen Wills Moody (1905-   ) did not charm the fans, but no one can deny she is probably the best American woman tennis player ever. She began playing tennis when she was thirteen, and was coached by her father. She was called "Little Miss Poker Face" because of her coolness on and off court.

Moody won the Forest Hills singles in 1923 when she was seventeen. Despite a back injury in 1934, she dominated women's international tennis from 1926 to 1938. During that time she won Wimbledon singles eight times, Forest Hills seven times, and the French Championship four times.

Moody was virtually unbeatable. From 1926 to 1932, she did not lose a single set in the United States.

She graduated Phi Beta Kappa from the University of California in 1927. She has published four mystery novels, and written features for United Press and newspapers.

Moody does not believe the women's tennis game has changed dramatically since her days on the circuit. "But," former Little Miss Poker Face adds, "the number of tournaments and the large prize money calls for the players today to be more serious about their game than we often were."

Navratilova: Wanted Freedom

Martina Navratilova (1957-   ) made her first big splash in 1975, when she came from Czechoslovakia to play at Forest Hills and never went home. "I did it to be free," she said. "I couldn't play the tournaments I wanted. Couldn't travel where I wanted."

The first year after Navratilova's defection was difficult. It is possible she will never see her parents again (the whole family plays tennis). But she seems to have stabilized her occasionally erratic game, and has settled into a new Texas home with professional golfer Sandra Haynie.

"My game needs work," Navratilova acknowledges. "I've got all the shots, I just don't use them as well as I should. I'm faster than Chris (Evert) — quicker, stronger, and I reach more shots. I'm just not that good yet."

In a year or two, Navratilova believes, she will be the number one woman tennis player in the world. She ranked number five in 1976, and won $128,535 in prize money. That's not bad for a young woman who considers herself "not that good."

Sutton: Wouldn't Default

In her prime **May Sutton** (1887-   ) was one of the world's best tennis players. She played into her eighties. But she endeared herself to historians forever in 1930 when she was in the final match against Hazel Hotchkiss Wightman at Forest Hills. During play, Sutton fractured her left leg and dislocated her right elbow. She refused to default, preferring a clean defeat, so she borrowed a crutch, put her racquet in her left hand, and completed the match. It was a consummate display of good sportsmanship.

Sutton was born in England and raised in California. At age 17, she made her debut at the U. S. National Championships, winning the women's singles without losing a set. She was the first American to win at Wimbledon (1904).

GOLF

Alcott: Promising Newcomer

Golf's 1975 Rookie of the Year, **Amy Alcott** (1956-   ), claims she got interested in her sport as a child because a golf show followed her Saturday morning cartoons. She found her mother's discarded clubs in the garage, and made herself a course by sinking soup cans into the front lawn of her home.

"I guess I had it tougher than the kids who grew up around country clubs," says Alcott. "But I had something more important. I had desire. I didn't care what people thought when they saw me hitting balls in my yard — that's the way I did it and I'm proud of it."

After winning the U.S. Junior Girls Championship, Alcott turned pro at eighteen. She won her first tournament, Miami's Orange Blossom Classic, one day after turning nineteen; she was the youngest golfer — male or female — to win a pro tournament. She continued her winning ways by placing in every one of her next eighteen tournaments.

In 1976, Alcott finished tenth among woman golfers on the money list with $52,800.

"The hardest thing," she says about adjusting to life on the pro circuit, "was being young and coming onto the tour right out of high school and a very close home environment. I think the thing I miss most is my mother's home-made soup."

Berg: No Bum

"Patty, you bum," golfer **Patty Berg** (1918-   ) used to mutter to herself when she flubbed an important shot. But her stunning career — including a lifetime record of eighty-one tournament victories — proves otherwise.

Minnesota-born Berg is a natural athlete. She was a high school track star, played quarterback on her brother's football team, and was runner-up in the National Girls' Speedskating Championships at age fifteen.

When her father gave her brother a golf club membership, thirteen-year-old Patty protested, "Just because I'm a girl is no reason not to give me one." She got her membership, along with four second-hand clubs, and seemingly came out of nowhere to reach the semi-finals of the Women's Amateur Championships three years later.

By the time she was twenty, Berg had won every major amateur title in the United States. She turned pro in 1940. For many years, Babe Zaharias was Berg's golfing nemesis, often beating her for top honors. Nevertheless, Berg won the Vare Trophy in 1953, 1955, and 1956. She won the U.S. Women's Open in 1946, and was three times the Associated Press Female Athlete of the year. She is the only woman to make a hole-in-one in the Open, and was founder and first president of the LPGA.

Blalock: Troubles Behind Her

Jane Blalock (1945-   ) gave up a teaching career — she graduated with a history and economics degree from Rollins College — because she thought golf might

be more profitable. It was: In 1976, after eight professional seasons, she had won $367,063.

But Blalock ran into some hard times along the way. In 1972, the LPGA accused her of cheating by moving her balls to better positions on the green. She denied the accusation, sued the LPGA, and won $13,000 in damages and $95,000 in legal fees. She was so elated by her vindication that she went out and earned another $10,000 the next day by winning the Karsten-Ping Open in Phoenix.

"It's only a matter of time," says Blalock, "before I end up on top. There's no reason I can't — I'm playing well, I'm happy, my troubles are all behind me now."

In the days when many other woman pros were snubbing Blalock, she renewed her old friendship with tennis great Billie Jean King. Now she hopes to emulate King by becoming a more militant voice for women golfers. "Billie Jean has rammed a lot of shots down the throats of the tennis establishment," says Blalock, "I can swing a wicked driver too, but golfing is a different game. I have to use more finesse."

Carner: Out Of The Slump

Joanne Gunderson Carner (1939-   ), known as "The Great Gundy," is one of the most popular women golfers among fans. She didn't turn pro until she was thirty-one, perhaps because she was doing so well as an amateur, winning every amateur title, including five U.S. Amateur victories.

But two years after turning pro, she entered into a two-year slump. "As an amateur I could hit the ball, but I didn't really know how," she recalled later. "I didn't know how to break down my swing and find out how to hit every shot. And at the same time I was thinking too much. . . . They tack on 'professional' after your name and you're supposed to know something."

She was helped back into the winner's circle by her teacher, golf pro Gardner Dickinson, and Billy Martin, ex-manager of the Texas Rangers baseball team. Martin advised her to save her analyzing of shots until the game was over. She started on the comeback trail with a tournament victory just one month later.

She won her second Women's Open in 1976 — the first was in 1971 — and placed third on the year's list of leading woman money winners.

Vare: Strictly Amateur

Glenna Collett Vare (1903-) has not tired of golf after playing the game for sixty years. She still gets in a few rounds every week.

Vare was an accomplished swimmer and diver by the time she was nine, and drove her first car at ten. Her father, a former champion bicycle racer, introduced her to golf when she was fourteen.

In 1922, Vare had her first successful tournament season. She won her first of six Women's Amateur Championships — a record that may never be broken. She won all but one of the 60 matches she entered in 1924.

Though she can boast a houseful of silver trophies, Vare has won not a penny for her golfing. She never turned professional. Of today's women golfers, she said recently, "There's only one difference now. I'm sitting here with all this silver. And they're chasing a pot of gold."

Mann: Highly Visible

Carol Mann (1941-) is among the most visible golfers on the women's tour. Not that she can help it — Mann stands 6-feet-3. Her achievements on the course (as fourth highest money winner on the tour) and off (as 1976 president of the LPGA) have also won her attention.

Mann started dreaming of a golf career at age eleven. "Theater people close their eyes and see their names in lights," she recalls. "I'd see mine on a locker-room plaque." She turned pro in 1961, won the Women's Open in 1965, and received the Vare Trophy for the best average in the LPGA in 1968. Mann was the first woman golfer to win more than $50,000 in a single year.

Mann's game fell down a bit in 1976 when she headed the LPGA. But, she said, "I decided that the sport was more important than any person." She is an outspoken fighter for bigger golf purses for women because she believes money is what gets recognition.

"Carol's unbelievable," young golfer Cathy Duggan says. "I don't think anyone else on the tour could do so much for the sport, keep her own game sharp, and still have time to care about other people."

Palmer: Not Arnie

"The Palmer in golf is no longer Arnie," declared *Sport* magazine in 1976 of the tenacious **Sandra Palmer** (1941-).

After a volatile, rootless childhood, Palmer settled on golf as her best friend. She took up caddying at thirteen, and saved up her earnings for her first pair of clubs. After a year of teaching high school biology and physical education, she joined the pro tour in 1964. She had four mediocre seasons, but finished among the top ten women money winners in 1968. She has remained on the list ever since. Her best season so far was 1975, when she won the U.S. Women's Open and the Colgate-Dinah Shore Winners Circle championship.

Palmer's slow start on the pro tour has been attributed to her height of 5 feet, 1 inch — a disadvantage in a sport that requires power and leverage. "At her height," explains her coach, "the stroke is flattened out, a tremendous obstacle. To compensate, she's had to develop more coordination and better timing."

Palmer is one of golf's hardest working players. "I don't have a secret," she says of her success. "I just like to work hard."

Rankin: Family Comes First

One of the most consistent golfers on the women's tour is **Judy Rankin** (1945-), the first woman to break the $100,000 annual earnings mark. She has not missed the cut in an LPGA tournament since 1965.

Rankin began playing golf at age six, scoring an unspectacular 84 for nine holes of play. Her game had improved considerably by the time she won the national Peewee title two years later.

Rankin joined the pro tour when she was seventeen, becoming one of the youngest women ever to do so. In 1976, she passed the $100,000 mark with a vengance, winning $150,734. She took over from Carol Mann as president of the LPGA that year.

Rankin's husband, Yippy, and her son, Tuey, travel with her on the golf circuit. "I'm nervous as hell no matter how Judy plays," says her husband. "If she's los-

"When I can get that super shot," says Judy Rankin, "It's indescribable."

ered won the English Ladies Championship in 1920. She held onto that title for five years straight. She came out of her first retirement to defeat American champion Glenna Collett Vare in the 1929 Women's British Amateur, a match still considered one of the greatest in women's golf history.

Wethered again came out of retirement in 1935 to tour the United States, golfing with such notables as Jones, Gene Sarazen, and Babe Zaharias. She defeated Zaharias in two outings.

Wethered, now Lady Heathcote-Amory, finds golf has changed a bit since her days of stardom. Not the least of the changes is in the players' style of dress. "We had to wear long skirts, and they were rather a nuisance," she recalls. "You took care they were not wider than they needed to be or they would swirl in the wind. And we didn't want them narrower than necessary because they would be constricting."

Whitworth: Top Money Winner
For **Kathy Whitworth** (1939-   ), perseverance paid off. She turned pro at nine-

ing, I'll try to help turn things around — I'll walk faster to slower, stop chewing gum, anything."

Marriage and motherhood improved her golf game, says Rankin, who admits to occasionally wanting to drop off the tour to keep house full time. "Despite all the success I've had on the tour," she once remarked, "if you were to ask what's most important in my life, I'd have to rank golf well behind my other careers as mother and wife."

Wethered: The Greatest Ever?
According to the knowledgable *Encyclopedia of Golf.* **Joyce Wethered** (1901-   ) is "the supreme woman golfer of her age, perhaps of all time." Golfing great Bobby Jones, after playing a match with Wethered, called her the best golfer, male or female, he had ever seen. Yet, her career lasted only nine years. "I wanted to do other things, and golf takes so much of your time," she explained.

A nineteen-year-old unknown, Weth-

As president of the LPGA, Kathy Whitworth fought for major prize money for women golfers.

teen, only three years after taking up golf. But she hated the pro tour, and dropped out to improve her game and lose weight. (She then tipped the scales at 225 pounds.)

Whitworth rejoined the tour in 1959, but was again on the brink of giving up after winning no money in three months of play. Another three months passed before she came into her first tournament money — $33.

By 1961, however, Whitworth was paying her own way on the circuit. She first captured the leading money winner title in 1965; she has relinquished the honor only four times since.

Whitworth has won more money than any other female pro golfer — $636,818 as of January 1977. She has also helped fatten the pocketbooks of her colleagues through her activities as LPGA president. She worked with its director, Bud Erickson, to improve the status of the tour. Thanks largely to her efforts, the minimum purse for an LPGA tournament was set at $40,000 in 1975.

Whitworth still has one more goal to achieve; she has yet to win the U.S. Women's Open.

Wright: Champ In Sneakers

Mickey Wright (1935-   ) is golf's little old lady in tennis shoes. Because of a painful disorder of her left foot, Wright has long worn tennis shoes — rather than the spiked shoes worn by most golfers — both on and off the course. Her unconventional footwear only troubles her, Wright claims, when she tries a long shot from a fairway sand trap.

Wright played her first round of golf at age eleven, scoring 145 for eighteen holes of play. She brought her score down to 100 at twelve, and to 80 one year later.

In 1956, Wright turned pro. It took her only two years to win her first of four U.S. Women's Opens. She is also a four-time winner of the LPGA crown. No other woman has won both tournaments in one year, but Wright has done so twice. In all, Wright has won 82 tournaments, more than any other player.

Wright left the pro circuit in 1965 to finish her education. Though she still plays in an occasional tournament, she spends most of her time "prudently" playing the stock market. "The market is so scary these days," she warns, "that you shouldn't think of doing a thing without spending three or four hours a day studying it."

Zaharias: Loved Golf Best

Sportswriter Grantland Rice once said that **Mildred 'Babe' Didrikson Zaharias** (1914-1956) was "without any question the athletic phenomenon of all time, man or woman." She was a superstar in a fistful of sports, and is listed here because she loved golf the most.

Zaharias was called "Wonder Girl" and a physical freak. The press called her "back-alley tough and barroom crude," and a "one-woman team." She deserved every adjective.

Zaharias grew up in Beaumont, Texas, the sixth of seven children. She was constantly working out in the gymnasium set up by her father in the backyard. Zaharias used the two-foot wide hedge in the front yard as a hurdle, developing the bent left leg style that distinguished her later hurdling.

Her family was musical, and at age seven Babe was a featured harmonica soloist on a Texas radio station. She was also a tapdancer. Zaharias was first-rate at everything she did, and had a burning ambition. Before a contest she would stroll up to her opponent and drawl, "Ah'm gonna lick yuh tomorrah."

In 1930, while she was playing forward in a basketball game she was spotted by M. J. McCombs, head of the Women's Athletic Program of the Employers Casualty Company in Dallas. She was hired to do office work, but she played on the company's nationally famous basketball team. During the two years she played on the team, she also established track and field records and won medals for swimming and figure skating. By the time she reached the 1932 Olympics she was called the greatest woman athlete in the world. That year she won gold medals in the javelin, the 80-meter hurdles, and the high-jump. She tore a tendon on her first javelin throw, but still set a world record and won the gold medal in the event. She was nineteen. Her amateur status was suspended by the Amateur Athletic Union (AAU) in December 1932 because she had endorsed an automobile. During the 1930s she toured as a professional golfer. In 1944, she regained her amateur status, at least with the U.S. Golfing Association (she never regained her AAU amateur standing). That year she won the Western Women's Open, the Texas Open, the Broadmoor Invitational, and was voted the Associated Press Female Athlete of the Year.

Zaharias won the USA National Women's Championship in 1946 by the biggest margin ever. In 1947, she won seventeen straight golf titles, including the British Women's Amateur (the first win for an American woman).

She went professional again in 1948 and, with Patty Berg, founded the Women's Pro Golf Association (WPGA). She dominated the professional tour circuit until 1951. In 1950 she was voted Outstanding Female Athlete of the Half Century by an Associated Press poll.

Zaharias learned she had cancer in 1953. Despite surgery and an apparent recovery — she won the U.S. Women's Open in 1954 — she died from the disease in 1956.

GYMNASTICS

Caslavska: Czech Symbol

When **Vera Caslavska** (1942-   ) won four gold medals and two silvers for her native Czechoslovakia in the 1968 Mexico Olympics, she became a symbol of the Prague Spring — Czechoslovakia's movement toward democratization under Alexander Dubcek.

After the Soviet invasion of Czechoslovakia in August 1968, she had been forced to go into hiding and had not been able to train. She had kept fit by lugging sacks of coal. Nevertheless, in October, she entered all six gymnastic events and brought in a medal in each one. She was the first to win four golds — for combined, parallel bars, horse vault, and floor exercises — in the summer Olympics. She presented her medals to the four leaders of the 1968 reform movement, including Alexander Dubcek.

Four years previously, at the Tokyo Olympics, Caslavska had won three gold medals in gymnastics.

For profile on Romania's 1976 Olympic gymnastic sensation, **Nadia Comaneci,** see "Girls."

Kim: Also Perfect

Occasionally forgotten in the clamor over Comaneci was the other new gymnastics star to emerge from the 1976 Montreal Olympics, the Soviet Union's **Nelli Kim** (1957-   ).

Kim, whose half-Korean father works as a roofing factory engineer, comes from the town of Chemkent, near Leningrad. She studied gymnastics at a special sports school from age nine. She claims that she practices her sport only one and one-half hours a day, considerably less than her teammates; she prefers to spend time at home with her family, sleeping late, and listening to Stevie Wonder records.

At the Montreal games, Kim won three individual medals (two golds and one silver), and earned perfect scores in the vault and floor exercises.

Kim seemed to lose interest in gymnastics after a 1976-77 tour of the United States with her Soviet teammates. She announced she would transfer from the Institute of Physical Culture, where she had been studying, to the Institute of Foreign Languages. Kim is reportedly engaged to a wrestler from her hometown.

Korbut: Everyone's Sweetheart

In 1972, 88-pound, 4-feet-10 **Olga Korbut** (1955-   ) stunned 800 million television viewers around the world with her breathtaking gymnastics performance. At the Munich Olympics, Korbut won one team gold, two individual golds, and an individual silver medal.

Korbut, who began gymnastics training at age nine, was the first to perform a "flik-flak," a half-back somersault from the top bar to the bottom bar of the uneven parrallels. But more amazing than her gymnastic feats was the rapport she established with her audiences. "Maybe they love me because they know I love them very much," she commented.

Between Olympics, Korbut made three gymnastics tours of the United States with her teammates. In the 1976 Montreal Olympics, she was upstaged by Comaneci and by her countrywomen, Kim and Ludmilla Tourischeva. Still, she won a team gold and an individual silver on the balance beam.

Inspired by Olga Korbut, U.S. woman gymnasts increased from 15,000 in '72 to 50,000 in '74.

Korbut made her final, sold-out tour of the United States with her team at the end of 1976, before retiring from competition. She has tentative plans to become a gymnastics coach, and has spoken vaguely of marrying. She bought a ready-made wedding gown on her last United States visit.

Latynina: Most Medals

Russian gymnast **Larisa Latynina** (1935-   ) has won more Olympic medals than any other competitor, male or female. At her first Olympics in 1956, she won a record four gold medals, along with a silver and a bronze. She won twelve more medals in the next two Olympics, the final six at the advanced age (for a gymnast) of twenty-nine. Her best event was floor exercise, in which she won three consecutive golds.

Latynina now coaches gymnastics in the USSR.

Rigby: Nimble As Peter Pan

American gymnast **Cathy Rigby** (1952-   ) weighed less than four pounds at her premature birth. She was frail for the first five years of her life, but grew stronger with the help and support of her crippled mother, a polio victim.

She progressed from doing her first trampoline back flips at age eight to entering her first Olympics at age fifteen. She won a silver medal in the 1970 World Championships, and a bronze in the 1971 World Games. At the 1972 Munich Olympics, Rigby placed tenth overall in the gymnastics competition.

After Munich, Rigby turned professional and toured the United States and Europe in a production of *Peter Pan,* playing the lead. She assisted with television commentary during the 1976 Montreal Games.

Tourischeva: "Goes For Perfection"

Despite Korbut's charisma and Comaneci's precocious virtuosity, the top female gymnast of the seventies is the

USSR's **Ludmilla Tourischeva** (1952-). An intense, disciplined performer, Tourischeva has been World champion four times: 1970, 1972, 1974, and 1976. She won two gold medals at the Munich Olympics in 1972.

After a serious back injury in 1974, Tourischeva recovered in time to win all five individual and all-around golds at the first World Cup championship. Though she came in third overall to Comaneci and Kim in Montreal, she took home silvers in the floor exercises and the vault.

During her competitive career that ended in 1976, Tourischeva bested Korbut in all but two competitions. "Olga tries for spectacular things," said one United States fan. "But Ludmilla goes for perfection."

TRACK AND FIELD

Blankers-Koen: "Flying Housewife"

Holland's **Fanny Blankers-Koen** (1918-) not only ran faster and jumped higher than any other woman in the world; according to her husband-coach, she also managed to "cook, clean, sew, knit, and take care of two children."

The couple met shortly before the 1936 Olympics, where she turned in an unspectacular performance. "The first thing I noticed about Fanny," her husband recalled, "was her long legs. That's the most important thing for an athlete — to have long legs and the will to do something."

But her future in competitive sports seemed doomed by World War II, which forced the cancellation of the 1940 and

Cathy Rigby posed atop the ticking crocodile while performing in *Peter Pan*.

1944 Olympics. Many assumed the 30-year-old Blankers-Koen was over the hill by the time of the 1948 London games. "One newspaperman wrote that I was too old to run — that I should stay at home and take care of my children," Blankers-Koen remembered. "When I got to London I pointed my finger at him and I said, 'I'll show you.'"

She did. Blankers-Koen became the first woman to win four golds in a single Olympics. She won the 100- and 200-meter dashes, set a world record in the 80-meter hurdles, and brought her team to victory in the 400-meter relay. Had she not been limited to entering three individual events, Blankers-Koen might also have won medals in the long jump and high jump. She held world records in both events at the time of the 1948 Olympics.

Cheng: Ran For Joy

"I run for joy," said **Chi Cheng** (1944-   ), who once broke five female world records in sprints and hurdles within a six-month period.

A painful thigh injury took the joy out of running for record breaker Chi Cheng.

The Taiwanese athlete began running competitively in high school. Cheng participated in the 1960 Rome Olympics, where her abilities brought her to the attention of Vincent Reel, who became her track coach and, later, her husband. Reel brought Cheng to the United States to train for the 1964 games. Cheng learned English quickly, and graduated from California Polytechnic University with straight A's.

She again represented Taiwan in the 1964 and 1968 Olympics, winning a bronze in the hurdles in 1968. Cheng's greatest year was 1970, when she won all 63 races she entered and broke or tied world records in the 100-yard and 100-meter sprints, the 200 meters, 222-yards and the 100-meter hurdles. The Associated Press named her 1970's Female Athlete of the Year.

But Cheng was increasingly plagued by an old thigh injury. Drugs, cortisone, and acupuncture failed to bring her relief. After surgery in 1972 and 1973 to remove the stiffened muscle, Cheng hung up her track shoes for good.

Hanson: Marathon Woman

Marathon record holder **Jackie Hanson** (1948-   ) is no superwoman in the Babe Zaharias mold. Hanson first took up running in high school to get out of other sports; she claims she still cannot do more than four push-ups.

She was a so-so middle-distance runner in 1972, when she attended her first marathon to provide moral support for a competing friend. Hanson was inspired to begin long-distance running herself, though she had never gone the full marathon distance before entering the Culver City, California, Marathon in 1973. Ignoring aches and blisters, Hanson won the race.

She has since won five more marathons, and set the women's world record for the marathon of 2 hours, 38 minutes, 19 seconds. She keeps in shape by running 90 to 100 miles a week. "I'm not saying marathons don't hurt," she admits, "they just hurt in a good way."

Frederick: "The Best"

According to decathlon champion Bruce Jenner, "the best female athlete in the world" is not Chris Evert, Nadia Comaneci, or another equally well-known sportswoman. Instead, it is pentathlete **Jane Frederick** (1952-   ).

Frederick, a *summa cum laude* graduate of the University of Colorado, and a UCLA graduate student, began long jumping in her native California when she was eleven. In March 1977, she won the AAU pentathlon championship in a tri-country meet (United States, USSR, Canada) despite an injury. She had gashed her ankle during the high jump and required eight stitches. (The women's pentathlon includes the 100-meter hurdles, the shot put, the high jump, the long jump, and the 200-meter dash.)

Frederick believes her academic activities — she has a 3.5 average and speaks five languages — have helped her on the athletic field. "They have taught me to be disciplined, to problem-solve and to be patient," she declares. "The body and mind actually are a lot alike — the more you condition them, the better they respond."

Lutz: Top Miler

Francie Larrieu Lutz (1952-   ), the sixth of nine children, began running at age thirteen in California. She was inspired to take up running when she saw an invitation to join the Junior Olympics on a box of Wheaties.

Married to fellow runner, Mark Lutz, she has been the best woman miler in the United States since 1969. Though she didn't make the finals in the 1976 Olympics, she began the 1977 track season with victories in both the one-mile and two-mile races at the AAU Indoor Nationals. A week later she repeated her triumphs in the U.S.-USSR-Canada track and field meet in Toronto.

Lutz — an attractive 5-feet-4, 105 pounds — was once asked by a track official to prove she was a woman. "What's the matter," she asked him with righteous indignation, "are you blind?"

McMillan: A Prediction Came True

When **Kathy McMillan** (1958-   ) was fourteen, her track coach predicted she would make the Olympic team one day — "if you work out winter and summer."

"He could have been kidding, but I believed him," the long jumper recalls. "I

didn't even know what the record was or how far I could eventually go."

McMillan worked as her coach advised, and added one to two feet to her jumps each year. By 1976, she well knew the U.S. women's long jump record — twenty-two feet, three inches — because she set it at the AAU national outdoor championships. McMillan went on to gain a spot on the U.S. Olympic team, and won a silver medal at Montreal for a jump just inches short of that of the first place finisher. The recent high school graduate was the first American to win a track and field medal at the 1976 games.

Rosenbaum: Wheelchair Superstar

Rarely does one athlete excel in such diverse events as shot put, table tennis, and "slalom." But **Ruth Broemmer Rosenbaum** (1945-   ) has won international medals for all three events and more without leaving her wheelchair.

Paralyzed by polio when she was six months old, Rosenbaum began serious wheelchair athletics in 1972. "At first, I didn't even know how to hold the shot," she admits. "There is a tremendous feeling of learning how to do things."

Rosenbaum won a gold medal in the slalom and two bronzes in the javelin and discus at the 1972 Para Olympics. (The slalom requires competitors to maneuver their wheelchairs through an obstacle course fraught with ramps, curves, and turns.) At the 1974 international games, Rosenbaum won four gold medals for slalom, shot put, discus, and javelin.

A computer programmer by profession, she is married to Richard Rosenbaum, a former swimming champion in wheelchair competition.

Rudolph: Black Gazelle

Wilma Rudolph (1940-   ) could not walk until she was eight years old. Nevertheless, in 1960 she became the only American woman to win three Olympic gold medals in track and field.

Rudolph grew up in Tennessee, the seventeenth of nineteen children of a porter and a domestic. She caught double pneumonia and scarlet fever when she was four, and one leg was crippled. But by high school, Rudolph was making up for lost time. She averaged thirty points a game for the girls basketball team, earning the

After the Rome Olympics, a fan stole Wilma Rudolph's shoes right off her feet.

nickname "Skeeter" because she "buzzed around the court like a mosquito." A basketball tournament brought Rudolph to the attention of Tennessee State University track coach Ed Temple, and she began to train as a sprinter. She made the 1956 Olympic team at sixteen, and earned a bronze in the 400-meter relay.

Rudolph stole the show at the 1960 Rome Olympics, winning golds in the 100- and 200-meter dashes and the 400-meter relay. "Running for gold medal glory," reported *Time*, "Miss Rudolph regularly got away to good starts . . . then smoothly shifted gears to a flowing stride that made the rest of the pack seem to be churning on a treadmill." Italians called her "La

Gazelle Nera" (the black gazelle), while the French dubbed her "La Chattanooga Choo Choo."

Tyus: Proud of Her Muscles

"I never ran just to win," says sprinter **Wyoma Tyus** (1945-   ). "I started running because I liked it. First around the house and then around the block and pretty soon in school."

At thirteen, Tyus came under the tutelage of Tennessee State's Ed Temple, and trained with Wilma Rudolph, five years her senior. Tyus made the 1964 Olympic team, and won a gold for the 100-meter dash and a silver for the 400-meter relay. Four years later, she became the first sprinter, male or female, to win gold medals for the 100-meter dash in two consecutive Olympics. She set a world record for women of 11.0 seconds in that event, and won another gold in the 400-meter relay.

Tyus believes it is finally becoming acceptable for women to participate in sports — even in the eyes of her mother and aunts who used to warn that running would make her unattractive. "I think they're starting to understand that it's okay for a woman to have muscles in her legs from running — that a man will still want her," says Tyus.

Walsh: Durable Athlete

"I don't think I ever walked," said **Stella Walsh** (1911-   ) of her childhood. She ran, instead.

Born Stanislawa Walasiewicz in Poland, she came to America at the age of ten months. Walsh broke her first world record at Madison Square Garden in 1930 by running the 50-yard dash in 6.1 seconds. Because of dual nationality, she represented Poland in the 1932 Olympics and won the 100-meter dash with a world record time of 11.9 seconds.

Walsh was a bitter rival of Babe Zaharias, and usually beat her in the long jump. Though not as versatile as Zaharias, Walsh was more durable.

The Polish-American athlete won the first of her forty U.S. titles when she was nineteen, and the last when she was thirty-seven. She was still competing in the taxing pentathlon at age forty-two.

White: Track's Grand Old Lady

"I have been the grand old lady of track for 20 years," **Willye White** (1940-   )

said after her fifth Olympics. The *New York Times* concurred: "Women's track and field began with Willye B. White."

White grew up on a Mississippi Delta plantation and picked cotton at the age of eight for $2.50 a day. She played on the high school varisity basketball team when she was in fifth grade. At sixteen, she ran track for Tennessee State University.

She held the world's record in the 60-yard dash and the long jump. She entered her first Olympic competition in 1956. She won a silver for the long jump in the 1956 Olympics and another silver medal in the 400-meter relay in the 1964 games.

White worked as a health administrator in Chicago, was named to the President's Commission on Olympic Sports in 1976, and was elected to the Black Hall of Fame.

SWIMMING

Babashoff: Olympic Medalist
Shirley Babashoff (1957-   ) has fulfilled her father's dreams. Her father always wanted his children to swim in the Olympics, something he could not afford to do when he was young. Shirley's parents went without furniture to pay for her training, and drove eighty miles round-trip to take her for coaching.

Babashoff began entering races when she was nine. At fifteen, she competed at the Munich Olympics and won two silver medals in the freestyle and a gold in the 400-meter relay.

To prepare for the 1976 games, Babashoff swam sixteen miles a day and lived on a diet of vegetables, salads and protein. Despite all her hours in the pool, she maintained a B average at California's Golden West College and was elected homecoming queen. She swam with the men's team at Golden West.

At Montreal, Babashoff shared a gold medal for the U.S. victory in the 400-meter freestyle relay. She came in second to her long-time rival, East German Kornelia Ender, in the 200-, 400-, and 800-meter freestyle.

Babashoff plans to become a marine biologist.

Chadwick: "Winners Never Quit"
"Winners Never Quit; Quitters Never Win" was the first thing **Florence Chadwick** (1918-   ) pasted in her scrapbook. Chadwick never lost sight of that motto, as she withstood cold, cramps, and close-by sharks to become one of history's greatest endurance swimmers.

In 1950, Chadwick made her first swim of the English Channel, becoming the thirteenth woman to do so. She broke Gertrude Ederle's existing record for women with a time of 13 hours, 20 minutes. "I feel fine, I am quite prepared to swim back," she announced upon emerging from the water.

She made the return trip one year later; she was the first woman to swim the Channel from England to France, against both wind and tide. But perhaps her greatest year was 1953, when she swam four channels — the English Channel, the Strait of Gibraltar, the Bosphorus, and the Dardanelles — in five weeks. She set speed records on each swim.

"I'm still swimming, but in the sea of finance," stock-broker Chadwick declared recently. She is also busy training young endurance swimmers to break her old records.

Coleman: Courageous Diver
One of diving's most courageous early stars was **Georgia Coleman** (1912-1940), Olympic springboard champion in 1932. She won the U.S. outdoor springboard and platform titles from 1929 to 1931. From 1929 to 1932 she was indoor 10-foot springboard champion, and 3-foot springboard champion in 1931.

Coleman contracted polio in 1937, but learned to swim again. She died of pneumonia in 1940.

Ederle: "America's Best Gal"
Gertrude "Trudy" Ederle (1906-   ), the first woman to swim the English Channel, was a genuine heroine whom President Calvin Cooldige called "America's best gal."

She was born in New York City, the daughter of a German-American butcher. Between 1921 and 1925 she held 29 different amateur national and world records for short distance swimming. In 1922, she broke seven world records in a single afternoon in a meet at Brighton Beach, New York.

Ederle competed in the 1924 Olympics

"Trudy" Ederle was greased to ward off the cold before swimming the English Channel in 1926.

and won three medals, including a gold for the 400-meter freestyle relay.

In 1925, at nineteen, she made her first attempt at the English Channel, but she became seasick and had to quit. Her second attempt, on August 6, 1926, succeeded, although a storm forced her to swim 35 miles for the 21-mile distance. Her time of 14 hours, 13 minutes, was more than two hours better than the existing men's record. When she returned to New York she was greeted with a ticker tape parade.

Ederle toured for two years in vaudeville as a swimmer, earning $2,000 a week. But because of the pressure, she had a nervous breakdown. Her hearing, which had weakened during the Channel swims, deteriorated into deafness. In 1933 she fell down a flight of stairs and spent the next four and a half years in a cast. Told she would never walk again, she refused to believe it. Six years and much hard work later, she was not only walking but swam in Billy Rose's Aquacade at the World's Fair.

In later years Ederle became a swimming instructor to deaf children.

Ender: History's Fastest Swimmer

Kornelia Ender (1958-   ), the fastest woman swimmer in history, is the product of the controversial East German push to produce the world's finest swimmers. The training allegedly includes injections of steroids and sex hormones to build up back and arm muscles.

Ender showed her promise when she was enrolled at the age of six in a special sports school. At fourteen, she won three silver medals at the 1972 Munich Olympics. Four years later, Ender won four Olympic gold medals — in the 100- and 200-meter freestyle, 100-meter butterfly, and medley relay — and a silver in the freestyle relay. She won two of her medals within twenty-five minutes of one another.

One of the most touching moments of the 1976 games occured when Ender was reunited with her grandmother, Rosalie Lehmann of Salina, Kansas. They had last seen each other when Ender was five months old, shortly before her grandmother defected to the West.

Ender has since retired from swimming to pursue a career as a pediatrician.

Fraser: "Granny" At Twenty-Seven

Australian **Dawn Fraser** (1937-   ) was called "Granny" by her teammates when, at the age of 27, she won her final Olympic gold medal. Her achievement was all the more spectacular because she had just recovered from an automobile accident in which her mother was killed.

Fraser was the fastest woman swimmer in the world between 1956 and 1964. She won the gold medal in the 100-meter freestyle in the 1956, 1960, and 1964 Olympics. She broke world records in that event twenty-seven times.

"She boldly and gaily dominates a sport that commonly verges on asceticism," *Sports Illustrated* once said of her. Fraser was apparently too bold and gay for the Amateur Swimming Union of Australia, which suspended her in 1965 for her antics at the 1964 Olympics. She had taken part in the opening parade despite orders not to (so that she could preserve her energy), had refused to wear the regulation swimsuit, and had swum the moat around the Imperial Palace to steal the Japanese flag as a souvenir. Fraser has retired from competitive swimming, and is now a wife and mother.

King: Diving Olympian

"I wasn't the one the boys asked to dance," recalls Olympic champion diver **Maxine "Micki" King** (1943-   ) of her childhood. "It was always, 'Let's go out and play catch.'" She was star goalie on the varsity water polo team of her alma mata, the University of Michigan. She was also three times the women's collegiate diving champion.

King entered the U.S. Air Force after graduation, and was allowed to continue training. Though she was expected to win a gold medal at the 1968 Olympics, she hit the board and broke her arm on the final dive. But she came back four years later to win the springboard diving gold medal at the Munich Olympics.

King then accepted an assignment as diving coach at the Air Force Academy at Colorado Springs. She was the first woman ever to coach an all-male college

Micki King, who took up diving for the fun of it at 10, in champion form at the '72 Olympics

team. "I've grown up in a man's world," she commented after taking the job. "I'm very comfortable with men. I can talk men talk."

Besides, commented one of her students, "It's really nice having a woman coach fix the cramp in your leg." King left the Academy to become director of women's intercollegiate sports at UCLA.

McCormick: Daredevil Diver

Pat McCormick (1930-   ) endured a lot of pain to become one of the world's great divers: a cracked spine, ribs, fingers, and jaw, as well as a cut and bruised body. The tough and determined Californian performed 100 dives daily, six days a week, for many years.

At the 1952 Olympic Games in Helsinki, McCormick won gold medals in both the highboard and springboard women's diving events. She repeated the feat in 1956, though she had been unable to train half the year while she was pregnant with her first child.

McCormick is one of four women to win the Sullivan Award (1956) for amateur athletics. In 1965 she became the first woman named to the International Swimming Hall of Fame in Fort Lauderdale, Florida.

Meyer: Narrowed The Gap

That women are narrowing the gap with men in athletic achievement was aptly illustrated by swimmer **Debbie Meyer** (1952-   ) at the 1968 Mexico City Olympics. Meyer beat the legendary Johnny Weissmuller's 400-meter freestyle record by thirty-three seconds, despite a twisted ankle, stomach ailment, and the high altitude of the site.

Meyer, a victim of chronic asthma, began swimming when she was eight. Four years later, her family moved to California, where she came under the tutalege of the hard-driving Sherm Chavoor. "I remember the first time I came out to practice and Sherm said, 'All right, do twenty laps to warm up,'" Meyer recalled. "I couldn't even do four."

But by the time she was fourteen, Meyer had set a world record, the first of fifteen. At the 1968 Olympics, she won three individual gold medals in the 200-, 400-, and 800-meter freestyle, breaking an Olympic record in each event. "The first time I was on the victory stand," said Meyer, "I kept thinking, 'Gee, I wish I was back in my room with my sunflower seeds, washing them down with warm ginger ale and talking with my roomie about boys."

Meyer resigned from swimming at twenty, just before the 1972 Olympics. "I didn't have a lot of friends," she once reminisced, "because a lot of the kids were sort of in awe of me."

SKIING

Fraser: First U.S. Medalist

The United States' first Olympic medals for skiing were won in 1948 by a skier many observers thought past her prime, thirty-one-year-old **Gretchen Fraser** (1917-   ).

Fraser, whose Norwegian mother was an enthusiastic skier, began skiing at age sixteen at her parents' ski resort in Mount Rainier, Washington. She married Don Fraser, a member of the 1936 Olympic ski team, and both qualified for the 1940 Olympics. But the games were cancelled because of the outbreak of World War II. During the war, Fraser taught skiing, swimming, and riding to amputees in Army hospitals.

Although an underdog because of her comparatively advanced years, Fraser qualified for the 1948 games. She won a silver medal in the combined Alpine — a downhill racing and slalom event since discontinued. In so doing, she gave the United States its first medal ever in skiing. She then won a gold in the special slalom.

In 1952, Fraser managed the women's ski team at the Oslo Olympics.

Kinmont: A Real Champ

Jill Kinmont (1937-   ) seemed to have everything going for her in 1955. The eighteen-year-old seemed certain of making the 1956 Olympic ski team and was being courted by fellow racer Bud Werner. Then a fall during the 1956 Snow Cup Race in Alta, Utah, left her paralyzed from below the shoulders down. She has limited use of her arms.

But that was not the end of Kinmont's troubles. Dick "Mad Dog" Buek, a friend who had reawakened her desire to live,

Gretchen Fraser won the U.S.'s first silver medal in skiing. Then she won its first gold.

was killed in a plane crash. Another crash took the life of Werner, with whom she had begun to renew her ties.

Kinmont did not admit defeat. Through rehabilitation therapy, she learned to paint and write. She earned an education degree at UCLA and became a teacher of remedial reading. She spends her summers in California's Sierra Nevadas teaching Indian children.

With profits from a 1975 film based on her life, *The Other Side of the Mountain*, she helped endow a "Jill Kinmont Indian Education Fund."

Lawrence: "Not Just Winning"

Andrea Mead Lawrence (1933-   ) did

not give off the aura of a fierce competitor. She was relaxed on the slope and off, and indulged in an occasional cigarette or glass of beer. "When I was racing," she later recalled, "people were always asking me the "how did I's", the "why did I's", and the "what for's" of competition, and I would spend hours and hours trying to explain that it was the involvement in skiing that gave me pleasure — not just winning."

Nonetheless, Lawrence was, at fifteen, the youngest member of the 1948 U.S. Olympic ski team. In the 1952 Oslo Winter Olympics, she won gold medals in the slalom and giant slalom. In the latter event, she fell on her first run but picked herself up and continued at a breakneck speed.

In 1956, six weeks after the birth of her third child, Lawrence competed in her final Olympics.

Mittermaier: Lucky At Last
"I'm very, very lucky," West German skier **Rosi Mittermaier** (1950-   ) contends. "I could have been killed several times in my life and here I am."

Other people wouldn't call it luck. Mittermaier barely survived birth, and nearly suffocated soon afterward when a goat climbed into her baby carriage and sat on top of her. A 1975 collision with a slalom pole almost blinded her, and she had just

Rosi Mittermaier was hoisted on the shoulders of teammates after winning the 1976 World Cup.

recoverd when she broke her arm in another slope accident.

A change in Mittermaier's fortunes was overdue by the time of the 1976 Innsbruck Winter Olympics. She won gold medals in the downhill and slalom, and came within twelve-hundredths of a second of winning a third gold in the giant slalom.

After adding a World Cup to her crown, Mittermaier left competitive skiing for such pursuits as writing her autobiography, recording a folk song album, and making a fortune from endorsing ski products.

Proell: Loves Speed
Five-time World Cup champion **Annemarie Proell** (1953-   ) loves speed, both down a ski slope and around an auto speedway. Proell's father whittled her first pair of skis; the family was too poor to buy them.

A self-taught skier, Proell won her first World Cup in 1970-71. She was disappointed at her second place finishes in slalom and downhill at the 1972 Sapporo Olympics. She affixed a plaque reading "Never Forget Sapporo" to the dashboard of the souped-up car that she was fond of driving at daredevil speeds along the mountain roads of her native Austria. Proell gave up fast driving after her marriage to soccer player Herbert Moser.

Proell retired in 1975, but emerged in 1977 to compete again for the World Cup. She lost to compatriot Lise-Marie Morerod.

SKATING

Albright: Skater Turned M.D.
"People tend to box little girls in," believes former champion skater **Tenley Albright** (1935-   ). "They teach them to sit properly and stand quietly and not attract attention. Sports is one place where girls can be free and enjoy the exhilaration of movement."

Albright acquired that freedom at age nine when she received her first pair of ice skates. She won her first title, the Eastern United States Junior Ladies championship, shortly after recovering from a mild case of polio which felled her when she was eleven. "Did you ever notice how many athletes my age once had polio?"

she asks. "I think it's because being paralyzed makes you aware of your muscles and you never want to let them go unused again."

She became the first American woman to win the figure skating World Championship in 1953. At the 1956 Winter Olympics, she became the first American woman to win a gold medal for figure skating.

Albright retired from competitive figure skating to become a surgeon. She still manages to skate at least three times a week.

Fleming: Ballerina On Ice

Peggy Fleming (1948-   ) owes her success on ice both to her own conscientiously developed talents and to the unselfish devotion of her family. Recognizing his daughter's potential, Albert Fleming moved his brood to Colorado Springs, where Peggy trained with resident pro Carlo Fassi. The elder Fleming worked overtime as a pressman to finance his daughter's training, while Mrs. Fleming helped cut costs by sewing all Peggy's costumes.

In 1964 Peggy Fleming became the youngest figure skater ever to win the national championship. Two years later, she became World Champion. But her victory was marred when she learned a few hours later that her father had died of a heart attack.

Fleming captured the gold medal at the 1968 Winter Olympics at Grenoble. "Peggy has no weaknesses," commented Gabriele Seyfert, a fellow competitor. "Peggy lands softly and everything she does is connected. It's pure ballerina."

Afterward, Fleming turned pro and performed with ice shows and on television until 1976.

Hamill: Eleven Years of Work

Dorothy Hamill (1956-   ) had just received her first pair of ice skates when she saw other children doing something on a frozen pond she couldn't do: skating backward.

Then eight, she begged her parents for lessons. By the age of twelve, she was engaged in a daily practice regimen that began at 5 a.m. Hooked on skating, she dropped out of high school at fourteen and

Dorothy Hamill trained for the Olympics six days a week. On the seventh she studied ballet.

was privately tutored so she could devote more time to the rink.

Eventually Hamill moved to Denver, Colorado, where she was trained by Carlo Fassi, Peggy Flemming's former coach. Hamill trained seven hours a day, six days a week, eleven months a year, at an annual cost of $20,000 to her father.

When she won the gold medal at the 1976 Winter Olympics at Innsbruck, it was the culmination of eleven years of dedication.

From Innsbruck Hamill went on to Sweden to win the World Championship. In April 1976, she turned professional and began a two-year contract with the Ice Capades.

Heiss: Kept Her Promise

Carol Heiss (1940-   ) put on her first pair of skates at the age of four. The daughter of a struggling baker, Heiss grew up in Ozone Park, New York, and was taken regularly by her mother to the Brooklyn Ice Palace.

Heiss made her first appearance in an amateur ice show when she was six. To help finance her training, her mother worked as a free-lance fabric designer.

At ten, Heiss won the mid-Atlantic and junior national titles. In 1956 she became world champion, the youngest up to that time.

Heiss' mother died of cancer shortly thereafter, and she took charge of the care of her younger brother and sister. She had promised her mother that she would not turn professional until she had won an Olympic gold medal. She kept her promise. In 1960 she won the gold at the Winter Olympics in Squaw Valley.

Henie: Artist on Skates

"Ours is not simply a sport, but also an art." So said **Sonja Henie** (1914-1969), who brought figure skating to the art it is today, and whose accomplishments in the sport have never been surpassed.

Born in Oslo, Norway, she began ice skating (and studying ballet) at six. She was Oslo Women's Champion at nine, Norwegian Champion from 1924 to 1929, and European Champion from 1929 to 1936. She was World Champion from 1927 to 1936. Henie won the gold medal at three consecutive Olympics — 1928, 1932, and 1936.

Following the 1936 Olympics, she became a professional skater. She starred in the Hollywood Ice Review, the first of the ice carnivals. She made ten movies and, at the peak of her career, ranked with Clark Gable and Shirley Temple in box office appeal. Her first movie, *One in a Million,* reportedly grossed $25 million.

Sonja Henie's lifetime earnings are put at $37.5 million. All of her awards, 257 medals, cups, and bowls, were insured for $200,000.

Ochowicz: Skater and Cyclist

Sheila Young Ochowicz (1950-   ) is the first American, male or female, to win three medals in a single winter Olympics. At the 1976 Winter Games at Innsbruck she won a gold medal in the 500 meter, a silver in the 1500 meter and a bronze in the 1000 meter.

That isn't all. She is the only athlete to hold world titles in two sports: skating and cycling. She got the double victory twice — in 1973 and in 1976. "I love the feeling of going fast," she explains.

Ochowicz was born in Birmingham, Michigan, the daughter of two expert cyclists. She began skating at nine and took up cycling at twelve to keep her legs in shape over the summer.

A natural competitor, she says training "isn't that much of a drudgery to me." Married to Olympic cyclist James Ochowicz, she has retired from competition.

A 1977 poll of skating coaches and officials rated Sonia Henie the greatest of all time.

Sheila Young Ochowicz believes it helps her style to wear no socks under her skates.

BOWLING

Costello: Bring On The Men

1976 Woman Bowler of the Year **Patty Costello** (1946-) is not content with a stunning 212 average and a record of seven wins in the sixteen tournaments she entered in 1976. She's fighting to take on the men. "I'd love to compete on the men's tour," says Costello. "I feel sure I would cash well, make the finals often, and have a good chance to win at least one tournament a year."

If any woman can succeed on the men's circuit, it is Costello. She set basketball and softball records in high school, before settling upon bowling. Her impetus for wanting to play with the men is partly financial; the top male bowler of 1976, Earl Anthony, took home $109,000 in prize money to Costello's $41,000. She plans to take the all-male Professional Bowlers Association to court, if necessary, to overturn a provision in its constitution barring women from its tournaments.

McCutcheon: Venerable Veteran

In 1927, a matronly, thirty-seven-year-old bowling veteran of four years accom-

Floretta McCutcheon bowled her last ball at a 1959 exhibition. It was a strike.

plished a feat that was recorded in Ripley's *Believe It Or Not*. **Floretta McCutcheon** (1888-1967) beat Jimmy Smith, the greatest exhibition bowler of all time, with a score of 704 to 697 in a three-game match — without a handicap.

The Iowa-born bowler achieved instant fame with her victory in a male-dominated sport. She toured the country giving exhibitions to put her daughter through college. In ten years of touring, she averaged 201 for 8,076 games.

McCutcheon bowled ten perfect games of 300. She had more than 100 three-game series with scores of 700 or better, and eleven with 800 or better. Many of her records remain unbroken.

In 1930, when she was 42, she finished fourth in a field of 254 male competitors at the 300 Club tournament in Cleveland, Ohio. That year she formed a partnership with promoter C.J. McCain and founded the Mrs. McCutcheon School of Bowling. By the time she retired in 1939, she had personally instructed over 250,000 bowlers.

Morris: Self-Assured Bowler

Betty Morris (1948-) started bowling at thirteen to acquire a little self-assurance. "I was shy, a real wallflower, when I was in high school," she recalls. "Then I started bowling with my dad. As I got better, it built up my confidence. Finally, I got this determination to be better than anybody else."

The Professional Women Bowlers Assication agreed Morris was the best in 1974 when it named her Bowler of the Year. She had won her first pro tournament in 1972, while six months pregnant.

Morris owns twenty different balls, to allow for varying lane conditions. With her husband, she operates "Bob and Betty's Bowlers Services" in Stockton, California.

Soutar: Bridesmaid To Bride

Judy Cook Soutar (1944-) had an unlucky string of thirteen second-place finishes before she won her first pro tournament — Tokyo's Pearl Cup — in 1973. "I'd be in a tight game and I'd be thinking to myself that the other girl knew she would win because she was bowling Judy Cook and Judy Cook always finished

Judy Soutar was a perennial bridesmaid on the bowling tour until she took up positive thinking.

second," she lamented. "I was the bridesmaid of women's bowling."

Her breakthrough was partly the result of reading a book on positive thinking recommended to her by fellow bowler June Llewellyn. "I learned that you can do anything your subconscious tells you to," Soutar said.

She also credited a pep talk by top male bowler, Dave Soutar, with improving her luck. The two married in 1974.

Judy Soutar was pro bowling's Woman Bowler of the Year in 1973 and 1975.

INVADING "MEN'S" SPORTS

Balukas: Pool Hall Sensation
In *The Music Man*, fast talking "professor" Harold Hill warns parents of "Trouble with a capital 'T' and that rhymes with 'P' and that stands for pool." Fortunately, there were no Harold Hills in Brooklyn when five-time women's pocket billiards champion **Jean Balukas** (1959-   ) was growing up.

Daughter of a grocer turned pool lounge owner, Balukas began playing the game when she was four. "I was barely tall enough to see over the table," she recalled.

Balukas won her first national women's championship at fourteen, and has successfully defended the title four times since. In winning her fifth consecutive championship in 1976, Balukas tied the record set by Dorothy Wise of Kansas City, Mo.

Pool is not the only sport in which Balukas excels. She came in second in a national junior bowling tournament at nine, played on her high school women's basketball team, and was runner-up in the 1976 and 1977 Women's Superstars competition. She plans to become a physical education teacher.

Guthrie: Lives Dangerously
Genevra Delphine Mudge, the first auto racer, probably set the cause of women in the sport backward rather than forward. Driving a Locomobile in an 1899 New York City race, she knocked down five spectators and stalled in the snow. Far more expert behind the wheel is **Janet Guthrie** (1937-   ), the first woman to drive in the prestigious Indianapolis 500 auto race.

Janet Guthrie calls herself "a race car driver who happens to be a woman."

Guthrie likes to live dangerously. She told her parents when she was a teenager that she wanted to learn to parachute. "I convinced them I was serious by jumping off the roof of our (one-story) home the summer I was sixteen," she recalled.

A graduate of the University of Michigan in physics, Guthrie passed the first series of tests for the astronaut program in the 1960s but was later rejected. In 1977, however, NASA announced that Guthrie was one of the women being considered for duty aboard an orbiting laboratory scheduled for launch in 1980.

Between 1964 and 1970, Guthrie finished nine times in the American Big Three endurance races: Watkins Glen at Watkins Glen, New York (6 hours), Sebring at Sebring, Florida (12 hours), and Daytona at Daytona Beach, Florida (24 hours).

"In company with the first lady every to qualify at Indianapolis, gentlemen, start your engines," announced the racetrack starter at the opening of the 1977 race. But Guthrie was plagued by mechanical difficulties, and came in twenty-ninth.

Guthrie has no intention of giving up. Of her progress in a male-dominated sport, she says, "I am a race car driver who happens to be a woman."

Hays: Cowgirl

"You don't really think about getting injured," says rodeo champion **Sue Pirtle Hays,** whose injuries on the rodeo circuit include a broken foot and hand, a concussion, a dislocated elbow, and separated vertebrae and pelvic bones. "You know there's a possibility of injury, but you can get hurt doing almost anything. That shouldn't stop you from doing what you like."

Hays didn't even let the impending birth of her son, Ty, interfere with her participation in the 1975 Girls Rodeo Association all-around championships. She finished fourth in the rodeo though she was eight months pregnant. "I wasn't out to prove anything," she commented. "I didn't want to miss one of the most important competitions in women's rodeo. And the doctor felt there wouldn't be any harm in my competing."

A fifteen-year rodeo veteran, Hays claims one of her rules for success is never

to accept riding advice from a man. After a brief maternity leave, Hays returned in 1976 to become the nation's top all-around female rodeo competitor. She was the year's top woman money winner in bareback riding, and second in bull riding and steer undecorating.

Harris: Basketball Star

In June 1977, **Lucy Harris** (1955-   ) became the first woman ever drafted by a men's professional basketball team. Though the action by the New Orleans Jazz was primarily a publicity device, it was also a sincere tribute to Harris's position as the nation's best offensive basketball player.

Harris grew up on a Mississippi farm, the seventh of nine children. "My older brothers and sister played basketball out back where they had set up nets and goals," she recalled. "They wouldn't let me play with them until I was good enough to score against them. I *had* to be good."

She was recruited by Mississippi's Delta State University, where she led its "Lady Statesmen" to a three-year, 50-game winning streak. Opponents are so wary of Harris, who scores an average of 31.2 points per game, that it is said the tops of her shoes wear out from being stepped on faster than do the bottoms.

Women's basketball was introduced to

Lucy Harris (45) attracted favorable notice from men's pro basketball scouts.

Joan Joyce rounds home to break a 0-0 tie at the 1965 Women's World Softball Tournament.

the Olympics in 1976, and U.S. team member Harris was the first player ever to score a basket at the games. The U.S. team finished in second place.

Joyce: Softball Superstar

Someone must have neglected to inform softball great **Joan Joyce** (1940-) that "pitchers can't hit." Joyce both pitches and hits better than any woman softball player in the world.

As a child, Joyce spent four to five hours a day throwing balls against the back of her Connecticut house. At thirteen, she joined the Raybestos Brakettes, an amateur softball team, as second baseman and outfielder. She was called upon to pitch in the 1958 National Women's Softball Tournament. Joyce said her most nervewracking moment of that game came in the seventh inning with her team leading 1-0. "I was then faced with the number two, three, and four men in their line-up," she recalled. "I was scared. What did I do? I pitched a no-hitter."

With Joyce on the mound, the Brakettes won twelve Amateur Association championships, ten in a 12-year period ending in 1975. Her win-loss record was 429-33, and included 105 no-hitters and 33 perfect

games. Meanwhile, Joyce's batting average was a respectable .327.

Along with tennis star Billie Jean King and sports promoter Dennis Murphy, Joyce helped found the International Women's Professional Softball Association in 1976. The league's first World Series was won in a four-game sweep by the Connecticut Falcons, led by none other than Joan Joyce.

Lind: Muscle Woman

"Once I didn't think muscles looked good on a woman," says rower **Joan Lind** (1953-). "Now I want all I can get." Preparing for the 1976 Olympics, where she won a silver in the single-scull event, Lind worked out eight hours a day — six in the water and two more lifting weights. She ate two-hour long dinners to keep up her strength.

Lind took up rowing at California State University, Long Beach when her then-boyfriend went out for the crew team. "I got into it by chance," she commented. "Then I got hooked." Over the next six years, she won thirteen national titles in four rowing events — singles, doubles, quad, and single dash.

One of Lind's greatest problems has

been a lack of American women rowers to race against. Another problem was financial; at some international races, she had to borrow a boat from her opponents.

"It's a beautiful sport," says Lind of rowing. "It's outdoors on a lake or on a river. And in the morning the water is like glass. You're moving fast and you get the greatest feeling of really being in shape."

Muldowney: Fast Woman

Shirley "Cha Cha" Muldowney learned street savvy behind the wheel of a car in Schenectady, New York, when she was a teenager. "I wanted to be the fastest woman in the world — in a manner of speaking," she says. As a drag racer she got her wish.

She is the second fastest drag racer in the world, having clocked 249.3 mph, second only to Don "Big Daddy" Garlits.

Ten years of professional driving have left literal and figurative scars. A fire in her car burned her face badly enough to require several operations. Her first marriage to Jack Muldowney (when she was sixteen) broke up.

"I am probably more comfortable when I get in that race car than I am any other time of the day," she says. It shows. She's the first woman named by the American Auto Racing Writers and Broadcasting Association to all-America status (1976).

Murdock: Modern Annie Oakley

"Some officials are still bothered by seeing a woman do anything," complained America riflewoman Margaret Murdock (1942-   ) at the Montreal Olympics. "They think this is a man's sport."

A nurse and mother, Murdock won a silver medal in the small-bore rifle, three-position (standing, kneeling, and prone) shooting competition at the 1976 games. She became the first woman ever to place in Olympic shooting, a sport in which men and women compete with one another.

But Murdock thought she deserved a gold medal, instead. Her score was the same as that of gold medalist Lanny Bassham — 1,162 points out of a possible 1,200 — but she lost by having fewer consecutive bulls eyes than her teammate. Though Bassham protested in Murdock's behalf, the judges were adamant in their refusal to allow the two to share first place honors. At the medal ceremony, Bassham helped Murdock onto the winner's stand, where they stood together while the national anthem was played.

Murdock distinguished herself in international compeition at the 1970 World Championships, where she won a gold in the standing event and placed seventh overall. Her victory was all the more remarkable because she was four months pregnant at the time. Shooting requires that the body be perfectly still, and a kicking fetus could easily have thrown off her shots.

O'Neil: Fearless

Kitty O'Neil (1948-   ) seems not to know the meaning of fear. As one of Hollywood's best stunt women, she has plunged 100 feet from a cliff and been doused with gasoline and set afire. She has traveled faster on land than any other woman in the world, and plans to break no fewer than six land and water speed records in 1977.

What makes Kitty run? "It's fun," she says. "It makes my heart flop."

O'Neil, the daughter of a Cherokee Indian mother and Irish father, has been deaf from birth. "My mother pushed me to read lips,' she recalled, "but she didn't push me in sports — I did that myself.

Daredevil Kitty O'Neil likes going fast because "it makes my heart flop."

Because I was deaf I had a very positive mental attitude. You have to show people you can do *anything*.''

O'Neil won 86 first-place trophies as an amateur diver, and was training for the 1964 Olympics when she contracted spinal meningitis. Doctors said she would never walk again, but she was back on her feet in time to just miss qualifying for the Olympic team.

Strapped into a three-wheeled rocket car, O'Neil set a new woman's land speed record of 512.70 miles per hour in December 1976. Only one man has ever gone faster.

Peppler: Volleyball Great

The United States volleyball team placed a dismal eleventh at the 1970 World Games in Bulgaria. But **Mary Jo Peppler** (1944-   ), star of the U.S. team, was voted the best player at the games.

Peppler played on a Southern California national championship volleyball team while she was in high school. When her parents moved to San Francisco, Peppler stayed behind because she feared the move would damage her fledgling career. She supported herself by selling encyclopedias door-to-door.

Peppler played on the 1964 Olympic volleyball team. She formed successful amateur teams in Los Angeles and Houston, and played for the co-ed El Paso-Juarez Sols of the professional International Volleyball Association.

Peppler won the first Women's Superstars competition, over such better-known athletes as Billie Jean King, Micki King, and Cathy Rigby. She was quickly dubbed the nation's — and perhaps the world's — greatest female athlete. Currently, she is developing a new athletic program at Utah State.

Women, believes Peppler, ''have things we can receive from sport as well as give to it that are different from what men offer and receive. Finesse and a striving for perfection as opposed to strength and aggressiveness.''

Ruffian: "Died In The Lead"

The greatest lady in horse race history was **Ruffian,** the high-spirited filly who died in 1975 after breaking her leg in a match race against the colt, Foolish Pleasure. The three-year-old filly was un-

beaten in ten starts, breaking or tying records in all but two of them, when the $350,000 challenge of the sexes pitted her against the year's Kentucky Derby winner.

Ruffian was ahead in the July 6, 1975 race, though Foolish Pleasure was narrowing the gap when both jockeys heard a snap — ''like when you break a stick,'' one said — as bones shattered in Ruffian's right foreleg. "She had been going so fast and was so full of herself — she was in the race of her life — that she kept running on the fracture, grinding, grinding the bones,'' her veterinarian reported. Though a team of doctors worked over her most of the night, they suspected from the start that Ruffian could not be saved. She was destroyed early the next morning. One of the Belmont Racetrack stablehands suggested an apt epitaph: "She died in the lead.''

Smith: Hollywood to Aqueduct

Robyn Smith is the greatest female jockey on the current track scene. She is the first woman jockey to win a major stakes race, and the first to ride three winners in one

Undefeated filly Ruffian died after breaking her leg in a 1975 challenge of the sexes race.

afternoon at a major New York track. The former Hollywood hopeful got her first mount in 1969 from the owner of the Golden Gate track near San Francisco. The *quid pro quo* for the publicity stunt was Smith's apprentice license.

She won several races in California, but the best she could do at the big-time tracks was to be exercise girl at Belmont Park in New York. She was allowed to race an underrated horse at Aqueduct in 1969, and she came in fifth. Since then she's had better mounts and many wins. She qualified for jockey (or journeyman) after winning 35 races — the qualification for promotion from apprentice.

In 1973, 5-feet-7, 105-pounder won the $27,450 Paumanauk Handicap, a major stakes race, aboard North Sea at Aqueduct. Nevertheless, she has still had to scrounge for mounts, but those she gets usually earn hefty annual purse totals. Says one admiring male jockey, "She's a better rider than a lot of guys anywhere."

Trimiar: "Tyger" in the Ring

"Women are supposed to be passive," says boxer **Marian "Tyger" Trimiar** (1953-   ). "But I'm not a passive person. I can't sit around and twiddle my thumbs."

Trimiar, who weighs in at 130 pounds, has been interested in boxing since childhood. "I used to watch it on TV all the time and I remember telling myself, 'That's what I want to do.'" She has trained at New York City's Gleason's Gym, where Mohammed Ali and Sugar Ray Robinson also worked out.

According to Trimiar, special rules have been imposed on women boxers. They cannot hit their opponents in the bust or below the belt. Special chest protectors — often rubber-lined bras — must be worn in the ring.

Trimiar believes boxing poses no greater danger to women than other sports. "Women have been brainwashed into thinking they aren't strong enough," she says. "With proper exercise, a woman won't get hurt."

Trimiar's shaved head is her ring trademark.

Williams: Ice Hockey Coach

Tiny, blonde **Barbara Williams** (1942-   ) won an Olympic silver medal for ice dancing. But she is even more remarkable for becoming, in 1977, the first woman coach in the rough and tumble world of professional hockey.

Williams was hired by the New York Islanders of the National Hockey League to improve members' "power skating" techniques. "In power skating," she explains, "you learn to use the edges of your skates, you learn where your body weight and balance should be, and how to increase your speed while you conserve your energy." One of the team's drills involves a hulking hockey player locking arms with Williams to try to push her down on the ice. Because of strong leg muscles and ability to dig her skates into the ice, Williams has yet to fall.

Though Williams wants her own daughter to take up figure skating instead of hockey, she believes the latter sport need not be violent. "A lot of the worst troublemakers are just frustrated because they don't know how to get from one place to another on the ice," she theorizes. "So they crack somebody over the head."

Wren: Woman Behind The Plate

Christine Wren (1949-   ) decided to become an umpire while playing for the Yakima, Washington, Webcats softball team in 1970. "I hit a line drive down the middle," she recalled, "but got called out while I was standing on first base. I figured that if he could call himself an umpire I could too."

Wren attended professional umpire school in California, and did so well that the Class A Northwest League signed her up. She became pro baseball's second female umpire. (The first, Bernice Gera, quit after one game in 1972, having committed the umpire's unpardonable sin of changing her mind.)

Wren suffered an occupational hazard not experienced by other umps. During a 1975 preseason game, a Portland player trotted onto the field and kissed her. "If this were a real game, I'd throw you out. No one is allowed to touch the ump," Wren sternly declared.

Well acquainted with the epithets fans frequently hurl at umpires, Wren says, "A ball player can't call me anything I haven't already called some other umpire when I was a player!"

Women at War

WOMEN IN COMBAT

"If the Navy could have used dogs or ducks or monkeys, certain of the older admirals would have preferred them to women," noted Virginia Gildersleeve, who helped create the U.S. Navy women's corps at the outset of World War II.

In seeking to bring women into the armed forces, Gildersleeve and her counterparts in the other branches of the service were bucking centuries of tradition.

Historically, societies have been far more inclined to give women bandage rolls than bayonets. With the exception of the Amazons — whose very existence is doubtful — ancient women were rarely depicted bearing lethal weapons, either for warfare or hunting. And, significantly, the few ancient heroines of combat were typically virgins, or at least childless. Diana, the Roman goddess of the hunt, was also the protector of chastity. Joan of Arc was called the "maid of Orleans."

Women have been denied the option of fighting in modern combat as well. Women "warriors" who entered the armed forces during World War II did so mainly because the male forces were not sufficient. Even in non-combat military roles, the employment of women has not had top priority.

Though barred from combat, Israel's female soldiers are trained to use firearms.

United States women are still prohibited by law from serving in combat. Even in Israel, where women's participation in the armed forces has been highly publicized, women have seldom fought in the front lines since statehood was achieved in 1948. Both Israeli and American female soldiers, however, receive battle training.

There are both cultural and biological arguments to the effect that women are simply not suited for combat. The biological argument states that physical aggression is primarily a male characteristic — though women are thought to be at least as aggressive verbally as men. In one experiment a female rhesus monkey was given male hormones while still in the womb; after birth she exhibited more threatening behavior than normal females.

Other studies, however, indicate that the amount and type of aggressiveness a person displays is more dependent on upbringing than biology. Anthropologist Margaret Mead studied one New Guinea tribe in which women were the aggressive sex, while men were docile.

The nature versus nurture controversy over aggression is far from settled. Yes, hormones play a definite role. But, as John Stuart Mill observed in 1869, "Women are what we have required them to be."

With luck the entire question of women — or men — at war will become moot. Still, it's interesting to look at the "warrior" roles women have played in the world's wars since ancient times.

FIGHTING WOMEN

By any yardstick, the most famous women warriors were the legendary Amazons. Their name comes from the Greek word *mazos,* meaning breast, and *a,* meaing to cut off. The Amazon women, according to some scholars, cut off their right breasts in order to draw their bows more easily.

There are several theories about the actual existence of the Amazons, or other exclusively female societies. First, some say, the Amazons developed from barbarian women who fought as auxiliaries to their warring men. Another theory is that it was simply a case of mistaken identity: the Amazons were smooth-shaven foreigners who attacked Greek colonies, and were mistaken for women. The third theory is that it is all pure fiction; a story evolved from the same cultural tendency that produced other examples of forceful Greek maidens.

The legend of the Greek Amazons stems from their supposed worship of the goddess Artemis, a huntress who carried bow and arrow, and spent her time in the forests. Her followers supposedly imitated Artemis by wearing short tunics and carrying bows and arrows.

A characteristic common to all Amazons, but beginning with the Greeks, is their avoidance of men. The Amazons dwelt as a family unit, but ruled with the firm hand of their own soliders. Men weren't allowed to be part of the tribal operations, and were used only for procreation and to raise children. Amazon women were said to have sexual intercourse with men from neighboring tribes, then they kept all female children and sent the males back to their fathers.

Several other tales of Amazons are prevalent, including reports of Amazons of Libya and Amazons of Asia Minor. But the only Amazon tribe that has been authenticated lived in Dahomey, West Africa late in the 19th century. The female force numbered some 2,500, officially including all wives of the king. The actual fighting force had 1,700 members, armed with knives, muskets, blunderbusses, duck guns, bows and arrows.

The purpose of these weapons was not to kill outright — they killed only in self defense — but to take slaves to be sold or to be used in the king's human sacrifices. (Some 5,000 "volunteers" were sacrificed annually to satisfy the king's religious beliefs.)

Boadicea: She Challenged Nero

Boadicea (also spelled Boudicca), who died about 60 A.D., was Queen of the Iceni, a tribe that lived in what is now East Anglia. The tribe was under the rule of Rome.

When Boadicea's husband, King Presutagus, died, he willed half his wealth to Nero in the hope of protecting his wife, daughters, and lands. Nero accepted the bribe, but gave no protection. His men beat Boadicea, raped her daughters, and enslaved the dead king's relatives. Enraged, Boadicea called her countrymen to arms with impassioned speeches about Roman atrocities. Her army held the Romans at bay for several days, but was defeated. On the last day of battle, Boadicea herself rode into the fray on a chariot, that also carried her daughters. Instead of being taken prisoner, she poisoned herself.

Zenobia: Queen of the East

Zenobia became Queen of Palmyra, an Arabian desert kingdom, upon the death of her husband in 266 A.D. Some historical sources suggest that Zenobia helped kill her husband.

Claiming the title Queen of the East, Zenobia tried to bring Syria, Western Asia, and Egypt under her command. She wore military garb and accompanied her troops. When Zenobia refused to make peace, she was captured by the Romans and was led, covered with jewels and golden chains, through the streets of Rome. After the show of Roman strength, Zenobia was permitted to retire to a quiet villa near Tivoli where she lived out her days.

Hind al-Hunud: Leader of the Pack

Hind al-Hunud was one of the prophet Mohammed's fiercest foes. She sprang from a mighty Arabian clan; her name meant "Hind of Hinds," or leader of the pack. A quick-witted woman of questionable virtues, she was one of the Quraish people who had long dominated the heathen city of Mecca.

Among Hind al-Hunud's people, there was a cult of The Lady of Victory, an aristocratic woman who incited frenzied patriotism in the male warriors. Accompanied by female followers, the Lady would stand near battlefields, singing and playing war songs on her lute until the battle was over. The men were expected to fight, win, or die. During the Quraish battles against Mohammed, Hind al-Hunud played this role. In spite of some victories, her husband eventually surrendered their city to Mohammed. She argued for her husband's death as punishment for his cowardice, but he won out, and Hind al-Hunud eventually became a Moslem. One of her daughters became one of Mohammed's wives.

Joan of Arc: Saintly Martyr

Few people have as romantic, respected, and awesome a foothold in history as **Joan of Arc** (1412-1431). The simple, illiterate daughter of a French plowman from Domremy, Joan was pivotal in ending the Hundred Years War (1337-1453) between the French and English. During her short life, she crowned a king, led countless battles to victory, served as a brilliant military tactician. She was tried, burned at the stake for heresy, and canonized.

At thirteen Joan began to hear the voices of St. Michael, St. Catherine, and St. Margaret, patron saints of her country, the French part of the Duchy of Bar. They urged her to avenge the wrongs dealt the French by the English following the Treaty of Troyes in 1420. The armies of the English King Henry VI occupied nearly all of the northern Kingdom, including Rheims, traditional city for French coronations. Charles VI, the Dauphin, could not be crowned until the city was liberated; Joan's mission was to see him become king.

Wearing men's clothing, and using her considerable guile and wits, Joan gained

At Joan's request, a priest held up a cross for her to look at as flames engulfed her.

an audience with the Dauphin. She persuaded him to permit her to lead a French army into battle against the English at Orleans. He wisely assented — the exhausted army, besieged at Orleans for months, responded to the adrenalin that the unprecedented leadership of a courageous woman inspired.

The English were routed and, at Joan's urging, the indecisive Charles went to Rheims for his coronation.

Joan witnessed Charles's coronation and his subsequent vacillation as well. He was not sensitive to the needs of military timing. Finally, Joan persuaded him to try to take Paris. But his advantage had been lost. In the battle of Compiegne in 1430, Joan was captured by Philip, Duke of Burgundy. The British cannily requested that she be handed over for trial by the church, since the French people would never have accepted her imprisonment unless first she, and then King Charles, were discredited.

Joan stood trial in Rouen in January of 1431. Among the seventy charges against her the most damaging was that she was a heretic because she gave her allegiance to God over the Church. Because of her relentless tenacity, she was chained to a wooden block and guarded by five English soldiers to prevent escape. She refused to reveal what she had said to Charles. She refused to deny her voices. And she was condemned to be burned at the stake.

Welsh: Searched for Her Husband

According to one observer, **Kit Welsh** (1667-1739) had "as much sex in her as you would find in a class devoted to the higher mathematics." Perhaps that accounted for her success in fighting in the British Army disguised as a man.

Welsh — also known as Trooper Christopher Welsh — entered the military in 1693 to search for her errant husband. Fighting in several battles of the War of the Spanish Succession, Welsh was twice wounded and once held prisoner by the French. She finally caught up with her husband in 1704; both remained with the army, though she now wore women's clothing and cooked more often than she fought. The stays of her gown saved her when she was hit, while searching the battlefield at Malplaquet for her husband's body. She retired in 1708 on a shilling-a-day pension, and was given a military funeral when she died.

Saragoza: Steadfast Spaniard

The brave Spanish woman **Augustina Saragoza** (1786-1857) shamed her countrymen to return to their guns during the 1808 siege of Saragossa by the French. Young Saragoza arrived at the Portillo gate to her city, where the fighting was heaviest, with food for the fighting men. But she found all the soldiers were dead or had abandoned their battle stations. She picked up a match from the hand of a dead gunner, and fired a 620-pound cannon.

The fiery young woman declared she would not leave the gun until the end of the siege. Inspired by her courage, the remaining soldiers returned to the fray. As promised, Saragoza stayed at her post until the bloody siege ended, fifty days later. Thanks in large measure to her perseverance, the Spanish rallied from near-certain defeat to repulse the attack.

Barry: Post-Mortem Surprise

Perhaps the best known case of a woman serving in the military as a man was that of **Dr. James Barry** (1795-1865), whose real name is not known. Said to be the granddaughter of a Scottish earl, Barry masqueraded as a man and studied medicine at the University of Edinburgh. Still disguised, she enlisted in the British Army in 1813, allegedly for love of an army surgeon. Barry had a distinguished military career, serving at Malta, Trinidad, and Cape Colony. she became Inspector General of the Army Medical Department.

Barry's sex was discovered only at her death.

Nightingale: Lady With the Lamp

The founder of modern nursing, **Florence Nightingale** (1820-1910) became a nurse over her family's objections, because she considered it God's will. In the mid-nineteenth century, it was not considered fitting for a woman of her refinement to become a sickroom drudge. Besides, many women who took up nursing were of dubious virtue.

Daughter of an aristocratic and wealthy Florentine family, Nightingale decided in 1844 to forego marriage for medicine and began visiting hospitals throughout

Aristocratic Florence Nightingale defied 19th century convention to become a nurse.

Europe. She became Superintendent of the Hospital for Invalid Gentlewomen in London in 1853. When Britain became embroiled in the Crimean War, the War Department asked her to nurse the wounded in Turkey. With thirty-two other nurses, she set up a hospital in a filthy Turkish barracks. Her tireless determination to create sanitary nursing conditions caused the death rate to decline. It was then that Nightingale earned the title, "The Lady With the Lamp."

After the war, she set up a school of nursing in London, and worked with the British Army to improve its hospitals and health care.

Amazons of the Seine

While the conquering Prussians waited outside the city in 1870-71 after the Franco-Prussian War, French radicals and moderates battled for control of Paris. Fighting with the radical faction were the Amazons of the Seine, called "petroleuses" (incendiaries) by opponents who accused them of setting fire to the city.

Initially, women participated in the conflict only as nurses. But Felix Belly, writing in *La Liberté,* called for ten battalions of "amazons" to be armed. Posters went up around town announcing thé plan, and about 1,500 women signed up. Wealthy women donated jewels and money to outfit the female troops in the distinctive uniform that became a target for political cartoonists: black trousers with orange bands, black wool blouse, black peaked cap trimmed in orange, and a cross-belted ammunition pouch. They were taught to use rifles and small arms, and fought shoulder to shoulder with men.

Cavell: "A Higher Duty"

The career of **Edith Cavell** (1865-1915), a colorless British Governess, took a new turn in 1895 when she returned home to care for her sick father. Her sickroom experience convinced her to become a nurse. In 1907 she organized a school of nursing in Brussels, Belgium.

Soon after the outbreak of World War I, Belgium was overrun by German troops. Saddened by the suffering of the Belgians under their captors, Cavell declared, "In times like these, when terror makes might seem right, there is a higher duty than prudence." She made her hospital a way station on an escape route for Allied soldiers imprisoned by the Germans. In 1915 German police raided her hospital and took her to the grim St. Gilles Prison. Realizing

that the men she had saved might return to fight them again, the Germans brought her to trial; she denied nothing, and was condemned to die by firing squad. A statue to Cavell stands today near London's Trafalger Square, inscribed with the magnanimous words she spoke shortly before her execution: "Patriotism is not enough. I must have no hatred or bitterness toward anyone."

Mata Hari: Agent Or Double-Agent?

The legendary spying activities of **Mata Hari** (1876-1917) are the stuff of high drama, and her life was dramatic from childhood on.

Born in Holland as Margaretha Zelle, she was expelled from convent school because she had allegedly slept with a priest. When she was eighteen she married forty-year-old Captain Rudolph MacLeod. They lived in Java, where she learned exotic dancing and gave birth to two children. The marriage was violent. One of her children died. She left MacLeod and moved to Paris where she worked in a brothel. Her career branched out when she became a belly dancer in the buff, adopting the name Mata Hari, ("Eye of Dawn").

She moved on to Berlin in 1905. There her lovers included the Crown Prince and the Kaiser's son-in-law. Another lover was Traugott von Jagow, commandant of the secret police, who persuaded her to

"Life is an illusion," announced Mata Hari as she prepared to meet the firing squad.

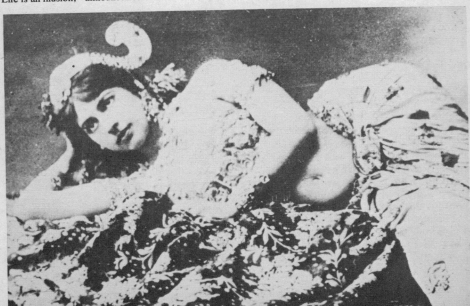

attend the German espionage academy headed by the infamous Fraulein Dokter.

Hari protested to her death that she had spied for the French against the Germans, but the evidence is against her. While vacationing in Madrid with the local chief of German intelligence, she delivered a message on German submarine activities to an official of the French embassy. She was instructed to go to Paris for payment. There she was arrested as a double agent, tried, and sentenced to death.

The explanation she gave for her ambivalent espionage was, "I love officers. I have loved them all my life."

Ibarruri: The Passion Flower

"It is better to die on your feet than live on your knees," exhorted **Delores Ibarruri** (1895-   ) to her compatriots during the Spanish Civil War. "They shall not pass!"

Ibarruri was raised in Spain's poor Basque mining country. "I know the terrible pain of days without bread, winters without fire, and children dead for lack of money for medicines," she recalled. She adopted her pen name, La Pasionaria ("the Passion Flower") when she began writing for a socialist weekly in 1918. Two years later she joined the Communist Party and became one of its most influential members.

During the Civil War she gave radio speeches urging Spaniards to resist the forces of General Francisco Franco. She advised housewives to prepare boiling oil to throw on the invaders, and led a woman's brigade that fought alongside men against the fascists.

She fled to the Soviet Union after the war, where she headed the exiled Spanish Communist Party. When the party was legalized by Franco's successor, King Juan Carlos, the 81-year-old Ibarruri made a triumphal return to her homeland.

Scholtz-Klink: Hitler's Ideal

"Woman has her battlefield," proclaimed Adolf Hitler. "With each child that she brings to the nation, she fights her fight for the nation." Helping to indoctrinate woman to procreate for the good of the Nazi state was **Gertrud Scholtz-Klink** (1902-   ), fueherin (woman leader) of the 50,000-member Women's Front, the Frauenschaft.

As Hitler's ideal of German womanhood, Scholtz-Klink was said to wield great influence over the women of Germany and German-occupied nations. "Frau Klink rules the lives of women in all things," said a half-Jewish German journalist after defecting to the West. "She tells them how many children they must have, and when; what they shall wear, what they shall cook, and how. What they shall say, laughing, to their husbands and sons marching to war. How they shall behave, smiling, when their men are killed."

Scholl: "White Rose" Leader

One of the few Germans who dared defy the Nazi regime was a young schoolgirl, **Sophie Scholl** (1921-1943). Sophie and her brother, Hans, organized the Weisse Rose ("White Rose") resistance group, which staged an anti-Nazi demonstration on the streets of Munich in 1943. Theirs was the first protest of its kind against the Third Reich.

The government did not take kindly to being denounced as a "dictatorship of evil" by the two courageous students and their organization. The Scholls were hauled away by the Gestapo, and Sophie's leg was broken during the interrogation which followed. After a hasty trial, the two were condemned to death.

Lubetkin: Warsaw Ghetto Heroine

Courageous **Zivia Lubetkin** (c. 1920-   ) freely chose to leave the relative safety of Soviet-occupied Poland to fight with her fellow Jews in the Warsaw Ghetto. Joining the five-member general staff of the Jewish Fighters Organization, she first had to convince her people of the Nazi peril. The Jews — 400,000 of whom had already been carted out of the Ghetto — were deluded into thinking they were being taken to labor camps, not to mass extermination chambers. Besides propagandizing, Lubetkin smuggled arms into the Jewish sector.

The Jews' battle against the Nazis began in April 1943 and lasted for ten days. Initially repulsed, the Nazis returned to set fire to the four corners of the ghetto to flush the fighters out. Lubetkin was appointed to lead a group to safety through the only possible escape route — the labyrinthian tunnels of the Warsaw sewer system. For twenty hours she and her party picked their way without resting through raw sewage that sometimes reached their knees. They escaped through a manhole to the street and were transported to the forest. However, their escape was detected, and other ghetto groups following them through the sewers were killed.

Lubetkin fought at the head of Polish partisan units until the end of the war. Afterward, she settled in Israel.

Tokyo Rose: Japanese Propagandist

There were many Tokyo Roses, but only one of them was punished for it: **Iva Toguri d'Aquino** (1916-   ).

D'Aquino was born in California. After graduation from UCLA in 1941, she traveled that year to her parents' homeland in Japan to visit an ailing aunt. The United States government would not give her a passport to return to the United States and, after the Japanese attack on Pearl Harbor on December 7, 1941, she was declared an enemy alien. She improved her Japanese at the Matsumiya Language School and got a job as a typist at Radio Tokyo. D'Aquino was one of thirteen women selected to read a prepared script on "Zero Hour," an English-language broadcast. Her introductions to musical numbers were Japanese propaganda.

At the end of the war, D'Aquino was arrested by the United States military police and imprisoned at Sugamo Prison for eleven months.

In 1946 she was released; the government did not prosecute her. Later she married and settled in Tokyo.

When her first child was born, she applied for a United States passport. Although she was legally entitled to it, public opinion was against her returning to the United States. On August 26, 1948, she was arrested and charged with treason and brought from occupied Japan to San Francisco for trial. Charged with eight counts, she was found guilty of one, that of speaking ". . . into a microphone concerning the loss of ships." She was sentenced to ten years in prison, fined $10,000, and lost her citizenship. In 1956 she was released, a citizen of no country. In 1977 she received a Presidential pardon.

AMERICAN WOMEN AT WAR

Colonial Era

Reed: Sewed Shirts

Ester Reed (1746-1780) was born in London, married Joseph Reed, and came to America in 1770. Her husband became a leader in the anti-Anglo movement, but Ester Reed's work was of greater historical importance. She led a campaign to raise money for General Washington's soldiers. When she presented him with $7,400 in specie, he asked that the money be used to buy linen shirts for his soldiers. Her committee sewed more than 2,000 shirts.

McCrea: Colonial Martyr

Jane McCrea's (1752-1777) value to the Colonial Army lay in her martyrdom. In the hope of seeing her fiance, who was serving with British General John Burgoyne's forces, McCrea remained in Fort Edward, New York, while others were evacuated. She was preparing for evacuation with her friend, Sarah McNeill, when the Fort was attacked by Indians. McNeill was delivered to the British, but McCrea's body, scalped and bullet-ridden, was discovered the next day near the Fort. Her death, which shocked both sides of the Atlantic became a propaganda tool. Neutral colonists rallied in her name to the Colonists' cause. Within three months of her death, Burgoyne surrendered to American General Horatio Gates.

Iva Toguri D'Aquino posed before the microphone she used for her World War II broadcasts.

Sampson: Cause Célèbre

The service of **Deborah Sampson** (1760-1827) as a soldier in the Revolutionary War was a *cause célèbre*.

Born in Massachusetts, she was an indentured servant until she was eighteen. She learned to read and write and became a school mistress. Wearying of the quiet New England life, she decided to sign up with the army. Her first effort was thwarted. Wearing men's clothing, she enlisted under the name of Timothy Thayer. Her identity was discovered during an enthusiastic celebration at a tavern.

The second time Sampson enlisted, again wearing a man's suit, she walked to Uxbridge and became Private Robert Shurtleff in the infantry volunteer Fourth Massachusetts Regiment. So discreet was she that her sex went undetected during her eighteen months of training at West Point (no physical examination was required) and during hand-to-hand combat at Tappan Bay. She was shot in the thigh at East Chester, but tended her own wounds. When she became ill with "brain fever" in Philadelphia, a nurse discovered her gender. Private Shurtleff was honorably discharged in 1783 and became Mrs. Benjamin Gannett a year later.

Sampson, soon the mother of three children, had to go on the road as a public speaker to support her family because her government pension was inadequate. She was a great success, particularly because she wore her uniform and performed military drills. Paul Revere interceded with the government in her behalf, and her pension was increased. A Liberty ship bearing the name *Deborah Gannett* was christened in 1944.

McCauley: "Molly Pitcher"

Mary Ludwig Hayes McCauley (1754-1832) served as a domestic until her marriage to barber John Hayes. When Hayes became a gunner for the Revolutionary army, she joined him in New Jersey where she performed campfollower chores. She got her nickname, **"Molly Pitcher,"** during the battle of Monmouth in 1778 when she carried water to the troops by pail and pitcher. When John was felled, either by bullet or the heat, she took his place at his cannon and fought to the end of the engagement.

"Molly Pitcher" at the cannon: "Her husband falls . . . she sheds no ill-timed tear."

A "tobacco-chewing, hard swearing woman," she was good-natured and courageous. For her services, she was awarded an annuity for life by the Pennsylvania legislature. After Hayes' death, she married John McCauley, who died in 1814.

Patton: Gunpowder Gift

Mary McKeehan (1751-   ) was born in England and emigrated to Pennsylvania. There she married John Patton. They moved to Carter County, Tennessee, where they ran a small gunpowder mill, a gift from her cousin Brig. Gen. Nathaniel Taylor. John joined the southern militia and Mary continued to make gunpowder. Her gift of 500 pounds of gunpowder enabled the Americans to defeat the British at the Battle of Kings Mountain. The battle was the turning point of the war in the southern colonies.

Ludington: Night-time Ride

On April 26, 1777, an exhausted army messenger appeared at the Ludington house in Connecticut. He was en route to get reinforcements to fight the British in Danbury, Connecticut. As he could ride no longer, sixteen-year-old **Sybil Ludington** took her horse on a 40-mile, night-time ride to get help from the local militia. Because of her courage the British were driven back to their ships. A statue of her on horseback stands in Carmel, New York.

Hart: Dinner Party Hostess

Nancy Hart (1735-1830) was big-boned, cross-eyed, and tough. She hated the British. During the war she was a spy and strategist. Her famous caper was "Nancy Hart's dinner party." Five Tories, who had just shot a neighbor, forced their way into her home, demanding a meal. Nancy Hart fed them a turkey and plenty of whiskey, and, while they were in a stupor, slid all but one of their weapons through a hole in the cabin wall. She said she would kill anyone who moved, and backed her words by shooting the one who did. Her husband, having been summoned by their daughter, arrived and Nancy Hart declared that shooting was too good for the Tories. They were hanged.

Darragh: Buttoned Information

Lydia Barrington Darragh, (1729-1789) born in Ireland, was a Quaker, midwife, mortician, and nurse. Since she lived in Philadelphia, across the street from British General William H. Howe, part of her house was commandeered by British officers. During one of their meetings, Darragh overheard plans to attack General Washington's army in two days at Whitemarsh where her son Charles was among the troops. She arranged for a message to be delivered to Washington warning him of the attack. There are several versions of how the message was delivered. One is that she sewed the message between the coat buttons of the jacket of her younger son, John, and he took it. Another says that she obtained a pass through the lines on the pretext of getting a sack of flour at Frankford Mill. Her intelligence report saved the American Army from a surprise attack.

Corbin: "Captain Molly"

When **Margaret Corbin** (1751-1800) was five, her father was killed by Indians and her mother was taken prisoner. She married John Corbin in 1772 and went with him to Fort Washington on Manhattan Island after he enlisted as a "matross" (artillery private). She was by his side when he was mortally wounded, and she took up his weapon, earning the reputation of the "first woman to take a soldier's part." She was wounded and lost the use of one arm. Margaret was voted the "heroine of Fort Washington" in 1779 by the Pennsylvania

Legislature. She was given a lifetime pension — half the monthly pay of a soldier — making her the first woman pensioner in the United States. She was buried at West Point.

The Civil War

Schuyler: $25 Million

Louisa Schuyler (1837-1926), great-granddaughter of Alexander Hamilton, lived in New York City where she established a committee of ninety-two prominent women to aid in wartime relief. At Cooper Union the women met to devise ways to assist the Union troops who were poorly housed, clothed, and fed. President Lincoln, responding to their request, established the United States Sanitary Commission. The Commission was staffed by volunteers and set up warehouses to collect food and medical supplies. During the War these women collected $25 million in supplies and services.

Livermore: Free Supplies

Mary Livermore (1820-1905) traced her hatred of the South to three years as a tutor on a Virginia plantation. She was born in Boston and married a minister in Leicester, Massachusetts. They moved to Chicago where Mary volunteered for the local Sanitary Commission. With Jane Hoge (see below) she organized four thousand midwestern groups to collect relief supplies which were shipped free of charge by the Illinois Central Railroad. In 1863, the women organized a sanitary fair in Chicago where they collected $72,000 by selling donated handiwork and household goods.

Hoge: Worked for Boys in Blue

Born in Philadelphia, Pa., **Jane Hoge** (1811-1890) and her husband Abraham, a merchant, moved to Chicago where Abraham set up an iron works. She founded the Home for the Friendless, a haven for widows and children, where she met Mary Livermore. She nursed the sick in her son's regiment, and, through the Sanitary Commission, helped distribute medical supplies to the sick and wounded western soldiers. With Livermore she toured front line hospitals and later gave speeches to rally citizens around the war effort. She wrote "The Boys in Blue" (1867), a tribute to the soldiers, and particularly to the women who assisted their military service.

Bickerdyke: Dirty Hands

Mary Ann Bickerdyke (1817-1901), variously known as "Mother Bickerdyke" and "the cyclone in calico," had remarkable energy and executive abilities. A widow at forty-three, she left her three children with neighbors in Illinois to begin four years of wartime work.

Working as a field agent for the Sanitary Commission (at $50 monthly), she was willing to get her hands dirty. Bickerdyke gathered up " . . . dirty, bloody and verminous underwear, blankets and bandages" and washed them in " . . . huge cauldrons filled with water, soap and carbolic acid." She persuaded the Commission to provide regular laundry service. She intimidated stingy supply officers into giving her materials, and once talked them out of one hundred cows and one thousand chickens to feed hospital patients.

General Grant issued a pass to her giving her authority to travel anywhere and take any supplies she wanted from Army quartermasters for her work. When her activities were questioned, General Sherman ruefully remarked, "She outranks me."

By war's end she had served on nineteen major battlefields, often picking through corpses in search of wounded, assisting in surgery, working in mud and freezing rain.

Edmonds: He's A She

Of the estimated 400 women who served in the Union Army disguised as men, one of the most famous was **Sarah Edmonds** (1841-1898). Born in Canada, she left home and, under the name Franklin Thompson, and wearing a suit of men's clothing, she became a traveling salesman. She went to Michigan, and when the War broke out she enlisted in the 2nd Michigan Regiment of Volunteer Infantry. Edmonds fought in the battles of Bull Run and Fredericksburg, but then retired.

She claimed that she left the army because her sex would have been discovered during an illness. Another story is that she deserted because she had fallen in love.

In later years she married and wrote *Nurse and Spy in the Union Army,* which sold 175,000 copies. When her military experience became known, she received a pension from the U.S. Congress.

Barton: Red Cross

Clara Barton (1821-12912) is most famous for founding the American Red Cross in 1881, but her work with the sick and wounded began during the Civil War.

A painfully inhibited child, she was later employed as a document copier for the U.S. Government. At the outbreak of the war she began to earn the title "Angel of the Battlefield." Circumventing the fledgling Sanitary Commissions, she organized her own group of women to take medical supplies to numerous battlefields, including Fredericksburg and Antietam, driving a four-mule team herself. She cheerfully assisted surgeons in the field. As the Sanitary Commission's activities increased, hers diminished. With the support of President Lincoln, Barton established a missing soldiers bureau at Annapolis, tracking down 13,000 missing, most of them dead.

Her work led to a physical and nervous breakdown. While recovering in Switzer-

Clara Barton, whose relief work began during the Civil War, helped found the American Red Cross.

land in 1869, she learned of the International Red Cross. In 1882 she persuaded Congress to ratify the international treaty protecting the Red Cross emblem and those who wore it. She served as president of the American Red Cross until 1903.

Tubman: Underground Conductor

That **Harriet Tubman** (1802-1913) wanted to serve anybody is a miracle, given the circumstances of her childhood. Born into slavery in Maryland, she was taken from her mother at age six to learn weaving. She was beaten several times a day for her refusal to do indoor work. At nine she was a field hand, hauling wood and splitting rails. At thirteen her skull was fractured when an overseer struck her on the head with a two-pound weight.

After marrying John Tubman, a free black, she escaped to Philadelphia. "For I had reasoned this out in my mind," she later said (Tubman was illiterate), "there was one of two things I had a right to, liberty or death. If I could not have one, I would have the other, for no man should take me alive. I should fight for my liberty as long as my strength lasted . . ."

Tubman fought for everyone's liberty.

After the War, Harriet Tubman financed black schools and started a home for the aged and poor.

She became a conductor on the Underground Railroad at the outbreak of the Civil War. In all, she made more than nineteen trips into Maryland to take slaves to Canada. She was called "the Moses of her people." Her ingenuity was considerable. Harriet would send coded messages in the form of spirituals to alert slaves of her arrival. Once she threw pursuers off her track by boarding a southbound train. She often stole the carriage of the plantation master to carry his own slaves North. At one time, a $40,000-reward was offered for her capture. John Brown consulted her in planning his ill-fated raid on Harper's Ferry. In 1862 she served as a nurse in South Carolina, advising blacks about escape. As a tactician and spy, Tubman was invaluable to the Union Army.

Boyd: Flirtatious Spy

Belle Boyd's (1844-1900) courage, to say nothing of her popular lectures about her wartime capers, insured her reputation as a *bona fide* heroine. For her, there wasn't enough action in raising money for the South. So, in 1861, she became a spy.

Boyd was a romantic, but she also had guts. When a Union soldier tried to raise the Stars and Stripes over her West Virginia home, she killed him. By flirting, she was able to extract important intelligence from Union soldiers posted in her home. She pulled off a great spying coup when she warned General Stonewall Jackson that the Union army was pulling back and burning its bridges. The bridges were saved and Jackson advanced almost as far as Washington, D.C.

Three times she was imprisoned. She went to England, ostensibly for her health, but actually to carry Confederate documents. She married a Union officer she met on the ship. But he died within a year. To support herself and her child, she became an actress. Later she extolled the unity of North and South in her popular lectures.

Greenhow: Wild Rose

"The Wild Rose of the Confederacy," **Rose Greenhow** (1817-1864) had a personality perfectly suited to notorious superspydom. In her youth, Greenhow lived with her aunt in an elegant boarding house in Washington, D.C., where she met and amused the most important politicians of the day. She married lawyer Robert Greenhow. After his death in 1854, she was again swept up in Washington social circles. The Confederacy enlisted her as a spy, and the results were remarkable. The Confederacy's first victory at Bull Run is attributed to her acquisition — probably in the boudoir — of advance plans. She set up an elaborate system of fifty spies — forty-eight of them women — between Washington and Texas.

Learning of the South's plans to attack Washington, she suggested that she and her cohorts cut crucial telegraph lines to speed the invasion. With the help of detective Allan Pinkerton, the authorities tracked her down. Greenhow ate the coded message she was carrying. News of Greenhow's arrest understandably gave several northern War Department officials, who had been habitués of her house, severe migraines.

Greenhow's spy ring flourished even when she was in prison. Her adventures continued after her release. In Europe she met Queen Victoria and Napoleon III. She wrote a book, and, on her trip home, wore a small purse containing her royalties in gold. When her ship was trailed by a federal gunboat, Greenhow decided to slip into a small boat to escape. The boat overturned and Greenhow drowned.

Van Lew: Distinguished Spy

Elizabeth Van Lew (1818-1900) was one of the Union's most effective spies, owing to her intelligence, cunning, and her distinguished Virginia family. Her parents were openly opposed to slavery, freeing their own, buying and freeing those of their neighbors. Van Lew took food and clothing to imprisoned Union officers. She helped many of these men escape North, and her operations went unnoticed because of her social standing.

She was able to "plant" Mary Elizabeth Boswer as a domestic (and spy) in Jefferson Davis' White House of the Confederacy. To cover her tracks, Van Lew feigned eccentricity, dressing and behaving strangely, and she became known as "Crazy Bet." Her network of spies included her own servants, who carried messages in their shoes. Van Lew herself carried messages in her watch.

When the Confererates were routed from Richmond, she raised the first southern Stars and Stripes since 1861 over her house. After the war she fought for women's rights by refusing to pay taxes — she was not, she said, being represented.

Trader: Southern Nightingale

Ella King Newsom Trader (1838-1919) was called "The Florence Nightingale of the South" with good reason.

A wealthy widow, she served as an extraordinarily able hospital administrator from the outbreak of the Civil War to its end. Although hospital work was considered undignified for a woman, her patience, persistence, charm, and social connections made her work successful. She set up hospitals throughout the South. A hospital in Chattanooga, Tennessee, the Newsom, was named in her honor.

Her postwar life was tragic. Trader lost her 1,100-acre plantation and her wealth because of Reconstruction confiscation and her second husband's ineptitude. In 1885, again widowed, she was nearly penniless and deaf and had a young daughter to support. But that year she got employment with the General Land Office.

FROM BANDAGE-WRAPPING TO SHARPSHOOTING

American women got official military status through the hospital door. After several wars of mopping brows and blood for nothing, in 1901, with the establishment of the Army Nurse Corps, they were able to serve officially for a little more than that. Women had proved themselves during the Spanish-American War by working skillfully in camp hospitals, on troop transports, and on the hospital ship USS Relief. The Navy got its own nurses in 1908.

Women made even greater inroads into the military during World War I. Some 21,000 military nurses saw active duty, but they did not hold military rank, nor did they receive pay or benefits equal to those of men in comparable positions. Yeomanettes — taken from their official tag (Yeomen F) — were a corps of 11,000 women who worked in Navy jobs previously held by men. most of their work was clerical, and they were posted to France, the Panama Canal Zone, Guam,

Hawaii, and the United States. During that war, there were also 300 "Marinettes" who fleshed out the Marines in stateside posts.

Women also filled many non-military jobs during the First World War. Masses of women obtained job training they couldn't have gotten during peacetime. More than 100,000 women worked in munitions factories, as streetcar conductors, elevator operators, and furnace stokers.

World War II Brings More Women

In World War II the military finally, officially, realized it could not live without women. Manpower shortages in and out of the services led to a big push in the recruiting offices. In 1942, the Women's Army Auxiliary Corps ("Auxiliary" was dropped a year later) was founded. More than 140,000 WACs worked in rear-echelon jobs during the War — as accountants, clerks, draftswomen, telephone operators, chauffeurs, cooks, librarians, truck drivers, postal clerks, and radio operators — all over the world. Not so rear echelon was WAC Colonel Mary Agnes Halleran, who was decorated for ferrying a contingent of soldiers across the English channel during the Normandy invasion.

The Navy's WAVES came into being in 1942. The acronym (Women Accepted for Volunteer Emergency Service) was the discreet invention of WAVE Commander Elizabeth Reynard. "I figure the word 'Emergency' will comfort the older Admi-

rals," she commented wryly, "because it implies that we're only a temporary crisis and won't be around for keeps." The Navy certainly hoped so. WAVES did not serve outside the borders of the United States. Still, their contribution was significant. More than 105,000 WAVES handled 80 percent of the Navy's mail service for the entire fleet. They held down 75 percent of the jobs at Radio Washington, the nerve center of Navy communications.

Female acronyms continued to multiply. SPARS (short for "Semper Paratus") was the Coast Guard's name for its 18,000 women. WAMS (Women Marines) numbered 22,000 during the War.

The 1,000 WASPS (Women's Air Force Service Pilots) were allowed to fly, but not in combat. Under the leadership of aviator Jacqueline Cochran, they ferried planes and trained pilots as an auxiliary of the Army Air Force. Still, they performed risky tasks, such as target towing for fire practice, and thirty-eight of them lost their lives. One of them, Cornelia Fort, was giving a flying lesson when the Japanese attacked at Pearl Harbor. She succeeded in outflying the Japanese fighter planes that fired on her, but she was later killed in a formation-flight accident.

The women who served as nurses during World War II took most of the flak. More than 73,000 of them served in the Army and the Navy. Half of the Army's

Women carved out a permanent place for themselves in the military during the Second World War.

Nurses, who were the first American women to reach foreign soil during the war, served overseas. Over 200 of them were killed. Five Navy nurses stationed in Guam were taken prisoner by the Japanese on the first day of World War II. The following year, eleven more were captured at Manila and imprisoned at Santo Tomas. Most of these nurses remained POWs until 1945.

Women spies regularly risked their lives. Under the auspices of the Office of Strategic Services, they were dropped behind enemy lines and engaged in sabotage and secret radio operations. One of them, who operated under the name Artemus, was landed on the Brittany Coast by ship because she had a wooden leg and couldn't jump.

"Rosie the Riveter," was an umbrella handle for more than 18 million women who held down war-related jobs between 1941 and 1945. They worked as switch-women on the Long Island Railroad, welders, and assembly workers in the ship-building industry, and produced aircraft, steel, artillery, and ammunition needed in the war. In addition, three million women worked for the Red Cross and two million worked in offices. Between 1940 and 1945 the number of women in the labor force increased from 25 percent to 45 percent. And they were in the work force to stay.

After the War

The Women's Armed Services Integration Act was passed (1948). It gave women permanent status in the regular Army, Navy, Air Force, and Marines. But the postwar military upper ranks continued to be filled by men only. Servicewomen were still nurses or clerks. If they married, they were automatically discharged. Equal military opportunity did not come about until 1967, with passage of Public Law 90-130. This law removed promotion restrictions, mandatory retirement, and the 2 percent force strength limitation. Currently, women constitute 5.4 percent of the nation's active duty force. In 1970 the Army named its first female generals: Mildred C. Bailey, then director of the WACs, and Lillian Dunlap, director of the Army Nurse Corps.

Today more women serve in the U.S. armed forces than in any country in the world. And more jobs are open to them in the military. In 1972 only one-quarter of the Army's military occupational specialties (MOSs) were open to women. Today women may enter 92 percent of the job classifications.

One bone of contention remains for military women: they are precluded by Congress from many top military assignments that involve combat or close-combat situations. However, according to law, career progression for women in all other career fields is comparable to that for male personnel.

Most Army and Navy women are still nurses or clerks, but some are performing non-traditional tasks. In 1973, one woman was a mechanic in the Army; today, nearly 200 women have their heads under the hoods. Army women are working as divers, nuclear power plant mechanic operators, policemen, and air traffic controllers. Navy women are serving as aviation anti-submarine warfare technicians, oceans systems technicians, and aviation fire control technicians. Legislation is pending that would permit Navy women to serve at sea.

Today women may marry, bear children, and stay in the service. Post nurseries and day-care centers have been established. And a 1973 Supreme Court decision ruled that families of servicewomen must receive the same benefits as those of servicemen.

Still, there is discrimination against female enlistees. Unlike the men, women must be high school graduates with "high moral standards."

Nevertheless, women are inching into top military ranks in a variety of ways. Beginning with the Air Force in 1969, the services have opened college ROTC (Reserve Officer Training Corps) programs to women. Completion of the program gives them a commission in the military as officers upon graduation. But the most prestigious route to stars and bars is via the service academies.

In 1976 all four service academies admitted women: U.S. Military Academy at West Point, 119 (in a class of 1,480); U.S. Naval Academy at Annapolis, 80 (in a class of 1,400); U.S. Air Force Academy at Colorado Springs, Colorado, 157 (in a class of 1,600); U.S. Coast Guard

Women in Service – Active Duty as of June 30, 1976

	Army	Navy	Air Force	Marines	Total
Officers	4,844	3,544	4,967	386	13,741
Enlisted Personnel	43,806	19,288	29,235	3,063	95,392
TOTAL	48,650	22,832	34,202	3,449	109,133

Academy at New London, Connecticut, 38 (in a class of 327). But coeducation has necessitated certain code changes. At West Point, women, like men, must have their hair cropped to collar length, but unlike the men, they take karate instead of boxing and wrestling. Their M-16 rifles are two pounds lighter than the men's M-14s. Barracks are integrated, but separate bathrooms have been built and everyone must wear bathrobes in the halls.

At Annapolis, visiting midshipmen of the opposite sex must keep their doors "open fully." Kissing and handholding in public are forbidden. First-year midshipmen can date only Cadets in their class.

Women midshipmen can't engage in body contact sports. At the Air Force Academy in Colorado Springs, women take physical fitness courses instead of boxing. To avoid corpulence, the women's meals are lower in calories than the men's. Women's uniform jackets do not have pockets, still a subject for debate, because a cadet carrying a shoulder bag and an M-16 looks a bit offbeat. Women plebes can date only cadets in their own class. And they cannot take pilot training courses or become navigators or missile-launching operators because they are combat or close-combat positions.

The Coast Guard Academy at New London, Connecticut, is run by the Department of Transportation and is not covered by the same law that integrated the other three academies. The Academy admits women voluntarily. The one difference in training for Coast Guard women as opposed to men is that they may not be stationed at sea.

The attrition rate of women in all the academies is higher than for men. Reasons generally given are homesickness and stiff competition.

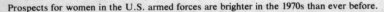

Prospects for women in the U.S. armed forces are brighter in the 1970s than ever before.

THE Lady from Maine MARGARET CHASE SMITH

FOR PRESIDENT

FOR PRESIDENT

Stateswomen

HISTORY'S POWERFUL WOMEN

Cleopatra: Femme Fatale

Cleopatra (69-30 B.C.), the second daughter of King Ptolemy XII, was the last ruler of the Macedonian dynasty. She considered herself the daughter of Ra, the sun god. Plutarch wrote of her: "Plato admits four sorts of flattery, but (Cleopatra) had a thousand".

Cleopatra, an ambitious, charming, and practical woman, married her brother, Ptolemy XIII, king of Egypt, when she was eighteen and he was fifteen. For the next few years, she worked to take his crown away by allying herself with Julius Caesar. She captivated Caesar as a means to increase her power; Caesar, in turn, wanted access to Egypt's great wealth.

Caesar led Cleopatra's successful war against her own brother. During his love affair with Cleopatra, he reportedly fathered her son, Caesarion. He installed Cleopatra in a villa near the Tiber in Rome and had a golden statue of her erected in the city. When Caesar was murdered in 44 B.C., Cleopatra returned to Egypt but was called back to Rome by Caesar's successor, Marc Antony. She sailed up the Nile on her way to Rome in a luxurious barge — made famous in Shakespeare's *Antony and Cleopatra* — and Antony, too, fell in love with her.

Antony followed Cleopatra back to Alexandria, where they reportedly lived a life of luxurious debauchery. After ten years and many political intrigues, Antony finally married Cleopatra, an act that united all of Rome against him. An enemy stole Antony's will from the temple of the Vestal Virgins and revealed that Antony intended to transfer the capital from Rome to Alexandria. In 31 B.C., the Roman Senate declared war against Cleopatra; in the middle of the naval battle, she abandoned Antony and his troops to return home.

She sent messengers to Antony to tell him she was dead. On hearing the news, he committed suicide, as Cleopatra had intended he should. Cleopatra then tried to seduce the new Roman victor, Octavian (later the Emperor Augustus), Caesar's adopted son, but failed. Rather than live as a humiliated queen, she, too, committed suicide, possibly through a poisonous snake.

Wu: From Concubine to Empress

Wu Hou (625-705 A.D.) rose from among the Chinese Emperor T'ai Tsung's harem of two hundred concubines to become the only empress in Chinese history. At the age of thirteen, she entered the emperor's harem, and quickly became his favorite. When he died, the emperor's heir, Kao Tsung — with whom she may have been already having an affair — fell in love with her. Through a series of intrigues, Wu gained the new emperor's favor, sent his childless wife to prison, and exiled or executed her other opponents. Kao Tsung raised Wu's family to the aristocracy so he could marry her.

Weak in character and in health, Emperor Kao Tsung began to rely on his wife more and more to run the country; during the last twenty-three years of his life, she was the real ruler of China. She was respected for her efficiency, courage, and ruthlessness. Her husband died in 683, and although her sons were the legal inheritors of the throne, she managed to depose them. By 690, at the age of sixty-five, she had usurped the title of emperor for herself. During her fifty years of power she was merciless toward opponents but also became a great patron of literature and encouraged religious tolerance. She extended the Chinese borders to include Korea, kept her country in a state of prosperity, and she also gave women greater freedom.

She helped stabilize China and paved the way for the rich T'ang culture that was to come. In February 705, while Wu was in ill health and under the influence of disreputable advisers, her leading ministers seized the palace and compelled her to yield power to her exiled son, Chung Tsung.

Isabella: Financier of Columbus

Isabella I, the Catholic, of Castile (1451-1504), became one of Spain's most renowned rulers when she inherited the territory of Castile from her half-brother, King Henry IV, following his death in 1474. In 1469, she had married Ferdinand, heir to the territory of Aragon, without the king's permission. Her right to succeed Henry IV was contested by Henry's daughter, Joan, but after a four-year war, Joan withdrew her claims. Isabella and

Ferdinand — known as the Catholic kings — brought Castile and Aragon under joint rule, a merger that lead the unification of Spain as a nation.

Isabella was a pious Catholic. In 1480, the Spanish Inquisition was organized to end the multiracial and multireligious character of the two kingdoms. It was the only institution common to both Castile and Aragon, and succeeded in expelling some 170,000 Jews in 1492. Isabella also began to reform the Spanish churches, encouraged scholars and education (she learned Latin at the age of thirty), and was the patron of Spanish and Flemish artists. The Catholic Kings also defeated Granada, the last Islamic kingdom in Spain, in 1492.

In 1492, Isabella gave Christopher Columbus financial support to explore the western Atlantic. With the discovery of the New World, Isabella saw yet another opportunity to spread Catholicism. However, when Columbus returned with Indians he had taken as slaves, she ordered them freed, and the moral problem of slavery became one of her major concerns until her death in 1504.

Elizabeth I: "Virgin Queen"

Queen Elizabeth I (1533-1603), daughter of King Henry VIII and Anne Boleyn, reigned from 1558 to 1603 and is admired today as one of the greatest of all English rulers. Prudent and shrewd, she could inspire devotion — a vast change from her immediate predecessors, her sickly brother Edward VI and her sister Mary Tudor ("Bloody Mary"), who had tried to reimpose Catholicism on the newly Protestant nation. During most of Mary's reign, Elizabeth had been locked up in the Tower of London, for her presence was a constant threat to the unpopular Mary.

Although Elizabeth extended the sway of Protestantism, those who practiced Catholicism were tolerated until 1570, when the Pope declared she was a false queen, a judgment that put English Catholics in the position of being potential political traitors. Nevertheless, despite harsher treatment, most Catholics continued to support Elizabeth. This national unity contributed to the English defeat of the Spanish Armada in 1558, one of history's decisive naval battles.

During much of her reign, Elizabeth had

Popular Elizabeth I claimed she had "the heart and stomach of a king" inside a woman's body.

to ward off repeated assassination plots by Mary Stuart, Queen of Scots, who was also a potential heiress to the English throne. After allowing Mary to live in confinement in England, plotting Elizabeth's murder, for eighteen years, Elizabeth was finally persuaded to sign her death warrant.

Elizabeth was often called the "virgin queen" for she never married. But she had a number of close male friendships, including those with Sir Walter Raleigh, the Earl of Essex, and Robert Dudley whom she named earl of Leicester. She remained devoted to Dudley for twenty-four years until his death in 1588. Hearing of his death, she shut herself up alone for so long that servants finally had to break down her door. Elizabeth's view of marriage may have been tainted by her father's treatment of his wives: when she was two, he murdered her mother, Anne Boleyn; when she was eight, he executed her cousin and stepmother, Queen Catherine Howard. Nevertheless, her refusal to marry probably reflected her sense of the political value of remaining available in the great European game of dynastic marriage.

Throughout her forty-five years in power, Elizabeth hesitated to draw England into unnecessary wars, a policy that brought stability and prosperity to the country. This in turn provided the secure society in which English literature began its greatest flowering.

Elizabeth loved her work and her people, and said: "I have but the body of a weak and feeble woman, but I have the heart and stomach of a king."

Mary: Queen of Scots

Mary, Queen of Scots (Mary Stuart 1542-1587), a Catholic with a precarious history as a ruler, was usually frustrated in her attempts to gain and hold power. She was the only child of King James V of Scotland, who thought the birth of a female heir was a disgrace. He died one week later, making the baby girl Queen of Scots. In 1558, Mary was wed to the dauphin, Francis II, who ruled France for only eighteen months before his death. Meanwhile, the queen of England, Mary I, had died, and Mary Stuart laid claim to that throne as well, pointing out that the new queen, Elizabeth I, had been declared il-

legitimate by her father. Mary Stuart's bid for power was the last hope for restoring Catholicism to England.

Mary returned to Scotland in 1561, hoping to form an alliance with Spain by marrying Don Carlos, the son of Philip II. Instead, she married Lord Henry Darnley, next in line after herself for the English throne. The marriage was unhappy, and she started an affair with her secretary, David Riccio. In 1566, Darnley had Riccio murdered. One year later, Darnley was in turn murdered in a mysterious explosion. It was generally believed that his wife had arranged it. A few weeks later, she allowed herself to be abducted by the earl of Bothwell, a Protestant, and she married him soon after.

The Scots were outraged. She was captured and forced to abdicate to her son, James VI. She tried to sail for France but was stopped. She finally fled to England in 1568. There she remained a virtual prisoner until, after several unsuccessful attempts to murder Queen Elizabeth I, she was executed on February 8, 1587.

Maria Theresa: Holy Roman Empress

Maria Theresa (1717-1780), daughter of Austrian Emperor Charles VI, was married and the mother of three when she became Holy Roman Empress in 1740 at the age of twenty-three. She had had only a superficial education and no political experience. She learned her job under trying circumstances: the treasury was empty, the army was in ruins, and Frederick the Great of Prussia threatened to invade her lands.

Aware of her own limitations, she placed able administrators in high positions and laid the foundation for government reforms that modernized and strengthened her empire. Industry was encouraged, primary education was made compulsory, and judicial procedures and punishments were standardized. Torture was abolished in 1776.

She became increasingly autocratic on the throne, but her marriage to Duke Francis Stephen of Lorraine, whom she had married for love in 1736, remained happy: they had sixteen children and ten survived to adulthood. When Francis died in 1765, the empress went into a cloister for a while; when she returned to rule, her devotion to Catholicism bordered on fanaticism. She shared her later rule in an uneasy truce with her son Joseph.

Catherine II: Russian Great

Catherine II, the Great, of Russia (1729-1796), established Russia as a great European power with its own national culture. During her thirty-four-year reign, which began in 1762, she replenished the state treasury by confiscating church-owned property, extended Russia by more than 200,000 square miles, organized twenty-nine new provinces, built more than one hundred new towns, and expanded trade.

Not Russian but German, Catherine had been married at the age of sixteen to Karl Ulrich, grandson of Peter the Great and heir to the Russian throne as Grand Duke Peter. The marriage was a total failure. Her husband was neurotic and paranoid; Catherine, in contrast, was considered enlightened and cultivated. She was, above all, ambitious. With the support of the army, the courts, and public opinion, she overthrew her husband in 1762 and proclaimed herself empress. Her husband was assassinated eight days later.

During her reign, she dealt with a devastating plague, a number of wars, and the greatest Russian revolution prior to 1917. She was witty and energetic but also cruel, egotistical, and domineering; by the end of her reign, most freedom had been taken away from the Russian peasants and serfs. A friend of Voltaire and Diderot, she established literary reviews, encouraged science, and collected art.

She was known to have many lovers, among them Grigory Potemkin, who annexed the Crimea from the Turks.

Victoria: A Sense of Duty

Queen Victoria (1819-1901) loved parties, a good laugh, and as little work as possible. But under the strong influence of her dour husband, Prince Albert of Saxe-Coburg-Gotha, she became hard-working and orderly. Honest and simple, Victoria was in many ways overwhelmed by her husband's more dominant personality.

Victoria's reign from 1837 to 1901 was the longest in English history. During it, she managed to restore dignity to the crown, bring security to the monarchy, and remain popular with the middle and

"Mysterious little Victoria" restored dignity and respect to the British Crown.

poorer classes. When her husband died in 1861, she was forty-two, a widow with nine children; she had a nervous breakdown. For the rest of her life, she had her husband's clothing laid out each day, and slept at night under his photograph, taken while he lay dead. Victoria continued the day-to-day business of the crown, but rarely appeared in public until Benjamin Disraeli, who had a profound influence over her, flattered her, cajoled her, and restored her self-confidence. At the time of her death in 1901, she had thirty-seven living grand-children, guaranteeing plenty of successors to her throne.

Victoria is best remembered not for any one political achievement, but for the dignity and respect she restored to the crown. Remarked writer Henry James upon her death, "We all feel a bit motherless today. Mysterious little Victoria is dead and fat vulgar Edward is king."

Bandaranaike: Ex-Prime Minister

At the time Sirimavo Bandaranaike (1916-   ) was defeated as prime minister of Sri Lanka, in July 1977, she was the only woman heading a government. Born of a wealthy aristocratic family, she was a housewife until her husband, prime minister from 1956 to 1959, was assassinated by a Buddhist monk for advocating Western-style medicine over herbal remedies.

Sri Lanka's Sirimavo Bandaranaike was a housewife until her politician-husband's assassination.

In 1960, she agreed to enter politics to rally supporters for the Sri Lanka Freedom party and implement her husband's nationalist programs. In 1961, she replaced English with Singhalese as the official national language. Her alliance with the Communists, and severe economic problems, led to her defeat in 1965; her successor fared no better and she was reelected in 1970 and 1975.

She maintained an uneasy alliance with the Communists, often disagreeing with them about trade union agitation. In general, she favored socialism and neutrality in international relations. The mother of three, she says: "I do not believe there is a single mother in the world who can bear to contemplate the possibility of children being exposed to atomic radiation and lingering death."

Perón: She Followed Husband
In July 1974, **Isabel Perón** (1931-) became the first woman chief of state in Argentina and in the Western Hemisphere, a title she held until she was forced out of office by a military junta in March 1976.

Isabel became president following the death of her husband, Juan Perón, who had returned to rule Argentina in June 1973 after eighteen years in exile. He had met Isabel, a professional dancer, in 1956 while she was performing in a Panama nightclub called Happyland after her ballet troupe had been stranded there during a tour. Isabel was twenty-five at the time, and Perón was sixty.

To provide stability and assure succession, the aging Perón quickly chose his wife Isabel as his vice-presidential running mate in the Argentine elections of September 1973. When he died of heart failure on July 1, 1974, she imposed a state of siege and suspended constitutional rights. She lacked the experience to handle the country's massive economic and violent political problems, and faced bitter resentment from many Argentinians who still worshiped Perón's first wife, Evita. Although she won an election, the country remained on the brink of anarchy. Organized labor forced her to resign in July 1975; she took a leave of absence, returned, tried to rule again, and was finally imprisoned in March 1976.

Charged with misusing government funds, Isabel lives under detention in a small house on a naval base, with a maid and two poodles. Commander of the Army Jorge Rafael Videla is now president.

Meir: Ardent Zionist
Golda Meir (1898-) was born Goldie Mabovitch in the Ukraine; she moved with her parents and seven brothers and sisters to Milwaukee, Wisconsin, in 1906. As a child, Meir remembered the pogroms that plagued the Jews of Czarist Russia. "If there is any logical explanation . . . for the direction which my life has taken . . . (it is) the desire and determination to save Jewish children . . . from a similar experience," she said. In Milwaukee, she became intrigued by Zionism and the Democratic Socialism of Eugene V. Debs. While a teenager, she started speaking on street corners for the Zionist cause and was soon convinced her future lay in the Jewish homeland. She married Morris Myerson in 1917; in 1921, they set sail for Palestine, where she was to become a leader in the creation of the state of Israel.

The Myersons had two children; she and her husband separated in 1928. Meir devoted her life to Zionism. In 1946, when the British arrested most of the top leaders of the Jewish Agency, Meir became acting head of the agency's political department — the top position of authority in Jewish Palestine. In 1948, she collected $50 million in the United States for Israel, and on May 14th of that year was among the signers of the proclamation of the State of Israel.

She was Israel's first minister to the Soviet Union. When she attended Moscow's only synagogue for Rosh Hashanah services, she set off a spontaneous pro-Israel demonstration by forty thousand Russian Jews. She was elected to the first Knesset (Parliament) in 1949, acting as architect of many social and economic programs, and in 1956 became minister of foreign affairs. In 1966, she resigned and became secretary general of the Israeli Labor party; following the heart attack of Premier Levi Eshkol in 1969, Meir was asked to serve as interim premier, a position she consolidated through elections. She served as premier for five years, until 1974, when she resigned because she was unable to form a coalition government.

Most of her time was spent strengthen-

Determination to create a good life for Jewish children inspired Golda Meir's political career.

ing Israel's borders and managing the country's economic problems. She was a pragmatic premier with a sense of humor. When a cabinet minister suggested that, since women were being assaulted on the streets after dark, a curfew for women should be imposed, she replied:"But it's the men who are attacking the women. If there's to be a curfew, let the men stay home."

Gandhi: Indian Raj

During her years as prime minister of India, from 1966 to 1977, **Indira Gandhi** (1917-   ) came under increasing attack for betraying the democratic principles of her father, Jawaharlal Nehru, who along with Mahatma Gandhi (no relation) had helped win India's independence from Great Britain in 1947. Indira Gandhi was an only child whose aristocratic parents were often imprisoned by the British for their support of independence. Left in the palace with only the servants, she amused herself by staging mock protest demonstrations with her dolls.

She studied history at Oxford University. In 1942, she married Feroze Gandhi, a young lawyer, against her father's wishes. The couple was imprisoned for thirteen months by the British. Britain's liquidation of its empire in 1947, forming India and Pakistan, resulted in massive bloodshed as Hindus and Moslems fought for property and revenge. Indira Gandhi arranged meetings between rival religious leaders and led a grassroots village-to-village campaign to restore peace.

When her father became India's first prime minister in 1947, she became his official hostess. He had never remarried following his wife's death in 1930. During the 1950s, Gandhi became the first woman member of the Congress party's eleven-member central election committee; by 1959, she was the party president. Nehru's health began to fail and for a while she handled all his important government work. After his death, she became minister of information and broadcasting. In 1966, she was asked to become prime minister in an effort to promote national unity.

Under Gandhi, India won a massive victory over Pakistan in the 1971 Bangladesh war. In 1974, India surprised the world by exploding its first atomic bomb.

Gandhi imposed a state of emergency in India in June 1975, a period of authoritarian rule that was to last nineteen months. The emergency rule was ostensibly designed to stop widespread conspiracy against her progressive reforms. In fact, the crisis had been precipitated by Gandhi's conviction on election fraud charges and an opposition campaign to drive her out of office. Under the emergency, Gandhi arrested and imprisoned thousands of political opposition leaders. Gandhi was finally pressured into calling an election and was soundly defeated in March 1977 by the opposing Janata party. "It's a relief to feel the big burden is off my shoulders," she said after her defeat.

REIGNING QUEENS

Margrethe II: Informal Queen
Queen Margrethe II (1940-   ) is the first woman to occupy the Danish throne in her own right and with the approval of the Danish voters. Female succession was approved by popular mandate as part of a new constitution in 1953. Margrethe became queen on January 15, 1972, one day after the death of her father, King Frederik IX.

She was born in Copenhagen one week after the Nazis invaded Denmark. Her mother, in symbolic defiance of the Germans, wheeled the infant in a carriage through the streets. From that time on, Margrethe was a symbol of freedom and hope for the Danes.

Margrethe is well-educated, fluent in several languages, and knowledgeable about archeology, which she studied at Cambridge University. The queen is informal: she prefers blue jeans in private; her friends call her "Daisy." She is sometimes brusque in public and is shy with strangers. She chain-smokes.

In 1967, Margrethe married Count Henri de Laborde de Monpezat, a former third secretary in the French embassy; they have two sons.

Juliana: Queen and Millionaire
The reign of **Queen Juliana** (1909-   ) of the Netherlands almost ended in 1976 after charges that her husband, Prince Bern-

hard, had accepted an illicit payment of $1.1 million from Lockheed Aircraft Corporation. The queen supported her husband and said if he were proven guilty she would abdicate rather than rule in disgrace; 90 percent of the Dutch people said they wanted Juliana to remain their queen, and the ruling Socialists who had brought the matter to public attention backed down.

As a compromise, the prince resigned all official posts and apologized to the country. Some friends felt that the prince's annual $262,000 allowance, set by his wife Juliana, was inadequate, making it easy for him to be lured by extra money; the queen's annual stipend is $1.34 million.

Juliana is the daughter of Queen Wilhemina and Prince Henry of the Netherlands. In 1937, she married German Prince Bernhard, who was screened carefully for any possible Nazi sentiment before her mother and the Dutch government approved the match. When Germany invaded Holland during World War II, the royal family fled the country. Juliana and her two children lived in exile in London and Canada for five years.

She became queen in 1948. In 1949, she granted independence to Indonesia, and Holland lost most of its empire in the East Indies. In 1953, floods threatened the economy of the country. Despite these obstacles, the nation under her rule rose from debtor to creditor status.

Juliana has a reputation for being a sensible, strong-willed queen. She keeps protocol at a minimum, has abolished the curtsy, encouraged leftists to participate in government, and supported almost all international cooperative efforts.

Elizabeth II: Outmoded Monarch?
A recent British survey shows that even though England did away with the notion of the "divine right" of kings three hundred years ago, one-third of all the subjects of **Queen Elizabeth II** (1926-   ) still believe she was chosen by God to rule. This explains, in part, why, even during severe economic crises, few complaints are heard about the queen's annual $3 million royal budget that helps maintain her four castles, planes, railroad cars, yacht, and staff of 463.

Despite Britain's decline as a world power, Elizabeth II remains beloved by her subjects.

The daughter of Prince Albert, duke of York, who later became King George VI, and Lady Elizabeth Angela Marguerita Bowes-Lyon, she became at an early age the empire's "favorite little girl," nicknamed Lilibet. Married in 1947 to Philip Mountbatten (now Prince Philip, duke of Edinburgh), she acceded to the throne following the death of her father in February 1952.

Although she was tutored privately as a child, her four children have gone to school with other youths. Elizabeth has a reputation for being frugal by royal standards, conscientious, sensible, well-informed, and blunt. She is the sixty-third ruler in a monarchy that goes back ten centuries.

MADAME PRESIDENT?

"I do not think we have yet reached the point where the majority of our people would feel satisfied to follow the leadership and trust the judgment of a woman as president," said Eleanor Roosevelt in 1934. Her opinion was borne out by a Gallup Poll three years later, which found that fewer than one American in three would vote for a woman for president.

During the 1960s, only about half the voting public said it would support a female presidential candidate. But by 1976, the ranks of voters who would consider a woman for president had swollen to 73 percent of the American electorate.

Groups most likely to support a female contender were nonwhites, the college educated, young people, big city residents, and persons of above average wealth. Republicans, Southerners, rural residents, older people, and those whose education stopped at the grade school level were most antagonistic to women candidates. Ironically, 4 percent more men than women would support a female presidential aspirant.

The Seventies: Decade of Change

Women's widening role in the business and professional world largely accounts for the shift to attitudes favoring a woman president. Especially significant are the increasing numbers of women running for office and staffing political campaigns at all levels of government.

The presidential election year of 1972 marked a breakthrough for women in politics. New reform rules brought more women than ever before to the year's political party conventions. At the Democratic National Convention, in particular, the women's caucus emerged as a force to be reckoned with; the women took their fights for better representation on predominantly-male delegations, abortion reform, and nomination of a female vice presidential candidate, Frances "Sissy" Farenthold of Texas, to the convention floor. Though their issues went down to defeat, the women succeeded in making things hot for the men running the convention.

Female delegates returned from the party gatherings inspired by the other political women they had met. Their new spirit was contagious; chapters of the new National Women's Political Caucus (NWPC) sprang up across the nation, and women taught one another the skills of successful politicking. The Women's Political Campaign Fund was established to attack a perennial problem of women in politics — lack of money.

In a roundabout way, Watergate helped women politicians because the break-in and cover-up were men-only affairs — except, perhaps, for Rose Mary Woods; women's reputation for political honesty soared. As pollster Peter Hart noted in 1974, "Every time we ask who's more honest, men or women, a plurality will say women."

By 1974, the number of women seeking state and national office had risen sharply to eighteen hundred. "Ever since Abigail Adams helped her husband write the Declaration of Independence, women have been active in politics," noted Barbara Mikulski, now congresswoman from Maryland, in 1974. "This is the year women decided not to be ghostwriters anymore. We're taking our own backgrounds, talents, and expertise, and working for ourselves."

When the year's results were in, the number of women in Congress had increased from fourteen to eighteen, and Connecticut's Ella Grasso became the nation's first woman governor who did not follow her husband into office.

Though the number of women seeking and holding public office held steady in 1976, their visibility and political sophistication increased. Democrat Barbara Jordan and Republican Anne Armstrong were mentioned seriously as vice presidential contenders at their respective parties' conventions. Women increased their numbers at the Republican National Convention, and the Democratic Committee pledged that equal representation of the sexes would be "promoted" at future conventions. Even the candidates' wives talked politics instead of recipes.

As feminist leader Gloria Steinem noted, "The big distance traveled since Miami (the 1972 Democratic Convention at Miami Beach) is from outside to in; from being odd-ball feminists in the wilderness to functioning inside the Democratic party as, at least, a recognized pressure group and occasionally a majority that wins."

Politics Becomes a Career

The decade of the 1970s has also seen a decline in the average age of women seeking office. For many years, women entered politics as an outgrowth of volunteer work after their children had flown from the nest. The typical female state legislator, for example, was until recently fifteen to twenty years older than her male counterpart. Today, however, women are making politics a career rather than a hobby; they are starting younger and aiming higher.

According to Gallup, even more Americans — better than four out of five — would vote for a woman for Congress, governor, or mayor than would support a female presidential candidate. From the ranks of women currently filling these jobs may well come the nation's first woman president. Or she may be a figure already known to the American public. A 1975 survey of seven hundred politically active men and women ranked Representative Jordan, Governor Grasso, Representative Shirley Chisholm, former Representative Martha Griffiths, former NWPC Chairperson Farenthold, and former Ambassador Armstrong as the women they would most like to see as president.

Though prejudices remain to be overcome, the election of a woman president may be no more than a decade away. Attitudes have changed remarkably since 1952, when Margaret Chase Smith responded when asked what she would do if one day, she woke up in the White House: "I'd go straight to Mrs. Truman and apologize. Then I'd go home."

PUBLIC WOMEN

Abzug: "A Very Serious Woman"

"There are those who say I'm impatient, impetuous, uppity, rude, profane, brash, and overbearing," admits former New York Congresswoman **Bella Abzug** (1920-). "But whatever I am . . . I am a very serious woman," she says.

Daughter of a Russian immigrant meat merchant, Abzug graduated from Columbia University Law School in 1947, after taking time out from her education to work in a World War II shipbuilding plant.

"Some came early, some came late, Bella has been there forever," said columnist Jimmy Breslin about Abzug's involvement in the peace movement. The same could be said about her work for a number of civil rights and civil liberties causes. In 1949, for example, she courageously ventured into Mississippi to defend a young black man appealing his conviction for raping a white woman. The courts refused to uphold Abzug's argument that the trial had been unfair because blacks could not then serve on Mississippi juries.

Abzug first threw her trademark wide-brimmed hat in the political ring in 1970, and became the first Jewish woman ever elected to Congress.

The Congresswoman was dubbed "Battling Bella" from her first day on Capitol Hill, when she defied the long-standing custom that new representatives are to be seen but not heard. She introduced a resolution calling for United States withdrawal from Indochina.

Abzug served three terms in the House before leaving for an unsuccessful try at a Senate seat. The Congressional achievements of which she is proudest are: working to end the Vietnam war, bringing new jobs to her state, chairing a subcommittee on government information and individual rights, and working "in and out of Congress" on behalf of women. In June 1977

Bella Abzug joined picketing against the arms race outside the White House in 1975.

she announced her candidacy for mayor of New York City.

Armstrong: "The Hen Delivereth"

"The cock croweth, but the hen delivereth the goods," is a favorite saying of **Anne Armstrong** (1927-   ), former ambassador to Great Britain.

After bringing up her family on her husband's 50,000-acre Texas ranch, Armstrong entered Republican politics. At the 1972 Republican convention, she became the first woman ever to deliver a keynote address.

She joined the Nixon administration in 1973 as Cabinet-rank presidential counsellor for youth, Latinos, and women. Thanks largely to her efforts, there were soon three times more women than ever before in government policy-making jobs.

Though she pressed inside the embattled White House for full disclosure of the Watergate affair, Armstrong defended former President Nixon until his resignation. "I sounded like the social director on the Titanic," she ruefully recalled later.

President Ford pressed Armstrong into service again as the nation's first female ambassador to Great Britain. At her February 1976 swearing-in Armstrong remarked that Abigail Adams, wife of America's first ambassador to the Court of St. James, "would have been just as excited as Betty Ford and I," about a woman holding the post.

Armstrong was popular and respected among Britons; newspapers dubbed her "Auntie Sam" and "London's Rose of Texas." As guest of honor at a party in London of the Anglo-Texan Society, she wore cowboy boots beneath her long, formal gown.

Armstrong was frequently mentioned in Republican circles as a possible running mate for Ford in 1976.

Boggs: Courageous Widow

House Majority Leader Hale Boggs disappeared in a small plane while campaigning for an Alaskan colleague in 1972. With the courage that had marked her quarter century as a Washington wife, **Corinne "Lindy" Boggs** (1916-   ) announced her candidacy for his Louisiana Congressional seat two months later. She won the 1973 special election with a stunning 81 percent of the vote.

Life with the brilliant but scandal-tainted Hale Boggs had not been easy for the former plantation belle who became his wife. His support of the civil rights movement won him many enemies among his Louisiana constituents; a cross was once burned in the yard of their home. When rumors about her husband's drinking problem spread, Lindy Boggs helped mend his fences. Her political acumen and willingness to take on jobs like chairing the Kennedy and Johnson inaugural balls gained her many admirers.

Lindy Boggs, in 1976, became the first woman to preside as permanent chairman over a political party convention. Her firmly-wielded gavel helped insure that the Democratic Convention that nominated Jimmy Carter was one of the most peaceful in recent memory.

Bolton: "A Congressman's Congressman"

When Ohio Congressman Chester Bolton died in 1939, his wife, **Frances P. Bolton** (1885-1977), was named to succeed him. Bolton assumed she was appointed to her late husband's seat because she knew his thinking. "Actually," she remarked later, "I didn't have the slightest idea what he thought.

Bolton's own thoughts and labors during her distinguished twenty-eight-year House career won her the accolade as "the Congressman's Congressman" from Eleanor Roosevelt.

Bolton was ranking Republican on the Foreign Affairs Committee and chaired its subcommittee on Africa. She was dubbed "the African Queen" in 1955 when she set off on a three-month fact-finding tour. At her own expense, the seventy-one-year-old Bolton journeyed 20,000 miles to study hospitals, schools, and missions in twenty-four African countries.

From 1953 to 1956, Bolton was half of the only mother-son team ever to serve in Congress. Her youngest son, Oliver, represented an Ohio district adjoining her own. Bolton lost her 1968 reelection bid.

Burke: Homemaker's Champion

Among the many "firsts" scored by California's **Yvonne Brathwaite Burke** (1932-   ) is being the first Representative granted maternity leave by the Speaker of the House. Burke gave birth to

Yvonne Burke became in 1973 the first member of Congress to be granted maternity leave.

her daughter, Autumn, in November 1973, one year after her election to Congress.

Daughter of a janitor at MGM Studios, Burke grew up in what she described as "an integrated slum" in East Los Angeles. She paid her way through college and law school by working in a garment factory and modeling for *Ebony*.

When rioting broke out in L.A.'s Watts ghetto in 1964 she organized a legal defense fund and was an attorney for the commission that looked into the causes of the riots. She worked with the NAACP to prepare a report on local housing conditions for blacks.

Burke entered public life in 1966 by winning election to the California General Assembly where she headed the Urban Development Committee. When court-ordered reapportionment created a predominantly black Congressional district in southwest L.A. in 1972, Burke ran for the new seat and won. During her campaign she married a constituent, businessman William Burke, and was vice chairman of the volatile 1972 Democratic Convention.

Burke's most talked-about Congressional effort is her Equal Opportunity for the Displaced Homemaker Act. The bill would establish federally funded training programs for long-time housewives who have lost their means of support through divorce or widowhood.

Chisholm: "Unbought and Unbossed"

Shirley Chisholm (1924-   ) was persuaded to run for Congress by a black welfare mother who arrived at her door with a campaign contribution of $9.62 in small change. If Chisholm made the race, the woman promised, she and her friends would put on weekly fund raisers to keep the campaign going. "Her gesture moved me to tears," Chisholm recalled.

No stranger to poverty, Chisholm grew up on her grandmother's primitive Barbados farm and in a cold-water Brooklyn flat. Extremely bright, Chisholm became an expert in early childhood education. Chisholm also found time to win prizes as an amateur ballroom dancer.

She won election to the New York State Assembly in 1964, battling the political establishment all the way. In her 1968 House race, she was opposed by civil rights leader, James Farmer. She scored an impressive upset victory.

The new Congresswoman quickly won a reputation as a fighter when the House leadership tried to appoint her to the Agriculture Committee. "Apparently all they know here in Washington about Brooklyn is that a tree grows there," she said, seeking an assignment of greater relevance to her poor, urban constituency.

In 1972, Chisholm again challenged the

Upon entering the presidential race, Shirley Chisholm proclaimed herself the people's candidate.

odds by announcing her candidacy for president. She won 151.95 votes out of a little more than three thousand cast at the Miami Beach Democratic Convention. But with a little money and organization, said her friend and rival Hubert Humphrey, "she might have defeated us all."

An ardent supporter of women's issues, Chisholm once commented, "I've suffered worse discrimination as a woman than as a black." Her autobiography is aptly titled, *Unbought and Unbossed.*

Douglas: Broadway to Capitol Hill

Helen Gahagan Douglas (1900-   ), wrote columnist Heywood Broun, "*is* the ten most beautiful women in the world." Besides looks, Douglas had acting and singing talent that won her acclaim from the Broadway stage to European concert halls. She also had a social conscience, awakened during an Arizona trip with her husband, actor Melvyn Douglas, shortly after their 1932 marriage. "We ran head-on into the migrants of those days, thousands of them, living in boxcars and caves dug out of the sides of the hills. . . . I was shocked, and I really came of age at this time," she recalled.

With what might have been the greatest years of her performing career still ahead of her, Douglas gave up the stage for politics. "I got into politics step by step," she said. "I always meant to stop." She won election to Congress in 1944 from a working class district of Los Angeles.

After three terms, during which the *New Republic* named her "the most courageous fighter for Liberalism in Congress," Douglas set her sights on a U.S. Senate seat. Her opponent was a fellow Congressman who had already made a name for himself as a foe of the left. After he had finished trying to paint Douglas red, the victorious Richard Nixon had a reputation as a gloves-off campaigner as well.

Douglas never again ran for public office.

Ferguson: Two For One

"Two governors for the price of one," was the slogan with which **Miriam "Ma" Ferguson** (1875-1961) sought the governorship of Texas in 1924.

Ferguson's husband, "Farmer" Jim,

Miriam "Ma" Ferguson was sworn in for the first of her two terms as governor of Texas in 1927.

had twice won election to the same office. He was impeached during his second term for misusing public funds and barred from again holding a "state position of honor, trust or profit."

So Miriam Ferguson dutifully entered the gubernatorial race to "vindicate the good name of my husband." Though a cultured woman with a staff of servants, she donned a calico apron and invited the press into the kitchen to watch her can peaches. She soundly defeated her opponent, the hand-picked candidate of the Ku Klux Klan.

At her inauguration in 1925, she made it clear she would depend on her husband for guidance. Her first official act was to sign an amnesty bill restoring Jim Ferguson's right to hold office. (The law was rescinded by her successor.) During the next two years, the governor granted executive clemency to more than 3,500 persons, many of them bootleggers. The official mansion became known as "the house of 1,000 pardons."

Defeated in tries for a second term in 1928 and 1930, Miriam Ferguson was finally returned to the Texas governorship in 1932.

Despite her reliance on Farmer Jim, Miriam Ferguson was no yes-woman. A visitor to the governor's mansion once came upon her scolding her husband.

"That man you told me to appoint was no good," she reputedly said, "and I told you he wouldn't be. I'm going to have him put out, and the next time you've got to be more careful."

Grasso: Undefeated

Aspiring politicians would do well to study the political career of Connecticut Governor **Ella Grasso** (1919-   ), who has never lost an election in a quarter century of public life.

Daughter of Italian immigrants, Grasso began her political involvement during World War II with membership in the League of Women Voters. "I am grateful to the League," she says, "because through the training I received there I developed a real understanding of issues. And, more than that, how to translate them into action."

Her second wise move was winning the friendship of Democratic boss John Bailey, who put her to work campaigning and writing speeches. In 1952 Grasso entered her first electoral contest for the state's House of Representatives. Early in her first term, Grasso hurried off the House floor when a Democratic caucus was hastily called. To her chagrin, she discovered the meeting was being held in a men's room in the Capitol. "I suddenly realized that I could never be an equal member of that body until some very basic changes were made," she recalled.

Grasso moved on to serve three terms as Connecticut Secretary of State and two in the U.S. House of Representatives. In 1974 Grasso became what she terms "the first lady governor who was not previously a governor's lady." Austerity has been the keynote of Grasso's administration; she even cut her own salary by $7,000 and gave up a chauffeured limousine for a less expensive state police car.

Griffiths: ERA Strategist

Had it not been for **Martha Griffiths** (1912-   ), the Equal Rights Amendment might still be languishing in the House Judiciary Committee, as it had been for twenty years. But the Congresswoman from Michigan devised the strategy that got the measure out of committee and through Congress in 1972. Her one-time Michigan colleague, former President Gerald Ford, has called the ERA "a monument to Martha."

Griffiths began working for the amendment in 1955, the year this former state legislator and judge came to Congress.

Her analytic mind and persuasive skills soon won her a host of admirers. She became the first woman member of both the Joint Economic Committee and the House Ways and Means Committee. She fought to equalize Social Security benefits for men and women, once telling her colleagues she was "tired of paying into a pension fund to support your widow but not my widower." She chaired Congress' first hearings on the status of women.

Griffiths left Congress in 1974 to spend more time with her husband, Hicks, who had talked her into seeking her first public office in 1946.

"My grandmother wanted to live long enough to vote for a woman president," Griffiths once remarked. "I'll be satisfied if I live to see a woman go before the Supreme Court and hear the justices acknowledge 'Gentlemen, she's human. She deserves the protection of our laws.'"

Harris: Black Trailblazer

Patricia Roberts Harris (1924-   ) has mixed feelings about being a trailblazer among women of her race, most notably as the first black woman to reach ambassado-

Congresswomen Martha Griffiths (left) and Leonor K. Sullivan worked out at the House gym in 1965.

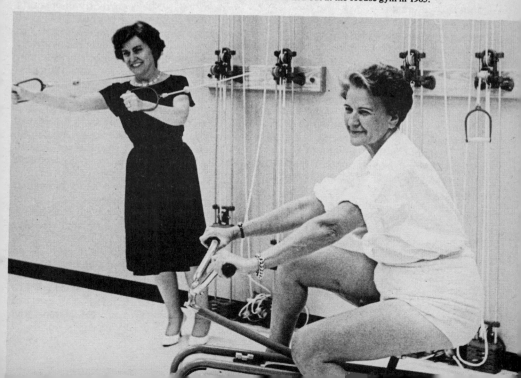

rial and cabinet rank. As she commented, when President Lyndon Johnson nominated her to be ambassador to Luxembourg in 1965, "I feel deeply proud and grateful . . . but also a little sad about being 'the first Negro woman' because it implies we were not considered before."

A descendant of slaves who worked to buy their freedom, Harris participated in one of the first civil rights sit-ins during her undergraduate days at Washington D.C.'s Howard University. With fellow students, she occupied the "colored only" section of a Washington restaurant.

After distinguishing herself as co-chairperson of the National Women's Committee for Civil Rights, and as a member of the Commission on the Status of Puerto Rico, Harris was tapped for the Luxembourg post. During her two years abroad she won praise for both charm and intellect.

Prior to being picked by then President-elect Jimmy Carter in late 1976 to head the Department of Housing and Urban Development, Harris was a partner in a Washington law firm. She had also been a board member of IBM, Scott Paper, and Chase Manhattan Bank, speaking out frequently for women's and minority interests.

Hills: Tennis Court to Cabinet

Attorney General Eliot Richardson flew to Los Angeles in 1973 to offer an assistant attorney general post to Roderick Hills. Though Hills turned him down, the trip was not in vain. Richardson was so impressed with Hills' wife, **Carla Anderson Hills** (1934-   ), that he subsequently offered her the job. She accepted, and rose in 1975 to be the third woman in U.S. history to head a Cabinet-level department, the Department of Housing and Urban Development.

Carla Hills was captain of the women's tennis team during her undergraduate days at Stanford University. With a classmate, she won the California intercollegiate women's doubles tournament. When she announced she wanted to go on to law school, her father refused to pay her tuition. So she financed her education herself, earning money during summer vacations by selling eggs.

In 1962 Hills and her husband helped found the Los Angeles law firm with which she practised until moving to Washington in 1974. She became the first female assistant attorney general since the early 1920s.

At his wife's urging to appoint more women to high government posts, President Gerald Ford tapped Hills to be Secretary of Housing and Urban Development in 1975.

Though she knew little about the housing industry when she took over HUD — a fact frequently harped upon by her early critics — Hills proved herself a quick learner. She won a reputation for cool efficiency; her greatest success was at moving the lethargic HUD bureaucracy to action.

Hobby: At Father's Knee

Oveta Culp Hobby (1905-   ) acquired political savvy early in life from her father, a member of the Texas legislature. She grew up reading the dry *Congressional Record* and became parliamentarian of the Texas House of Representatives at twenty.

She branched into journalism after marrying William Hobby, a former Texas governor and publisher of the *Houston Post,* in 1931. (She is currently the paper's editor and chairman of the board.)

Hobby went to Washington in 1941 to head the women's division of the War Department public relations office. She participated in planning for the Women's Army Corps, and became its first director in 1942. Believing the WACS "a serious job for serious women," she decreed that its recruits' frilly pink undies be replaced with regulation Army khaki.

President Dwight Eisenhower named Hobby in 1953 to head a government agency in charge of health, education, and social and economic assistance. Later that year the agency was upgraded to Cabinet status and Hobby became the first Secretary of Health, Education, and Welfare. Hobby implemented the president's budget-trimming designs, cutting back on school lunch, migrant education, and disease research programs. Her actions led political cartoonist Herblock to award her the title, "The Secretary of Not-Too-Much Health, Education, and Welfare."

Writer Jimmy Breslin ranked Liz Holtzman's 1972 win among the century's most important elections.

Holtzman: "Lion Killer"

Shy young **Elizabeth Holtzman** (1941-   ) became "Liz the Lion Killer" in 1972 by scoring an upset primary victory over long-time incumbent Congressman Emanuel Celler, mighty head of the House Judiciary Committee. It was not Holtzman's first election victory. Running under the slogan, "Win With The Twins," Holtzman and her brother, Robert, were elected vice president and president, respectively, of their high school student government.

After graduation from Harvard Law School — one of fifteen women in a class of more than five-hundred — Holtzman worked in private practice and as New York Mayor John Lindsay's liaison with the parks and recreation department. She chose "Time For A Change" as the theme for her 1972 Congressional bid; ironically, it was the same slogan Celler had used when he first won the seat in 1922. Pressed for funds, Holtzman ran a "shoe leather" campaign in subway stations and supermarkets. "I found mothers taking their daughters up to meet me," she recalled. "They wanted their daughters to have a different conception of the possibilities for them."

Holtzman edged out the complacent Celler and her Republican general election opponent. Securing appointment to Celler's old Judiciary Committee, she won national fame during its 1974 hearings on the impeachment of Richard Nixon.

Jordan: Not "Run Of The Mill"

Texas Representative **Barbara Jordan** (1936-   ) stands a good chance of becoming the nation's first woman Supreme Court justice — if not its first woman president. "I always wanted to be unusual," says Jordan of her childhood. "I never wanted to be run of the mill." Her father, a warehouse clerk and Baptist preacher, spurred her on. He was critical if her report cards contained any grade lower than A.

Jordan captained Texas Southern University's victorious debate squad, and became the first black admitted to Boston University Law School. Following graduation in 1959, she set up practice on her parents' dining room table until she could afford an office.

After two unsuccessful campaigns, Jordan was elected to the Texas Senate in 1966. She garnered national notice in 1967 when President Lyndon Johnson sum-

Barbara Jordan brought down the house as 1976 Democratic Convention keynote speaker.

moned her to the White House for a briefing on his new civil rights program. Jordan, he said, "proved black is beautiful before we knew what it meant."

With the help of her old mentor, Jordan won a House seat in 1972 with 81 percent of the vote. She became the Old Confederacy's first black Congresswoman.

Jordan's reputation for eloquence was made in 1974 during the House Judiciary Committee's impeachment hearings. "My faith in the constitution is whole, it is complete, it is total," she declared in a voice that commanded attention.

Despite a solidly liberal voting record, Jordan has proven herself adept at reaching accommodation with the more conservative members of her party.

Jordan unwinds after a hectic legislative week by singing and playing the guitar; she favors spirituals, gospel, and folk tunes.

Keys: Ways and Means Romance

It had all the makings of a successful situation comedy. Attractive Congresswoman and handsome Congressman clash during debate on a tax bill. Serving on the same committee, they gain mutual respect. After many furtive kisses in the dignified halls of Congress, the two marry and live happily ever after serving the people who sent them to Washington.

But many of the Kansans represented by Congresswoman **Martha Keys** (1930-) did not find her 1976 marriage to Indiana Representative Andrew Jacobs quite so romantic. It was bad enough, they said, that Keys and her husband of twenty-six years had divorced only six months earlier. But, they added, a woman's place is with her husband; by marrying Jacobs, Keys had switched her loyalties from Kansas to Indiana.

Keys was then wrapping up her first term in Congress. A housewife and music teacher before her election, she had won high marks from her fellow members of the House Ways and Means Committee for her clear grasp of complex economic issues. For some time, the only obstacle between Keys and Jacobs was Abner Mikva, an Illinois Congressman who sat between them during Ways and Means sessions. He was eventually persuaded to change seats.

Key's private life caused her a tough

reelection battle in 1976, despite her protestations that her first marriage had been long dead and her second had no impact on her commitment to Kansas. She won narrowly, while Jacobs coasted to victory, *his* constituents apparently little concerned about the marriage.

Kreps: Feminist in the Cabinet

Juanita Kreps (1921-) did not gush with gratitude when Jimmy Carter chose her to be his Secretary of Commerce. Instead, she promptly took her new boss to task for failing to appoint more women to high government posts. To Carter's excuse that few qualified women could be found for such positions, Kreps suggested he do a "better job of looking."

Kreps grew up in Kentucky's mining country and worked her way through Berea College, a small school for the disadvantaged. There she delved into the study of economics.

Kreps went on to earn her master's degree and doctorate from Duke University, where she began her teaching career in 1955. She was the school's vice president at the time she was named to Carter's Cabinet.

Recent legislation has extended the power of Kreps' Commerce Department. The department, for example, recently began to oversee ocean floor mining,

Juanita Kreps has written five books, including *Sex in the Marketplace: American Women at Work*.

Clare Boothe Luce called President Truman "a gone goose" at the 1948 Republican Convention.

coastal development, and the 200-mile fishing limit.

Kreps is quick to acknowledge the difficulty of juggling the demands of husband, children, and career. "I'm a very ordinary cook," she admits, "and my house is not all that clean." When her two daughters once asked why she did not stay home and bake cookies like other mothers, Kreps laughingly responded, "I don't make very good cookies."

Luce: Superwoman
"There is nothing **Clare Booth Luce** can't do," once wrote *Collier's* columnist Frank Genvasi. "She might even get to be President or Vice President." Indeed, the achievements of **Clare Booth Luce** (1903-   ) as writer, reporter, Congresswoman, ambassador, and consummate political phrasemaker would seem sufficient for any five women.

Born into what she termed "genteel poverty," Luce had a brief, unspectacular career as a child actress. She understudied for Mary Pickford in the play, *The Good Little Devil,* but Pickford never missed a performance.

Her first political venture came in 1922 as a propagandist for the National Woman's Party. Donning leather helmet and goggles, she scattered from an airplane leaflets announcing the seventy-fifth an-

niversary of the Seneca Falls women's convention.

She turned her talents from magazine editing to playwrighting after her 1935 marriage to Henry R. Luce, founder of Time, Inc. The most successful of her plays was *The Women,* a study of bitchiness among the idle rich. She visited Europe, Asia, and Africa for *Life* early in World War II; she was the last woman out of Warsaw before the Nazi invasion.

Believing the Democratic Party under Franklin Roosevelt was mismanaging the war, Luce campaigned for the Republicans in 1942. She dazzled a Madison Square Garden political rally with her rhetoric, and was picked to run for Congress from Connecticut two years later.

Luce became her state's first female Representative, and won a seat on the important Military Affairs Committee.

She left Congress in 1949, but returned to public life when President Eisenhower appointed her Ambassador to Italy. She served in that post for four years, and helped negotiate the division of Trieste.

McCormack: Anti-Abortion Candidate
"If things have gotten so bad that a housewife from Merrick (Long Island) says she is running for president, then it's time for a change," said **Ellen McCormack** (1926-   ), a housewife from Merrick, in

late 1975. The issue that got McCormack
fired up was abortion, which she vehemently opposes. At the request of the
Long Island-based Pro-Life Committee,
she entered the 1976 Democratic presidential race.

Aside from a childhood post in the Girl
Scouts, McCormack had never held public
office.

Following her graduation from high
school, McCormack was a legal secretary.
She married a New York City Police inspector. The McCormacks have four children. She joined the anti-abortion movement in 1970 by helping found Women
for the Unborn, a group that sought to
focus more media attention on the pro-life
position.

McCormack freely admitted she was a
one-issue candidate, though she came out
for day care centers and gun control,
while opposing capital punishment and the
ERA. She disliked the nitty gritty of politics.

Though lacking money and organization. McCormack did not give up her campaign. Roughly nine months after she took
to the stump. McCormack's name was
placed in nomination at the Democrats'
Madison Square Garden convention; she
received twenty-two delegate votes out of
the more than three thousand cast.

Mesta: "Hostess With The Mostess"

The reputation of **Perle Mesta** (1889-1975)
as America's "hostess with the mostess"
may never be surpassed.

Mesta aspired to a concert singing
career before her marriage to a wealthy
Pittsburgh manufacturer. She began her
Washington party-giving as a Republican
during World War I, and was said to have
been courted after her husband's death by
Charles Curtis, vice president under Herbert Hoover. Mesta later decided that
Democrats had more fun, and emerged as
the capital's premier hostess during the
administration of her long-time friend,
Harry Truman.

She was rewarded in 1949 by being appointed U.S. envoy to Luxembourg. One
of her greatest challenges in the post was
the bad feeling created by U.S. servicemen who visited the tiny country on leave
and got roaring drunk. Mesta persuaded
the GIs to make her residence their local

Luxembourg was Perle Mesta's reward for befriending
Harry Truman and raising funds for his campaign.

headquarters, and provided entertainment
and moderate refreshment until it was time
for them to return to their barracks.

Mesta arrived back in Washington in
1953 and resumed her gaily informal party
giving. She was the inspiration for Irving
Berlin's musical, *Call Me Madam*.

Perkins: "Be Ye Steadfast"

Proper daughters of wealthy New England
Republicans did not frequent tenements,
sweatshops, and picketlines. But **Frances
Perkins** (1882-1965) nonetheless cast pro-
priety aside to become a leading champion
of the nation's working class.

Though her family frowned upon
women working outside the home, they
permitted Perkins to take a job teaching
chemistry in Chicago, following her
graduation from college. She soon found
her way to Jane Addams' Hull House,
where she lived and worked among immigrant women. After witnessing the needless deaths of 146 women in New York
City's 1911 Triangle Shirtwaist Company
fire, Perkins devoted herself to lobbying
for laws to protect workers. She took her
cause to the state capitol at Albany, where
she became a protege of Governors Al
Smith and Franklin Roosevelt.

When President-Elect Roosevelt began
forming a team to guide the nation out of

Frances Perkins carried her fight for the working class from Hull House to White House.

Depression, he quickly decided upon Perkins to head the Department of Labor. She became, in 1933, the first woman in a president's cabinet. Laws establishing Social Security, minimum wages, maximum hours, and labor's right to organize were helped along by Perkins.

One of the two Cabinet members who remained in Roosevelt's administration until his death, Perkins was often a lonely figure. Labor distrusted her because she was not one of their own. Right-wingers sought her impeachment over her reluctance to deport a leftist labor leader. She silently agonized over her alcoholic, manic-depressive husband, whom she loyally refused to divorce.

Perkins took solace in the verse from I Corinthians that she adopted early in life as her personal creed: "Be ye steadfast, unmovable, always abounding in the work of the Lord, forasmuch as ye know your labor is not in vain."

Rankin: "I Cannot Vote For War"

"I want to stand by my country," declared Congresswoman **Jeannette Rankin** (1881-1973) in April 1917. "But I cannot vote for war." That conviction cost her, not one political career, but two.

Women could vote in very few states when Rankin campaigned for one of Montana's at-large House seats in 1916. "I am deeply conscious," she said after her hard-won victory, "of my responsibility as the first woman to sit in Congress. I will represent not only the women of Montana, but also the women of the country."

She helped lead the battle in Congress for the suffrage amendment, and proposed a maternity and infant health bill that became law in 1921. But she received most attention for voting to oppose U.S. entry into World War I. Though forty-nine Congressmen voted with her, Rankin was singled out for abuse.

After a futile run for the U.S. Senate, Rankin left Congress in 1919 to work as a lobbyist for consumer and peace groups.

Her brown hair had turned white by 1940, when she was elected to a second House term. Ironically, another declaration of war came before that Congress in December 1941. But this time, only Rankin voted no. It was said her political career as good as ended that day. She did not seek re-election.

Emporia (Ks.) Gazette Editor William

Jeannette Rankin twice committed political suicide by voting against resolutions of war.

Allen White was one of the few contemporaries to give Rankin points for courage: "The *Gazette* entirely disagrees with the wisdom of her position," he wrote, "but, Lord, it was a brave thing! And its bravery somehow discounted its folly."

Rankin never gave up the fight for peace. In 1968, she led a "brigade" of several thousand women on a peace march to the steps of the Capitol.

Ray: Nonconformist Governor

"If I don't conform to the image of what a governor should be or act like, I'm sorry," says Washington's **Dixy Lee Ray** (1914-   ). "But I'm not going to spend hours agonizing over it." In truth, Ray seems not at all apologetic for the unconventionality that has characterized her from birth.

Ray's parents were so convinced she was going to be a boy that they had no girl's name selected for her. Listed on her birth certificate as "Baby Ray," the child soon won the title "Little Dickens" for her antics. The nickname was shortened to "Dick" and later to "Dixy." ("Lee" came from distant relative Robert E. Lee)

Ray spent much of her childhood out of doors, acquiring a love of nature that inspired her to choose a career in marine biology. She came to public attention in 1972, when President Richard Nixon appointed her to the Atomic Energy Commission. She became head of the AEC one year later. Then the most powerful woman in the federal government, Ray opened up the AEC's activities to public scrutiny. The AEC was split into two new agencies in 1974, and Ray moved to the State Department as assistant secretary for oceans and international environmental matters. When Secretary of State Henry Kissinger failed to consult her as much as she though appropriate, Ray resigned. Some suggested the stuffy State Department was not the place for Ray, who dressed in tweeds and knee socks and lived in a twenty-eight-foot trailer with her two dogs.

Ray returned to her native Washington, and surprised state politicos by jumping into the 1976 gubernatorial race. She swept into office despite a late start and haphazard organization, promising fiscal austerity and government streamlining.

Ross: "No Bad Memories"

Wyoming was both the first state to give women the vote and the first to inaugurate a woman governor. She was **Nellie Tayloe Ross** (1876-   ).

Ross, mother of three, who had never before given a public speech, was elected in 1924 to fill out her late husband's gubernatorial term. She ran for reelection in 1926, but lost in a close race. Some said she had been too cautious.

Ross became a state legislator and vice-chairman of the 1928 Democratic National Convention. There she seconded the presidential nomination of Governor Al Smith, and herself received thirty-one votes for vice president.

She directed the women's division of Franklin D. Roosevelt's 1932 presidential campaign, and was appointed by the new president to head the U.S. Mint. The first woman to hold the post, she served from 1933 to 1953. When the nation began coming out of the Depression, the demand for coins broke all previous records. Ross distinguished herself with hard work, and she kept the mint turning out money twenty-four hours a day, seven days a week.

One of the few women of her generation in politics, Ross recalled as her hundredth birthday neared, "I have no bad memories. People always treated me well."

Schroeder: "I'm That Nut"

When first running for Congress in 1972, a grinning **Pat Schroeder** (1940-   ) began her speeches: "Hi! I'm that nut you've been hearing about . . . the one who leaps over barricades uttering obscenities, the one who keeps the kids in the freezer." Coloradoans saw the ludicrousness of similar innuendos about women politicians and elected Schroeder to the House.

Both Schroeder and her husband, Jim, are attorneys; they met in the Harvard University Law Library. Mother of two, she was counsel for Planned Parenthood of Colorado before her election to Congress.

Schroeder's first battle after reaching Washington was for a seat on the powerful House Armed Services Committee. The staunchly pro-military committee was hardly prepared for any woman, let alone one who made no secret of her frequent opposition to the Pentagon. "Defense

Pat Schroeder's only regret about going to Congress was having to give up blue jeans for dresses.

people say they are protecting women and children," says Schroeder. "As a woman with children I want to be able to say there are other things we can do to protect us than build bases."

Smith: Woman of Conscience
During her first Senate campaign in 1948, **Margaret Chase Smith** (1897-   ) slipped on an icy pavement in Bangor, Maine and broke her arm. But she was back on the campaign trail later the same afternoon. Smith had little tolerance for any obstacle — whether it was a broken arm, anti-Communist hysteria, or the fact that a woman had never done it before — that threatened to stand in her way. Yet she remained as cool as the fresh rose she placed in her lapel each day.

Smith's maiden speech after winning election to the Senate — she had already spent more than eight years in the House — was a courageous "declaration of conscience," critical of Senator Joseph McCarthy's red witch hunts. "The American people," she said, "are sick and tired of being afraid to speak their minds lest they be politically smeared as 'communists' or 'facists' by their opponents." She was the first Senator to speak out against McCarthy.

Smith sought the vice-presidential nomination at the 1952 Republican con-

vention. She claimed she had 250 delegates pledged to her through supporters of former presidential candidate Thomas Dewey. But, she said, Dwight Eisenhower learned of her strength and ordered his lieutenants: ". . . by no means let her name come to the floor." Instead, Richard Nixon became the Republican vice presidential nominee.

Twelve years later Smith made a try for the nation's highest office by running in two presidential primaries. She became the first woman ever placed in nomination for president at a major party convention.

Smith lost her bid for election to a fifth Senate term in 1972.

Sullivan: Consumer Crusader
Signing into law the Consumer Credit Protection Act of 1968, President Lyndon B. Johnson praised "that able Congresswoman from Missouri" who fought "— and I say 'fought' — for a strong and effective bill when others would have settled for less." He was speaking of **Leonor K. Sullivan** (1904-   ), a leading voice for consumers during her twenty-four year Congressional career.

"I remember what it was like when I arrived," she said. "Those of us interested in consumer legislation could have caucused in an elevator." But she succeeded in winning her colleagues' support for many consumer laws, including federal inspection of poultry, protesting of chemical food additives, prohibiting the sale of foods with cancer-causing ingredients, and stronger controls on pep pills, barbiturates, and other drugs.

Many low-income families have Sullivan to thank for the food stamps that enable them to eat better for less. Sullivan began fighting for the food stamp plan in her first Congressional term, and lobbied three presidents before the program was extended nationwide in 1964.

Wallace: Uncomplaining Wife
The deeds of **Lurleen Wallace** (1926-1968) may never win her a place alongside the statesmen in John F. Kennedy's *Profiles in Courage*. But she was a woman of great personal courage, nonetheless.

At sixteen, she was tending a variety store cash register when George Wallace, a law student awaiting induction into the

Army Air Corps, came in to buy a nickel chocolate bar. They were married soon after, and she accompanied him to a New Mexico base, where they lived in a converted chicken coop.

Aside from fishing, riding horseback, and learning to fly, she remained at home while her husband built up a reputation as the South's most outspoken foe of integration. During George Wallace's 1962 campaign for governor, her innate shyness was considered a political liability.

But when Alabama law prohibited George Wallace from seeking a second term in 1966, he announced Lurleen would run instead. On the campaign trail, she surprised Alabamians with her polish and vivacity. When reporters noted she looked wan as election day neared, she dismissed them with, "I've been dying of cancer for five years, if you believe the rumors." She had had a malignant tumor removed only weeks before launching her campaign.

Though she deferred to her husband on most issues, the decision to increase funding for state mental hospitals was credited to Lurleen Wallace, alone.

She underwent a second cancer operation six months into her term, and died the following year. Many Alabamians still revere Lurleen Wallace, who stoically bore her pain out of devotion to her husband.

BECOMING POLITICAL

From the halls of Congress to the local PTA, women are flexing their political muscles as never before. But for the woman whose life has been preoccupied with family, job, or school, the leap into politics can seem frightening.

It need not be if she takes it one step at a time. Political activism can mean everything from staying abreast of current events to running for president.

Make the news a family affair. It's never too early to begin teaching children the importance of staying informed.

Inform Yourself
The first step on the path to political savvy is learning about local, state, national, and international affairs. Try to set aside some time each day for reading the newspaper.

Find out when local governing bodies — such as school board, city council, or planning commission — meet, and attend some of their sessions to observe democracy in action. Check in advance to ascertain whether there are interesting items on the agenda.

It's challenging to compare your political views with those of family, friends, and neighbors. You might organize a weekly coffee and political conversation group for the women in your neighborhood.

Write A Letter
You might also wish to convey your political views to your elected representatives. The offices of most local officials are listed under the city and county headings in your phone book. State legislators can be addressed in care of your state capitol. Mail for U.S. representatives and senators can simply be marked "U.S. Capitol, Washington, D.C." The zip code is 20515 for House members and 20510 for senators.

Busy elected officials usually prefer to hear from constituents by letter rather than by phone. Keep your message clear, direct, and short; maximum length should be one page. Be sure to state precisely what you want the official to do about the problem you raise: Should he or she introduce a bill? Make a speech? Vote a particular way on a bill already under consideration? Cover only one topic per letter. The more professional your letter appears, the more likely it is you will receive a prompt, solicitous answer. Messages typed on letterhead or plain white paper convey an aura of authority. Be sure to include a return address so that the officeholder can respond to the points you raise. Don't feel miffed if you do not receive an answer by return mail; some senators receive almost as much mail as Ann Landers.

Scrutinize the Candidates
Being well informed is especially important at election time when political charges and countercharges fill the air.

The League of Women Voters urges you to look through the smokescreens of phony issues and personal smears that some candidates create. Beware, for example, of such techniques as name calling, rumormongering ("Although everyone says my opponent is a crook. I have no personal knowledge of any such wrong-doing.''), and guilt by association (''My opponent has the support of a bunch of long-haired weirdos.''). Decide which candidates address the important issues affecting their constituents. There is nothing wrong with a candidate who occasionally admits to not knowing the solution to a problem; far more suspect is the person who prescribes miracle cures.

After you view a paid political ad on television, the league advises that you ask yourself: ''What did the agency-tailored, custom-made product tell me about Candidate X? Did the ad change my attitude? If so, was it because of the music, the scenery, the snappy script, or did I learn something about an issue — something important?''

Likewise, scrutinize a candidate's leaflets and ''personalized'' letters to see if he or she is speaking about the real issues, rather than about lodge membership, pet dogs, or vague support of motherhood and apple pie. Investigate the reliability of polls and group ratings that candidates cite in their behalf.

Attend meetings and rallies prepared to ask tough questions. Also, feel free to pose questions to campaign workers who appear on your doorstep distributing a candidate's literature; if they do not know the answer to your query, they should pass it along to somebody at campaign headquarters who does.

As election day nears, the league advises that you make your decision on the basis of the issues of greatest importance to you and how you believe they should be handled. Note the candidates' stands on those issues, and vote for the person whose views most closely match your own regardless of looks, political party affiliation, or marital status.

Well in advance of the election, be sure to check on your community's voter registration laws. Generally, first-time voters must make formal application, declaring that they are U.S. citizens aged eighteen or above who have lived at their current address for a specified period of time. If you did not vote in the last general election or have since moved or changed your name, you are usually required to re-register.

Check local voter registration laws. Usually you can't vote unless you're signed up.

Work for a Candidate

Women have long been the foundation of political campaigns. Most high-ranking politicians owe much of their success to a loyal female corps of envelope stuffers, telephoners, and party givers. Recently, women have also begun to move into such visibility jobs as campaign manager, press secretary, and advance person.

For the political novice, the best place to enter a campaign is at the volunteer level. Contact the person heading the campaign in your area and offer your services. Be sure to mention any special abilities that might make you valuable to the campaign; for example, your singing talents might be put to good use at a fund raiser or your writing skills might get you a speechwriting post. Don't despair if your first tasks seem mundane; there are always plenty of advancement opportunities for eager volunteers.

During the political off-season, you might wish to continue your involvement through membership in local political clubs or community service organizations. Meet as many people as possible. Learn what issues other women are concerned about. Discover how deals are made and promises extracted. Volunteer to take on tough projects that will demonstrate your mettle. By the time the next campaign rolls around, you might well find yourself in a position of considerable clout. Many political volunteers have moved up to permanent paying jobs in advertising, public relations, lobbying, or campaign management. If your candidate is victorious, you might win a job on his or her staff.

Join A Club

The political club is no longer the domain of the cigar-chomping ward heeler. Two predominantly female political organiations are emerging as good proving grounds for aspiring women politicos.

Though the League of Women Voters is hardly an infant — it was founded in 1920 by feminist Carrie Chapman Catt to educate recently enfranchised women voters — it gained new stature in 1976 by organizing the presidential and vice presidential debates.

The league — now 160,000 members strong — is strictly nonpartisan, meaning that it neither runs nor endorses candidates. Instead, it concentrates on researching issues, monitoring government performance, and lobbying for measures ranging from tax reform to the Equal Rights Amendment. The league's voter service arm sponsors citizen education projects, arranges candidate forums, participates in voter registration campaigns, and publishes information on candidates and issues.

For further information, contact the League of Women Voters of the U.S., 1730 "M" Street, N.W., Washington, D.C. 20036. Or check the telephone directory for your local league chapter.

While the league is nonpartisan, the 35,000-member National Women's Political Caucus calls itself "multi-partisan." The primary objective of the increasingly sophisticated caucus is to involve more women in politics both as campaign workers and as candidates. Founded in 1972 as "the political arm of the women's movement," the caucus has encouraged women candidates of all political persuasions. It has worked to change the practices that kept women in menial positions in the party structure, has forged coalitions of women delegates to the 1976 Republican and Democratic National Conventions, and has bargained with the Carter administration to get more women into top federal jobs.

The caucus's national offices are at 1411 "K" Street, N.W., Washington, D.C. 20005.

Into The Ring

The final stage in becoming political is running for office yourself. Before taking the leap, suggests Congresswoman Pat Schroeder, "Assess critically your own qualifications; examine carefully the real base of your support; build credibility; develop a strong grass-roots organization; use innovative and hard hitting media; be issue oriented."

Start out small. Many a prominent woman politician has begun her career as PTA president or precinct committeewoman.

Get your family behind you from the start. Explain to them that the campaign must take priority for a certain number of weeks or months.

Women often dislike asking for money. But, like it or not, dollars can make or break a campaign. The first person you recruit to your cause should be a talented fund raiser. While you're raising money, make a plan for how to spend it. Don't spend all your funds on campaign buttons — you may be left high and dry when it's time to buy radio advertising.

Volunteers can often be vital. Start with your friends and political contacts, and ask them to pass the word to others. High school and college students can be indefatiguable helpers — many are now assigned to spend time campaigning as part of their political science studies.

Be sure to contact political organizations and women's groups for advice, volunteers, and money.

Open a headquarters, even if it is initially nothing more than a handy basement or garage. Furnish it with sturdy tables and chairs, a telephone and someone to answer it, information on your district, precinct maps, your position papers, and lists of registered voters and volunteers.

Let the news media know you are off and running. Seek out somebody with press experience to work at getting you free publicity. Speak before any organization willing to listen, whether it has five members or five hundred. Each speaking engagement will make your next outing that much easier.

Most of all, prepare yourself psychologically for the campaign and its outcome. Politics is a tough business, and opponents are not always honest and fair in the charges they level against you. It is especially important for women to learn to keep their cool — and that includes fighting back even the most justified tears. And remember that few politicians since George Washington have won every race they entered.

THE WOMAN'S VOTE

When women won the vote in 1920, some pundits foresaw a string of matinee idol-presidents more notable for their looks than their intelligence. The Gallup Poll's findings on women's voting behavior would surprise them. The two most handsome presidential candidates of recent times — John F. Kennedy and Jimmy Carter — would not have been elected had women voters had their way.

Much to the chagrin of idealistic feminists like Carrie Chapman Catt — and much to the relief of political bosses and interest groups — women have consistently voted much like men. Variables such as education, income, and race are more significant than sex in predicting how an individual will vote.

Still, there are differences in men's and women's voting behavior. Women tend to favor the more moderate candidate; hence, extremists like Barry Goldwater in 1964 and George Wallace in 1968 were rejected by more women than men. Women are less likely to change a fairly respectable horse in midstream, a trait that may have led them to support Gerald Ford over Carter in 1976.

Women pay less attention than men to a candidate's political party or ideological label. Instead, they give greater weight to character and personal life. It is commonly thought that women favored Dwight D. Eisenhower over Adlai Stevenson in 1952 and 1956 because of the former general's "father image" and his opponent's divorce.

Kennedy's youthful brashness and Catholicism caused him to lose women's votes to Richard Nixon in 1960. However, women narrowly favored Hubert Humphrey over Nixon in 1968, perhaps because they saw the Democratic candidate as more closely sharing their own interests in peace and civil rights.

Women started out favoring George McGovern, the peace candidate, in 1972. But Nixon's international achievements, his portrayal of McGovern as an indeci-

Vote By Groups in Presidential Elections Since 1952

	1952		1956		1960			1964
	Stevenson %	Ike %	Stevenson %	Ike %	JFK %	Nixon %	LBJ %	Goldwater %
Total	44.6	55.4	42.2	57.8	50.1	49.9	61.3	38.7
Sex								
Male	47	53	45	55	52	48	60	40
Female	42	58	39	61	49	51	62	38

	1968			1972		1976		
	HHH %	Nixon %	Wallace %	McGovern %	Nixon %	Carter %	Ford %	McCarthy %
Total	43.0	43.4	13.6	38	62	50	48	1
Sex								
Male	41	43	16	37	63	53	45	1
Female	45	43	12	38	62	48	51	*

Based on Gallup Poll Survey Data

sive radical, and the mismanaged Eagleton affair brought women back to the Republican fold.

On the issues, other studies have shown women to be more inclined than men to favor spending for domestic purposes rather than for military hardware or space shots. More women support environmental, consumer, and civil rights measures. However, women are less likely than men to accept busing, which many of them see as a threat to their children's safety. Women are more inclined to oppose capital punishment.

Women as a whole go to the polls less frequently than men. In the 1920 election — the first balloting after suffrage was ratified — only one-third of the eligible female voters participated. By 1972, women's participation rate had risen to 62 percent, compared with 64 percent for men.

Between 75 and 95 percent of women are said to vote like their husbands, though who is telling whom how to vote remains a matter of conjecture. A 1972 poll revealed that 64 percent of women and 60 percent of men believed women did not necessarily vote as their husbands told them.

AMERICA'S ROYAL FAMILIES

Traditionally one of the most admired women in the land is the president's wife. Even Lady Bird Johnson and Pat Nixon, whose husbands at times were unpopular with the American people, remain beloved public figures.

Long before Eleanor Roosevelt, first ladies did far more than shake hands and pour tea. Today, first ladies have proven themselves eloquent representatives of their husbands — and effective "pillow talk" lobbyists for women's concerns.

Here are the forty-one women who married presidents:

"I sometimes think the arrangement is not quite as it ought to have been," wrote **Martha Washington,** early in her husband's administration, "that I, who had much rather be at home, should occupy a place with which a great many younger and gayer women would be prodigiously pleased." Yet she laid her homesickness aside to enliven the then New York capital with sparkling teas, popular among George's friends and foes alike. The weekly fetes often came to an abrupt halt upon Martha's announcement that her husband's 9 p.m. bedtime was long past. A widow, and a year his senior, Martha dubbed her husband, "Old Man."

While deliberating the fate of the American colonies at Independence Hall, Continental Congressman John Adams received an unsolicited bit of advice from home: freedom from tyranny should extend to women as well as men. His strong-minded wife, **Abigail Adams,** took time off from running the family farm to write, urging that he "remember the ladies" in designing the new government. The Adamses were the first family to occupy the White House, a structure Abigail found dark, chilly, and unfinished. Ever resourceful, she strung a clothesline across the stately reception room to hang out the wash.

Thomas Jefferson described his marriage to the former **Martha Wayles** as "ten years of unchequered happiness." The couple often made music together, she singing and playing the harpsichord, while he fiddled. Her death at thirty-three drove him to pace the floor of his bedchamber for three weeks, stopping only to fall upon a pallet in complete exhaustion. Jefferson never married again, though he later had a forty-year liaison with Martha's mulatto half-sister, Sally Hemmings, a slave who was freed after his death.

Charming **Dolley Todd,** an attractive Philadelphia widow, could not make up her mind about Congressman James Madison's marriage proposal. Much to the indecisive young woman's embarrassment, Martha Washington summoned her to the president's residence to confer her blessing on the "engagement." For probably the first — and last — time in her life, Dolley was at a loss for words. After marrying Madison, she quickly gained a reputation as Washington's nineteenth century "hostess with the mostess." She was first lady for a record sixteen years, eight of them as hostess for widower Thomas Jefferson. She won her place in history in 1814 by saving valuable state documents and George Washington's portrait when the British advanced upon the White House.

Dolley Madison saved George Washington's portrait from British matches during the War of 1812.

Tiny but regal **Elizabeth Kortright Monroe** overcame chronic ill health to accompany her husband on diplomatic missions abroad. Stationed in Paris soon after the French Revolution, Elizabeth was credited with saving the life of the imprisoned Marchioness de Lafayette, wife of America's Revolutionary War benefactor. "La Belle Americaine," as Elizabeth was known, insisted upon visiting Madame Lafayette on the day the Frenchwoman was to be beheaded, and helped secure her release.

Daughter of an American envoy to London, **Louisa Johnson Adams** was the only first lady born outside the United States. She continued the family tradition by giving birth to one her four children in Berlin, and to another in the old Russian capital of St. Petersburg. When her husband became Secretary of State, Louisa entertained Washington society with weekly salons and fortnightly dinner dances. One newspaper wrote a lengthy poem after an especially lavish party she gave for war hero Andrew Jackson, each stanza ending with the refrain, "Belles and matrons, maids and madames, All are

gone to Mrs. Adams'." Louisa was plagued with ill health during her White House tenure, frequently succumbing to fainting spells, hysteria, and depression.

The most hotly debated issue of the 1828 Presidential campaign had nothing to do with the growth of the young nation and its increasing influence in the world. Instead, the crucial issue was the notorious first marriage of **Rachel Robards Jackson.** Rachel originally wed Andrew Jackson in 1791, mistakenly believing that a divorce from her first husband had already been granted. Though the Jacksons were married a second time after the divorce took effect, charges of adultery persisted. "Old Hickory" killed a man in a duel over his wife's honor. "Ought a convicted adulteress and her paramour husband to be placed in the highest offices of this free and Christian land?" asked Jackson's opponents in 1828. True, their mudslinging failed to defeat the popular war hero, but Rachel suffered a mental breakdown and died before her husband took office.

Although Martin and **Hannah Hoes Van Buren,** whom he fondly called "Jannetje," grew up together and spent twelve years as husband and wife, she received not a word of mention in his autobiography! She died at thirty-five, nineteen years before he became president. Little more is known of her than the description on her gravestone: "A sincere Christian, dutiful child, tender mother and most affectionate wife; precious shall be the memory of her virtue."

The widowed Van Buren took up residence in the White House with his four bachelor sons. Aghast that the mansion had no official hostess, Dolley Madison introduced the eldest son to her cousin, Angelica Singleton. The president soon had a daughter-in-law and the White House a new mistress.

Like many a father, Judge John Symmes did not think William Henry Harrison good enough for his daughter, **Anna Symmes Harrison.** When the Judge asked the young Army lieutenant how he intended to support Anna, Harrison replied, "My sword is my means of support, sir." Strong-minded Anna would not be deterred by her father's objections: during his absence from home, she called in Harrison and a justice of the peace and had the wedding performed. Wife of one president and grandmother of another (Benjamin Harrison), Anna never made the White House her home. Her husband caught cold during the inauguration, which was traditionally held outdoors, and died before Anna could join him in Washington.

Letitia Christian Tyler was in declining health by the time her husband reached the presidency. She appeared in public only once after his swearing in, at the White House wedding of her daughter. Nonetheless, all of Washington's elite attended her East Room funeral, and even the newspapers fiercely opposed to her husband published glowing eulogies.

Tall, dark, and flirtatious, **Julia Gardiner Tyler** married the widowed President when she was a mere twenty-four. She claimed Tyler had proposed to her at a costume ball which she attended dressed as a Greek maiden. "I said 'No, no, no' and shook my head with each word, which flung the tassel of my Greek cap into his face with every move," she recalled. After changing her mind, Julia held court at the White House like a queen. She introduced French cooking, dancing, and the playing of "Hail to the Chief" to the White House. An avid supporter of Texas statehood, she lobbied Senators and their wives to annex the Lone Star Republic.

The gaiety White House visitors enjoyed during Julia Tyler's reign was short lived. **Sarah Childress Polk,** a strict Presbyterian, deemed dancing, card playing, and refreshments "respectful neither to the house or the office" and banned them from public functions. Besides handling the customary domestic chores, the childless Sarah became her husband's skilled confidential secretary, often working alongside him ten to twelve hours a day. Of all America's Presidents, the stiff, humorless Polk is credited with the most romantic dying words: "I love you, Sarah. For all eternity, I love you."

Zachary Taylor boasted that his wife, **Margaret Smith Taylor,** was a better soldier than he. For thirty-five years, the plantation-bred Margaret followed him from one isolated army post to another. Dismayed that they could not retire in peace, she urged her husband not to seek the presidency. Taylor would have done well to heed her advice.

Like many schoolboys, Millard Fillmore fell head over heels in love with his first teacher, **Abigail Powers.** But Fillmore, too poor to attend school as a child, had the advantage of being a decade older than his classmates. Seven years later, his ex-teacher became his wife. Abigail, then an invalid, carried her love of learning to the White House. Astonished at not finding a single book in the mansion, she persuaded Congress to establish a White House library. She died after catching cold during the inauguration of her husband's successor. Fillmore was remarried after Abigail's death to Caroline McIntosh.

Jane Appleton Pierce was not eager for her husband to become president; she fainted promptly upon receiving word of his nomination and taught her son, Benny, to hope for his father's defeat. Benny was killed in a freak train accident shortly before Pierce's inauguration. The tragedy, which Jane considered divine compensation for her husband's election victory, cast a pall over the Pierce administration. The melancholy Jane spent her White House tenure dressed in black, writing letters to her dead son.

James Buchanan was America's only bachelor president, though he was briefly engaged to wealthy Ann Coleman in 1819. It was rumored that the conscientious Buchanan devoted too much time to his young law practice and not enough to Ann. She broke off the engagement and died of a drug overdose a few months later. Buchanan's White House hostess was his niece, **Harriet Lane Johnston,** whose extensive accumulation of paintings today forms the core of the National Collection of Fine Arts.

Like her beau, Abraham Lincoln, **Mary Todd** had a lively interest in politics. So lively that Lincoln almost had to fight a duel with a politician his future wife had ridiculed in a letter to the editor. Southern-born Mary suffered vicious press attacks during her husband's administration for her rumored Confederate sympathies and extravagant tastes. The latter charge was more valid than the former; Mary, who once purchased 86 pairs of gloves on a single shopping spree, accumulated a personal debt estimated at between $30,000 and $70,000. Mary's ec-

Extravagant Mary Lincoln eventually had to sell her White House finery to pay her bills.

centricities were aggravated by the premature deaths of her husband and three of her four children. Her sole surviving son had her briefly committed to a mental institution.

"There goes my beau," remarked **Eliza McCardle,** upon first spying the young tailor who would soon set up shop in her Tennessee village. True to her prophecy, she married Andrew Johnson a year later. Eliza taught her husband to write, and hired a man to read to him as he went about his stitching. Johnson continued to rely on her wise counsel during his White House years. Eliza never had to darn her husband's stockings; the self-reliant Johnson continued to sew his own clothing, even in the White House.

Julia Dent Grant was self conscious about her crossed eye, but her husband would not let her have it corrected. He said he loved her just as she was. After years of poverty and camp-following, Julia luxuriated in a garishly redecorated White House. She was enraged when her husband turned down a third term without consulting her. As consolation, he took

her on an round-the-world tour which included a barge on the Nile and the palaces of China, where they dined on a seventy-course dinner, including soles of pigeon's feet. Julia hesitated about descending into a Nevada gold mine they were visiting, but persevered bravely upon learning Grant had bet a dollar her fear would keep her above ground.

"Lemonade" **Lucy Hayes,** so called because lemonade was the strongest drink served at the White House during her tenure, was the first president's wife to graduate from college. She received her diploma from Ohio Wesleyan Women's College in 1851. Lucy silently endured her husband's unusually close relationship with his sister during the early years of their marriage. "You are Sister Fanny to me now," he told his wife after Fanny died in childbirth. Mother of a daughter and seven sons — Hayes once said the couple was in "the boy business" — Lucy initiated the traditional Easter egg roll on the White House lawn.

Lucretia "Crete" Garfield, a school teacher before her marriage to her childhood sweetheart, had a mother-in-law problem: her husband James' mother, who lived with the couple throughout most of their married life, even got the first kiss after his inauguration. though herself recuperating from a near-fatal case of malaria, Lucretia steadfastly remained at her husband's bedside during his lingering death, after he was felled by an assassin's bullet.

Daughter of a Navy hero who explored the Amazon, vivacious **Ellen Herndon Arthur** was an acclaimed soprano. Ellen died of pneumonia a year before her husband became president. Washington rumormongers thought a presidential wedding was in the offing when word leaked out that a woman's portrait adorned Arthur's bedchamber. But the picture turned out to be of Ellen; the president took time from the duties of his office to place fresh flowers beside it each day.

One of Grover Cleveland's few presidential actions to receive near-universal approval was his marriage to **Frances Folsom,** the young and beautiful daughter of his late law partner. Twenty-eight years his wife's senior, Cleveland had given her parents the carriage she rode in as a baby!

The newlywed Clevelands· were pursued on their honeymoon by an over-zealous press, which kept a spyglass trained on the couple's resort cottage. (Cleveland's long bachelorhood had not passed without affairs. During his first presidential campaign, he publicly assumed responsibility for fathering a child out of wedlock.) Five years after Cleveland's death in 1908 Frances married an archaeologist and professor.

While courting minister's daughter **Caroline Scott,** Benjamin Harrison spent so much time on her father's front porch that he came to be called the "pious moonlight dude." During her husband's administration, Caroline oversaw a major renovation of the White House; for the first time the presidential family had more than one bathroom. She helped found the Daughters of the American Revolution, and was its first regent. Caroline died two weeks before her husband lost his 1892 reelection bid. Harrison later married Caroline's niece, Mary Dimmick, who had taken the ailing Caroline's place as official hostess during the last two years of his administration. At age sixty-four, Harrison became a father for the third time.

After the early deaths of her two children, the distraught **Ida Saxton McKinley** developed epilepsy, then an uncontrollable affliction. Despite frequent convulsions, Ida insisted upon accompanying her husband to all social engagements. The devoted McKinley became adept at covering his wife's face with a handkerchief to cover her blank eyes and salivating mouth. The American public never knew of her illness. Even in the moments after he was shot by an assassin, McKinley's thoughts turned to Ida. "My wife," he exclaimed to his secretary, "Be careful . . . how you tell her — oh, be careful."

Double tragedy struck Theodore Roosevelt in 1884: his mother, Martha, and wife, **Alice Lee,** died within two days of one another. He never mentioned Alice's name again, not even to her namesake born days before her mother's death. TR's second wife, **Edith Carow Roosevelt,** treated her ebullient husband like a small child. After the birth of the couple's fourth son, she remarked, "Now I have five boys." If the president ever tried to stay at his desk past 10:30 p.m. Edith's "Theo-

dore!" firmly reminded him it was bedtime. Edith's stepdaughter, Alice, was as frisky as her father; her youthful escapades included jumping fully clothed into a swimming pool, over indulging in wine on a visit to China, smoking on the White House roof when her father forbade her to do so inside, and entertaining young men by dancing in her chemise. Commented Roosevelt, "I can either run the country or control Alice, not both." Today in her nineties, Alice Roosevelt Longworth is still entertaining Washington society with her antics and sharp tongue.

Strong-willed **Helen Herron Taft** had greater expectations for her good-natured, slow-moving husband than he had for himself. During a visit to the White House as a teenager, the future first lady announced she liked the mansion so well that she intended to preside over it one day. Her son Robert, and grandson Robert Jr., represented their native Ohio in the U.S. Senate. "Nellie" Taft dutifully accompanied her husband to public functions, including Cabinet meetings, prepared to place an elbow in his ample side when he invariably began dozing off. She preceded Lady Bird Johnson in beautifying the nation's capital; the cherry trees lining Washington's tidal Basin were her idea.

A talented painter, **Ellen Axson Wilson** worked as first lady to improve the capital's slum neighborhoods. She took Congressmen on tours of the city's worst alleys until they passed a badly needed housing bill. The President could scarcely be consoled when Ellen died midway into his first term. To ease Wilson's depression, his doctor introduced him to the woman who would become his second wife, wealthy widow **Edith Galt.** When Wilson suffered a disabling stroke late in his administration, Edith came closer than any other woman to being president. For seventeen months she helped run the government in Wilson's name from behind the door of his sickroom. Contrary to her critics' claims, Edith was not power hungry, she simply sought to keep up the pretense that her husband was doing his job. Though resignation was contemplated, Wilson's doctors feared it would kill his will to live, and Thomas R. Marshall, the vice president, was generally thought an unfit successor.

Nicknamed by her husband "The Duchess," stern faced **Florence Kling Harding** ruled the business department of his newspaper, the Marion *Star* (Ohio), with an iron fist. She was stingy with raises, but generous with spankings for newspaperboys who loafed on the job. Florence was determined to make her husband president, though the affable, lazy Harding pleaded with her to let him abandon the race when he fared poorly in the early rounds. "Well, Warren Harding," she remarked after the election was won, "I have given you the presidency; what are you going to do with it?" (She was said to always call him "Warren Harding.") Florence refused to permit an autopsy when Harding died on a cross-country excursion, fueling rumors that she had poisoned him. Immediately after the funeral, she set about burning most of her husband's official papers, many of which alluded to his extramarital affairs and other shenanigans.

Grace Goodhue Coolidge, as effusive as husband "Silent Cal" was terse, worked at a school for the deaf before her marriage. "Having taught the deaf to hear, she might perhaps teach the mute to speak," her taciturn fiancé once joked. Grace's early culinary efforts were not always successful. After choking down a piece of her

Newlywed Edith Wilson helped run the government in her husband's name from his sickroom.

first apple pie, Coolidge suggested to a guest, "Don't you think the road commissioner would be willing to pay my wife something for her recipe for pie crust?"

A Stanford University geology laboratory was the unlikely meeting place of **Lou Henry** and Herbert Hoover. After becoming the first woman ever to receive a geology degree, she married Hoover and embarked upon a life of travel. Their first home was in China, where she nursed the wounded during the Boxer Rebellion. Later, while living in London, the couple translated a sixteenth century Latin metallurgy classic, Agricola's *De Re Metallica;* Lou was fluent in five languages. Despite the worsening Depression, each presidential dinner under Hoover was a black tie, seven-course affair, complete with liveried butlers, footmen, and buglers. But White House guests questioned whether the speed with which the president wolfed down his food left him adequate time to appreciate Lou's menus.

A shy, gawky youngster whose family derisively called her "Granny," **Eleanor Roosevelt** metamorphosed into an energetic and compassionate "First Lady of the World."

When FDR was stricken with crippling polio, Eleanor successfully battled his mother's plan to retire him to his country estate. Eleanor became her husband's eyes, ears, and legs, bringing cheer to Depression breadlines and overseas military bases. The indefatigable first lady gave weekly press conferences, wrote a newspaper column, broadcast a radio show, and once kept two White House receptions running simultaneously. On one occasion she sneaked off from a White House dinner to take a late-night flight with aviatrix Amelia Earhart; afterward, she wanted to take flying lessons, but her husband would not permit it. (While Eleanor roamed the world, Roosevelt enjoyed a thirty-year affair with her former secretary, Lucy Mercer Rutherford. Lucy was with the president in Warm Springs, Georgia when he died.)

In widowhood, Eleanor continued her political and humanitarian activities, serving as delegate to the newly-formed United Nations, traveling widely, and speaking courageously for the causes in which she believed. Adlai Stevenson, UN

Eleanor Roosevelt was her husband's eyes, ears, and legs. His heart belonged elsewhere.

ambassador and former presidential candidate, said, upon her death in 1962, "She would rather light candles than curse the darkness, and her glow has warmed the world."

A sandlot baseball pitcher in her youth, **Elizabeth Wallace Truman** indulged her passion for the sport by attending Washington Senators games whenever her schedule as first lady permitted. Harry Truman had first met his Bess when she was five; "She had golden curls . . . the most beautiful blue eyes," he recalled years later. They were married in 1913, after a ten-year courtship. To plain-speaking Truman, Bess was "the Boss" and daughter Margaret, "the Boss's Boss." An adoring father, HST fired off a threatening letter to music critic Paul Hume when he panned Margaret's Washington singing debut.

Vivacious **Mamie Doud** was a society belle in both Denver and San Antonio, her summer and winter homes, when she met "Ike" Eisenhower. The young army lieutenant had to ask her for a date a month in advance. A lifelong army wife — she once estimated she had moved twenty-seven times in her first thirty-seven years of marriage — Mamie considered the White House her first real home. She quickly redecorated the presidential bedroom in her favorite pink, adding a king-sized bed "so I can reach over and pat Ike on his old bald head any time I want to." Holidays were faithfully observed in the Eisenhower White House. Wives of presidential staffers were startled upon arriving at an October luncheon to find paper witches and skeletons hanging from the dignified State Dining Room's ceiling.

Not the least of John Kennedy's political assets was his lovely wife, the former **Jacqueline Bouvier,** who had little liking for politics. The couple met over asparagus at the home of a matchmaking friend when Jacqueline was "The Inquiring Camera Girl" for the *Washington Times-Herald* and Kennedy the capital's most eligible bachelor.

Returning home from a European goodwill tour the year he took office, the president proudly described himself as "the man who accompanied Jacqueline Kennedy to Paris." Viewing politics as "my enemy as far as seeing Jack was concerned," Jacqueline preferred to spend long weekends foxhunting in Virginia, waterskiing off Cape Cod, or sailing the Mediterranean on the yacht of friend Aristotle Onassis. She made only one purely political trip with the president: his fateful November 1963 foray into Texas.

Jacqueline and her children remained in the public spotlight long after Kennedy's assassination. The nation watched daughter Caroline grow from a toddler playing "dress-up" in her mother's shoes (size

Jacqueline Kennedy considered politics "my enemy as far as seeing Jack was concerned."

10), to a free spirited young woman who once shaved off an eyebrow because she thought her face too symmetrical. After the death of second husband, Onassis, Jacqueline returned to work in New York as an editor for a publishing firm.

A $2.50 Sears Roebuck ring cemented the 1934 marriage of Lyndon Johnson and **Claudia "Lady Bird" Taylor.** (The future first lady got her unique nickname from her childhood nurse, who thought her "cute as a little lady bird.") The couple's fortunes turned upward after their marriage, thanks in large measure to Lady Bird's management of their ranching and broadcasting properties. Lady Bird took firm charge of her husband as well, directing everything from his perpetual diet to his surprise resignation speech. "I felt ten pounds lighter, ten years younger, and full of plans," she said upon LBJ's annoucement that he would not seek another term in 1968.

Lady Bird crusaded for a more beautiful countryside with the same enthusiasm Jacqueline Kennedy had brought to the job of White House restoration. Johnson christened a 1965 law restricting billboards on interstate highways "The Lady Bird Act."

The two Johnson daughters led the press and Secret Service on a merry chase. "Watusi Luci" ducked out of the White House in a blonde wig to spend a weekend at a Midwest university, during which time she met future husband Patrick Nugent. The quieter Lynda Bird acquired a glamorous new image when she began dating actor George Hamilton. Both daughters were married during their father's administration.

Thelma "Pat" Ryan Nixon, who met her husband in an amateur theatrical production, never slipped out of the role of dutiful and efficient political wife. Richard Nixon dedicated his book, *Six Crises,* to her, writing, "To Pat: she also ran."

Some thought the Nixon marriage was less tranquil than it appeared; Carl Bernstein and Bob Woodward suggested in *The Final Days* that Pat nearly filed for divorce in 1962, and had not slept with her husband since. Friends and family were quick to deny the report, and Nixon once pointedly observed that his wife had suffered her 1976 stroke only days after she

Rosalynn Carter emerged as a trusted spokesperson for her husband early in his political career.

had read the Woodward-Bernstein book. The first lady hinted at the difficulty of her life as a politician's wife when a reporter inquired whether she would want daughter Tricia to marry a politician. "I would feel sorry for her if she did," Pat responded.

Tricia, a petite blonde in the Alice in Wonderland mold, lived reclusively in the White House until her 1971 Rose Garden wedding to Edward Cox. Extroverted daughter Julie, wife of President Eisenhower's grandson, David, was the most spirited of the Nixons in defending her father against charges of official misconduct. She became an author in 1977 with her *Special People*.

"Elect Betty's Husband" read a popular political button of the 1976 presidential campaign. many voters said they would have preferred **Elizabeth Bloomer Ford** to either her husband or his opponent.

The soft-spoken former dancer-model won public approval for daring to speak out in favor of legalized abortion and the Equal Rights Amendment. "I'm the only First Lady to ever have a march organized against me," she cracked, after ERA opponents massed in front of the Ford White House. Though her more rock-ribbed husband gulped, Betty said she would not be surprised if her sons smoked marijuana or her daughter had a premarital affair. Betty's candid discussion of her breast cancer surgery early in her husband's administration was credited with saving the lives of thousands of women, including Second Lady Margaretta "Happy" Rockefeller.

Teenage daughter Susan was familiar with the White House floor plan before her father took office, having sold guidebooks of the mansion during the Nixon Presidency. Under the tutelage of White house photographer David Kennerly, Susan became adept with a camera, often joining the press corps in scrambling for pictures of her famous father.

When **Rosalynn Smith Carter** took to the stump for husband Jimmy — appearing in as many as seven cities a day — reporters asked her about more than recipes, children, and clothes. Rosalynn's soft Southern drawl answered the same tough questions on foreign policy, economics, and abortion that were posed to her husband. Painfully shy in her youth, Rosalynn's first reaction to giving a political speech was, "I just can't." But she learned that she could, earning the description "a magnolia made of steel." Her admiring husband calls her "my secret weapon." The first lady's gymnastics were not limited to the verbal; she once vaulted over the locked door of a public toilet.

At eight, freckle-faced Amy Carter was not enthusiastic about her father's election victory; like Martha Washington nearly two hundred years before, she preferred the familiarity of home to the new sights and sounds of the distant capital. But also like Martha, Amy adjusted to her new life in the limelight — especially after receiving a treehouse on the White House grounds, in which she was permitted to camp overnight.

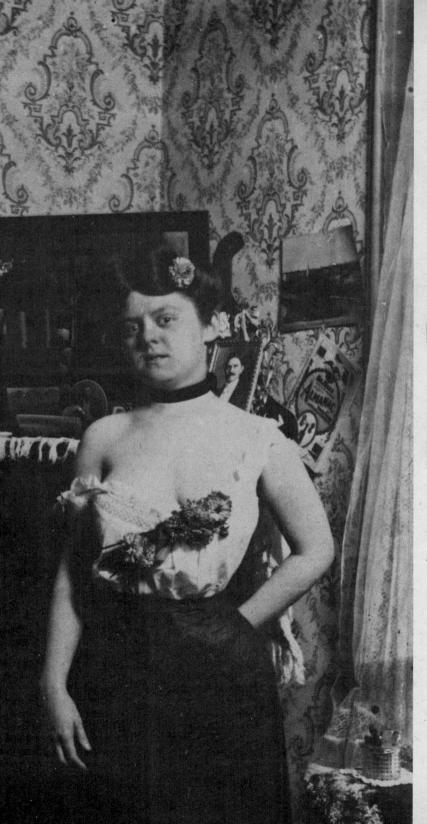

Badwomen

Chicago women rounded up in 50s vice raid. Women criminals have usually been used by men.

WOMEN AND CRIME

The crime rate has not changed significantly in recent years, but the number of women involved in violent crimes has increased. Today the most publicized criminals are those associated with male-dominated groups; the Charles Manson cult, the Symbionese Liberation Army, and the Weather Underground. But, the more significant crime increase for women has been seen in such areas as embezzlement, fraud, forgery, and counterfeiting.

Historically, women and violence are often connected. Women have been known to murder their own children out of frustration, greed, or ignorance. As anthropologist Margaret Mead points out, "Females have been accustomed, over the centuries, to fight only to save their young, and so they fight to kill."

But today, women are involved in many other kinds of crimes as well. According to the FBI Uniform Crime Reports for 1975, larceny accounts for most female arrests (24 percent). During the period 1970 to 1975, all arrests of males increased 30 percent, according to the FBI, but all arrests of women were up 56 percent. This continues a long-term trend.

The FBI also reports that women offenders account for 10 percent of violent crimes. This rate has remained fairly constant since 1942.

While most women in prisons today are from minority groups, poor, unemployed, and barely literate, the women who receive most of the attention do not come out of the ghettos. They are instead middle-class daughters of suburban parents, who have become "revolutionaries."

New York psychiatrist Herbert Hendin says he sees many such women college students. "Outwardly they are anxious to please their parents, but inwardly they are raging — at their parents, their parents' values and often at themselves," he says. Many, like Sara Jane Moore, an FBI informer who tried to kill President Ford, have social profiles identical with male political assassins.

These political crimes are sporadic. A more important trend appears in the number of women arrested for property offenses. Almost one-third of the people arrested for embezzlement, larceny, and fraud are now women. If this upward swing continues, equal numbers of men and women will be arrested for these crimes by the 1990s.

Women may be more involved in financial offenses because they are more desperate than ever before for money. More women live alone, with dependent children, yet in 1976 men who worked full-time earned 74.8 percent more than full-time women workers. Women's unemployment rates are higher than men's, and often their fraud and forgery offenses are related to welfare checks and other government payments. Other factors are the greater opportunities women have to commit white-collar financial crimes as they move up the business ladder.

Indeed, it has been suggested that feminism, which has altered the status of many women, may also play a role in female crime. Women are encouraged to feel and act more independent — and thus they are more willing to take risks.

But most women criminals, far from being liberated in any sense, are often the most oppressed and exploited of American females. Milton Burns, assistant superintendent of the Purdy Treatment Center for Women in Washington, D.C., says: "We have seen very little of the woman who is the leader of the crime, or who commits crime on her own without a man having led her or forced her into it. Even in drug-related crimes, women are used by men — they forge drug prescriptions for men, or they become prostitutes to get money for men."

Nevertheless, arrest statistics are unreliable. Are women really committing more crimes, or are the police more willing to arrest them now than they were a few years ago? Most agree that police attitudes are changing toward all kinds of female crimes. A Los Angeles police captain says of street crimes: "In the past, police were reluctant to search women on the streets. Now they get frisked like everybody else — we can't afford to take chances anymore."

Today, most women are arrested for social, rather than violent crimes: for drugs, prostitution, drunkenness, theft, disorderly conduct, and fraud. Nearly one-third of the women in New York State correctional facilities, for example, are serving time for narcotics. Many were caught working for men, in behind-the-scenes jobs like heroin-bagging. About half the women in prison today are black, and 15 percent are Hispanic. Their average age is twenty-nine, and most have dependent children. Almost all have no relatives or friends willing to aid them.

'Misguided' Rather than Dangerous

A woman who has broken the law is often considered misguided rather than dangerous, and is labeled "cheap" or "loose" because she has violated accepted female roles.

In addition to the moral flaws imputed to a woman criminal, men and women are also viewed differently when it comes to conviction and sentencing. In several states, women now serve longer sentences than men charged with the same crime; this is apparently based on the contradictory theory that women are more responsive than men to rehabilitation, but might require longer confinement.

But, this theory falls apart in practice. Women in prison receive little or no vocational training. The average number of vocational programs in each female institution is 2.7; the average number in each male institution is ten.

There is little to prepare a female convict for a decent job or healthier family ties once she gets out of jail. Because most prisons for women are in rural, isolated areas, visits from children are almost impossible. Seven states have no female prisons, and women are sent to nearby states, reducing even further the chance for family contact. After release, a woman is also faced with the emotional burden of caring for children who have lived without her for a long time and may no longer accept her as an authority figure.

Women also face prison humiliations that men usually do not suffer. Only 12 percent of all people involved in correctional work are women. Thus, in many prisons, women must appear partially clad before male guards assigned to the places where they sleep, go to the bathroom, and receive medical attention.

BADWOMEN

Tudor: Bloody Mary

Mary Tudor (1516-1558) ruled England from 1553 until her death. The first woman to rule England in her own right, "Bloody Mary" is remembered mainly for burning more than three hundred Protestants at the stake in a vain effort to preserve Catholicism as the national religion.

Mary Tudor was the daughter of King

Catholic "Bloody Mary" burned more than 300 English Protestants at the stake.

Henry VIII's first wife, Catherine of Aragon. When the king defied the pope, broke with the Roman church and married Anne Boleyn, the nine-year-old Mary was declared illegitimate and forced to act as lady-in-waiting to Boleyn's and the king's baby daughter, Elizabeth. Later, when the king tired of Boleyn, Mary Tudor regained favor, and eventually succeeded her brother Edward VI to the throne. Despite pressure from her father, Mary never relinquished her Catholicism. In 1554, she married Philip II of Spain in an attempt to bring the church of Rome back to her people. A Protestant insurrection broke out, and for three years rebel groups roamed the countryside. The queen's popularity deteriorated even further when she joined Spain's war against France and lost Calais, England's last possession on the European mainland. Gradually her marriage deteriorated, and Mary Tudor died in 1558.

Bonney and Read: Pirate duo

Anne Bonney and **Mary Read** gained notoriety on the high seas in the late 1700s. They had a remarkable childhood circum-stance in common. Both had been dressed as boys when they were small. When Mary Read's mother needed money, she concocted a scheme to disguise Mary as her younger brother, who had died, and take her to London to visit her grand-mother. The scheme worked: grand-mother was so pleased to see her "grand-son" again that she promised money to help rear him. When still young, Mary Read went to sea as a crewman, passing as a man; later, she was an infantry soldier and then a cavalry trooper. In Flanders, she fell in love with a Flemish soldier, re-vealed her true sex, and married him. For the first time, she wore women's clothing. Her husband, however, died soon after their marriage, and widow again donned male garb, joined the Dutch army, and sailed for the West Indies. During the voyage, the ship was attacked by British pirates. Thinking Read was an En-glishman, they invited her to join them. From then on, Read reportedly wielded "a cutlass, pistol, and [had] every outward appearance of a daring sea robber."

In 1719 she met Anne Bonney, who was also passing for male on a pirate ship. Bonney, the illegitimate child of an Irish-American lawyer and his maid, had been moved into her father's house dis-guised as a boy, so neighbors, and his wife, would not suspect she was really the out-of-wedlock daughter they all knew ab-out. Eventually, the wife discovered the farce, but Anne Bonney had already learned to enjoy being treated like a boy.

She was married, briefly to a sailor named Bonney, but in Providence, R.I., she was lured away by a pirate named John Rackam ("Calico Jack"). She dressed in men's clothing once again and joined his crew. Bonney was reported to be so strong that "when a young fellow would have lain with her, against her will, she beat him so that he lay ill of it a con-siderable time." She supposedly fell in love with the handsome Mary Read when they met. After each learned the other's sex, they became good friends.

In an attack on their ship in 1720, the crew scurried below decks, leaving the two women topside to fight it out. Bonney fired a pistol below to flush the crew out, killing one man and wounding several others. Despite their attempts to save the ship, it was captured and all its crew taken in chains to Jamaica. Both women were sentenced to hang, but the sentences were changed to life in prison when it was learned both women were pregnant.

Butterworth: Kitchen Counterfeiter

Mary Butterworth (1686-1775) was a housewife who led a highly successful counterfeiting ring in Plymouth Colony, Massachusetts. In 1716, she began copying the pound 'bills of credit' issued by Rhode Island, using a hot iron and a piece of starched muslin to transfer the image from a real bill to a blank piece of paper. With the help of friends, she filled in the images with crow quill pens. The bills sold for half their face value; a local justice helped to pass them. The law caught up with her in 1723, but she and six others pleaded innocent. No evidence against them could be found, and they were released.

Silver: Ax Killer

In the North Carolina mountains, grizzly legends have grown up around another infamous woman, **Frankie Silver**. Three days before Christmas in 1831, she supposedly hacked her husband Charlie to death with an ax as he slept in front of the fireplace, cut his body into small pieces, and burned all but the unburnable portions. Those she stuffed in a hollow log behind the house. But the unburned parts were soon discovered, and a Morganton jury convicted her of murder. Her uncle and father helped her escape jail by cutting her hair, dressing her like a boy, and driving her out of town. She was apprehended, and on July 12, 1833, Frankie Silver became the first and only white woman ever hanged legally in North Carolina.

But the story does not end here. Many residents of Morganton claimed that the truth behind the Frankie Silver story was quite different from the legend: that, in fact, her husband had come home drunk and attacked her, and that she swung the ax in self-defense.

Because married women at that time were not allowed to take the witness stand in their own defense, no one ever heard Frankie Silver's story.

Walker: Criminal Trousers

Another audacious woman, **Dr. Mary Walker** (1832-1919), committed the crime of wearing trousers in public. Walker graduated from Syracuse Medical College in 1855, only six years after Elizabeth Blackwell had become the nation's first female physician. Her preference for male attire developed during the Civil War, when she worked in the fields as an assistant surgeon in the Union army. She was the only woman ever to receive the Medal of Honor, and she wore the medal with pride everywhere. The honor was withdrawn near the end of her life, however, when a government review board decided it had been awarded improperly.

The first of her several arrests for wearing a frock coat and trousers on the street, occurred in New York City in the late 1860s. She declared at the time that her attire was healthier than corsets, which she called "coffins," and more respectable than hoop skirts, which revealed much of one's leg on a windy day. In court, she claimed the right to dress as she pleased "in free America, on whose tented fields I have served for four years in the cause of human freedom." She was not without sympathizers: the judge admonished the policeman for arresting her, and she left the courtroom amid applause. Nevertheless, she was often hissed on the streets, but she persevered, and was active in The Mutual Dress Reform and Equal Rights Association.

Mandelbaum: Female Fagin

One criminal who died rich was **Fredericka Mandelbaum** (1818-1889), affectionately known as "Marm," who became the most successful fence of all time. She apparently led a quiet life as a housewife and mother until 1862, when she bought a house in New York City. Within two years, she had safely sold $4 million in stolen goods and become a millionaire. She taught other female criminals how to improve their trades; and two of her "graduates," Sophie Lyons and Black Lena, became famous con women. Marm also taught youngsters how to pick pockets and, as they grew older, how to burgle and blackmail.

In 1884, indictments were drawn against her, and she fled to Canada with an estimated $10 million. She lived the rest of her life in quiet luxury.

The murder of hard-living, hard-loving outlaw Belle Starr has never been solved.

Starr: Bandit Queen

Meanwhile, the Wild West was breeding its own brand of wicked woman. **Belle Starr** (1848-1889) nicknamed the "bandit queen," moved with her family from Missouri to Texas, where she joined the outlaws by falling in love with them: first with Cole Younger, a handsome member of the James Gang, who made her pregnant and then left her; next with Jim Reed, who invited her to ride with his outlaw band. Her father locked her in a closet to prevent her elopement with Reed, but she escaped through a window and "married" him in a mock ceremony.

By 1873, Belle was a full-fledged outlaw; she supposedly tortured an old Indian prospector until he revealed where he had buried his $30,000 in gold; she wore two six-shooters at her waist and led a band of cattle rustlers and horse thieves who made regular raids on Oklahoma ranches. She finally married Sam Starr, a Cherokee, and together they stole livestock. They were arrested twice and spent six months in jail. After Sam Starr was killed in a gun fight in 1886, Belle took another lover, Jim July, and insisted he change his name to Starr. She continued to evade the law and, in 1881, sheltered Jesse James in her hideout. Belle Starr was killed by an unknown gunman while riding alone, in 1889. Some said her killer must have been one of her ex-lovers; others accused her son, with whom she was said to be having an incestuous relationship.

Cannary: Calamity Jane

"Calamity Jane" was born Martha Jane Cannary (1852-1903), probably on a farm near Princeton, Missouri, and was orphaned at the age of fifteen. She spent the next few years drifting through construction camps and cow towns from Missouri to Wyoming, and took jobs working as a dance hall girl — work that usually included prostitution. She may have acquired her nickname after she warned men who offended her that they were courting calamity.

While still a teenage she is believed to have married an army officer, in 1867. But she soon left him and, dressing in men's clothing, took to gambling and drinking in saloons. Calamity bragged that she was the only person in the West who had both worked in and patronized brothels, claiming she could deceive any prostitute. (In those days, even in houses of prostitution, sex usually took place in the dark with most clothing left on.)

Most of the later legends about Calamity Jane's exploits as an Indian fighter, army scout, and stagecoach driver are believed to be untrue. They were probably written in 1896 to promote her as the star attraction of a traveling dime museum. She was never accused of killing anyone. It is known that she worked as a mule-skinner, but was fired when she got drunk and revealed she was a woman. She also hired out as a bullwhacker, to whip the ox teams that hauled freight wagons across the South Dakota plains.

She seemed to be a woman who rushed in where others feared to tread, and in 1878 she was dubbed the "angel of mercy," for being the only person willing to nurse back to health the victims of a smallpox epidemic in Deadwood, South Dakota. When necessary, she obtained food for the ill at gunpoint. By the end of her life, in 1903, her eyesight had begun to fail, possibly due to venereal disease.

the film *Butch Cassidy and the Sundance Kid*. Her name was **Etta Place**, a tall stately woman who usually dressed in black. She was a Fort Worth housewife and school teacher before she met Harry Longbaugh, the notorious "Sundance," at a community dance. She joined him and, at first, was only a witness to his crimes. But when she learned that the robbery of a Union Pacific train outside Tipton, Wyoming, had netted Sundance and Butch Cassidy only fifty dollars, she decided to assume responsibility for future heists. During the robbery, the gang invaded a bank with a skunk they had found along the way and took off with $30,000.

In 1901, pursued by the law, she left with the men for South America; in Argentina, the trio stole almost $30,000. Cassidy was said to have been killed in Bolivia, although his death was never confirmed. Place and Sundance returned to the United States in 1907, and parted soon after in Denver.

Calamity Jane's life was as brutal as it was exciting; she was an alcoholic by age 24.

Place: 'Sundance' Woman

At the turn of the century, there was a real "Sundance" woman, equal in good looks to Katharine Ross, who portrayed her in

Barker: Mastermind Ma

Ma Barker (1872-1935), another frontier legend, was never arrested for any crime; but she was the mastermind behind the robberies, kidnappings, and murders committed by her four sons Herman, Lloyd, Arthur, and Fred. As a child, Ma Barker read the Bible, played the fiddle, and worshipped Jesse James, whom she

Bodies of Ma Barker and son Fred were displayed following their 1935 shoot-out deaths.

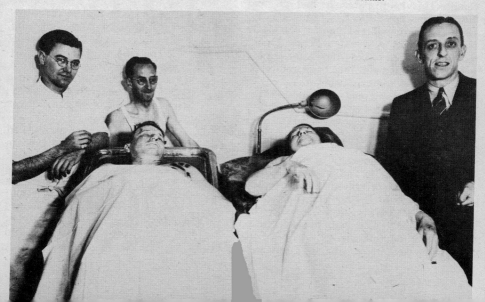

saw once. She married George Barker, a sharecropper, in 1892. With her sons, Barker accumulated at least $3 million by robbing payrolls, post offices, and banks, in Missouri.

Until 1922, Ma Barker managed to keep her sons out of jail. But eventually their luck ran out. Herman was either shot by police, or committed suicide when he was stopped as a robbery suspect; Lloyd got twenty-five years in Leavenworth; Arthur ("Doc") was charged with killing a night watchman and got life in prison, but was later released when someone else confessed to the murder; Fred got a five-to-ten year prison sentence.

In 1931, Freddie was released from prison and the Barker clan moved to Minnesota, where they ran the Green Lantern Saloon and recruited new gang members from their customers. Ma Barker planned the kidnapping of wealthy brewer William A. Hamm and, later, of banker Edward G. Bremer. But during the Bremer kidnapping Arthur left behind a fingerprint, and was captured shortly afterward. A map in his apartment led the FBI to a house in Lake Weir, Florida, where Ma Barker and Fred were hiding. Both were killed in the shoot-out: Ma Barker was hit three times by bullets; one, shot directly through her heart, was said to have been self-inflicted.

Botkin: Candy Killer
One of the most imaginative murderers in American history is probably **Cordelia Botkin** (1854-1910). After she had left her husband and moved to San Francisco, in 1895, Botkin met John Dunning, the local bureau chief of Associated Press. Dunning was married but eventually moved in with Botkin; his wife, Elizabeth, returned to her parents' home in Delaware.

In 1898, Dunning ended his affair with Botkin and left to cover the Spanish-American War. Botkin was furious, certain he would return to his wife once the war was over. To prevent this, she purchased some arsenic and a box of candy, poisoned the candy, and sent it to Dunning's wife with a note: "With love to yourself and baby." Believing the candy had been sent by a close San Francisco friend, Elizabeth, along with her sister, ate enough of it to kill them.

Dunning went immediately to Delaware

and verified that the note had been written by Botkin. She was sentenced to life imprisonment in 1898 but was permitted to leave the prison two days a week in return for giving her wardens sexual attention.

Borden: Forty Whacks
Lizzie Borden (1860-1927) is famous for the plot to murders commemorated in a childhood rhyme:

> Lizzie Borden took an ax
> Gave her mother forty whacks;
> When she saw what she had done
> She gave her father forty-one.

In 1892, her father and stepmother were found hacked beyond recognition, in their home in Fall River, Massachusetts. No one had been seen entering or leaving the house, so the blame fell on one of two people: Bridget Sullivan, the housemaid; or thirty-two-year-old Lizzie Borden, who lived at home. It was known that Borden hated her stepmother, and it was later learned that she had exchanged only a few words with her father in the two years before he died.

In the end, however, Borden was found innocent of the murders. She was well-

Lizzie Borden inherited a fortune after the ax murders of her parsimonious parents.

respected in Fall River. She was active in the church, visited the sick, and belonged to the Women's Christian Temperance Union. Her cause was taken up by leading feminists of the day, including Lucy Stone and Mary Livermore. She was acquitted: the prosecution was unable to produce a witness or a murder weapon, although a broken ax, that had been washed recently and dipped in ashes so as to appear dusty, was found in the Borden's cellar several days after the murder.

For the rest of her life, she remained a recluse in the opulent home her inheritance had bought her. Some people, including her sister and a niece, were said to know that Borden had, in fact, been the murderer.

Mallon: Typhoid Mary

Typhoid Mary, born **Mary Mallon** (1870-1938), was a carrier of typhoid fever and knowingly spread her illness around the New York City area, causing at least fifty-three cases of typhoid and three deaths. Mallon worked as a cook; in every household where she was employed, people contracted the disease and she would quietly disappear. Her activities went unnoticed until 1906, when George A. Soper, a health department official, was called in to investigate the cause of typhoid in the Charles Henry Warren family. His attention focused eventually on the cook, Mallon, who had left three weeks after the sickness began, and he quickly discovered the disease had followed her everywhere for the last ten years.

She evaded health department attempts to locate her until March 18, 1907, when she was caught and, after a fierce struggle with police, taken to the Willard Park Hospital for Contagious Diseases. There, it was learned that her body discharged a continual stream of typhoid germs, but she refused to take any precautions to prevent the spread of the disease. For three years, she was confined to Riverside Hospital on an island in the East River. After legal battles and much publicity, she promised hospital officials she would take needed precautions and would no longer work as a cook. They released her and she vanished for five years, drifting from job to job under aliases.

In 1915, she took a job as cook in the Sloane Hospital for Women, and twenty-five people were stricken with typhoid. Once again Soper was called in to investigate; he identified Typhoid Mary from handwriting the cook had left behind. Outraged, Soper tracked her down and on March 27, 1915, she was again confined to Riverside Hospital, where she was kept under supervision and given a job that didn't threaten lives.

Nesbit: Swinger

A femme fatale of another sort was **Evelyn Nesbit** (1884-1967), who moved to New York from Pittsburgh at the age of sixteen, and soon afterward became the mistress of millionaire Stanford White, the famous architect. Three years later, not content with the fame and wealth already lavished on her, she married multimillionaire Harry K. Thaw. Thaw and his new wife tormented each other about her love affair with White.

He made her refer to White as "the bastard." During an ocean cruise, he grew so jealous that he chained her to the bed and whipped her until she confessed every sexual act she and White had performed. She told Thaw in detail how White had plied her with champagne, stripped and raped her, and made her swing naked on a red velvet swing hanging from the ceiling of his apartment.

Distraught with jealousy, Thaw vowed revenge. On June 25, 1906, along with the rest of high society, including White, the couple attended a musical play on the roof of Madison Square Garden, a building White had designed. During the performance, Thaw rose calmly from his chair and fired three shots into White, killing him instantly. Thaw was found not guilty by reason of insanity.

Gunness: Cleaver Killer

To her neighbors in LaPorte, Indiana, **Belle Gunness** (1860-1908?) appeared to be a respectable, hard-working widow. True, she was tried for killing her husband with a cleaver, but the jury ruled his death accidental, and she continued to care for her home and three children as before. Gunness, however, was leading a double life. She placed ads in Chicago newspapers, looking for a new husband with money.

504

Several men answered the ads and, after a brief courtship, each disappeared.

On April 28, 1908, the Gunness farmhouse burned to the ground, apparently with Gunness and her three children inside. But the sheriff discovered that the woman in the charred ruins was decapitated, and was not Gunness. He suspected someone had killed this unknown woman and then set fire to the house. One of Gunness' lovers, Ray Lamphere, who had worked for her as a handyman had been fired shortly before the blaze. A few days earlier, she told several people he had threatened to burn down her house. Lamphere was arrested as the most obvious suspect.

Meanwhile, the brother of Gunness' last suitor became suspicious and insisted on a search of the ruins of the Gunness home. By the time the searchers finished, they had unearthed fourteen bodies; each of the bodies had been chopped into pieces. Gunness had apparently lured them with promises of marriage, bilked them of an estimated total of $30,000, and then killed them. Lamphere swore that it was Gunness who had killed the unknown woman and then set fire to the her own house. He was found guilty of setting the fire, however, and died in prison. Gunness, if she was still alive, was never heard from again.

Snyder: Dumbbell Death
On March 19, 1927, **Ruth Brown Snyder** (1895-1928), along with her lover, Henry Judd Gray, committed what would become known as the Dumbbell Murder. Snyder, bored with being a housewife and mother, spent most of her time reading romantic novels. She tried to poison her husband several times but always failed to kill him. Finally she sought help from Gray. He hid in her husband's bedroom and, once her husband was asleep, tried to kill him with a dumbbell. The blow did little damage and Ruth — determined to succeed this time — grabbed the dumbbell from him and crushed her husband's skull with it.

They tried to make the murder look like part of a bungled robbery committed by outsiders, but no one believed them. Soon they were blaming each other. The jury took only ninety-eight minutes to find

"Dumbbell" murderer Ruth Snyder peered out of her cell four days after her husband's death.

them both guilty of murder and sentenced them to death. Ruth Snyder went to the electric chair on January 12, 1928.

Parker: Clyde's Bonnie
Nineteen-year-old **Bonnie Parker** (1911-1934) met Clyde Barrow in a Dallas cafe, where she worked as a waitress. She was married but independent: her husband was serving ninety-nine years in prison for murder. She moved in with Clyde and when he was arrested for a burglary in Waco, Texas, she helped him escape from jail by slipping a .38 Colt revolver through the bars of his cell. He was caught again, and served two years. When Clyde was released in 1932, Bonnie and Clyde began stealing, robbing, and killing in Texas, New Mexico, and Missouri. Their heists never brought in much money; their largest haul was $1,500.

During his prison stays, Clyde had become a homosexual; male accomplices who joined them in their sprees, including Roy Hamilton and W. J. Jones, served as lovers to both Clyde and Bonnie, who reportedly was a nymphomaniac. Much publicity surrounded their exploits, and Bonnie was nicknamed "Suicide Sal." In 1933, they were joined by Clyde's brother, Buck, and his wife, Blanche. Buck was

Despite all the attention Bonnie and Clyde received, they never made off with much money.

were caught in an ambush in Louisiana and their bodies riddled with bullets.

Judd: Cut 'em up

Winnie Ruth Judd, (1905-   ) a doctor's wife, was twenty-three when she committed her crime: in the fall of 1932 she killed two women, dismembered one of them, and tried to ship their bodies from Arizona to Los Angeles in a trunk. A baggage attendant became suspicious when he saw something red dripping from her luggage, and asked her for the keys. Instead, Judd got in her car and drove off. She turned herself in later, saying she had killed in self-defense. She was found guilty and committed to an Arizona mental hospital, from which she escaped seven times. The last time, in 1962, she lived presumably at large for eight years before she was discovered. In 1969, she was declared sane and sent to prison. She was paroled on December 22, 1971.

Fugate: Teenage Killer

On January 28, 1958, fourteen-year-old **Caril Fugate** (1944-   ) watched her boyfriend, Charles ("Little Red") Starkweather, murder her mother, stepfather, and two-year-old sister in their

soon killed and Blanche was captured in a police trap in Joplin, Missouri. On May 23, 1934, Bonnie and Clyde were set up for capture by a friend, Henry Methvin. They

The law caught up with Winnie Ruth Judd when she tried to ship two dead bodies in a trunk.

Nebraska home. The couple fled the house two days later, and within forty-eight hours murdered seven people: a seventy-year-old farmer, a teenage couple, a traveling salesman, and a wealthy industrialist, his wife, and maid.

They were finally arrested when Fugate ran toward a squad car screaming: "Help! Starkweather's going to kill me! He's crazy!" At first, Starkweather claimed she had been his hostage, but later he told the jury she was a willing participant in the murders and could have escaped a number of times when he left her alone with loaded guns. Starkweather was executed, and Fugate was sentenced to life in prison.

In 1973, Fugate began seeking a reduction of sentence. She was released on June 20, 1976, after eighteen years in prison. Asked about her plans, she said: "I'd just like to be an ordinary dumpy housewife."

TERRORISTS

A new breed of woman criminal — dedicated to terrorism for political causes — has sprung up in the last few years. In West Germany, **Angela Luther,** the daughter of a Hamburg lawyer, ranks among the country's most wanted terrorists. She is one of the few members of the leftist guerrilla Baader-Meinhof gang still at large. The gang has been charged with five murders, fifty-four attempted murders, and a number of robberies. In February 1975, she drove the getaway car during the kidnapping of West Berlin mayoral candidate Peter Lorenz.

In Japan, another woman terrorist, **Fusako Shigenobu** ("Auntie") is considered to be the brains behind the Japanese Red Army, a leftist guerrilla band of about thirty-six members. She is credited with recruiting thirty Japanese militants for the Palestinians and for plotting the 1972 massacre at Israel's Lod Airport, where twenty-eight people were killed, including her husband, Tsuyoshi Okudaira, another leftist. She hijacked a jumbo jet in 1973, seized the French embassy in The Hague in 1974, and helped coordinate the occupation of the United States embassy in Malaysia in 1975. When the "revolution" is over, she says she wants to become "a teacher dealing with juvenile delinquents."

MANSON'S WOMEN

In America, the Manson women became a cultural phenomenon of the late 1960s and the 1970s, causing psychiatrists, sociologists, and parents everywhere to wonder how young, middle-class girls could become so emotionally enslaved to a man that they would eagerly kill for him. In 1970, three of these women — **Susan ("Sadie") Atkins, Patricia ("Katie") Krenwinkel,** and **Leslie Van Houten,** along with their leader, Charles Manson — went on trial for the 1969 ritual murders of actress Sharon Tate and six other people. All were found guilty and given life sentences. Van Houten, whose attorney was murdered during her trial, has won a re-trial. A fourth woman, **Linda Kasabian,** was promised immunity for turning state's evidence.

Manson's female followers lived with him at the secluded Spahn ranch in the Santa Susanna Mountains, near Los Angeles where they reportedly believed that Manson was Jesus Christ and obeyed all his orders without question. He told them where and what to steal, what to wear, whom to sleep with (all were required to have sex with Manson), and whom to kill. Manson believed racial warfare was inevitable and wanted to speed up the process by carrying out "helter skelter," a plan of random murder of whites that would, he apparently thought, be blamed on blacks.

WOULD-BE ASSASSINS

During Manson's trial, other women disciples kept vigil in front of the Los Angeles Hall of Justice, shaved their heads, and copied Manson's actions: when he carved an X on his forehead, so did they. One of those disciples was **Lynette Alice ("Squeaky") Fromme,** who met Manson when she was a seventeen-year-old runaway from the Los Angeles suburbs. She was attracted to him, she explained, because "a dog goes to somebody who loves it and will take care of it."

On September 5, 1975, Fromme aimed a .45 caliber pistol at President Ford, outside the statehouse in Sacramento, California. Although there was no bullet in the firing chamber, she became the first woman convicted of attempting to assas-

Would-be assassin Lynette "Squeaky" Fromme appeared at her trial in long, red robes.

sinate a president. It was believed she did it to please Manson. Until the attempt, she had shared a Sacramento apartment with other Manson women: they had begun to wear long red robes and turbans, proclaiming a new religious order devoted to Manson's miraculous return to freedom. Now she is serving a life sentence at the San Diego Metropolitan Correctional Center. Her letters are carefully screened as a result of threatening mail she sent to executives of the Environmental Protection Agency.

Another woman, **Sara Jane Moore,** was convicted of trying to shoot President Ford, in San Francisco's Union Square, on September 22, 1975. Moore, who is forty-seven, was born in Charleston, West Virginia (as was Charles Manson), has been married four times, and has abandoned three children. In the 1960s, she became a radical groupie in the San Francisco Bay Area, and then an FBI informer. When arrested, she said assassination is "a valid political tool, when used selectively." She is now serving a life sentence at the Terminal Island Federal Correctional Institution, in Los Angeles. Those who knew her felt she was a misfit rather than a radical. A former employer recalled: "She wanted to be something she wasn't. She wanted attention."

PATTY HEARST'S KIDNAPPERS

Radical women shared leadership of the Symbionese Liberation Army, which on February 5, 1974, kidnapped nineteen-year-old **Patricia Hearst** — granddaughter of one of the country's most powerful publishers, the late William Randolph Hearst — from the Berkeley apartment she shared with fiancé Steven Weed.

The SLA grew out of the black culture program at Vacaville State Prison, but most of its leaders were white. In addition to the Hearst kidnapping, it took credit for the murder of Marcus Foster, Oakland's black school superintendent. The SLA symbol was a seven-headed cobra, and its credo a blend of Marxism and terrorism.

The women of the SLA, who were killed in a shoot-out with police, were:

• **Nancy Ling Perry** ("Fahizah"), twenty-six, a Goldwater supporter in 1964 and, later, an English literature major at Berkeley, where she turned to the radical left. She lived with Russell Little, a philosophy graduate and prison reform activist. Their home became the first SLA headquarters, and she became its spiritual and doctrinal leader.

• **Patricia Soltysik** ("Mizmoon"), daughter of a pharmacist, a scholarship student at Berkeley when she met Donald DeFreeze, the "field marshal" of the SLA who was also an escaped convict from Soledad Prison. In 1973, she broke all ties with her family and asked them to burn all photographs of her. She was reportedly the chief theoretician of the SLA.

• **Camilla Hall,** twenty-nine, the daughter of a Minneapolis Lutheran minister. She graduated from the University of Minnesota with a degree in humanities and began her radical activities in Berkeley after she met and fell in love with Patricia Soltysik.

• **Angela Atwood,** twenty-five, a former Indianapolis school teacher, who moved in with two other SLA members, William and Emily Harris, after her marriage broke up in 1973.

Donald DeFreeze, and William Wolfe (a doctor's son whom Patty Hearst said she loved), were also in the house.

On May 17, 1974, police laid seige to the house. Within seventy minutes they had pumped more than 5,000 rounds of ammunition into it. The house eventually burned to the ground, with all six people in it. DeFreeze had apparently committed suicide. The rest died of gunshot wounds, burns, and smoke inhalation.

Two remaining members, the Harris couple, both graduates of Indiana University, continued to help hide Hearst for a while; They then went off on their own, and eluded capture until 1976. While her daughter was still in hiding, Emily Harris's mother sobbed to a church usher: "She's wrong, she's wrong, but she's ours." The Harrises were found guilty of three counts of kidnaping, armed robbery and car theft; and were sentenced to serve eleven years to life in prison. They still face federal charges for their part in the 1974 Hearst kidnapping.

THE FBI'S MOST WANTED WOMEN

Only six out of 342 people, on the FBI's "Ten Most Wanted" list, have been women — since the list was created in 1950. All of the six appeared among the top ten between 1968 and 1970, and most were involved in the radical political movement in the United States.

On December 28, 1968, **Ruth Eisemann-Schier,** a native of Honduras and a graduate of the National University of Mexico, received the dubious honor of becoming the first woman to make the list. She was sought for kidnapping Barbara Jane Mackle from a Decatur, Georgia, motel and burying her alive. She and her partner, Gary Steven Krist, also demanded a $500,000 ranson from Florida land developer Robert F. Mackle for his daughter's safe return. Barbara Jane was found alive after eighty hours. Eisemann-Schier escaped, but was arrested two months later in Norman, Oklahoma, where she was working as a car hop.

Marie Dean Arrington appeared on the list on May 29, 1969, when she escaped from a Florida prison. She had been in

Since her 1972 acquittal, Angela Davis has resumed her teaching and political activities.

WANTED BY THE FBI

INTERSTATE FLIGHT - MURDER, KIDNAPING
ANGELA YVONNE DAVIS

FBI No. 867,615 G

Photograph taken 1969   Photograph taken 1970

Alias: "Tamu"

Never a 'Himicane'

Storms are like women: fickle, and no two are exactly alike. At least, so said one weather forecaster in trying to explain why, since 1953, the National Weather Service has given women's names to hurricanes and typhoons. The first major storm of each year is called by a woman's name beginning with A, and the names progress through the alphabet until the new year, when a new alphabetical list of names is used. The lists are repeated every ten years.

This system equates acts of nature with a distinct female personality, and the implications can be rather macabre: in 1963, for example, "Flora" killed 6,000 Cubans and Haitians; in 1969, "Camille" destroyed 19,467 homes and killed 258 people in the southwestern United States; in 1972, "Agnes" left 330,000 people homeless, destroyed 2,400 farm buildings and 5,800 businesses, damaged 25 cities, and killed 118 people in the northwestern United States.

Women have, from the beginning, objected to this arbitrary use of their names for killer storms. On March 3, 1954, four women named Edna called their local radio station to protest the naming of Hurricane Edna. The weatherman was so upset that he scratched the name from his weather report and replaced it with his own name: Howard. In January 1972, a Miami, Florida, woman called the National Weather Service to suggest it use the names of United States senators instead of women because, "senators delight in having things named after them."

Ten Most Damaging Hurricanes Named After Women

Hurricane	Deaths	Date
1. Flora	6,000	October 4-8, 1963
2. Fifi	2,000	September 19-20, 1974
3. Janet	500	September 22-28, 1955
4. Audrey	430	June 27-30, 1957
5. Diane	400	August 18-19, 1955
Hattie	400	October 31, 1961
6. Hazel	347	October 12-16, 1954
7. Inez	293	September 24-30, 1966
8. Camille	258	August 17-18, 1969
9. Hilda	200	September 19, 1955
10. Agnes	118	June 19-20, 1972

prison for murdering two persons, including a Florida legal secretary who had been shot repeatedly and then run over several times by a car. She was not recaptured for 2½ years, when FBI agents found her in New Orleans and returned her to prison.

Angela Yvonne Davis was added to the list on August 18, 1970, for allegedly furnishing the weapons involved in a shootout, in the Marin County, California, courthouse, on August 7 of that year. During the shootout, Jonathan Jackson, brother of Soledad Brother George Jackson, tried to free several black prisoners; a judge and three prison inmates, including Jonathan, were killed. Although not present at the shootout, Davis was charged with kidnapping, murder, and conspiracy.

Davis, born in 1944 in Birmingham, Alabama, studied French literature at Brandeis University and spent her junior year of college at the Sorbonne, in Paris, where she studied Marxism. She graduated magna cum laude, Phi Beta Kappa, from Brandeis, studied philosophy in West Germany, and completed her master's degree at the University of California in San Diego, where she worked with Herbert Marcuse, an American Marxist professor. In California, Davis began working with the San Diego Black Conference, the Black Panther party, and the Communist party. She was hired as an acting assistant professor of philosophy at UCLA; subsequent attempts to fire her for her political activities were declared unconstitutional. In 1970, however, charged with "inflammatory speeches" on behalf of the Soledad Brothers, she was barred from teaching.

On October 13, 1970, Davis was arrested in New York City on charges stemming from the Marin County shootout. She spent two months in the New York Women's House of Detention, and was then extradited to California's Marin County Jail. In June 1972, after thirteen weeks of testimony by ninety-five witnesses, she was acquitted of all charges.

Bernadine Rae Dohrn was put on the FBI's top ten list on October 14, 1970, after she failed to show up in Chicago to face charges from the "days of rage" confrontation between the radical Weathermen and Chicago police in June 1969. She was indicted for violating federal anti-riot laws and for conspiring to bomb buildings in Detroit, Chicago, New York, and Berkeley. On December 7, 1973, Dohrn was dropped from the ten most wanted list, after state charges against her were dismissed, but she is still wanted for other charges.

Dohrn was born in 1942 in Chicago, and from the age of eight grew up in Whitefish Bay, Wisconsin, an affluent suburb of Milwaukee. She earned a master's degree in history from the University of Chicago, and graduated from law school in 1967. Dohrn never took her bar exams; and those who knew her at the time felt her radicalization was due, at least in part, to the sex discrimination she had faced in law school.

On October 17, 1970, **Katherine Ann Power** and **Susan Edith Saxe** joined the list for their alleged involvement in a Boston bank robbery, in which the robbers netted $26,000 and killed a Boston patrolman. After the robbery, police found weapons and an arsenal of ammunition in Power's apartment. It was generally agreed that the two women, and one of their accomplices, Stanley Bond, had stolen the money to finance radical causes. Both women had graduated from Brandeis University: Saxe was involved on campus with the feminist movement and the Black Panthers; Power took part in demonstrations organized by the Students for a Democratic Society. After almost five years in hiding, Saxe was arrested in Philadelphia, on March 27, 1975. Power is still at large and is currently the only woman on the FBI's list.

Women and Law

WOMEN AND AMERICAN LAW

It is difficult for a woman today to realize the extent discrimination plagued her female ancestors during the early history of the United States. Women today vote, own property, insist on equal pay, and have complete responsibility for their own financial affairs. None of this was possible for their great-great-great-grandmothers of the eighteenth century.

The Civil War brought the first widespread interest in women's rights, as women started to fight for enfranchisement along with the Negro, first for an end to black slavery, then for votes for the freedmen. But progress in suffrage and other areas of women's rights was painfully slow, because the legal system reflected the country's attitude that women were inferior to men.

Although women won the right to vote in 1920, it has been only in the last decade that laws have been passed to give women more truly equal opportunity in a male business and financial world.

History of women's legal rights

In the early history of our country, a married woman could not manage her own property, enter into contracts, or bring

Scene from an 1870 British divorce court. Most American law originated in mother England.

Changing Your Name

The assumption that a woman takes her husband's name in marriage is no longer automatically made. The feminist movement has spurred many women to rebel against giving up their own names when they marry.

Although one reason is political — women do not want to lose their identity in marriage — another reason is practical. As more women pursue careers before they marry, they often retain their maiden names for continuity in their professional lives.

Some women opt to use both maiden name and husband's name with a hyphen in between. This works well with short names, like Kathy Cole-Kelly, but can be unwieldy with longer names.

Other women refuse to keep their maiden names at all, noting that those are names their mothers took upon marriage, and actually belong to their fathers' lineage. They choose a wholly new name, whether they marry or not. In another switch, one woman changed her surname from Silverman to Silverwoman.

The law allows any person to adopt any name he or she chooses, as long as it's not for illegal purposes. In the United States, only Hawaii and Puerto Rico require a woman to use her husband's last name. Some states assume adoption of the husband's name, unless papers are filed to the contrary. (A fee is often charged for the filing.) Other states require an already-married woman to bring a lawsuit to get the court's permission to revert to her maiden name.

If you want to change your name, check the requirements of your state. Most states require a Petition for Change of Name to be filed with the appropriate court, along with a fee. The petition asks your current name, address, age, new name sought, and your reason for wanting the change.

legal suits. Her husband could claim all her wages, as could his creditor, to settle his debts. Connecticut law gave a man title to his wife's property, excepting her necessary clothing.

Before 1840, Massachusetts law prevented women from handling money matters; it even stipulated that a man be responsible for the treasury of a women's sewing club.

In the courts, a married woman was not subject to a lawsuit unless her husband was also made a party. A wife operating under her husband's supervision could not be convicted of a crime, as the courts presumed she was coerced. She was also considered incompetent to testify in court (as were slaves, mental incompetents, etc.).

Single women were afforded more rights than married women, but not as many as men. They could draft legal documents, retain sole ownership of their property, and have access to the courts through a deputy. However, daughters did not have the right, as sons did, to be named as beneficiaries in a father's will.

Married women from wealthy families could protect their money to some extent by drawing up prenuptial agreements and making trust arrangements before they were married.

Beginning around 1840, a glint of recognition emerged of the glaring injustice that befell most women when they married. Most state legislatures started to pass Married Women Acts, which separated husbands and wives in the eyes of the law and allowed women to hold title to their own property, retain wages, and conduct their own legal business.

But the new laws did not change the legal presumption that husbands were the heads of households, and many laws forbade women to dispose of their own property without a husband's consent. The presumption exists even today in Alabama.

Perhaps nowhere has sex discrimination been more insidious than in the working world. The Industrial Revolution, with its often appalling working conditions and hours, in dirty and unsafe factories, induced many states to pass "protective legislation," aimed at regulating working conditions and hours for women.

The Supreme Court generally struck down much of this legislation, claiming it violated workers' rights to enter into individual contracts of their own choosing. It did, however, uphold one law in a 1908 case, *Muller vs. Oregon*. In this one instance, said the Court, protective legislation for women was proper because they had delicate natures.

This type of "protective legislation," which was subsequently passed by other states, was double-edged. While — on the books — protecting women from exploitative working conditions, it also kept them from competing equally with men in the employment marketplace. By restricting their hours and heavy work a woman could handle, the laws made some women ineligible for jobs they could do.

No Equal Protection
Women tried to strike down "protective" legislation on the grounds that it violated the Equal Protection clause of the Fourteenth Amendment, one of the post-Civil War amendments, which stated: "No state shall . . . deny to any person within its jurisdiction the equal protection of the laws."

In deciding questions involving equal protection, the Supreme Court has developed separate tests for two classes of discrimination, suspect or not. To discrimination on the basis of race and national origin, the Court gave "suspect classification" status. This means that, because of the long history of racial and ethnic discrimination, any laws that resulted in such discrimination were immediately "suspect," and were struck down, unless very compelling evidence was produced to show that they were necessary for the greater good of society.

Sex discrimination, however, was *not* given this "suspect" status. Instead, if there was a "rational basis" for a sex discrimination law, the law would stand. "Rational basis" could be interpreted by a court to mean anything from a feeling that women were the weaker sex and needed protective legislation, to the idea that men deserved to earn more money than women because they supported families.

In 1873, upholding a sexually discriminatory law, Supreme Court Associate Justice Joseph P. Bradley used the

"Studies in Expression: When Women Are Jurors," 1906. Even after suffrage, women's service on juries was limited. Women were often passed over for jury duty unless they notified the court they wanted to serve. Not until 1975 were such requirements declared unconstitutional.

following "rational basis": "Man is, or should be, woman's protector and defender. The natural and proper timidity and delicacy which belongs to the female sex evidently unfits it for many of the occupations of civil life."

The "rational basis" test has continued to be applied to sex discrimination cases through this century. In 1948, the Supreme Court upheld a (now-repealed) Michigan law which forbade women from working as bartenders, unless the bar was family-owned. The "rational basis" for upholding the law was that women should be protected from the social and moral problems associated with bars.

In 1961, the Supreme Court upheld a Florida law that excluded women from jury duty, the "rational basis" being that women were the center of the home and family life, and should be protected from the supposedly unseemly atmosphere of a criminal trial in a courtroom.

In fact, although the court decisions of the 1970s began to rule in favor of women's rights, in 1973 the Supreme Court still refused to adopt the "suspect classification" rules in sexual discrimination cases.

Legal progress for women

"Rational basis" notwithstanding, in the 1970s women began winning court battles against sex discrimination under the old Equal Protection clause. The U.S. Supreme Court struck down, in Reed vs. Reed, in 1971, an Idaho law which mandated the preference of a male parent over a female parent in administering a deceased child's estate. Also found discriminatory under the Equal Protection clause was a law requiring more stringent standards for a woman Air Force officer applying for housing and medical benefits for her spouse, than those required a male officer (Frontiero vs. Richardson, 1973).

Since that decision, twice as many cases involving women's rights have come up as in the preceding 100 years. The Court's rulings against sexually discriminatory laws showed women that at last the time had come for challenging such laws successfully.

In other cases before the Supreme Court, female workers won retroactive pay increases to give them the same salaries as men holding the same jobs. When a group of women with pre-school children was refused employment by a major corporation, they took the company to court and won the right to jobs, unless men with preschool children were also considered unemployable.

In 1973, the Court upheld a Pittsburgh municipal ordinance prohibiting newspapers from publishing job offerings in sex-segregated classified advertisements, and the ordinance was quickly adopted throughout the country. The Court also struck down company rules against the employment of women with illegitimate children, when no such rule was applied to men.

In the education field, where there are many women teachers, numerous sex discrimination cases have been brought to the courts. As recently as 1940, the Supreme Judicial Court of Massachusetts upheld a local school board rule which prevented married women from being hired as teachers. Soon after, because of the shortage of men due to World War II, such rules were ignored.

But many boards of education retained employment strictures affecting women only. In 1974, the Supreme Court took up the case of two female junior high school teachers who challenged a school board rule requiring all pregnant school teachers to take maternity leave, without pay, at least five months before the expected birth of the child.

The two pregnant teachers wanted to avoid the unpaid maternity leave and finish out the school year, as their babies weren't due until the summer. The Court declared that the school board's rules were unconstitutional because procreation was a fundamental right within the right to freedom of personal choice.

The rights of pregnant women remain a source of controversy. The Supreme Court, in 1974, upheld a California disability disability insurance program which refused disability insurance to a woman who was absent from work because she was having a baby.

Applying the "rational basis" test, the Court determined that there could be no sex discrimination when a law applied to traits particular to one sex. The decision implied that if a *man* got pregnant, he would not receive disability benefits either!

Anti-sexist legislation

While the courts have been reevaluating the rights of women in our society and have struck down a number of sexual discriminatory laws, Congress, too has responded to the feminist movement and to increasing demands for equal legal treatment for both sexes.

Since 1963, Congress has passed six major laws and one amendment aimed at eliminating sex discrimination.

The Equal Pay Act of 1963 was the first federal law which prohibited sex discrimination. An amendment to the 1938 Fair Labor Standards Act, this law requires employers to pay men and women the same rates for equal work, and covers all employees within the minimum wage laws, plus executive, administrative, professional, and outside sales personnel. The Act is administered by the Wage and Hour Division of the U.S. Department of Labor, which, in 1974, found that over 30,000 women had been underpaid.

The Fair Labor Standards Act, of which the Equal Pay Act is a part, prescribes the minimum wage employers under the law's jurisdiction may pay. In 1974, it was amended to include most private household workers, the majority of whom are women.

Title VII of the Civil Rights Act of 1964, supplemented by the 1972 Equal Employment Opportunity Act, is the most comprehensive anti-discrimination statute in the federal arsenal. It makes it unlawful for employers and labor unions to discriminate on grounds of race, color, religion, sex or national origin.

The Equal Employment Opportunity Commission (EEOC) enforces Title VII, which, among other things, makes it illegal to fire a woman because of pregnancy or marriage. In 1976, more than 20,000 sex discrimination charges were filed with the EEOC.

Title IX of the Education Amendments of 1972 was a very controversial law when it was passed. The law, which prohibits sex discrimination against employees or students of an education institution posed a threat to many school, or school-related, single sex events. (Single sex volunteer youth service groups, like the Girl Scouts and the Young Women's Christian Organization, were exempted from the law.) But, when the Department of Health, Education, and Welfare, which had been authorized to enforce the statute, banned such parent-child activities, it was overruled by the president.

Also controversial was the effect on school sports programs. The law mandated that the same amount of money be spent on girls' sports as on boys' sports.

Title IX did not, however, prevent the Supreme Court from upholding single-sex schools. A girl refused admission to an all-male high school in Philadelphia brought suit, claiming that the all-boys' high school was better than the all-girls' school to which she was assigned. In April 1977, an equally-divided Supreme Court allowed the sex-segregated high schools to remain so. Colleges and universities can restrict their undergraduate curricula to one sex, but graduate programs must be open to men and women alike.

The Women's Education Equity Act of 1974 authorizes the Secretary of Health, Education and Welfare (HEW) to spend money to end discrimination based on sex in vocational and career counseling, sports education, and other programs.

In an effort to stop discrimination against women in housing, in 1974 Congress passed amendments to the 1968 Fair Housing Act. By prohibiting discrimination against women getting rental and housing loans, the amendments seek to aid single and divorced women, female roommates, and women with children who have a hard time finding housing.

The most recent and ambitious anti-discrimination law on the books is the Equal Credit Opportunity Act of 1974. Written to end decades of severe discrimination against women trying to establish credit, the law requires all financial institutions to make credit equally available to credit-worthy customers, regardless of sex or marital status.

Specifically, the Act prohibits creditors from: asking the sex of the credit applicant; asking about the use of birth-control procedures or the applicant's childbearing plans; differentiating between male and female heads of households. They are also barred from insisting a married woman's charge accounts be held in her husband's name, terminating credit or imposing new conditions based on a change of marital status, and requiring a credit cosigner of a woman when one would not be asked of a man.

The only questions a creditor can ask an applicant are those bearing directly on ability and willingness to pay.

The Act offers two recourses to aggrieved consumers. They may file a civil action suit against the alleged violator asking up to $10,000 in damages. Or they can file a complaint with the appropriate fed-

eral agency. If they are complaining about a bank, the Federal Reserve System hears the complaint. In all other cases, the complaint is referred to the Federal Trade Commission (FTC). One problem with this alternative is that agencies will not take any action until several complaints about a particular creditor are received.

Equal Rights Amendment

The most volatile legal issue involving women and the law today is the Equal Rights Amendment. Despite popular assumptions, it is not a new amendment.

Drafted in 1923 by feminist Alice Paul who, with her followers, had just won the right to vote, they saw the need to further broaden women's rights by another such constitutional guarantee.

The bill had been introduced into Congress every year, until 1972, when it passed both houses. Then began the fight for its ratification as the 27th Amendment. Ratification by 38 states is required. This must occur by March 1979. As of April 1977, 35 states had ratified the amendment. (Thirteen states already have ERA's in their state constitutions.)

What does it say?
The ERA reads:
Section 1. Equality of rights under the law shall not be denied or abridged by the United States or by any State on account of sex.
Section 2. The Congress shall have the power to enforce, by appropriate legislation, the provisions of this article.
Section 3. This amendment shall take effect two years after the date of ratification.

ERA proponents, which include most major women's organizations, from the League of Women Voters and the Young Women's Christian Association to the National Organization for Women, feel that ERA will give impetus to the fight for equality. Without it, proponents argue, an unfavorable Supreme Court could reverse *all* the legal rights women have won in recent years.

Proponents also claim that passage of the ERA would lead to more vigorous enforcement of existing sex discrimination laws. The ERA would make sex a "suspect classification" in the eyes of the court, as are racial and ethnic groups, forcing judges to consider allegations of equal protection violations based on gender with the most scrupulous objectivity.

Opponents of the ERA, like Phyllis Schlafly, head of STOP ERA, the National Council of Catholic Women, and others, feel that ERA would accomplish little more than present sex discrimination laws, and that the few benefits it would bring about are far outweighed by the changes it would cause.

Most threatening to ERA opponents is the fear that the amendment would destroy the rights and the role of homemaker. Certain family laws would change under the ERA. Widowers would receive equal rights with widows, who now have certain monetary and tax advantages. Alimony laws would be based on need rather than sex. (Twenty-eight states already provide alimony payments for needy husbands.) Custody rights would still be based on the child's best interests, but there might be a reevaluation of the tradition that often automatically gave the mother custody. But ERA would have no jurisdiction over social customs, personal relationships, or laws based on sexual differences.

Another charge made by ERA opponents is that the amendment will make women eligible for the draft and combat duty. ERA would subject women to the draft under the same terms as men: under a renewed draft, men with families would probably be exempted; so would women. Combat assignments would be made on an ability basis. The ERA would also force changes in military regulations which currently discriminate against women.

ERA is not designed to radically change our laws. Its purpose is only to insure that whatever is given or denied men by law should also be given or denied women.

If ERA is ratified, the state and federal government will have two years to revise discriminatory laws.

Choosing an attorney

You can serve as your own attorney in a court case, if you wish, but it's not recommended. Court procedures can be very complex, because of technical requirements varying interpretations of almost every law; an attorney is most often indispensable to guide you through the intricacies. A lawyer's knowledge of legal technicalities in a courtroom can win you a case that you might lose on your own.

Because so much depends on your attorney, selecting the right one can be very important. Start by asking friends, business associates, and relatives, for names of competent lawyers they have used. Check the Better Business Bureau, your county attorney's office, local legal clinics, and lawyer referral services of local bar associations. The latter often have representatives who, for a fee of from $5 to $15, will advise on choosing the right lawyer.

Check the experience of the lawyers in whom you are interested, both for their familiarity with the local court personnel and procedures, and for their specialties. It makes no sense to hire an expensive divorce lawyer to handle your civil suit against a moving company that damaged your furniture. Bar associations' referral services break down their membership by specialties, which will help you narrow the field.

Make sure you have good rapport with your lawyer. You should be able to discuss a situation frankly, especially a sensitive, personal one, like divorce. You shouldn't be intimidated by a lawyer, or feel that he or she disapproves of your actions.

It is very important to establish the fee, and what it includes at the beginning of your relationship with the lawyer. You and your lawyer should draw up and sign a written agreement covering services to be performed, how much time the work is expected to take, and what the approximate or maximum fee will be. You can always renegotiate the agreement if things change, but you should keep abreast of the costs and what they cover.

RAPE

One of the side effects of the feminist movement in the past several years has been a focus on the ancient crime of rape.

Rape has a sordid history. Traditionally, rape was not considered a crime against women, but rather an insult to the men of their family. The honor of the men was involved. Women were raped as part of the booty when soldiers captured a town.

Today, the situation has changed. Until recently, the victim's story had to be corroborated by one or more witnesses in order to convict. Because there are few witnesses in rape cases, there were few convictions. Most states have changed that requirement, and rape today often carries a penalty of long-term imprisonment.

Most rape laws, which are state rather than federal laws, define rape as the penetration, without consent, of the vagina by the penis. Because (under such laws) the sexual act is only criminal when there is no consent, it is the *only* crime which requires proof of the victim's state of mind, in addition to the usual requirement of the intent of the accused.

The Federal Bureau of Investigation reports that rape is the fastest growing crime in the country, but this could be due to the fact that more rapes are reported now as a result of more enlightened procedures.

In 1975, there were 56,090 forcible rapes reported. One year later the number had increased by 9 percent. Over the past fifteen years, rape increased by 165 percent, the FBI reports. Despite the growing tendency to report rapes, however, the trauma and guilt that still accompany rape for many women lead some experts to estimate that there are three to four times more rapes each year than are reported. Unfortunately, only 59 percent of all persons arrested for rape are prosecuted. Of these, 46 percent are acquitted, 42 percent are found guilty, and the remaining 12 percent are convicted on a lesser charge.

Rape is a particularly traumatic crime because it is sexual, and often has more damaging psychological than physical effects. In addition to the very real dangers of venereal disease, pregnancy, and often brutal bodily damage, a woman may feel embarrassed, angry, humiliated or, in many cases, guilty for not having been about to do something to stop the rapist.

Police have been criticized in recent years as insensitive and lax in handling rape victims. The Law Enforcement Assistance Administration reported in October 1976 that the response of police, prosecutors, and hospitals to rape victims is poorly coordinated and inadequate. But change is on the way. Today, every major police department in the nation has established special sexual offense units with the expertise necessary to assist rape victims.

Because of the potential sensationalism of a rape trial, it can be rough on a victim, who must look at her alleged assailant and relive the crime in the courtroom before strangers. Because there are usually no witnesses to a rape, it's the victim's word against the alleged rapist's. A defense attorney can do a very biased, but effective job of trying to damage the victim's credibility and shatter her nerves before the jury. Because defense lawyers have so routinely used the techniques of blackening the victim's reputation, most states now forbid any court inquiries into the complainant's sex life.

In 1975, Congress passed the Health Revenue Sharing and Health Services Act. This authorized establishment of a "national center for the prevention and control of rape." When it opens, it will be a clearing house for rape information and a reference center for gauging the effectiveness of rape laws.

There are a number of preventive measures you can take to protect yourself from rape, as well as recommended behavior if you are attacked.

Prevention of Rape
In the home: Quite frequently, rapes occur in the victim's home, where she feels most secure and least suspicious. To cut down chances of being raped at home: keep entrances and hallways well lit; securely lock windows and doors; *never* open a door to a stranger. Give the impression that you aren't alone when responding to a knock on the door. Call out, "I'll get it, Bob," or the like.

If an unexpected repairman turns up, tell him to slip his identification under the door, then *call the company* for confirmation *before* admitting him. Never allow a stranger in to use your telephone. If he says it's an emergency, make the call for him, *while he waits outside*. Avoid entering an elevator alone with a stranger.

In addition, women who live alone or

with other women should use their first initials rather than first names on mailbox, in a telephone listing, or apartment directory.

When walking alone walk at a steady pace, exuding confidence, because a rapist looks for vulnerable victims. Keep your hands as free of packages and boxes as possible; don't walk in dark places; avoid short cuts through alleys and empty parking lots.

Keep away from bushes, alley entrances, and other dark places where an assailant might hide. If you think you're being followed, don't go home. Head for a place where you'll get assistance, like a nearby police station, a neighbor's house, or a lighted restaurant, pharmacy, or taxi stand. If you feel you are in imminent danger from a stalking stranger, scream "Fire!" instead of "Help!"

In the car: Don't park in dimly lit places; always lock the car; keep your vehicle in good condition to avoid breakdowns; *check the back seat* for a hidden attacker *before* entering car; keep the doors locked while driving, especially at night.

Returning home at night: Leave a light on inside the house and at the entranceway; have your keys ready before reaching the door; if someone drove you home, have them wait until you are safely indoors.

In Case of Attack

Experts don't agree on a single strategy to follow if you are attacked. The circumstances, the options of the victim, the personality and physical power of the rapist — especially one with a knife or gun — all drastically modify the reaction. Police frequently advise against fighting back, because that may lead to more violence or death. But failure to put up some resistance may render criminal prosecution difficult.

Some people recommend self-defense courses for women, or suggest women carry weapons. If you do carry a weapon, make sure you know how to use it efficiently — you'll probably only get one chance to try. Also remember, it's not a good idea to carry something your attacker can grab from you and use against you.

If you decide to act aggressively, do it right the first time, because you probably won't get another chance and the rapist will probably become much more violent. Some experts, claiming that a rapist is less self-confident at the beginning of an attack, recommend that a victim fight and scream at the outset of an assault. But fighting may also antagonize the attacker, making him angrier and more violent.

Many women have had success by speaking calmly to the rapist. This may throw him off guard and allow you to escape.

Don't fight or struggle with a rapist if he has a weapon. Your only recourse here is to try to escape, if the opportunity presents itself. If you think it feasible, push him off balance, and run; try kneeing him *hard* in the crotch — then flee — simultaneously screaming your head off.

The Aftermath

If you have been raped, don't take a bath or change clothes. Your clothes will be required as evidence in a rape trial, and you must have a medical exam to prove you've been raped.

Report the rape to the police immediately, or, if you are terribly upset, see if there is a rape crisis center in your area and call it. Many have opened in the past few years. Most centers are staffed by trained women, who will tell you exactly what to do.

If you go to the police first, you may be referred to a special rape unit, which most major city police departments now have. If you are nervous about reports that police are insensitive to rape victims, *take a friend with you* who will help you be calm and stand up for your rights.

Don't answer any questions about your past sex life. It has nothing to do with the rape, and most states now forbid evidence in court about a victim's past sex life.

Take a friend with you when the police send you to a doctor or hospital to have a medical exam. One of the most frequent complaints rape victims make is about the rude and abrupt medical exams they are given by police doctors. Your friend can help you insist on courteous treatment. You should also go to *your own doctor* for examination and help afterward, and *get an anti-pregnancy pill*.

If your rape case should go to trial, some advise that you get your own lawyer whom you can trust to stand up for your rights. There are special rules of evidence in rape cases that are designed to protect you, the victim, from unfair questions that damage your credibility, especially in the area of your sex life.

WIFE BEATING

Wife beating has long been a closet crime. While technically illegal, it has been condoned as one of the least savory but permitted prerogatives of men over their wives. It is estimated that as many as twenty-eight million women in this country are physically abused by their husbands.

The typical battered wife client, according to one attorney, is thirty-five to forty years old, married ten years with several children, and has no marketable skills, no money of her own, no job, and no credit. Her economic dependence keeps her in her husband's power.

Further, if her husband has been abusing her regularly, she usually has little feeling of self-worth. She also feels guilty because she thinks she is to blame for her husband's beatings — she has nagged him or made too many demands on him.

Help Now Available

Today, battered wives no longer need suffer in silence. In the past few years, police, courts, and society have moved to help abused women escape from threatening situations and start new lives. The most practical step has been the opening of centers where women and their children can escape from violent husbands. They are housed, fed, counseled, and comforted for about a month in the centers.

Also, police departments are beginning to recognize wife beating as a public issue rather than a private problem. Legislatures are reviewing their laws about wife beating and moving toward stiffer penalties for wife abuse.

Courts, too, are favoring tougher penalties. A California court recently upheld the felony conviction of a wife beater. In most states, wife beating has traditionally been treated as a misdemeanor.

What should a woman do to bring criminal charges against her husband after a beating? As soon as she can, she should get out of the house, go to a neighbor, and call the police — the more witnesses the better. As soon as possible, she should go to a doctor or hospital and have pictures taken. Then she should file a charge against her husband at the police station.

If she feels she should get a divorce, as many professionals in the child abuse field recommend, she should get a lawyer and under no circumstances contact her husband or go back to her house without the lawyer's legal advice. By returning home, she may be condoning her husband's behavior in the eyes of the law.

SISTERS IN THE LAW

Brent: Colonial Attorney

Margaret Brent (1600-1671) was the first woman lawyer in the colonies and probably the first feminist. She came to Maryland in 1638 and, because of her family's connections, was given the first land grant ever vested in a woman.

Eventually, because of other acquisitions, she became one of the largest landowners in the colony and was the proprietor of a manor, an estate of more than a thousand acres. Such land holdings earned her the title of lord and the right to conduct business and sign contracts, rights held by no other woman of that time.

Brent became active in politics and a close ally of Governor Leonard Calvert, who named her sole executor of his will. The court also appointed her attorney for his estate. Again, no other women had these rights.

In 1648, she went before the Maryland Assembly, demanding the right to two votes in the legislature, one vote as the lord of her manor, and one vote as the attorney for Calvert's estate. She was denied the votes because she was a woman.

During her years in Maryland, she was involved in more lawsuits than anyone else in the colony, usually acting as an attorney for her relatives and neighbors. From 1642 to 1650, her name appeared 124 times in the court record.

Lockwood: Fought for Women

Lawyer, politician, feminist, **Belva Ann Bennett Lockwood** (1830-1917) probably

Belva Lockwood, first woman to practice before the Supreme Court, ran for President in 1884.

did more than any other woman to advance the national status of women attorneys.

Married at eighteen and widowed six years later with a small child, she graduated with honors from Genesee College (later Syracuse University) at age twenty-seven and took a teaching job at an upstate New York school.

In the mid-1860s, she moved to Washington, D.C., where she married again and opened one of the capital's first coeducational schools.

She also began studying the law, under a local attorney after she was refused admission to three Washington, D.C. law schools on grounds that she would distract the young male students. Eventually, she was admitted to National University Law School (later part of George Washington University), but got her diploma only by petitioning the school's ex-officio president, President Ulysses S. Grant.

In 1873, she was admitted to the District of Columbia bar, but the federal court refused to hear a woman attorney. She lobbied for a congressional bill to break down the barrier; with its passage, she was, in 1879, the first woman admitted to the Supreme Court's bar.

An ardent feminist, Lockwood founded Washington's first suffrage group and lobbied among congressmen for feminist legislation, including passage of a law she had drafted guaranteeing equal pay for women in the civil service.

In 1884, she ran for president on the Equal Rights ticket, despite the disapproval of Susan B. Anthony and other leading suffragists. She polled only four thousand votes and ran again in 1888 with

even less success. But her prominence won her a State Department delegate's seat to the International Congress of Charities, Correction and Philanthropy in Geneva in 1896.

In 1906, at the age of seventy-six, she was back in the Supreme Court, arguing successfully on behalf of the Eastern Cherokee Indian tribe in a case that won her clients $5 million.

Bradwell: Legal Publisher

Myra Colby Bradwell (1831-1894), founder of the first weekly legal newspaper in the West, was a successful advocate of laws giving women legal rights; however, she never practiced law herself.

She had been a schoolteacher while her husband and brother were partners in a successful Chicago law firm. Then in 1861, when her husband was elected county judge of Cook County, she began to work in the law office to ease the load on her brother. She learned a lot of law but could not appear in court or practice in her own right.

In 1868, she founded the *Chicago Legal News.* Her husband, by then a member of the state legislature, pushed through special acts enabling her to be the president of the publishing company, despite prohibitive laws against married women, and making the publication of opinions, notices, and laws in the newspaper admissible evidence in court.

The newspaper was an enormous success, and Bradwell used it as a sounding board for advocating judicial and legal reform. Many of her suggestions became law, including Chicago's first zoning ordinances, regulation of large corporations, compulsory retirement of judges, and the

Myra Bradwell battled for women's rights on the pages of her *Chicago Legal News.*

formation of bar associations. She also won endorsement of the Chicago legal community for women's suffrage.

Her own legal battles were not as successful. Although she passed the Illinois bar exam in 1869 with distinction, she was denied admittance to the bar because of her sex and because she was married; the U.S. Supreme Court would not intervene in the decision. Although subsequent state legislation, urged by her husband, abolished sex discrimination, she never again applied for the bar. In 1890, the Illinois Supreme Court, acting on its own initiative, admitted Bradwell to the bar, but she never practiced.

Instead, she turned her energies to removing legal disabilities plaguing women. Through the *Chicago Legal News* and other lobbying efforts, she drafted successful bills securing married women the right to their own wages, permitting them to hold school board offices, and allowing them to serve as notary publics.

Allen: Lawyer by Chance

Florence Ellinwood Allen (1884-1966) was the first woman to sit on a high federal court but came to the law field only by chance. She was initially bent on a career as a concert pianist, but a nerve injury that prevented her from playing the piano forced her to turn to other pursuits, one of which was the law.

Although admitted to the bar in her home state of Ohio, she couldn't get a regular legal job because she was a woman. Instead, she worked for a number of social causes, including the women's suffrage movement in Ohio.

In 1919, she became the first woman appointed assistant county prosecutor in her Ohio home county. Within a year, she was elected a judge in the Court of Common Pleas, and two years later was elected to the Ohio Supreme Court.

In 1934, President Franklin D. Roosevelt appointed Allen to sit on the Sixth Circuit of the U.S. Court of Appeals, one notch below the U.S. Supreme Court. The appointment made her the first woman to serve as a judge in a federal court of general jurisdiction. She was later appointed chief justice of the circuit court.

Perhaps her most influential work while serving on the court was her majority opin-

ion in the controversial Tennessee Valley Authority case, which affirmed the constitutionality of the government project.

Hughes: She Swore in LBJ

Judge **Sarah Tilghman Hughes** (1896-   ) became known to the world when she administered the oath of office to Lyndon B. Johnson minutes after the assassination of President John F. Kennedy in Dallas in 1963. But the eighty-year-old dynamic woman had already been well-known in legal and political circles for many years.

After graduating from Goucher College and holding a number of jobs, including that of a Washington, D.C. policewoman, she earned her law degree in 1922 from George Washington University. She married a fellow law student, and they moved to Dallas to practice.

Mixing law with politics, she was elected to the Texas legislature in 1930. During three terms, she worked major revisions into the Texas divorce law. Her first judgeship came in 1935 when the governor nominated her to the bench of the Fourteenth District Court of Dallas County. Despite opposition from a number of male Texas senators, she was confirmed. While on the bench, she lobbied for and won the right of women to serve on juries.

In 1961 President Kennedy appointed her to the U.S. District Court for the Northern District of Texas, where she still serves.

Sarah Hughes administered the oath of office to Lyndon B. Johnson on November 22, 1963.

In 1971, while sitting on the court, she ruled a Texas bank had been guilty of sex discrimination in its refusal to hire a woman because she had an illegitimate child.

"It is common knowlege that it is easier to determine if a woman has illegitimate children than men," she said.

Hufstedler: Prominent Justice

Shirley Hufstedler (1926-   ) is the highest ranking woman judge in the United States. She sits on the United States Court of Appeals for nine western states and Guam. The Denver-born lawyer, who has practiced for twenty-seven years, is an avid reformer. Her proposals have included offsetting the high cost of legal fees with an "economy court," where a single, court-employed attorney would represent both sides of a dispute.

A graduate of the University of New Mexico and Stanford Law School, Hufstedler began her law career in Los Angeles in private practice with her husband. She prospered during her ten years in private practice and, in 1961, was appointed to her first judgeship at the Los Angeles County Superior Court.

After five years, her reputation as an incisive judge gained her the appointment to the Court of Appeals of California. In 1968, the late President Lyndon B. Johnson appointed her to her present high judgeship, where she has won praise for her opinions.

Bird: Progressive Judge

Rose Elizabeth Bird (1936-   ), chief justice of the California Supreme Court, is the first woman to serve on that seven-judge-court.

Growing up with her widowed mother who worked in a factory, Bird learned early to work hard to gain self-sufficiency. She graduated cum laude in 1958 from Long Island University in New York and planned a career as a teacher or foreign correspondent.

But while earning a graduate degree at the University of California at Berkeley, she worked as a legislative aide in the state legislature and became fascinated with the law. She switched into law school, graduating in 1965, and was subsequently hired as the first female law clerk in the Nevada Supreme Court.

A year later, she became the first woman to work in the Santa Clara County public defender's office, where she successfully argued a case before the U.S. Supreme Court.

In 1975, California Governor Edmund G. Brown, Jr. tapped Bird to be the first woman to serve in the state's cabinet. As secretary of agriculture and services, Bird became one of the governor's most trusted advisers, drafting a controversial farm-labor law that restored peace to California agriculture.

In 1977, Brown appointed her to her present position as chief justice, considered especially significant because the California court has the reputation of being the most innovative and authoritative state court in the United States.

Sharp: Legal Trailblazer

Another woman chief justice of a state supreme court is **Susie Marshall Sharp**, (1907-   ) who in 1974 was named to the post in the North Carolina Supreme Court; she had served for twelve years as an associate justice.

A legal trailblazer among women for many years, Sharp, a native of Rocky Mount, North Carolina, was the only woman in her class at the University of North Carolina Law School in 1926. In 1949, she was appointed the first woman special judge on the state's superior court, where she earned a reputation as a compassionate and incisive legal scholar. In 1962, she was elected to the state's supreme court, where she is now chief justice.

She has voted against reinstating the mandatory death penalty, upheld the state's right to use tax funds to bus school children in urban areas, and ruled against the use of state bonds for private industrial development.

"One of the finest compliments I ever got," Sharp once said, "was when a lawyer was asked how it felt to appear before a woman judge, and he replied, 'I have not been conscious of appearing before a woman judge!'"

Wary of juggling a career and a marriage, Sharp has remained single. "A woman has got to draw up a blueprint. She has got to budget her life," she says.

Norton: Free Speech Advocate

As chairwoman of New York City's Human Rights Commission for seven years and a former lawyer for the American Civil Liberties Union (ACLU), **Eleanor Holmes Norton** (1937-   ) has been an articulate and effective advocate of the right of free speech.

During her five years at the ACLU, Norton, who is black, defended every kind of person and group, from civil rights activists to Ku Klux Klansmen to politicians to feminists. In one highly publicized case, she won promotions for sixty women employees of *Newsweek* who had accused the magazine of sex discrimination in jobs.

She specializes in cases involving freedom of speech, believing that the First Amendment has contributed to "almost every social change in the twentieth century." Her clients have included black Georgia State Representative Julian Bond, who was denied his legislative seat for his outspoken anti-Vietnam War views, and Alabama Governor George Wallace. When then presidential candidate Wallace was denied a permit for a political rally in New York City in 1968, because Mayor John V. Lindsay feared civil unrest, Holmes took on Wallace's case and won.

"If people like George Wallace are denied free expression, then the same thing can happen to black people," she explained to one interviewer.

As New York City's human rights commissioner, she had won more liberal maternity benefits for women workers, forced the 21 Club and the Biltmore Hotel Men's Bar to open their doors to women, and promoted revision of outdated federal and state laws regulating workmen's compensation and minimum wages, abortion laws, and the establishment of day centers.

In 1977, Norton was named to head the Equal Employment Opportunity Commission.

Volner: Watergate Lawyer

A rising star on the government legal scene is thirty-three-year-old **Jill Wine Volner** (1943-   ), known to many for her skillful cross examination of former President Nixon's secretary, Rose Mary Woods, at the Watergate trial.

As a trial attorney at the famed trial, she became nationally known, as much for her mini skirts as for her legal footwork. She still waxes enthusiastic about her Watergate work: "It was a fantastic experience. I worked with marvelous lawyers on both sides and learned a lot."

Volner was brought up in Chicago and went to the University of Illinois, graduating in 1964 with a journalism degree. Eager to become a political reporter, she found that newspapers were unwilling to hire a woman in that slot; she decided to go to law school to buttress her journalistic background.

At Columbia Law School, Volner found she was more interested in the law than in journalism and interested enough in fellow law student Ian Volner to marry him. They moved to Washington, D.C., where he had gotten a job and she, deciding to pursue criminal law, was hired as a trial attorney by the Department of Justice.

Following her Watergate success, ABC-TV offered her a job as a political reporter. After much thought, she took instead a job as an associate in a prominent law firm.

Most recently, President Jimmy Carter tried to persuade her to take an administrative post in the Justice or Treasury Departments. She finally accepted a position as general counsel to the Department of the Army, a job previously held by two of Carter's current cabinet officers.

Army General Counsel Jill Wine Volner admits she objects to being called "a lady lawyer."

WOMEN JURORS AND LAWYERS

Women, like men, have many roles to play in our legal system — defendant, plaintiff, lawyer, judge, or juror. Traditionally, their participation in any of these roles has been limited and, although women are more involved now than ever before, they are still treated much differently than men.

Women did not serve on juries at all before they were enfranchised, as potential jurors' names were taken from voter registration lists. After the passage of the Nineteenth Amendment granting suffrage to women, other state legislation limited their service on juries. For example, a woman was ineligible for jury duty unless she officially notified the court that she wanted to serve. Not until 1975 were such requirements declared unconstitutional by the Supreme Court.

Juries still tend to be male-dominated, but lawyers try to get women jurors when they feel it will help their clients. Common wisdom in the legal profession has it that women jurors will favor the handsome, young, male defendant, as well as his male lawyer. On the other side of the coin, female jurors are supposed to distrust other women, and lawyers may try to select women jurors if the opposition's main witness is a woman.

When a woman is a defendant, her looks as well as her gender have an effect on the jury. According to a University of Maryland study, juries in most criminal cases tend to believe a good-looking female defendant more often than a homely one. The exception is in crimes involving a swindle, when a pretty defendant is at a disadvantage. Women defendants also receive better treatment at the hands of an all-male jury.

The result is that sexual attitudes and prejudices often play as important a part in a trial as the evidence.

Women Lawyers

Until this decade, women lawyers were rarities. In the nineteenth century, a woman could learn law only by studying in the office of a male lawyer, usually a relative. In 1870, Ada Kepley became the first woman awarded a law degree, earned at Union College of Chicago. But as recently as the 1940s, women were not admitted to most law schools — Harvard Law School admitted no women until the mid-1950s. Nor were women encouraged to practice law, either in private law firms or in government jobs.

In 1967, only 3 percent of the 300,000 lawyers in the United States were women, and they earned approximately two thousand dollars a year less than male lawyers. After nine years of experience the gap between men's and women's salaries widened to eight thousand dollars. As recently as 1969, women made up less than 7 percent of the law student population.

Today, however, women are entering the law field in droves. Women now make up a third of all classes entering law school, and they are pursuing successful legal careers in private business, government, and on law school faculties. They have their own firms and sit as judges on all levels of courts except the United States Supreme Court.

Public Interest Law

In 1976, Susan Estrich was the first woman elected president of the Harvard Law Review, a scholarly publication edited by the school's most respected students. Many women, after graduation from law school, have been successful in public interest law. In President Jimmy Carter's new administration, one in six appointees at the cabinet, sub-cabinet, federal-agency and White House-staff level has been a woman. A third of the women have been lawyers — generally in their thirties.

But there is still progress to be made before women reach full equality, in terms of attitude and actual jobs.

Most women are desk lawyers, handling research, estate and trust work; few are criminal lawyers who argue aggressively in the courtroom.

Recent successes in the courts may help them. A major New York law firm settled a 1976 discrimination suit by establishing a quota system requiring the offer of jobs to women lawyers at 20 percent higher than the percentage of women graduating from the law schools where the firm recruits. The settlement also called for equal pay and advancement without regard to sex. A number of other firms have been forced to make similar agreements.

LEGAL STATUS OF HOMEMAKERS

Little has been written to inform the homemaker of her legal rights in marriage, divorce, and widowhood; therefore, the National Commission on the Observance of International Women's Year Committee on Homemakers, chaired by former Congresswoman Martha Griffiths, sponsored a series of papers to explore the status of homemakers in each state from the viewpoint of the woman not employed outside the home. These informational papers point to little known aspects of domestic relations law and emphasize laws and judicial precedents that fail to give proper recognition to the value of the homemaker and the welfare of children.

The following chart extracts from the homemaker papers parts of the state laws that are of special interest, and those which are either grossly unfair to homemakers or unique to a particular state. The material offered is of general interest and should not be used by researchers writing precise legal papers. It may not reflect changes in family law made in recent months. The chart was prepared by Sheryl Swed and reviewed by Roxanne Barton Conlin.

Copies of the legal status of the homemaker papers for each state are available for $1.25 each from: Superintendent of Documents, U.S. Government Printing Office, Washington, D.C. 20402.

ALABAMA

RIGHTS: Women may marry with their parents' consent at age 14 and at age 18 without it. Men are not allowed to marry until age 17 with parental consent or at 19 without it. Alabama requires a woman to take her husband's name upon marriage. If a woman has written a will before marriage, it is automatically revoked after her marriage without regard to her wishes. This law does not apply to husbands. A man who finds his wife in the act of adultery with another man and immediately kills her is not guilty of murder, (punishable by death or life imprisonment) but of manslaughter only, (punishable by one to ten years imprisonment). There is no such defense for a woman who murders her husband under similar circumstances.

PROPERTY: The only state that requires a husband give his wife permission to sell her own separate real estate. He must actually sign the deed with his wife as if he owned it.

INHERITANCE: If a husband dies without a will, the widow must divide the personal property of the husband with the children equally. Children are entitled to inherit real estate from their father even ahead of their mother.

RAPE: It is not a crime for a man to force sexual intercourse on his wife, even if not living together or if one has filed for a divorce.

ALASKA

SUPPORT: It is estimated that fewer than 50% of the women in Alaska who are supposed to be receiving child support are actually receiving it. A married homemaker has no civil right to a share of the family's income short of seeking to end the marriage by divorce or putting her husband in jail. Courts refuse to intervene in an ongoing marriage to assure that the wife and children are provided with the necessities of life. The wife must depend on her husband's good faith and sense of responsibility.

PROPERTY: A wife is free to buy, sell, or lease her separate real property without interference from her husband. Both spouses are personally and solely liable for their own separate debts incurred either before or during marriage.

ABUSE: If a wife beater is arrested, he is likely to be released quickly on $25 bond. The sentence for a convicted wife beater is usually a fine of $25-$50 which may be suspended. Separate reporting of wife beating is not required; thus data is limited. The average total time spent by police on each wife-beating complaint is 17 minutes.

INHERITANCE: If a husband dies without a will, the wife receives the first $50,000 of the estate but only ½ of the remainder if there are children or parents of the husband.

ARIZONA

SUPPORT: Because of the refusal of the courts to interfere in a continuing marriage, the homemaker dependent on her husband's earnings has no access to them except through her husband's sense of fairness. Arizona permits courts to award support beyond the age of 18 for mentally or physically disabled children. Court ordered child support payments may not be retroactively decreased.

PROPERTY: Either spouse separately may acquire, manage, control or dispose of community property or bind the community. A wife has all the legal power over community property that her husband has.

DISSOLUTION/DIVORCE: The only ground for dissolution is the allegation that the marriage is "irretrievably broken." Essentially a divorce may be obtained at the will of one of the spouses.

INHERITANCE: All of a couple's property, whether separate or community, goes to the survivor if a will has not been written. A wife is protected even if her spouse decides to write a will giving all his property away, since half of the community is hers, and he cannot will her half away.

RAPE: Rape is not a crime when perpetrated by a husband on a wife even if the parties are separated or one has filed for a divorce.

ARKANSAS

PROPERTY: The homestead right is the husband's, not the wife's and the husband can choose and abandon a homestead at will without the wife's consent. Once the homestead is abandoned by the will of the husband, it can be sold by him without his wife's consent. The law presumes that all personal property, such as money, household furnishing and the like, belong to the husband. In order to protect her personal property from sale by her husband without her consent or attachment by his creditors, a married woman must file a schedule of her separate property with the county recorder. If she does not, the burden is on her to prove that she bought the property out of her separate funds. No such burden is ever placed on the husband.

DISSOLUTION/DIVORCE: The property division allowed depends on fault and does not take into account a spouse's contribution as homemaker.

INHERITANCE: If a husband dies without leaving descendants, and has been married at least three years preceding his death, then all property goes to his widow. If he is not survived by descendants and has been married less than three years, his widow receives one-half of all his property plus statutory allowances and homestead rights. If the husband is survived by descendants, then regardless of the length of the marriage, the widow receives only statutory allowances, homestead rights, and dower, and all remaining property is divided among the descendants.

CALIFORNIA

SUPPORT: The right to support depends on need rather than sex. 75% of all welfare recipients are women. Women receiving assistance must register for employment when youngest child is 6.

PROPERTY: Community property — Since 1975 both spouses have had an equal power of management and control over community property.

ABUSE: Wife and child beating are covered under the same section of the penal code; statistics are compiled jointly. Charges of abuse are generally not brought because local authorities view incidents as personal matters.

DISSOLUTION/DIVORCE: In a divorce situation community property is divided equally. However, the husband's earning power or capacity is not viewed as a property asset of the community and is never divided equally. Both spouses are eligible for alimony and have an equal right to custody of the children and an equal duty to support them.

INHERITANCE: If there is no will, all of the community property goes to surviving spouse and at least 1/3 of the separate property goes to surviving spouse.

RAPE: A husband cannot be charged with raping his wife even if they are separated and awaiting divorce.

COLORADO

LEGAL RIGHTS: Women may sue or be sued in regard to their property, person or reputation. They may carry on their own business and their earnings are their sole property. A married woman has the same right to sue for loss of consortium as her husband.

SUPPORT: Both spouses are liable for the reasonable and necessary expenses of the family and both are equally liable for the support of children. Any purchases made by husband or wife which are for use of family and which are appropriate to their station in life may be charged to both the husband and the wife or to either separately. Child support continues as a duty after the death of the person owing that support and may be handled by maintaining life insurance on the person owing support.

ABUSE: Assault and battery by a husband is a crime but no real remedy is available to Colorado's wives. Law enforcement officials are not anxious to intervene in "domestic squabbles"; few shelters are available to battered wives seeking protection.

DISSOLUTION/DIVORCE: All property acquired during marriage, no matter whose name it is placed in, is subject to division by the court. A Colorado statute requires the court to consider the contribution of a homemaker in dividing marital property. The law provides for the appointment of an attorney for the child in custody cases.

RAPE: A husband may be charged with rape if the spouses are living apart.

CONNECTICUT

SUPPORT: Husband and wife are jointly responsible for family expenses.

PROPERTY: "Common law" property system: whatever income you earn and whatever property you accumulate during marriage is yours, and your spouse has no control over it.

ABUSE: Husbands and wives can be arrested for assaulting their spouses, for threatening them, or for recklessly endangering their life or for health. However, the police do not want to be involved in "domestic squabbles."

DIVORCE: Has a partial no-fault system where a divorce is granted if the marriage has irretrievably broken down or if the parties have been living apart for 18 months and there is no chance of reconciliation. The law now does not require that the court consider the value of the homemaker's work in awarding alimony and in dividing marital property. The law permits a judge to assign to either the husband or wife all or any part of the estate of the other. Financial security for a child is playing an increasingly important role in courts' decisions to award custody.

INHERITANCE: If the husband or wife dies without a will, the surviving spouse is entitled to the first $50,000 of the estate plus one-half of the remainder.

RAPE: A wife has no legal protection against sexual assault or rape by her husband even if she is separated from him and has filed for divorce.

DELAWARE

PROPERTY: A man and wife may enter into an agreement before marriage to determine what rights each shall have in the other's estate.

ABUSE: Assaults between spouses are referred to the family court which may hear only third degree assault, that is the least degree of assault, no matter how extensive the injuries inflicted. Thus the charge and punishment against a wife beater are lessened.

DISSOLUTION/DIVORCE: The unwillingness of one party to be divorced is not grounds for denial of the petition. There is no authority by statute or under case law to award permanent alimony. In making a division of marital property the court is obligated to consider the contributions of a homemaker. The duty to support minor children rests equally upon both parents and the non-monetary contribution made by the custodial parent is to be considered in equating the amount to be contributed by the non-custodial parent. Where a man is simultaneously liable for the support of more than one dependent, a statutory scheme for determining priority among dependents exists.

INHERITANCE: A woman who has been given a small portion or none of her husband's estate may refuse the inheritance and receive one-third of the estate, or $20,000, whichever is less.

DISTRICT OF COLUMBIA

SUPPORT: Unless a woman is willing to end her marriage, she has no enforceable means of requiring her husband to support her.

ABUSE: A married woman may not sue her husband for physically abusing her.

DISSOLUTION/DIVORCE: A divorce may be granted where the parties have been voluntarily separated for 6 months or where they have been separated for one year even though one spouse may not have consented to the separation. Unless the parties have made a valid agreement concerning their respective property rights acquired during marriage, the court may distribute as it deems just all property acquired during the marriage (other than by gift, bequest, etc.), whether the property is held in the name of both parties or one. While a wife may lose alimony as a result of her misconduct, the courts specifically reject using alimony to penalize a man for his misconduct.

INHERITANCE: If a husband dies without a will, the widow will inherit the whole estate only if there are virtually no living relatives, including brothers, sisters, nieces, nephews, parents, children or grandchildren.

RAPE: Consent to marital relations cannot be retracted while the marriage is legally intact, even though the parties are living separate and apart even if one has filed for divorce.

FLORIDA

LEGAL RIGHTS: A wife has the right to sue a person who has injured her husband for loss of her husband's companionship, affection, and consortium, including sexual relations.

PROPERTY: A full-time homemaker can be effectively prevented from securing any part of the property acquired during marriage if her wage-earning husband places all property in his name.

ABUSE: If a woman files an action for dissolution of marriage she may secure a mutual restraining order to keep her husband from molesting her; however, enforcement of the order is difficult. Authorities see wife abuse as a "domestic dispute."

DISSOLUTION/DIVORCE: Under a no-fault dissolution, the court may consider the adultery of the spouse seeking alimony, which is usually the wife, although court interpretation of this law is not consistent. Although alimony is given in only a small percentage of cases, rehabilitative alimony is available to assist a divorced person thorugh vocational or therapeutic training or retraining. The dissolution statute does not specifically require the courts to consider the economic contribution of the homemaker to the marriage.

INHERITANCE: If a husband dies without a will, the wife takes the entire estate only if the husband left no surviving lineal descendants, that is children or grandchildren.

GEORGIA

SUPPORT: A wife can bring no legal action to enforce support unless she separates from husband.

PROPERTY: Separate property state. The house occupied by the family belongs only to husband, even if wife is the wage earner, and makes the payments. A child is, by law, under the control of his/her father who has the sole right to his or her services and the proceeds of his or her labor when the parents are living together.

ABUSE: Abuse may be prosecuted as a simple battery or aggravated battery. However, police officials have been reluctant to become involved in these cases.

DISSOLUTION/DIVORCE: Upon separation of husband and wife, the obligation to pay alimony and child support falls only upon husband. Although husband is legally obligated to provide support for family during marriage, if his wife provides for the needs of herself and children, upon divorce she may be forced to continue to be self-supporting.

INHERITANCE: If there is no will, upon the death of husband without children, the wife is sole heir and takes all his estate. If there are children in the marriage, the wife and each child take equal shares, except that in no event will the wife take less than a 1/5 share.

RAPE: Wives are not protected against forcible sexual acts of their husbands. Sexual intercourse is deemed a right until marriage is dissolved. Refusal of sexual relations may be grounds for divorce or desertion.

HAWAII

LEGAL RIGHTS: A married woman by statute in Hawaii is not liable for her husband's debts. Law establishes a parent-child relationship regardless of the marital status of the parents. Unmarried parents are permitted to file the names of both parents on a child's birth certificate, thereby in effect legitimizing the child.

SUPPORT: A wife is liable for the support of her children where the husband is unable or absent and her property and earnings can be taken to provide for them.

PROPERTY: Common law property state where property belongs solely to the person whose name is on the title.

ABUSE: Permits a wife to charge her husband with assault. However, if a woman is injured by her husband and incurs medical expenses, loss of wages and other damages, she cannot sue him for those expenses.

DISSOLUTION/DIVORCE: "No-fault" state. All that is required is proof that "the marriage is irretrievably broken." In contested divorces, the court has the discretion to divide all the marital property, regardless of its source or characterization.

INHERITANCE: If a man dies and leaves a will which excludes his wife, or which gives her only a small share of his estate, she has the right to elect to take against the will and receive one-third of his net estate.

IDAHO

LEGAL RIGHTS: A wife or husband may sue each other in Idaho for injuries either family resources. Both spouses are equally liable for family expenses and either may be sued separately by a creditor for those debts.

SUPPORT: In general, courts refuse to interfere in an on-going marriage to insure support. As long as the parties live together, the wife is entitled to only what the husband chooses to give her or what she herself earns.

PROPERTY: All property or income acquired after marriage, except inheritances and gifts, belong to the husband and wife equally, regardless of who earns it, and each spouse has an undivided half interest in everything. Since 1974 both husband and wife have had the right to manage and control the community property.

DISSOLUTION/DIVORCE: Where a husband seeks a divorce from his wife or where divorce is granted on a "no-fault" ground, no alimony of any kind is awarded.

INHERITANCE: When a married person dies, the surviving spouse is entitled to one-half of the property and money acquired by the couple during the period of their marriage. Therefore, only half the community property may be disposed of in a will or is subject to inheritance taxes. If a spouse dies without a will, Idaho law provides that the half of the community property of the deceased spouse passes to the survivor.

RAPE: It is possible for a wife to charge her husband with rape if she has filed for divorce or separation or if she has not lived with her husband for six months.

ILLINOIS

SUPPORT: The courts refuse to intervene in an on-going marriage to allocate family resources. Both spouses are equally liable for family expenses and either may be sued separately by a creditor for those debts.

PROPERTY: Common law property system under which property acquired during a marriage belongs to whoever holds the title.

DISSOLUTION/DIVORCE: One of the few remaining states without no-fault divorce. In making an award of alimony the court is not required to take into account the value of a homemaker's unpaid labor. A wife who is "at fault" will not get alimony except under special circumstances. However, in making an award of alimony, the court may not consider a husband's misconduct. No statutory standards governing the disposition of marital property. The law does permit conveyance of property held solely in the name of one spouse to the other spouse, in the court's discretion.

INHERITANCE: If a man dies without a will, his widow will get all the estate if there are no children and one-third of the estate if there are children, with the remaining two-thirds going to them.

RAPE: Illinois law defines rape as sexual intercourse with a woman who is not the wife of the perpetrator, forcibly and against her will.

INDIANA

LEGAL RIGHTS: A homemaker's domicile does not necessarily have to be the same as her husband's.

PROPERTY: A wife has no power to prevent a husband from disposing of his real and personal property; he may do so without her consent and without her knowledge.

ABUSE: A homemaker cannot recover medical expenses or other damages from her husband for injuries caused by his physical abuse.

DISSOLUTION/DIVORCE: The most frequently used statutory ground for dissolution of marriage is the no-fault "irretrievable breakdown of marriage." No provision for on-going spousal support after a dissolution. The effects of the combination of no-fault divorce and no alimony are disastrous for a homemaker. In dividing property, the court must consider the contribution of a spouse as homemaker.

INHERITANCE: Neither spouse may completely disinherit the other. If the surviving spouse is a second or other subsequent spouse and did not have children by the deceased, then the surviving spouse shall take only a life estate in one-third of the real estate of the decedent and the remaining interest shall vest at once in the children of the decedent's former marriage.

RAPE: A man cannot be charged with sexually abusing his wife even when the parties are not living together or where one has filed for a divorce.

IOWA

SUPPORT: Both spouses are liable for the reasonable and necessary expenses of the family and for the support of the children. Any purchases that either the husband or wife make which are for the use of the family and which are appropriate for their station in life may be charged to both the husband and wife or to either separately. Nothing requires a creditor to seek payment first from the husband and then from the wife.

ABUSE: Figures from a recent survey indicate nearly one of four married women are beaten by their husbands. A wife may charge husband with assault which carries a penalty up to 30 days in jail or a fine of $100 or both.

DISSOLUTION/DIVORCE: Iowa law prevents either spouse from removing the other from the homestead until after divorce is granted. In 90% of divorce cases that come before the Iowa courts, no alimony is awarded. In 1973, 73% of all child support payments were between $10 and $20 per week; in 20% of the cases involving children, no child support of any kind was allowed.

INHERITANCE: If a deceased spouse leaves a will, surviving spouse may decide to take what is granted by its terms or may take a ⅓ interest in all the real estate, all personal property of the family, and ⅓ of the other personal property.

RAPE: A husband may be charged with raping his wife if he injures her or threatens her with a weapon even if they are living together.

KANSAS

SUPPORT: A person has a duty to support spouse and can be criminally charged if s/he does not. Duty is based upon ability to support and is limited to necessary items only. No legal tools are in place to enforce support.

PROPERTY: A married woman may sell and convey real and personal property or contract regarding her property in the same manner and extent as a married man.

ABUSE: Women may press criminal charges but probably will face lack of cooperation from legal officials who do not want to interfere in "domestic disturbances."

DISSOLUTION/DIVORCE: During a divorce proceeding, all real and personal property is under control of divorce court. If a woman has co-signed on a debt with her husband, she is still liable even if husband has been ordered to pay the debt.

INHERITANCE: A man may not disinherit his wife. She will receive at least ½ of her husband's property despite terms of will. If divorced prior to death, alimony and child-support awards do not extend past death and cannot be claimed against the estate.

RAPE: No legal protection to a woman against sexual assault by husband, even if she is separated or in the divorce process.

KENTUCKY

LEGAL RIGHTS: A married woman may sue her husband for negligent acts he may commit against her. Children born to a man and woman who are married must be given the surname of the father, even though both husband and wife want to name the child with the mother's surname.

SUPPORT: A husband is not responsible for the wife's debts before or after marriage, except to the extent he received property from the wife as a result of the marriage. The husband is legally required to furnish only the wife's "necessaries" during marriage.

DISSOLUTION/DIVORCE: Under a new divorce law, courts must consider the economic contribution of the wife, including domestic services, in a division of property. However, up to now the wife's role as a homemaker has not been as highly valued as that of the breadwinner. The general rule of thumb is that the wife gets approximately one-third of jointly held property if she has been a homemaker and up to a maximum of one-half if she has been a wage-earning participant in the accumulation of property.

RAPE: Although the law does not specifically exempt a husband from being charged with rape of his wife, there is a possibility that a husband cannot be found guilty of committing this offense against his wife.

LOUISIANA

SUPPORT: A wife may file a criminal neglect of the family charge for non-support but such cases require that the husband provide no money for six weeks in order to show intentional neglect.

PROPERTY: A husband has the power to sell and mortgage community property including home without consent or knowledge of wife. Creditors may seize both husband's and wife's interest in community property when the husband defaults on a debt. Community property system contemplates equal share for husband and wife of all that is earned and accumulated during the marriage. However, law says that husband has "total control and charge of all community affairs and all property belonging thereto." Earnings are included in community and are subject to husband's control.

DISSOLUTION/DIVORCE: Alimony is not granted on the basis of past services of wife or length of marriage but on present need and ability to pay of husband. To receive alimony wife must prove separation was not her fault, that she needs support and that husband can pay; but in no case can wife receive more than ⅓ of husband's income.

INHERITANCE: A wife is not heir to husband's half of community unless he writes a will to this effect. Wife cannot receive husband's half of community if husband has children or living parents since they are forced heirs and must receive a share in his estate regardless of provisions in the will.

MAINE

PROPERTY: If a husband and wife jointly run a business the profits are the property of the husband. Although the law recognizes the married woman's right to hold and manage property, the courts have demonstrated a readiness to find that the husband is his wife's agent for management of her property. If a husband earns most of the income, that income, and any family assets purchased with it will be the husband's property. Because a married woman's contribution to the family partnership economy is in services rather than money, the law does not recognize the real value of her contribution.

DISSOLUTION/DIVORCE: A wife may receive a lump sum payment in lieu of alimony. When dividing marital property, the court is required to consider the contribution made by the homemaker.

INHERITANCE: If a husband leaves no will, the share of the widow in the husband's estate (after payment of funeral costs, debts, taxes and estate administration costs) will range from something more than 33⅓% to 100%; the exact percentage depending on a complex of factors involving size of the estate, existence of children or close relatives, and the nature of the property left.

MARYLAND

LEGAL RIGHTS: One spouse cannot sue the other for such civil offenses as intentional or negligent infliction of emotional distress, slander, libel, or assault and battery.

PROPERTY: There is no Maryland law that imposes an obligation on a husband to permit his wife to share in the control of family resources. Courts and administrative agencies generally assume ownership of marital property by the husband in the absence of proof of ownership by the wife. A wife has no claim on property in the husband's name, even the family home or personal property, unless she has made a financial contribution which the court chooses to recognize. Maryland courts have not recognized the performance of a wife's duties as a contribution to the marriage.

ABUSE: While it is possible in Maryland to have one's husband prosecuted under criminal law for assault and battery, in practice this remedy accomplishes little. When a husband is prosecuted and found guilty, often the result is merely unsupervised probation. Rarely is a husband incarcerated or offered counseling.

DISSOLUTION/DIVORCE: In granting alimony, the court will consider the wife's conduct even though the divorce itself is based on non-fault grounds.

INHERITANCE: If there is no will, or where there is a will and wife renounces it, a wife will inherit the entire estate only if there are no surviving children, parent or brother or sister of the deceased.

MASSACHUSETTS

PROPERTY RIGHTS: Retains a form of property ownership known as a tenancy by the entireties, which is available only to a husband and wife. The property is owned jointly by both spouses, but only the husband has the right to manage and control it and to receive any profits from it.

WIFE ABUSE: A woman may sue her husband if he injures her intentionally or negligently and may recover her medical expenses and other damages from him.

DIVORCE/DISSOLUTION: No such thing as a "legal" separation. Massachusetts has both no-fault and traditional fault grounds for divorce, such as adultery and desertion. By statute, the right to custody of children is equal in the absence of parental misconduct and the welfare and happiness of the children is the determinate. Child support payments may be awarded even beyond the age of majority, which is 18, up to the age of 21. The court is not required to consider the contribution of a homemaker to the acquisition of marital property.

INHERITANCE: Neither spouse may totally disinherit the other. A surviving spouse will receive at least one-third of the real and personal property of the deceased spouse.

RAPE: A man cannot be charged with the rape of his wife, even if he and his wife are separated and she has filed for divorce.

MICHIGAN

SUPPORT: Theoretically a husband is bound to furnish his wife a home and other needs to the extent of his ability and in return a wife owes her husband her services as a homemaker. However, courts will not interfere in an on-going marriage to insure support.

PROPERTY: Contracts and promissory notes between spouses are void under Michigan law and unenforceable.

ABUSE: Under the Criminal Compensation Act, if a husband causes his wife injury, she may sue him for damages. Under the Criminal Compensation Act, she is ineligible for any payment except for medical expenses.

DISSOLUTION/DIVORCE: There is one no-fault ground for divorce. It is nearly impossible for one spouse to prevent the other from getting a divorce if he or she wants it. No-fault divorce was enacted without providing economic protections for the homemaker. The court may divide the parties' property; however, there are no standards for such division and there is no requirement that the court recognize homemaking as a contribution.

INHERITANCE: If a husband dies without a will, the widow takes from one-third to all of his real and personal estate depending on whether there are children or other relatives.

RAPE: A woman can charge her husband with sexual assault if they are living apart and one of them has filed for divorce.

MINNESOTA

LEGAL RIGHTS: A woman may sue her husband for damages if he negligently injures her. A woman may seek damages for loss of consortium, that is loss of companionship, services, and sex due to injuries inflicted upon the spouse.

SUPPORT: Within the context of the marriage the wife has no legal right to support beyond that which her husband is willing to voluntarily provide for her. Husband and wife are both liable whether jointly or separately for all necessary goods and services furnished to and used by the family.

ABUSE: Assault and battery is a crime; however, the police respond slowly and indifferently to calls involving "domestic quarrels."

DISSOLUTION/DIVORCE: Joint property of the parties is divided as the court shall determine to be just, with wide discretion granted the court. The court may award up to one-half the value of a spouse's separate property to the other. Courts are not required to recognize the value of the services provided by the homemaker when dividing marital property.

INHERITANCE: The law will not presume joint ownership with survivor's rights unless this is specifically stated in the deed to the property.

RAPE: A husband may be charged with rape only if the parties are living apart and one of them has filed for a divorce or for separate maintenance.

MISSISSIPPI

LEGAL RIGHTS: Even though a woman works eight hours a day for six days a week and earns twice as much as her husband, she cannot be considered as her husband, the head of the household under the law. A wife and husband may sue each other in certain circumstances, but the law prohibits them from suing each other for personal wrongs, such as assault and a battery or negligence.

SUPPORT: In order to require a husband to support his wife and family, a wife must separate from her husband and engage in legal action. Courts will not interfere in an ongoing marriage as a matter of policy.

PROPERTY: The law requires the signature of both spouses in any conveyance of the homestead.

ABUSE: Even though it is technically a crime for a man to beat his wife, law enforcement officials tend not to treat it as a serious matter.

DISSOLUTION/DIVORCE: In determining whether alimony and/or division of the property is necessary after the marriage ends. State courts are not required to consider the contribution made by the homemaker to the family and the community. There is no absolute right to alimony in Mississippi.

INHERITANCE: If a husband dies without leaving a will and does not have any children or descendants of children, the wife is entitled to his entire estate after all debts are paid. If he leaves children or descendants of children, a wife is entitled to a share equal to each child's part of his estate.

MISSOURI

LEGAL RIGHTS: When a wife engages in activities which earn money but which are performed in the home or in conjunction with her husband, she may find that those earnings are not considered hers but are her husband's as a matter of legal right.

SUPPORT: Although the husband has a legal duty to support his wife, it is an obligation defined and controlled solely by him and not enforceable by the wife. If the husband is the only wage earner, the wife has no claim on his wages or assets during the marriage.

DISSOLUTION/DIVORCE: Any property acquired by either spouse during the marriage other than gift or inheritance to one spouse, no matter in whose name it is titled, is subject to being divided between the two spouses as the court deems just. Courts are to consider the contribution of each spouse to the acquisition of the marital property, including the contribution of a spouse as homemaker, when dividing property.

INHERITANCE: If there is no will and no children, parents or siblings of the deceased spouse, the survivor will inherit all of the property. If there are children or grandchildren, the surviving spouse inherits half while the other half of the estate is divided among these others.

RAPE: Although a husband may force intercourse, due to the marital relationship, this cannot be defined as the crime of rape.

MONTANA

SUPPORT: Both the husband and wife have a duty to support each other. The noncompensated services of a spouse acting as homemaker are specifically included in the definition of support.

ABUSE: A wife who is assaulted by her husband may not sue him civilly, and husbands and wives may not sue each other for any intentional or negligent injury.

DISSOLUTION: The court may apportion all the property of either party regardless of when and how it was acquired and regardless of marital fault. In apportioning the property the court is required to consider, among other things, the contribution of a spouse as homemaker or as wage earner to the family unit. No law requiring full financial disclosure under oath by both parties to a divorce.

RAPE: Montana law exempts from the definition of rape all forcible intercourse between husband and wife even if the spouses are no longer living together.

PREGNANCY: A pregnant woman cannot be required to terminate her employment because of her pregnancy. She must be allowed to take reasonable leave of absence for her pregnancy and childbirth. The law requires that disability caused by pregnancy and childbirth must be treated the same as any other disability in any policy of disability or leave benefits or the like maintained by an employer.

NEBRASKA

SUPPORT: A wife has a legal right only to what her husband chooses to give her. If it is insufficient to meet her needs, or her children's needs, her only legal recourse is divorce.

PROPERTY: A creditor must sue a husband first before he attempts to collect a debt for necessities from a wife. A married woman may contract with her husband, but not for domestic services. Domestic services are considered to be a duty of the wife and she therefore cannot legally be compensated by her husband for their performance, except by a "gift" from him.

ABUSE: Although a great number of wives report that they are beaten by their husbands and although a man can be criminally charged if he beats his wife, no cases have been found where a wife has filed a complaint against her husband for assaulting or threatening her.

INHERITANCE: A widow is entitled to a share of her husband's property if he dies without a will or he makes a will which excludes her.

DISSOLUTION/DIVORCE: In dividing marital property, the court is obliged to consider the history of the contributions to the marriage by each party, including contributions to the care and education of the children and interruption of personal careers and educational opportunities. The court may not modify or cancel already accrued alimony amounts that are in arrears.

NEVADA

SUPPORT: The husband is supposed to support the wife with necessaries but there is no legal machinery in the state to force him to do so except if a woman files a complaint in court for separate maintenance or to file for a divorce.

PROPERTY: A wife has equal management and control of the community property with her husband. The law recognizes written agreements between husband and a wife as to the nature of their property.

ABUSE: It is not police policy to arrest a wife abuser unless the battering is enough to charge the husband with a felony, i.e., assault with a deadly weapon.

DISSOLUTION/DIVORCE: Nevada has three no-fault grounds for divorce: incompatibility, separation without cohabitation for one year, and defendant's insanity for two years. The court has jurisdiction over community property but none over separate property of the husband or wife, except that the court may set aside separate property of one or the other to assure payment of court ordered child support or alimony.

INHERITANCE: A husband and wife may each will away his or her half of the community property to anyone. The other half belongs to the surviving spouse and is not subject to administration in the deceased spouse's estate. The separate property of any person may be willed to anyone. A decedent may even disinherit spouse or children.

NEW HAMPSHIRE

LEGAL RIGHTS: If a woman lives with a man to whom she is not legally married for a period of three years, during which time they acknowledged each other as husband and wife and are generally reputed as such, she shall be deemed legally married upon the death of one involved and entitled to inherit, assert homestead claims and receive social security payments to the same extent as any other surviving spouse.

SUPPORT: A court can order a husband to provide "suitable support" for his wife and/or children, but there are no cases recorded where action was brought when the husband and wife were living together.

PROPERTY: Any property, real or personal, that a wife accumulates prior to marriage remains hers during marriage unless she voluntarily transfers title to her husband. Any personal property a wife earns, acquires, or inherits during marriage is exclusively hers free from any interference or control by her husband. If a wife co-signs on her husband's obligations and he defaults, the loan company can proceed against the wife whether or not they first seek to collect from the husband.

ABUSE: Penalties for wife beating or simple assault range from a verbal warning to a small fine.

DISSOLUTION/DIVORCE: Law does not require the court to consider the contribution of a spouse as a homemaker in dividing marital property. The trial judge exercises almost absolute discretion in making financial awards and property settlements.

NEW JERSEY

SUPPORT: Traditionally courts have been hesitant to intervene in an on-going marriage to assure that a wife is being provided adequate support.

ABUSE: A wife who has been physically abused by her husband can file a complaint against him in the municipal court which is then registered as an assault and battery, depending upon the degree of the injury. There is no statistical breakdown in court reports for assault and battery against a spouse.

DISSOLUTION/DIVORCE: Real and personal property owned by a couple is divided by the court upon a judgment of divorce or separation. When making an equitable distribution of property the court is not required to recognize the economic value of the services of a homemaker. During the 1973-1974 term in N.J. 19,628 divorces were decreed.

INHERITANCE: If a husband dies without a will and the family residence is in his name alone, title to the house descends to the children. In a case where a husband deliberately makes a will which excludes his wife, she is entitled only to her dower interest which is a one-half life estate in the real property of the husband. That means that while she may occupy the property, or collect and use the profits, she may not sell it or otherwise dispose of it without the consent of other heirs and distribution to them.

NEW MEXICO

INHERITANCE: In 1973 the New Mexico legislature voted to allow wives in the state to will their halves of the community property to anyone they choose, just as their husbands could. However, the legislature specifically provided that this law would only apply to wills made after July 1, 1973.

PROPERTY: Community property acquired primarily through the earnings of either the husband or wife after marriage, including all increases in the value of those earnings as well as any property purchased with either the husband's or wife's earnings, belongs to both marriage partners. However, if a husband puts his paycheck into his own account, the wife would have no way of helping to manage this part of the community property.

ABUSE: The City Attorney's Office in Albuquerque has an official policy of not prosecuting any complaint by a wife who is still living with her husband. There are no shelters for abused women in New Mexico.

DISSOLUTION/DIVORCE: New Mexico law does not prevent a husband from transferring part of the community property to someone else when a divorce is pending. In a division of community property at divorce, the earning capacity of the husband, which has often been developed at the expense of the wife's own earnings and career potential, is not considered. A woman has no legal interest in the retirement rights of her husband unless those rights have "vested" before the divorce. This is so even though part of his salary, which is legally community property, went into a retirement fund.

NEW YORK

SUPPORT: A husband has a legal duty to provide his wife and children with necessaries. Ordinarily this duty may not be enforced while the parties are living together. Parents have a duty to support their children until they are 21.

PROPERTY: What a husband has purchased with his money and put in his name alone, is his.

ABUSE: A divorce is not automatically granted in all cases of wife beating: evidence of a pattern of violence or a concerted course of conduct by the husband against the wife must be shown.

DISSOLUTION/DIVORCE: Housewives' services are not given monetary value in a division of property. A new law requires both parties in a divorce action to disclose all of their assets.

INHERITANCE: Through large debts, trust funds, life insurance, and gifts or savings bonds to other people, a husband may decrease the amount of a wife's inheritance to almost nothing. When a person dies without a will, law distributes the estate among the surviving relatives. A wife with no children would get $25,000, plus one-half of the residue, with the remainder going to the husband's father and mother. A wife with one child would take $2,000, plus one-half of the residue, with the remainder going to the child.

RAPE: A husband cannot be convicted of raping his wife, even when they are not living together.

NORTH CAROLINA

SUPPORT: A recent study indicated that 47% of all court-ordered support payments are not met by husbands.

PROPERTY: When real property is owned jointly, the wife is usually not entitled to manage or control the property. The husband is entitled to full possession, control and use of the estate, and to the rents and profits arising therefrom to the exclusion of the wife during their marriage of property held in tenancy of the entirety. The domestic services of a wife, while living with her husband, are presumed to be gratuitous, and the performance of labor and work beyond the scope of her usual household and marital duties, in the absence of a special contract, is also presumed to be gratuitous.

INHERITANCE: It may be possible for a husband to disinherit his wife or limit the inheritance passing. A husband may provide for his widow in such a way as to deprive her of control of her inheritance by willing his property to a trustee who is directed to invest the property and pay the income from these investments to the widow.

RAPE: A husband is legally incapable of raping his wife or assaulting her with intent to commit rape, even while they are separated and/or in the process of getting a divorce.

NORTH DAKOTA

SUPPORT: A husband must support wife by his property or labor, but he alone decides in what manner and to what extent he will provide support. A wife must support husband by separate property if he is too ill to support himself and has no funds to do so. No ability to sue for support in on-going marriage. Both husband and wife are liable for family debts which are for food, clothing, shelter, fuel and education for the minor children.

PROPERTY: Separate property state. If property is in husband's name, wife has no rights to it. A wife's contribution to the family unit as a homemaker is not recognized by the law. A married woman has the same rights in making contracts and owning property as if she were single.

ABUSE: A wife may bring assault charges; however, many times such cases are not taken seriously by law enforcement officials. There are very few places where a woman may seek protection.

DISSOLUTION/DIVORCE: Most divorce actions are brought on the grounds of irreconcilable differences. There is little a wife can do under "no fault" law to prevent husband from divorcing her.

INHERITANCE: If husband has a will, wife may take what is given in the will or ⅓ of the total estate. If there is no will she will get the entire estate only if there are no children or husband's parents.

OHIO

SUPPORT: The level of support a husband is required to maintain for his wife is totally discretionary with him.

PROPERTY: Upon marriage, the rights of the spouses merge and each must obtain the other spouse's signature to sell any real estate during the time the marriage exists, regardless of whether the property was individually owned before the marriage took place. The law permits a husband to act as his wife's agent in transactions involving her separately held real estate and she is personally liable for expenses incurred.

ABUSE: There are no Ohio statistics on the problem of the battered or sexually abused wife and there seems to be reluctance by the authorities to discuss the matter.

DIVORCE: Under a modified no-fault statute, a divorce may be granted if the parties live apart for two years. In determining whether to award alimony and in what amount, the court is required to consider the contribution of a spouse as homemaker.

INHERITANCE: Upon marriage each spouse relinquishes the right to disinherit the other and must leave the other spouse at least one-half of her or his estate if there are no children or only one child.

RAPE: The statutes cover the rape of a wife by her husband when the parties are legally separated or one has filed for separation or divorce.

OKLAHOMA

SUPPORT: A husband must support his wife but there is no practical means for enforcing the law. Courts refuse to intervene in an on-going marriage. A homemaker has the "right" only to what her husband chooses to give her. If purchases are not necessities a wife is liable for separate debts before and after marriage.

PROPERTY: Oklahoma is a common law state with separate property. A wife has no interest in property acquired by her husband in his name.

DISSOLUTION/DIVORCE: Oklahoma pioneered joint or split custody of children. Oklahoma has twelve fault grounds for divorce, including incompatibility which is the most frequent ground used.

INHERITANCE: If the husband dies without leaving a will and has been married only once and has only one child, the wife and child each receive half of the estate according to a statutory formula.

RAPE: A man may not be charged with raping his wife even when they are not living together or are in the process of getting a divorce.

OREGON

LEGAL RIGHTS: Either spouse may sue the other for any damages suffered from negligent or intentional harm. A wife may enter into contracts with others and her husband. Any labor a wife performs for her husband is presumed to be gratuitous, even when it is outside ordinary household duties.

SUPPORT: A husband must support his wife but there is no practical means for enforcing the law. Courts refuse to interstate even to appear on the scene unless a divorce proceeding has begun and a restraining order has been secured.

LEGAL RIGHTS: Oregon law refuses to recognize common law marriages and provides no jurisdiction for domestic relations; judges to hear matters in dispute between persons who are living together without formal ceremony.

SUPPORT: For practical purposes, a wife's right to support from her husband is unenforcible except upon separation or dissolution of the marriage.

ABUSE: Police departments view domestic quarrels skeptically and hesitate even to appear on the scene unless a divorce proceeding has begun and a restraining order has been secured.

DISSOLUTION/DIVORCE: If a party has paid support for a former spouse for more than ten years under a court decree, and if the former spouse has not made reasonable effort to become financially self-supporting, the party paying support may ask the court to set aside the portion of the decree which allows support for the former spouse.

INHERITANCE: If a husband dies without a will, with surviving children and a wife, his wife receives one-half of his estate. If she survives him and there are no children, she is granted all of the net estate.

RAPE: It is not possible for a man to commit the crime of rape upon his wife.

PENNSYLVANIA

PROPERTY: Married couples may own property under "tenancies by the entirety," where both parties own the entire property, and neither can rent, sell, mortgage, or otherwise dispose of it without the other's consent. When one party dies the other automatically owns the whole. A wife is not entitled to an accounting of assets held in tenancies by the entirety which are controlled and managed by her husband.

ABUSE: A wife who has been beaten by her husband cannot sue him for the medical expenses she incurs in treating her injuries. She is ineligible for assistance under Crime Victim's Compensation Act.

DISSOLUTION/DIVORCE: Pennsylvania divorce laws are the worst in the nation for homemakers; there is no permanent alimony and no real property division. There are no "no-fault" grounds for divorce.

INHERITANCE: If a husband dies without a will, his widow is entitled to a proportion of his separate estate and automatically becomes the sole owner of entireties properties. The surviving spouse inherits the entire estate only if there are no surviving children, parents, siblings, nieces, nephews, grandparents, uncles and aunts.

RAPE: A wife who is the victim of sexual assault by her husband can charge him with a crime if they are living in the same residence but are legally separated by agreement or court order.

RHODE ISLAND

SUPPORT: There is not a single reported case in R.I. in which any court ordered a husband to pay any amount to a wife or child for support when the parties were still living together and were not also seeking a divorce or separation. As a matter of public policy, the courts will not involve themselves in disputes within ongoing marriages. A homemaker's security depends solely on her husband's sense of commitment and good will and not on the law.

DISSOLUTION/DIVORCE: In 1974 there were 11,009 children whose mothers had to go to court to obtain support from their fathers. Although the legislature has established irreconcilable differences as a no-fault ground for divorce, the law requires the court to consider fault in determining awards of alimony and child custody.

INHERITANCE: If a husband leaves a spouse and children and has no will, the wife would receive ½ of the husband's personal property and the children would get the other half. The wife would have a life estate (that is, use of the property until her death) in his real estate and the children would inherit the remaining interest. If a husband leaves a will which excludes his wife, she may elect to take ⅓ of the real property for life only.

SOUTH CAROLINA

LEGAL RIGHTS: A wife who is injured by her husband can sue him in civil court for the damages he causes her. Wife has obligation to be tolerant, within reason, of the husband's shortcomings.

SUPPORT: Any able-bodied man must support his wife and minor children by providing a place to live at the location of his choosing, food and some clothing. The husband is not required to pay for anything else as long as they reside together.

PROPERTY: Common law property state. Property is owned by whomever holds the title, whether that property is acquired before or after marriage.

ABUSE: If a woman flees home because of abuse and files for divorce, she must prove that the physical cruelty endangered her life and also that she did not "provoke" the conduct of which she complains.

DISSOLUTION/DIVORCE: A woman is absolutely precluded from receiving alimony if she is found guilty of adultery. Alimony may not be used to punish an errant husband.

INHERITANCE: A married man can't will more than ¼ of his property to his mistress or illegitimate children, if he has a wife living and legitimate children. A woman forfeits her dower rights (to own for her life ⅓ of all the real estate her husband acquired during the marriage) by her misconduct, and also forfeits the estate part she would receive if there were no will. There is no similar provision requiring the forfeiture of a man's right to wife's property.

SOUTH DAKOTA

LEGAL RIGHTS: A husband and wife cannot contract with each other to alter the legal relations that are spelled out by statute.

SUPPORT: Unless a wife wants to file for separate maintenance or divorce, her right to support during marriage is limited to what her husband chooses to give her. A wife is responsible for the support of her "infirm" husband but she is not liable for his debts contracted prior to or during marriage out of her separate earnings or separate property.

DISSOLUTION/DIVORCE: Not a no-fault state. When a divorce is granted for the fault of either party, the court may make an equitable division of all the property, whether the title to the property is in the name of the husband or the wife. Marriage and divorce between reservation Indians may be governed by individual Tribal Codes.

INHERITANCE: South Dakota is one of the few states which allows either spouse to completely disinherit the other spouse. There is no "forced share." Since 1953 S.D. has presumed that husbands and wives have made equal contributions towards the acquisition of joint tenancy property and therefore taxes only one/half of the property upon the death of either.

TENNESSEE

PROPERTY: There is no legal principle by which family income from whatever source can be regarded as equally owned by both partners. At present, a wife cannot enforce a right to one-half of the marital assets, nor does she have any legal recourse if her husband uses marital assets held in his name without her permission, or even without her knowledge. The services of a homemaker have always been assumed to be "gratuitous."

ABUSE: A wife has no legal remedy in damages for physical injury at the hands of her husband. Facilities to shelter abused women have been virtually nonexistent although a few private efforts are beginning.

DISSOLUTION/DIVORCE: Divorce courts have so much discretion that awards and even decisions fluctuate almost with the temperment of the judges. Statute on child support is not sex-specific and a wife can be ordered to pay. If alimony is involved only a husband will be affected. There is no specific provision compelling strict financial disclosure by parties to a divorce action.

TEXAS

SUPPORT: Husband has duty to support wife. Wife has duty to support husband if he is unable to support himself. However, courts will not interfere in an on-going marriage to enforce support.

PROPERTY: Community property state. Each person manages own separate property and own earnings.

ABUSE: Police are "reluctant to interfere in family disputes." "Substantial physical injury" is necessary for any conviction.

DISSOLUTION/DIVORCE: Each person manages own earnings. Thus a homemaker who makes no salary may have no management rights in family money. In a divorce settlement a spouse is not entitled to future earnings of other spouse. No permanent alimony or maintenance provision. Retirement benefits may be awarded to a wife in a divorce settlement if and when received by the husband. If a woman has co-signed on a debt with her husband, she is still liable to the creditor even if the husband has been ordered to pay the debt in a divorce decree.

INHERITANCE: If there is no will, portions of estate go to children and widow.

RAPE: A husband cannot be found guilty of raping his wife.

UTAH

SUPPORT: The expenses of the family and the education of the children are the responsibility of both husband and wife. A married woman's obligation to support her husband in times of need is terminated upon divorce, but a woman separated from her husband pending divorce could find herself liable for his support.

ABUSE: Laws against assault are systematically not enforced when violated in a family context.

DISSOLUTION/DIVORCE: The "fault" concept of divorce is maintained. The courts are not required to consider the wife's contribution as a homemaker in making a division of debts and marital property. The wife is presumed to be the most fit person to have custody of young children.

INHERITANCE: If a husband does not leave a will, the widow will receive all of the property only if there are no lineal descendants, and no parents, siblings, nieces or nephews, or grandnieces or grandnephews.

RAPE: A married woman cannot sue her husband for rape, even where the parties are separated and one of them has filed for divorce.

CREDIT: Arbitrary decisions based on sex and marital status are being used to deny credit to women. Many businesses refuse to grant a woman credit in her own name, even if she never assumed her husband's surname in marriage. These practices are illegal.

VERMONT

LEGAL RIGHTS: Vermont permits a woman to enforce contracts with her husband, but not for her services as a homemaker. Vermont allows legal actions by one spouse against the other.

PROPERTY: Property acquired during marriage belongs to the spouse who has title. However, a deed for real property to a married woman must explicitly exclude her husband, or the property is not her sole property. When couples own their property jointly, the husband has the right to purchase goods and services for the upkeep of the jointly held property, even without the wife's consent or knowledge.

DISSOLUTION/DIVORCE: If a husband is granted a divorce because of the wife's adultery, her own separate property may be given to her husband. The husband is entitled to his, no matter how adulterous. Disclosure of real and personal property cannot be compelled for property division or for child support allocation but only when alimony is considered. When support is ordered to be paid for a wife, the court may appoint a trustee and require all payments to be paid through that person. No similar provision exists to prevent a husband from having full and free access to money awarded to him.

INHERITANCE: A court may prevent a woman from breaking her husband's will; however, the court has no right to make this kind of a determination if the surviving spouse is male.

VIRGINIA

SUPPORT: The principal that a husband has a "natural and legal duty" to support his wife is enunciated only in cases where there has been a breakdown of the marital relationship and the parties are not living together.

PROPERTY: Common-law property state. Each party owns and controls own earnings and property. However, an exception to the law presumes the husband is the owner of all property. Therefore a wife's property may be taken to pay for her husband's debts, while a husband's property cannot be taken to pay his wife's debts. The presumption is that whatever the wife owns she received because of something furnished by her husband.

ABUSE: A wife does not have the right to sue her husband for damages resulting from his physical attack on her.

DISSOLUTION/DIVORCE: The court cannot divide a couple's property upon divorce, which therefore requires a second legal action for partition. A new law requires that the courts consider the value of a homemaker's unpaid labor in setting alimony.

INHERITANCE: If a husband leaves a will, a wife in Va. can choose to take what she is granted by its terms or she may "break the will" and take what she would have received if he had died without a will which is a one-third life estate in the real property.

RAPE: A husband cannot be convicted of the crime of rape if he forces his sexual attentions on a wife even when they are living separately.

WASHINGTON STATE

PROPERTY: Community property state: each spouse has a one-half ownership interest in the community property. Both spouses have the power to manage the community property.

DISSOLUTION/DIVORCE: The basis for a dissolution of marriage is that the marriage be "irretrievably broken." The court will divide property only when the parties do not agree on the disposition of it. If a child has not completed her or his education, the court may order child support beyond the age of majority (age 18). Even though a dissolution decree divides the debts between the parties, creditors are not bound by it and can collect from either spouse.

INHERITANCE: Neither spouse may devise or bequeath by will more than his or her one-half of the community property, but each may dispose of separate property in any ways he chooses. If a spouse dies without a will, the surviving spouse receives the decedent's share of the community estate. Distribution of the separate estate depends on whether the decedent is survived by children, parents, or brothers and sisters.

RAPE: A man may not be charged with raping his wife even if the parties are separated or one of them has filed for a dissolution.

WEST VIRGINIA

LEGAL RIGHTS: In spite of a statute which states that earnings of a married woman belong to her, the courts have decided that when a wife earns money working in her husband's business, those earnings belong to the husband.

SUPPORT: The homemaker whose husband earns an income and simply refuses to share it has little recourse unless she wishes to, divorce him or to charge him with a crime. Creditors have the right to proceed against either husband or wife when a debt is contracted for family purposes.

PROPERTY: If title to property is in the husband's name only, and the couple divorces, the wife has no claim to any part of it. A woman who does not work outside the home and who has no separate estate, has no right to assets accumulated during the marriage in her husband's name.

DISSOLUTION/DIVORCE: The courts cannot take property owned by one spouse and give it to the other in a divorce proceeding.

INHERITANCE: If a person dies without making a will, any interest in real estate he or she has will pass to his or her children and their descendants. If there are no children, or descendants of children, only then does the real estate pass to the wife or the husband. A surviving spouse, be it a man or a woman, is entitled to dower, that is a life estate in one-third of all real estate of the deceased.

WISCONSIN

LEGAL RIGHTS: Although a married woman may own and control her own earnings, her husband has control of earnings "from labor performed for her husband, or in his employ or payable by him."

PROPERTY: Separate property state where property acquired by either spouse during marriage belongs to the one who acquires it, that is, the one who pays for it. If the husband is the only spouse earning money, all property acquired during the marriage is paid for and owned by him. The law does not recognize the value of the homemaker's contribution.

ABUSE: Wife beating may be a misdemeanor or a felony carrying fines and jail terms. However, the district attorney and judges may treat cases superficially.

DIVORCE: Still requires proof of "fault" for divorce, the "no-fault" grounds being limited to cases of voluntary separation for a year or the mental illness of one spouse. Alimony, child support and property division are set at the discretion of the trial court.

INHERITANCE: If a husband leaves no will, the wife is the sole heir and receives everything if there are no children.

RAPE: It is a crime for a man to rape his wife if they are living apart and an action for annulment, legal separation, or divorce has begun.

WYOMING

SUPPORT: A husband and wife are both liable jointly and separately for the necessary expenses of the family and for the costs of educating the children. A creditor may sue either the wife or husband or both to collect debts.

DISSOLUTION/DIVORCE: Although statutes provide a plaintiff with 11 grounds, the most commonly used ground is "irreconcilable difference." Courts do not generally award alimony. Though the statute does not require it, courts presume that a mother is best able to care for young children.

INHERITANCE: A widow cannot be divested of her husband's total estate. If the deceased spouse deprived the living spouse of more than half the estate in a will, the living spouse may elect to take half the estate. If a spouse does not leave a will, the surviving spouse is entitled to the entire estate only if there are no lineal descendants, parents, brothers, sisters, nieces or nephews. If a deceased husband was in debt at death, creditors have the right to sell a homestead worth more than $6,000 and divide the excess over $6,000.

RAPE: Because it is not unlawful for a man to have carnal knowledge of his wife, either forcibly or not, a man can never be convicted of raping his wife, even if they are not living together or have started divorce proceedings.

Feminists

FROM THE MAYFLOWER TO SENECA FALLS

The American girl born while our nation was still young entered a tightly circumscribed world. She was taught to be a butcher, baker, candlemaker, and much more, in the home, but she was usually denied any intellectual education, personal rights, or political participation. It was a man's world outside, and a woman's place was in the home.

From the landing of the Mayflower to the first formal women's rights meeting in 1848 in Seneca Falls, New York, women fought an uphill battle for the rights given men. They did so while contributing enormously, by dint of plain old hard work, to the growth of the colonies and then the republic.

Fifteen of the twenty-four women landing with the Pilgrims at Plymouth survived the first winter. The mortality rate for the women immigrants who followed was not as high, which was fortunate, because the colonies would not have survived without their labor and the children they bore.

With their children, they did everything, including working in the fields at harvesttime. They cared for livestock, maintained a kitchen garden, prepared and preserved foods by smoking and drying — there were no shortcuts in the kitchen then. They spun, wove, sewed, washed, ironed, made soap. But, like black slaves, they had fewer rights than male indentured servants.

"There are but three States of Life, through which they [women] can pass," wrote a man in 1737 in a work entitled *The Whole Duty of a Woman: Or, The Infallible Guide to the Fair Sex,* "*viz.* Virginity, Marriage, and Widowhood, two of them are States of Subjections, the First to the Parent, the Second to the Husband, and the Third . . . a Condition the most desolate and deplorable."

Women who never passed beyond the first state, i.e., remained single, were considered particular failures. "Old maids," wrote a sea captain, "are useless trouble to all the human flesh."

Given this atmosphere, it is remarkable that any women spoke up for a fairer shake, but there were pioneer voices.

In the 1630s, one **Anne Hutchinson** insisted to her Boston Puritan brothers that a woman had a right to express herself on church matters, that God exists in every human being, and that all people, including women, could communicate with God in his or her own way. The all-male Puritan hierarchy, however, would not suffer a wilderness Joan of Arc, and Hutchinson was banished to the Long Island wilderness. Her loyal family went with her, and all but her youngest daughter were killed by Indians.

The Puritan churchmen were backed up in their opinion by St. Paul, who wrote, "Let the woman learn in silence with all subjection. But I suffer not a woman to teach, nor to usurp authority over the men, but to be in silence."

In Maryland, in 1647, **Margaret Brent,** executrix for her late brother and Lord Baltimore, her late suitor, shocked the Maryland House of Burgesses when she requested two votes, one for Lord Baltimore as executrix of his will and one for herself.

Denied, she asked that proceedings of the Council session be declared invalid. She lost, but continued to be an acknowledged power behind the scenes in the colonies.

Ironically, at the time Brent was denied her vote, there were no written sex restrictions on voting — it was simply an unwritten assumption that women were second-class citizens.

The state of Virginia was the first state to explicitly exclude women from the franchise. At the time of the Revolutionary War, New Jersey was the only state where women could vote, because its constitution read "all inhabitants." Women were disenfranchised in that state in 1807.

1776: No Freedom for Women

The Revolutionary War freed the colonies from Mother England but not the American mothers from the colonial fathers. Colonial women worked hard in the War of Independence, however. The Daughters of Liberty organized anti-tea leagues, brewing herbal "Liberty Tea" to make their point.

To further implement the boycott of British goods, patriotic American women manufactured their own cloth and garments. The headquarters for cutting army garments was the Philadelphia home of Sarah Bache, daughter of Benjamin Franklin, where, in a single day, twenty-two hundred shirts were counted for shipment.

In 1777, **Abigail Adams**, wife and mother of presidents, wrote to her husband, John, the famous letter asking that women's rights be recognized in the new republic:

"In the new code of laws . . . I desire you would remember the ladies and be more generous and favorable to them than your ancestors. Do not put such unlimited power into the hands of the husbands. Remember, all men would be tyrants if they could. If particular care and attention is not paid to the ladies, we are determined to foment a rebellion, and will not hold ourselves bound by any laws in which we have no voice or representation."

Although Abigail Adams' promised rebellion didn't start until 100 years later, her other cause, that women should receive an education equal to men to make them better mothers and citizens, did see some progress as the century turned.

Knowledge to the Woman

With the independence of America came the new notion that perhaps women should receive some education. The idea initially seemed to stem more from patriotism than from any concern about women themselves.

Dr. Benjamin Rush said that in this newly established republic, "the equal share that every citizen has in the liberty . . . and government of our country, make it necessary that our ladies should be qualified to a certain degree of a peculiar and suitable education, to concur in instructing their sons in the principles of liberty and government."

At the same time, some women began to challenge the concept of male intellectual superiority.

Judith Sargent Murray wrote an essay on this theme, published in 1790, asking, "Is it a fact of nature that she hath yielded to one half the human species so unquestionable a mental superiority?"

In 1792, Englishwoman Mary Wollstonecraft's famous work *A Vindication of the Rights of Woman* appeared in the United States and London. She charged,

---

Wollstonecraft: Treat Us as People

It is not surprising that Englishwoman **Mary Wollstonecraft** (1759-1797) became a feminist and wrote the first major work which asserted that woman, like men, are human beings and should be treated as such. She had a drunkard for a father, a brother-in-law who mistreated her sister, and a lover of her own who made her so unhappy she tried to drown herself.

A Vindication of the Rights of Woman, published in London and in the United States in 1792, refuted Jean-Jacques Rousseau's dictate that a woman's only role is to please and be useful to men — "What nonsense," she said. Women, she wrote, have a right to be educated for their own purposes. Wollstonecraft advocated free, coeducational day schools for boys and girls.

"Independence is the grand blessing of life," she wrote. Wollstonecraft learned her independence early and fiercely protected it. She bore an illegitimate daughter and supported her. When she became pregnant a second time she agreed, reluctantly, to marry her lover, William Godwin. She bore Godwin a daughter, Mary, but died soon after, at the age of thirty-eight of complications from the birth. Her daughter, Mary Godwin, married Percy Bysshe Shelley and wrote "Frankenstein."

---

among other things, that male writers had implanted the idea that "the whole tendency of female education ought to be directed to one point: to render them pleasing."

A decade later, a well-educated and well-traveled Scotswoman, Frances Wright, began a ten-year stint as a lecturer, charging that men degraded themselves by imposing inferiority on women.

Wright stirred audiences with her thesis that everything — friendship, marriage, parenthood — would suffer until women were recognized as equal. She urged workingmen also to demand free public education.

Her forthrightness earned her the backlash of antifeminists. She was accused of promoting atheism and free love, and opponents used the epithet "Fanny Wrightist" to refer to women's rights advocates.

School Days

Visiting mothers swooned when they saw their daughters studying the circulation of the blood with charts of the female body at Emma Hart Willard's Female Seminary, Troy, New York, in 1821. Any mention of a feature of the female body was considered a gross indelicacy. But Willard had opened her school, the first endowed institution for educating women, to give her students the same education as men.

The country's first coeducational college, Oberlin, in Oberlin, Ohio, opened in 1833, but the curriculum was different for men and women.

In addition to the appearance of formal educational facilities for women, many women started "female improvement societies," which included reading aloud "useful" books while they worked at church-sewing circles.

The societies led many women's fingers from sewing to writing, and in 1840 feminist Lucy Stone's Literary Society decided, "Ladies ought to mingle in politics, go to Congress."

Black women had their own "female literary societies" in the North and West. The goal was education of their children. Outspoken leaders Maria W. Steward, Harriet Tubman, Frances E. W. Harper, Sarah Remond, and Sojourner Truth recognized the relationship between Negroes' and women's slavery and their equal need for emancipation.

The world opened up to other women through employment in the textile factories which the Industrial Revolution brought to nineteenth century New England. For many women in the 1830s, factory work provided good pay, female comradeship, and exposure to new ideas. With the influx of cheap, immigrant labor in the 1850s, wages went down and working hours in textile towns like Lowell, Massachusetts, increased to as many as thirteen hours a day.

Some Male Allies

Not all men sneered at the need for women's rights. John Quincy Adams, Abigail Adams' son, stood before Congress in 1838 and said what his father had not, that women should have the right to vote. The Congress, however, insisted that suffrage was a states matter.

Other men — Henry Blackwell, Robert Dale Owen, John Neal, Judge Hurlburt — also supported women's rights. Judge Hurlburt, in fact, had written a paper against women's rights, then found he could refute his own argument. So he published a second pamphlet, "Human Rights," which was widely circulated.

Women and Slavery

Many women, sensitive to their own needs for equal rights, adopted the cause of antislavery. While all-male antislavery units in the North rallied to William Lloyd Garrison's famous cry "I will be heard!" in his weekly newspaper, *The Liberator*, some two hundred women from ten states formed the First National Female Anti-Slavery Society.

Feminists Sarah and Angelina Grimké, daughters in a South Carolina slave-owning family, told their firsthand tales of slavery to large and mixed abolitionist audiences in Massachusetts. Attacks upon them for "unwomanliness" illuminated the similarities between their lack of freedom and the lack of freedom of the black slaves.

In 1840, Elizabeth Cady Stanton and Lucretia Mott, antislavery activists, attended the World Anti-Slavery Convention in London, where they were ignored by the men, but they discovered Mary Wollstonecraft's works on women's rights. They returned, determined to pursue their own cause of equal rights.

Evils of Liquor

The picture of a tight-lipped matron, shaking her finger primly while lecturing on the evils of liquor, is familiar — and

Stanton: Eloquent Suffragist

A heckler at an 1871 suffrage meeting suggested women should confine themselves to marriage and motherhood. Why? Because his wife had borne him eight children.

"I have met few men, in my life, worth repeating eight times," fired back **Elizabeth Cady Stanton** (1815-1908).

Herself the mother of seven, the diminutive, white-haired Stanton hardly fit the nineteenth century's stereotype of a feminist rabble rouser. But she ranks alongside Susan B. Anthony as one of the founding mothers of American feminism.

After a strict Presbyterian upbringing in rural New York, Stanton attended the famous Troy Female Seminary. She married abolitionist Harry Stanton, and immediately after the wedding, they set off for the 1840 anti-slavery convention in London., It was there Stanton's feminism was aroused after women were excluded from the sessions.

Stanton, and fellow American Lucretia Mott, decided to hold a women's rights convention in the United States. It took place eight years later at Seneca Falls.

In 1851, Stanton met Susan B. Anthony, and the two began their

work for women's rights. They were well-matched, Anthony was a good behind-the-scenes administrator, and Stanton an eloquent speaker.

Stanton helped edit the feminist newspaper, *The Revolution* and was first president of the National Woman Suffrage Association.

In 1895, when she was eighty, Stanton published her controversial *Woman's Bible* to refute clergymen's opposition to women's suffrage.

---

laughable — to many. But for women in the temperance movement, abolishing drink was no joke.

The male, drunk or sober, had all the rights. He could beat his wife and children, gamble away his earnings, and sell his wife's property without her knowledge. Since the law saw husband and wife as one person — the husband — there was no legal recourse for the woman.

By working for state and local regulation of liquor, tens of thousands of women became politically active. The letters they wrote, the petitions they carried, and the meetings they held would hold them in good stead when it came time to fight for the vote.

Feminism Begins

Margaret Fuller's *Woman in the Nineteenth Century*, published in 1845, capped off the struggle for women's rights in the first half of the nineteenth century. It was the first full-length feminist philosophical treatise published in the United States.

Fuller, a Transcendentalist, urged women to cultivate their minds and eschew emotions and domestic routine.

It was this kind of clear thinking and exciting writing that paved the way for women's active pursuit of the vote in the last half of the nineteenth and early part of the twentieth centuries, beginning in 1848 in Seneca Falls, New York.

THE SUFFRAGE STRUGGLE

It was the height of the haying season in upstate New York in July 1848, when an advertisement appeared in a small rural newspaper, the *Seneca County Courier,* inviting women to a women's rights convention.

But hay was far from the minds of the three hundred men and women who gathered in the Wesleyan Chapel in Seneca Falls on July 19. Stirred by the ringing speeches of a young, earnest feminist named **Elizabeth Cady Stanton** and anti-slavery advocate **Lucretia Mott,** the convention became the first body in the nation's history to declare that women should have the right to vote.

The resolution was one of twelve adopted as the Seneca Falls Declaration, which was patterned after the Declaration of Independence. It is considered the single most important document of the nineteenth-century American women's movement, laying out a blueprint for women's equal rights.

Anthony: Napoleon in Petticoats

"Men, their rights and nothing more; women, their rights and nothing less," was the motto of the feminist newspaper edited by **Susan B. Anthony** (1820-1906). It was also the proposition to which she dedicated the last fifty of her eighty-six years.

Born into a family of Quakers — the one religion which did not discriminate against women — Anthony was an individual of indomitable will, spirit,

and ability. Beginning in 1852, when she attended her first women's rights convention, she and her lifelong associate, Elizabeth Cady Stanton, organized petitions, conventions, canvasses, and lectures to press for the cause of women.

More than any other suffragist, Anthony was the victim of masculine ridicule. But she ultimately came to earn the respect — however begrudging — of her critics. By the 1870s, a St. Louis newspaper conceded, "No longer in the bloom of youth — if she ever had any bloom — hard featured, guileless, cold as an icicle, fluent and philosophical, she wields today tenfold more influence than all the beautiful and brilliant female lecturers that ever flaunted upon the platform . . ."

Anthony never married; she never found a man with enough "moral spine."

The month before her death, Anthony attended her last women's conference and left her admirers with the message, "Failure is impossible."

Declaration of Sentiments and Resolutions (Excerpted)
Adopted by the Seneca Falls Convention, July 19-20, 1848

When, in the course of human events, it becomes necessary for one portion of the family of man to assume among the people of the earth a position different from that which they have hitherto occupied, but one to which the laws of nature and of nature's God entitle them, a decent respect to the opinions of mankind requires that they should declare the causes that impel them to such a course.

We hold these truths to be self-evident: that all men and women are created equal; that they are endowed by their Creator with certain inalienable rights; that these are life, liberty, and the pursuit of happiness. . . .

The history of mankind is a history of repeated injuries and usurpations on the part of man toward woman, having in direct object the establishment of an absolute tyranny over her. To prove this, let facts be submitted to a candid world.

He never permitted her to exercise her inalienable right to the elective franchise.

He has compelled her to submit to laws, in the formation of which she had no voice.

He has made her, if married, in the eye of the law, civilly dead.

He has taken from her all right in property, even to the wages she earns.

He has made her, morally, an irresponsible being, as she can commit many crimes with impunity, provided they be done in the presence of her husband. In the covenant of marriage, she is compelled to promise obedience to her husband, he becoming to all intents and purposes, her master — the law giving him power to deprive her of her liberty, and to administer chastisement.

He has so framed the laws of divorce, as to what shall be the proper causes, and in case of separation, to whom the guardianship of the children shall be given, as to be wholly regardless of the happiness of women — the law, in all cases, going upon false supposition of the supremacy of man, and giving all power into his hands.

After depriving her of all rights as a married woman, if single, and the owner of property, he has taxed her to support a government which recognizes her only when her property can be made profitable to it.

He has monopolized nearly all the profitable employments, and from those she is permitted to follow, she receives but a scanty renumeration. He closes against her all the avenues to wealth and distinction which he considers most honorable to himself. As a teacher of theology, medicine, or law, she is not known.

He has denied her the facilities of obtaining a thorough education, all colleges being closed against her.

He allows her in Church, as well as State, but a subordinate position, claiming Apostolic authority for her exclusion from the ministry, and, with some exceptions, from any public participation in the affairs of the Church.

He has created a false public sentiment by giving to the world a different code of morals for men and women, by which, moral delinquencies which exclude women from society, are not only tolerated, but deemed of little account in man.

Now, in view of this entire disfranchisement of one-half of the people of this country, their social and religious degradation — in view of the unjust laws above mentioned, and because women feel themselves aggrieved, oppressed, and fraudulently deprived of their most sacred rights, we insist that they have immediate admission to all the rights and privileges which belong to them as citizens of the United States.

Stanton's Defense

The resolution on voting was controversial. While members unanimously passed all the other resolutions, it took a stirring defense by Stanton, then an inexperienced orator, assisted by black abolitionist and scholar Frederick Douglass, to push through the suffrage resolution by a narrow margin.

The first formal demand for women's suffrage met the same reaction that would greet suffrage demands for the next sixty years — ridicule and disdain.

The Seneca Falls convention was "unnatural," and "the most shocking incident ever recorded in the history of womanity," and nothing more than the "Petticoat Rebellion," said newspaper editors, clergymen, and politicians.

Unnatural or no, Seneca Falls sparked another convention two weeks later in Rochester, New York, where women resolved to petition the state legislature annually for women's suffrage until they won. They also pledged to establish legal rights for widows, wives, and mothers, including the right to make decisions about their children's welfare.

Other conventions followed, as did the formation of small women's rights groups and statewide women's organizations. In 1850, delegates from nine states attended the first National Woman's Rights Convention in Worcester, Massachusetts.

In 1851, Elizabeth Cady Stanton and Susan B. Anthony met and began a close friendship and working relationship that became the bedrock of the women's suffrage movement.

It soon was clear that women had become a force to be reckoned with, though the Civil War, internal dissension and formidable public opposition delayed their success. Women's advocates, however ridiculed, could no longer be ignored.

Ridicule was easy to come by. The people who dubbed Seneca Falls the "Petticoat Rebellion" were unwittingly accurate. Women were hampered by petticoats and hoops, fringes, tight armholes, and rigid whalebone corsets. The attire of a properly dressed woman could weigh over twelve pounds, making the simplest movements a challenge.

But when Elizabeth Cady Stanton in the 1850s adopted a completely free form of dressing in the then popular European style of pantaloons, a belted tunic, and just-below-the-knees skirt, newspaper illustrators had a field day caricaturing her clothes. No fool, Stanton refused to muddle her cause with clothes and gave up the outfit.

Slaves Freed; Not Women

The Civil War freed the slaves from bondage, but unfortunately did not free women from theirs. With the war's outbreak in 1861, women's rights advocates were urged to abandon their "selfish" cause and devote their energies to war work.

So Union women, as the United States Sanitary Union, set up hospitals, worked in them, collected medical equipment, sewed, cooked, and did the work of the absent men on the farms and in businesses.

In the middle of the war, women's rights advocates joined abolitionists to form a strong antislavery lobby. In 1865, thanks in large part to the work of the National Woman's Loyal League, led by Stanton and Anthony, the Thirteenth Amendment to the United States Constitution, abolishing slavery, was ratified.

The antislavery forces then began pushing for two more amendments to insure the citizenship and voting rights of the newly freed blacks. Women abolitionists proposed that the latter amendment also give the vote to women. But their pleas for support fell on deaf ears. The women were told it was the "Negroes' hour" and that their demands were "complicating the real issue."

As a result, neither the Fourteenth (1868) nor the Fifteenth (1870) Amendment made mention of women.

During the national debate on the Fifteenth Amendment, disagreement about whether to fight for co-enfranchisement with the Negro, created havoc within the women's suffrage organization. That, coupled with the movement's concentration on the war effort at the expense of their own cause, destroyed the united front women had forged in the 1850s.

The woman's rights movement split into two factions in 1869. The National Woman Suffrage Association, formed by Anthony and Stanton, was the more radi-

Truth: 'Ain't I A Woman'

Born a slave in New York State, and mother of thirteen children who were sold into slavery, **Sojourner Truth** (1797-1883) was a natural orator. When New York freed its slaves in 1827, Sojourner Truth came to New York City and became a revivalist minister, active in abolitionist and women's rights causes.

Her "Ain't I a Woman?" speech at the 1851 Women's Convention in Akron, Ohio, awed her audience, including the white minister who had preceded her on the podium and had opposed women's rights.

"The man over there says women need to be helped into carriages, and lifted over ditches, and to have the best place everywhere. Nobody ever helps me into carriages or over puddles, or gives me the best place . . . and ain't I a woman?"

She bared her arm, (she was six feet tall) and thrust it high. "I could work as much and eat as much as a man — when I could get it — and bear the lash as well! And ain't I a woman?" She told of

bearing thirteen children, seeing them sold into slavery, crying, "with my mother's grief, none but Jesus heard me. And ain't I a woman?"

Her speech was the highlight of the convention. The chairwoman, Frances Gage, wrote, "She had taken us up in her strong arms, and carried us safely over the slough of difficulty, turning the whole tide in our favor."

cal. The NWSA continued to favor enfranchisement of women through an amendment to the U.S. Constitution.

The rival American Woman Suffrage Association reflected the more conservative views of feminists like Lucy Stone and Julia Ward Howe. The AWSA favored working for woman's suffrage on the state level. The domineering personality of the NWSA's Anthony also helped bring about the schism.

Many feminists also believed Anthony and Stanton did the cause no good by allying themselves with Victoria Woodhull. They charged that Woodhull's outspoken views on "free love" and a woman's right to control her body hardly helped the suffrage movement.

Renewing Interest

Perhaps every important cause needs to slow down temporarily to allow society to catch up with it. In the 1890s, as if awakening from a long sleep, the suffragists seemed refreshed and renewed their pleas, and if the country was not yet receptive, it was no longer so hostile.

Women's rights had taken some steps forward, especially in the West, since the Civil War. Wyoming gave women equal rights in 1869, and when it won statehood in 1890, it became the first state to grant women suffrage. Colorado followed suit. By 1890, women could vote in school elections in nineteen states, school politics apparently being thought suitable for women.

Stone: Kept Her Name

Supplying the origin of the term "Lucy Stoner," for a woman who keeps her maiden name after marriage, **Lucy Stone** (1818-1893) was a feminist and magazine editor during the early years of the feminist movement.

Like Elizabeth Cady Stanton, Lucy Stone grew up in a traditional household where education for women was not considered necessary. When she insisted on going to Oberlin College in Ohio, her father refused to pay her tuition as he had done for her brothers, although he later relented.

While Stone was in college, she began campaigning for women's rights, and in 1850 organized the first national women's conference in the United States.

Lucy Stone married Henry Blackwell in 1855, but kept her married name — "A wife should no more take her husband's name than he should take hers." At their marriage they read a statement protesting laws which gave the husband custody of his wife's person and vowed that marriage is an equal partnership.

Stone and her husband founded the *Woman's Journal*, the leading magazine promoting women's suffrage, in 1872. She also helped found the American Woman Suffrage Association.

Woodhull: "Mrs. Satan"

Polite society denounced her as "Mrs. Satan." Sister feminists kept their distance. Moralists had her thrown into jail on a libel charge. But beautiful and quick-witted **Victoria Woodhull** (1838-1927) refused to be intimidated.

Woodhull and her sister, Tennessee Claflin, enchanted septuagenarian Commodore Cornelius Vanderbilt with their professed magnetic healing powers. He set them up in a Wall Street brokerage business, which netted them profits of $700,000 in three years.

With their fortune, the sisters started *Woodhull and Claflin's Weekly*, a periodical which dared endorse women's suffrage and financial independence, short skirts, vegetarianism, free love, licensed prostitution, and birth control.

Woodhull was thus already notorious when she declared her candidacy for President in 1872 on the Equal Rights ticket. Respectable feminists scoffed. Her running mate, abolitionist Frederick Douglass, refused to campaign. They won only a few thousand votes and Woodhull spent election night in jail for exposing the adulterous affair of the supposedly rock-ribbed Rev. Henry Ward Beecher in print.

After her acquittal, Woodhull moved to England, where she married a wealthy banker and continued lecturing and writing until the end of her eighty-nine years.

Women of the St. Louis Equal Suffrage League campaigned for the vote in a small Missouri town.

In a renewed spirit of cooperation, the two formerly feuding women's groups merged into the National American Woman Suffrage Association (NAWSA). Elizabeth Stanton was the first president, followed by Susan Anthony in 1892, and by Carrie Chapman Catt in 1900. Catt was the only one of the three to live to see suffrage granted to women.

The suffragists, however, did not win over all their old enemies. Politicians detested them. They had no use for female intrusions into their male domains or for high-minded investigations into their government operations, which feminists promised to do.

The clergy, leaning heavily on unclear or censored translations of the Old and New Testaments and on antifeminist St. Paul, preached consistently against women's suffrage, which, they claimed, would remove women from their "proper sphere." (Stanton, to rebut the clergy's charges, prepared a two-volume *Woman's Bible*, which reinterpreted allegedly antifeminist opinions. But many feminists, who disagreed with some of her dramatic revisions and feared further alienation of

the church, disassociated themselves.)

Immigrant men went along with their party bosses in sneering at suffragists. That these men, largely ignorant of the democratic process, could vote while women could not infuriated the suffragists.

Liquor interests contributed handsomely to campaigns against woman's suffrage.

Perhaps most unsettling were the complaints of other women who declared the suffragists "unladylike." These women insisted that they were not capable of voting and that men knew best anyway.

Near the Voting Booth

But the times finally caught up with the suffragists, and the turn of the century brought them to the last leg of their journey to the voting booth.

In the early 1900s, immigrant and working-class women began to join their middle-class sisters in the struggle for women's rights. Organizations like the Women's Political Union, the Young Women's Christian Association, the National Women's Trade Union League, and

This cartoon by feminist Blanche Ames unmasks the villains of the pro-suffrage forces.

Catt: Victory At Last

Carrie Chapman Catt (1859-1947) belonged to the second generation of American feminists: practical, political, and professional.

Raised in Iowa, Catt graduated at the top of her class from Iowa State Agricultural College. She intended to read law, but poverty forced her to take work as principal of an Iowa school. Two years later, she was superintendent

of schools, a position of rare authority for a woman.

After her first husband died, only three months after their wedding, Catt went to work as a journalist. Her second husband was sympathetic to women's rights; their marriage contract allowed her four months a year to campaign for suffrage.

Catt worked under Susan B. Anthony, who groomed her for a top job in the suffrage organization. When Anthony resigned the presidency of the National American Woman Suffrage Association in 1900, she named Catt her successor. Catt crusaded for suffrage until it was won, only taking time off to care for her dying husband.

Three years after the Nineteenth Amendment was ratified, Catt wrote, "It is doubtful if any man . . . ever realized what the suffrage struggle came to mean to women . . . How much of time and patience, how much of work, energy, aspiration, how much faith, how much hope, how much despair went into it. It leaves its mark on one, such a struggle."

the National Consumer League helped bridge the gap between the two groups.

Women won the vote in referenda in Washington state (1910), California (1911), Oregon, Arizona, and Kansas (1912), and Nevada and Montana (1914).

Debate on the Susan B. Anthony amendment was revived in Congress in 1913 when two women, Alice Paul and Lucy Burns, became chairwomen of NAWSA's Congressional Committee and introduced activist tactics like parades, outdoor rallies, and hunger strikes to publicize their point. Troops were often called to restore order, which brought more attention to the suffragist cause.

While shrewdly reaping results from the drama Paul and Burns created, Catt would not commit NAWSA to their methods. The two women left NAWSA to start the Congressional Union and, in 1917, began picketing the White House.

Every day for eighteen months two teams of women from the activist group stood as ''silent sentinels'' in front of the White House.

When the country declared war on Germany in 1917, the Congressional Union, now called the National Woman's Party, remembered the ground suffragists lost during the Civil War and continued fighting for suffrage.

While keeping their vigil at the White House, they were attacked by bystanders and in the subsequent melee, 218 women were arrested and 97 jailed, although their sentences were later revoked — they'd been guilty only of blocking the sidewalk.

These activist tactics were a great help to NAWSA, now two million members strong. Catt presented her party, in contrast to the Woman's Party, as one of persuasion and compromise. While the more radical group protested with pickets, she was reminding President Wilson of the bravery of American women nurses on the front and of women's competence in assuming business and family responsibilities for their absent husbands.

On January 1, 1919, President Wilson informed Congress that he favored the Nineteenth Amendment. The House of Representatives passed it the next day, the Senate, the following June. On August 26, 1920, it was ratified by the thirty-sixth state, Tennessee, and it became part of the United States Constitution.

It only took, by Carrie Chapman Catt's calculations:

- 52 years of campaigning,
- 56 referenda to male voters,
- 480 efforts to get state legislatures to submit suffrage amendments,
- 277 campaigns to get state party conventions to include women's suffrage planks,
- 47 campaigns to get state constitutional conventions to write women's suffrage into state constitutions,
- 30 campaigns to get presidential party conventions to adopt women's suffrage planks into party platforms,
- 19 successive campaigns with 19 successive Congresses.

Victory was almost in sight when New York City women paraded for the vote in May, 1913.

SUFFRAGE ABROAD

While the American women's suffrage movement was, true to this country's character, a boisterous display of democracy — numerous women's conventions, many resolutions, countless attempts at legislative action, and attendant newspaper ridicule — the suffrage movement in England, the only other country that had any feminist activity at the time, was a somber and ultimately more violent affair.

Because Englishwomen were fighting a much deeper tradition of meager educational opportunities and a more entrenched class society and male dominance than their Amendment counterparts, their battle was more difficult, slower to start, and more bitter when it erupted.

An Englishwoman is credited with writing the first strong women's rights treatise — **Mary Wollstonecraft** (1759-97).) She published *A Vindication of the Rights of Woman,* a rousing work which examined and condemned the servile role women were taught to play in society and called for equal education and rights for women.

Her work was dismissed as ridiculous — Horace Walpole called her "a hyena in petticoats" — but her radical new thinking inspired American feminists in the nineteenth century, who used her work as a jumping-off point for their cause.

Wollstonecraft's fellow Englishwomen, however, did very little fighting for women's rights in the century following her death. Only the pens of a few outstanding writers, Harriet Taylor and her husband, John Stuart Mill, kept the feminist cause alive in England.

In the early 1900s, however, the feminist movement burst into England in the form of the **Pankhurst** family — mother Emmeline and daughters Christabel and Sylvia. These women formed the activist Women's Social and Political Union to fight for women's rights.

Led by the Pankhursts, hundreds of women crashed windows, slashed pictures, and assaulted the police. They chained themselves to iron gates outside the homes of important men. When jailed, they went on hunger strikes and were brutally force-fed.

Their violent tactics, combined with the sympathy they earned for their work during World War I, finally put women on the road to the vote.

In 1918, all women over thirty who were householders or wives of householders were enfranchised. In 1928 the voting age was reduced to twenty-one, and women were given voting parity with men.

Although the women's suffrage movement originated in the United States and England, New Zealand won the international suffrage sweepstakes, granting women the vote in national elections in 1893.

Australia was next, introducing women's suffrage in 1902, followed by Finland in 1906, and Norway in 1913. By 1918, all but three Canadian provinces gave women the vote in that country — Quebec held back full suffrage for women until World War II.

From 1914 to 1939, women achieved the vote in national elections in twenty-eight more countries.

In 1977, women were denied the franchise in only three countries — Jordan, Kuwait, and Nigeria.

THE SILENT YEARS (1920–60)

If ever there was a year that American women should have been euphoric about their progress, it was 1920. That year the Nineteenth Amendment was ratified, ensuring women's suffrage, new women's groups were pushing for further reforms, and women were holding skilled labor and administrative jobs that before World War I had always been held by men. Even the ratification of the Prohibition Amendment, the year before, had been due to women's lobbying efforts.

And women were delighted with themselves. Sporting new, short skirts, smoking cigarettes, they thought they had won the battle for emancipation and could now settle down and have some fun. Causes were out as the booming prosperity of the 1920s rolled in.

Dedicated feminists, ever vigilant, worried at this attitude. Said **Emily Newell Blair** to a young suffragist in 1920, "I am sorry for you young women who have to

Paul: Early Militant

Had **Alice Paul** (1885-1977) joined the women's movement sixty years later than she did, WITCH or the Radical Feminists — not the more staid NOW — would have been the group for her. Paul was a militant. Using hunger strikes and marches — even burning President Woodrow Wilson in effigy — she focused attention on the suffrage struggle.

Born and educated in the United States, Paul went to England in 1906 to work in a settlement house. There she learned the militant tactics employed by the British suffragists.

She brought those methods home with her, putting them to use first as head of the National American Woman Suffrage Association's Congressional Committee, and later as head of her own Congressional Union. In 1913, she organized a suffrage parade of eight thousand women in Washington, D.C. She and her fellow marchers were spat upon, slapped, tripped, and insulted.

Paul orchestrated demonstrations in front of the White House until President Wilson endorsed the suffrage amendment in 1919. Imprisoned in 1917 for her activities, she went on a hunger strike that lasted twenty-two days.

Paul did not give up the fight when the Nineteenth Amendment was ratified. Though she returned to school to study law, she saw to it that an Equal Rights Amendment was introduced in Congress in 1923.

---

carry on the work for the next ten years, for suffrage was a symbol, and now you have lost your symbol."

Her words were prophetic. Indeed, the giddiness of the 1920s obscured some of the realities of the decade. In some cases women who had replaced men in industry were demoted or fired when the men returned to the work force. The progress made by women in the work force was offset by severe wage discrimination against them.

The loss of the "symbol" of suffrage affected the inner circle of serious feminists as well. With the vote guaranteed, they began to focus on separate, special interests, breaking off into new organizations with varying goals.

The largest new group was the League of Women Voters, founded in 1920 as an outgrowth of the National American Woman Suffrage Association (NAWSA). Determined to continue reform for women, state chapters of the League were successful in eliminating some local discriminatory marriage and property laws. They also succeeded in repealing laws that prohibited women from serving on juries or holding office — laws that some legislatures had passed after ratification of the suffrage amendment.

When the elections of the early 1920s revealed only a light turnout of eligible women voters and showed their voting patterns to be no different from men's, the League leaders decided that education of women, rather than fighting for reform of the political system, should be their primary function. Instead of using the education to proselytize for feminist goals, the

League assumed a conservative, fact-finding, nonpartisan approach to educating women.

The reorganized National Woman's Party under the direction of Alice Paul took a more activist tack.

In 1923, the party unsuccessfully introduced in Congress the Equal Rights Amendment, which its members felt would be much more effective in ending discrimination against women than the League's education method. They continued, unsuccessfully, to reintroduce ERA in every congressional session. The League initially opposed ERA, not wishing to overturn hard-fought protective laws for factory workers.

Depression and World War II

Feminism, hailed for its modernity in 1919, became a scapegoat for the country's ills as the Depression closed its grip on Americans in the 1930s. Many argued that women, by going to work and taking needed jobs away from men, had caused the Depression. By leaving home, they had weakened the moral fiber and created a crisis of spirit.

In 1936, a Gallup poll showed that nearly four out of five Americans felt that wives should not work if their husbands were employed — 75 percent of the women questioned agreed.

Women, however, remained in the work force during the 1930s in the same proportions as in the 1920s, although the ratio of women to men in the professions fell.

Women's groups worked together during the Depression to prevent backsliding on issues they had fought for in earlier years. The Business and Professional Women's Clubs, the League of Women Voters, and other organizations lobbied together successfully to defeat twenty-six state bills that proposed prohibiting the employment of married women who were not heads of households. The League also protested federal legislation that disallowed the employment of both husband and wife in the federal civil service — legislation that led to the firing of many women employees.

However, the League still maintained its first allegiance to social rather than feminist reforms. During this period it was responsible for extending the merit system within the civil service and the improvement of public-school education. The League also promoted the Social Security Act of 1935 and lobbied for the passage of the Food, Drug and Cosmetic Act in 1938.

Said one League leader, "We of the League are very much for the rights of women, but . . . we are not feminists primarily; we are citizens."

Another product of the Depression decade was the availability of birth-control information. By 1940, every state except Connecticut and Massachusetts had legalized its distribution. Family-planning clinics had increased from 28 to 746 nationally between 1930 and 1941, a third of them federally funded.

With World War II came a brief improvement in the status of women. As they had done in World War I, women took over men's jobs at home while the soldiers went to the front. Between 1940 and 1945 the percentage of women in the work force increased from 25 to 36 percent.

However, the advances they made, including equal pay with men and federally funded day-care centers, were considered part of the war effort rather than a permanent aid to women. All federal funds allocated for day care were discontinued in 1946, and between 1945 and 1947, the percentage of women in the work force dropped from 36 to 28 percent.

Many women would have preferred to work. A Women's Bureau study in 1944 found that 80 percent of the women working during the war wanted to continue in their jobs. Black women, in particular, were helped by the labor shortage, moving in substantial numbers from domestic work to factory labor. And after 1947, women did begin to return to the work force, so that in 1951 31 percent of the work force was women. As a group, however, they were not much heard from for the next twenty years, as the country headed into the postwar baby boom and the era of the full-time housewife.

Women After the War

The word "feminism" seemed to simply disappear from the country's vocabulary from World War II until 1960. Young couples, yearning for security after the war, married, moved to the suburbs if they

Friedan: Critic of the Mystique

Betty Friedan (1921-   ), mother of modern American feminism, was a suburban housewife when she wrote *The Feminine Mystique* in 1963. Her book exploded the 1950s myth of the happy homemaker by reporting on the unhappiness and boredom of many full-time housewives.

In her book, Friedan identifies "the problem that has no name" which results from the "feminine mystique" — propaganda designed to lull women into giving up their search for an individual identity and submerging themselves in their home, husband, and children. The result is a feeling of emptiness at middle age, which sends many women to psychiatrists with "mysterious ailments."

The success of *The Feminine Mystique* catapulted Friedan into the forefront of the burgeoning women's movement in the 1960s. She separated from her husband, and moved from suburb to city. Friedan was one of the founders of the National Organization for Women (NOW), the National Women's Political Caucus, and New York's First Women's Bank. She helped set up the successful Women's Strike for Equality in 1970.

"I'm very unbored," says Friedan. "I'm nasty, I'm bitchy, I get mad. But, by God, I'm absorbed in what I'm doing."

could, and women immersed themselves wholly into family life.

One important feminist book, Simone de Beauvoir's *The Second Sex,* which discussed the subjection of women, was published during this period, but the time was a quiet one for most women's groups.

Lack of membership and disagreement over the Equal Rights Amendment considerably weakened the women's movement. The Woman's Party, BPW, and the National Federation of Women's Clubs supported the ERA, but the League of Women Voters, the Women's Bureau of the U.S. Labor Department, and women in the labor movement opposed it. They argued that it went against their best interests.

The ERA, though passed twice in the 1950s in the Senate, was defeated both times in the House by an anti-ERA lobby organization.

It would take the new spirit of the sixties and seventies to revitalize the weakened feminist cause by uniting women to fight discrimination that still plagued women on almost every level.

FEMINISM NOW

The country seemed to catch fire when John F. Kennedy was inaugurated in 1961. The forty-three-year-old President was armed with energy and the promise of social reform for blacks, who had been agitating for civil rights during the 1950s, and for women. Before the year was out, he ushered in a progressive new decade for women's rights by creating the Presidential Commission on the Status of Women, the first body of its kind.

In the next four years, two new laws were passed prohibiting pay discrimination against women and banning sex discrimination in employment. Many states established commissions to improve the status of women.

American women, who had been relatively docile during the quiet Eisenhower years, began to respond to the changing atmosphere. In 1963, **Betty Friedan,** a housewife from a suburb outside of New York City, published *The Feminine Mystique*. The document challenged the prevailing idea that all women were happiest as homemakers.

She accused advertisers, educators, sociologists, and psychologists of selling the American woman the myth of the "feminine mystique," that women could find total fulfillment through childbearing and homemaking, and said that the latter was boring. The result of the "mystique," she claimed, was that many women lacked a sense of identity because they had abandoned their own goals to live through their families.

The Feminine Mystique became a best seller, was excerpted in national women's magazines, and has since been translated into thirteen languages.

Interest in women's rights grew during the next several years until, in 1966, a group of women delegates to a meeting of state women's commissions organized a lobby, the National Organization of Women (NOW), to ensure adoption and enforcement of women's rights legislation. "The absolute necessity for a civil rights movement for women had reached such a point by 1966," wrote Friedan, one of NOW's founders, "that it only took a few of us to get together to ignite the spark — and it spread like a nuclear chain reaction."

NOW, which grew from three hundred members at its founding to forty-eight thousand members in 1974, has used the law in its fight to end discrimination. By petitioning government agencies and through test court cases, it ended sex-segregated want ads in newspapers (1968), won back pay and ended sex discrimination for employees of the Southern Bell Telephone and Telegraph Co. (1968) and of the American Telephone and Telegraph Co. (1973), and drafted and saw passed the Equal Credit bill (1974).

Other women's groups were formed after NOW, including the Women's Equity Action League (WEAL, 1968), which lobbies against discrimination in employment, education, and taxation; the Women's Political Caucus (1972), which pressures political parties in favor of women's interests, and Federally Employed Women (FEW, 1968), a lobby group for women in the federal government.

Women's Liberation

While NOW and similar organizations followed the traditions of nineteenth-century women's groups that worked primarily to improve the legal and economic status of women, the 1960s saw the birth of women's groups dedicated to bettering the political and social status of women.

Called women's liberationists ("libbers," or "bra burners" by their critics), women in these groups were either convinced that women were oppressed politically, in the sense of workers being oppressed in a capitalist society, or in a societal way, in that they were conditioned by men to think of themselves as second-class citizens. The latter idea was particularly potent because it publicly questioned and thus threatened the existing, very personal structure of men-women relationships.

The ideas were not new — English feminist Mary Wollstonecraft had written of many of the same things in 1792 — but more women were ready to act on them than ever before.

This was because many of the women liberationists had grown up in an era of social activism and had worked in civil rights and Vietnam War protests. Challenging society's attitude toward themselves, a process dubbed "consciousness-raising," was just the next step for them. (In many cases they had to challenge sexist attitudes within their own protest groups — women's liberation advocates were pelted with tomatoes and thrown out of a 1966 Students for a Democratic Society convention.)

Their methods, like their politics, were more radical and flamboyant than those of the more traditional NOW. Instead of arguing law, they took to the Atlantic City boardwalk in 1968 to protest the Miss America Contest as sexist. A live sheep was crowned Miss America, and symbols of femininity — bras, girdles, hair curlers — were thrown in a trash can (no bras were burned here, but were at later demonstrations, hence the term "bra burners").

By the end of the 1960s the women's liberation movement sprouted everywhere. Offbeat protests were held all over the country, like the "Burial of Traditional Womanhood" at Arlington Cemetery in 1968. Women formed consciousness-raising groups to explore

The Sexist ABC's

A is for St. Thomas **A**quinas who said that woman is "defective and accidental . . . a male gone awry."

B is for Dr. Edgar **B**erman, who said "raging hormonal imbalances" make women unfit to be president.

C is for **C**onfucius who said, "Men have their respective occupations and women their homes."

D is for the **D**ouble Standard.

E is for **E**masculate which self-assured women are said to do to men.

F is for Sigmund **F**reud who advanced the "penis envy" theory to explain female behavior.

G is for **G**olf courses — Like Maryland's Burning Tree Country Club — which bar women from teeing off.

H is for radical Abbie **H**offman, who declared, "the only alliance I would make with the women's liberation movement is in bed."

I is for the Jewish prayer, "**I** thank thee, Oh Lord, that thou hast not created me a woman."

J is for the U.S. **J**aycees, who refuse to open their ranks to women.

K is for **K**uwait, one of the three nations in which women cannot vote.

L is for "**L**adylike," which women's rights advocates are perennially accused of not being. Or for "**L**esbian," which they are perennially accused of being.

M is for **M**achismo, which has kept Latino women "in their place."

N is for **N**ational Airlines' "Fly Me" advertising campaign.

O is for "**O**bey," a wedding vow traditionally asked of women, only.

P is for **P**layboy centerfolds.

Q is for **Q**ueen Victoria, who declared, "We women are not made for governing — and if we are good women, we must dislike these male occupations."

R is for **R**ape.

S is for **S**top ERA.

T is for **T**opless bars.

U is for "**U**nder My Thumb," a rock ditty by the Rolling Stones.

V is for **V**eils which still are a necessity for many Arab women.

W is for **W**olf **W**histles.

X is for **X**XX-rated movies.

Y is for Henny **Y**oungman, who owes his career to the "wife joke."

Z is for **Z**oos in Saudi Arabia, which admit men and women on alternate days.

— Barbara McDowell

their changing role in society, and books were published discussing everything from women's role in literature to female sexuality: Kate Millett's *Sexual Politics* (1969), Robin Morgan's *Sisterhood Is Powerful* (1970), and Germaine Greer's *The Female Eunuch* (1971).

Legalized Abortion

The emotional question of whether abortions should be legalized became a symbol of, and rallying point for, the women's movement in the early 1970s in the same way the suffrage amendment had united women's groups earlier in the century.

The first abortion laws were passed in the 1820s to protect women from the hazards of surgery and unskilled abortionists (medical techniques in the nineteenth century were primitive, and any kind of operation was avoided if possible). Before that time, abortions were legal before the first movement of the fetus.

More limits were placed on abortions during the century as each of the states passed various laws forbidding abortion or allowing it only to save the life of the mother. After the Civil War, a number of omnibus laws banned almost everything sexual — including talking about sex — and restricted abortion.

Although the American Law Institute drafted an abortion reform proposal in 1959, there was little talk in favor of abortion until 1962, when Sherry Finkbine, an Arizona woman, tried to get an abortion in this country after she learned a drug she had taken, Thalidomide, would cause severe deformity in her baby. Permission was denied, so she and her husband flew to Sweden where she had an abortion.

Colorado was the first of twelve states between 1967 and 1970 to reform abortion laws, allowing abortion in certain circumstances, including rape, incest, or if the mother's life was endangered.

In 1970, women's liberation and organizations like the YWCA and the Board of Trustees of the American Medical Association began fighting to repeal the laws completely, so that women could have abortion on demand.

But abortion's foes were as adamant as its proponents. "Right-to-life" advocates, claiming that human life begins at the moment of conception, denounced abortion as murder.

Women's groups, however, had found a rallying point in the abortion issue. In August 1970, the Women's Strike for Equality focused attention on three feminist goals: abortion on demand, equal job and educational opportunity, and twenty-four-hour child care. The strike, marked by parades, pickets, rallies and teach-ins across the nation, was the largest demonstration ever for women's rights.

Three years later in January 1973, after more lobbying and demonstrations, the Supreme Court overruled all state laws restricting or prohibiting a woman's right to an abortion during the first three months of pregnancy. The Court also ruled that during the next six months of pregnancy the state may "regulate the abortion procedure in ways that are reasonably related to maternal health" and that during the last ten weeks any state may prohibit abortions, except where it is necessary to preserve the mother's life.

The Sex of the Future

"I have seen the sex of the future, and it is women," wrote columnist Art Buchwald at the turn of the decade. Indeed, his jesting remark seemed true in the early 1970s, as women's liberation groups successfully pursued their goals to repeal abortion laws and end sex discrimination.

In 1970, according to a Virginia Slims American Women's Opinion Survey, only 40 percent of women interviewed favored efforts to strengthen women's status in so-

ciety. In 1974, the figure had grown to 57 percent. Another survey which sampled the opinions of 120,000 young, relatively affluent and well-educated women in 1973 showed that only 2 percent believed their total fulfillment could come solely from being wives and mothers.

Women were doing very well for themselves. Because of new legislation and court cases, they were being recruited for and promoted to higher business positions than they had ever held. There were attacks on sexism at all levels, in many publications from publishers' guidelines for nonsexist children's books to the use of "Ms." instead of "Miss" or "Mrs."

Ms., a feminist magazine, was started in 1972, and its first issue of three hundred thousand copies sold out in eight days instead of the eight weeks it was supposed to take. **Gloria Steinem,** one of the magazine's founders, became a cult heroine, and young women took to her trademark, aviator glasses.

The Equal Rights Amendment, which had been introduced annually in Congress since 1923, with varying degrees of success, was ratified by the House of Representatives in October 1971, by a vote of 350 to 15. The following March the Senate ratified the amendment by a vote of 84 to 8. Twenty-two states ratified the amendment in 1972.

Women's liberationists were at the peak of their power, but there were setbacks, as the energy and motivation proved hard to sustain.

Discord began to weaken the movement. Diverse groups of women, who had joined forces to fight for abortion, drifted apart to pursue more specialized interests.

At the same time, women who had been opposed to abortion repeal or to the women's movement itself, organized themselves as an efficient lobby, which hurt the women's liberation causes.

The ERA felt the first impact of these changes. Between 1972 and 1975, twelve states had ratified the amendment; between 1975 and January 1977, only one state ratified ERA. ERA is currently three states short of the thirty-eight needed for ratification by 1979. Fifteen states have rejected the amendment, and three states have voted to rescind their earlier approval.

Steinem: More Than Glamour

Gloria Steinem (1934-   )
comes by her feminist sympathies
naturally. Her grandmother was
president of the Ohio Women's
Suffrage Association from 1908 to
1911.

Raised in a rat-infested Toledo
slum, Steinem studied at Smith
College before setting off for New
York to make her career as a
writer. She ended up — albeit
briefly — as a Playboy bunny.
Steinem spent a month in rabbit
ears, cotton tail, and little else,
gathering information for a
magazine exposé on Playboy Club
operations.

Steinem was recruited to the
feminist cause in 1968, when she
attended a women's liberation
meeting to obtain material for her
New York magazine political
column. She quickly became one
of the movement's leading
fund-raisers and speakers. In 1972,
she helped found the feminist
monthly *Ms.* of which she continues
as an editor.

Tall, attractive, with long
blond-streaked hair, and
ever-present aviator glasses,
Steinem has often been called the
movement's "glamour girl." She
shrugs off the description with, "I'm
not going to walk around in Army
boots and cut off my hair."

Glamour girl or no, she has
emerged as one of modern
feminism's most visible and
articulate spokeswomen.

Fighting the ERA

Spearheading the anti-ERA campaign is
Phyllis Schlafly, author, politician, housewife, and mother of six, who has worked
since 1972 to defeat ERA.

Schafly calls the ERA a "fraud," and
claims women are already protected under
existing laws granting equal job, educational, and credit opportunities, a charge
disputed by ERA proponents who say the
ERA is needed to ensure equal opportunity for women. Her efforts are credited
with the recent backlash against ERA, including the defeat of New York and New
Jersey state ERA amendments — both
states had previously ratified the federal
ERA amendment.

The middle 1970s have not been without
some progress. In 1974, a large coalition of
women's organizations, including such diverse groups as the Camp Fire Girls, the
Future Homemakers of America, the
Gray Panthers (a lobby group for older

people), the National Association of
Women Lawyers, and the United Auto
Workers International Women's Department, worked with the Women's Action
Alliance to produce a blueprint for further-
ing women's rights, called the U.S. National Women's Agenda.

The eleven-point agenda, which was
approved by the National Women's Political Caucus, includes: Working to elect
legislators who will support the Agenda's
principles; enforcing equal education
laws; recognition of importance of
homemaking; improving the treatment of
rape victims; wider coverage of women's
issues as hard news; and tax deductions
for child-care expenses.

Another feminist landmark was the
United Nations' designation of 1975 as International Women's Year, highlighted by
an impressive two-week conference in
Mexico City, attended by more than one
thousand delegates from 133 nations.

Schlafly: ERA's Bitterest Foe

Not every woman wants a string of college degrees, an income of her own, and a calling that takes her away from the kitchen. Equal Rights Amendment opponent **Phyllis Schlafly** (1924-   ) has all those things. But she is fighting hard on behalf of women who don't have them — and don't want them.

Schlafly is chief spokeswoman for the Stop-ERA forces, which have so far succeeded in thwarting the proposed constitutional amendment.

Daughter of a "poor" salesman and his librarian wife, Schlafly worked her way through college by testing bullets in a World War II ammunition factory.

Since then Schlafly has had little time for the coffee klatch and bridge club circuit. She has six children and has written seven books, including *A Choice, Not An Echo,* a 1964 best seller supporting conservative Senator Barry Goldwater's Presidential campaign.

More than 11,000 Americans subscribe to the monthly *Phyllis Schlafly Report,* which has concentrated since 1972 on criticism of the Equal Rights Amendment, which, she claims, "will take away from women the rights they already have."

The delegates, 20 percent of whom were men, unanimously adopted a forty-nine-page "World Plan of Action," which stressed the need for women's participation in government and set goals for increased literacy, employment, and civic, social, and political equality, to be checked at the next women's conference, planned for Iran in 1980.

CONSOLIDATING GAINS

Some saw in the passing of the pickets, the marches — even the bra burnings — the decline of the feminist movement. Nothing could be further from the truth. The most visible signs of protest are gone, but only because they have served their purpose of attracting attention to women's concerns. The action has moved indoors from the Atlantic City boardwalk to the voting booth, the court room, and the executive suite. Women's liberation continues to score new victories each day: the teenager who stars on the girls' basketball instead of cheering for the boys' squad, the woman with grown children who summons the courage to get her first job, the new mother who chooses to leave her job to be with her baby.

A 1976 Gallup poll found that one third of American women of all ages, races, and socioeconomic groups firmly believe they are better off than they were five years ago, and more than half feel the lot of women has improved at least a bit.

Nearly half of the women who think their sex is better off now give women's groups a "great deal" of the credit. Eight out of ten of the women give the liberation movement a "fair amount" of the credit.

Finally, nine out of ten of these women call themselves "fairly happy" with their lives, and half of that number are "very happy."

The battle for women's rights is far from won. A movement described by one of its leaders, former NOW President Wilma Scott Heide, as "the most profound universal behavioral revolution the world has ever known" takes time. It also will require women's continued vigilance, patience, and courage.

PHOTO CREDITS

Chapter Opening Photos: p. 95: Grandma Moses; p. 227: Gwendolyn Brooks; p. 263: Helen Thomas; p. 285: Bessie Smith; p. 325: Mae West; p. 359: Maria Mitchell (left) and Mary Whitney; p. 393: Aimee Semple MacPherson; p. 409: Mildred "Babe" Didrikson Zaharias; p. 459: Margaret Chase Smith; p. 539: Alice Paul unfurls Women's Party banner.

Photo Credits. Abbott Laboratories: p. 17; Alinari/Scala: p. 215, 216 (2), 218, 221 (2), 399; Amalgamated Clothing Workers of America: 174, 179; American Cancer Society: p. 19; American Dental Association: p. 32; Association for the Advancement of Psychoanalysis of the Karen Horney Psychoanalytic Institute and Center: p. 37; Bancroft Library, University of California, Berkeley: p. 43; The Bettmann Archive: p. 12, 14, 114 (2), 116, 117, 164, 187, 190, 381, 400, 406, 489, 511, 539, 545; Brown Brothers: p. 46, 108, 268, 313, 380, 448, 479; Chicago Historical Society: p. 233 (Art Sheet Music Cover, Uncle Tom's Cabin No. 2, The Slave Mother by George Linley, London, undated), 388; Culver Pictures, Inc.: p. 13, 53, 93, 109, 149, 156, 178, 210, 285, 314, 323, 325, 333, 336, 341, 352, 372, 463, 491; Ewing Galloway: p. 68, 119; Fall River Historical Society: p. 502; Girls Scouts of the U.S.A., p. 55; The Granger Collection, p. 218; Greensboro Historical Museum: p. 487; The Hirshhorn Museum: p. 224; Houghton Library, Harvard University, p. 250, 376; Kansas State Historical Society: p. 175; Library of Congress: p. 45, 50, 60, 78, 115, 123, 132, 143, 144, 157, 160, 161, 168, 207, 208, 377, 403, 411, 412, 451, 521; Malloy Gallery, New York: p. 407 (2); Manchester Historic Association: p. 173; Margaret Mead, American Museum of Natural History: p. 366; The Metropolitan Museum of Art: p. 110 (Museum Excavations, 1919-20; Rogers Fund and contribution of Edward S. Harkness), 111 (Rogers Fund, 1909), 113 (Bequest of Isaac D. Fletcher, 1917); Minnesota Historical Society: p. 171; Missouri Historical Society: p. 548; Mount Holyoke College Library: p. 155; Movie Star News: p. 118, 232, 235 (2), 236, 241, 287, 306, 321, 326, 327, 328 (2), 329, 331, 332, 333 (Ball), 334, 335, 336, 337 (2), 339 (2), 340, 343, 344, 345, 346, 347 (2), 348, 349, 350, 351, 353, 354 (2), 356, 358; The Museum of Modern Art: p. 219; The National Archives: p. 453; National Periodical Publications: p. 281; National Portrait Gallery: p. 51; National Woman's Christian Temperance Union: p. 377; Nevada Historical Society: p. 378; New York State Historical Association, Cooperstown: p. 65; Oklahoma Historical Society: p. 500; Planned Parenthood: p. 28, 41, 77, 82, 87, 169; Providence Public Library: p. 495; Schlesinger Library, Radcliffe College: p. 245, 369; Schomburg Center for Research in Black Culture, New York Public Library: p. 454; Sophia Smith Collection, Smith College: p. 26, 257, 260, 267, 543, 547, 548 (Woodhull), 550 (2), 551; State Historical Society of Missouri: p. 222; State Historical Society of Wisconsin: p. 176; United Press International: p. 31, 47, 48, 54, 57, 62, 66, 88, 95, 96, 100, 103, 104, 105, 119, 121, 133, 134, 135, 136, 138, 441, 159, 165, 186, 188, 192, 205, 209, 212 (2), 213, 225, 227, 249 (2), 252 (2), 255, 256, 259, 265, 267, 269, 272, 275, 276, 278, 279 (Van Buren), 280, 286, 287, 288 (2), 289, 291, 292 (2), 293, 294, 296, 297, 298 (2), 300 (2), 301, 303, 305, 306, 307, 308, 310, 311, 312, 316, 317, 318 (2), 319, 320, 324, 360, 362, 364, 365 (2), 366, 371, 373, 380, 382, 383 (2), 384, 385, 386, 387, 388, 390, 391, 393, 396, 398, 401 (2), 405, 409, 413, 415 (2), 417, 421 (2), 424, 425, 426, 428, 430, 431, 432, 433, 434, 435 (2), 436, 437 (2), 438, 439, 441, 443, 444, 447, 450, 456, 458, 459, 464, 465, 467, 469, 471, 472, 473, 475 (2), 477, 478, 479, 492, 493, 494, 496, 501 (Barker), 504, 505 (2), 507, 508, 509, 522, 524, 553, 555, 560; Vassar College Library: p. 359, Western History Collections, University of Oklahoma Library; p. 501; Wide World Photos; p. 226, 264.

Cover photo (left): Bernard Nagler, Black Star.